DEVELOPMENT ECONOMICS

THE PEARSON SERIES IN ECONOMICS

Abel/Bernanke/Croushore
*Macroeconomics**

Bade/Parkin
*Foundations of Economics**

Berck/Helfand
*The Economics
of the Environment*

Bierman/Fernandez
*Game Theory with Economic
Applications*

Blanchard
*Macroeconomics**

Blau/Ferber/Winkler
*The Economics of Women,
Men and Work*

**Boardman/Greenberg/
Vining/Weimer**
Cost-Benefit Analysis

Boyer
*Principles of Transportation
Economics*

Branson
*Macroeconomic Theory
and Policy*

Brock/Adams
*The Structure of American
Industry*

Bruce
*Public Finance
and the American Economy*

Carlton/Perloff
*Modern Industrial
Organization*

Case/Fair/Oster
*Principles of Economics**

Caves/Frankel/Jones
*World Trade and Payments:
An Introduction*

Chapman
*Environmental Economics:
Theory, Application,
and Policy*

Cooter/Ulen
Law & Economics

Downs
*An Economic Theory
of Democracy*

Ehrenberg/Smith
Modern Labor Economics

Farnham
Economics for Managers

Folland/Goodman/Stano
*The Economics of Health
and Health Care*

Fort
Sports Economics

Froyen
Macroeconomics

Fusfeld
The Age of the Economist

Gerber
*International Economics**

González-Rivera
*Forecasting for Economics
and Business*

Gordon
*Macroeconomics**

Greene
Econometric Analysis

Gregory
Essentials of Economics

Gregory/Stuart
*Russian and Soviet Economic
Performance and Structure*

Hartwick/Olewiler
*The Economics of Natural
Resource Use*

Heilbroner/Milberg
*The Making of the Economic
Society*

Heyne/Boettke/Prychitko
*The Economic Way
of Thinking*

Hoffman/Averett
*Women and the Economy:
Family, Work, and Pay*

Holt
*Markets, Games and Strategic
Behavior*

Hubbard/O'Brien
*Economics**

*Money, Banking,
and the Financial System**

Hubbard/O'Brien/Rafferty
*Macroeconomics**

Hughes/Cain
American Economic History

Husted/Melvin
International Economics

Jehle/Reny
Advanced Microeconomic Theory

Johnson-Lans
A Health Economics Primer

Keat/Young/Erfle
Managerial Economics

Klein
*Mathematical Methods
for Economics*

Krugman/Obstfeld/Melitz
*International Economics:
Theory & Policy**

Laidler
The Demand for Money

Leeds/von Allmen
The Economics of Sports

Leeds/von Allmen/Schiming
*Economics**

Lipsey/Ragan/Storer
*Economics**

Lynn
*Economic Development:
Theory and Practice
for a Divided World*

Miller
*Economics Today**

*Understanding Modern
Economics*

Miller/Benjamin
The Economics of Macro Issues

Miller/Benjamin/North
*The Economics of Public
Issues*

Mills/Hamilton
Urban Economics

Mishkin
*The Economics of Money,
Banking, and Financial Markets**

*The Economics of Money,
Banking, and Financial Markets,
Business School Edition**

*Macroeconomics: Policy
and Practice**

Murray
*Econometrics: A Modern
Introduction*

Nafziger
*The Economics of Developing
Countries*

O'Sullivan/Sheffrin/Perez
*Economics: Principles,
Applications and Tools**

Parkin
*Economics**

Perloff
*Microeconomics**

*Microeconomics: Theory and
Applications with Calculus**

Phelps
Health Economics

Pindyck/Rubinfeld
*Microeconomics**

**Riddell/Shackelford/Stamos/
Schneider**
*Economics: A Tool for Critically
Understanding Society*

Ritter/Silber/Udell
*Principles of Money, Banking
& Financial Markets**

Roberts
*The Choice: A Fable of Free
Trade and Protection*

Rohlf
*Introduction to Economic
Reasoning*

Roland
Development Economics

Ruffin/Gregory
Principles of Economics

Sargent
*Rational Expectations
and Inflation*

Sawyer/Sprinkle
International Economics

Scherer
*Industry Structure, Strategy,
and Public Policy*

Schiller
*The Economics of Poverty
and Discrimination*

Sherman
Market Regulation

Silberberg
Principles of Microeconomics

Stock/Watson
Introduction to Econometrics

Studenmund
*Using Econometrics: A Practical
Guide*

Tietenberg/Lewis
*Environmental and Natural
Resource Economics*

*Environmental Economics
and Policy*

Todaro/Smith
Economic Development

Waldman
Microeconomics

Waldman/Jensen
*Industrial Organization: Theory
and Practice*

**Walters/Walters/Appel/
Callahan/Centanni/
Maex/O'Neill**
*Econversations: Today's
Students Discuss Today's Issues*

Weil
Economic Growth

Williamson
Macroeconomics

*denotes MyEconLab titles   Visit **www.myeconlab.com** to learn more

DEVELOPMENT ECONOMICS

Gérard Roland
University of California, Berkeley

PEARSON

Boston Columbus Indianapolis New York San Francisco Upper Saddle River
Amsterdam Cape Town Dubai London Madrid Milan Munich Paris Montreal Toronto
Delhi Mexico City Sao Paulo Sydney Hong Kong Seoul Singapore Taipei Tokyo

Editor in Chief	Donna Battista	**Cover Photos**	Top left: OutdoorPhoto/Fotolia; top right: Living Legend/Fotolia; bottom left: Gianliguori/Fotolia; bottom right: Tony Karumba/AFP/Getty
Executive Acquisitions Editor	Adrienne D'Ambrosio		
Editorial Project Manager	Sarah Dumouchelle		
Executive Marketing Manager	Lori DeShazo	**Text Design and Project Management**	Gillian Hall, The Aardvark Group
Managing Editor	Jeff Holcomb	**Composition and Artwork**	Laserwords
Senior Production Project Manager	Nancy Freihofer	**Printer/Binder**	Edwards Brothers
Operations Specialist	Carol Melville	**Cover Printer**	Lehigh-Phoenix Color/Hagerstown
Cover Designer	Jonathan Boylan	**Text Font**	Palatino

Credits and acknowledgments borrowed from other sources and reproduced, with permission, in this textbook appear on the appropriate page within text.

Chapter opener photo: Ssguy/Shutterstock

Library of Congress Control Number: 2013942162

10 9 8 7 6 5 4 3 2 1

www.pearsonhighered.com

ISBN 10:   0-32-146448-6
ISBN 13: 978-0-32-146448-4

Brief Contents

Chapter 1   **The Development Gap**   1

Chapter 2   **Poverty and Inequality**   27

Chapter 3   **Population Growth**   55

Chapter 4   **Economic Growth**   82

Chapter 5   **Structural Change and Development Strategies**   113

Chapter 6   **International Trade and Exchange Rates**   145

Chapter 7   **Institutions and Economic Development**   175

Chapter 8   **Markets and Hierarchies**   203

Chapter 9   **Political Institutions**   232

Chapter 10   **Legal and Fiscal Institutions**   264

Chapter 11   **Culture**   288

Chapter 12   **Rural Land Rights and Contracts**   312

Chapter 13   **Property Rights and Efficiency in Urban Areas**   340

Chapter 14   **Market Development**   366

Chapter 15   **The Role of Credit Markets in Development**   394

Chapter 16   **Health Care Delivery in Developing Countries**   422

Chapter 17   **Delivering Education in Developing Countries**   455

Chapter 18   **Delivering Infrastructure in Developing Countries**   485

Chapter 19   **Corruption**   508

Chapter 20   **Conflict**   537

Appendix   **Econometric Appendix**   561

             Glossary   581

             Index   593

Contents

Chapter 1 **The Development Gap** 1

Facts about the Development Gap 4
   The Income Gap 4
   The Poverty Gap 6
   The Health Gap 7
   The Education Gap 10
   The Urbanization Gap 11
   Why Is There a Development Gap? 13

The Evolving Development Gap 13
   Differences in Economic Growth 14
   Population Growth 16

Stories of Economic Catch-Up and Decline 17
   The Historical Catch-Up of Japan and
      Germany 18
   Economic Decline 21
   Important Questions 24

Chapter Summary 25 • Key Terms 25 •
Review Questions 25

Chapter 2 **Poverty and Inequality** 27

Poverty Measurement and Comparisons 28
   Measuring Poverty 28
   How to Compare Poverty Levels 33
   Poverty Rates in Practice 36

**Measurements and Comparisons of Income
Inequality** 38
   Measuring Income Inequality 38

Economic Determinants of Inequality 44
   Education and Income Inequality 44
   Land Ownership and Income Inequality 45

Inequality, Growth, and Development 46
   The Kuznets Hypothesis 46
   Income Inequality and Economic Growth 49
   Inequality over Time 50

Chapter Summary 53 • Key Terms 53 •
Review Questions 54

Chapter 3 **Population Growth** 55

**Population over Time and the Demographic
Transition** 56
   An Exponentially Growing Population 56
   The Evolution of Population Growth Rates 58

The Determinants of Population Growth 60
   Fertility, Mortality, and Birth and Death Rates 60
   Age Distribution 61

The Determinants of Fertility Rates 63
   The Economics of Fertility Choices 63
   Fertility Choices and Institutions 69
   Fertility Choices and the Demographic
      Transition 73

Family Planning and Population Growth 77
   Family Planning Policies 77
   Externalities and the Economics of Family
      Planning 78

Chapter Summary 79 • Key Terms 80 •
Review Questions 80

Chapter 4 **Economic Growth** 82

Growth and Factors of Production 83
   Factors of Production 83
   The Production Function 84
   Factor Productivity 85
   Factor Shares 86
   Growth Accounting 87

The Neoclassical Solow Growth Model 88
   Constant Returns to Scale and Diminishing
      Marginal Products 89
   Equilibrium in the Solow Model 90
   The Steady State in the Solow Growth
      Model 91
   Growth Inside and Outside the Steady State 92
   Technological Progress and the Steady
      State 93
   The Effect of Different Savings Rates 94
   Differences in Human Capital 95
   Income Convergence 96

Endogenous Growth Theory 97
   Boundless Knowledge-Based Growth 97
   Knowledge as a Non-Rival Good 98
   Basic Equations of the Romer Model 100
   The Romer Model versus the Solow Model 100
   Intellectual Property Rights and Technology
      Transfers 101

Empirical Analysis of Economic Growth 102
   Geography and Growth 104
   Institutions and Growth 105

Chapter Summary 111 • Key Terms 111 •
Review Questions 112

Chapter 5 **Structural Change and Development Strategies** 113

Structural Change 114
   From an Agricultural to an Industrial Economy 114
   From an Industrial to a Service Economy 114
   Structural Change across Industrial Sectors 115

The Lewis Model of Structural Change 116
   The Traditional and Modern Sectors 116
   Transfer of Labor from the Traditional to the Modern Sector 118
   The Lewis Model in Practice 120
   The Role of Institutions 122

The Harris-Todaro Model of Rural to Urban Migration 123
   The Harris-Todaro Model and the Migration Equilibrium 123
   The Implications of the Harris-Todaro Model 126

Development Strategies: Sectoral Growth 128
   Balanced and Unbalanced Growth 128
   Big Push Theories 130

Development Strategies: Import Substitution versus Export Promotion 132
   Import Substitution and the Prebisch-Singer Hypothesis 133
   Industrialization and the Protection of Infant Industries 134
   Export Promotion and the Asian Miracle 135

The Foreign Aid Controversy 139
   Sachs and the Argument for Foreign Aid 140
   Easterly and the Skeptics' View 140
   What Conclusions Should We Draw about Foreign Aid? 141

Chapter Summary 142 • Key Terms 143 • Review Questions 143

Chapter 6 **International Trade and Exchange Rates** 145

World Trade Evolution and Developing Countries 145
   The Increased Openness of Developed and Developing Economies 146
   A Diverse Trade Performance across Regions 147
   The Evolution of Trade Specialization in Developing Countries 148

The Theory of Comparative Advantage 148
   The Benefits of Exchange and Specialization 150

   Japanese DVD Players and Chinese Shirts: Comparative Advantage in Action 151
   Factor Endowments and Comparative Advantage 152
   Comparative Advantage and Patterns of Trade 154
   Trade Specialization and Export Price Risk 154

The Politics of Trade 156
   Winners and Losers in International Trade 156
   Collective Action Failure 157
   "Give and Take" 157

The Costs of Trade Barriers 158
   Protectionism and Tariffs 158
   Nontariff Barriers 159

Trade Institutions: Bilateral versus Multilateral 161
   Multilateral Trade Avoids Trade Diversion 161
   Multilateral Trade Agreements Are Politically Easier to Achieve 162
   The World Trade Organization 163

Exchange-Rate Policies in Developing Countries 165
   Degrees of Convertibility 166
   Fixed and Floating Exchange-Rate Regimes 168

Chapter Summary 172 • Key Terms 172 • Review Questions 173

Chapter 7 **Institutions and Economic Development** 175

What Are Institutions? 176
   Formal Institutions 176
   Informal Institutions 177
   Interactions between Institutions 178

What Do Institutions Do? 178
   Informational Problems 179
   The Hold-Up Problem 185
   The Commitment Problem 187
   The Cooperation Problem 190
   The Coordination Problem 195

The Persistence of Inefficient Institutions 198
   The Functionalist Fallacy 198

Chapter Summary 200 • Key Terms 201 • Review Questions 202

Chapter 8 **Markets and Hierarchies** 203

The Central Planning Debate 204
   The Theoretical Argument against Central Planning 205
   Lange's Rebuttal 206
   Hayek's Fundamental Criticism 207

The Central Planning Experiment   208
  Managerial Incentives under Central
    Planning   208
  Central Planning and Shortage   213
  Economic Behavior under Shortage   215
  Worker Behavior   220
  Complexity, Coordination, and the Slow Demise
    of Central Planning   222

Prices versus Quantities   224
  Coordination Mistakes Using Price and Quantity
    Signals   224

Institutions and the Boundaries of the Firm   228
  The Trade-Off between Efficiency and
    Holdup   229
  Less Vertical Integration with Better
    Institutions   229

Chapter Summary 230 • Key Terms 230 •
Review Questions 231

Chapter 9   **Political Institutions**   232

Political Regimes   233

**Economic Effects of an Autocracy versus a
Democracy**   235
  The Theory of Autocracy   236
  The Theory of Democracy   238
  Autocracy and Democracy Compared   240

Political Institutions in a Democracy   244
  Presidential and Parliamentary
    Democracies   244
  Electoral Rules   245
  The Economic Effects of Democratic
    Institutions   246

Political Institutions in an Autocracy   249
  Communist Regimes   249
  Nazism and Fascism   250

Waves of Democratization   251

Theories of Democratization   254
  Income and Democracy   254
  Education and Democracy   255
  Inequality, Social Conflict, and
    Democracy   257

Chapter Summary 262 • Key Terms 263 •
Review Questions 263

Chapter 10   **Legal and Fiscal
Institutions**   264

Legal Institutions   264
  Differences between the Common-Law and
    Civil-Law Systems   265

The Economic Effects of Different Legal
    Systems   268
  Controversies over the Importance of Common
    and Civil Law   272

Fiscal Institutions   275
  Taxation in Developing Countries   275
  Determinants of Tax Structure   280
  Why Does Taxation Differ between Developed
    and Developing Countries?   283

Chapter Summary 285 • Key Terms 286 •
Review Questions 286

Chapter 11   **Culture**   288

Measuring Culture   289
  The World Values Survey   289
  Schwartz's Cultural Mappings   293
  Hofstede's Index of Individualism and
    Collectivism   294

Culture's Effect on Institutions   297
  Culture and the Quality of Democracy   297
  Culture and Norms of Governance   300
  Culture and Contract Enforcement   301

Cultural Obstacles to Economic Development   303
  Egalitarian Norms and Development   303
  Religious Taboos on Interest   304
  Islam and Inheritance Laws   305

The Effects of Culture   307
  Religiosity and Growth   307
  Religious Beliefs and Trust   308
  Culture and Thrift   308
  Pitfalls to Avoid in Research on Culture   309

Chapter Summary 310 • Key Terms 311 •
Review Questions 311

Chapter 12   **Rural Land Rights and
Contracts**   312

**Worldwide Land Distribution and Land
Contracts**   313

Properties of Land Contracts   316
  Farmer Ownership   317
  Communal Ownership   318
  Fixed Land Rental   318
  Sharecropping   320
  Labor Contracts   320

Economic Effects of Land Contracts   323
  Communal and Private Ownership   324
  Sharecropping Compared to Privately Owned
    Farms   326
  Sharecropping Compared to Fixed Rental
    Contracts   327

Plantations and Slave Labor   327
Plantations and Privately Owned Family
    Farms   328
Institutions and Patterns of Land Inequality and
    Land Contracts   329

Land Reform   330
The Experience of Land Reform   330
Obstacles to Land Reform   333
Effects of Land Reform   335

Chapter Summary 338 • Key Terms 338 •
Review Questions 339

Chapter 13   **Property Rights and
Efficiency in Urban Areas**   340

Property Rights and the Informal Sector   341
The High Transaction Costs in the Informal
    Sector   342
Institutional Obstacles to Entry in the Formal
    Sector   343
The Economic Effects of Titling   345

**Institutions and Property Rights Protection: Lessons
from Transition Economies**   347
The Informal Sector and Institutional
    Quality   347
Property Rights, Investment, and Market
    Development   349

Privatization   352
From Nationalization to Privatization   352
Privatization Goals and Problems   353
Methods of Privatization in Developing
    Countries   356
Privatization Outcomes   357

Chapter Summary 364 • Key Terms 364 •
Review Questions 364

Chapter 14   **Market Development**   366

Institutions and Market Development   367
Taking Markets for Granted   367
Specific Problems of Market Development in
    Poor Countries   368
Business Networks in Development   370

**The Emergence of Markets in Transition
Countries**   371
The Output Fall in Central and Eastern
    Europe   372
China and the Dual-Track System   374
Lessons from the Effects of Transition on Market
    Development   376

Rural Markets and the Monopsony Problem   376
Monopsony and the Hold-Up Problem   377
Monopsonies in Developing Countries   378
Possible Solutions to the Monopsony
    Problem   379

Market Integration   381
Communication Obstacles to Market
    Integration   382
Transportation Obstacles to Market
    Integration   384
Regulatory Obstacles to Market
    Integration   386

Famines   388
Amartya Sen's Analysis of Famine   388
Famines and Democracy   390

Chapter Summary 391 • Key Terms 392 •
Review Questions 392

Chapter 15   **The Role of Credit Markets
in Development**   394

**The Demand for Credit in Developing
Economies**   395

**The Theory of Credit Markets in
Development**   396
Financing an Entrepreneur in Mumbai   396
Adverse Selection and Credit Rationing   398
Moral Hazard and Collateral   400
Moral Hazard and Monitoring   401
Monitoring and Variation in Interest Rates   402
Dealing with Default   403

Credit Constraints in Developing Countries   404
The Difficulty of Measuring Credit
    Constraints   404
Exploiting the Indian Priority Lending
    Reform   405

Microfinance   409
How Does Microcredit Work?   409
Incentive Properties of Microcredit   410
Other Forms of Microfinance   413
Is Microfinance Profitable?   415
Evaluating Microfinance   418

Chapter Summary 419 • Key Terms 419 •
Review Questions 420

Chapter 16   **Health Care Delivery in
Developing Countries**   422

**A Historical Perspective: The Epidemiological
Transition**   423

Measuring Health   424
Self-Reported Health Status   424
Self-Reported Symptoms   425
Reporting Daily Activities   425
Nutrient Intake   425
Anthropometric Measures   426
Disability Adjusted Life Year (DALY)   427

Diseases and Development   428
HIV   429

Diarrheal Diseases   432
Malaria   433
Worms   437
Tuberculosis   440

Cheap Drugs and Development   441
Why Pharmaceutical Companies Spend So Little on Developing Countries   442
An Advance Market Commitment   442
The Costs of Vaccine Commitments for Developing Countries   443

Health and Income   444
Does Better Health Lead to Higher Incomes?   444
Does More Income Improve Health?   446

Institutions and the Provision of Health Care   447
Variable Quality of Health Care Systems   447
Corruption in the Health Care Sector   448

Chapter Summary 452 • Key Terms 453 • Review Questions 454

Chapter 17   **Delivering Education in Developing Countries**   455

Measuring the Education Gap   456
The Primary School Gap   456
The Secondary-School Gap   458
The Educational Gender Gap   458
Educational Achievements   459
The Issue of Education Quality   462

The Returns to Education in Developing Countries   464
Externalities of Education   465
The Role of Government in Education   466
Empirical Estimates of the Returns to Education   467

Institutions and Education in Developing Countries   470
Why Is There Child Labor and Should It Be Banned?   470
The Indian Caste System and Educational Choices   473

What Reforms Can Improve Education?   476
Fighting Teacher Absenteeism   476
Are Incentives for Teachers Effective?   477
Decentralization   478
Vouchers   479
Reducing Education Costs   480
Reducing the Educational Gender Gap   481

Chapter Summary 482 • Key Terms 483 • Review Questions 484

Chapter 18   **Delivering Infrastructure in Developing Countries**   485

The State of Infrastructure in Developing Countries   486
Inequality of Access to Infrastructure   486
Institutions for Infrastructure Provision   488

Development Effects of Infrastructure Investment   489
The Effect of Infrastructure Investment on Growth   490
The Benefits of Transportation Infrastructure   491
The Costs and Benefits of Dams   494
White Elephants   497

Investment Risk and the Cost of Capital in Infrastructure   498
The Cost of Capital   499
Estimates of the Cost of Infrastructure Investment   500

Geography and Infrastructure   501

Institutional Aspects of Infrastructure   502
Regulatory Reform   502
Decentralization   503
Fighting Corruption in Road Construction   504

Chapter Summary 505 • Key Terms 506 • Review Questions 507

Chapter 19   **Corruption**   508

What Is Corruption?   509

Measuring Corruption   510
Objective Measures of Corruption   511
Subjective Measures of Corruption   513

Greasing the Wheels or Rotting the Fruit Basket?   515

Corruption and Growth   517

Why Are Some Countries More Corrupt than Others?   518
Development and Corruption   519
Political Institutions and Corruption   520
Legal Institutions and Corruption   522
Natural Resources, Trade, and Corruption   522

Culture and Corruption   523
Different Cultures, Their Various Social Norms, and Corruption   523
Disentangling Culture from Other Institutional Causes of Corruption   525

The Difficulty of Fighting Corruption   527
Few Success Stories, but Can We Generalize?   527

Higher Pay for Civil Servants: Does It Work?   528
Why Is Fighting Corruption So Difficult?   529

Chapter Summary 530 • Key Term 530 •
Review Questions 531 • Appendix 532

Chapter 20   Conflict   537

Theoretical Explanations of Conflict   538
Misjudging Your Rival   539
Deals That Aren't Worth the Paper on Which
They Are Written   540

The Empirical Determinants of Conflict   541
Why Do Civil Wars Start?   542
Greed versus Grievance   545
What Is the Causal Link between Conflict and
Development?   550

The Economic Effects of Conflict   551
The Long-Term Effects of War   552
The Long-Term Effect of Hiroshima and
Nagasaki   553
The Long-Term Effects of Bombing
Vietnam   554
Sierra Leone's Civil War   556

Chapter Summary 559 • Key Terms 559 •
Review Questions 559

Appendix   Econometric Appendix   561

Some Basic Statistical Concepts   562
Mean, Variance, and Standard
Deviation   562
Covariation between Two Variables   564
Bivariate Regression Analysis   565

Causal Inference   567
The Treatment Effect and Selection Bias   568
Randomized Evaluations   569
Ordinary Least Squares and Causal
Inference   569
Bias from Omitted Variables   570
Panel Regressions   571
Fixed Effects and Difference-in-Differences
Estimation   572
Instrumental Variables   574
A Regressions Table   577

Glossary   581

Index   593

Introduction

The economics of development is one of the most exciting fields in economics. It asks the same questions Adam Smith raised when he founded the study of economics: Why do some countries develop earlier than others? Why do some countries fail to develop while others are successful?

While we have learned a lot about what the wrong answers to those questions are, we have also made progress in recent years in finding the correct answers. Some of the most innovative advances in economics in the past 15 years have been in development economics and they have changed this field tremendously.

Two New Research Directions in Development Economics

Two notable research directions have reshaped the way we think about economic development. The first of these focuses on the fundamental role of institutions in understanding development and growth. Institutions, or the rules of the game in society and the economy, play a big role in determining how costly or inexpensive it is to pursue economic transactions such as buying or selling goods and services, or getting a loan to start a business. In some countries, institutions make economic transactions easier and establish a climate in which property rights are protected and the rule of law prevails. Such institutions have a positive effect on development. In other countries, institutions make economic transactions very difficult: property rights and investments are not protected, corruption is rife, abuse of power by politicians is the norm, and laws are either flawed or not well enforced. These institutions have a negative effect on economic development.

This undergraduate textbook is the first that comprehensively takes stock of the exciting new research that has taken place in recent years to gain an understanding of the role of institutions in economic development. We devote special chapters to particular sets of institutions—legal, political, and fiscal—as well as cultural and social norms. We examine the effect of institutions on growth, property rights, market development, and the delivery of public goods and services. Finally, we explore issues of institutional change such as democratization or property rights reform.

The second research direction that has completely changed the face of development economics is the rapid introduction of randomized evaluation of development projects. Randomized evaluation, now widely used in medical research, initially faced resistance from the medical community: people objected that if a new treatment existed, researchers should not randomly choose who might benefit from it, but give everyone access to the therapy. The disadvantage of this approach was that often only those who were the most health conscious chose to follow the new treatment. As health-conscious people are generally healthier than individuals who are less concerned with their own health, the studies based on that population therefore tended to overestimate the effects of a particular medical treatment. Randomized evaluation is necessary to evaluate medical treatments scientifically.

In recent years, development economists have wholeheartedly adopted the randomization approach to program evaluation in development projects. Entrepreneurial development economists such as Michael Kremer at Harvard, Abhijit Banerjee and Esther Duflo at MIT, Edward Miguel at UC Berkeley, and many others have convinced nongovernmental organizations (NGOs) to use randomized evaluation to assess the effects of various development and aid programs, and answer such questions as: What is the effect of deworming drugs on school participation and learning? What are the best methods for keeping water clean and preventing diarrheal diseases? How effective are bed nets in fighting malaria? What are the most successful tools to enhance the quality of education in poor countries, textbooks, school meals, smaller class sizes, or scholarship programs? Program evaluation enables researchers to figure out which programs are most effective and which policies have the best cost-to-benefit ratio in terms of achieving the goals of health, education, and social welfare, among other measures of development. This book provides a comprehensive study of the recent research in program evaluation in development economics.

The spread of randomized evaluations in development economics has also been associated with great improvements in empirical analysis. For obvious ethical reasons, researchers cannot analyze issues such as assessing the effects of abduction and the horrors of war on child soldiers or understanding the causes of armed conflicts using randomized evaluations, nor can they use these methods to answer the "big" questions about the effects of institutions on development. Nevertheless, researchers in recent years have developed very rigorous and innovative empirical methods for answering these and other questions about the causal effects of economic, social, and political variables.

While different in their focus, research on the role of institutions and on the use of randomized controlled trials to evaluate development policies are quite complementary. Randomized controlled trials are focused on precisely measuring the effect of particular policy interventions in local settings. Research on the role of institutions is more often done in a wider setting and analyzes differences in institutions across countries and, sometimes, across regions in large countries. Knowledge of a particular country's history is often crucial to understanding the origin and evolution of that country's institutions. However, both of these new directions in research share a common dedication to using the highest econometric standards and appropriate empirical methods to measure causal effects.

In this book, we take a broad view of economic development. The field is not confined simply to the study of poverty and underdevelopment, but it also examines how countries become successful in development. In the last decades, parts of East Asia followed by China and India, have been experiencing significant success in economic development. It is crucial that we try to understand the reasons for their success. We pay particular attention to development in

China and we also examine various aspects of economic history to provide a historical perspective on development successes and failures.

Organization of the Book

The comprehensive and flexible nature of the book's contents is designed so that instructors may pick and choose topics according to their specific interests and they can teach chapters in the order that works best for their students.

Part I introduces all the main issues in economic development and covers traditional contributing factors such as poverty and inequality, demographic issues, economic growth, structural change, development strategies, trade, and foreign aid and debt.

Chapter 1 presents data about the development gap, the huge difference in income per capita as well as in other measures of development, between the world's rich and poor countries. It presents the core focus of the book: why some countries grow out of poverty while others do not. It includes a number of maps to present the data so that students can visualize where poverty and underdevelopment are prevalent.

Chapter 2 considers poverty and inequality and how to measure these conditions. In addition, we discuss the evolution of poverty and inequality in the world over time and some of the underlying factors that drive changes in poverty and inequality.

Chapter 3 examines population growth, which has traditionally been an important issue in development. We examine trends in population growth in developing countries and discuss the theory of fertility choices and how it applies to development. We discuss family-planning policies and the reasons why population growth has begun to slow down in developing countries, a phenomenon called the demographic transition.

Chapter 4 covers growth theory. We consider the main theories of growth, both the Solow model and the model of endogenous growth. We also discuss the empirical literature on growth, a subject that many development textbooks do not address. A very important topic in this chapter is the role of institutions in explaining long-term growth. We also discuss alternative explanations for growth such as human capital and geography.

Chapter 5 focuses on issues of structural change. We discuss the traditional Lewis model of structural change as well as the Harris-Todaro model of rural-to-urban migration. We discuss some of the development strategies from the past 50 years such as big-push theories, balanced versus unbalanced growth theories, and import substitution and export promotion strategies.

Chapter 6 discusses globalization and the important international economic issues relevant to development. We offer a simple and thorough explanation of the theory of comparative advantage, and we discuss the political economy of trade and the critical role of multilateral institutions such as the WTO in maintaining free trade agreements. We explain how the WTO's basic rules of reciprocity and nondiscrimination help to sustain and expand multilateral agreements. We also cover exchange-rate issues as well as the topics of foreign debt and aid. In particular, we discuss recent controversies about how useful foreign aid actually is for development.

Part II focuses on institutions and their role in economic development.

Chapter 7 provides precise definitions of various institutions and explains in detail how they help solve a number of important problems that occur in economic transactions. These may be informational problems relative to the quality of goods and services or the reliability of the parties participating in a transaction; commitment problems and incentives to cheat or to renege on promises; collective-action problems and the difficulties faced by communities that attempt to make decisions or take actions that benefit their members as a whole; and coordination problems and the difficulties encountered by economic agents in developing common, efficient norms of behavior. This chapter is critical to understanding, at the microeconomic level, the role that institutions play in solving the various problems that arise in transactions between individuals and within communities.

Chapter 8 examines a topic important for the role of institutions in economic development: the role of markets versus hierarchies in the allocation of resources. In all economies, some goods and services are provided through the market while others are rendered through a hierarchical command system usually run by the government. In the 20th century, some countries even tried to achieve faster development by relying on central planning instead of free markets to allocate most resources in the economy. We discuss the incentive problems in central planning and large bureaucracies, and explain why central planning proved inferior to the capitalist market system.

Chapter 9 compares political institutions in the context of development. We compare the basic political institutions of democracy and dictatorship as well as different forms of both. Political institutions have an important effect on many indicators of economic performance such as growth or the delivery of public goods and services. This chapter also discusses theories and studies of democratization.

Chapter 10 covers legal and fiscal institutions. We present comparative research on legal systems, in particular common- and civil-law systems, and their effect on the development of financial markets. Fiscal institutions are also important because it is more difficult to raise tax revenues in developing countries than in developed countries. This is particularly the case in many countries where a large part of the economy operates in the unofficial sector.

Chapter 11 studies the role of culture in development. Students are introduced to the different methods by which researchers attempt to measure culture, understood as values and beliefs. We also present results from emerging research on the effects of culture on an economy.

Part III covers the core issues that development economists have been working on. The chapters on property rights, corruption, and conflict are unique to this text.

Chapter 12 examines issues of property rights and contracts in rural contexts. It analyzes the types of land contracts that exist on different continents and their economic effects, as well as how a country's institutions can influence these contracts. We also consider the history of land reforms and their economic effects in developing countries.

Chapter 13 discusses issues of property rights in urban contexts and it explores both the effects that result from the absence of legal titles to property in many developing countries and the differences across countries in terms of the protection of property rights. We also provide a detailed analysis of the issue of privatization policies in developing countries.

Chapter 14 considers market development in poor countries and the link between institutions and the development of markets in those countries. An important problem for rural market development is monopsony; farmers often face a single buyer who will only pay a very low price for their goods. This leaves farmers with little incentive to make investments that would increase their agricultural productivity. We also study the experience of transition economies; because free markets did not exist under central planning, the experience of these economies is useful to our understanding of how markets develop. We analyze issues of market integration as well as the obstacles to it in developing economies, and we consider famines and the market problems associated with these devastating events.

Chapter 15 looks at the role of credit markets in development. Here, we build on the issues discussed in Chapter 7. Informational and commitment problems are crucial issues in credit markets. In developing countries, the low levels of collateral and high costs of monitoring loans make these problems more serious. We discuss issues of credit constraints that firms can face and we also study microfinance, an innovative institution that has emerged to deal with some of the specific transaction costs of credit in developing countries.

Chapter 16 presents pertinent facts about health issues in development and how they have evolved over time. We explain the different ways economists measure health and we examine the relationships between health and development, health and income, and health and long-term growth. We also survey the results provided by randomized evaluations of health interventions in poor countries. In addition, this chapter discusses the issue of how to create access to cheap drugs in poor countries as well as the institutional factors relevant to the provision of healthcare services in developing countries.

Chapter 17 discusses the provision of education in developing countries and offers an overview of its progress and failures. We also survey the results of all the different randomized experiments undertaken to improve the quality of education. We discuss the various institutional problems in education such as the allocation of funds between the private and public sector; the allocation of funds to primary, secondary, and tertiary education; the persistent effects of corruption; and the educational gender gap and the programs designed to deal with this problem.

Chapter 18 examines the delivery of infrastructure in developing countries. It is difficult to attract infrastructure investment in poor countries because of their weak protection of property rights. Infrastructure decisions by politicians are not always efficient and scarce funds are often used to finance "white elephant" projects that are economically inefficient, but bring benefits to politicians. We also discuss various other problems developing countries face in relation to infrastructure investment, such as the economic effects of dams or the allocation of responsibility over infrastructure between different levels of government.

Chapter 19 focuses on corruption in the context of development. We explain the pros and cons of the measures of corruption that economists use. There is a direct link between the quality of institutions and the level and persistence of corruption, with cultural aspects playing a significant role. We survey the research on the causes and consequences of corruption and discuss policies to prevent and eradicate it.

Chapter 20 covers the issue of conflict in development. This is an important topic that is often neglected in other textbooks. Because most conflicts since World War II have taken place in developing countries, we present both theoretical and empirical analyses of the causes and consequences of these conflicts.

For those instructors who have a strong preference for traditional development themes, we recommend beginning with Part I, Chapters 1–6, which cover standard development issues. We then recommend Part II, Chapters 7–11 for those who are not very familiar with the economics of institutions. Finally, we recommend concluding with Part III, Chapters 12–20.

For an institutional approach, you may move from Chapter 1 directly to Chapters 7–11. After covering Chapters 12–15, add one chapter from Chapters 16–18, then return to Chapters 4, 2, and 6, and end with Chapters 19 and 20.

For those most interested in microeconomic issues of development, we recommend Chapters 1–4, Chapter 7, one chapter from Chapters 8–11, and then Chapters 12–20.

For those interested in a comparative approach to development, all chapters should be of interest, but if they cannot all be covered, a possible course could be Chapters 1, 2, and 4 followed by Chapters 7–15, and ending with Chapters 19 and 20.

For those instructors who would like to focus on the political economy of development they should also be interested in all chapters, a possible order could be Chapters 1–4, Chapters 6–11, and Chapters 16–20.

There are obviously other ways to structure a course using this textbook and we have made every effort to provide ample material for a variety of approaches.

Other Specific Features

Each chapter contains boxes on numerous topics related to the chapter's content. There are end-of-chapter summaries and review questions, many of which ask students to gather and analyze relevant data using critical thinking skills.

The book contains a wealth of data and figures on all the issues covered in the chapters. It is important for students interested in development economics to become familiar with these types of data in order to develop a quantitative grasp of the main issues in development such as poverty, differences in income per capita across the world, literacy rates, and infant mortality among others.

In order to understand development issues, undergraduate students not only need to be able to read descriptive tables, but they must also be familiar with regression tables. While they need to know the basic econometric methods used in economics, they do not need to know how to perform econometric analysis (this is reserved for graduate school). They must, however, learn to read and understand econometric tables that report results based on the most frequently used econometric techniques. We try to make this reading of econometric tables as easy as possible. In the chapters that include econometric tables, we explain the results in an intuitive way so that students can understand them as such. The book provides a special Econometric Appendix that explains some of the principle econometric concepts and methods. All the methods used in the book's various tables are included in this appendix, which is useful for students who want to know more about the concepts and methods, and a better understanding of them will be both illuminating and rewarding. However, this text was written to present frontier research in development economics in an accessible way to students studying traditional economics or other social sciences, as well as to anyone interested in understanding development.

As far as theory is concerned, our general approach has been to include mathematical models in text boxes and to provide explanations in the main text. The models in the text boxes also help students to achieve a more rigorous understanding of the economic theory and we strongly encourage students to read these boxes. Chapter 4 on economic growth is the only chapter in which models are included in the main text because it is usually difficult to understand growth theory without the use of production functions and basic models such as the Solow model. Even in this chapter, however, we try to focus on the essential components of theory and devote sufficient space to discuss the empirical literature on growth, which has delivered many new insights about economic development in the last 20 years.

Supplements

Instructors can download many useful teaching resources from the Instructor Resource Center, www.pearsonhighered.com/roland, or from the catalog page for *Development Economics*. The Instructor's Manual provides solutions for all of the end-of-chapter exercises.

The Companion Website, by Sandra Trejos, Clarion University, features key concepts, multiple-choice quizzes, and graphing and quantitative exercises for each chapter.

The book's PowerPoint® presentation, by Jeff Werling, University of Maryland, provides instructors with a set of comprehensive lecture slides.

Acknowledgments

I am very grateful to Oleksiy Shvets who has provided extremely helpful assistance to me since I started working on this book. Oleksiy did tremendous work in helping me with data collection and presentation as I worked on the first version of the book. I would also like to thank James Zuberi, who provided great research assistance and helped me with the preparation of the overall manuscript. I also received research assistance from Brian Scholl and Sarath Sanga.

I benefited tremendously from all those who read and commented on various parts of the manuscript. Particular thanks go to my colleague Pranab

Bardhan who went through all chapters and gave me many useful suggestions. I am also very grateful to my colleague Fred Finan who helped me to improve the econometric appendix. I wish to thank the many reviewers solicited by Pearson who commented on various chapters:

Berhanu Abegaz, College of William & Mary
David A. Anderson, Centre College
Raj Arunachalam, University of Michigan
Robert Beekman, University of Tampa
Valerie R. Bencivenga, University of Texas–Austin
Jeffrey T. Bookwalter, University of Montana
Kristie Briggs, Creighton University
Lisa D. Cook, Michigan State University
Christopher J. Coyne, West Virginia University
Ian Coxhead, University of Wisconsin–Madison
Eleanor D. Craig, University of Delaware
John Deal, Manchester University
Can Erbil, Brandeis University
Erwin F. Erhardt, III, University of Cincinnati
Evangelos M. Falaris, University of Delaware
Amanda J. Felkey, Lake Forest College
Andrew D. Foster, Brown University
Andres Gallo, University of North Florida
Ira Gang, Rutgers University
Godfrey Gibbison, Georgia Southern University
Chris D. Gingrich, Eastern Mennonite University
Abbas P. Grammy, California State University–Bakersfield
Kwabena Gyimah-Brempong, University of South Florida
Denise Hare, Reed College
Andrew Healy, Loyola Marymount University
Norman Hicks, George Washington University
Seema Jayachandran, Stanford University
Vibha Kapuria-Foreman, Colorado College
Elizabeth Katz, University of San Francisco
Sherif Khalifa, California State University–Fullerton
Tung Liu, Ball State University
Ricardo A. Lopez, Brandeis University
Frank McIntyre, Rutgers Business School

Michael A. McPherson, University of North Texas
Hiranya K. Nath, Sam Houston State University
Camille Soltau Nelson, Oregon State University
Quynh Nguyen, University of Maryland
Ozgur Orhangazi, Roosevelt University
Oluwole Owoye, Western Connecticut State University
Stephen Pollard, California State University–Los Angeles
Michael A. Quinn, Bentley University
Bee Y. Roberts, Penn State University
Rati Ram, Illinois State University
Margarita M. Rose, King's College
Naveen Sarna, University of Maryland
Yochanan Shachmurove, University of Pennsylvania
Stephen L. S. Smith, Gordon College
Christodoulos (Chris) Stefanadis, University of Piraeus
Radoslaw (Radek) L. Stefanski, University of Oxford
Emma C. Stephens, Pitzer College
Gordon Streeb, Emory University
Vasant A. Sukhatme, Macalester College
Radek Szulga, Carleton College
Simge Tarhan, Colby College
Sandra Trejos, Clarion University of Pennsylvania
Evert Van Der Heide, Calvin College
Randal Verbrugge, Georgetown University
Nancy Virts, California State University, Northridge
Jeffrey Werling, University of Maryland
Lisa Wilder, Albright College
John Willoughby, American University
Dean Yang, University of Michigan
Bassam Yousif, Indiana State University

Roxanne Hoch-McCarley convinced me to write this book with Pearson. At a later stage, I received great help from Adrienne D'Ambrosio, Deepa Chungi, and Sarah Dumouchelle. Deb Thompson edited the whole manuscript in the final stage. I am grateful to all of them and all those at Pearson who worked on the book.

Finally, I wish to thank my wife, Heddy, and my entire family who put up with me and my anxieties as I was working on the various versions of the book. They are also glad that it is finished. I wish to dedicate this book to the memory of my parents Yves Roland and Mimy Leclercq, who passed away during the final revision of the book, as well as to the memory of my brother Damien Roland who worked tirelessly in his short life to defend the interests of mineworkers on all continents and who had a keen interest in enhancing working conditions in developing countries.

Gérard Roland
Berkeley, May 2, 2013

The Development Gap

Students who are interested in studying development economics may have various motivations for doing so. They might have idealistic motivations and want to help eradicate poverty and disease in poor countries. They may intend to work for a non-governmental organization (NGO) or an international development aid agency to achieve these goals. Better knowledge of development economics can provide more useful solutions to help the poor in developing economies. Students might also have intellectual motivations and want to understand why poverty can be so persistent and how development economics can contribute to finding solutions to poverty. Why can our planet produce enough food to feed all its inhabitants, yet hundreds of millions of people still suffer from hunger? Which economic policies work best, at the regional, national, urban, and village levels, to help people escape poverty, achieve higher living standards, receive better health care and education, and live longer? How can development economics provide answers to those questions?

There is no better way to introduce the topic of economic development than with some striking pictures. Figures 1.1a, 1.1b, and 1.1c show three different world maps produced by Mark Newman, at the Department of Physics and the Center for the Study of Complex Systems at the University of Michigan. The first map displays the landmass of the world's countries. The second map represents the size of countries as proportional to their population; for example, China and India appear much larger than on standard maps since they have populations, respectively, of 1.3 and 1.2 billion people. Japan and Indonesia also appear larger. Notice how Russia and Canada appear much smaller than on standard maps. On the African continent, South Africa, Nigeria, Egypt, and Ethiopia appear larger, while on the North American continent, Mexico also appears larger.

In the third map, the size of a country appears as proportional to its gross domestic product. Here, the United States, Europe, and Japan appear very large, and Germany appears nearly as large as China. Notice how Central and South America and Africa have become tiny.

These three maps clearly illustrate the challenges of economic development in the world. The overwhelming majority of the world's population lives in developing countries, while most economic activity takes place in a few rich countries such as the United States, Japan, or the nations of Western Europe. Most people on the planet still have very low living standards and roughly one billion people live in conditions of great poverty, surviving on less than a dollar a day. The study of economics should not, therefore, view the issues of economic development as a marginal or exotic subject. It is *the* most important economic problem on our planet and development economics thus has the potential to make a significant positive impact on the lives of people around the world.

FIGURE 1.1a   The Actual Land Mass of the World's Countries

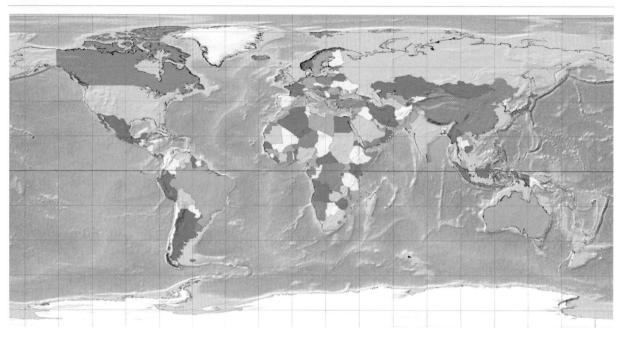

FIGURE 1.1b   A World Map Representing a Country's Size as Proportional to Its Population

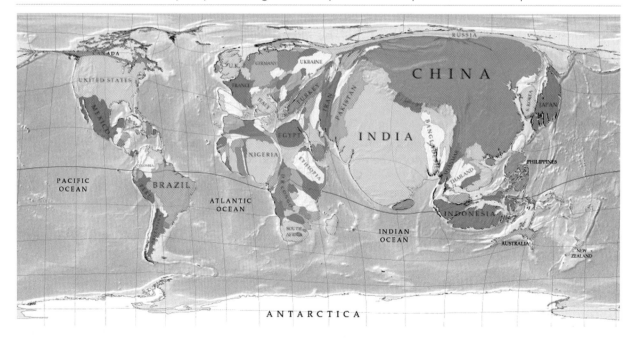

FIGURE 1.1c   A World Map Representing a Country's Size as Proportional to Its Gross Domestic Product

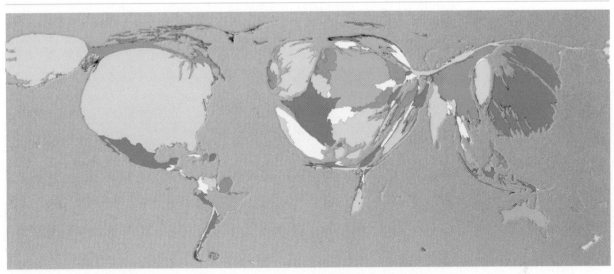

In the first map, country sizes are proportional to their landmass; in the second map, they are proportional to their populations; and in the third map, they are proportional to their gross domestic product.

Source: Printed with permission from Mark Newman, University of Michigan. http://www-personal.umich.edu/~mejn/cartograms/.

In this chapter, we examine some of the most important facts about economic development and consider some of the main questions studied in development economics. We first learn about the **development gap**, the differences in economic development between the advanced economies of the United States, Japan, and the Western European nations and the poorer economies of Africa, Asia, Latin America, and Eastern Europe. We review measures of the development gap in terms of income, life expectancy, health, education, and level of urbanization, which will provide a fresh and precise perspective on the scope of the development gap between the richest and poorest countries in the world.

This gap has been evolving over time, decreasing for some countries while increasing for others. For example, in recent decades some Asian countries such as China and India have successfully undertaken a vigorous process of development and have begun to close the gap with the richest countries. Obviously there is still a long way to go, but it is encouraging to see that there are some major success stories in developing nations, and they may help us better understand why the development gap has unfortunately increased in many other poor countries. Another important fact we must consider is that development is not irreversible: rich countries can be engaged in a process of economic decline. Argentina was among the richest countries in the world at the beginning of the 20th century, but over the next 50 years, it experienced a significant downturn in its economy. Development economists have primarily focused on the success or failure of development in poor countries; they have paid less attention to the phenomenon of the decline of countries who had already achieved success in economic development. It is critical to understand economic decline in order to prevent it.

Facts about the Development Gap

There are different ways to measure the gap in economic development between rich and poor countries. We will look at the income gap, the health gap, the education gap, and the differences in rates of urbanization across the world.

The Income Gap

The first and most obvious way to measure the development gap is to measure the income gap between developed economies and poor countries. A common measure of income is **gross domestic product (GDP) per capita**. This is a measure of the value of output produced per inhabitant of a country during a given year. Gross domestic product per capita is a good approximation of average annual per capita income. The only difference is that annual per capita income adjusts for income flowing into or out of the country, as well as for foreign aid and remittances. Of course, these can be significant for poor countries. Nevertheless, GDP is the single most widely used measure of a country's economic size. In order to compare across countries, we need to express GDP per capita in U.S. dollars (or some other common currency). In development economics, it is important to use exchange rates based on **purchasing power parity (PPP)** when converting GDP per capita in the local currency to U.S. dollars. Purchasing power parity exchange rates are based on the prices of all goods and services, and are constructed such that the same basket of goods in one country has the same dollar value in all countries.

Let us look at GDP per capita across countries in 2010 using purchasing power parity. Luxemburg is the richest country in the world with a GDP per capita of $86,000. The world's poorest country is the Democratic Republic of Congo (formerly called Zaire) with a GDP per capita of only $350. This is a very large difference, close to 1:250. Other rich countries include the United States, Norway, Singapore, Qatar, and the United Arab Emirates with a gross domestic product (GDP) per capita around $50,000. Most European countries have a GDP per capita between $20,000 and $40,000. In contrast, 12 countries, including Congo have a GDP per capita lower than $1,000. These include Burundi, Liberia, Eritrea, Niger, the Central African Republic, Sierra Leone, Malawi, Timor-Leste, Mozambique, Madagascar, and Togo. Apart from Timor-Leste in Southeast Asia, all of these countries are in sub-Saharan Africa. Figure 1.2 shows a map of GDP per capita based on purchasing power parity.

Comparing Per Capita Incomes across Countries Using Purchasing Power Parity (PPP) Exchange Rates

Using PPP to measure a country's GDP (or any other statistical data) means that we must use an exchange rate based on purchasing power parity instead of the market exchange rate to obtain a dollar measure of GDP for that country. The purchasing power parity measure computes exchange rates between currencies of different countries so that *the same basket of goods in any two different countries has the same dollar value.* This is difficult to do but is important for making international income comparisons. One dollar will typically buy less in a rich country than in a poor country if we use existing exchange rates. For example, one U.S. dollar was exchanged internationally in 2012 at roughly 55 Indian rupees. However, 55 Indian rupees will typically buy more things in India than will one U.S. dollar in the United States. The purchasing power parity exchange rate will thus be lower than 55 rupees per dollar, probably closer to 40 rupees or even less. The world's poorest people live on less than one dollar a day. Even though they live under conditions of extreme poverty, they can typically buy more with one dollar in their country than a resident of New York, Tokyo, or London can purchase with that same dollar.

The reason why market exchange rates do not equalize purchasing power parity is that exchange rates are based only on the prices of tradable goods and do not take into account non-tradables, i.e., goods and services that are not traded internationally. Non-tradable goods are usually less expensive in poorer countries. Many of these non-tradable goods are services and their price is related to the cost of labor, which is lower in poorer countries. For example, the price of a haircut is usually lower in poorer countries. The technology for cutting hair is basically the same everywhere and the cost is essentially the wage of the hairdressers. A haircut is a non-tradable service because people do not typically travel across countries to get a cheaper haircut.

As we can see from Figure 1.2, most of the world's poorest countries are in Africa. South Africa is the richest country on the continent with slightly over $10,500 per capita. However, most countries in sub-Saharan Africa are much poorer and have a GDP per capita that is closer to the $1,000 range. Many Asian countries are still very poor; Nepal and Afghanistan have a GDP per capita of roughly $1,200 Bangladesh and Myanmar are below $2,000, and Cambodia, Laos, Pakistan, Vietnam, India, the Philippines, Mongolia, and Indonesia are below $5,000.

Russia and the nations of Latin America and Eastern Europe are among the middle-income countries with a GDP per capita in the range of $5,000 to $15,000. Brazil, for example, has a GDP per capita slightly above $11,000, which is around the Latin American average. Some of the former Soviet republics are quite poor. Tajikistan and Kyrgyzstan have a GDP per capita close to $2,000, roughly the level of Cambodia. Uzbekistan and Moldova have a GDP per capita slightly above $3,000 and are poorer than Vietnam or India. During the Communist period of the 20th century, we would not have classified Soviet republics as developing countries. However, since the fall of Communism, it is clear that many former Soviet republics are actually quite poor. Even

FIGURE 1.2   GDP Per Capita in 2010 (Purchasing Power Parity in Dollars)

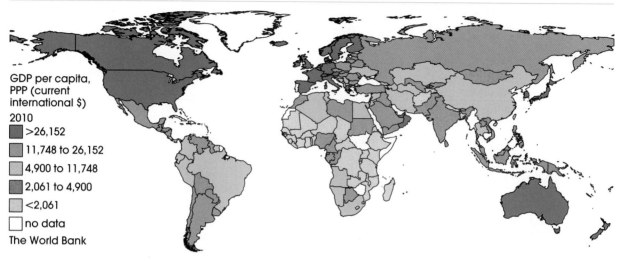

The world's poorest countries are concentrated in Africa.

Source: The World Bank, World Development Indicators, http://databank.worldbank.org.

Russia must now be seen as a middle-income country with a GDP per capita of $19,000, which is closer to that of Mexico ($14,500) than to that of the United States ($47,000).

The Poverty Gap

The income gap shows that an overwhelming proportion of the world population lives on less than $10,000 a year. However, this measure does not give an accurate idea of the extreme poverty that exists in the world. Figure 1.3 shows the poverty headcount ratio at $2 a day measured in purchasing power parity. This represents the percentage of the population that lives on less than $2 a day and it is a measure used by the World Bank to gauge extreme poverty. We will talk more about measurement of poverty in Chapter 2. As Figure 1.3 demonstrates, slightly over 70% of the population in South Asia (Afghanistan, Bangladesh, Bhutan, India, Maldives, Nepal, Pakistan, and Sri Lanka) fits that definition of poverty, while nearly 70% of the population in sub-Saharan Africa lives below that poverty line. As a result, those two regions represent a strong concentration of extreme poverty, with 1.2 billion people in South Asia and 600 million people in sub-Saharan Africa living on less than $2 a day. In East Asia and the Pacific, 33% of the population, or roughly 730 million people, live below that poverty line. Overall, a bit less than half of the human beings on the planet live on less than $2 a day.

Measures of income and poverty are crucial indicators of development, but they are not the only ones. We will next look at other factors that can give us an idea of economic development and living conditions.

FIGURE 1.3   Poverty Headcount Ratio in 2008 at Poverty Line of $2 a Day in 2005 Prices (Purchasing Power Parity)

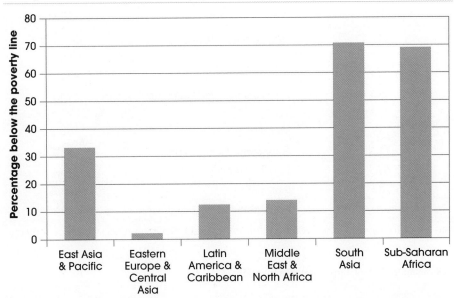

More than two-thirds of the population in sub-Saharan Africa and in South Asia live on $2 a day.

Source: The World Bank, World Development Indicators, http://databank.worldbank.org/.

The Health Gap

There is an important health gap between rich and poor countries. People in developing countries are more prone to diseases, they do not live as long as people in developed countries, and many of their children die at a young age.

Differences in life expectancy. In 2010, a child born in Japan could expect to live until 83, while a child born the same year in Sierra Leone in Africa could only expect to reach the age of 47. **Life expectancy** is defined as the average number of years a newborn infant would live if health and living conditions at the time of its birth remained the same throughout its life. It reflects the health conditions in a country and the quality of health care its people receive. Life expectancy is closely correlated with income, but it is instructive to look at the numbers on life expectancy in different regions of the world shown in Table 1.1. For each region that includes developing countries, the table identifies the countries with the lowest and the highest life expectancies. Life expectancy in North America is given for comparison.

As the table indicates, life expectancy is the lowest in sub-Saharan Africa by more than 10 years compared to South Asia, and by more than 20 years compared with other regions in the world. All countries outside sub-Saharan Africa have a life expectancy above 50, except for Afghanistan, but 11 African countries have a life expectancy below 50. As we will see in Chapter 16, AIDS is a big factor in reducing life expectancy in many African countries, but it is

TABLE 1.1   2010 Life Expectancy (Years) at Birth in Regions of the World and in Selected Countries

Region, country	Life expectancy	Region, country	Life expectancy
Sub-Saharan Africa	**54.2**	**East Asia and Pacific**	**73.3**
Lesotho	47.3	Timor-Leste	62
Cape Verde	73.77	Japan	83
South Asia	**65.3**	**Latin America and Caribbean**	**74.1**
Afghanistan	48.3	Haiti	61.8
Sri Lanka	74.7	Costa Rica	79.2
Middle East and North Africa	**72.5**	**Europe and Central Asia**	**75.7**
Iraq	68.5	Turkmenistan	64.9
Qatar	78.1	Switzerland	82.2
		North America	**78**

There are marked differences in life expectancy across the world. It is the lowest in sub-Saharan Africa where poverty is the highest.

Source: The World Bank, World Development Indicators, http://databank.worldbank.org/.

not by any means the only factor contributing to a low life expectancy. Many mothers die giving birth, diseases such as yellow fever and tuberculosis are often fatal, and parasitic diseases and malnutrition make people more vulnerable to illness, leading to an early death.

Outside Africa, other countries with a low life expectancy are Haiti (61.8), Timor-Leste (62), Papua New Guinea (62.4), Cambodia (62.5), Myanmar (64.6), India (65.1), and Pakistan (65.2). Conversely, there are some rather poor countries where life expectancy is quite high. For example, life expectancy in Cuba (79) is higher than in Chile (78.9) and, for that matter, higher than any other country in Central or Latin America. As a comparison, life expectancy in the United States (78.2) is lower than in Cuba or Chile. In China, life expectancy is 73.3 years. Countries from the former Soviet Union have a relatively low life expectancy; Russia's is 68.8, which is lower than Indonesia (68.9). Turkmenistan has a life expectancy of only 64.9, which is below India or Pakistan. Kazakhstan has a life expectancy of 68.3, which is lower than Nepal (68.4) or the Philippines (68.5).

Differences in infant mortality rates. The **infant mortality rate** measures the probability that a child will die before reaching age 1. It is computed as the number of children dying before age 1 per 1,000 live births in the same year. One has to divide this rate by 10 to compute the probability of dying before age 1.

As Figure 1.4 shows, infant mortality rates are the highest in sub-Saharan Africa and South Asia, the regions in the world where there are also the highest poverty rates. For the sake of comparison, the figure shows infant mortality rates for high income countries that are members of the Organization for Economic Co-operation and Development (OECD).

FIGURE 1.4   Infant Mortality Rates in 2010 (Per 1,000 Live Births)

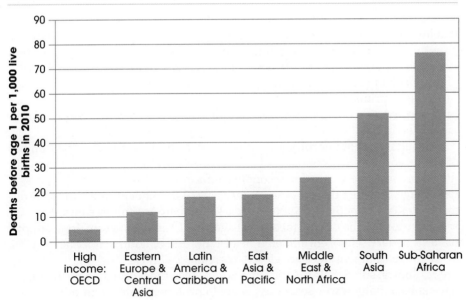

Infant mortality rates are measured as the number of deaths before age 1 per 1,000 live births.

Source: The World Bank, World Development Indicators, http://databank.worldbank.org/.

In Africa, Sierra Leone has an infant mortality rate of 134 per 1,000, Congo has 112, Somalia 108, and the Central African Republic has 106. These are the four countries with the highest infant mortality rates in the world. The 20 countries with the highest infant mortality rates are all in Africa, except for Afghanistan (103). Haiti has a mortality rate of 70.4 per thousand, Pakistan 69.7, Tajikistan 52.2, and Myanmar 50.4. Behind all these numbers are human dramas. Every year, 9 million children die before they have reached the age of 5, leaving grief-stricken families. Most of these unnecessary deaths could be avoided by reducing poverty and improving health care in these developing nations.

Some developing countries have low infant mortality rates demonstrating that health care policies can make a difference. Cuba has an infant mortality rate of only 4.6 per thousand, the same rate as the United Kingdom and a lower rate than the United States (6.5). Korea (4.2), Malaysia (5.6), Montenegro (7.2), Chile (7.7), Russia (9.1), Uruguay (9.2), and Thailand (11.2) are some of the other countries with low infant mortality rates.

Policy interventions can be quite effective in reducing child mortality. Between 2005 and 2010, Kenya reduced its infant mortality rate by 8% each year, perhaps the fastest reduction observed among developing countries. A key factor seems to be a policy that encourages the spread of insecticide-treated bed nets as a way to fight malaria, one of the main causes of infant mortality in tropical and sub-tropical areas. In 2003, only 8% of Kenyan households used such bed nets, but by 2008, treated bed nets were used by more than 60% of households.

The Education Gap

Access to education is another factor affecting the development gap. Countries that invest in good education can realize high productivity gains and economic growth. Unfortunately, poor countries often cannot afford a good education system, a deficit that contributes to the perpetuation of the development gap.

Important progress has been made in the last decades to introduce universal access to primary school, but in poorer countries, many children still do not have access to secondary education. Figure 1.5 gives 2009 figures for enrollment in secondary school in the principal regions of the world.

Secondary school enrollment rates are measured by dividing the number of pupils enrolled in secondary school, regardless of age, by the population in the theoretical age group for secondary education. This measure, given as a percentage, is called the gross secondary school enrollment rate. Gross enrollment rates can sometimes be above 100% when there are children enrolled who are above and/or below the theoretical age. The United Kingdom, for example, has a secondary school enrollment rate of 178% and Belgium has a rate of 160%.

School enrollment rates are closely correlated with GDP per capita. As Figure 1.5 shows, sub-Saharan Africa and South Asia, the world's poorest regions, have substantially lower secondary school enrollment rates than other developing regions in the world.

African countries have the lowest secondary school enrollment rates. Niger has only 12%, the Central African Republic 14%, and Burkina Faso 19%. Twelve

FIGURE 1.5   Gross Secondary School Enrollment in 2009, by Region

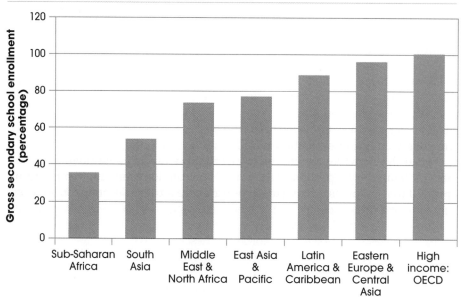

Large differences in secondary school enrollment rates still exist across the world. In most regions, gross school enrollment rates are above 75%. They are nevertheless below 40% in sub-Saharan Africa and below 60% in South Asia.

Source: The World Bank, World Development Indicators, http://databank.worldbank.org/.

African countries have secondary enrollment rates below 30%. Pakistan has the lowest enrollment rate outside Africa with 33.6%. In comparison, Bangladesh has 49% and India has 60%. Other countries in Asia having low enrollment rates are Cambodia (45%), Myanmar (53%), Timor-Leste (58%), and Bhutan (60.8%). In contrast, China has an enrollment rate of 80%. In Latin America, El Salvador (63%) has the lowest enrollment rate followed by Paraguay (67%). Costa Rica, Colombia, Peru, Uruguay, and several Caribbean island nations have rates above 90%. In sub-Saharan Africa, the countries with the best enrollment rates are South Africa (93%), Cape Verde (85%), and Botswana (80%). Clearly there is considerable variation in school enrollment across continents and even across countries.

A big success story in education is South Korea, a nation that used to be very poor. In the 1960s, its income level was comparable to Afghanistan, but it currently has a GDP per capita comparable to Israel or New Zealand. In a few years, it could even catch up with Japan. The South Korean education system is an even bigger success story, excelling beyond those in some of the most advanced economies and it is certainly an important factor behind South Korea's economic success. South Korea now tops all other countries in the world in terms of the proportion of young people who have completed secondary school. Currently, 97% of South Koreans between the ages of 25 and 34 have achieved secondary education. This is better than Norway and Japan, where slightly more than 90% have achieved that goal. South Korea is among the top countries in the world in terms of the proportion of young people entering university. In an international comparison of math skills, Korean teenagers placed second behind Finland. South Korea has not only consistently invested in education, but it has also managed its education system quite efficiently.

The Urbanization Gap

Rich countries are typically very urbanized. The Industrial Revolution developed in cities as workers came from the countryside to the city to earn a better living in factories rather than continue to toil on the land. Even today, the large service sector in rich countries is primarily located in cities. Typically, we tend to think of poorer countries as having a low level of urbanization and a larger share of the population that still lives in rural areas and works on the land. As we will see below, this situation is changing.

Figure 1.6 provides an overview of **urbanization rates** worldwide. These rates measure the proportion of a country's population living in urban areas as opposed to rural areas. Many small countries are strongly urbanized, but even large countries like the United States and Canada, with great expanses of land, have high urbanization rates, even into the 80% range.

Africa is the continent with the lowest level of urbanization. Burundi, Uganda, Niger, Ethiopia, and Rwanda have urbanization rates below 20%. However, some African countries are highly urbanized; for example, Djibouti and Gabon have urbanization rates close to 90%. Libya has an urbanization rate of 78%, while Liberia, Cape Verde, Botswana, South Africa, the Republic of Congo, Angola, Cameroon, Gambia, Ghana, Cote d'Ivoire, and Nigeria have urbanization rates above 50%.

In Asia, the least urbanized countries are Nepal (18.2%), Cambodia (22.8%), Afghanistan (24.8%), Bangladesh (28.1%), and Vietnam (28.8%). India has an

FIGURE 1.6   World Urbanization Rates, 2010

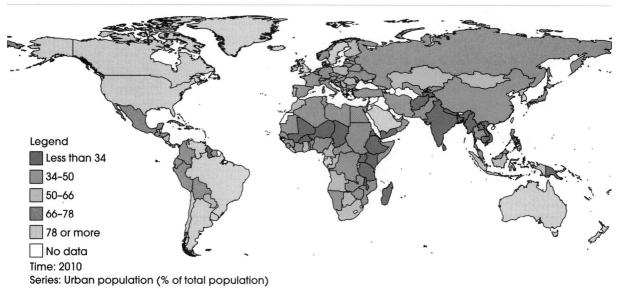

Legend
- ■ Less than 34
- ▨ 34–50
- ▨ 50–66
- ▨ 66–78
- ☐ 78 or more
- ☐ No data

Time: 2010
Series: Urban population (% of total population)

While urbanization rates are lower in Africa and in South Asia, large portions of the world have rates above 50%.

Source: The World Bank, World Development Indicators, http://databank.worldbank.org.

urbanization rate of 30.1% and China's rate is 44.9%. Many Asian countries have become highly urbanized; for example, South Korea has an urbanization rate of 81%, higher than Japan's (67%).

In Latin America, Guyana is the least urbanized country, but it still has an urbanization rate of 28.5%. Many Latin American countries have very high urbanization rates, with Venezuela at 93%, Uruguay 92.5%, Argentina 92.4%, Chile 89%, Brazil 86.5%, and Mexico 77.8%.

These rates clearly demonstrate that the planet is becoming more and more urbanized. Since 2010, more than half of the world's population lives in urban areas. Worldwide, a majority of countries now have urbanization rates over 50%, with all rates increasing rapidly.

In contrast to historic trends, current higher levels of urbanization are not necessarily equivalent to higher levels of income as many migrants now move from the countryside to live in urban slums under conditions of extreme poverty with no basic infrastructure such as water, gas, electricity, transportation, and sewage systems. Today, developing countries have some of the largest cities in the world. Mexico City has nearly 23 million inhabitants; Sao Paulo (Brazil) and Mumbai and New Delhi (India) have around 20 million inhabitants; Shanghai (China) has 18 million; Jakarta (Indonesia) has over 16.5 million; Kolkata (India) and Cairo (Egypt) have close to 16 million; and these numbers keep going up. Out of the 20 largest cities in the world, only three are in advanced industrialized countries (Tokyo, New York, and Los Angeles).

These high urbanization rates in the developing world mean that when we consider policies to alleviate poverty, we should think of both rural and urban areas. How can we bring decent housing, basic infrastructure, health, and education to the large cities of the developing world?

One success story in urban development is that of Naga City in the Philippines. This is a mid-size town with 175,000 inhabitants. Until the late 1980s, like many other cities in the developing world, it was heavily indebted, corruption was rampant among city officials, and public services were in disarray due to the corruption of the Philippine government led by President Ferdinand Marcos, who ran the country as a dictatorship. After a popular uprising in 1986 that removed him from power and the election of Corazon Aquino that year as the new president of a democratic Philippines, people all over the country hoped for change. In 1988, Jesse Robredo ran for mayor of Naga City on a platform of reform. Because his opponent was linked to the old Marcos regime, people voted Robredo into office. He started by cracking down on illegal gambling, strip clubs, and prostitution. He reduced the city's budget deficit by threatening businesses with higher taxes and court action if they continued to evade paying the taxes they owed. His most critical reform was to bring more transparency and citizen participation to city governance. For example, citizen representatives were encouraged to participate in local government committees, voicing their opinions and monitoring decision-making processes, an innovation that resulted in improved municipal services. When a corrupt provincial governor imposed an ineffective police chief on the city, Robredo instituted a vice squad staffed by volunteers from the city and members of the police force who were empowered to arrest criminals engaged in illegal gambling, prostitution, and other corrupt activities. In a few years, Naga City became a model of participatory governance, winning many awards worldwide. Its experience has been studied by local politicians and urban experts from all over the world. The key lesson of Naga City's renewal is that more citizen participation in local governance was a key factor in the eradication of corruption and mismanagement. As we will see throughout this book, governance is a critical issue in economic development.

Why Is There a Development Gap?

As we can see from the different measures of development analyzed above (GDP per capita, poverty, health, education, and urbanization), there are significant differences worldwide in terms of the level of development. The development gap is the first and most important stylized fact in the economics of development and it raises one of the most, if not the most, important questions in the economics of development: Why did some countries develop earlier than others?

The Evolving Development Gap

To get a clear idea of development issues, it is not enough simply to try to understand the development gap, which would give us only a static view. We also need a dynamic view. How is the development gap evolving over time?

The answer is that the gap has closed dramatically for some countries while it has increased for others. There are notable examples of developing economies closing the gap with wealthier nations, but there are also nations experiencing stagnation and decline. We first look at data on economic growth and population dynamics.

Differences in Economic Growth

It is helpful to look at the growth rates of different groups of countries. Figure 1.7 shows average growth rates of GDP per capita (measured in purchasing power parity or PPP) across different developing regions of the world between 1980 and 2010.

As Figure 1.7 reveals, the East Asia and Pacific region has had very strong growth in GDP per capita rates in the last 30 years, at over 4% per year. Growth in South Asia has also been very strong. In contrast, growth in sub-Saharan Africa has been close to zero and in the MENA region (Middle East and North Africa) and in Latin America and the Caribbean, it has been lower than 1%.

On average, China has been growing at over 8% a year, the highest growth rate over that period for any single economy in the world. This means multiplying income per capita by more than a factor of 10 over that period! Other Asian countries such as South Korea, India, Thailand, and Singapore have been growing at a very healthy pace as well—all with an average growth rate above 4% per year. As a consequence, the gap between Asian economies and the advanced industrialized economies has definitely been declining in the last 3

FIGURE 1.7   Average Annual Growth Rate (1980–2010) of GDP Per Capita (PPP) in Constant 2005 Prices

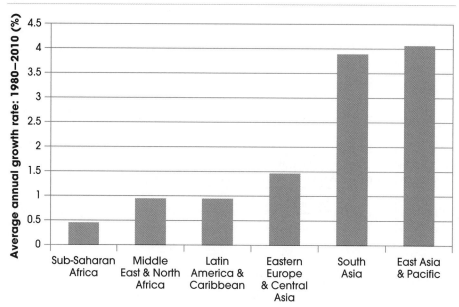

Growth rates of GDP per capita in the last 3 decades have been high in East Asia and the Pacific and South Asia, and low in sub-Saharan Africa, the Middle East and North Africa, and Latin America and the Caribbean.

Source: The World Bank, World Development Indicators, http://databank.worldbank.org.

decades. The fast-growing Asian economies have been often called the "Asian tigers." Figure 1.8 gives average growth rates for a selected number of countries over the same period.

FIGURE 1.8   Average Annual Growth Rate (1980–2010, in %) of GDP Per Capita (PPP) in Constant 2005 Prices for Selected Countries

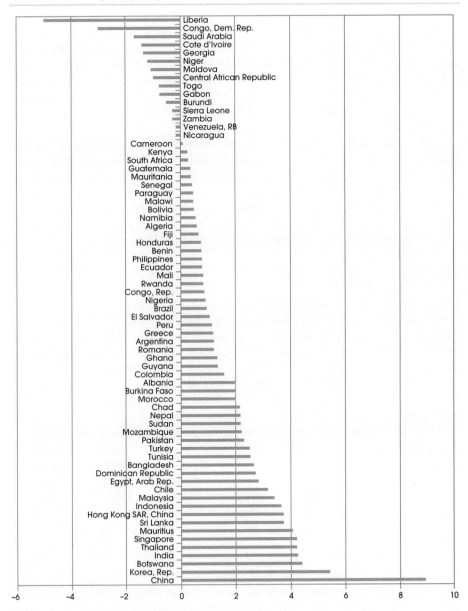

China has had by far the largest growth rate in the last 30 years, while several African countries have had a negative growth rate.

Source: The World Bank, World Development Indicators, http://databank.worldbank.org.

In sub-Saharan Africa, some countries have had very respectable growth rates. This is the case for Botswana and Mauritius, which have had average growth rates of over 4% per year during that period. However, growth rates for most other countries are either around the 1% level, on average, or are even experiencing a negative rate. Many of the poorest countries in the world have not only become poorer relative to the richer countries, but they have also become poorer than they initially were in 1980. This includes some large African countries such as the Democratic Republic of Congo.

Countries in the Middle East and North Africa have had rather low growth rates. Saudi Arabia has had a negative growth rate despite the surge in oil revenues resulting from the 1973 oil embargo placed on Western nations by the Organization of the Petroleum Exporting Countries (OPEC), from which Saudi benefited tremendously. Algeria and Mauritania have had growth rates close to zero. Egypt and Morocco have had the fastest growth, but only at an average of 2.8% and 2% per year respectively.

Latin America has had a lackluster growth performance in the last 30 years with Chile (3.15%) and the Dominican Republic (2.7%) being the only exceptions. Most countries in the region have had an average growth rate between 1% and –1%. The 1980s have often been referred to as a lost decade for Latin America because the region struggled with large foreign debts in a decade of high real interest rates and many countries underwent structural adjustment programs supervised by the International Monetary Fund (IMF).

Population Growth

When considering the evolution of the development gap, population growth is also a relevant variable. Population growth should contribute to GDP growth because a larger population increases the labor force. However, if output growth is slower than population growth, GDP per capita will tend to fall. In addition, if population growth is larger in the poorer countries, the proportion of the poor in the world population will increase more over time. In other words, there will be more and more people on the wrong side of the development gap.

Figure 1.9 shows the population in various regions of the world in 2010 as a multiple of the population in 1960. The world's poorest region, sub-Saharan Africa with a current population of 854 million, has had the highest population growth. In 2010, its population was 3.7 times larger than 50 years ago. The Middle East and North Africa, with a population of 383 million, had the next highest population growth, increasing by more than 250% in 50 years. South Asia, which includes India, has a population of 1,633 million, an increase of 185% in 50 years. East Asia and the Pacific, which includes China, is the most populated region in the world with a combined population of over 2.2 billion. The population growth rate in that region is slightly more than half that of South Asia but still higher than in the Organisation of Economic Co-operation and Development (OECD) countries. Eastern Europe and Central Asia, while covering a large proportion of the planet's territory, only increased their population by 33% in 50 years. These regions currently have a total population of only 890 million. The growth rates show that population growth is highest in the poorest regions of the world, in particular in sub-Saharan Africa,

FIGURE 1.9   Total Population in 2010 as a Multiple of the Population in 1960

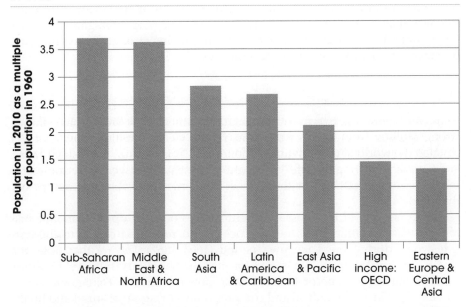

Population growth in the world is highest in the poorer regions.

Source: The World Bank, World Development Indicators, http://databank.worldbank.org.

and because countries in that region have also had less economic growth, this means that the development gap has been increasing there.

To summarize, the development gap has been increasing primarily in Africa, which is already the poorest continent on earth, while the development gap has been decreasing for Asian countries, including China and India. However, a few African countries seem to have been much more successful than others in reducing the gap. Countries in the Middle East and Northern Africa or in Latin America and the Caribbean have had too low a growth rate to be able to catch up with the more advanced industrialized countries. While the development gap has been growing in many of these countries, it has been decreasing in others. How do we explain these significant differences?

Our discussion leads us to formulate another very important question that development economics must confront: Why have some poor countries started to catch up in terms of development while others have failed?

Stories of Economic Catch-Up and Decline

The development gap emerged because some countries developed earlier than others. The British economy took off in the late 18th century, while significant growth in the American economy and most continental European economies began in the 19th century. Some countries, such as Japan and Germany, were subsequently able to catch up on the early developers while others were not. When trying to understand catch-up and decline, it is important to take a historical perspective and look not only at what happened in the past decades, but also at economic evolution over the last centuries. In this section, we analyze some historical success stories of economic catch-up: Japan and Germany. We also analyze historical stories of decline: China, Argentina, and Turkey's Ottoman Empire. These countries have been growing strongly in recent years, but have experienced significant economic decline in the past.

The Historical Catch-Up of Japan and Germany

China and India, the two most populated countries in the world, have shown strong signs of economic catch-up in recent years, but they have not yet equaled the world's most advanced economies. This was not the case for Japan and Germany; during the late-19th century, these nations were very successful in their efforts to catch up with the most economically developed countries of that time.

Japan has one of the most successful stories of catch-up in economic history. It was, traditionally, a feudal society and remained closed to the outside world during the Tokugawa period (1603–1867). During that time, the country was ruled by a dynasty of *shoguns*, or hereditary military dictators. In 1867, the Meiji emperor took back the power from the Tokugawa *shogun* and engaged in a very radical and comprehensive program of social and political reforms. Japan's rigid feudal system, with its division of society into four caste groups (*samurai*, which was the aristocratic warrior class, farmers, artisans, and merchants) was abolished, and the traditional power of the *samurai* was dismantled. The emperor sent missions to Europe and the United States to study the institutions of industrialized countries. Students were sent abroad for education and thousands of Western teachers were hired to instruct Japanese students.

The Japanese government made large infrastructure investments; it built extensive railroad and road systems, and electrification spread rapidly throughout the country. The government vigorously promoted industrialization by financing investments in large factories, setting corporate taxes at a low level, and instituting initiatives to help businessmen create networks of business relationships and associations. Large conglomerates, i.e. business groups known as the *zaibatsu* and composed of various firms that spanned different sectors of the economy (Mitsubishi, Sumitomo, and Nissan are names still familiar today), began to emerge. These conglomerates contributed to vigorous economic growth until World War II. The *zaibatsu* enjoyed large economies of scale and provided a useful structure to firms within the conglomerates for financing investments.

After its defeat in World War II and the destruction of a large part of its infrastructure, Japan recovered quickly and underwent several decades of very spectacular growth based on high-quality and low-cost manufacturing. Massive quantities of Japanese cars, motorcycles, and electronics were exported to markets around the world. Figure 1.10 shows the catch-up process of the Japanese economy. It displays economic historian Angus Maddison's estimate of Japan's per capita income over time as a percentage of that of the United Kingdom and the United States. The United Kingdom was the first country to industrialize and was the most advanced economy in the world during most

FIGURE 1.10   Japan's Per Capita Income as a Percentage of Levels in the United Kingdom and the United States

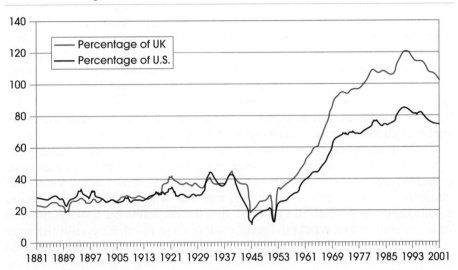

Until World War II, income per capita in Japan was below 40% of the levels in the United Kingdom and the United States. Between 1945 and 1990, Japan caught up with the United Kingdom and reached 80% of the U.S. level.

Source: Maddison, A., "The World Economy: A Millennial Perspective," Organisation for Economic Co-operation and Development, 2007.

of the 19th century. The robust American economy became the world's largest only toward the end of the 19th century. As we can see, in the first decades after the Meiji restoration, Japanese income per capita was less than 30% that of the United Kingdom or the United States. By the beginning of the 1930s, it was over 40%. After a large dip following World War II, a very impressive catch-up process began and by the end of the 1970s, Japan had overtaken the British economy, which had a less-impressive growth rate in the decades following World War II. In the first 2 decades after the war, Japanese income per capita also rose strongly relative to the United States and reached a peak of over 80% around 1990. However, the 1990s were a decade of stagnation for the Japanese economy.

Another example of successful catch-up is that of the German economy. Germany has existed as a country only since 1871. Before that, there were many independent German states. In the 19th century, Germany lagged behind the United Kingdom in its industrialization process. It is only after the unification of Germany that Bismarck, the German chancellor, launched a large-scale industrialization program that focused on the development of heavy industry. German unification itself contributed greatly to the development of markets, as tariffs between German states were abolished. The industrialization process also included the rapid development of railways and the importation of various technologies from the United Kingdom such as steel production. A new type of bank emerged, the **universal bank**, i.e., a financial institution that both lent money to firms but also held equity in industrial enterprises. Universal banking played a very powerful role in using a bank's assets to finance large investments that allowed German industry to enjoy the economies of scale and grow very rapidly. As Figure 1.11 shows, German income per capita was around 60% of the UK level until the last decade of the 19th century when it started to increase, reaching close to 80% by World War I. After World War II, the German economy recovered very quickly from the devastation that followed Hitler's defeat and started growing faster than the British economy, overtaking it by the end of the 1960s. The German economy began to slow down relative to the United Kingdom around the time of the fall of the Berlin Wall in 1989 and German unification in 1990.

The famous economic historian Alexander Gerschenkron, who studied the history of industrialization processes, put forward the idea of "the advantages of backwardness."[1] His thesis was that although latecomers to the industrialization process would have to compete with the early industrializers who did not face any competition, they could nevertheless achieve a faster process of industrialization that would eventually allow them to catch up with the early industrializers. First of all, a latecomer could imitate already existing technologies. Then, if that country could achieve the necessary economies of scale, it

FIGURE 1.11 German Per Capita Income as a Percentage of Levels in the United Kingdom

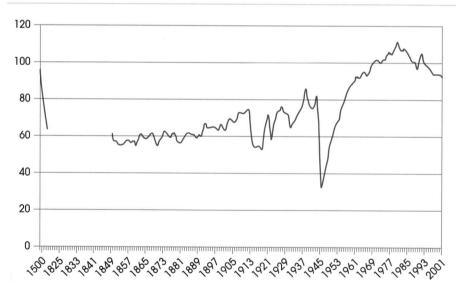

After German unification in 1871, Germany began to catch up economically with the United Kingdom and overtook it during the 1960s.

Source: Maddison, "The World Economy," 2007.

---

[1]Alexander Gerschenkron, *Economic Backwardness in Historical Perspective* (Cambridge, MA: Belknap Press of Harvard University Press, 1962).

could very quickly reach the **industrial frontier**, i.e., a situation in which the most advanced technologies are used in various industrial sectors. The necessity to achieve these economies of scale and the incentive to catch up required sufficiently large amounts of capital, which were provided either by the private sector or by the government. In Germany, universal banks helped finance large-scale investments, while in Japan, this role was played by the *zaibatsu*. State intervention also played an important role by providing the necessary infrastructure investment, opening domestic markets to competition, or shielding infant industries from foreign competition. In both Germany and Japan, the state often directly provided part of the capital necessary for accelerated industrialization. However, while there can be significant advantages to economic backwardness, not all countries are able to use these advantages to their benefit. The data provided earlier in this chapter on the increasing development gap shows that most countries are not able to do so.

The examples of economic catch-up show that the development gap is not necessarily inevitable. It is not true that once a country lags behind, it cannot catch up. While this gives us reasons to be optimistic, the evidence on catch-up does not in itself give us an explanation of how and why it may or may not occur.

Economic Decline

When we look at the big questions of development, it is possible to overlook the fact that certain developing countries were not always poor. Historically, some countries were among the richest in the world, but they descended into poverty or stagnated. The best known example is China.

China was the richest country in the world for at least several centuries. Many modern inventions, such as gunpowder, the crossbow, the abacus, the wheelbarrow, and the compass originated in China. The Chinese invented iron casting and were the first to harness draft animals, which greatly improved agricultural productivity. They invented paper, ink, and printing. The first seismoscopes to register earthquake tremors were built in China.

Figure 1.12 gives estimates by Maddison on GDP per capita in China and Europe at different times in history. Gross domestic product per capita is measured in 1990 international dollars, i.e. using purchasing power parity exchange rates based on 1990 U.S. dollars. Obviously, these numbers are very approximate and represent very imperfect measures of GDP per capita. However, it seems clear that China had higher average living standards than Europe until at least the 14th century or even the beginning of the 17th century. China had higher average living standards than Japan until about the early 19th century. The country then experienced a long period of economic stagnation under the Ming dynasty (1368–1644) and the Qing dynasty (1644–1912). The British colonized China in the 19th century and the country experienced several civil wars in the 19th and early 20th centuries, first between warlords and later between the Nationalists and the Communists who fought for power after the last Qing emperor was deposed. The Chinese economy experienced turbulent years under Mao Zedong (1949–1976) and it was only in 1978 that it started growing economically again once the transition process from socialism to capitalism was initiated.

FIGURE 1.12   Estimates of GDP Per Capita in China and Europe in 1990 International Dollars

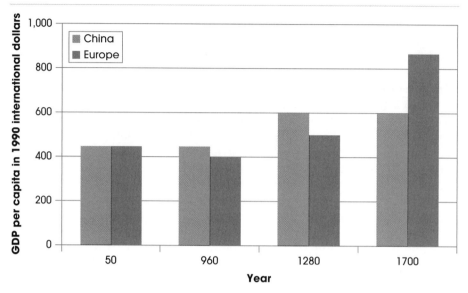

China was richer than Europe until the 17th century.

Source: Maddison, "The World Economy," 2007.

Throughout history, China was not the only country to experience periods of superior economic development as compared to Europe. After the fall of Constantinople (1453), most of Eastern Europe was dominated by the Ottoman Empire, which was for several centuries, militarily superior to most of the contemporaneous European nations. The Ottoman empire controlled not only modern-day Turkey, the Middle East and large parts of Northern Africa, but also most of the Balkans and what constitutes modern Greece, the whole of the former Yugoslavia (apart from Croatia), Romania, Bulgaria, and parts of Hungary, the Crimea and most of the area around the Black Sea. Estimates of living standards are hard to calculate but economic historians Suleyman Ozmucur and Sevket Pamuk have computed statistical time series for the wages of unskilled construction workers in Istanbul, London, Paris, and Vienna from the 15th to the 19th centuries.[2] Wages in Istanbul were always about a third lower than in Western Europe, but in the 19th century they started to decline as these European nations began to industrialize. The Ottoman Empire subsequently declined throughout the 19th century and eventually collapsed during World War I.

Argentina was one of the 10 richest countries in the world in the early 20th century. However, at the end of the century, Argentina had declined relative to all other wealthy countries. Figure 1.13 shows Argentina's GDP per capita as

---

[2]Suleyman Ozmucur and Sevket Pamuk, "Real Wages and Standards of Living in the Ottoman Empire, 1489–1914," *The Journal of Economic History* 62, no. 2 (June 2002): 293–321.

FIGURE 1.13   GDP Per Capita of Argentina as a Percentage of Levels in the United Kingdom and the United States

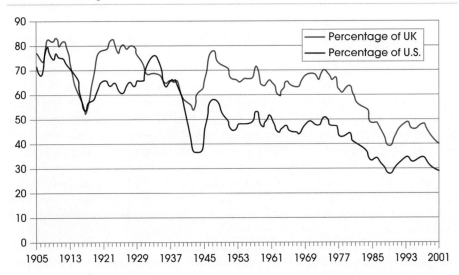

Argentina was one of the richest countries in the world in 1900, with a GDP per capita of 80% of the world's wealthiest countries, the United Kingdom and the United States. However, it experienced continuous decline throughout the 20th century.

Source: Maddison, "The World Economy," 2007.

a percentage of levels in the United Kingdom or the United States throughout the 20th century. Around 1900, Argentina had reached 80% of the levels in the United States and the United Kingdom, but it declined continuously throughout the 20th century. By the year 2000, Argentina's GDP per capita had shrunk to 40% that of the United Kingdom and to 30% that of the United States.

China, Turkey, and Argentina are not the only examples of relative economic decline. Spain was presumably the wealthiest country in the world in the 16th century, but it did not participate in the industrialization process and became one of Europe's poorer economies.

There are other historical examples of economic decline. The Arab Caliphate, the Muslim empire created by Muhammad and his descendants under the Umayyad and Abbasid dynasties, controlled North Africa, most of Spain to the northwest, the Arab peninsula, the Middle East, and large parts of Central Asia. It was a very rich civilization, arguably more advanced than Western Europe at the time, which was undergoing a period of cultural and economic decline during the Dark Ages that followed the fall of the Roman Empire. Throughout what was called the Islamic golden age that lasted more or less until the Crusades (11th and 12th centuries) or the Mongol invasions of Europe (13th century), there was a blossoming of science, culture, and technology. The Arabs made important breakthroughs in medicine, architecture, engineering, and science, in particular mathematics and astronomy. They preserved and expanded knowledge from the ancient Greek and Persian civilizations, which was ultimately passed on to the Europeans during the Renaissance. Commerce was vibrant throughout the Mediterranean and the Middle East during the Islamic golden age. Baghdad was for centuries one of the richest and most culturally sophisticated cities in the world.

There were other civilizations that realized regional or global economic supremacy. Ancient Egypt was probably the wealthiest country in the world from 3200 BCE to 332 BCE, the longest known period of economic supremacy in history. At its height in 500 BCE, the Persian Empire controlled the Middle East and parts of North Africa and Central Asia until Alexander the Great defeated its army in 330 BCE. The Roman Empire and later the Byzantine Empire were both technologically and economically very advanced. It was not until the 15th century that Western Europe achieved the living standards that existed under the Roman Empire a thousand years before. When the Roman Empire split in two in 395 CE and Rome was invaded by barbarian hordes, the Eastern Roman empire, Byzantium, continued to develop rigorously, and was a dominant regional power, only rivaled by the Arabs between the 6th and 11th centuries.

Certainly there are other examples of civilizations that rose and fell before the Industrial Revolution, which permanently changed economies from predominantly rural to predominantly urban and industrial. Apart from Argentina, we probably have not yet witnessed long-term declines in industrialized countries because the history of industrialization is still young and spans only about 250 years. However, it is interesting to note that the United Kingdom, the first country to industrialize, went through a period of relative decline in the 20th century. While it was clearly the richest country in the world in the 19th century, its economic supremacy was lost in the 20th century and it is only toward the end of the 20th century that the British economy began to bounce back. Even within industrialized countries there are whole regions that go through periods of long-term economic decline. This discussion leads us to the following question: Why do some wealthy countries begin to decline and ultimately become poor?

This is obviously a question that concerns both developing countries as well as prosperous economies. The fear is often raised that competition from dynamic developing countries such as China and India might eventually undermine the economies of the richer countries (the Western European nations, the United States, and Japan), resulting in their economic decline.

Important Questions

In this chapter, as we examined the facts that contribute to the development gap, we have asked three important questions:

1. Why did some countries develop earlier than others?
2. Why have some poor countries started to catch up economically while others have failed to develop?
3. Why do some rich countries decline and ultimately become poor?

In this chapter, we have mainly reviewed the factors that contribute to the development gap; as a result, we have not yet tried to provide answers to these questions. Finding answers is what we will attempt to achieve in the chapters that follow. Obviously, these are not the only questions studied in development economics. However, the three questions raised here, especially the first two, are at the crux of most other questions that development economists try to answer. It is critical to keep them in mind as we progress through the book.

Chapter Summary

Facts about the Development Gap

We have presented data on the development gap that shows the differences in income, health, education, and level of urbanization across countries in the world. These data give us a better sense of what we are dealing with when we consider development issues, and they help to inform us about the economies of different countries. The development gap is greatest in sub-Saharan Africa and South Asia. We presented some success stories in health (the Kenyan experience with treated bed nets and the fight against malaria), education (the South Korean education system), and urban development (the experience of Naga City in the Philippines).

The Evolving Development Gap

We examined data on economic growth in the different countries and regions of the world and discussed the fact that some developing countries, mostly in Asia, have been growing rapidly and have begun to close the development gap. Other countries, in particular in Africa, have unfortunately seen the development gap increase in recent decades.

Stories of Economic Catch-Up and Decline

We presented some historical data on the process of economic catch-up that took place in Japan and Germany since the end of the 19th century. We have also seen examples of the opposite tendency, that of decline, in particular the case of Argentina, clearly not the only case of economic decline in history.

Key Terms

development gap
gross domestic product (GDP) per capita
industrial frontier
infant mortality rate
life expectancy

purchasing power parity (PPP)
secondary school enrollment rates
universal bank
urbanization rates

Review Questions

1. Go to the following World Bank webpage: http://www.app.collinsindicate.com/worldbankatlas-global/en-us

   In the search box in the upper right corner of the page, enter the following: GDP per capita, PPP (current international $). A map of the world will appear. If you click on the Play button in the center below, you will see the evolution of the map since 1980. Record your three most important observations and give reasons for your selections.

2. Go to the following World Bank webpage: http://databank.worldbank.org/ddp/home.do

   In the Database section, select the first row, "World Development Indicators." As a new page appears, click "Select all" for countries. As a new page appears, in the list of series, select "GDP per capita, PPP (current international $)." Click the "Select all" button for years. Click "Next." Click the "Map" button. As you can see, there are no data for 1960. Select "1980" in the "Time" box. Do this for other years. Carefully observe the results and note your observations. You can choose other series and other years to display maps of development data.

3. Go on the following World Bank webpage: http://databank.worldbank.org/ddp/home.do

   In the Database section, choose the first row, "World Development Indicators." As a new page appears, click "Select All" for countries. As a new page appears, in the list of series choose "GDP per capita, PPP (current international $)." Click the "Select all" button for years. Click the "Download" button. As a new page appears, click "Excel." You should be able to open the downloaded series as an Excel file, either on a Mac or a PC. Build a chart for 2005. Select the best chart format to present your data.

4. Follow the same steps as in Question 3 above and download for 2005 the series for "Poverty Headcount ratio at $1.25 a day, PPP (% of population)" and "Life expectancy at birth, Total (years)." Display the two variables in a scatter point chart with one variable on the horizontal axis and the other on the vertical axis. What are your main observations? Are there countries with high poverty and high life expectancy? Are there countries with low poverty and low life expectancy?

5. In the May 19, 2012 issue of *The Economist* (www.economist.com), read the article "African child mortality. The best story in development." Find documentation elsewhere about policies that reduce child mortality and discuss through which channels this occurs. What is your opinion on the best policies to address the issue?

6. Read Chapter 2 in Angus Maddison's "The World Economy: A Millennial Perspective" OECD, 2007. What lessons do you take from it on the effects of Western expansion on countries in Asia, Latin America, and Africa?

7. Choose a developing country and look up the data analyzed in this chapter on GDP per capita, the poverty headcount ratio, life expectancy, infant mortality, secondary school enrollment, urbanization, and population for that country. How have these data evolved in the last 20 years? Interpret these evolutions.

8. In *Poor Economics: A Radical Rethinking of the Way to Fight Global Poverty* (Public Affairs Book 2012) by Abhijit Banerjee and Esther Duflo, read Chapter 2. How do you relate the story of Pak Solhin's descent into poverty to the issues we have just discussed in this chapter? What is the main lesson from Banerjee and Duflo's chapter on hunger among the poor in developing economics?

9. Look up the Programme for International Student Assessment (PISA) data base on international student assessment at http://pisa2006.acer.edu.au.

   Look up scores for reading, math, and science at the grade 7 level. In each category, which are the five developing countries (non-OECD countries) that do best and the five that do worst? Do you see patterns in your results? How do you interpret these results?

10. In Daron Acemoglu and James Robinson's *Why Nations Fail* (Crown Business Publishers, 2012), read Chapter 3. Does the theory in that chapter help explain the development gap? How?

Poverty and Inequality

Roughly one quarter of the world population currently lives on less than 1 dollar a day. About half of the world population lives on less than 2 dollars a day. How can families live on such a meager amount? Picture life in Beru village in the southwest corner of Haiti. The terrible earthquake of 2010 that hit Port-au-Prince, the capital of Haiti, is still vivid in the residents' memories and media coverage of the disaster revealed to the world the conditions of extreme poverty in Haiti. Beru village is a day-and-a-half hike from the town of Les Anglais and it is very difficult to reach. Although the villagers enjoy views of nature's beauty, poverty is pervasive. People live in small tin-roof or thatched-roof huts with walls made out of woven wood and surfaced with a mixture of dung and mud. These 200-square-foot huts house extended households that average 10 people. There is no electricity, no plumbing, and the nearest source of water is a polluted spring 2 hours walk from the village. Avocadoes are one of the main sources of food, so hunger is less prevalent in the village than in the slums of Haitian cities where, even before the earthquake, children were fed mud-laced cakes to ease their hunger. In Beru, the school is nothing more than a tin roof on concrete pillars with a partial wall. The children sit on the dirt floor. They have neither school materials nor even a teacher. They sit there for the duration of the school day and the older children take care of the younger ones.

Haiti is one of the poorest countries in the world, but its richest citizens have been enjoying living standards that are equivalent to those of the most affluent Americans. Living in secluded villas, rich families have, in the past decades, been able to accumulate large fortunes. Most of their wealth was sent abroad and deposited in foreign banks during the ultra-repressive regimes of the Duvalier family, first that of father "Papa Doc" who ruled between 1957 and 1971 and then that of his son "Bébé (Baby) Doc" between 1971 and 1986, until he was overthrown by a popular uprising. Jean-Bertrand Aristide, a priest who tried to defend the interests of the poor, was elected president in 1991. However, the rich families of Haiti were still very powerful and were able to oust Aristide through a military coup. He was again elected president in 2001 and overthrown yet again in 2004. This is an example of how extreme poverty and income inequality contribute to instability and political unrest in poorer nations.

Economists have been studying poverty for many years and have devoted great effort to developing tools to measure poverty accurately. In the first part of this chapter, we will examine the tools for defining and measuring poverty on our planet. We will ask: How has poverty evolved over time? What are the trends in various geographic regions?

In the second part of this chapter, we will examine economic inequality in developing countries. On a global scale, the richest 2% of the world population own more than 50% of its wealth.[1] What about inequality on a country-by-country basis? While some poor countries have a relatively egalitarian distribution of wealth and income, other countries are much more inequitable than the United States (which, among the advanced economies of the world, is one of the most inequitable).[2] How do we measure inequality? What determines the gap between the rich and the poor, and why does it vary across countries? Does inequality tend to increase or decrease over time? Is inequality good or bad for growth? We will see that while inequality has increased in many countries, the spectacular growth in China, India, and other Asian countries has led to a decline of overall income inequality worldwide.

Poverty Measurement and Comparisons

In order to fight poverty, international organizations, governments, and **nongovernmental organizations (NGOs)** have worked to establish policies that support and aid those in need on the planet.[3] To identify those who are in need, we need to be able to measure poverty in a meaningful way and compare poverty levels among various countries.

Measuring Poverty

While it may seem easy to recognize poverty, it is difficult to define and measure it properly so as to make meaningful international comparisons. In this section, we examine the main methods used to measure poverty.[4]

Poverty measurements are usually based on survey data. A **survey** is a sampling of data based on questionnaires asked of a limited but representative subset of the population to be assessed.

Local poverty assessments. Researchers trying to survey poverty in developing countries sometimes ask the people in villages who among them is poor. These questions usually receive the typical answers: the poorest in a village are often the disabled, the ill, the elderly, the widows, and the weaker members of the community who do not get enough support from their families. However, when villagers find out that the surveys will be used to target poverty relief,

---

[1]James B. Davies, Susanna Sandström, Anthony Shorrocks, and Edward N. Wolff, "The World Distribution of Household Wealth," 2008 UNU-WIDER Discussion Paper No. 2008/3.

[2]In 2001 in the United States, 10% of the population controlled 69.8% of the wealth. Davies et al., "The World Distribution of Household Wealth," 2008.

[3]Nongovernmental organizations (NGOs) are voluntary private associations pursuing nonprofit motives such as promoting health, education, or peace. They are mainly funded through gifts and grants. They may receive money from a government, but are not under any form of government control.

[4]A very complete and informative survey on the definition and measurement of poverty can be found in Angus Deaton, "Measuring Poverty in a Growing World (or Measuring Growth in a Poor World)," *Review of Economics and Statistics* 87, no. 1 (February 2005): 1–19.

they tend to declare that the whole village is poor. In these situations, the incentives faced by villagers may cause surveys to overestimate the extent of poverty.

Calorie counting. Another approach for estimating poverty involves **calorie counting,** determining the minimal cost of 2,000 calories worth of food per day, the average daily number of calories humans need. Because poverty has always been associated with hunger, obtaining enough food to survive is the very first economic priority for poor households. How does a poverty calculation based on calorie counting work? First, the researcher determines the caloric value of an ounce of food, be it rice, beans, or chicken. Then, the researcher finds the calorie count of a dollar's worth of these different types of foods to see how many calories a dollar of rice buys, how many calories a dollar of chicken buys, and so on. For example, an ounce of chicken contains roughly 50 calories. Say that a dollar buys a pound (16 oz) of chicken. A dollar thus buys $16 \times 50 = 800$ calories. The next step is to take the foods that buy the most calories for the same price and calculate how much it costs to buy the equivalent of 2,000 calories. In other words, economists try to find the diet that "buys" 2,000 calories the cheapest. This then determines a level of income below which people are considered poor. This calorie count is sometimes adjusted for gender and the type of work people do. For example, men doing hard physical work farming or fishing may need more than 2,000 calories per day, while women who work in the service sector may need less.

The calorie counting approach to measuring poverty puts significant constraints on people's diets. The cheapest way to get 2,000 calories is a mixture of beans and rice (or other legumes or cereal grains). While this combination might be the cheapest way to evade hunger, we cannot expect people to live on such a diet every day of their lives, and must take into account nutrition, food preferences, availability of diverse food choices, and eating habits.

Poverty line. A less stringent approach than calculating the cheapest basket of food that provides 2,000 calories is to look at the food basket people actually buy and calculate how much income is necessary to buy the equivalent of 2,000 calories of those foods. The **poverty line** is the income required to purchase 2,000 calories of food, taking into account food habits and preferences. Those families or individuals with income below the poverty line are considered poor, whereas those with income above that line are not. A related statistic is the **poverty headcount,** the number of people in a given population who are below the poverty line. The **poverty headcount ratio** is the proportion of that population that is below the poverty line. If N is the population of a country and Q is the poverty headcount, the poverty headcount ratio, denoted as H, is $H = Q/N$. The poverty line is a useful measure because all of those people below the poverty line are expected to be the most vulnerable to increases in food prices that can threaten their very survival.

In practice, the calculation of the income necessary to purchase 2,000 calories of food is rarely updated on a regular basis. Instead, the poverty line is typically updated by adjusting for inflation. In other words, if the cost of living increases by 5%, economists will increase the poverty line by 5%. This is not an accurate method because the basket of goods used to calculate the consumer price index is typically not the same as the basket of goods used to calculate the poverty line. If the prices of basic foodstuffs used in the poverty line calculation increase by 8% and the consumer price index increases only by 5%, then a 5% adjustment to the calculation of the poverty line will be too low by 3%. In some countries, the price adjustment of the poverty line is done more accurately by taking into account only the prices of the basket of foods bought by the average poor. However, even in that case, the basket itself is rarely updated to take into account changes in the consumption habits of the poor.

Another challenge in measuring poverty using the poverty line is that with urbanization and the decline of agriculture, people tend to need less calories. Using the same calorie standard in cities as in rural areas tends to overestimate the poverty line in cities relative to the countryside. In principle, research should adjust for a lower calorie count in cities, but there is no exact way to do this.

A related issue is that people in cities tend to be better organized politically and are closer to the sites of power than those in the countryside. The

The Effect of the 2008 Food Price Hikes on the World's Poor

For people living at or near the poverty line, an increase of 10% in the price of food means roughly a decrease of 10% in the amount of food they can afford. Large price swings can easily plunge hundreds of millions of people into acute hunger or even starvation.

In 2008, the price of many basic food items in developing countries increased substantially, leading to episodes of hunger and food protests. The international price of wheat roughly doubled within a year and the price of rice doubled or tripled in many places, leading various Asian governments such as Indonesia and India to suspend their exports of rice. In June of that year, the price of wheat in Pakistan went up by more than 25%. The increased cost of rice and cereals in the world contributed to pushing 120 million people into hunger in 2008. The price of meat and dairy products also went up dramatically, making meat, in particular, unaffordable for most poor people.

In Haiti, one of the poorest countries in the world, the 2008 crisis was particularly devastating. The price of rice, beans, fruit, and condensed milk went up by 50% during the first half of 2008. The most vulnerable were Haiti's children, dozens of whom died of malnourishment at the height of the food crisis. In order to quell their hunger, people were eating "dirt cookies," made from a combination of clay, soil, and salt, that had no nutritional value and contained toxins and parasites that caused illness. The crisis became worse after storms flooded fields in late summer and destroyed a large part of the harvest. Emergency food aid from the international community avoided widespread starvation.

In 2010, a 7.0 earthquake hit Haiti and killed at least 100,000 people, causing even more devastation to the already impoverished country and its minimal infrastructure. The nation's extreme poverty was one of the reasons for the high number of casualties resulting from the earthquake: in its aftermath, undernourished people were living in unsafe dwellings with little or no sanitation or medical facilities. Emergency aid from the international community was again organized to alleviate the consequences of this natural disaster. Three years later, in 2013 more than 300,000 Haitians were still living in temporary shelters.

urban poor would resist any attempt to lower the poverty line because of the negative effect such a measure might have on government decisions to redistribute income toward those living at or below the current line. As a result, it is difficult to keep politics out of the determination of the poverty line.

The poverty gap. Another problem with determining a definition for the poverty line is that someone with an income 1 cent above the poverty line would not be declared poor, while someone with an income 1 cent below the poverty line would be. Common sense suggests that these people have roughly the same income, but how can one be declared poor and not the other? If a government were judged by how much it reduces poverty, it could theoretically give very small transfers of aid to those who are slightly below the poverty line to get them barely above the line. Theoretically, it could even take assistance away from the very poor to finance small transfers to those who are slightly below the poverty line. This process, targeting the "richest" of the poor, would only improve the country's poverty score on paper without doing much to alleviate actual poverty.

A solution to this problem is to measure the **poverty gap** (also called the total poverty gap) that, unlike the poverty headcount, takes into account the degree of poverty, or the distance to the poverty line. The poverty gap assesses people below the poverty line according to their distance from the line. For example, an individual with an income equal to 90% of the poverty line would be counted with a weight of 10% (10% below the poverty line), while someone with an income equal to 10% of the poverty line would be counted with a weight of 90% (90% below the poverty line). In practice, it is difficult to obtain exact data on the income of all those below the poverty line, but researchers can compute the poverty gap by multiplying the poverty headcount Q by the average distance of the poor from the poverty line, in proportion to the poverty line. Calling y_q the average income of the poor who are below the poverty line and z the poverty line, the poverty gap PG is thus calculated as follows:

$$PG = Q(z - y_q)/z$$

A related calculation is the average poverty gap APG, obtained by dividing PG by N the population:

$$APG = (Q/N)(z - y_q)/z = H(z - y_q)/z$$

This calculation can be compared with the poverty headcount ratio because it gives a measure of poverty relative to the general population.

Table 2.1 illustrates how we calculate the average poverty gap. We take a very simple numerical example and assume a poverty line of 1 dollar a day. Take two countries, A and B, that have total populations of 200 million each with 100 million below the poverty line, i.e., with a poverty headcount ratio of 50%. A close look at Table 2.1 shows, however, that in country B, 80 million people have a daily income of less than 50 cents while in country A, only 20 million people have a daily income below 50 cents. In other words, country B has a larger concentration of people with an income below 50 cents compared to country A, even though both countries have the same poverty headcount

TABLE 2.1   An Example of the Poverty Headcount Ratio and the Average Poverty Gap

Income distribution below poverty line (daily income)	Between 0 and 25 cents	Between 25 and 50 cents	Between 50 and 75 cents	Between 75 cents and 1 dollar	Poverty headcount ratio (in %)	Average poverty gap (in %)
Country A (millions of people)	10	10	40	40	50	17.5
Country B (millions of people)	40	40	10	10	50	32.5

Country A and country B both have 50% of the population below the poverty line. However, there is more extreme poverty in country B than in country A. The average poverty gap takes this difference into account.

ratio. We can use the data in this example to compute the average poverty gap in each country.

In country A, $H = 50\%$, $z = 1$, and $y_q = [(20 \times 0.25) + (80 \times 0.75)]/100 = 0.65$. We thus find that $APG = 50\%(1 - 0.65)/1 = 17.5\%$. Another way of looking at this is as follows: 10 million people have a daily income between 0 and 25 cents, and 10 million people have a daily income between 25 and 50 cents. In other words, 20 million people, or 10% of the population, have an average distance of 75 cents from the poverty line. Similarly, we can see that 80 million people, or 40% of the population, have an average distance of 25 cents from the poverty line. The average poverty gap is:

$$(10 \times 0.75) + (40 \times 0.25) = 17.5\%.$$

Turning to country B, we see that

$$H = 50\%, z = 1, \text{ and } y_q = [(80 \times 0.25) + (20 \times 0.75)]/100 = 0.35$$

As a result, $APG = 50\%(1 - 0.35)/1 = 32.5\%$. From a different perspective, 40% of the population has an average daily income of 25 cents and 10% of the population has an average daily income of 75 cents. The average poverty gap is thus

$$(40 \times 0.75) + (10 \times 0.25) = 32.5\%,$$

which is higher than in country A.

An easy interpretation of the average poverty gap is the percentage of the population to which one would have to give a dollar a day in order to make sure nobody lives below the poverty line (of 1 dollar a day). This is, of course, a fictitious transfer, but it reflects the fact that people below the poverty line are counted with weights according to the distance between their income and the poverty line. Note that the average poverty gap is by definition smaller than the poverty headcount ratio. These measures would be equal only if those living below the poverty line had an income of zero.

Table 2.2. gives both the poverty headcount ratio and the average poverty gap for selected countries. Take Bangladesh and the Democratic Republic of the Congo, referred to henceforth as Congo. Both have a poverty headcount

TABLE 2.2   The Poverty Headcount Ratio and the Average Poverty Gap for Selected Countries

	The poverty headcount ratio in 2005 (in %)	The average poverty gap in 2005 (in %)
Bangladesh	49.6	13.1
Bolivia	19.6	9.7
Cambodia	40.2	11.3
Democratic Republic of the Congo	54.1	22.8
Nigeria	65.9	29.6
Peru	8.2	2.0

The poverty headcount ratio shows the percentage of the population of the selected countries that lives below the poverty line (here, 1 dollar a day). The average poverty gap indicates what percentage of the population would have to receive a transfer equivalent to 1 dollar a day in order for poverty to be eradicated in those countries.

Source: United Nations, http://millenniumindicators.un.org/unsd/mdg/SeriesDetail.aspx?srid=580 and http://millenniumindicators.un.org/unsd/mdg/SeriesDetail.aspx?srid=584.

ratio around 50% (49.6% for Bangladesh and 54.1% for Congo). However, the average poverty gap in Congo is nearly twice that in Bangladesh, suggesting that among those living below the poverty line, there is more extreme poverty in Congo relative to Bangladesh.

Even though the average poverty gap gives a more accurate view of poverty than does the poverty headcount ratio, it is not always possible to compute the poverty gap accurately, as we need data on the income distribution of those below the poverty line.

How to Compare Poverty Levels

Our next task is comparing measures of poverty across countries. The poverty line varies from country to country. Most of the poor in the United States would not qualify as poor in India. For comparisons across countries to be meaningful, we need to compare poverty only across developing countries, excluding the wealthy developed nations.

Poverty lines and exchange rates. One method that compares poverty across countries takes a particular country's poverty line and converts it into other countries' currencies. For example, we can take the poverty line of India in rupees and the poverty line in Thailand in baht and convert them into dollars using current exchange rates. With the Indian and Thai poverty lines expressed in U.S. dollar terms, we can make an objective comparison.

A problem arises with this method because exchange rates between currencies only reflect the prices of exported and imported goods. All goods that are not exported and imported are called **non-tradables.** These goods are very important for the poor because in developing countries, the poor are unable to buy expensive imported goods. As a result, currency conversions of poverty lines based on exchange rates may give a misleading comparison of living standards across countries.

Poor countries usually have low prices for non-tradable goods because of the low wages in those countries. We know that the price of a haircut is a common example because the technology and skills needed for a haircut are roughly the same all over the world. The price of a haircut in richer countries is more expensive than in poor countries because the wages of a barber or hairdresser, the main cost, are higher compared to the wages in poorer countries. For example, the price of a haircut in the United States is about $20, but in India you can easily get a haircut for 20 rupees, which is roughly 45 cents using the market exchange rate of 45 rupees for 1 dollar. This example of the significant difference in the prices of non-tradable goods in developed and developing countries explains why it is impossible to live anywhere in the United States for 1 dollar a day, while in the poorest countries, it is possible to purchase more goods and services with the equivalent of 1 dollar in local currency. Tourists traveling to poor countries often find that goods and services are "cheap" relative to their home country for this same reason. The same is true when comparing prices of non-tradable goods between developing countries. For example, the prices of non-tradable goods are likely to be higher in Brazil than, say, in Congo because income per capita is higher in Brazil. A comparison of Brazil's and Congo's poverty lines using the exchange rate would thus tend to underestimate Brazil's poverty headcount or overestimate Congo's poverty headcount because the prices of non-tradables are lower in the latter country.

Purchasing power parity. Because the market exchange rates of poorer developing countries are based only on imports and exports do not incorporate differences in the prices of non-tradable goods, how can we meaningfully compare living standards of the poor across countries? We can address this problem in part by computing **purchasing power parity (PPP) exchange rates**, which are calculated so that a typical basket of goods in two countries, including non-tradables, would have the same value when using the PPP exchange rate.

In practice, PPP indices are based on a large basket of goods and services that are representative of people's average expenditures: lodging, food, transport, education, health, etc. The idea of purchasing power parity is that the same basket of goods should have the same value in two countries. For example, if a basket of goods is worth $1,000 in the United States and worth 1,500 ringgit in Malaysia, then the PPP exchange rate between the U.S. dollar and the Malaysian ringgit should be 1.5 ringgits for 1 dollar. In May 2012, the market exchange rate was 3.03 ringgits per dollar, suggesting an undervaluation of the ringgit relative to the PPP exchange rate.

Thus, when making international comparisons of poverty lines, it is best to use PPP indices rather than market exchange rates. That said, PPP exchange rates have limitations, too. They only reflect average living standards in a given country. The actual basket of goods and services consumed by the poor is, in general, very different from the average basket of goods and services consumed in that country, even if it is a developing country. Because of this, PPP exchange rates may not accurately reflect the living standards of the poor. Ideally, we need to compare baskets of goods and services consumed by the very poor across developing countries, but this information is not yet available on a large enough scale. In addition, the cost of living is lower in rural areas than in urban areas.

Other international challenges of surveys. Even if we were able to find a good exchange rate with which to compare the living standards of the poor, international comparisons are still an issue because surveys to determine the poverty line are done differently in different countries. In some countries, people are asked about their incomes, while in others, they are asked to report their expenditures. However, expenditure reports can differ from income reports in as many ways as people save, borrow, receive money, and sometimes hide income. Moreover, it may be more difficult for people to remember accurately their expenditures rather than their income. Unfortunately, there is no straightforward way to convert income into expenditures without doing additional surveys.

Other problems arise from the type of information on which the surveys focus. For example, estimate what you spent in the last week. Now think of what you spent in the last month. Are your weekly expenditures exactly one-fourth of your monthly costs? Probably not. Asking about expenditures over a longer period provides a clear idea of people's average purchases. If asked to report only over a 7-day period, people might have bought more or less during that period than what they would on average. Over a period of 1 month, the error is likely to be smaller. However, over a 1-month period, people are very likely to forget many of their expenditures.These differences can be quite substantial. In India, surveys typically cover expenditures over a monthly period. However, in an experiment to see how monthly and weekly numbers varied, some people were randomly chosen to report over a monthly period, while others were randomly chosen to report over a 7-day period. On average, households reported roughly 30% more food purchased over the 7-day reporting period and 18% more on other expenditures. Such a measurement error could cut the poverty headcount in India by half![5] All of these issues should make us aware that the data gathered on poverty are necessarily very imperfect.

One dollar a day. The 1-dollar-a-day methodology that the World Bank has pioneered and used defines an international poverty line. In an early study, Martin Ravallion from the World Bank and two co-authors noticed that national poverty lines in developing countries tended to be clustered around 1 dollar a day.[6]

The World Bank, in its annual World Development Report for 1990, used the 1-dollar-a-day-standard as the international poverty line. The 1-dollar–a-day definition of extreme poverty was subsequently adopted at the 2000 Millennium Summit, where world leaders met at the United Nations

---

[5] Angus Deaton, "Measuring Poverty," 2005 and Abhijit Banerjee, Roland Benabou, and Dilip Mookherjee, eds., *Understanding Poverty* (Oxford: Oxford University Press, 2006): 3–16.

[6] Martin Ravallion, Gaurav Datt, and Dominique van de Walle, "Quantifying Absolute Poverty in the Developing World," *Review of Income and Wealth*, 37 no. 4 (December 1991): 345–361.

headquarters in New York to define the Millennium Development goals. The first Millennium Development goal aims at halving the proportion of people living on less than 1 dollar a day. The World Bank has since then been in charge of measuring how many people live under 1 dollar a day. However, while the 1-dollar-a-day definition is an easy headline grabber, the value of 1 dollar varies over time. Moreover, poverty surveys are not conducted frequently and are fraught with measurement errors, as seen above. In 2001, the World Bank decided to use PPP exchange rates based on the prices of 1993. It also decided to use a definition of $1.08 a day as the international poverty line. Since then, it has systematically used national household surveys in developing countries to find out how many people were living under this international poverty line. Efforts are contiuing to refine and update the definition of the international poverty line as are the World Bank's efforts to make national poverty surveys as comparable as possible.

Poverty Rates in Practice

Poverty rates provide critical information for policymakers. If a nation's poverty rates are increasing, we know that some of its policies are falling short and we should determine how to reverse that trend. If the poverty rate is decreasing, that means a nation's policies are effective. If we can determine the causes of the decrease, then we can shape existing policy to reduce poverty even more.

Here again, we face measurement issues. The basic challenge is how to compare poverty across time. The World Bank uses the well-known measure of 1 dollar a day to measure the poverty line, but prices vary over time. Using 1993 prices, one dollar a day in 2001 represents an income of $340 for that year, but using 1985 prices yields an income of $495 for that same year. While significant research has been done in this area over recent years, there is, unfortunately, still no method for measuring the evolution of poverty over time on which everyone agrees.

Chen and Ravallion's data. Shaohua Chen and Martin Ravallion were the first researchers to publish an authoritative study on international poverty following the definition of the Millennium Development Goals in 2000.[7] They are considered among the world's best experts on the subject of poverty and have done many of the World Bank's studies on the subject. The Chen and Ravallion estimates are generally considered the most accurate and the most detailed among poverty studies because they are the only ones that rely solely on household consumption surveys. As we discussed above, these surveys are often not conducted in the same way and their comparability across countries is not perfect. However, the national accounting and income data from developing countries, which had been used very frequently in the past to measure poverty, are now considered by researchers to be even more unreliable than consumption surveys.

---

[7]Shaohua Chen and Martin Ravallion, "How Have the World's Poorest Fared since the Early 1980s?" *World Bank Research Observer* 19 no. 2 (2004): 141–169.

The latest estimates from the Chen and Ravallion team are from 2008.[8] They use a poverty line of $1.25 a day based on 2005 PPP exchange rates. The data were constructed using 675 household surveys across 116 developing countries spanning the period 1981–2005. Over 1.2 million randomly sampled households were interviewed for the 2005 estimate, a sample that is representative of 96% of the population of the developing world. Table 2.3 gives Chen and Ravallion's estimates of the number (poverty headcount) and percentage of the population (poverty headcount ratio) in different regions of the world.

In the bottom-right row of Table 2.3, in 2005, we can see that 25.19% of people on the planet were living below the poverty line, down from 51.87% in 1981. Reduction in poverty was the greatest in East Asia and the Pacific. In 1981, we see that 77.67% of the region was below the poverty line (over a billion people), while in 2005, only 16.78% (slightly over 300 million people) were below the line. In a quarter of a century, poverty has significantly declined in East Asia. A major factor in this decrease is the growth miracle in China. In 1981, we see that 84.02% of the Chinese population was below the poverty line, while in 2005 that percentage was reduced to 15.92%.

After East Asia, the Middle East and Northern Africa have had the biggest reductions in poverty. The poverty headcount ratios (expressed in percentages) decreased from 7.87% in 1981 to 3.6% in 2005, making poverty very marginal in that part of the world.

TABLE 2.3   The Poverty Headcount and Headcount Ratio Based on $1.25 a Day

	Poverty headcount (in millions)			Poverty headcount ratio (percent)		
	1981	1993	2005	1981	1993	2005
East Asia and Pacific	1071.49	845.26	316.21	77.67	50.77	16.78
China				84.02	53.69	15.92
Europe and Central Asia	7.06	20.05	17.29	1.67	4.26	3.65
Latin America and the Caribbean	47.08	46.64	45.25	12.87	10.1	8.22
Brazil				17.1	12.97	7.76
Middle East and North Africa	13.66	9.85	10.99	7.87	4.07	3.6
South Asia	548.29	559.42	595.58	59.35	46.94	40.34
India				73.17*	58.46	50.91
Sub-Saharan Africa	212.25	317.36	388.38	53.37	56.87	50.91
Total	1899.82	1798.57	1373.69	51.87	39.19	25.19

Table 2.3 shows the number of people (in millions) living on less than $1.25 a day in different regions of the world between 1981 and 2005, the most recent year for which those measures exist. The same data are also shown as a percentage of the populations of the different regions.

Source: The World Bank, http://iresearch.worldbank.org/PovcalNet/povDuplic.html.
*1977 instead of 1981.

[8]Martin Ravallion, Shaohua Chen, and Prem Sangraula, "Dollar a Day Revisited," *World Bank Economic Review*, 2009: 163–184.

South Asia has also had a decline in poverty rates. In 1981, the headcount ratio was 59.35% and by 2005, it had decreased to 40.34%. This reflects the reduction in poverty rates in India, the biggest country in South Asia. Given that the decline in poverty rates is less spectacular than in East Asia and that more than half of the planet lives in Asia, South Asia is currently the region of the world with the largest number of poor people. Moreover, the total number of South Asian people below the poverty line has increased from 548.29 million people in 1981 to 595.58 million people in 2005.

In Latin America and sub-Saharan Africa, poverty has declined more slowly than in other regions. In sub-Saharan Africa, nearly 51% of the population was still below the poverty line in 2005, hardly a change from 53.37% in 1981. Sub-Saharan Africa had a lower poverty headcount ratio in 1981 than did East Asia, but by 2005, sub-Saharan Africa had by far the highest poverty rate of any region of the world.

Europe and Central Asia is the only region in the world to have had both a relative and absolute increase in poverty, with the poverty headcount ratio increasing from 1.67% in 1981 to 3.65% in 2005. This is the result of the transition process from socialism to capitalism, which has significantly increased poverty primarily in the countries of the former Soviet Union such as Russia, the Ukraine, Kazakhstan, Uzbekistan, and Turkmenistan. These increased poverty levels are the result of both a substantial fall in economic output and a large increase in income inequality following the introduction of the market economy in these nations.

Measurements and Comparisons of Income Inequality

Research on income inequality describes the differences in income and wealth between the poor and the rich. Few people are indifferent to income inequality. Some think it is very important to fight it, while others consider it is a necessary evil for economic development. The causes and consequences of income inequality have been the focus of significant economic research. We will begin our discussion with how to measure it.

Measuring Income Inequality

Measuring income inequality is not straightforward. How can we compare the situation of a developing country in which 80% of a population is poor but its richest citizens are not much richer than middle-class people, to another developing country in which only 40% of the population is poor but the top 10% are extremely rich and have a "jet-set" lifestyle? Determining which country has the most income inequality is not easy to do.

The answer depends on many factors. We need to look at the income distribution as a whole in each of the countries we are examining. Ideally, we would like to use as much information as possible from a country's income distribution. At the same time, we also want to express inequality in terms of a single number in order to compare inequality across countries and time easily.

Researchers have a variety of different tools for measuring inequality, but we will only cover the most frequently used.

Quantile measures. To divide the population of a country into income categories, researchers use **quantile measures**. Particular examples of quantiles are quartiles (4 groups), quintiles (5 groups), and deciles (10 groups). Researchers frequently compute a **quantile ratio**, a ratio of the average income in the highest quantile over the average income in the lowest quantile. For example, the ratio of the richest decile over the poorest decile measures the ratio of the average income of the top 10% of incomes over the average income of the bottom 10% of incomes. Similarly, we can compute a quintile ratio (the top 20% over the bottom 20%) or a quartile ratio (the top 25% over the bottom 25%). In Brazil, for example, the quintile ratio is 30, which means that the average income of the top 20% is 30 times higher than that of the bottom 20%.

Although quantile measures are easy to compute, they do not use all the available income distribution information. The decile ratio will only use information on the income of the top and bottom 10%, neglecting the 80% who are in between. The quartile ratio uses more information (the top and bottom 25%), but the information is more diluted as it hides information about income distribution among the top or bottom 25%. The bottom 10% might be very poor while the next 10% above them might have a decent income; the average will hide this discrepancy. However, although quantile ratios do not efficiently use income distribution information, they are very useful when information about the whole range of income distribution is poor or unreliable. For example, in some countries, only the wealthy report their incomes and pay income tax; as a result, researchers have then no other choice than to rely on survey data to gather information about the incomes of the poor in order to compute quantiles. For a variety of reasons, using surveys to estimate the incomes of the middle class would likely be even more tricky than for the poor for various reasons. They may be reluctant to accurately report their income or their expenditure patterns are more complex than those of the poor, so they may make more mistakes in reporting expenditures.

The Lorenz curve. Economists present information on income distribution graphically with the **Lorenz curve**, which plots the cumulative income share of different quantiles for the whole range of income distribution, as shown in Figure 2.1.

On the horizontal axis, we rank incomes from the poorest to the richest using quintiles (5 income categories). The Lorenz curve indicates the cumulative share of income held by the cumulative share of the population.

In Figure 2.1, starting from the bottom left, the first coordinates tell us that the bottom 20% of the population only have 5% of total income. The bottom 40% have 15% of total income, which means that the second quintile has 10% of total income. The bottom 60% have 35% of total income, which means that the third quintile has 20% of total income, and so on.

How unequal is the income distribution illustrated in Figure 2.1.? How can we use the Lorenz curve to evaluate income inequality in a country?

FIGURE 2.1   The Lorenz Curve

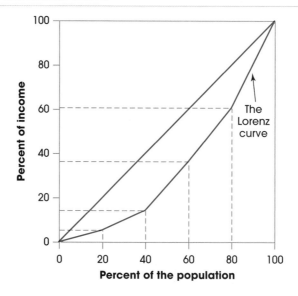

The Lorenz curve plots the share of income (on the vertical axis) held by the poorest quintile to the richest quintile of the population.

Equal versus unequal income distribution. Consider two extremes, a completely equal and a completely unequal distribution of income, extremes that are depicted in Figure 2.2. With a perfectly equal income distribution, everybody would have the same income. In that case, 20% of the population would have 20% of total income, 40% would have 40% of total income, and so on. The Lorenz curve would be identical to the diagonal line in Figure 2.2.

What does a highly unequal distribution of income look like? Imagine that the first 99% of the population have no income and that all the income was held by 1% of the population. In that case, the Lorenz curve would be completely flat until it reached the 99% population threshold, at which point it would spike up to 100%, as shown in Figure 2.2. In other words, it would look like a flat horizontal line followed by a vertical line just before 100%. In reality, we will never encounter these extreme forms of income distribution. Nevertheless, they give us an idea of what an equal and an unequal distribution of income would look like on the Lorenz curve.

The Gini coefficient. How can we use the information provided by the Lorenz curve to compare different distributions of income in different countries? Suppose that one Lorenz curve is close to the diagonal and that another is a more horizontal line. We know that the latter represents a more unequal distribution of income. However, comparing two countries might be more difficult if the Lorenz curves cross each other. How do we determine which country has a more unequal income distribution? How can we use all the information about income distribution to compute a single number that enables us to compare inequality across countries?

FIGURE 2.2   Lorenz Curve with Extremely Equal and Unequal Income Distribution

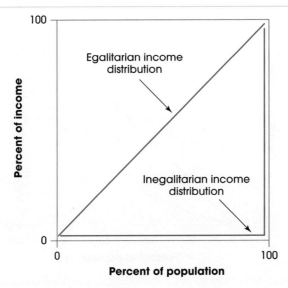

If everyone in a given population has the same income (fully equal income distribution), then the Lorenz curve would follow the diagonal line. If all income were held by the wealthiest 1% of that population (completely unequal income distribution), the Lorenz curve would be a flat horizontal line between 0 and 99% of income and a vertical line thereafter.

We can use the Lorenz curve to construct such a number, which is called the **Gini coefficient**. It is defined as twice the area between the diagonal and the Lorenz curve. In the extreme case of a completely equal distribution of income, the Lorenz curve will coincide with the diagonal. The Gini coefficient will thus be equal to zero. Now, consider the case of a completely unequal distribution of income. Because the Lorenz curve coincides with the rectangular kink formed by the horizontal axis and the right-hand side vertical axis, the surface below the diagonal thus forms a triangle of surface ½ (1 times 1 times ½). Indeed, both the vertical and the horizontal axes have a measure of 1 (respectively 100% of income and 100% of the population). The Gini coefficient will thus take a value between 0 and 1 (or 0 and 100% if expressed as a percentage). Countries with low inequality of income distribution will have a low Gini coefficient and countries with high inequality of income distribution will have a high Gini coefficient.

We can calculate the Gini coefficient in a straightforward way using the information we have on income distribution, as shown in Figure 2.3. Call S the area below the Lorenz curve. The area between the diagonal and the Lorenz curve is equal to $0.5G$, where G stands for the Gini coefficient. The triangle below the diagonal is equal to ½. Thus, we have $0.5G + S = 0.5$. The formula for G is thus:

$$G = 1 - 2S.$$

FIGURE 2.3   The Lorenz Curve and the Gini Coefficient

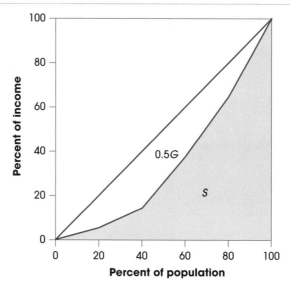

The Gini coefficient G is equal to twice the area between the diagonal and the Lorenz curve.

Figure 2.1 contains information on the quintile distribution of income with the first quintile having 5% of income, the first two having 15%, the first three having 35%, and the first four having 60%, with the richest quintile holding the remaining 40%. The area S is formed from one triangle and four trapezoids. The triangle has an area $0.5(0.2 \times 0.05) = 0.005$. Recall that the formula of a trapezoid is its base multiplied by half of the sum of its two heights. Given that all four trapezoids have the same base, their area is equal to:

$$0.2[(0.05 + 0.15)/2 + (0.15 + 0.35)/2 + (0.35 + 0.6)/2 + (0.6 + 1)/2]$$
$$= 0.2(.05/2 + 0.15 + 0.35 + 0.6 + 1/2) = 0.325.$$

S is then equal to $0.325 + 0.005 = 0.33$. The Gini coefficient is equal to $1 - 2 \times 0.33 = 0.34$. We can calculate Gini coefficients once we have information on the quantiles of income distribution.

Real-world Gini coefficients. Figure 2.4 provides Gini coefficients (expressed in percentages between 0 and 100) for a selected group of countries, primarily from 2010, but also from various other years.[9] The Gini coefficients shown in Figure 2.4 take values between 25 for Sweden on the low end, and 59 for Haiti on the high end. Latin American countries, African countries, and China have relatively high income inequality. India's Gini (33.4) is nearly 10 percentage points lower than that of China (42.5). The United States is among the most inegalitarian wealthy countries with a Gini of 40.8. Russia's income

---

[9]These Gini coefficients were calculated in different years, but because income inequality does not change that much over the course of two or three years, this does not impact our purposes.

FIGURE 2.4   Income Inequality in Selected Countries

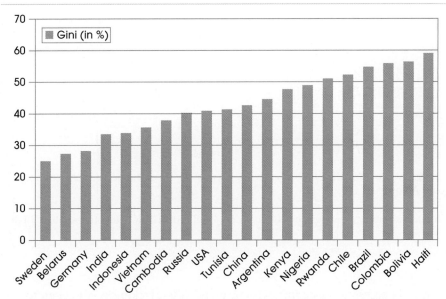

Gini coefficients (in percentages) are shown for a selected group of countries. A low Gini coefficient means low income inequality and a high Gini coefficient means high income inequality.

Source: The World Bank, World Development Indicators, http://data.worldbank.org/indicator/ SI.POV.GINI.

distribution is roughly that of the United States with a Gini of 40.1. The average for developed OECD countries is around 35. The other countries shown in Figure 2.4 have a relatively equal distribution of income. Sweden, Belarus, and Germany all have a Gini below 30.

Are there any specific geographic patterns of inequality, especially in the developing world? Table 2.4 gives us the answer.[10] The first column shows the Gini coefficient and the second column shows the decile ratio (top 10% average income over bottom 10% average income). We see that the highest Gini coefficient is in Latin America and the Caribbean. Sub-Saharan Africa also has a high degree of income inequality. All other regions have a Gini below 40%. Note that the decile ratio gives the same ranking. It is striking to see that the decile ratio is 2 to 3 times higher in Latin America than everywhere else. It is well known that the very wealthy in many Latin American countries live like their affluent counterparts in the United States, enjoying private jets, huge properties with armies of servants, and access to all the best amenities available in any fully developed country. However, the poor in Latin America, especially the indigenous populations, live in extreme poverty, barely making ends meet,

---

[10]The numbers presented in Table 2.4 are averages based on country data. Care must be taken when interpreting them. The Gini coefficient for Latin America cannot be calculated by taking the average Gini coefficient for countries in that region. Nevertheless, a high average Gini coefficient for a region compared to others will tend to show that inequality is higher in that region.

TABLE 2.4   Income Inequality in Different Regions of the World (1995–2006)

	Gini index (percentage)	90th/10th percentile ratio
Sub-Saharan Africa	46	6.63
Middle East and North Africa	37	5.12
Latin America and Caribbean	50	14.42
South Asia	33	4.12
East Asia and Pacific	39	4.92
Eastern Europe and Central Asia	31	4.17
High-income OECD	31	4.09

Regional averages for the Gini coefficient and the ratio of the 90th to the 10th percentile of the population are shown here. Inequality is the highest in Latin America.

Source: The World Bank, World Bank data base, http://siteresources.worldbank.org/DATASTATISTICS/Resources/table2_7.pdf.

with little access to basic infrastructure and often lacking access even to safe drinking water and electricity.

Economic Determinants of Inequality

Why are there large differences in inequality across the world? What are the underlying economic forces that generate more inequality in some countries and less in others? We explore these questions in this section.

Education and Income Inequality

The first potential determinant of differences in income inequality across countries is variable access to education. Some countries have broad access to education while others do not. The idea of a link between education and income inequality is fairly straightforward: people with limited access to education will acquire less skills and consequently will earn lower wages than those with broader access. Countries that provide a solid education to their populations will have less income inequality because skills will be abundant and there will be fewer differences in wages. People with limited education are also less likely to participate in the political process than their educated peers. The illiterate are not able to read party platforms. If poor and uneducated people do not participate in the political process, there will be less pressure for income redistribution to the poor, which would reduce income inequality. Low education thus perpetuates educational and income inequality.

Table 2.5 provides some broad data relative to income inequality and education (measured by literacy rates) that indicates some relation between the two, though perhaps not as strong as we might expect. Africa has high income inequality and also one of the lowest literacy rates while East Asia has a high

TABLE 2.5 Education and Income Inequality

	Literacy rate in 2009	Gini Coefficient (in percentage) 1995–2010
Sub-Saharan Africa	62.3	46
Middle East and North Africa	74.4	37
Latin America and Caribbean	91	50
South Asia	61	33
East Asia and Pacific	93.5	39
Eastern Europe and Central Asia	97.9	31
High-income OECD	98.8	31

Higher average years of schooling tend to be associated with lower income inequality as expressed by a lower Gini coefficient; however, the relationship is not strong.

Source: For the Gini coefficients, see Table 2.4 and for the literacy data, The World Bank, World Development Indicators, http://databank.worldbank.org.

literacy rate and a lower income inequality rate. Note, however, that South Asia has even lower literacy rates than Africa but a much lower rate of income inequality. Latin America, which has the highest rate of income inequality, also has a high literacy rate.

Even if there is some relationship between education and income inequality, the reason is unclear. Unequal education may lead to unequal incomes as argued above. However, one can also claim that income inequality generates educational inequality, as the poorest households cannot afford to invest in education. A negative correlation between income inequality and education therefore does not tell us whether low education causes more income inequality or the other way around. Causality between education and income inequality could work both ways.

Land Ownership and Income Inequality

Another determinant of income inequality is the historic inequality of property ownership. There are significant differences in the patterns of land ownership across continents, with Latin America having an extremely inequitable distribution of land while land distribution in Asia is more equitable. The distribution of land ownership is very important in the context of developing countries in which agricultural production still plays an important role in their economies. As we can see in Figure 2.5, there is a clear positive correlation between the land Gini, which expresses inequality in land ownership, and the income Gini. Inequality of wealth leads to inequality of income. Those owning relatively large amounts of land will have a very high income while those owning little or no land will have a very low income. Note that many land Gini coefficients are extremely high, suggesting that a very small proportion of the population owns a large part of the land.

FIGURE 2.5   Income and Land Inequality

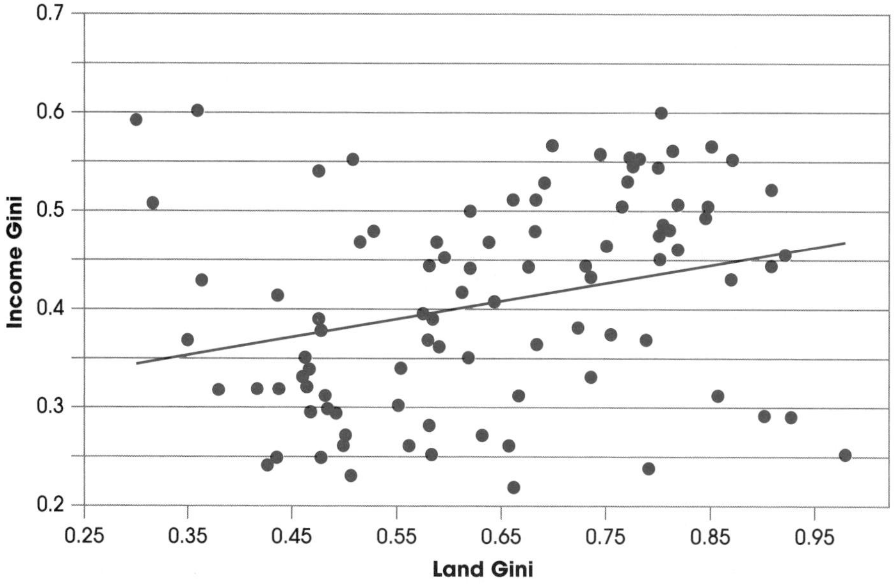

There is a strong correlation between inequality in land ownership as expressed by the land Gini and income inequality as expressed by the income Gini.

Source: Income Gini (the data span the late 1990s to 2010): The World Bank, World Development Indicators, http://databank.worldbank.org. Land Gini, E.H.P. Frankema, "The Colonial Origins of Inequality: Exploring the Causes and Consequences of Land Distribution" (working Paper, Groningen Growth and Development Centre, University of Groningen, Groningen, Netherlands, 2006). For some countries, the data span the period from 1960 to the late 1990s.

Inequality, Growth, and Development

What is the relationship between economic development and income inequality? Is income inequality good or bad for growth? Conversely, how does economic growth affect income inequality? If we can identify a relationship between income inequality and economic growth, what is the direction of causality? How has income inequality evolved in the world? We will address these questions in this section.

The Kuznets Hypothesis

We must first analyze the evidence from economic literature for a relationship between economic development and income inequality. A famous hypothesis developed in 1955 by Simon Kuznets, an American economist who received the Nobel Prize in 1971, states that income inequality at first increases with economic development but later decreases as countries become wealthy. The reason why income inequality increases first is that only part of society grows out of poverty at initial stages of economic development. As some people become richer and others remain poor, income inequality must inevitably increase. Eventually, however, the effects of economic growth "trickle down" to the poor, whose living standards also increase, and inequality declines as a result.

Another way to illustrate this relationship is to associate economic development with industrialization. Countries begin their economic development primarily with agricultural production. The industrial sector starts small but it is the source of economic growth and modernization. As the industrial sector grows, income inequality increases as incomes in the industrial sector are higher than those in the agricultural sector. When the industrial sector becomes dominant in the economy, income inequality begins to decrease. Thus, according to the Kuznets hypothesis, income inequality is a non-linear function of income with an inverted U-curve relationship between economic development and income inequality.

Figure 2.6. illustrates the idea of the Kuznets curve with initial data from Kuznets's research that was published in 1955. Figure 2.6 expresses income inequality as the share of the 20% richest over the 60% poorest in a population.

Cross-sectional analysis. Since Kuznets, many researchers have asked whether the Kuznets curve is still relevant and extensive studies in the 1990s examined that question. Usually, a Kuznets curve could be based on cross-sectional studies of world income distribution data. In other words, a researcher would rank countries from the poorest to richest in terms of income on the horizontal axis, and then plot income inequality data on the vertical axis. Middle-income countries tend to have higher income inequality than low- or high-income countries. The middle-income countries are generally from

FIGURE 2.6   The Kuznets Curve

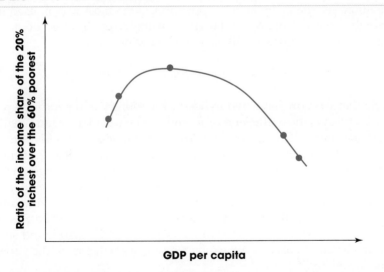

Kuznets mapped GDP per capita on the horizontal axis and a measure of inequality for which data were available for a few countries: the ratio of the income share of the 20% richest over the 60% poorest. He found that inequality first increases with economic development and then decreases, forming an inverted U-curve.

Source: Simon Kuznets, "Economic Growth and Income Inequality," *American Economic Review*, 45, no. 1 (1955): 1–28. Printed with permission of American Economics Association.

Latin America, which is a notoriously inegalitarian region. The equation for performing the analysis with a cross-sectional regression is as follows:

$$Inequality_i = a + by_i + cy_i^2 + error_i$$

where y_i is income per capita. There is a Kuznets curve or an inverted U-curve between income per capita and income inequality if coefficient b is significant and positive, and coefficient c is both significant and negative.

Cross-sectional analysis assumes that all countries go through the same economic development process and that income per capita is the only variable determining income inequality. These assumptions warrant questioning. As Asian countries develop economically to reach the income levels of Latin America, why should they have the income inequality levels of Latin America? Similarly, can we expect that as Latin American countries develop to reach the income levels of Europe those levels will become as equal as Europe's? There are many country-specific determinants of income inequality, so comparing countries is like comparing apples and oranges. This is a general problem of cross-sectional regressions.

Panel regression. It is important to distinguish between the cross-sectional data and the time series evolution. If the same country, say Brazil, goes through an inverted U-curve of inequality as it develops, this trend would be more convincing evidence for the Kuznets curve than would a comparison of income inequality in Mali (a low-income country), Brazil (a middle-income country), and Germany (a high-income country). A **panel regression**, a regression technique that analyzes data variation across countries and across time (for more information, see the Econometric Appendix), is the most widely used method to make this comparison. A panel regression analyzing the effect of income per capita on income inequality will have the following form:

$$Inequality_{it} = a_i + b_i y_{it} + c_i y_{it}^2 + error_{it}$$

Note that we now have two indices: i for country and t for time. We also have country-specific coefficients a_i, b_i, and c_i. In particular, b_i and c_i will be the country-specific coefficients for the Kuznets curve. If these coefficients are significant and have the expected signs (b_i positive and c_i negative), then we can be sure that as the same country develops, inequality goes through an inverted U-curve. A study by Klaus Deininger and Lyn Squire found no evidence of an inverted U-curve based on such a panel regression.[11] However, the time span of their data was relatively short, as available data for most countries only go back to 1970 or 1980. In a more recent study, Robert J. Barro found some evidence of a Kuznets curve, but it explained only a small part of the variation in income inequality.[12]

---

[11]Klaus Deininger and Lyn Squire, "A New Data Set Measuring Income Inequality," *World Bank Economic Review* 10, no. 3 (1996): 565–591.

[12]Robert J. Barro, "Inequality and Growth in a Panel of Countries," *Journal of Economic Growth* 5, no. 1 (March 2000): 5–32.

Income Inequality and Economic Growth

What about the relationship between income inequality and economic growth? We begin by determining their relationship, as shown in Figure 2.7. It plots long-term growth rates of GDP per capita expressed in purchasing power parity between 1960 and 2005 against income inequality as measured by the Gini coefficient. The data show some dispersion, but there is a negative correlation: countries with a higher Gini tend to have lower growth rates.

Since the early 1990s, there has been a near-unanimous consensus among economists that income inequality is bad for economic growth. This consensus is based on empirical research and on various theories predicting that more income inequality is expected to lead to less economic growth.

Consider Latin America and Asia. Latin America, the region with the most income inequality, has generally had a rather poor economic growth record in recent decades. Compared to most other regions, it had very low growth in the 1980s and 1990s. Asia, on the other hand, has been relatively more equitable than the rest of the world, both in terms of the distribution of land and the distribution of income, and has experienced very impressive economic growth in recent decades. What are the theoretical explanations for why income inequality may be bad for economic growth?

Credit market imperfections. One explanation is related to credit market imperfections. If a country's poor are numerous and unable to borrow in order to engage in entrepreneurial activities, economic growth will be limited. Consider two economies, one that has very unequal income distribution with many poor who cannot borrow, and another with fewer poor and a larger pool of people who are able to borrow. Because people in the economy with more

FIGURE 2.7   Income Inequality and Economic Growth

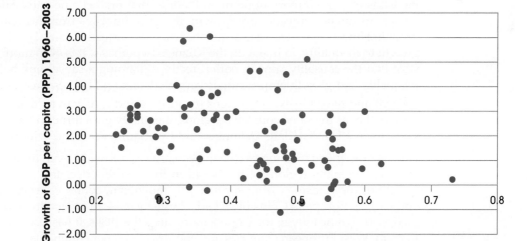

Countries with a higher income inequality (a higher Gini coefficient) also have a lower long-term growth rate of GDP per capita.

Source: Gini: see Figure 2.5. GDP per capita, PPP (constant 2000 $): The World Bank, World Development Indicators.

equal income distribution have access to more credit, they are better able to expand their economic activities than those in the more unequal economy.

Political economy. Another explanation for income inequality negatively impacting economic growth is based on political economy, the interaction between economics and politics. The basic political economy argument emphasizes the negative consequences of greater pressures for income redistribution, especially in democratic countries where a majority of poor people can vote to tax the rich. Pressures for redistribution can also take place through strikes, protest movements, trade union actions, etc. If a high initial level of income inequality leads to a high level of income redistribution, there will thus be more economic distortions associated with such redistribution. For example, if redistribution is financed from income taxes, a high tax on labor income will decrease labor supply because labor supply in the economy generally increases with income. Similarly, a high tax on capital income may lead to decreased investment or capital flight. These distortions will then have a negative effect on growth. More income inequality may simply lead to resentment that results in social unrest and instability in the form of protests and riots, especially if bad economic shocks hit the poor. This could also have a negative effect on economic growth.

Note that there can be countervailing forces to the political economy argument. Instead of voting to redistribute money from the rich to the poor, people may vote for more public services such as education, health, or infrastructure improvements that benefit the poor but may also encourage economic growth. More money for education may increase the general level of human capital, making people more productive and thus leading to more growth in the economy. However, if this argument is valid, then more public services should eventually lead to less income inequality. Higher economic growth related to initial inequality would then eventually lead to less inequality. This reasoning leads us to an important point: in theories that predict a negative effect of income inequality on economic growth, the causality runs from inequality to growth. However, we can also argue that there is, instead, a causal chain from growth to inequality, in line with the Kuznets hypothesis. It is even more plausible that the causality runs in both directions. Finding a causal link between inequality and growth empirically is very challenging. That research question is still wide open.

Inequality over Time

Has income inequality increased or decreased worldwide over time? It has increased in many regions of the world in the past few decades. As a consequence of the transition from socialism to capitalism, countries from Central and Eastern Europe to China have had a large increase in inequality and it has increased significantly in the United States since the 1980s. It has also increased in many West European countries and countries on other continents.

Instead of looking at income inequality within specific countries, an alternative approach is to determine whether it has increased or decreased worldwide. This requires examining the world distribution of income as if the world were one country. Take the examples of the United States and China. Income inequality has increased in both countries. However, living standards have grown much faster in China than in the United States over the past 30 years. Even though inequality has increased in both countries, combining the data for China and the United States suggests that there has probably been a net decrease in income inequality because of the rise in living standards in China.

Economist Xavier Sala-i-Martin has examined the evolution of inequality across the world.[13] His series for the world distribution of income combines information on GDP per capita, a measure of average income, with data from household surveys. This exercise is imprecise by nature, given the data on which it is based. Household surveys are done quite irregularly and are certainly not available for every year or even for every country. For missing years, Sala-i-Martin has used interpolation techniques.[14]

Figure 2.8 shows Sala-i-Martin's estimate of the evolution of the world distribution of income between 1970 and 2000 as measured by the Gini coefficient,

FIGURE 2.8   The Evolution of the World Gini Coefficient

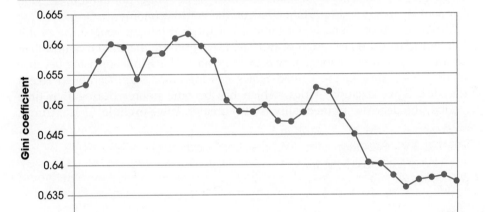

According to Sala-i-Martin, inequality in the world's income distribution has decreased since 1970. The main reason for this trend is the strong growth in China and India, where incomes have been catching up with those of richer countries.

Source: Xavier Sala-i-Martin, "The World Distribution of Income: Falling Poverty and . . . Convergence, Period," *Quarterly Journal of Economics* 121, no. 2 (2006): 385.

---

[13]Xavier Sala-i-Martin, "The World Distribution of Income: Falling Poverty and . . . Convergence, Period," *Quarterly Journal of Economics* 121, no. 2 (2006): 351–357.

[14]Say for a given country we have surveys for quintile shares for 1995 and 2000. We then assume a linear trend between those years to estimate values for 1996, 1997, 1998, and 1999. Suppose the share of income of the 20% richest is 40 in 1995 and 50 in 2000. Linear interpolation will give 42 in 1996, 44 in 1997, 46 in 1998 and 48 in 1998. We can justify this technique for short intervals because income distribution does not change rapidly. In some countries, only one survey for quintile shares may be available, which makes interpolation impossible. In that case, Sala-i-Martin uses information on the evolution of income distribution from neighboring countries to estimate an evolution. He also uses the same method for countries for which no surveys are available.

the latest data he used in his study. We see that there was an upward trend until the 1980s, but that there has been a continuous downward trend since then. How can we explain this downward trend? The answer has to do mainly with the process of economic growth in China and India. As these countries are so important in terms of the world population, their income growth has pulled hundreds of millions of people out of poverty and reduced income inequality worldwide. The economic reform process started in China in 1978 and it is exactly around that time that the world Gini coefficient began to drop.

Figure 2.9 illustrates the evolution of the Gini coefficient by excluding some countries or continents to gauge the effect of the growth of different countries. Note that in the figure, the vertical axis is scaled down so that the evolution of world income inequality looks flatter than in Figure 2.8. Nevertheless, we do see the same downward trend. For example, when we exclude China, we see that the world Gini has tended to increase from .62 to .648. The growth process in China has thus played a crucial role in reducing income inequality worldwide. China represents more than one-fifth of the world population, so what happens there has an important effect on the world economy.

The growth of China is not the only factor that has influenced the evolution of the world distribution of income. If we exclude the United States, then the decrease in income inequality is even greater. This is not suprising because income inequality in the United States has increased significantly in recent decades. If we exclude Africa, which has become poorer during that time period, the decrease in inequality is also greater. If we exclude Africa, China,

FIGURE 2.9   Evolution of the World Gini Coefficient (1970–2000), Excluding Various Countries

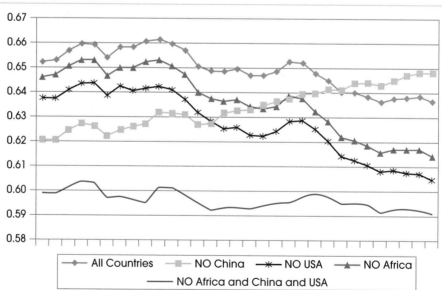

Excluding China, income inequality worldwide has increased over time. Excluding Africa, China, and the United States, it has remained stable.

Source: Sala-i-Martin, "The World Distribution of Income," 387.

and the United States, we nevertheless continue to see a tendency of reduced income inequality.

Overall, the economic growth process in China and other parts of Asia has thus reduced income inequality worldwide in recent decades. This result is consistent with the analysis of poverty early in this chapter that showed extreme poverty has tended to decline everywhere except in Africa.

Chapter Summary

Poverty Measurement and Comparisons

International measures of poverty are based on poverty lines. They are calculated as the income necessary to purchase the daily amount of calories necessary to survive, taking into account the usual eating habits of a population. The poverty headcount measures the number of people who are below the poverty line. The poverty gap is calculated by multiplying the poverty headcount by a population's average distance below the poverty line. Internationally comparable measures of poverty are difficult to determine because the exchange rates between currencies do not accurately reflect differences in the cost of living across countries. Therefore, purchasing power parity exchange rates are preferable to market exchange rates as measures of poverty, although they, too, are not perfect because they reflect average costs of living in a given country rather than the cost of living of the poor. Poverty has tended to decline in the last decades in most regions of the world except Africa. The impressive growth performance of China, India, and Asia as a whole has lifted hundreds of millions of people out of poverty.

Measurements and Comparisons of Income Inequality

Two concepts are most often used to measure inequality: the quantile ratio, which measures the ratio of income between the top quantile and the bottom quantile, and the Gini coefficient, which assumes values between zero and 1. A low Gini coefficient means a relatively equal distribution of income, while a high Gini coefficient means a highly unequal distribution of income.

Economic Determinants of Inequality

Low access to education is associated to high income inequality. Inequality in land ownership is also an important determinant of income inequality.

Inequality, Growth, and Development

The Kuznets hypothesis states that a country may first become more unequal in income distribution as it grows out of poverty and then it will become more equal again as it becomes rich. The international evidence for the Kuznets curve is weak. Economists have put forward theories based on credit constraints and political economy considerations that indicate income inequality may be bad for economic growth. While inequality has increased over time in many countries in the last 30 years, income inequality worldwide has tended to decrease. The main reason is that as China and India, in particular, have had very strong economic growth, the incomes of billions of people have increased, thereby reducing worldwide income inequality.

Key Terms

calorie counting
Gini coefficient
Lorenz curve
nongovernmental organizations
non-tradables
panel regression
poverty gap

poverty headcount
poverty headcount ratio
poverty line
purchasing power parity (PPP) exchange rates
quantile measures
quantile ratio
survey

Review Questions

1. Explain how to calculate a poverty line.

2. What is the poverty gap? What is the advantage of this measure over the headcount ratio?

3. Calculate the poverty gap for a country in which 80% of the population is below the poverty line of 1 dollar a day. In that country, 20% of the population has a daily income below 20 cents, 15% has a daily income between 20 and 40 cents, 15% has a daily income between 40 and 60 cents, 10% has a daily income between 60 and 80 cents, and 20% has a daily income between 80 cents and 1 dollar.

4. Explain some difficulties encountered by researchers seeking to develop internationally comparable data on poverty.

5. What is the Lorenz curve and how do you construct it? Draw a relatively equal and a relatively unequal Lorenz curve. Explain the difference.

6. How do you calculate a Gini coefficient? How does the Gini coefficient reflect high or low income inequality and why?

7. Draw the Lorenz curve and calculate the Gini coefficient for two countries based on the following decile income share data, where the poorest decile is on the left and the richest is on the right. What can you infer from the comparison of the Gini coefficients between these two countries?

| Country A | 30 | 20 | 15 | 10 | 5 | 5 | 5 | 5 | 3 | 2 |
| Country B | 20 | 15 | 10 | 10 | 10 | 10 | 10 | 10 | 4 | 1 |

8. Give three theories for why income inequality can be bad for economic growth. Provide your own view on this question.

9. Read the article by Branko Milanovic and Lire Ersado "Reform and inequality during the transition: An analysis using panel survey household data, 1990–2005 (downloadable at http://mpra.ub.uni-muenchen.de/7459/1/MPRA_paper_7459.pdf). On the basis of that paper, what are the reasons why income inequality has increased in transition countries?

10. Go to the World Bank's website on global poverty: http://iresearch.worldbank.org/PovcalNet/povcalNet.html

    Select "All" in the box for regions, select "national" in coverage, use the >> button to add all countries to the right panel, click the box "Aggregate over selected countries on a selected poverty line," and click "Continue." Enter 2005 for the reference year and $45 for the monthly poverty line and submit. Note the numbers for the poverty headcount and the poverty gap. Go back and select $60 for the monthly poverty line and submit. Note the numbers. On the basis of the information you have, how many people live on a monthly income between $45 and $60? Choose your own numbers using the PovcalNet website to get a better grasp of poverty. For example, compare the number of poor in the world living on a monthly income below $45 between 2005 and 2008.

Population Growth

We saw in Chapter 1 that population growth tends to be high in the poor developing countries of the world, especially in Africa. An important concern for development economists is whether continued high population growth may keep poor countries mired in poverty, which will be the case if a country's population grows faster than its national income. There are also more general concerns about the expansion of the world population. Growing populations consume the planet's finite resources—oil, minerals, and even water—at rapid rates. Population growth strains resource utilization worldwide, affecting both developed and developing countries.

In 1970, Tunisia, a small country in North Africa, was a typical example of a poor country with high population growth. In the 1960s and 1970s, women on average gave birth to between six and seven children. Thanks to medical progress, infant mortality rates had gone down substantially, and most children survived their first year. As a result, Tunisia's population, similar to the fast-growing populations in other developing countries, grew rapidly. In 1970, 69% of the population was below the age of 30. The Tunisian government, however, was one of the first developing countries to see the necessity of addressing the country's population challenges. With the support of the country's Islamic religious leaders, the government decided to launch an extensive education program on contraceptives and family planning that reached even the most remote villages. The program provided young people confidential access to family planning services and the government simultaneously raised the legal age for marriage and legalized abortion. To date, an average of more than 10 million dollars has been spent each year on family planning policies. The education and empowerment of women have also played critical roles in the government's policy. Women in Tunisia enjoy a high level of education; roughly 70% of women of working age are active in the Tunisian economy's formal sector. Currently, women have, on average, two children, which is closer to the norm of birth rates in developed countries and certainly much less than in the neighboring countries of Morocco, Algeria, Libya, and Egypt. Because of these very successful family planning policies, Tunisia's population growth since the turn of the millennium has been around 1% per year and life expectancy has increased from less than 50 years in the 1950s to above 70 today. The example of Tunisia shows that active family planning policies can significantly reduce population growth while increasing the health, education, and financial well-being of the population through specifically targeted policies.

In this chapter, we will address the trends of population growth in developing countries. We will see why population tends to grow faster in these nations compared to developed countries. We will also see why population growth slows down when a country becomes richer. We will also examine the important role of family planning policies in curbing population growth in developing countries.

Population over Time and the Demographic Transition

Concerns over a rapidly growing world population are not new. Thomas Malthus (1766–1834) voiced his concerns as early as the 1700s when he put forth the idea that in the absence of wars, famines, and natural catastrophes, population would grow exponentially. As a result, increases in food supplies could not keep up with population growth, which would have to be curbed dramatically to avoid famine and misery.

Currently, the general concern is that if a country's income grows at a slower rate than its population, income per capita (the ratio of income to the population) will decline over time. In other words, population growth would be associated with poverty instead of prosperity, which is a trend we have seen in developing countries. Does this mean that population growth always has a negative effect on a country's economy? Not necessarily. Population growth is a direct source of both a country's productive capacity and overall demand for products and services. If the population in a country stagnates, or starts to decline, there will be little addition to the labor force. That population would also start to age, and there would not be enough young people to replace older workers leaving the workforce. Moreover, market demand would develop more slowly, which would slow down the expansion of economic output.

In this section, we provide a baseline for our discussion of the effects of population growth by looking at population trends over time, and especially in the last few centuries.

An Exponentially Growing Population

For most of human history, there was a maximum of just a few hundred million people on the planet. The population started increasing quickly during the Industrial Revolution, as shown in Figure 3.1. In 1800, the world population was just below 1 billion. In the last 200 years, it has gone from 1 billion to over 7 billion people. In 1965, the world population was already double that of 1900. In a little more than 40 years, between 1960 and 2000, the world population doubled once again. Since the Industrial Revolution at the end of the 1700s, the world population has been growing as never before in human history.

The curve that charts the evolution of the world population in Figure 3.1 resembles a hockey stick. It is very flat until the 1800s and then increases exponentially with a nearly vertical slope by the end of the 1900s. Roughly every 4 days, the world population increases by 1 million! Every year, it increases by roughly 90 million, which is nearly one-third of the U.S. population and more than the population of either the United Kingdom, France, or Germany.

Figure 3.2 shows the initial population level for each continent in 1950 and the population increase between 1950 and 2010. We see that in Asia, Africa, and Latin America, the population increase has been higher during those 60 years than those regions' initial 1950 population levels. Note, however,

FIGURE 3.1   Evolution of the World Population since 1000 BCE

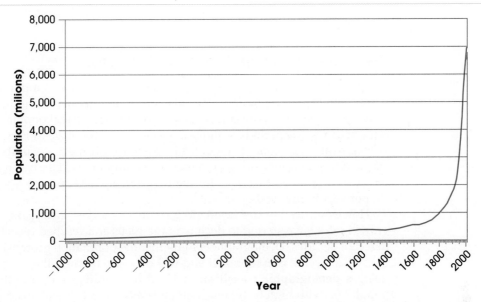

The world population has grown exponentially since the beginning of the Industrial Revolution at the end of the 18th century.

Source: For the years before 1920, Colin McEvedy and Richard Jones, *Atlas of World Population History* (New York: Penguin, 1978); after 1920, *United Nations Statistical Yearbook,* available online from 1950 onward, at http://esa.un.org/wpp/Excel-Data/ population.htm.

FIGURE 3.2   Population in 1950 and Population Increase (1950–2010) per Continent

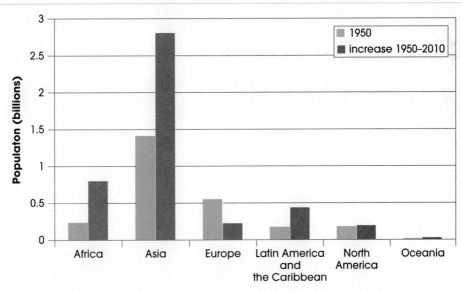

The population increase between 1950 and 2010 has been higher than the 1950 population levels in Africa, Asia, and Latin America. Population growth in the last 60 years has been the highest in developing countries.

Source: United Nations, http://esa.un.org/wpp/Excel-Data/population.htm.

that this is not the case in Europe and North America. The largest population increases in the last 60 years have clearly been taking place in developing countries.

The Evolution of Population Growth Rates

The **growth rate** of the population, which is the increase in a population as a percentage of that population, has also expanded greatly since the Industrial Revolution. Figure 3.3 provides estimates of average annual population growth rates over 50-year periods in the last 3,000 years. The curve in Figure 3.3 looks very similar to the one in Figure 3.1, though with more volatility. Until the late 1700s, the growth rate of the world population was below a meager 0.2% per year. It only reached 0.5% for the first time in 1800 and quickly climbed to 2% per year in the 1900s.

However, despite the dramatic growth of the last 200 years, population growth rates have started to decline in the 1960s and reached rates below 1.5% in recent decades. Demographers think that the population growth observed in the last 200 years is exceptional and will decrease because the world is undergoing a **demographic transition**, defined by a shift from a stabilized global population with high birth and high mortality rates to a stabilized population characterized by low birth and low mortality rates. Demographers believe that this demographic transition has been occurring over the last 300 years and they expect it to finish before the end of the 21st century.

FIGURE 3.3 Estimated Average Annual Population Growth Rates since 1000 BCE

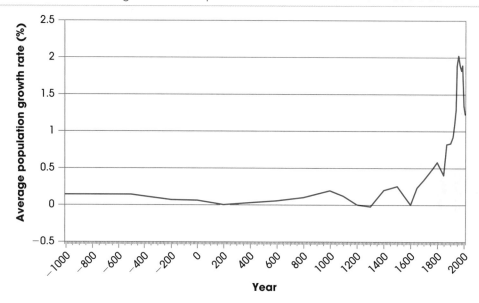

Population growth rates have been below 0.2% per year for most of human history, but they have grown enormously since the beginning of the Industrial Revolution at the end of the 18th century. Population growth rates started to decline in recent decades because of the demographic transition.

Source: McEvedy and Jones, *Atlas of World Population History*, 1978; United Nations Statistical Yearbook, http://esa.un.org/wpp/Excel-Data/population.htm.

Economists characterize the demographic transition by a significant reduction in mortality rates due to economic growth and improved medical care, while fertility rates remain high. Because of these parameters, birth rates climb and death rates decline. The result is the severe population growth we have witnessed over the last few centuries and continue to witness today in developing countries. The demographic transition ends when fertility rates decline to match the much lower mortality rates. In the end, population growth should stabilize at around zero. Demographers expect the world population to stabilize at 8 to 12 billion at the end of the transition.

Population growth in developed countries was very high in the 18th, 19th, and first half of the 20th century, but it has slowed down in the last 40 years, and has stabilized near zero if we exclude immigration rates from developing countries. Two centuries ago, a European family would routinely have six to eight children, but parents would need a minibus to transport eight children in Europe today! Currently, fertility rates have become so low in most advanced economies that without immigration from poorer countries, their populations would shrink. Looking at the demographic transition in developed countries may help us predict what is likely to happen to their populations during this century.

Figure 3.4 suggests that the demographic transition might also be taking place in developing countries, although the process may be somewhat slower when compared to developed nations. Indeed, population growth has declined on all continents in the last 2 decades relative to the period 1950–1990. Population growth was also lower worldwide in the 2000–2010 decade as compared

FIGURE 3.4 Average Annual Population Growth Rates per Continent during Recent Decades

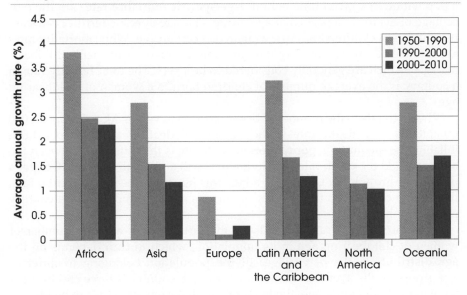

Population growth rates have declined worldwide since 1990.

Source: United Nations, http://esa.un.org/wpp/Excel-Data/population.htm.

to the 1990–2000 decade, with the exception of Oceania (Australia, New Zealand and surrounding countries and islands), which has experienced large migration inflows in recent years, and also Europe. Population growth continues to be higher in developing countries, but in Asia and Latin America, recent population growth was not much higher than in Europe or North America for the period 1950–1990.

Figures 3.1 through 3.4 raise various questions. Why was population growth so low until the last 2 centuries and why did it accelerate so much after the Industrial Revolution? One simple answer is that agricultural, economic, and technological progress has increased living standards and increased food supplies, making it possible to sustain a larger population on the planet. However, this cannot be the whole answer. If this were the case, the richest countries would have higher population growth rates than poor countries, but in the last 50 years the opposite has happened. Why then has population growth been highest in the poor regions of the world and lowest in the developed regions? Finally, why have we seen a reduction in population growth everywhere in the world in recent decades? To answer these questions accurately, we need to look closely at the determinants of population growth.

The Determinants of Population Growth

We begin our discussion of the determinants of population growth with some basic demographic vocabulary. We then examine the dynamics of population growth based on demographic variables.

Fertility, Mortality, and Birth and Death Rates

Population growth is largely determined by how many people enter and exit a population in a given time period. **Age-specific mortality rates** are the percentage of deaths in a particular age group, and **age-specific fertility rates** are the number of children born to a woman of a certain age. While mortality rates are counted at any age, fertility rates are only counted for women's childbearing ages, which are generally considered to be 15–44. The **total fertility rate** in a country is the average number of children born to a woman of childbearing age.

The **birth rate** is the number of babies born each year in a country per 1,000 inhabitants. The **death rate** is the number of deaths each year per 1,000 inhabitants. A country's **population growth rate** is the difference between the birth rate and the death rate (we divide the birth and death rates by 10 to get a percentage growth rate). We must adjust this figure for the **net migration rate**, the difference between the number of persons entering and leaving a country per 1,000 inhabitants.[1]

A country's birth rate depends on the fertility rates and the number of women of childbearing age in its population, which in turn depends on the **age distribution**, the percentages of the population belonging to different age groups. If the average total fertility rate in a country is three children per woman of childbearing age, the birth rate in that same country can be high or

---

[1]We will not discuss international migration in this chapter.

low depending on whether the proportion of women of childbearing age in the population is high or low. The same is true for the death rate. If a country has many young adults and relatively few old adults, the death rate will tend to be low (and vice versa) because the frequency of deaths is higher among older people compared to young people. Age distribution is thus a key factor in explaining birth and death rates as well as population growth.

Age Distribution

Age distribution percentages vary greatly across countries. Developing countries, such as Uganda, Somalia, or Afghanistan, typically have a high proportion of young people, while developed countries, such as Japan or Germany, typically have a high proportion of elderly people.

Age distribution directly affects population growth. Take two countries, A and B, with populations of 100 people each and the same age-specific fertility rates among the young and age-specific mortality rates among the old. Assume that in each age group there are an equal number of men and women. Today's young become old in the second period when all the old die. In each country, we assume that the mortality rate among the young is 10% (meaning 10% of today's young die before becoming old). We also assume fertility rates of 2.2. In other words, every young woman will give birth to 2.2 children in the second period. The only difference we assume between country A and country B is the initial age distribution: A has 70 young and 30 old, while B has 50 young and 50 old. The first three columns of Table 3.1 summarize these details.

In country A, there will be 77 young people in the second period (2.2 times 70/2 = 77). On the other hand, 10% of 70 die before becoming old, leaving 63 old for the second period. The total population of country A in the second period is then 77 + 63, or 140. In other words, the population has grown by 40%.

Country B's young in the second period will be 55 (2.2 times 50/2 = 55). On the other hand, 10% of 50 will die before becoming old, which means that the next generation's old will be 45. The population in country B in the second period is 55 + 45, or 100; its population has not grown at all. This example illustrates that even if mortality rates and fertility rates are the same in different countries, the population growth can be very different because of the differences in the age distribution of the population.

TABLE 3.1 The Effect of Age Distribution

	Initial age distribution in A and B	Fertility rate	Mortality rate (%)	Population second period
Young in A	70	2.2	10	77
Old in A	30	0	100	63
Young in B	50	2.2	10	55
Old in B	50	0	100	45

Countries A and B have identical fertility and mortality rates but country A is younger than country B. The population in country A therefore grows by 40%, while the population in country B does not grow at all.

Age distribution is often displayed graphically with population pyramids. In Figure 3.5, showing Brazil's population pyramid, we can see the age group with the largest share is that of people ages 15–19. The shares of older groups gradually become smaller. Note that the slope of this pyramid is quite flat, meaning that younger age groups are much more numerous than older age groups. Note also that the share of the groups below age 15 is less than that of the age 15–19 group. This means that there were, on average, fewer babies born per year between 1986 and 2000 than between 1981 and 1985.

Demographic trends, the evolution of populations over time, tend to have considerable inertia. Take a **stationary population**, defined as a population that has zero growth over time, in which fertility and mortality rates have been very

FIGURE 3.5   Brazil's Age Pyramid in 2000

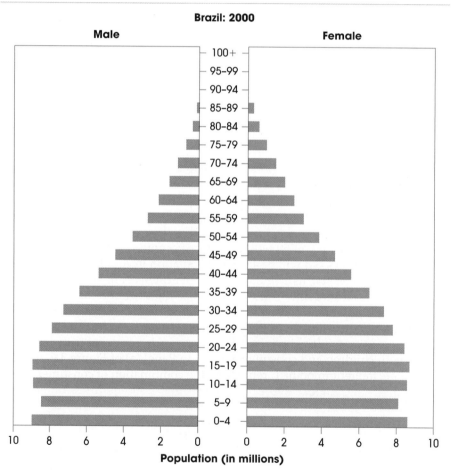

The largest shares of Brazil's population are the young below the age of 25. This reflects a young population.

Source: Data from http://www.census.gov/ipc/www/idb/pyramids.html.

stable, generation after generation. Assume that suddenly a somewhat high fertility rate is observed during one generation such as the U.S. baby-boom phenomenon after World War II. Once these children grow up and become young adults, even if their fertility rate goes back down to that of previous generations, they will still have more children than their predecessors because of their greater numbers and the population will grow as a result. Birth rates will also be higher, even though the fertility rate has gone back to normal. If there are more young than old, the general death rate in the population will be lower as well, since the young have a lower mortality rate. If the birth rate increases and the death rate decreases, there will be population growth even though fertility rates have gone back to normal, and age-specific mortality rates have never changed. A one-time increase in the fertility rate will thus lead to an increase in population growth for a long time afterward. Because of this, population growth has significant inertia.

Because of this inertia in population growth, measures taken to control population growth will only take effect many years after their initiation, probably an entire generation later. Family planning policies affect the fertility rates, but in a country with a young population, a decline in fertility rates will not immediately result in lower population growth for the reasons we just outlined. Therefore, when evaluating the effects of family planning policies, policy makers must take this inertia into account.

The Determinants of Fertility Rates

The number of children families chose to have varies greatly across countries. In this section, we examine the economic reasons behind differences in fertility choices across countries.

The Economics of Fertility Choices

Raising children is costly. Their basic needs include food, shelter, clothes, medical attention, and education, the cost of which vary country by country. Social norms across countries and social groups also affect the cost of raising a child, whether for the expense of a private school education or for health care.

If people love children but also like consumer goods, what is their budget line for both children and consumer goods? In Panel (a) of Figure 3.6, the first budget line, tangent to point 1, represents the combination of consumer goods and children that a household can afford. If that household has no children and spends all its income on consumer goods, then it can afford an amount of consumer goods equal to the intersection of the budget line with the vertical axis. If the household spends all its money on children, then it can afford a number of children equal to the intersection of the budget line with the horizontal axis.

Any combination of number of children and consumption level that is on the budget line of Panel (a) in Figure 3.6 is the maximum a household can afford given its budget. Assume that the choice is point 1, where the budget line is tangent to the indifference curve between consumer goods and children. The choice is a number of children n_1 and a number of consumer goods c_1.

Shifts in the cost of children. If the cost of raising children decreases due to the introduction of a good public school system or free health services, for example, the budget line will rotate upward. Because the cost of consumer goods has not changed, the intersection of the budget line with the vertical axis has not moved. Due to the reduction in the cost of having children, the intersection of the budget line with the horizontal axis has moved to the right in Panel (a) of Figure 3.6. We see that the new fertility choice is at point 2 with fertility choice n_2 and consumer good choice c_2. Note that the amount of choice for both has increased. The reduction in the cost of having children has a similar effect to an increase in income and families can afford both more children and more consumer goods.

As we know from microeconomic theory, a reduction in the price of a good leads to two effects: an income effect and a substitution effect. The income effect means that the reduction in the price of one good makes it possible to afford more of all goods. The substitution effect means that families will tend to consume more of the relatively cheaper good. If the income effect dominates the substitution effect, consumption of all goods increases. This is the case illustrated in Panel (a) of Figure 3.6.

What insights can we gain from Panel (a)? A reduction in the cost of having children, such as education reform, may result in people having more children. We can use this insight to compare fertility choices across countries or across regions, such as in rural versus urban areas of developing countries. The cost of having children in poor rural areas is often less than in urban areas because rural parents use the land to feed and clothe their children. Moreover, children work on the land to help their parents, which further reduces the cost of raising children. If the cost of having children is lower in rural areas, then the number of children per household in rural areas should be higher compared to urban areas, which is typically the case.

Shifts in the cost of consumer goods. In Panel (b) of Figure 3.6, we focus on a reduction in the cost of consumer goods, rather than a reduction in the cost of having children. Because of the decreased cost of consumer goods, the budget line rotates upward on the vertical axis, meaning that families can afford more consumer goods and more children. Thus, the reduction in the cost of consumer goods also acts like an increase in income. When comparing point 1 with point 3, the choice after the reduction in the cost of consumer goods, we see that while c_3 is higher than c_1, n_3 is lower than n_1. In other words, the decrease in the cost of consumer goods leads to a reduction in the number of children desired.

Why might that be? The answer is related to the relative importance of the income and substitution effects. In the example illustrated in Panel (a), the income effect dominates and a reduction in the cost of having children led to an increase in both children and consumer goods. In the example illustrated in Panel (b), the opposite occurs and the substitution effect (choosing more of the cheaper consumer goods and less of the relatively more expensive children)

FIGURE 3.6   The Determinants of Fertility Choices
Panel (a) A Reduction in the Cost of Children

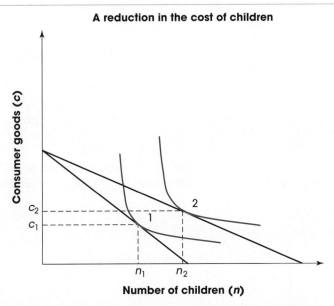

With an initial choice of consumer goods and number of children at point 1, a reduction in the cost of children shifts the budget line on the horizontal axis and leads to an increase in the demand for consumer goods and number of children (point 2).

Panel (b) A Reduction in the Cost of Consumer Goods

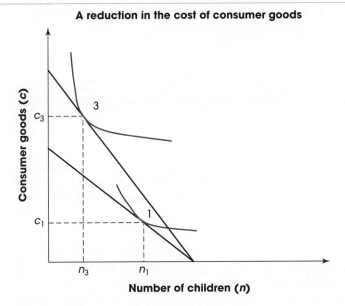

Starting from an initial choice of consumer goods and number of children at point 1, a reduction in the cost of consumer goods leads to an increase in the demand for those goods and a reduction in the demand for children (point 3).

dominates the income effect (a family can afford more of both). We see that availability of cheaper consumer goods leads to a reduction in the desired number of children. High levels of consumerism are often associated with a choice for fewer children.[2]

Shifts in income. If income increases, making it possible to afford more consumer goods and more children, families may in some cases choose fewer children. This is the case illustrated in Figure 3.7 as the budget line expands outward in a parallel direction, making it possible to have more children and more consumer goods. The choice of children and consumer goods then shifts from point 1 with c_1 and n_1 to point 4 with c_4 and n_4. There, an increase in income leads to more consumer goods but fewer children.

Why might an increase in income lead to families choosing to have fewer children? The answer is not straightforward. In microeconomic theory, when

FIGURE 3.7   Fertility Choices and Increases in Income

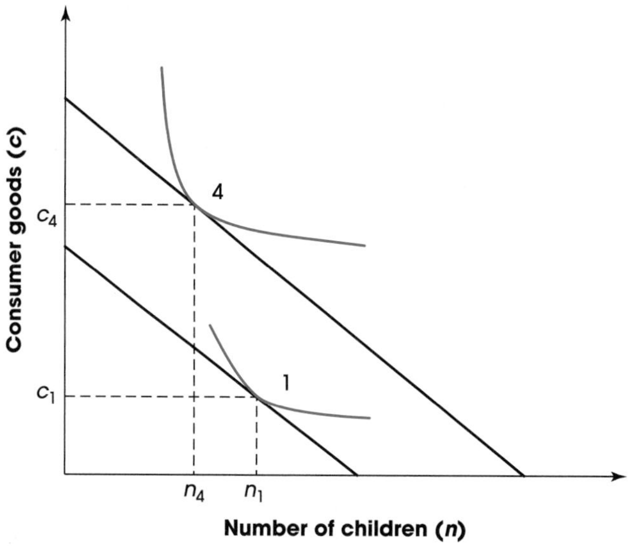

Starting from an initial choice of consumer goods and number of children at point 1, an increase in income leads to an increase in the demand for consumer goods and a reduction in the demand for children. The latter effect is due to a quantity-quality tradeoff in the choice of children. As incomes increase, the opportunity cost of time also increases and parents prefer to invest in child quality rather than in child quantity, spending more time and money on a smaller number of children.

---

[2]Note that these are only illustrative examples. Whether the income of the substitution effect dominates depends on the change in the slope of the budget line and on the slopes of the indifference curves. We can also construct examples in which either the substitution effect dominates when the cost of raising children is reduced or the income effect dominates when the cost of consumer goods goes down.

people choose to have less of a good as a result of an increase in income, we refer to the good with decreased demand as an **inferior good**. Examples of inferior goods include potatoes, bread, rice, or millet. Normally, an increase in income should cause people to choose more of all goods. A good for which consumption goes up as income goes up is a **normal good**.

This leads us to the following puzzle: are children inferior goods in the sense of microeconomic theory? Families in rich countries typically have fewer children than families in poor countries as shown in the examples illustrated in Figure 3.7. The cost of raising children is nevertheless higher in rich countries than in poor countries and we could argue that this is the reason why families in rich countries have fewer children. However, in order for children *not* to be inferior goods in the sense of microeconomic theory, we would have to argue that the cost of raising children is *relatively* higher in richer countries than in poor countries. In other words, if a rich family from a developed country has an income that is 100 times higher than that of a family from a developing country, the cost of raising children would have to be more than 100 times higher in the rich country relative to the poor country. This might be the case, but it also might not.

Should we then consider children as "inferior goods" in the sense of microeconomic theory? That would seem unreasonable. Economists have considered different ways of amending the standard economic theory of fertility choices to explain why people in richer countries have fewer children than do people in poor countries without assuming that children are inferior goods. One possible explanation is based on two ideas: 1) raising children requires time on the part of parents and the opportunity cost of time, especially for women, increases drastically with economic development; and 2) there is a quantity-quality trade-off in fertility choices. Instead of opting to have more children, parents can choose to have fewer children but to invest more time and money in each child. The first part of the argument is a restatement of the idea that the cost of childrearing increases with income. The second part of the argument, however, leads to a convincing story of why parents choose to have fewer children when income rises: given that the opportunity cost of women's time increases with income, households prefer to choose a higher quality over a higher quantity as their income increases. This is a view that has been expressed first by Nobel Prize–winner Gary Becker.[3] By integrating the quantity-quality trade-off in fertility choices, Becker's theory explains that an increase in parental income will lead to an increase in demand for "child quality," as quality is increasingly preferred to quantity, making the demand for children a normal good again. Thus, Becker's explanation reveals why people choose to have fewer children when income increases and it is not based on the assumption that children are "inferior goods" in the sense of microeconomic theory.

Shifts in preferences. Figure 3.8 shows yet another way to explain why economic development causes people to choose to have fewer children. The analysis in previous figures emphasized the cost variables that are relevant in fertility choices: the cost of having children and the cost of consumer goods in combination with the relevant levels of income.

---

[3]Gary S. Becker, *A Treatise on the Family* (Cambridge: Harvard University Press, 1981).

Using Twins to Test the Quantity-Quality Theory of Fertility in India and China

How do we test Becker's theory of the quantity-quality theory in fertility choices? It is not obvious. We could test whether families with fewer children invest more in each child, but this would not be an accurate measure of the quantity-quality trade-off because families choose both quantity and quality at the same time. In addition, these choices depend on family characteristics that are not easily observed, such as parents' inherent preferences for children versus other choices in life. Families who care more for children may, for example, have both more children and more investment in each child compared to families who care less for children and decide to have fewer children for that reason.

Development economists Mark Rosenzweig and Kenneth Wolpin found a clever way to estimate the quantity-quality trade-off by looking at twins in India.[4] Say that parents want to have two children. If, however, the second pregnancy produces twins, the household will end up having three children instead of two as desired. In accordance with the quantity-quality theory, because of the unexpected additional child, the child quality or investment in each child should be lower. In families with twins, the exact number of children is not chosen but is exogenous, which makes it possible to estimate its effect on quality investment.

Rosenzweig and Wolpin used data from a national sample of 2,939 farm families in India, collected between 1969 and 1971 by the National Council for Applied Economic Research in New Delhi. They found that an index of educational attainment per child was lower in families with twins than in families without twins, showing evidence of a quantity-quality trade-off. However, they failed to find that having twins had a significant effect on purchases of consumer durables.

Hongbin Li, Junsen Zhang, and Yi Zhu did a similar exercise for families in China.[5] In their study, they were able to control for birth order effects because educational investment in children tends to decline with birth order. They found that having one more child reduces the probability of being enrolled in (or not dropping out of) school by 4 percentage points. Interestingly, the effect is only valid in rural areas and not in urban areas.

Costs and income are, however, not the only variables that matter in fertility choices. The benefits of having children may change, too. Figure 3.8 illustrates an example of changes in preferences, more precisely a situation in which there is a reduction in the benefits of having children. Analyzing the case of a shift in preferences makes it possible to determine the variation in the benefits of having children while the cost and the budget line remain the same. The change in the relative benefits of having children translates into a change in the shape of indifference curves between consumption and children. The indifference

---

[4]Mark R. Rosenzweig and Kenneth I. Wolpin, "Testing the Quality-Quantity Fertility Model: The Use of Twins as a Natural Experiment," *Econometrica* 48, no. 1 (January 1980): 227–240.

[5]Hongbin Li, Junsen Zhang, and Yi Zhu, "The Quantity-Quality Trade-off of Children in a Developing Country: Identification Using Chinese Twins," *Demography* 45, no. 1 (February 2008): 223–243.

FIGURE 3.8   Reduction in the Benefits of Having Children

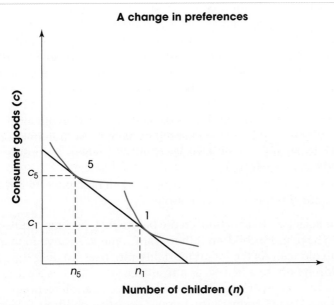

Starting from an initial choice of consumer goods and children at point 1, changes in preferences lead to an increase in demand for consumer goods and a reduction in the demand for children. These changes in preferences are related to the development of pension programs and urbanization that eliminate the need to have children who will ultimately have to care for their aging parents, points that we discuss below.

curve has now become flatter at n_1, the initial choice of children. This means that families have an increased preference to reduce the number of children in order to acquire more consumer goods. Since the trade-off has changed at the existing budget line, families will end up choosing more consumer goods and fewer children. Therefore, a reduction in the benefits of having children results in fewer children and more consumption. This change in preference is represented by point 5.

In the next section we look at what factors might cause a change in the economic benefits of having children.

Fertility Choices and Institutions

The benefits of having children are usually–though not exclusively–related to differences in institutions across countries. In societies or economic sectors with no social security programs or poor medical care, children are an investment for old age. This is especially true in rural societies. When people become too old or too disabled to continue to work on the land, they risk starving to death if nobody is there to care for them. In agricultural societies, caring for the elderly usually implies providing food and shelter for them. This is exactly what children have been doing for millennia in the agricultural-based regions of the world. Children are thus an insurance policy for old age.

Financial security. The concept of social security, as we know it today, did not exist a century ago and still does not exist in the countryside for poor peasants in the developing world who, until 2007, constituted the majority of the global population. Saving for private pensions is hard enough in advanced economies; it is not even an option for most people in many developing countries. This is because most of the income earned by poor people is in the form of agricultural output, which cannot be stored over a lifetime given the perishable nature of agricultural goods. Throughout history, relying on children has been the best, if not the only, option for securing basic needs in old age. The old-age insurance motive is an important benefit of having children in poor countries. This motive is usually absent in richer countries, where governments or businesses fund old-age pensions.

This need for security in old age, coupled with high poverty rates, increases the demand for children for three reasons.

1. In poor societies, many children die before they become adults. Parents need to have more children if they want some to survive to take care of them in old age. As the infant mortality rate rises, so does the number of children born to a family; as a result, each family has a greater chance that a larger number of children will survive to adolescence.
2. Children vary in productivity. In poor societies, children are less likely to be educated and able to generate enough income to take care of their aging parents. If only a small percentage of children receive an education or vocational training, parents will tend to have more children, in the hopes that at least one of them will be able to get an education and be successful enough to support them in their old age.
3. In cases of extreme poverty, children might move away from their parents, taking any income and support with them. A family needs to have more children to ensure that at least some of them remain at home to take care of the elderly when they can no longer take care of themselves. As the old-age insurance motive grows stronger with increased poverty levels, so does the benefit of having more children.

The need for support and care in old age is thus a driving force behind having many children in developing countries.

Commitment and cultural values. The necessity for children to care for their elderly parents does not guarantee that children take on this responsibility. Children might be opportunistic and abandon their parents or not take adequate care of them. Once the parents are dependent on their children, they usually do not have the means to protect themselves from poor care.

In advanced economies, parents can use the promise of an inheritance as an incentive to make sure their children take good care of them. In rural societies, the legal structure that governs inheritance laws may not exist, parents may not be aware of it, and most importantly, there is usually not much for children to inherit in terms of wealth or property. Children can abandon their parents without suffering any consequences. Once these children become elderly, however, they could then be subject to the same treatment by their own children. Societies are eventually better off if there is a caring and responsible relationship between the younger and older generations.

CHAPTER THREE   Population Growth

Unfortunately, there is no obvious mechanism to enforce such a commitment. In the absence of legal constraints, a social norm guiding people's behavior is the only way to enforce a support system for the elderly. Social norms have developed to promote arrangements in which children take care of their old parents and thereby solve this important commitment problem. Respect and obedience for the elderly, ancestor worship, moral duty to continue a family's lineage, and social prestige or good fortune associated with having many children are all cultural values and beliefs that work to sustain commitment to parental care in old age.

Social norms of gender bias. Social norms also differ among societies and can influence fertility choices. In societies with a strong male gender bias, for example, it is not the total number of children but the total number of boys a family has that is important. In many rural societies, girls are valued less than boys are; once the girls marry, they belong to their husbands' families and are not available to take care of their own parents in old age. This is the case in most of rural India and China for example. Girls are also valued less than boys are because they have less physical strength or their household duties prevent them from working for wages to support the household. These social norms have ancient origins but persist to the present day. Preferences for boys over girls imply that parents take better care of boys than they do girls. This preference may go as far as female infanticide, the killing of baby girls at birth.

Social norms that value boys over girls can vary greatly in different societies. Figure 3.9 shows population sex ratios across different continents; in

FIGURE 3.9   Population Sex Ratios in 2010

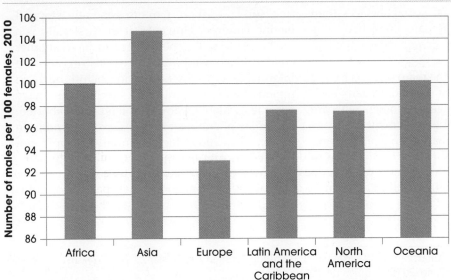

The sex ratio (the number of males per 100 females) is the highest in Asia and the lowest in Europe. Among other factors, this reflects differences in preferences for boys over girls in various regions of the world.

Source: United Nations, http://data.un.org/Data.aspx?q=world+population&d=PopDiv&f=variableID%3A13%3BcrID%3A900.

general, from a purely biological perspective, there should be slightly less males than females in a population. This is generally the case on most continents, except in Asia where there were estimated to be 104.8 males per 100 females in 2010. While there are many reasons why this ratio may vary, social norms and a strong gender bias for boys are likely to play an important role in explaining these differences.

The Missing Women

In 1990, Amartya Sen, Nobel Prize winner in economics, was among the first to write about the abnormal male to female sex ratio in Asia and other regions of the world.[6] If Asia had the same male to female ratio as do other regions of the world, in China alone there would be 50 million more women, and a total of 100 million more women in Asia and North Africa. The numbers behind the "missing women" phenomenon tell a terrible story of discrimination against women and extreme inequality leading to neglect and higher female mortality. In South Asia and North Africa, women receive less health care, food, and social services than men do. Surprisingly, female mortality rates are not higher for all age groups below the late thirties.

Sen thinks that one of the main reasons for the weak bargaining power of women in many societies is the low percentage of women who are able to engage in gainful employment and earn wages. This lowers the bargaining power, and more generally, the social position of women in a household.

In China, the one-child policy is clearly to blame for the "missing women phenomenon" because it led in many cases to infanticides of baby girls and neglect of young female children. Emily Oster, a Chicago economist, came up with an intriguing and unheard of explanation of the missing women phenomenon in China. She claimed that the main reason for the unbalanced sex ratio in China was the prevalence of hepatitis B, which is known to lead to a higher male to female birth ratio.[7] This finding was criticized by Avraham Ebenstein, who showed convincingly that it was related to the one-child policy.[8] If the first child is a boy, parents generally stopped having children. However, if the first child is a girl, parents will generally try to have another child until a boy is born. There is also evidence of infanticide and of sex selection before birth; in regions where ultrasound techniques have become available, baby girls tend to be aborted. A similar phenomenon is observed in India. In India as in China, doctors are, in principle, not allowed to divulge the sex of a baby *in utero*. However, this rule is often not enforced.

---

[6]Amartya Sen, "More Than 100 Million Women Are Missing," *New York Review of Books* 37, no. 20 (December 1990).

[7]Emily Oster, "Hepatitis B and the Case of the Missing Women," *Journal of Political Economy* 113 no. 6 (2005): 1163–1214.

[8]Avraham Ebenstein, "The 'Missing Girls' of China and the Unintended Consequences of the One Child Policy," *Journal of Human Resources* 45, no. 1 (2010): 87–115.

If social norms play a prominent role in fertility choices, can we expect to see some inertia in those choices as incomes increase? In societies where the social norm calls for large families, people would continue to have many children, at least for a couple of generations, even when governments introduce old-age pensions and the old-age insurance motives for having children disappear.

Fertility Choices and the Demographic Transition

At the beginning of this chapter, we discussed the demographic transition using the economic theory of fertility choices and taking into account institutions and social norms that produce inertia in those choices. Indeed, without inertia in fertility choices, demand for children should decrease immediately as the economic and institutional reasons for having many children disappear. In that case, a population should stabilize very quickly at a lower level, even taking into account the momentum effects of demographics we also discussed. However, this has not been the case and the expected changes in fertility choices have been much slower.

Demographic transition in developed countries. In the 20th century, incomes in developed countries increased as did the costs of having children relative to the price of mass-produced consumer goods. Countries became more urbanized and government-financed pensions to care for the elderly were introduced. As a result, families gradually chose to have fewer children. These social changes eliminated the old-age-insurance motive for having numerous children and led to a reduction in family size.

Reduced demand for children does not automatically adjust to these social and economic changes. Social norms for family planning choices take time to adapt to the evolving economic and social trends. It usually takes several generations for social norms to adapt and for families to want fewer children. Major medical innovations of the 20th century have led to a significant decrease in mortality rates in both developed and developing countries. The rational response of families to decreasing mortality rates would be an immediate and corresponding decline in fertility rates because higher survival rates for children would result in the need for fewer children in order to achieve an adequate number of surviving offspring.

Social norms do not change overnight, however, as can be seen from the experience of developed countries over the past 200 years. As we have seen, change is much more gradual. As people become more urbanized, the norms that call for large families tend to change for two reasons:

1. Costs and benefits change: Because urban schools, shelter, food, and clothing are more expensive, the costs of having children rise. Urban areas may also provide more support for elderly citizens, and the benefit of having many children to care for aging parents declines.
2. Social norms evolve or disappear: When people migrate to urban environments, they may feel uprooted and are more likely to adjust their social norms to their new circumstances than if they were still living in more traditional rural areas.

Demographic transition in developing countries. The same phenomenon that has taken place in advanced economies is already starting to take place in developing countries. As we saw earlier in this chapter, total population growth on the planet is already starting to decline. Fertility rates are declining slowly and are likely to decline further, due to the gradual shift in social norms.

These changes have only just begun; the end of the demographic transition in developing countries is not yet in sight. We do not yet know how quickly social norms will adjust and lead to a reduction in fertility rates that would stabilize the world population.

Demographic transition and future population growth. The demographic transition contradicts the dire predictions of Malthus on the future of the planet. Malthus assumed that the exponential growth of the world population would continue indefinitely until the growing scarcity of food would lead to famine, which would then curtail population growth. If developing countries' fertility choices reflect those we have described in advanced economies, then the world population will indeed stabilize. When this shift happens, however, a large group of elderly people will require care because reductions in fertility rates lead, over time, to an aging population.

Population Growth and Aging Populations

In developed countries such as the United States, large elderly populations are increasing. However, during the Great Depression and World War II, fertility rates were rather low. Between 1929 and 1945, the total fertility rate in the United States was, on average, 2.49 children for women ages 15–44.[9] After the end of World War II, however, there was a baby boom and between 1946 and 1964 the total fertility rate was 3.4 children.

Because there was a significant decline in fertility rates after the baby boom (they have been consistently below 2.1 children since 1980), the retirement of the baby-boom generation has begun to create a problem for younger generations. A simple number that helps us to understand this issue is the **old-age dependency ratio**, usually defined as the ratio of the retired population above the age of 65 over the active population defined as those from ages 16 to 64. We multiply this ratio by 100 to express it in percentages. The higher the old-age dependency ratio, the greater the percentage of retired people in the population who depend on those still in the labor force to support them financially.

In 1975, the old-age dependency ratio in the United States was 47%.[10] This means that there was roughly one retiree for 2 workers. By 2006, the old-age dependency ratio was already at 71% and it is projected to increase over time as the baby-boomer generation continues to retire through 2029. In addition, increases in life expectancy rates result in increases in the old-age dependency ratio.

Any reduction in population growth in developing countries will eventually result in a similar problem as that created by the baby-boomers in the United States. If population

---

[9]For U. S. fertility rates, see http://www.cdc.gov/search.do?action=search&query Text=fertility+rates.

[10]For data on the old-age dependency ratio in the United States, see http://www.bls.gov/emp/emplab10.htm.

growth declines, there will be fewer working people to take care of aging retirees who were born in times when population growth was larger. China is a good example. In 1980, its old-age dependency ratio was 8%; it is expected to grow to 36–39% by 2040 and 39–45% by 2050.[11] The reason for this shift is the one child policy China introduced in 1978, which led to a significant reduction in birth rates. This future increase in the old-age dependency ratio will pose an important challenge to financing pensions and health care for the elderly. Figure 3.10 shows the population pyramid for China in 2000, with projections for 2050. In 2000, the proportion of the population over 65 was quite small, but this proportion is projected to increase greatly in the future while the proportion of the young is projected to decrease.

FIGURE 3.10   China's Population Pyramid in 2000, with Projections for 2050

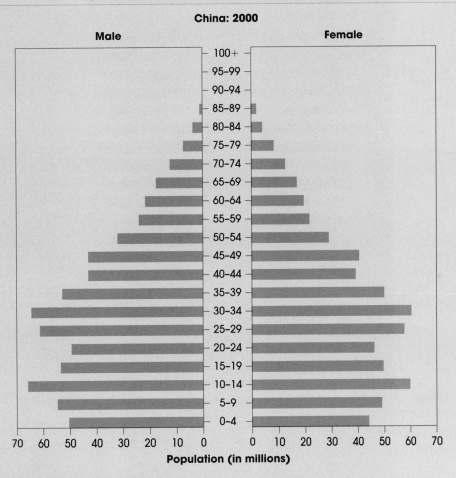

Source: U.S. Census Bureau, International Data Base.

(Continued)

[11]For data on the dependency ratio in China, see http://data.un.org/Data.aspx?d=Pop Div&f=variableID%3A44.

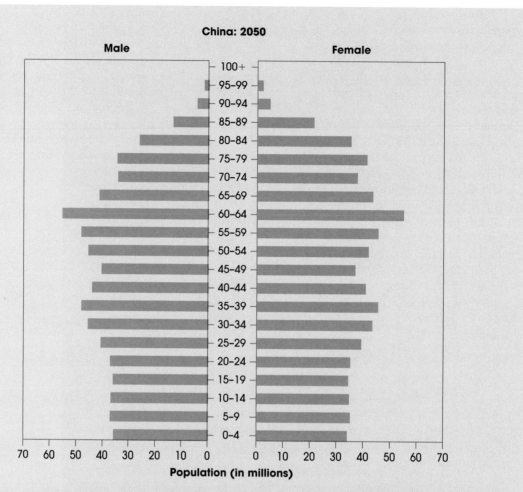

China: 2050

Male — Female

Population (in millions)

The one child policy will lead to a rapid aging of China's population. In 2000, the largest shares of the population were among those younger than 35. After 2050, they will be among those older than 60. The proportion of the old will increase and the proportion of the young will decrease, reflecting a drastic shift in the age distribution of the population.

Source: U.S. Census Bureau, International Data Base.

If, because of the demographic transition, the population growth rate continues to decline to 0.7% a year, which is the rate in developed countries, the world population would still grow by roughly 450 million per year, a number roughly equal to about 150% of the current population of the United States. Limited resources and available space on the planet will still be critical problems even as population growth declines.

Family Planning and Population Growth

Can developing countries afford to wait for the demographic transition to lower their population growth rates? Governments in some developing countries are not passively anticipating that fertility rates will drop, but are implementing family planning policies to speed up the demographic transition and reduce those rates.

Family Planning Policies

Family planning policies vary greatly across countries. China stands out as a country that took family planning to extreme measures. After the Cultural Revolution (1966–1976), Chinese leaders decided to curb population growth dramatically. By implementing a "one child" policy in 1978, the government prohibited parents from having multiple children. There were harsh punishments (career consequences, loss of housing, and/or no health and education coverage for the first child's siblings) and the implementation of the policy was quite ruthless in the cities. In rural areas, the policy's enforcement was not always as harsh, but it had tragic consequences for baby girls, as discussed earlier in this chapter. Rural families believed that if a family was to have only one child, it should be a boy. Parents often killed first-born daughters in order to have the chance of producing a male heir. When ultrasound technology became widely available, the selective abortions of female fetuses were a result. Because of this gender imbalance, in many villages over time, the great majority of young people were male. The gender imbalance made it very difficult for young boys from rural areas to find wives. At the same time, the dramatic reduction in the number of women of childbearing age resulted in a decrease in population growth.

In China's urban areas, other social phenomena occurred. Parents tended to spoil their only child regardless of gender, and the term "little Buddha" was coined to characterize an only child, many of whom were often obese due to their pampered upbringing.

On occasion, India has also implemented drastic family planning policies by means of active campaigns to sterilize people. When Indira Gandhi was prime minister (1966–1977), many people underwent forced sterilization or were sterilized without their knowledge. In other cases, sterilization was voluntary and people received a radio or other minor compensation for agreeing to undergo the procedure.

Other developing countries have generally been less aggressive and more respectful of human rights in their family planning policies. In the rural areas of some nations, family planning centers inform people of the advantages of having fewer children and government workers distribute contraceptives (condoms, birth control pills, etc.) free of charge. The ease with which women can obtain an abortion in many countries also plays an important role in family planning policies. However, it is very challenging to find good scientific studies that evaluate family planning policies and it is unfortunate that most of the available literature on this subject has been politicized.

Externalities and the Economics of Family Planning

Family planning policies have often been controversial for religious reasons. Because most current religions date back to times when mortality rates were very high and when social norms encouraged high fertility rates, many faiths oppose any form of family planning and continue to support social norms that promote high fertility. If we put religious debates and ethics aside, what are the economic justifications for various family planning methods? The answer, as is often the case in economics, depends on **externalities**, the impacts that economic transactions have on others who are not part of those transactions. In the case of a family's fertility choices, externalities refer to the impact of those choices on the welfare of the rest of the population. Even if it is rational for a family and in its best interests to have many children, these fertility choices still impose negative externalities on others. In other words, the choice to have many children could result in negative externalities on society as a whole.

Natural resources. The use of natural resources is a good example of a negative externality. When having children, families rarely take into account the high levels at which humans consume natural resources. This can lead to critical shortages of those resources for whole communities. For example, in parts of India, water utilities force overcrowded middle-class housing developments to turn off their water supplies every other day in order to compensate for the high number of tenants using the scarce reserves of clean water.

Congestion. A second negative externality relates to **congestion effects** in the provision of public services, such as health, education, and various types of infrastructure (water, sewer, transportation, etc.), which are very costly and particularly difficult to establish in developing countries. Families usually do not take into account the congestion effects of their fertility choices on the provision of public services.

How do large families contribute to congestion effects? For example, say there is only one school and one hospital for every 10 villages in Africa. If the populations in those villages increase while the number of schools and hospitals remains the same, the quality of the services they provide deteriorates. Classes become too large and queues at hospitals get longer. The influx of students and patients forces teachers and doctors to care for an increasing number of people using a fixed amount of time and resources. In the large megacities of poor countries, traffic congestion is far more extreme than in their developed counterparts. Traffic jams in Bangkok, Seoul, and Cairo are much worse than in Los Angeles, New York City, and London.

Emigration. A third negative externality relates to emigration. As population numbers increase in poor countries and jobs become scarcer, many people leave their countries to better their lives in rich nations, even if they must do so as illegal immigrants. This worldwide phenomenon can create problems for the host countries.

The emigration of rural inhabitants from developing countries to wealthier developed nations is a phenomenon similar to the rural–urban migration problem within developing countries, an issue that we will discuss in Chapter 5.

The externalities described above are the same in terms of congestion effects in the provision of public services and in terms of natural resource consumption. These externalities are often not as extreme in the case of emigration to rich countries as they are in the case of rural–urban migration within a developing country. There are several reasons for this.

1. Rich countries provide more and better public services, and congestion effects are likely to be smaller given the more extensive networks of schools and hospitals in those countries.
2. Emigration to rich countries has positive effects for the host countries. The immigrants contribute to the workforce, which creates a more dynamic labor market with a diverse set of skills that benefit booming economies.
3. In rich countries where birth rates are declining, younger immigrants add to the working population. This influx of young workers helps to ease the financial burden of funding pensions for the older members of society.

   To summarize, there are certainly good economic reasons to implement family planning policies and curb population growth in developing countries, while there may also be cultural, religious, or ethical reasons to oppose family planning. In this chapter, we have only discussed the economic rationale for family planning policy. It is important to keep in mind that even if they are well implemented, family planning policies take a long time to produce their effects fully because of the inertia in population growth related to age-distribution effects.

   In concluding this chapter, note that we have reasons to be optimistic about the question raised at the beginning of this chapter about the dangers of population growth. The world population may be on its way to stabilization, but whether this happens depends largely on whether the world economy continues to grow and incomes continue to increase. Even then, whether we can use the planet's scarce resources more efficiently so as to accommodate this larger stabilized population is still an open question. The topic of economic growth will be the subject of the next chapter.

Chapter Summary

Population over Time and the Demographic Transition

The world population has dramatically increased following the Industrial Revolution. Since 1800, it has gone from less than 1 billion to over 7 billion people. Since about 1950, most of the population growth on the planet has taken place in developing countries. Even though this growth is impressive, there are signs of a demographic transition to lower fertility rates and lower population growth. Since the 1960s, population growth rates have declined from 2% per year to less than 1.5%. Although the demographic transition has been progressing over many decades in advanced countries, there are signs that it has also started in developing countries. Population growth has been declining in the last 2 decades on all continents.

The Determinants of Population Growth

The growth rate of the population is the difference between the birth rate (the number of newborn babies per year per 1,000 inhabitants) and the death rate (the number of deaths per 1,000 inhabitants) both multiplied by 10. The birth rate depends on the total fertility rates (the average number of children born to a woman of child-bearing age, i.e., ages

15–49) and the number of women of child-bearing age, which depends on the age distribution, i.e., the shares of the population formed by the different age groups. The death rate depends on the mortality rates (the percentage of deaths in a particular age group) and the age distribution of the population.

The Determinant of Fertility Rates

The simple economics of fertility choices explains how families react to an increase in income, to a variation in the costs of having children, and to variations in the prices of consumer goods. Parents choose not only the number of children they will have but also how much time and money they will invest in each child. In addition, institutional factors help to explain some of the changes in the economic benefits of having children. With the development of government-financed pension programs and urbanization, the motive for having children as old-age insurance loses its importance and reduces the demand for them. Social norms regarding the desirable number of children adjust to these changed circumstances and lead to the demographic transition. This transition has already taken place in developed countries and is beginning to occur in developing countries.

Family Planning and Population Growth

The fertility choices families make can result in externalities in terms of resource use and the effects of congestion on the provision of public services. These externalities provide an economic justification for family planning policies. Developing countries have implemented various types of family planning policies, the most drastic being China's one child policy, which has been in place since 1978.

Key Terms

age distribution
age-specific fertility rates
age-specific mortality rates
birth rate
congestion effects
death rate
demographic transition
demographic trends
externalities

growth rate
inferior good
net migration rate
normal good
old-age dependency ratio
population growth rate
stationary population
total fertility rate

Review Questions

1. Who was Malthus and what was his theory? Did his theory prove correct? Why or why not?

2. A younger country (with a larger percentage of young people) will have a higher population growth rate than an older country (with a larger percentage of old people) even if both countries have exactly the same fertility and mortality rates. Explain this phenomenon using an age pyramid for a young country and for an old country.

3. Read Imran Rasul, "Household bargaining over fertility: Theory and evidence from Malaysia," *Journal of Development Economics* 86, no. 2 (June 2008): 215–241. What are the main ideas about bargaining over fertility choices developed in that article? What are the themes developed in the article that are not mentioned in this chapter? What kinds of marriage institutions affect bargaining over fertility choices within the household? Explain.

4. Choose two developing countries. Research and discuss their family planning policies. Have they been successful? Why or why not?

5. Why do fertility rates decline as countries become wealthier?

6. What is the role of social norms in explaining the demographic transition?

7. Explain the economic rationales for family planning policies.

8. Suppose there is a country in which 40% of people are below age 20, 40% are between ages 20 and 40, and 20% are between ages 40 and 60.

Assume no one lives above age 60 and the fertility rate is 4. The initial population size is 100.

(a) Compute the proportion of young, adult, and old after 20, 40, 60, 80, and 100 years.

(b) Calculate the population growth rate over each period of 20 years.

(c) Assume a country with the same population composition but with a fertility rate of 2 as a consequence of family planning policies. Do the same exercise as in (a) and (b) above. What is the effect of family planning policies after 20, 40, 60, 80, and 100 years on i) population growth and ii) the composition of the population?

9. Do the same exercise as in Question 8 but assume initially that 20% of people are below age 20, 20% are between ages 20 and 40, and 60% are between ages 40 and 60. Compare the answers to both questions and discuss the effect of the age distribution of the population on family planning policies.

10. Go on the website of the U.S. Census Bureau International Data Base. In 2013, it was at http://www.census.gov/population/international/data/idb/informationGateway.php. Find the projected age pyramid for Tunisia for 2000, 2025, and 2050.

(a) How does the pyramid evolve?

(b) What does this evolution tell us about the demographic transition?

(c) What does it tell us about aging of the world population?

(d) Answer questions (a)–(c) for a country of your choice.

4 Economic Growth

Until 250 years ago, income disparities between countries were much smaller than they are today. Some, like China, were wealthy, but most countries were relatively poor. However, in the last 250 years, the world economy has changed dramatically; some countries have grown vigorously while others have retained living standards from centuries ago.

In the second half of the 18th century, Great Britain industrialized its economy, followed in the 19th century by the United States and Europe. Japan, which had been isolated from the rest of the world for centuries and deeply mired in its feudal traditions, started growing very rapidly at the end of the 19th century. As a result of its economic strength, it was able to create a powerful military that defeated Russia's tsarist army in 1905 and went on to invade and occupy China and large parts of Asia in the 1930s and 1940s. After Japan's defeat in World War II, its economy continued to develop very rapidly, with GDP growing at 9% on average between 1950 and 1970. Other Asian countries (Taiwan, South Korea, Hong Kong, and Singapore) experienced rapid growth in the 1960s and 1970s by following the Japanese model of an export-oriented economy. Since the 1980s, China, the most populous country in the world, has had GDP growth of nearly 10% per year. As the Chinese "miracle" has unfolded over the past decades, income per capita has increased by a factor of 10. India has also started to grow vigorously since the end of the 20th century. Underscoring the power of these two emerging economies, India and China together include more than one-third of the world population.

It is important to distinguish between economic development and economic growth. **Economic development** refers to improvements in living standards and in the quality of life, while **economic growth** measures only growth in economic production. Economic growth may not accurately reflect all aspects of economic development because growth often results in negative effects on the quality of life such as pollution and urban congestion. Nevertheless, economic development cannot take place without economic growth. Growth is thus fundamental to development.

In this chapter, we introduce some important economic concepts to consider when discussing economic growth. We then review two very important theories of economic growth that explain the capital accumulation process. We will show that these theories, and others, based on capital accumulation explain only a small part of the differences in growth among countries. We then discuss the empirical evidence for the main causes of growth and highlight two important explanations for why some countries are so wealthy and others are so poor: geography and institutions. Currently, economists believe that institutions are central to understanding economic performance and economic growth in developing countries. The impact of institutions on growth will continue to inform our discussion of institutions throughout the remainder of the book.

Growth and Factors of Production

When we analyze the sources of economic growth, the first thing we must consider is the contribution made by the factors of production.

Factors of Production

Consider the output of a firm producing T-shirts. The firm generates output by combining labor and capital (machines, buildings, trucks). Labor and capital are critical factors in the creation of value and in the production of output in an economy. In our example, not a single T-shirt could have left the workshop floor without the combination of labor and capital, which are **factors of production**.[1] Factors of production are fundamental determinants of output. More labor and more capital allow for more production and contribute to growth.

What about the inputs (raw materials, energy, etc.) used to produce the T-shirts? Shouldn't they also be seen as factors of production? The inputs are not part of the value created by that firm. We define the concept of **value added** as the value of output minus the value of inputs used in production. The value added in this example is the value of the T-shirts minus the value of the inputs necessary to produce them. Value added is the basis for measuring production in the economy. If we do not subtract the value of inputs from the sales value of the T-shirts, we will count the cotton twice, first as output in the cotton factory and second as input in the T-shirt factory. By calculating the value added of all firms in the economy, we get the value of output produced in the economy as a whole and avoid double counting.

Increased output is not simply the result of providing additional labor and capital. An increase in labor will not result in more output in a highly mechanized industry, such as a car factory, while it will generate more output in a firm that uses labor as its primary resource, such as a bakery. The productivity of each factor of production depends on the quantity of the other factor of production used in production.

The combination of factors of production not only differs across firms and economic sectors, but also across countries because of differences in **factor abundance**, the relative availability of the different factors of production. In highly developed countries, capital is usually more abundant than labor and production thus relies more heavily on capital, while in poor countries labor is usually more abundant than is capital. Poor countries have less capital and it is usually of lower quality.[2]

A good example that illustrates this difference between developing and developed countries is road construction. In advanced economies, all the steps involved in building roads require the use of specialized machines that create flat surfaces, compact the ground below the road, transport and spread gravel, and

---

[1]In agriculture, land is also a very important factor of production. However, we will not discuss land in this chapter.

[2]For example, many used and outdated machines, trucks, and cars often find their way to developing countries, where they receive a second life. The quality of these machines and vehicles is often so bad that they break down and require frequent repairs.

mix, pour, spread, and smooth the asphalt. Since about 2000, China has undertaken an intensive road construction program. However, on many construction sites, hundreds of workers, instead of complex machines, break rocks into gravel while others spread the gravel on the roadbed. Many of the operations that are mechanized in advanced countries are performed by manual labor in developing countries like China because capital is scarce but labor is quite abundant.

The Production Function

The **production function** is a mathematical expression of the joint effect of the factors of production on output. Call K_t the stock of capital in the economy during year t, call L_t the amount of labor, and call Y_t output in the economy. The production function is:

$$Y_t = F(K_t, L_t) \tag{1}$$

This production function expressed in equation (1) is quite general. In this chapter, we will repeatedly use the Cobb-Douglas production function, which takes the following form:

$$Y_t = A_t K_t^\alpha L_t^{1-\alpha} \qquad 0 \le \alpha \le 1 \tag{2}$$

Note that this function takes into account the interdependence of the factors of production, more specifically their interaction. If a firm had either no labor or no capital, its output would be equal to zero, however much it had of the other factor. This is due to the multiplicative character of the function. Note also that A_t is a scale factor that links units of labor and units of capital to dollars of output.[3]

The Cobb-Douglas production function is a useful function for various reasons. First, it easily models the interaction between capital and labor. Second, as we will see below in more detail, it readily provides expressions for the returns to capital and labor, and for their contribution to the growth process. More importantly, it is a good approximation of the relationship between the factors of production and output at the macroeconomic level.

This production function exhibits **constant returns to scale**, meaning that if we multiply each factor by the same number, output is also multiplied by that number. Suppose we double the size of the labor force and the capital in our T-shirt production example. The assumption of constant returns to scale means that output is also doubled. We could also have a case of **increasing returns to scale** (output is multiplied by more than 2 if labor and capital are multiplied by 2) or **decreasing returns to scale** (output is multiplied by less than 2). Mathematically, the assumption of constant returns to scale means that if we multiply all factors by a constant z, then output is also multiplied by z:

$$A_t(zK_t)^\alpha(zL_t)^{1-\alpha} = z^{\alpha+1-\alpha}A_t K_t^\alpha L_t^{1-\alpha} = zY_t$$

To understand economies of scale, take the example of a shipping business. It has a boat that can carry a cargo of 1,500 tons. With two boats of the same

---

[3]Later in this chapter, we will see that other elements than scale enter into A_t.

size, the firm can ship twice as much cargo, or 3,000 tons. This is an example of constant returns to scale. However, assume that with the same amount of steel and materials used for two vessels, the firm instead builds a boat twice their size. Doubling the length, width, and height of the boat increases the volume by 8 and the business can thus ship much more than twice the amount of cargo. This is an example of increasing returns to scale.

Factor Productivity

The production function helps us analyze **factor productivity**, the contribution of each factor of production to output. There are different types of factor productivity, including **average productivity** and **marginal productivity** as well as **total factor productivity**, all terms that we explain in turn.

Average labor productivity. A common measure of economic performance is average labor productivity obtained by dividing national output by total employment in the economy, Y_t/L_t.[4] This number tells us how much, on average, one worker contributes to national output in a given year. We can express labor productivity in terms of the production function:

$$\frac{Y_t}{L_t} = A_t K_t^{\alpha} L_t^{1-\alpha-1} = A_t \left(\frac{K_t}{L_t}\right)^{\alpha} \tag{3}$$

Notice that average labor productivity is a function of K_t/L_t, the **capital intensity**, which tells us how much capital there is per worker. Rich countries that have abundant available capital have higher capital intensity in production than do poor countries.

Marginal productivity. Another measure economists often use in economic analysis is marginal productivity, the output increase caused by an additional unit of labor (or capital) in the economy. Newspapers rarely report this measure, but marginal productivity is nevertheless a fundamental concept. We use it in reference either to labor or to capital, calling it the **marginal productivity of labor**, or the **marginal productivity of capital**, respectively.

We can express the marginal products of labor (MPL) and capital (MPK) as the partial derivatives of the production function with respect to labor and capital.[5] We obtain this partial derivative by taking the derivative of the production function with respect to labor (or capital). It tells us by how much output increases if we add one unit of labor or capital to the economy. Mathematically, we obtain these expressions as follows:

$$MPL = \frac{\partial Y_t}{\partial L_t} = A_t K_t^{\alpha}(1-\alpha)L_t^{1-\alpha-1} = (1-\alpha)A_t \left(\frac{K_t}{L_t}\right)^{\alpha} \tag{4}$$

---

[4]In some countries where good access to employment data is not available, economists divide output by the population of working age.

[5]Note that since the production function is a function of both capital and labor, the derivative with respect to labor or capital is a partial derivative.

$$MPK = \frac{\partial Y_t}{\partial K_t} = A_t \alpha K_t^{\alpha-1} L_t^{1-\alpha} = \alpha A_t \left(\frac{L_t}{K_t}\right)^{(1-\alpha)} = \alpha A_t \left(\frac{K_t}{L_t}\right)^{-(1-\alpha)} \qquad (5)$$

Note that the marginal product of labor decreases when labor increases. L_t is in the denominator of the expression for MPL, so MPL declines when L_t increases. The same thing can be said for the marginal product of capital: MPK declines when K_t increases. Economically, this means that labor and capital have a **diminishing marginal productivity**: the more labor (or capital) added to the economy, the smaller the additional output that will be generated.

Another useful tool generated by the production function is the "cross-derivative," or the derivative of the marginal product of labor with respect to capital:

$$\frac{\partial Y_t}{\partial K_t \partial L_t} = A_t \alpha K_t^{\alpha-1}(1-\alpha)L_t^{-\alpha} > 0 \qquad (6)$$

This expression is positive, which means that the marginal product of labor increases when there is more capital in the economy. Adding a worker in a more mechanized firm will add more output than will adding a worker in a less mechanized firm. Similarly, incorporating more mechanization in a firm will make existing workers more productive.

Factor Shares

Another important concept in production is that of **factor shares**, the share of national income used as payment for the share of capital (or labor) in production. How do factor shares relate to the production function? In a competitive economy, we know that each factor will be paid its marginal product and that a firm will want to hire labor as long as the marginal product of labor is higher than the marginal cost of labor, or the wage rate. We can use the same reasoning for capital. A firm will want to invest, or add capital, as long as the marginal product of capital is higher than the *opportunity cost* of capital, the interest rate.[6] Indeed, as long as the marginal product of capital is higher than the interest rate, we get a higher return by investing more capital in the firm than by putting it in the bank. Of course, wages and the interest rate adjust in the economy in response to supply and demand on the labor and capital markets, but in equilibrium, the marginal product of labor and capital will adjust to be equal to the wage rate and the interest rate respectively. Therefore, at the economy-wide level, total wage payments should be equal to the marginal product of labor times the total amount of labor. Total payment to capital should similarly be equal to the marginal product of capital times the stock of capital in the economy. The shares of labor and capital are thus the payments to labor and capital divided by national income: $MPL \times L_t/Y_t$ and $MPL \times K_t/Y_t$.

---

[6]The opportunity cost of capital is the interest rate, because instead of investing capital in the firm, we can put it in the bank and earn the market interest rate.

When we calculate factor shares using the Cobb-Douglas production function, we get quite striking and simple results:

$$\frac{MPK.K_t}{Y_t} = \frac{A_t \alpha K_t^{\alpha-1} L_t^{1-\alpha}.K_t}{Y_t} = \frac{\alpha A_t K_t^{\alpha} L_t^{1-\alpha}}{A_t K_t^{\alpha} L_t^{1-\alpha}} = \alpha \qquad (7)$$

$$\frac{MPL.L_t}{Y_t} = \frac{A_t(1-\alpha)K_t^{\alpha} L_t^{-\alpha}.L_t}{Y_t} = \frac{(1-\alpha)A_t K_t^{\alpha} L_t^{1-\alpha}}{A_t K_t^{\alpha} L_t^{1-\alpha}} = (1-\alpha) \qquad (8)$$

Notice that the share of capital is equal to its exponent α in the production function and the share of labor is equal to $(1 - \alpha)$. The result is simple and easy to remember: the wage rate and the interest rate may vary over time, and the quantity of labor and capital in the economy may all fluctuate, but in the end, the shares of capital and of labor are given by very stable parameters. This is not simply a result of the particular Cobb-Douglas form for the production function. In reality, factor shares are also very stable. In advanced economies, the share of capital is roughly one-third of total income and the share of labor is roughly two-thirds of total income. The share of capital tends to be somewhat higher in many developing economies. In China, the share of capital has been rising over the years and has been above 40% for many years. In India, it has also been around 40% in recent years.

We can use factor shares to estimate key variables of the production function for which there is no systematic data collection, such as parameter α. Because we also usually have data from national economies for L_t, K_t, and Y_t, we can also use these data to estimate MPL and MPK.

Growth Accounting

The production function is a very useful tool in **growth accounting**, which estimates what percentage of an economy's growth rate we can explain using the growth rate of the labor force, the growth rate of the capital stock, and residual factors.

Take the Cobb-Douglas production function, but replace A_t with e^{at}. This is an exponential function. It assumes that A_t grows at a constant rate a over time. The production function is then:

$$Y_t = e^{at} K_t^{\alpha} L_t^{1-\alpha} \qquad (9)$$

Take the logarithm of that function, remembering that the logarithm of an exponential function is its exponent:

$$\text{Log } Y_t = at + \alpha \log K_t + (1 - \alpha)\log L_t \qquad (10)$$

If we take the derivative of the logarithm with respect to time (assuming time is continuous), we obtain growth rates:

$$\frac{d\log Y}{dt} = a + \alpha \frac{d\log K_t}{dt} + (1 - \alpha)\frac{d\log L_t}{dt} \Rightarrow$$

$$g_Y = a + \alpha g_K + (1 - \alpha)g_L$$

We can decompose the growth rate of national output ($g_Y = dY_t/Y_t dt$) into three elements:

1. the growth rate of capital multiplied by weight α;
2. the growth rate of the labor force multiplied by weight $(1 - \alpha)$; and
3. parameter a, called the **growth rate of total factor productivity**.

Total factor productivity is defined as the part of output that labor and capital cannot explain. It is usually thought to be the result of technological progress. Indeed, if innovations allow the production of twice as much of a given product with the same quantity of labor and capital, the innovations would show up in the estimate of total factor productivity. A higher level of output not caused by capital or labor may also be the result of institutional reforms or other aspects of the economy unrelated to capital accumulation and population growth. While technical progress may indeed lead to increases in factor productivity, it is not necessarily the only or even the main cause of increases in factor productivity. As we will see later in this chapter, institutional improvements may be a major cause of increases in total factor productivity.

Growth accounting makes it possible to estimate total factor productivity in a country year after year. If we know g_Y, g_K, g_L, and the capital share α, we can compute a. Take the case of China between 2000 and 2005. Its GDP grew at an average rate of 9.5%. Capital grew at an average rate of 12.6% and labor at a rate of 1%. Given an estimated share of capital of 50%, TFP growth is equal to $9.5 - .5 \times 12.6 - .5 \times 1 = 2.7$. In other words, 2.7% of the 9.5% growth rate, nearly one-third, is explained by total factor productivity.

Total factor productivity tells us a lot about a country's growth. Some countries have a very high capital accumulation but small growth in total factor productivity, while others have an opposite situation. Capital accumulation and population growth are without doubt an important source of growth in most countries, but, as we will see later in this chapter, the biggest variation among countries is total factor productivity.

To understand growth further, we need to consider all three sources of growth. We do this by looking both at the main theories of growth and at empirical research on growth as a means to determine why growth rates vary so much across countries.

The Neoclassical Solow Growth Model

Robert Solow developed the neoclassical growth model for which he received the Nobel Prize in Economics in 1987.[7] It is called the neoclassical growth model because it assumes competitive markets and a diminishing marginal product of capital. It easily links the production function with savings, investment, population growth, and technical change.

[7]Robert M. Solow, "A Contribution to the Theory of Economic Growth," *The Quarterly Journal of Economics* 70, no. 1 (1956): 65–94.

Constant Returns to Scale and Diminishing Marginal Products

To introduce the Solow model, let us return to the Cobb-Douglas production function assuming for now that $A_t = A$, i.e., it is constant over time:

$$Y_t = A K_t^\alpha L_t^{1-\alpha}$$

If we divide both sides of the equation by L_t we get:

$$Y_t/L_t = A K_t^\alpha L_t^{1-\alpha-1} = A(K_t/L_t)^\alpha$$

Using the notations: $y_t = Y_t/L_t$ and $k_t = K_t/L_t$, we then have the following equation relating average labor productivity and capital intensity:

$$y_t = A\, k_t^\alpha \tag{11}$$

This simple equation says that labor productivity increases with capital intensity. This relationship is important for development because it points to the critical role of capital accumulation in increasing labor productivity. We can obtain this relation between labor productivity and capital intensity because of the assumption of constant returns to scale.[8]

Figure 4.1 shows this relation, which highlights a key feature of the Solow model: average capital productivity ($Y_t/K_t = y_t/k_t$ when one divides both sides by L_t) decreases as capital in the economy increases. Figure 4.1 shows this

FIGURE 4.1   The Solow Model

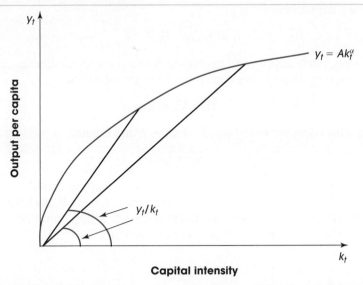

Output per capita y_t is expressed as a function of capital intensity (capital per worker). The slope y_t/k_t represents average productivity of capital. This slope decreases as capital intensity increases, meaning that average capital productivity decreases as capital intensity increases.

---

[8]Try inserting parameter β either larger or smaller than $1 - \alpha$ as an exponent of L_t in the production function and you will see that you cannot get rid of L_t in the numerator.

relationship graphically, as the angle going from the origin to the production function gets smaller as k_t rises on the horizontal axis. Average productivity decreases because of diminishing marginal productivity: the slope of y_t flattens as capital intensity increases.

Equilibrium in the Solow Model

What insights can we derive from the Solow growth model? Let us start with an equation that defines the allocation of national income Y_t between consumption C_t and savings S_t:

$$Y_t = C_t + S_t \tag{12}$$

Equation (12) is simply an accounting equation stating that all income not consumed is saved. In the next equation, we assume that national savings S_t are a constant share of income, with a savings rate s:

$$S_t = sY_t \tag{13}$$

It is clear that savings increase or decrease with income. However, we could also assume that savings vary with other variables, such as the interest rate or expectations of future income streams, so this is a simplifying assumption.

On the expenditure side, assuming a closed economy (with no exports or imports) and no government, the components of aggregate demand are consumption and investment I_t. Investment is the addition to the capital stock (assuming a depreciation rate δ):

$$I_t = K_{t+1} - K_t + \delta K_t \tag{14}$$

When aggregate supply and aggregate demand are in equilibrium, national income is then spent on either consumption or investment.

$$Y_t = C_t + I_t \tag{15}$$

Using equation (15), we have $C_t + S_t = C_t + I_t$ and obtain:

$$S_t = I_t \tag{16}$$

In a macroeconomic equilibrium (aggregate supply equals aggregate demand), the available funds for investment provided by household savings have to be equal to aggregate investment demand. Using equations (13) and (14), the equilibrium condition equation (16) becomes:

$$S_t = sY_t = I_t = K_{t+1} - K_t + \delta K_t \tag{17}$$

Rearranging terms, we get:

$$K_{t+1} = (1 - \delta)K_t + sY_t \tag{18}$$

This equation states that next period's capital stock will be equal to this period's capital stock that has not depreciated plus the investment generated from the savings in the economy.

Assume for simplicity that everyone works and that the population grows at rate n, meaning today's population is equal to yesterday's population plus the addition population, nL_t:

$$L_{t+1} = L_t(1 + n) \tag{19}$$

Now divide the capital stock equation (18) by L_t:

$$K_{t+1}/L_t = (1 - \delta)K_t/L_t + sY_t/L_t \tag{20}$$

Taking into account the fact that $y_t = y_t/L_t$ and $k_t = K_t/L_t$, and using the population growth equations (11) and (19), we have:

$$(1 + n)k_{t+1} = (1 - \delta)k_t + sA\, k_t^\alpha \tag{21}$$

This equation describes how capital intensity evolves over time. With k_{t+1} on the left-hand side of the equation and k_t on the right-hand side of the equation, the capital intensity at $t + 1$ is a function of capital intensity at t. Capital intensity evolves just like capital in the capital stock equation (18), except that we must add nk_{t+1} to k_{t+1} to correct for the fact that the population is growing at rate n. Seen differently, if we put nk_{t+1} on the right-hand side of equation (21), we have capital intensity at $t + 1$ that is equal to capital intensity net of depreciation at t plus savings per capita minus the negative impact of the population growth rate on capital intensity at $t + 1$.

The Steady State in the Solow Growth Model

What is the dynamic of capital intensity and income per capita over time? Figure 4.2 includes two functions representing both the left- and right-hand sides of the capital intensity equation (21) as two functions of k_t. The left-hand side $(1 + n)k_{t+1}$ is a straight line with slope $(1 + n)$ and the right-hand side $(1 - \delta)k_t + sy_t$ is the sum of a linear function of $(1 - \delta)k_t$ and of a concave function sy_t, $= sA\, k_t^\alpha$. As we can see from Figure 4.2, both functions intersect at a point where $k_{t+1} = k_t = k^*$, i.e., capital intensity, and thus output per capita, remain the same over time. This intersection point is called the **steady state**. In the steady state, the population grows at rate n, the savings rate is s, and the depreciation rate is δ, but capital accumulation is such that the level of capital intensity remains the same period after period.

We solve algebraically for the steady state equation by replacing in equation (21) k_{t+1} and k_t by k^* (and y_t by y^*). We get $(1 + n)k^* = (1 - \delta)k^* + sAk^{*\alpha}$:

$$k^* = \left(\frac{sA}{n + \delta}\right)^{\frac{1}{1-\alpha}} \rightarrow y^* = \frac{1}{A^{1-\alpha}}\left(\frac{s}{n + \delta}\right)^{\frac{a}{1-\alpha}} \tag{22}$$

Note from steady state equation (22) that the steady state capital intensity increases with the savings rate s and total factor productivity A, and decreases with the growth rate of the population n and the depreciation rate of capital δ. Higher population growth reduces capital intensity by definition. Moreover, a higher depreciation rate also leads to lower capital intensity as more capital is depreciated.

FIGURE 4.2   Steady State in the Solow Model

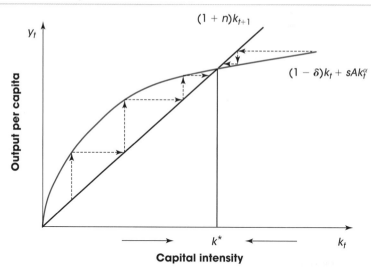

If capital intensity is below or above steady state capital intensity k^*, the economy adjusts and moves along the arrows, with output per capita and capital intensity varying until the steady state k^* is reached.

Why should we be interested in the steady state of the Solow model? The steady state is a way to characterize an economy in the long term. In the Solow model, capital intensity will converge over time to the steady state. Why is that? Returning to Figure 4.2, we start with a level of k_t that is lower than k^*. That level of k_t corresponds to the level of the curve $(1 - \delta)k_t + sy_t$. Take a straight vertical line from k_t to the $(1 - \delta)k_t + sy_t$ curve. We know from equation (21) that the point reached will correspond to a number $(1 + n)k_{t+1}$. Since these numbers are equal, we draw a horizontal line until we reach the $(1 + n)k_{t+1}$ line. The point reached corresponds on the horizontal axis to next period's capital intensity level k_{t+1}. We can now draw a vertical line until we reach again the curve $(1 - \delta)k + sy$. The new number will be equal to $(1 - \delta)k_{t+1} + sy_{t+1}$. From there, we can draw a horizontal line to the line $(1 + n)k$ to reach point $(1 + n)k_{t+2}$. Continuing in this manner, we converge toward the steady state k^*. We can repeat the same exercise if we start from a point k_t that is above k^*. We will also converge toward the steady state.

Growth Inside and Outside the Steady State

How do we represent the economic growth process with the Solow model? Because productivity stays constant in the steady state, the growth rate of income is necessarily equal to the rate of population growth. Population growth is thus the only variable that affects the growth of the economy in the steady state. This conclusion seems counterintuitive. However, we must remember that it is only true in the steady state. To understand economic growth in the Solow model fully, it is best to think of growth on the path *toward* the steady state, or the *transition growth path*. Returning to Figure 4.2, observe the horizontal moves we make as we progress from an initial low level of k_t toward the steady state k^* to the right. These are the period-by-period increases in capital intensity. These increases get smaller and smaller as we approach the steady state. The lower the initial level of capital intensity, the larger the *initial* increases. As capital intensity determines income per capita, large increases in capital intensity result in high increases in income per capita. Growth is thus higher the lower capital intensity is relative to steady state capital intensity, and it decreases gradually as it gets closer to the steady state. The economic reason for this decrease relates to the diminishing marginal product of capital. The marginal product of capital is higher in economies where capital is scarce and capital intensity low. Consequently, growth should be higher in economies where the initial level of capital intensity is low. Diminishing returns to capital thus influence the growth path of a country.

Technological Progress and the Steady State

An increase in total factor productivity in the Solow model can offset declining growth rates as capital intensity increases. To represent this case, we assume that A increases over time instead of remaining constant. We saw in steady state equation (22) that the steady state capital intensity increases with total factor productivity. Figure 4.3 illustrates this case. An increase in A from A_1 to A_2 leads to an increase in steady state capital intensity from k_1^* to k_2^*. We can understand this shift from A_1 to A_2 as technological progress that arrives exogenously. Technological progress means the introduction of new machines, new equipment, or new forms of organization that make it possible to increase output at a lower cost. In terms of the Solow model, if the economy is at a level of capital intensity k_t below k_1^*, then the increase in technical progress makes the economy move further away from the steady state, leading to higher growth.

FIGURE 4.3 Technological Progress in the Solow Model

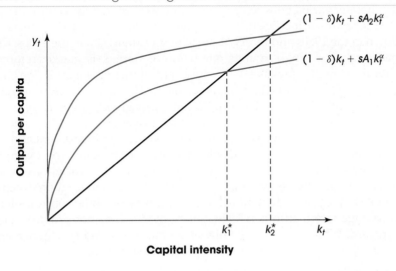

Technological progress in the economy leads to a shift from A_1 to A_2, which leads to an increase in steady state capital intensity from k_1^* to k_2^*.

The Effect of Different Savings Rates

Another prediction of the Solow model is that an increase in the savings rate leads to an increase in the steady state. Assume two countries, 1 and 2, that differ only in terms of their savings rate (the two countries have the same A, n, and δ). Assume country 1 saves 5% on average of its national income and country 2 saves 15% of its national income and assume α is equal to 1/3. Using equations (11) and (22), we get the following ratio of income per capita y_1/y_2 between the two countries:

$$\frac{y_1}{y_2} = \left(\frac{s_1}{s_2}\right)^{\frac{a}{1-\alpha}} = \left(\frac{5}{15}\right)^{\frac{1}{2}} = .577$$

Looking at the ratio y_1/y_2, we see that due to its lower savings rate, country 1 would end up in steady state having an income per capita that would be 57.7% of country 2.

Do some countries grow faster than others due to higher savings and investment rates? The Asian economies (Japan, South Korea, Taiwan, Hong Kong, Singapore, and now China) have traditionally had high savings and investment rates, and they have been growing rapidly in the last decades. Alwyn Young, among others, says that this is the main reason for the Asian growth miracle.[9] Technological progress has not necessarily been higher in those countries compared to the United States or to European economies, but their high savings rate can account for their higher growth rates.

For many years, economists thought that differences in savings and investment rates were the key to development and the Solow model is consistent with this view. However, in reality, countries with high investment rates do not necessarily have higher growth rates. The best example is that of the Soviet Union, which was a centrally planned economy until 1991. Investment rates in the Soviet Union were higher than in most of the rest of the world, hovering around 30% between 1930 and 1980, while investment rates across the world generally varied between 15% and 25%. Unfortunately, central planners allocated investment inefficiently and economic growth started an increasing slowdown in the 1960s and the 1970s, reaching virtually 0% in the 1980s. China also had a relatively high savings rate before it started its market reforms in 1978, but its growth rate was low because central planners were just as inefficient as Soviet planners in allocating investment. The savings rate in the reform period (since 1978) has still been quite high, but growth rates have become spectacularly high, consistently close to 10% for over 30 years. This is because market reforms resulted in a substantial improvement in investment allocation in agriculture, light industry, and manufacturing in general. The example of China before and after its market reforms shows that the efficiency of investments can vary greatly depending on the particular economic environment.

Even if savings rates do matter for growth, why do some countries have a higher savings rate than others? The Solow model does not provide insights in this regard. While it shows that higher savings rates lead to a higher steady state level of income, the savings rate is exogenously given.

---

[9]Alwyn Young, "The Tyranny of Numbers: Confronting the Statistical Realities of the East Asian Growth Experience," *The Quarterly Journal of Economics* 110, no. 3 (1995): 641–680.

Differences in Human Capital

When analyzing differences in growth, the accumulation of physical capital is not the only relevant variable. Another important variable is **human capital,** or the knowledge embodied in people. People in rich countries are generally more highly educated than are people in poor countries.

What can the Solow model tell us about differences in human capital? To explore this question, we need to modify the Cobb-Douglas production function and introduce a human capital parameter h to take into account the idea that those who are more educated are more productive. In other words, a country with more human capital will have more effective labor than one with less human capital. Parameter h, representing the average level of human capital, will be higher in countries where people are better educated:

$$Y_t = AK_t^\alpha(hL_t)^{1-\alpha} = (Ah^{1-\alpha})K_t^\alpha L_t^{1-\alpha} \tag{23}$$

The expression on the right-hand side shows that we can analyze the model with human capital in a similar way as the above model: parameter A has now been replaced by $Ah^{1-\alpha}$. Using our expression for the steady state, we simply replace A with $Ah^{1-\alpha}$; we then get:

$$y^* = \left[(h^{1-\alpha})A\right]^{\frac{1}{1-\alpha}}\left(\frac{s}{n+\delta}\right)^{\frac{\alpha}{1-\alpha}} = hA^{\frac{1}{1-\alpha}}\left(\frac{s}{n+\delta}\right)^{\frac{\alpha}{1-\alpha}} \tag{24}$$

Steady state income per capita depends directly on the level of human capital. If two countries, 1 and 2, differ only in terms of human capital, then their income ratios should be equal to h_1/h_2.

Differences in human capital are a better predictor of differences in income per capita than are investment rates. However, differences in human capital cannot be the whole story behind differences in growth and development. For example, the level of human capital was quite high in the former socialist countries under central planning, but growth still lagged. When the transition to a market economy started, economists were very optimistic about the prospects of growth for those countries because of the very high initial level of human capital, but that optimism faded when the GDPs of those countries began to decline. For some, the output fall lasted only a few years, but in the former Soviet Union, it lasted for the better part of the 1990s. The level of human capital also started to decline in the former Soviet Union following the fall in output. This means that increased education expenditures might not only be the cause of growth but also the result of growth. Countries that grow fast may be able to afford a better education. The direction of causality between human capital and growth is unclear.

Apart from the question of causality, differences in human capital are not extreme enough to explain the differences in development between countries. Differences in education should predict that Mali, one of the poorest countries in the world, would have roughly one-third of the income per capita of the United States.[10] In reality, it has only 3% of U.S. income per capita.

---

[10]Data from Robert E. Hall and Charles I. Jones, "Why Do Some Countries Produce So Much More Output Per Worker than Others?" *The Quarterly Journal of Economics* 114, no. 1 (1999): 91.

Income Convergence

The most basic prediction of the Solow model is **income convergence**: poor countries should grow faster than rich countries because they have a higher marginal product of capital. Eventually, the income gap should tighten and countries should all converge to the same steady state. Of course, this is only the case if all countries have the same savings rate, depreciation rate, population growth rate, and total factor productivity. Everything else being equal, the model predicts income convergence. A whole body of economics literature has developed to examine whether or not we can observe convergence in income per capita.[11]

There is not much evidence of income per capita convergence. Figure 4.4 plots the GDP per worker in 1960 and the vertical axis shows the real annual

FIGURE 4.4   Growth of Income Per Worker (1960–2008) and 1960 Initial GDP Per Worker

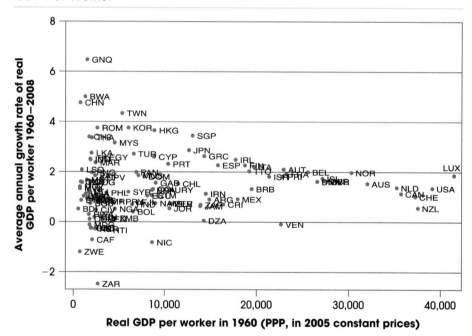

There is no negative relation between GDP per capita in 1960 and growth of GDP per capita between 1960 and 2008. If there were convergence, countries that were poorer in 1960 would have had higher rates of growth. On the contrary, poorer countries have had volatile growth, with some experiencing a lower growth than rich countries and some having a higher growth.

Source: Alan Heston, Robert Summers, and Bettina Aten, Penn World Table Version 7.0, Center for International Comparisons of Production, Income and Prices at the University of Pennsylvania, May 2011: http://pwt.econ.upenn.edu/php_site/pwt_index.php.

---

[11]See, for example, Robert J. Barro, "Economic Growth in a Cross Section of Countries," *The Quarterly Journal of Economics* 106, no. 2 (1991): 407–443; and Danny T. Quah, "Twin Peaks: Growth and Convergence in Models of Distribution Dynamics," *The Economic Journal* 106, no. 437 (1996): 1045–1055.

average GDP per capita growth rate between 1960 and 2008 for the 189 countries included in the Penn World tables.[12] Notice that countries that were poorer in 1960 have not necessarily had a higher growth rate than richer countries. Some did, but others did not. There is no negative correlation between initial GDP per worker and growth, contrary to what the Solow model predicts. Some countries have been catching up, but other countries have not seen much growth for decades. As we can see in Figure 4.4, some countries like Zimbabwe (ZWE), the Central African Republic (CAF), the Democratic Republic of the Congo (ZAR), Haiti (HTI), Nicaragua (NIC), or Venezuela (VEN) have even had, on average, negative growth.

Could we explain the absence of obvious convergence by differences in technological change across countries? The Solow model cannot explain such differences because technological progress is exogenous. Higher rates of technological progress in rich countries may offset a lower marginal product of capital, but we would still have to explain why some countries have experienced more technological progress than others. In other words, we would have to have an endogenous explanation for technical change rather than a less satisfactory exogenous explanation. This is what we investigate next.

Endogenous Growth Theory

Endogenous growth theory proposes a drastic alternative to the Solow growth model in both its components and its predictions. Contrary to the Solow model where technology is exogenous, **endogenous growth theory** suggests that growth is generated by endogenous technical change resulting from entrepreneurial innovation. This theory generated great excitement in the economics profession when it was introduced in a now-famous model by Paul Romer.[13] This model and a closely related, well-known paper by Philippe Aghion and Peter Howitt have initiated a whole body of economics literature.[14]

Boundless Knowledge-Based Growth

Endogenous growth theory is optimistic about the possibilities of economic growth and development. One of its important predictions is that growth can be boundless. Just as people in the 16th century could not imagine how we would live in the 21st century, endogenous growth theory envisions a world in which future generations may benefit from advances in technology that we cannot even grasp today. Endogenous growth theory does not deny that resources are finite or that the planet is facing serious ecological problems, but states that economic incentives have the potential to bring about technological change that significantly reduces our use of finite resources and helps us transition to the use of renewable resources.

---

[12]The Penn World Tables give purchasing power parity estimates of GDP and GDP per capita.

[13]Paul M. Romer, "Endogenous Technical Change," *The Journal of Political Economy* 98 no. 5 (1990): 71–102.

[14]Philippe Aghion and Peter Howitt, "A Model of Growth through Creative Destruction," *Econometrica* 60, no. 2 (March 1992): 323–351.

One of the key ideas of endogenous growth theory is the difference between human capital and knowledge. Because human capital can only exist in people, in the long term it cannot grow much faster than the population. In a country where the educational level is low, progress made in providing the population with a better-quality education will lead human capital to grow faster than the population, but in a country where high-quality education is already widespread, human capital cannot grow faster than the population. When people die or become unproductive because of old age or disability, their human capital will become idle.

Knowledge, unlike human capital, is not necessarily embodied in people. It exists in books, files, archives, patents, computer code, and in various other forms that humans can store. In principle, knowledge can grow boundlessly and can accumulate indefinitely. The only constraint to the accumulation of knowledge is that people have to produce it through research. Growth of knowledge is thus constrained by the number of people doing research.

Production of knowledge depends on the existing body of knowledge. Modern medical researchers who exploit the latest advances in genetics are more productive than were medical researchers at the beginning of the 20th century who did not even know about antibiotics. Research productivity can thus increase because new ideas develop from the existing body of knowledge. In endogenous growth theory, the more knowledge there is in the economy, the higher its growth rate.

Knowledge as a Non-Rival Good

Knowledge is not just any type of economic good; it is a **non-rival good**, or a good that can still be consumed by the seller even after it is sold. Most normal economic goods are rival goods; once they are sold, the seller can no longer consume them. In contrast, the seller of knowledge still keeps it even after selling it. However, knowledge is also an **excludable good**, which means a seller can exclude others from its consumption. Many public goods are both non-rival and non-excludable. A country's army provides the public good of defense. One cannot exclude particular members of the public from the good provided by that defense. People can, however, be excluded from access to knowledge. Secrecy rules, patents, and intellectual property rights are all means to prevent access to knowledge. Keeping knowledge hidden from others is not always easy. For example, music can circulate illegally even when it is protected by copyright laws. The same is true for computer software programs and all other forms of knowledge.

The possibility of excluding others from access to knowledge is important to understanding how the creation of knowledge works. Knowledge in the economy progresses via incentives to innovate. Entrepreneurs develop an idea that will improve a particular technology by either lowering costs for producers or delivering a new product to consumers. Entrepreneurs innovate in the hope of receiving the maximum amount of money from their innovations. This maximum profit is possible only if they can prevent others from copying their innovations and making money from them. Copyright and patent laws protect the knowledge created by innovators by preventing others from using this knowledge.

For innovation incentives to work properly, innovators must expect **monopoly rents**, i.e., extra profits derived from monopoly status. Perfect competition would otherwise eliminate the incentives to innovate. What does this mean? Suppose that an entrepreneur wants to invest in research on a new household refrigerator that requires very little energy and is relatively inexpensive. We can easily imagine that there would be a large market for such a product. However, the entrepreneur must take significant risks and invest large sums of money in research before a good product design is developed. The research may not be successful and, even in case of success, the demand may be disappointing. Assume that in case of a successful design, other firms will immediately copy it and enter the market for the new refrigerator. The innovating firm and the competing firms will both offer lower prices to consumers up to the point where they are barely breaking even. This is usually what happens in a situation of perfect competition. If such future cutthroat competition is to be expected, the entrepreneur may decide that it is not worth investing the money in research for the new product because there will not be adequate future profits to recover the fixed cost of investment. If, on the other hand, in case of successful research, the innovating firm receives a patent giving it exclusive rights to produce the new refrigerator for a number of years, the firm will reap monopoly profits during that period. The prospect of those monopoly profits will make it worthwhile to invest in research and innovation. Acquiring temporary monopoly rights leads to imperfect competition but provides incentives to innovate.

The idea that imperfect competition is necessary for innovation was put forward by Joseph Schumpeter, the famous Austrian economist (1883–1950) who taught at Harvard in the 1930s and 1940s. Schumpeter saw innovation by entrepreneurs as the most positive force of capitalism and the source of economic growth, and he understood that the search for monopoly profits was a key motivation of entrepreneurs. It is important to note another important difference between the Solow neoclassical growth model and the endogenous growth model: the Solow model assumes perfect competition, in which factors are paid according to their marginal productivity and capital accumulates until the marginal product of the last unit of capital invested is equal to the interest rate or rental price of capital. In the endogenous growth model, innovators are motivated by the possibility of generating monopoly profits with their innovation. Imperfect competition is *necessary* for growth in the endogenous growth theory.

Monopoly profits associated with innovations are usually temporary. Society has to strike a fine balance between the incentives of innovators and the benefits to society from making technological knowledge widely available. One thing is certain: not protecting innovations or protecting them for too long are not optimal situations. The time frame for temporary protection of innovations is studied in the theory of industrial organization or in the theory of intellectual property rights.[15]

---

[15]See, for example, Jean Tirole, *The Theory of Industrial Organization* (Cambridge, MA: MIT Press, 1988); and Suzanne Scotchmer, *Innovation and Incentives* (Cambridge, MA: MIT Press, 2006).

Basic Equations of the Romer Model

Endogenous growth models are mathematically more complex than the Solow model. In this section, we examine a partial and simplified version of the Romer model to provide a sense of how it works.

We start by dividing the total number of workers in the economy L_t between the labor force working in the productive sector L_{Yt} and the labor force working in the research sector L_{At}:

$$L_t = L_{Yt} + L_{At} \tag{25}$$

The production function differs slightly from that in the Solow model. Human capital in the productive sector is equal to $A_t L_{Yt}$, the product of the stock of knowledge A_t and productive labor. The production function takes the following form:

$$Y_t = K_t^\alpha (A_t L_{Yt})^{1-\alpha} \tag{26}$$

Note that A_t varies over time, is endogenous, and depends on innovation. Growth of knowledge in period t is given by:

$$g_{At} = \Delta A_t / A_{t-1} = \delta L_{At}$$

Another way of reading that equation is to multiply both sides by A_t:

$$\Delta A_t = A_{t-1} \delta L_{At}$$

The increment to knowledge $\Delta A_t = A_t - A_{t-1}$ is then given by the stock of knowledge multiplied by the labor force in the research sector and parameter δ, which can be interpreted as an indicator of the efficiency of research. The insight that additions to knowledge increase with the stock of knowledge is important because countries with a higher stock of knowledge will add more to knowledge than countries with a lower stock of knowledge.[16] Note also that a key implication that derives from these assumptions is that if A_t grows just as do K_t and L_t, there are increasing returns to scale in the economy.

The Romer Model versus the Solow Model

The Romer model's predictions are different from those of the Solow model in several important ways:

1. In the Romer model, imperfect competition is necessary for innovation and growth, while the Solow model is based on the neoclassical model of perfect competition.
2. Innovation is endogenous in the Romer model and depends on the stock of knowledge and research and development. It is exogenous in the Solow model.

---

[16]One component of the model that we will not develop here is that the innovation sector that produces knowledge and that sells patents to a sector in which there is monopolistic competition. The latter sector produces inputs for the competitive consumer goods sector. In equilibrium, the labor force in the productive and research sector is then allocated in such a way that the return to labor in both sectors is the same. Note that if labor in the innovation sector grows, knowledge growth will also be higher in the economy.

3. In the Romer model, rich countries should grow faster than poor countries because of their higher existing stock of knowledge.[17] The model predicts divergence between poor and rich countries, not convergence. The Solow model predicts that poorer countries with low capital intensity should experience higher growth rates and converge at the income level of richer countries. If the Romer model is a better description of reality than the Solow model, then we must be very concerned about whether poor countries will be able to catch up with rich countries.

Intellectual Property Rights and Technology Transfers

Development economists focus primarily on the divergence result of the Romer model. This result, however, ignores trade and circulation of information between rich and poor countries. According to the logic of the Romer model, even though the rich countries are most productive at research, technology transfers from the rich to the poor countries could avoid economic divergence between them. An implication of this proposition is that the protection of intellectual property rights at the international level is not beneficial to poor countries because it hinders technology transfers that would reduce divergence between rich and poor countries.

The WTO and Property Rights Protection

At the international level, intellectual property rights are an important source of disagreement between rich and poor countries. In the World Trade Organization (WTO), the United States is fighting for the protection of intellectual property rights. For example, it has raised complaints about Chinese companies that have pirated software from Microsoft and other technologies from various companies. The Chinese seem to excel at taking apart Western products and reproducing cheaper versions that sell very successfully in mainland China and other Asian markets. Because American companies put the money and time into developing and producing the original products, they claim that it is unfair that the Chinese are making profits from copying their ideas.

The economic argument for the strict enforcement of intellectual property rights is that the prospect of temporary monopoly profits is necessary to create incentives for innovation. In the end, poor countries will benefit from the availability of more effective drugs, better cars, and advanced computers, as these goods will be cheaper to buy and of better quality. Thus, strict enforcement of property rights should also be in their interests.

There are also powerful arguments against overly strict enforcement of property rights at the international level. First, poor countries may directly benefit from technological transfers at the lowest possible price. These transfers counter the tendency toward divergence in economic development and give poor countries an opportunity to catch up. Second, by granting poor countries easy access to advanced technologies and thus helping them to achieve higher growth rates, the demand for products from innovating firms and rich countries will increase.

(Continued)

---

[17]However, empirical research has shown that the Romer model is too extreme in terms of its treatment of the research sector. See, for example, Charles I. Jones, "R&D-Based Models of Economic Growth," *Journal of Political Economy,* 103, no. 4 (August 1995): 759—784.

Third, developing countries can achieve better economic outcomes if they have quicker access to technological transfers, even if there is a price in terms of reduced incentives to innovate in the richer countries. From the economists' point of view, knowledge externalities mean that overly strict enforcement of property rights is not optimal in terms of encouraging development in poor countries. There is an optimal trade-off between lower profits for innovating firms (and maybe a slightly lower innovation rate) and the benefits to developing countries from technological transfers. While it is hard to believe that Microsoft has less incentive to innovate because China and other developing countries pirate its software products, a total lack of enforcement of intellectual property rights is not the way to go either. As always, the difficulty is finding that optimal trade-off in practice.

This discussion leads us to ask this question: Are advanced industrialized countries insisting on too much enforcement of intellectual property rights in WTO negotiations? Perhaps poor countries have a valid point by organizing to impose an agenda at WTO meetings that would be friendlier toward the interests of developing countries.

Empirical Analysis of Economic Growth

According to the growth theories we discussed above, the accumulation of physical and human capital, technological progress, and population growth play important roles in explaining a country's growth rate. In this section, we analyze the determinants of growth empirically. We start by asking what drives the main differences in the levels of income between rich countries that historically have had high growth and poor countries that have had lower growth.

Table 4.1 shows 1) output per worker in different countries as a ratio of the U.S. level; 2) the contribution of capital (calculated here from the Cobb-Douglas production function as the capital output ratio to the power of one-half);[18] 3) the contribution of human capital; and 4) total factor productivity when the latter is computed residually as in growth accounting. The data are from 1988 and taken from the Penn World Tables. They are measured in purchasing power parity. Output per worker is very highly correlated with long–term growth and thus can be seen as a measure of that growth. In Table 4.1, we also see that Canada has about 94% of the productivity of the United States. It has about the same capital output ratio and the same level of total factor productivity, but a lower level of human capital. Differences in human capital are thus the main determinant of the difference in productivity between Canada and the United States.

Let us look now at the data for developing economies: differences in total factor productivity are the main reason for differences in output per worker (labor productivity) with the United States. Take China. Its productivity level in 1988 was about 6% of that of the United States (in purchasing power parity terms). The contribution of capital was close to 90% that of the United States and its level of human capital was about two-thirds that of the United States. Its total factor productivity

---

[18]This is derived from a model including human capital in which $y_t = \left(\frac{K_t}{Y_t}\right)^{\frac{\alpha}{1-\alpha}} h_t A_t$, where $h_t = H_t/L_t$ is human capital per worker, and where $\alpha = 1/3$.

TABLE 4.1   Decomposition of Productivity Differences (Ratios to the United States)

Country	Y/L	Contribution from $(K/Y)^{\alpha/(1-\alpha)}$	H/L	A
United States	1.000	1.000	1.000	1.000
Canada	0.941	1.002	0.908	1.034
Italy	0.834	1.063	0.650	1.207
West Germany	0.818	1.118	0.802	0.912
France	0.818	1.091	0.666	1.126
United Kingdom	0.727	0.891	0.808	1.011
Hong Kong	0.608	0.741	0.735	1.115
Singapore	0.606	1.031	0.545	1.078
Mexico	0.433	0.868	0.538	0.926
Argentina	0.418	0.953	0.676	0.648
USSR	0.417	1.231	0.724	0.468
India	0.086	0.709	0.454	0.267
China	0.060	0.891	0.632	0.106
Kenya	0.056	0.747	0.457	0.165
Zaire (today Congo)	0.033	0.499	0.408	0.160
Average, 127 Countries	0.296	0.853	0.565	0.516
Standard Deviation:	0.268	0.234	0.168	0.325

Differences in measures of accumulation of physical and human capital explain only a small part of the differences in output per worker between the poorest countries in the world and the United States. The largest discrepancy is explained by differences in total factor productivity.

Source: Robert E. Hall and Charles I. Jones, "Why Do Some Countries Produce So Much More Output per Worker than Others?" *The Quarterly Journal of Economics* 114, no. 1 (1999): 91.

was, however, only 10% that of the United States. Neither capital accumulation nor human capital accumulation can explain the difference in output per worker in China relative to the United States. We can reach the same conclusion looking at India, Kenya, or Zaire (today called the Democratic Republic of the Congo). Accumulation of physical and human capital would predict a much smaller difference in output per worker than is the case in reality. We also see that the standard deviation of total factor productivity is very high across the world.

If we cannot explain differences in levels of economic growth using only capital accumulation and differences in human capital, and if variations in total factor productivity are the main driver of differences in output per worker, then what explains those differences in total factor productivity? We now discuss two competing hypotheses that seek to provide an answer: geography and institutions. The geographical view emphasizes differences in climate and geographical isolation as a cause of differences in economic growth rates. The institutional view postulates a causal effect of institutions on growth: countries that have strong institutions to protect property rights and investment will grow and develop faster than countries with weak institutions.

Geography and Growth

In a series of articles, Jeffrey Sachs, a Columbia University economist, and his various coauthors have emphasized the role of two important geographical facts relevant to growth: the importance of latitude (distance to the equator) and geographical isolation.[19]

A first striking fact is that there are very few rich countries between the tropics of Cancer and Capricorn. The poorest countries of the world are located in those tropical latitudes closest to the equator, while the rich countries tend to be located in the more temperate zones outside the tropics. Most of the African continent is located in the tropics, along with most of the poorest countries in the world. Parts of Mexico, all of Central America, and most of South America are also in the tropics. Southeast Asia and a large part of South Asia are located within the tropics as well; the only rich country in the tropics is Singapore.[20]

As far as geographical isolation is concerned, there is in general much less population density in landlocked areas. Large parts of Africa are landlocked and most African rivers are not navigable. Significant areas of Russia are landlocked as well as most of Central Asia. The U.S. Midwest and extensive regions of northern Canada are also landlocked and very lightly populated, while landlocked areas of Africa, Central Asia, Northern India, and Russia are somewhat more densely populated than the latter. Note also that while large parts of China are not landlocked because of a long coastline and the presence of two very large rivers that cross China (the Yangtze and the Yellow River), there are still areas of China that are both densely populated and distant from major waterways.

Economic reasons for the importance of geography. Why does geography matter for growth and development? The key reasons are as follows:

1. The areas within the tropics are less hospitable because of tropical diseases and the intense heat. Tropical diseases have tended to increase mortality and have negatively impacted the general health of the population. Moreover, the extreme heat makes hard physical labor outdoors, especially farming, difficult.
2. Significant volatility in rainfall amounts is prevalent in tropical countries. Tropical areas receive a lot of rain, which should be good for agriculture, but there is too much rainfall volatility to allow stable agricultural production. Many areas in India, for example, will not have any rain for months, but during the monsoon season, the daily rainfall will often cause deadly floods.
3. Landlocked areas have high transportation costs. Easy access to coastal areas facilitates trade, as ships can carry large amounts of goods between international seaports and ports on navigable rivers.

The role of geography in practice. Because geography is a factor that is truly exogenous to the economic system, it seems quite plausible that it should play a role in development. However, there are reasons to question whether geography is the main cause of differences in development across the world today. If geography played a major role in development, then the countries

[19]John Luke Gallup, Jeffrey D. Sachs, and Andrew D. Mellinger, "Geography and Economic Development," *International Regional Science Review* 22, no. 2 (August 1999): 19–232.
[20]Northern Australia is located in the tropics.

that were disadvantaged by climate and geography should have always been poorer than the countries that were located in more fortunate places, but this is not the case. Before the 1500s, the Mughal civilization of India, the Aztecs in Mexico, and the Inca in Peru were among the most developed civilizations in the world. Now, those same regions are among the poorest in the world.

In a well-known article, Daron Acemoglu, Simon Johnson, and James Robinson have documented a trend that they call "reversal of fortune," in which there is a negative correlation between development in 1500 and development today.[21] We do not have measures of GDP per capita for 1500 because no one collected those statistics at the time. We have, however, rather good proxies for development, one of which is the level of urbanization. There has always been a relatively strong correlation between economic development and level of urbanization. In the past, only societies with a minimum level of productivity in agriculture and a well-developed system of commerce and transport could sustain large cities. Because agriculture is the basic source of food for a population, the more productive agriculture in a society is, the larger the fraction of the population that does not need to live off the land because farmers can produce enough for themselves and for those in the cities.

Figure 4.5 shows the correlation between urbanization in 1500 in territories of what would later become European colonies and the log of GDP per capita in 1995 (PPP). Urbanization is measured as the fraction of the population living in urban centers of more than 5,000 inhabitants. GDP per capita is measured in logs to make the differences look smaller and also because differences in logs represent growth rates. In 1500, Europe had not yet started to colonize the world and to take over the Americas, Africa, Oceania, and large chunks of Asia. European colonization in the centuries that followed thoroughly destroyed American Indian civilizations such as the Aztec and the Inca. The slave trade in Africa also had a profoundly destructive effect on existing civilizations on that continent.[22] The most adverse affects of colonization by European powers were in those areas of the world that were the most economically developed. We can see a clear negative correlation between urbanization rates in 1500 and GDP per capita in 1995. A similar picture also emerges if development is measured by population density instead of by urbanization. This negative correlation suggests that colonization had, in the long run, a deeply adverse effect on the economic development of the colonized countries.

This negative correlation sheds doubt on the idea that geography is the key to understanding differences in development. What are the causes of this reversal of fortune? The question leads us to another—and more promising—explanation for differences in development across the world: the role of institutions.

Institutions and Growth

Douglass North, Nobel Prize winner in economics, has argued for many years that institutions are the key to understanding why some countries developed earlier than others. Recent research has shown strong evidence of a causal link

---

[21]Daron Acemoglu, Simon Johnson, and James A. Robinson, "Reversal of Fortune: Geography and Institutions in the Making of Modern World Income Distribution," *The Quarterly Journal of Economics* 117, no. 4 (November 2002): 1231–1294.
[22]See Nathan Nunn "The Long-Term Effects of Africa's Slave Trades," *The Quarterly Journal of Economics* 123, no. 1 (2008): 139–176.

FIGURE 4.5   Log GDP Per Capita in 1995 among Former European Colonies and Urbanization Rate in 1500

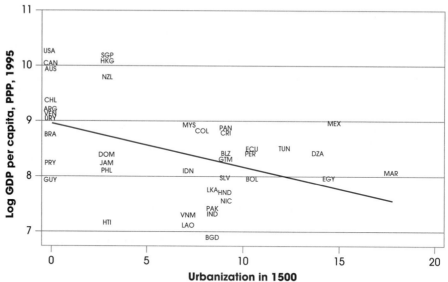

There is a negative correlation between economic development in 1500 (represented by urbanization rates measured by historians) and modern economic development as measured by log GDP per capita in 1995. If geography were the main cause of underdevelopment, we should, instead, see a positive correlation.

Source: Daron Acemoglu, Simon Johnson, and James A. Robinson, "Reversal of Fortune: Geography and Institutions in the Making of Modern World Income Distribution," *The Quarterly Journal of Economics* 117, no. 4 (November 2002): 1231–1294.

between institutions and growth. This research was described in another famous paper by Daron Acemoglu, Simon Johnson, and James Robinson.[23]

The correlation between institutions and growth. Acemoglu and his colleagues take a measure of institutions from an indicator called "protection against expropriation risks" averaged between 1985 and 1995. These are data from the International Country Risk Guide produced by a private company, *Political Risk Services,* to assess the risks that investments will be expropriated in different countries. These survey data are based on subjective perceptions of businesspeople. Many economists use them as a measure of institutions because the data are comprehensive and available for a very large number of countries in the world. The data are, nevertheless, not an ideal measure of institutions because perceptions of a country's institutions might be tainted by its economic performance. In other words, the observation of poor economic performance in a country might lead the people surveyed to give an overly negative view of institutions in that country. Conversely, the observation of strong economic performance might lead to surveys that are too positive.

---

[23]Daron Acemoglu, Simon Johnson, and James A. Robinson, "The Colonial Origins of Comparative Development: An Empirical Investigation," *The American Economic Review* 91, no. 5 (2001): 1369–1461.

As we can see from Figure 4.6, there is a strong positive correlation between log GDP per capita and protection against expropriation risks. Note that because we are looking at log GDP per capita and not directly at growth rates, we are capturing growth in the long term, that is, over centuries rather than over decades. In fact, taking log GDP per capita as a measure of long-term growth is equivalent to measuring growth with an initial level of GDP per capita close to zero, which is a good approximation of what it was many centuries ago.

Even though there is a strong correlation between institutions and growth, correlation is not causation. It is not clear that institutions cause growth. The causality could go the other way. One could indeed argue that poorer countries cannot afford good institutions and that they can introduce better institutions only after achieving a certain level of development. Even if reverse causality is not convincing, there could be omitted variable bias: a third variable that explains both the quality of institutions and growth.

One of the reasons why the article by Acemoglu, Johnson, and Robinson became so famous is that they were able to demonstrate empirically a causal effect of institutions on growth using the instrumental variable technique (see the box on page 110) by showing that institutional differences in developing countries have their origins in different rates of settler mortality at the time of colonization.

FIGURE 4.6 Average Protection against Risk of Expropriation and Log GDP Per Capita

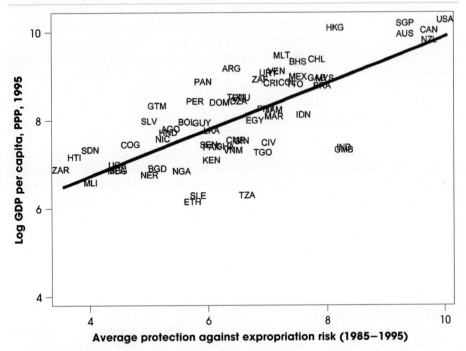

Countries in which economic agents are better protected against the risk of expropriation, an indicator of the quality of institutions, have a higher level of economic development as measured by log GDP per capita.

Source: Daron Acemoglu, Simon Johnson, and James A. Robinson, "The Colonial Origins of Comparative Development: An Empirical Investigation," *American Economic Review* 91, no. 5 (2001): 1380. Printed with permission of American Economics Association.

Settler mortality and institutions. When European colonizers spread out to conquer the world, they found that some areas were more inhospitable than others. The Congo, with an abundance of rubber and copper, had very valuable natural resources, but malaria and other tropical diseases were so widespread that it was extremely challenging for Europeans to settle there. Settler mortality was extremely high in the Congo, making it nearly impossible for colonizers to settle down for long periods. The colonizers (in this case, the Belgians) were only interested in extracting the natural resources to sell on the world market. Therefore, they set up **extractive or predatory institutions** that were intended to exploit the country's resources. The Belgian colonizers enslaved the Congo's native peoples and forced them to work on large rubber plantations under harsh conditions that soon caused disease and death among the Africans.

While the colonial institutions in the Congo are a clear example of predatory institutions, Europeans also found more hospitable locations for colonies, where settler mortality was lower, such as parts of North America, Australia, New Zealand, and Argentina. Immigrants from all over Europe came to settle in these new territories in the 18th and 19th centuries. Here, the intention was not to steal the natural resources, but rather to put down roots and develop agriculture, commerce, and industry. Because the new settlers emigrated in the hope of improving their own fortunes and those of their children, they sought to establish institutions that would be beneficial for economic development. They did this by improving the institutions of their home countries. For example, the drafters of the U.S. Constitution were very concerned about not reproducing the institution of the monarchy in the newly independent United States. As a result, they established a system of checks and balances to prevent the emergence of an excessively powerful executive branch of government that could expropriate private businesses.

Acemoglu and his colleagues argue that differences in settler mortality among the European colonies led to the establishment of different types of institutions. Predatory institutions were established in those areas where settler mortality was high and institutions protecting property rights were established in areas more hospitable to settlers. This difference in the type of institutions established at the time of colonization has had a long-lasting effect on growth in those former colonies.

The work by Acemoglu, Johnson, and Robinson has quickly become the dominant view on explaining growth. It has brought institutions to the mainstream of economics. Because of this research, much of the current research in economics tries to understand the role of institutions and their effects on different measures of economic performance.

A Causal Effect of Institutions on Growth

The best way to produce evidence of causality of institutions on growth is to find an instrumental variable—a variable that is correlated with the independent variable (institutions) but not with the dependent variable (log GDP per capita)—and to perform instrumental variable regression.

This method, explained more at length in the Econometric appendix to this book, allows us to estimate a causal effect from the independent variable to the dependent variable. In a first stage, the independent variable is regressed on the instrumental variable. This gives an estimate of the part of the variation of the independent variable that is explained by the variation of the instrumental variable. Because the latter is not correlated with the dependent variable, we can then be confident that the part of the variation of the independent variable predicted by the instrumental variable is truly independent from the dependent variable. In a second stage, we then regress the dependent variable on the part of the independent variable predicted by the instrumental variable. The estimation coming out of this second stage gives us an estimate of a true causal effect from the independent to the dependent variable.

Why can settler mortality be a good instrumental variable? Acemoglu et al. first argued that settler mortality centuries ago could not have had a direct impact on today's level of economic development. In other words, settler mortality is uncorrelated with the dependent variable (log GDP per capita). On the other hand, as we saw in Figure 4.7, there is a negative correlation between settler mortality (measured in logs) and protection against expropriation. In other words, countries that had high settler mortality at the time of colonization have weak institutions today.

The regression analysis in Table 4.2 gives the evidence for the institutional theory of growth. The basic result is in the first column of the table. Look first at panel C, which gives the ordinary least squares regression of log GDP per capita against protection from expropriation. Notice that the coefficient is equal to 0.52 (with a standard error of 0.06 in parentheses below). Look now at panel A, which is the instrumental variable regression called the second stage. Here, the coefficient is larger (0.94 with a standard error of 0.16). Finally, panel B gives the first-stage regressions, i.e., the

FIGURE 4.7   A Negative Correlation between Settler Mortality and Protection against Expropriation

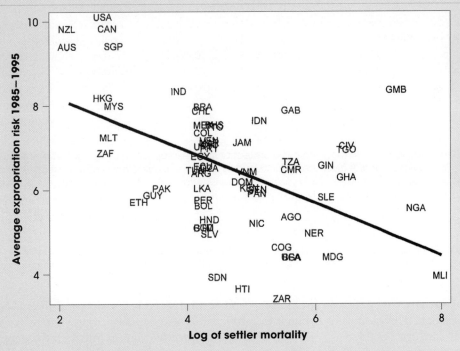

The early mortality of European colonial settlers several hundred years ago is negatively correlated with the quality of institutions at the end of the 20th century.

Source: Acemoglu, Johnson, Robinson, "The Colonial Origins of Comparative Development: An Empirical Investigation," 2001: 1384. Printed with permission of American Economics Association.

(Continued)

TABLE 4.2   Regressions of Log GDP Per Capita on Average Protection against Expropriation Risk

	Base Sample (1)	Base Sample with Latitude (2)	Base Sample without neo-Europes (3)	Base Sample without Africa (4)	Base Sample with Continent Variables (5)
Panel A: Two-Stage Least Squares					
Average Protection Against Expropriation Risk 1985–1995	0.94 (0.16)	1.00 (0.22)	1.28 (0.36)	0.58 (0.10)	0.98 (0.30)
Latitude		−0.65 (1.34)			
Asia					−0.92 (0.40)
Africa					−0.46 (0.36)
"Other" Continent					−0.94 (0.85)
Panel B: First Stage for Average Protection against Expropriation Risk 1985–1995					
Log European Settler Mortality	−0.61 (0.13)	−0.51 (0.14)	−0.39 (0.13)	−1.20 (0.22)	−0.43 (0.17)
Latitude		2.00 (1.34)			
R-squared	0.27	0.30	0.13	0.47	0.30
Panel C: Ordinary Least Squares					
Average Protection Against Expropriation Risk 1985–1995	0.52 (0.06)	0.47 (0.06)	0.49 (0.08)	0.48 (0.07)	0.42 (0.06)
Number of Observations	64	64	60	37	64

The dependent variable is log GDP per capita in 1995. "Average protection against expropriation risk" is measured on a scale from 0 to 10, a higher score meaning more protection from expropriation by the government. The data are from *Political Risk Services*. Panel A gives the second-stage instrumental variable regressions of log GDP against "average protection against expropriation risk," where the latter is instrumented by the log of early settler mortality (and also latitude in column 2) and panel B gives the first-stage regressions where "average protection against expropriation risk" is regressed on the instrumental variable. Panel C gives the ordinary least square regression of log GDP per capita against "average protection against expropriation risk."

Source: Acemoglu, D., S. Johnson and J. Robinson "The Colonial Origins of Comparative Development: An Empirical Investigation," *American Economic Review* 91, no. 5 (2001): 1386. Printed with permission of American Economics Association.

effect of the log of settler mortality on protection against expropriation. The coefficient is equal to −0.61 with a standard error of 0.13.

The second column introduces the absolute value of latitude as an independent variable by measuring distance to the equator. Its coefficient has large standard errors both in the first-stage and second-stage regression and thus is not significant. It also has the wrong sign, as we would expect a positive sign in line with the geography explanation of growth: the higher the distance from the equator the higher the growth. The coefficient in the instrumental variable regression is not very different from the first column.

The third column does the same as the first two columns except that now the "neo-Europes"—United States, Canada, Australia, and New Zealand—are excluded from the regression. The results are unchanged, showing that they are not driven by those countries. The fourth column performs the same analysis excluding Africa, to see if the results are entirely driven by that continent. The coefficients remain significant, though the coefficient of the effect of institutions on log GDP per capita is now somewhat lower. The fifth column introduces dummy variables for continents and the results are still unaffected.

Chapter Summary

Growth and Factors of Production

The production function relates output to factors of production labor and capital: $Y_t = F(K_t, L_t)$. It allows us to derive different measures of productivity: average productivity of capital (Y_t / K_t) and labor (Y_t / L_t), marginal productivity of capital ($\partial Y_t / \partial k_t$) and labor ($\partial Y_t / \partial L_t$) as well as total factor productivity, the part of output that is not explained by capital and labor. We have learned how to do growth accounting and we can decompose growth into the contribution of factor accumulation and total factor productivity: growth of output g_Y is the sum of total factor productivity growth a and a combination of the growth of capital g_K and the growth of labor g_L.

The Neoclassical Solow Growth Model

The Solow model assumes a diminishing marginal return to capital. We derive a steady state capital intensity $k^* (= K^* / L^*)$ and a steady state level of output per capita that depends on the savings rate s, population growth n, the depreciation rate δ, total factor productivity A and the share of capital in total income α. The Solow model predicts that poorer countries should grow faster than rich countries.

Endogenous Growth Theory

Endogenous growth theory derives economic growth as based on endogenous technical change determined by the innovation incentives of entrepreneurs. Innovation gives partial monopoly rights to entrepreneurs. Endogenous growth predicts that rich countries should grow faster than poor countries because their knowledge base is larger. Poor countries can only catch up if they benefit from technological transfers.

Empirical Analysis of Economic Growth

Empirical analysis of growth shows that capital accumulation and human capital accumulation do not adequately explain the large differences in income levels between the richest and the poorest countries in the world. The role of geography as an explanation for large differences in income across the world is based on two arguments: 1) economic activity is more difficult in tropical areas because of the heat and tropical diseases, and 2) landlocked areas are more isolated and have less access to trade opportunities. A problem with the geography explanation for growth is that there is a negative correlation between economic development in 1500 and today. If geography were the main explanation for differences in development, this correlation should be positive.

Research has found a convincing causal effect from institutions to growth. Countries with institutions that are more protective of property rights have become richer and countries with inadequate protection of property rights have remained poor. Using settler mortality as an instrumental variable for institutions, we find that this is a causal effect, not a mere correlation.

Key Terms

average productivity
capital intensity
constant returns to scale
decreasing returns to scale

diminishing marginal productivity
economic development
economic growth
endogenous growth theory

excludable good
extractive or predatory institutions
factor abundance
factor productivity
factor shares
factors of production
growth accounting
growth rate of total factor productivity
human capital
income convergence
increasing returns to scale

knowledge
marginal productivity
marginal productivity of capital
marginal productivity of labor
monopoly rents
non-rival good
production function
steady state
total factor productivity
value added

Review Questions

1. Go to the Penn World Tables website, https://
pwt.sas.upenn.edu. Click on PWT Data Download for the latest version of the data. On the
next page, click on Data Download. Select China
(version 2) and Argentina, the variable "PPP
Converted GDP per capita" (rgdpl) for 1980
and 2000. Calculate average growth rates for
each country. Which one is the largest? Select
the same variable for the same countries for each
year between 1980 and 2000, and build a graph
with the data. What do the figures show that you
cannot see in the figure for average growth rate?

2. Read Paul Krugman's article "The Myth of Asia's
Miracle," *Foreign Affairs* 73, no. 6 (Nov./Dec.
1994), pp. 62–78 (see also http://www.jstor
.org/stable/20046929). Explain Krugman's
arguments using the Solow model and the
Cobb-Douglas production function. What is
your own view? Provide arguments and facts
not included in the article to support your view.

3. What are expressions for the factor shares of
labor and capital using the Cobb-Douglas production function? In quantitative terms, what
are the usual estimates of these shares?

4. What is total factor productivity growth? Give
its expression with the help of a Cobb-Douglas
production function with $A = e^{at}$.

5. How can you compute total factor productivity growth using observable statistics? Take
a growth rate of 6%, a growth rate of labor of
3%, a growth rate of capital of 8%, and a share
of capital of 40%. Calculate total factor productivity growth. You can go to the Penn World
Tables to do a similar exercise for a country of
your choice. However, you will not find series
for the stock of capital and you will have to

make an assumption for the growth of capital.
Can you use the available series in the Penn
World Tables to estimate the growth of the
capital stock? Justify your answer.

6. Derive the steady state level of capital intensity and labor productivity in the Solow model
with a Cobb-Douglas production function,
assuming macroeconomic equilibrium (equality of savings and investment), a depreciation
rate δ of capital, a constant savings rate s, and a
zero growth rate of the population.

7. Endogenous growth theory claims that growth
can, in principle, be unbounded. How can that
be? Is this claim incompatible with a scarcity
of resources on the planet? Justify your answer
based on economic concepts.

8. In general, economists insist on the importance
of respecting property rights. However, they
are usually against the strict enforcement of
intellectual property rights. Is this a contradic-
tion? Use economic concepts to formulate your
answer. How does this relate to the discussion
of endogenous growth theory?

9. Acemoglu, Johnson, and Robinson have established a causal relationship from institutions
to growth. Explain. Why can they claim it is
causal?

10. Read "What Is China Doing to Its Workers?"
by Arvind Subramanian, http://www.iie.com/
publications/opeds/oped.cfm?ResearchID=885.
The author states that dictatorial regimes tend
to have a higher capital share, while democracies have a higher labor share. Discuss. What
kind of research would you do to test this
proposition? Find an article that has already
tackled this subject.

Structural Change and Development Strategies

5

Economic development is associated with important changes in the structure of an economy. In the late 18th century and into the 19th century, the British economy industrialized as textile production moved to factories, manufacturers began to use the steam engine, and large steel mills were constructed. These new technologies devoured coal and iron ore in the production of rails, locomotives, and large industrial machines. Millions of people left the countryside to work in modern factories. Soon after England industrialized, other European countries followed. Germany, in particular, developed very impressive steel and chemical industries. At the end of the 19th century, the expanding U.S. economy, recovering from a devastating civil war, also developed a strong industrial sector. The industrial extraction of oil through the use of drilling rigs and wells in Pennsylvania led to many manufacturing applications, products, and materials, and it fueled the nascent car industry in the early 20th century.

More than 100 years later, the modern Chinese economy, which had been predominantly rural, is now following a similar path, becoming one of the world's most important manufacturing bases. Millions of China's rural inhabitants have left their fields and small village workshops to migrate thousands of miles away to urban areas with modern factories that produce shirts, jeans, dresses, television sets, computers, radios, and microwave ovens for export.

How did these countries manage the change from agriculture-based to manufacturing-based economies? How did they find the capital to build new mills and factories? How were they able to attract the necessary labor force from the countryside? How did this structural change facilitate the development and growth of their countries? In this chapter, we take a closer look at the processes by which countries change their production structure from primarily agricultural to industrial, how this structural change results in the migration of the work force from the countryside to the cities, and what strategies and government policies make this structural change possible. How can growth in one sector promote growth in other sectors? Should countries insist on protecting their domestic industry to create their own manufacturing base or should they instead emphasize the development of a competitive export sector? What is the role of foreign aid in development strategies? These are some of the critical questions we will address as we consider structural change and development strategies.

Structural Change

When some sectors in an economy expand while others shrink, we refer to this as **structural change**. In the context of economic development, the structural change we discuss in this chapter is the shift from a predominantly agricultural economy that relies on traditional farming methods, to a predominantly urban economy that relies on modern industrial technologies. This change is fundamental to the process of economic development as it results in high economic growth rates when workers leave behind less productive rural jobs to work for urban firms that are more productive.

We saw in Chapter 1 how a low level of development is associated with a low level of urbanization and, conversely, a high level of development tends to be associated with a higher level of urbanization. When countries undergo structural change, they experience a reduction in agricultural employment and an increase in urban employment, whether in industry or services. In addition to the change from an agricultural to industrial economy, there are various other types of structural change relevant to development and growth, such as a transition from an industrial to a service-based economy, or an industrial structural change as certain industrial sectors expand and others contract. We will now take a closer look at each of these types of structural change.

From an Agricultural to an Industrial Economy

The most significant structural change is from a predominantly agricultural economy with low productivity, to a predominantly industrial economy with high productivity. Today's advanced economies underwent this process between the 18th and 20th centuries, while many Asian economies, such as China, are going through it now.

Figure 5.1 illustrates this shift in the Chinese agricultural labor force from 1978 to 2011. The share of the agricultural labor force, measured as the share of the agricultural population in the total population, declined from 75% to 60%.[1] If China continues to follow in the steps of other industrialized countries, agricultural workers will continue to leave rural areas and move into the urban job market.

From an Industrial to a Service Economy

Another type of structural change occurs with the transition from a predominantly industrial economy to one that is service-based. The service sector includes roughly all non-industrial urban sectors, such as banking, insurance, retail, education, health, entertainment, restaurants, and hotels. In the world's most advanced economies, including the United States, Europe, and Japan, the change from a predominantly industrial economy to a service-based economy has only taken place in the last 5 decades.

Developing countries are likely to make this shift as well and many may even take a shortcut. In recent years, India, with its large agricultural sector,

---

[1]To be correct, this measure is based on the assumption that the share of the active population is the same in agriculture as outside agriculture.

FIGURE 5.1   The Percentage Share of China's Agricultural Labor Force, 1978–2011

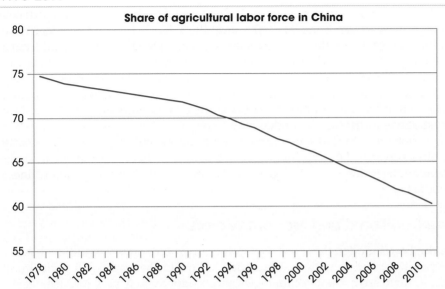

The share of China's agricultural labor force has been continuously declining since 1978 as millions of workers have left farms and rural villages for employment in the manufacturing sector.

Source: Food and Agriculture Organization of the United Nations (FAO), http://faostat.fao.org.

has developed a vigorous service sector that has become the economy's main source of growth. The growth of Indian call centers, in which employees answer service calls from all around the world, has mushroomed. Call center employees work around the clock, taking phone calls from all time zones: Australia in the morning, the United Kingdom and Europe in the evening, and the United States at night. India's software-producing sector is also developing rapidly; software engineers are writing computer code for companies all around the world.

Structural Change across Industrial Sectors

There are other, more modest, types of structural changes, such as shifts across industrial sectors. For example, South Korea has been moving in the direction of high-tech industry, following in the footsteps of Japan. In the 1960s, South Korea was specializing in capital-intensive, low-technology industries such as steel and chemicals, while Japan was moving toward the automobile and electronics industries. Since the 1980s and 1990s, however, South Korea has also developed strong automobile and electronics industries. Shifts to high-tech industry and to the service sector usually take place during later stages of development, while the shift from a predominantly agricultural to a predominantly industrial economy is the most important structural change at earlier stages of development.

The Lewis Model of Structural Change

Arthur Lewis's theory of structural change formed the basis of economic development research from the late 1950s until the 1980s.[2] He won the Nobel Prize in 1979 for his theory that addresses the question at the heart of the shift from a traditional, agricultural economy to a modern, industrial economy: how can we encourage structural change to achieve growth and development?

Even though his theory was developed in the early 1950s, the structural change that has taken place in China since 1978 is probably one of the best illustrations of the Lewis model. Hundreds of millions of peasants have left the countryside to find jobs in the modern manufacturing sector. The nearly endless supply of labor has helped keep wages low, thereby leading to a booming manufacturing sector that has flooded the world with low-priced Chinese products.

The Traditional and Modern Sectors

In the Lewis model, there are two sectors in an economy: a traditional sector (agriculture) and a modern (industrial) sector. In the traditional agricultural sector, there are no new technologies and productivity is very low. The Lewis model states that in the traditional sector, the marginal product of labor is equal to zero up to a certain point. In other words, it is possible to withdraw a large amount of labor from the traditional agricultural sector without losing any output.

Figure 5.2 illustrates the difference between production technology in the traditional and modern sectors. The production functions are shown as levels of output (agricultural or industrial), a function of labor working in the sector. The slope of such a production function indicates the marginal product of labor, i.e., the extra output that can be obtained by an extra unit of labor. Because the production function is concave, its decreasing slope means that the marginal product of labor is declining.

Surplus of agricultural labor. Even though the production functions in the traditional and modern sectors are both concave, there are some key differences between them. The first difference is that the marginal product of labor in the agricultural sector is equal to zero beyond level L_A^*. For higher levels of agricultural labor, the slope of the production function is equal to zero. This means that adding more labor beyond level L_A^* does not lead to any increase in output.

How can the marginal product of labor be equal to zero in traditional agriculture? It is a result of the huge surplus of labor in that sector. People have lived off the land for millennia. Because agriculture was the only source of subsistence and their main priority was survival, not efficiency, family members shared agricultural output. Coupled with large families, due to the fertility choices we discussed in Chapter 3, a surplus of labor in the traditional

---

[2]W. Arthur Lewis, "Economic Development with Unlimited Supplies of Labour," *The Manchester School* 22, no. 2 (May 1954): 139–191.

FIGURE 5.2 The Production Function in the Traditional Agricultural and Modern Industrial Sectors

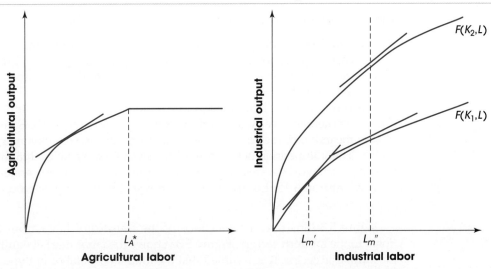

In the traditional agricultural sector, output increases with agricultural labor: the marginal product of labor, the slope of the production function, is positive and declining. However, past point L_A^*, agricultural output stays flat as more labor is added: the marginal product of labor is equal to zero. In the modern industrial sector, even though the marginal product of labor declines with industrial labor (it is smaller at L_m'' compared to L_m'), capital accumulation shifts the production function upwards, from $F(K_1, L)$ to $F(K_2, L)$, and increases the marginal product of labor. For the same amount of labor L_m'', the marginal product of labor is higher with the level of capital K_2 compared to the smaller level of capital K_1.

sector developed over time. If the marginal product of labor is equal to zero, this means that it is possible to withdraw people from agriculture without any negative effect on agricultural output. This is one of the key insights of the Lewis model.

Capital accumulation in the modern sector. A second difference between the two sectors is that the industrial sector is assumed to become more productive as it receives more capital. Note that in Figure 5.2, we have two production functions in the industrial sector, $F(K_1, L)$ and $F(K_2, L)$. When the level of capital in the sector increases from K_1 to K_2, two things happen: 1) with a higher level of capital, we can produce more output with the same amount of labor, and 2) at any given level of labor, the marginal product of labor rises with the addition of more capital.[3]

Let us examine in depth the implications of the second point. Suppose that the market wage for labor is equal to the marginal product of labor at L_m' on $F(K_1, L)$. When the level of capital increases to K_2, we can achieve the same marginal product of labor at a higher level of labor, L_m'' on $F(K_2, L)$ in Figure 5.2. This means that enterprises in the industrial sector will hire more labor, up to L_m'', if the wage level remains the same as before.

---

[3]Recall from Chapter 4 that the marginal product of labor increases when there is an addition of capital. This is the complementarity between capital and labor.

Transfer of Labor from the Traditional to the Modern Sector

The following three assumptions are made in the Lewis model:

Assumption 1 Labor can be moved away from the traditional sector at no cost. In other words, labor can be induced to move from agriculture to industry at a wage level that is equivalent to the subsistence wage in agriculture.

Assumption 2 The labor market in the modern sector is competitive so that workers are ready to bid down their wages to get a job. Enterprises in the industrial sector can thus benefit from the excess labor in agriculture. This competition between workers lowers the wage level to the point at which workers are indifferent to working in agriculture versus industry.

Assumption 3 Profits from the modern sector are reinvested only in that sector.

Figure 5.3 illustrates Lewis's idea of the transfer of labor from the traditional to the modern sectors. Figure 5.3a shows the labor market equilibrium in the industrial sector. It is assumed that the total level of labor in the economy is composed of labor in agriculture and in industry. When labor leaves agriculture, it becomes available for the industrial sector. Figure 5.3b reproduces the production function in the traditional agricultural sector from right to left (instead of from left to right).[4] An increase in agricultural labor means a move from right to left on the horizontal axis.

Assume that w^* is a wage level in the industrial sector that leaves workers indifferent to staying in agriculture versus working in the modern sector (at a very low subsistence-level wage corresponding to their living standards in the rural economy). Assume that the level of capital in the industrial sector is at K_1. That level of capital corresponds to a demand for labor schedule $L^d(K_1)$ in Figure 5.3a. The labor market equilibrium in the industrial sector will be at the intersection between $L^d(K_1)$ and the labor supply curve, with an equilibrium wage at w^*.

Increasing the level of capital beyond K_1, as more labor starts moving away from agriculture to industry, the labor market equilibrium remains at w^* until capital accumulation in the industrial sector has reached K_2. The wage does not increase before that point because the labor supply curve in the industrial sector is completely flat and labor supply is perfectly elastic.[5] It is perfectly elastic because labor can move away from the agricultural sector to the industrial sector at wage w^* without causing a fall in agricultural output. This is the basis for Lewis's notion of unlimited supply of labor.

At this point, our analysis shows that capital accumulation in the modern sector can continue to absorb labor from the traditional sector at subsistence wage w^*. If the wage level remains low, the level of profitability in the modern sector will be very high and there can be rapid capital accumulation and expansion.

---

[4]The reason for this switch is to help us see the impact of migration from the traditional agricultural sector (Figure 5.3b) to the industrial sector (Figure 5.3a).

[5]Recall from introductory economics that a horizontal supply curve means a perfectly elastic supply. In other words, a slight increase in the wage leads, theoretically, to an infinite increase in supply. However, note that in Figure 5.3a, supply of industrial labor is only perfectly elastic until point L_A^* is reached in agriculture.

FIGURE 5.3   Labor Market and Capital Accumulation Equilibrium in the Industrial Sector

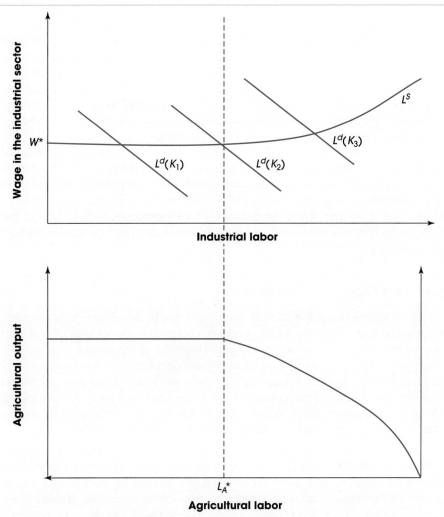

As labor leaves agriculture (L_A moves from left to right in the lower panel of Figure 5.3), and supplies more labor to the modern industrial sector (movement from left to right on L^s in the upper panel of Figure 5.3), labor supply L^s is perfectly elastic (horizontal slope) until L_A reaches L_A^*. This is because the marginal product of labor in agriculture is equal to zero (flat slope of the production function). As long as L^s remains perfectly elastic, the industrial wage remains at level w^*. The low wage level in the industrial sector allows for large profits and rapid capital accumulation, leading labor demand L^d to shift to the right from $L^d(K_1)$ to $L^d(K_2)$. When labor in the agricultural sector falls below level L_A^* (moves to the right of L_A^* in the lower panel of Figure 5.3), the marginal product of labor in agriculture becomes positive and labor will be prepared to move to the modern sector only if the wage becomes higher than w^*. Therefore, labor supply becomes upward-sloping and labor market equilibrium at the intersection between L^s and $L^d(K_3)$ is at a higher wage than w^*.

Once capital accumulation in the modern sector continues beyond K_2 to, say, level K_3, total labor employed in agriculture falls below level L_A^*. With agricultural labor at levels to the right of L_A^*, agricultural output will then begin to fall and the marginal product of labor in agriculture will become positive. As labor continues leaving the traditional sector, the marginal product in agriculture will increase and workers in the agricultural sector can now find jobs that pay more than the subsistence level w^*. The labor supply curve in the industrial sector therefore begins to slope upward. In order to attract labor away from the agricultural sector, enterprises in the industrial sector will thus be required to pay a higher wage than w^*. Subsequently, the new labor market equilibrium in the industrial sector will also be higher than w^*, as we can see in Figure 5.3.

The main idea of the Lewis model is that as long as the marginal product of labor in agriculture is equal to or close to zero, it is possible to attract workers to the modern sectors at a low wage level. This makes it possible for capital in the modern sector to accumulate rapidly. Structural change occurs as the agricultural sector shrinks while the industrial sector expands. Labor shifts to the more productive modern sector and as a consequence of this structural change, the economy grows.

The Lewis Model in Practice

The Lewis model has played a very important role in development economics. In the 1960s and 1970s, one of the primary concepts in development was that massive aid was needed to finance the development of the modern sector. This vision was very optimistic. In countries where development has been successful, such as China in recent decades, the Lewis model is a good approximation of reality. However, in most countries that have remained poor, this structural change has not taken place. When we hold the Lewis model up to economic realities, we can better understand the limitations of its assumptions.

Scarcity of capital. Today, the mainstream opinion in economics is that the modern sector does not draw labor from the traditional sector very easily because of the initial scarcity of capital in developing countries. If there were enough capital, the modern sector could hire massive numbers of workers. Unfortunately, the level of capital necessary to even jumpstart the process is not readily available in many developing countries. It is because of this scarcity that international aid in the 1960s and 1970s aimed at providing that capital to developing countries in order to jumpstart their modern sectors, but the results were very mixed. Indeed, scarcity of capital is not the only reason the predictions of the Lewis model may fail to materialize.

Reinvestment of profits in the domestic economy? Even if there had been adequate initial capital to jumpstart the modern sector in developing economies, it is not clear that the profits would have been reinvested domestically. In many cases, firms in very profitable sectors simply did not reinvest income into the domestic economy. For example, when oil-producing countries such as Saudi Arabia and other Gulf states earned windfall revenues as a consequence of the oil shocks of 1973 and 1979, they invested their profits in the global economy.

When they channeled their investment profits back to the domestic economy, it was, for the most part, only to finance the consumption habits of the rich.

Inefficient industrial sectors. Contrary to the Lewis model, the modern industrial sectors in developing economies have often been unable to make large profits due to inefficient management. They were, therefore, unable to perform their expected roles in developing the economy. In some cases, investment came from government. This was the case of India's state-owned enterprises, while in Latin American nations, government subsidies helped to create domestic industries. Unfortunately, the governments in these countries operated these industries inefficiently.

In many cases, unions organized workers to obtain higher wages.[6] Remember that the Lewis model assumes competitive labor markets in which excess labor bids down wages. Because the marginal product of labor is high in the modern sector, strong trade unions could organize workers and threaten to strike unless they earned wages closer to, or even higher than, the value of the marginal product of labor in industry. If trade unions were able to impose high wages on the industrial sector, the return on capital accumulation would be lower and there would be less capital accumulation and growth.

Urban migration in practice. The effect of migration on development has been unequal at best. In countries such as China, the mobilization of the surplus labor in agriculture has contributed to a booming manufacturing sector. In most other developing countries, however, enormous rural-urban migration has led to the development of shantytowns, such as the Brazilian *favelas,* and an increase in the size of the **informal sector**, the economic sector that operates outside the formal legal system. Members of the informal sector do not have business licenses, do not declare their income, and do not pay taxes on their informal income. The informal sector includes those who work as street peddlers, as well as the employees of the sweatshops and workshops that manufacture goods for global export. Even though many of the people who migrate from the agricultural sector to the manufacturing sector ultimately work in the informal sector, the informal sector is not particularly productive. The move from the agricultural to the informal sector represents a shift from rural poverty to urban poverty. Moreover, not all who migrate from agriculture find urban employment, even in the informal sector; there is high unemployment in the big cities of the developing world.

Contrary to the predictions of the Lewis model, the population shift from rural to urban areas has had little overall effect on development and growth. Figure 5.4 plots the change in the urbanization rate for a set of 153 countries between 1980 and 2010 on the horizontal axis, and the average annual growth of GDP per capita for the same period on the vertical axis. We can see that there have been large, rapid increases in urbanization rates during that period, but countries that have higher changes in urbanization rates do not necessarily have higher average growth rates.

---

[6]This was especially the case in Latin America, at least until the 1970s. See, for example, Charles S. Maier, *In Search of Stability: Explorations in Historical Political Economy* (Cambridge: Cambridge University Press, 1987).

FIGURE 5.4   The Relation between Change in Urbanization and Growth

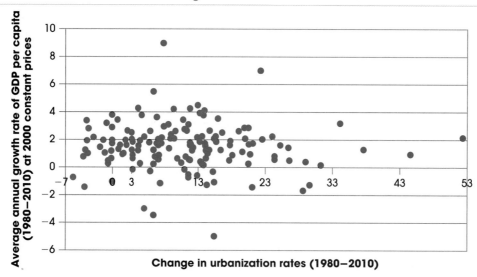

There is no correlation between increases in urbanization rates across the world between 1980 and 2010, and average annual growth of GDP per capita in the same period. The Lewis model suggests that there should be a positive correlation.

Source: The World Bank, World Development Indicators, series urbanization rate; GDP per capita (constant 2000 $).

The Role of Institutions

For years, the outcomes that contradicted the predictions of the Lewis model surprised economists. Development economists now see that many of these outcomes relate to the roles institutions play in the transition from agricultural to urban sectors.

We saw in Chapter 4's discussion of institutions and growth that the quality of institutions is a key determinant of growth in an economy. The return to capital is depressed when property rights are not sufficiently protected and when there are weak institutions. In those circumstances, wealthy citizens in developing countries find it more profitable to engage in **capital flight**, investing their capital in worldwide markets instead of in the domestic economy. High barriers to entry and inefficient institutions result in a large informal sector in which the necessity of hiding a firm's enterprises and profits makes it difficult to introduce modern and efficient technologies.

Many governments in developing countries erroneously expected that the state would spearhead urban industrial development and invest heavily in state industries. These sectors became opportunities for politicians to engage in **patronage**, the creation of inefficient jobs as a way to buy votes. Politicians also distributed all sorts of privileges, perks and funds to trade union leaders and bureaucrats.

The Harris-Todaro Model of Rural to Urban Migration

While the capital accumulation predictions of the Lewis model were, for the most part, not verified, economists have seen confirmation of one of its predictions, the migration of workers from the traditional rural areas into urban areas. Unfortunately, because the modern sector does not usually develop as the Lewis model predicts, these rural migrants often join the large mass of urban unemployed or occasional workers in the informal sector. If this is the case, why does the work force continue moving away from rural areas only to land in urban shantytowns? One explanation to this puzzle can be found in the Harris-Todaro model of rural to urban migration.[7] As with the Lewis model, it is concerned with migration from rural to urban areas; however, in contrast to the Lewis model, which focuses on capital accumulation in the modern sector, Harris and Todaro focus on the puzzle of why people in rural areas may move to join the army of the urban poor and unemployed.

We begin our discussion of the Harris-Todaro model by examining the rural to urban migration decision from the individual's point of view. Imagine you are working in the countryside and are certain to live the impoverished life of your parents and grandparents, toiling hard on the land but barely able to feed your family. Your community has a weak basic infrastructure, with little or no water, electricity, gas, telephone, or television, and few public goods such as hospitals and schools. Going to the city might be tempting, but it is a risky proposition. You may be lucky, land a well-paying factory job, and be able to afford modest lodging with better amenities, a denser network of hospitals and schools, a television, and maybe even a car. If your children receive a good education, they may be able to improve their situations even further. On the other hand, you may join the mass of urban unemployed, living a life that may be even worse than what you left in the countryside. If the expected outcome that results from luck is high enough, then it might be worth taking the risk to migrate. The **Harris-Todaro model** formalizes this line of reasoning by analyzing workers' migration decisions based on a comparison of lifetime-expected income in the rural areas versus that of urban areas.

The Harris-Todaro Model and the Migration Equilibrium

The Harris-Todaro model contains the following features:

1. The decision to migrate is based on a comparison between the expected lifetime income in a rural area and the expected lifetime income after migrating to an urban area. Once an individual migrates, it is assumed that he or she will not go back to the countryside.[8]

---

[7]John R. Harris and Michael P. Todaro. "Migration, Unemployment and Development: A Two-Sector Analysis," *American Economic Review* 60, no. 1 (1970): 126–142.

[8]This will be the case in particular if the individual sells his or her land to finance the costs of migration. Note, however, that we assume away the cost of migration in the model to simplify the exposition.

2. There is considerable risk involved in migrating. Migrants may get a well-paid job in an urban industry, but may also end up unemployed. The probability of becoming unemployed is assumed to increase with the unemployment rate.

3. There will be excess migration if wages in urban areas are higher than rural income. Excess migration will lead to urban unemployment.

Figure 5.5 provides a simplified presentation of the Harris-Todaro model in two steps. Figure 5.5a looks at the migration decision when there is full employment and full wage flexibility in the urban sector. Figure 5.5b looks at migration in the presence of labor market rigidities in the urban sector and urban unemployment. To simplify the analysis, we look at a one-period model in which income is given by the wage rate. Migration is assumed to be costless.

In Figure 5.5a, the total labor force (agricultural and urban) is the length of the horizontal axis. At any point on the horizontal line, labor in the traditional agricultural sector L_A is measured by the distance between that point and the intersection with the left vertical axis, while the labor force in the modern manufacturing sector L_M is measured by the distance between that point and the right vertical axis. Increase in L_A is thus represented by a movement from left to right on the horizontal axis, while an increase in L_M is represented by a movement from right to left. At the extreme left point, where the horizontal axis intersects with the left vertical axis, all labor would be in manufacturing, with zero labor in the agricultural sector. At the extreme right point, where the horizontal axis intersects with the right vertical axis, all labor would be in agriculture. Curves D_A and D_M represent labor demand curves in both sectors as a function of wages in the sectors, where the wage levels w_A and w_M are on the left and right vertical axes, respectively. Demand for labor in each sector

FIGURE 5.5a   The Harris-Todaro Model: Migration with Full Employment

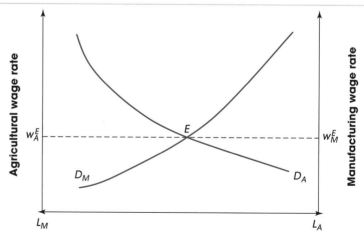

D_A and D_M are the labor demand curves in agriculture and manufacturing, respectively. With full wage flexibility, the migration equilibrium is at point E. At point E, workers are indifferent to leaving or staying in agriculture as the wages in agriculture and manufacturing are equal and there is no urban unemployment.

FIGURE 5.5b   The Harris-Todaro Model: Migration with Urban Unemployment

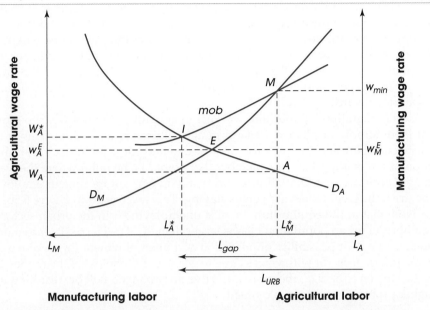

If the wage rate in manufacturing cannot fall below w_{min}, the migration equilibrium is at point I on the intersection between curves D_A, the demand for labor in agriculture and the curve mob of points (w_A, L_{URB}) where workers are indifferent between wage w_A in agriculture and income w_{min} received with probability L_M/L_{urb} (the ratio of labor in manufacturing over urban population) and income zero when unemployed, received with probability $1 - L_M/L_{urb}$. In a migration equilibrium, labor in manufacturing is at L_M^* and agricultural labor is at L_A^*. The difference L_{gap} between L_A^* and L_M^* is the urban unemployment rate.

declines as the wage increases. The curve D_M is inverted because L_M is measured on the horizontal axis from right to left.

How do we determine the migration equilibrium? Note first that at L_M^*, the agricultural wage that would absorb the rest of the labor force is at point A on D_A. If, however, there is a wage gap between agriculture and manufacturing, and people can move freely from one sector to the other, many people in agriculture will want to move to the city to get a job at the higher wage w_{min}. Not all the migrants will be able to get a job at that higher wage; the lucky ones will earn w_{min} and the unlucky ones will earn zero. L_{URB} represents the total labor force that, in equilibrium, migrates to the city (see the arrow with L_{URB} in Figure 5.5b). Because not all migrants will get a job, there will be a "labor gap" represented by the distance $(L_{URB} - L_M^*)$ indicating the difference between the total number of migrants and those who get a job in the manufacturing sector. Assume that the probability of getting a job is the same for everybody and equal to $L_M^*/L_{URB}(\leq 1)$. The migration equilibrium is a situation in which no one wants to move to the city.

To find the equilibrium, we first construct the mobility curve mob, which includes all the points (w_A, L_{URB}) at which agricultural workers are indifferent to a wage w_A in agriculture versus moving to the city where they get w_{min} with probability L_M/L_{URB} and 0 with probability $1 - L_M/L_{URB}$. How do we construct this curve? Start with point M in Figure 5.5b. This is a point where $L_{URB} = L_M^*$

and where w_A would have to be equal to w_{min} in order to leave agricultural workers indifferent because no one moving to the city would be unemployed. Point M is thus on the *mob* curve. Now increase L_{URB} by moving toward the left in Figure 5.5b. Because L_M^* is fixed, there is now a positive probability of not finding a job in the city. Therefore, workers in agriculture would be willing to stay in agriculture at a wage w_A below w_{min} and be indifferent to moving or not. The more L_{URB} increases, the more unemployment there will be and the lower the w_A that keeps workers in agriculture indifferent. Therefore, the *mob* curve slopes downward.

In the migration equilibrium, workers in agriculture do not want to move, but labor supply and labor demand in agriculture are also equal. This is the intersection between the *mob* curve and the demand curve for agricultural labor, or point I. It is important to remember that point I is the point where the wage in agriculture is such that all those who stay in agriculture remain employed and are indifferent to leaving versus staying. This wage is w_A^* in Figure 5.5b.

Note that in the equilibrium, there is unemployment in the urban sector as equilibrium urban population L_{URB}^* is larger than L_M^*. The Harris-Todaro model predicts the joint possibility of migration and unemployment (or employment in the informal sector with wages close to zero). In the context of the model, the higher the level of w_{min}, the more attractive an urban job will be, resulting in a higher probability of unemployment.

The Implications of the Harris-Todaro Model

Contrary to the Lewis model of structural change that we found did not fit the reality of most developing countries, the Harris-Todaro model currently remains the most convincing theory for understanding the most common patterns of rural to urban migration in developing countries. Several important implications of the Harris-Todaro model underscore the complexities of that migration.

Excess migration. The Harris-Todaro model indicates that there will be excess migration because free mobility, combined with wage rigidity in urban areas, leads to urban unemployment in equilibrium. Thus, the high urbanization rates that we have seen in the world in the last decades are not necessarily a sign of healthy economic development. They may, to a large extent, reflect excess migration.

Urban planning. Excess migration has consequences for urban planning. Too many migrants from the countryside create congestion in terms of the provision of public services such as health, education, and various types of infrastructure. In other words, they contribute to crowding in hospitals and schools, and on roads and other forms of transportation.

Adverse effects of rural education. The Harris-Todaro model implies that rural education programs may have adverse effects. We generally tend to see a high level of education in rural areas as a good thing. However, the Harris-Todaro model indicates that this can lead to increased migration to the cities and to higher urban unemployment. Rural youth who have received an education will indeed strive for better jobs in the city, hoping that their education will benefit them in the urban job market. Until the urban sector can provide jobs at the same pace as rural children receive an education, many educated rural youth will move to the cities and face unemployment.

Higher unemployment. It would seem that the creation of urban jobs would be the simple answer to high urban unemployment. The government, possibly with the help of international aid organizations, could create new jobs in the public sector or encourage the creation of jobs through public spending programs, subsidies, and tax cuts for enterprises hiring urban labor. Unfortunately, job creation programs can actually lead to more unemployment. For every position created in urban areas, many new immigrants will migrate from the countryside with the hope that an urban employer will hire them for that position. The total number of unemployed in the cities may rise as new jobs are created. In other words, job creation programs intended to decrease unemployment might actually cause unemployment to increase.

Rural to urban migration policy. The Harris-Todaro model's findings of excess migration and high unemployment show the complexities of dealing

China's Internal Immigration Policy

China's agricultural reforms of 1978, which replaced collective ownership of land with the "Household Responsibility System" (whereby households could sign 15-year land leases) significantly increased the efficiency of agricultural production. This made it possible to release the excessive labor that existed in the countryside.

The surplus labor generated by the reforms was first absorbed by so-called "township village enterprises" (TVEs), small industrial firms or workshops owned by local governments. The TVEs were the main engine of growth in the Chinese economy in the 1980s and early 1990s, and brought relative affluence to the countryside in the first phase of reforms. The employment opportunities provided by the TVEs prevented many rural Chinese workers from looking for work in urban areas.

In addition to the TVEs, Chinese policy severely restricted internal migration. Under the rigid household registration system called *hukou*, rural residents were required to register with local authorities and they did not have the right to become urban residents even when they lived and worked in a city. The *hukou* system was a policy specifically designed to prevent rural to urban migration.

In practice, many people have ignored the migration prohibitions. Millions of illegal migrants have filled the cities and augmented the urban and informal labor forces. Illegal migration to the cities continued to increase throughout the 1980s, but since the 1990s, the government has eased the policy restrictions and it has become somewhat easier for a rural resident to obtain an urban residency permit. These permits are temporary and they often come at a very high price (in the Beijing area, they cost around $10,000, more than 5 times an urban worker's annual average salary).

Without residency permits, migrant workers do not have access to social services, health care, or schools for their children, and police can deport any illegal migrants back to the countryside. These illegal migrants have become second-class citizens who resent their pariah status.

with the problem of rural to urban migration. Most countries do not restrict migration and pay the price of having high levels of urban unemployment. Ideally, urban unemployment would not exist if there were no wage rigidities in the urban sector. However, if it is difficult to do away with those rigidities, then unrestricted migration will lead to excess migration. China, for example, has chosen to restrict internal migration to deal with this problem.

Reducing urban unemployment by restricting migration from the countryside seems like an unnecessarily proscriptive policy to those of us for whom freedom to move is a fundamental human right. Our instincts on these matters, however, are not always consistent. We are shocked by restrictions to mobility within a country, but are less shocked by restrictions to mobility across countries. Are these restrictions different? Shouldn't the same principles that make us defend freedom of migration within a country lead us to also defend freedom of migration across countries? There is no easy answer to these questions.

The main policy conclusion to draw from the Harris-Todaro model is that more should be done in developing countries for the economic development of rural areas, both to create attractive income opportunities (both farm and non-farm income) in the countryside, and to improve the delivery of public services such as health care and infrastructure, reducing the likelihood that people will migrate to cities. A poor countryside will create poverty in the cities, while a more developed countryside will reduce urban poverty.

Development Strategies: Sectoral Growth

So far, we have discussed how the transfer of labor from the traditional agricultural sector to the modern industrial sector may take place. We have not discussed what strategies governments follow in order to develop the modern sector. These development strategies differ in terms of which of them are given priority, whether efforts are concentrated on one sector or on many sectors at the same time, and what methods are used to manage the spillover effects of growth in a particular sector on other sectors.

We first examine different theories related to **sectoral growth**, the expansion of specific sectors of the economy, and ask whether it is better to encourage equal growth across the different industrial sectors or, instead, to promote the growth of particular industrial sectors at the expense of others. We then take a closer look at the idea that a large-scale investment in one industrial sector will result in the growth of related and interconnected sectors.

Balanced and Unbalanced Growth

A continued focus of discussions on structural change since the 1950s and 1960s has been whether we should favor **balanced growth**, in which all economic sectors grow at the same rate, or **unbalanced growth**, in which sectors grow at different rates. With balanced growth, supply and demand remain in equilibrium over time in all sectors. Take the example of an economy with a steel sector and a coal sector. As the steel sector expands, its demand for coal will also increase. If both sectors grow at the same rate, then the growing supply of coal for the steel sector will match the growing demand for coal by the steel sector. In an economy with unbalanced growth, if the steel sector grows faster than the coal sector, the increased demand for coal by the steel sector may not be met by the supply of coal from the domestic coal sector. Unbalanced growth results in excess supply in some sectors and excess demand in others.

Balanced growth. The main argument for balanced growth is that an economy has a higher growth rate if it is in equilibrium, that is, if supply and demand across sectors grow in sync. Mathematical models developed in the 1950s and 1960s, including those by mathematical genius John von Neumann, indicated that growth was fastest along a balanced growth path.[9] Although these were quite sophisticated models, we can see the logic behind them in the following metaphor: A straight stretch of road represents balanced growth with all the wheels of a car traveling at the same speed. A curve in the road represents unbalanced growth as some of the car's wheels must slow down in order to maintain its balance on the curve. The larger the turn, the more slowly the car will go in order to maintain its balance. Structural change in an economy is similar to a curve in the road. The economy must make a "turn" in its **sectoral composition**, a change in the weight of each sector in terms of the economy's output, such as the weight of agriculture, the steel industry, the textile industry, etc. A car that follows a straight line travels faster than a car that turns, just as an economy in which all sectors grow at the same rate grows faster than an economy in which the sectoral composition undergoes change.

In the coal and steel example considered above, if the capacity of the steel industry grows at a faster rate than that of the coal industry, the limited supply of coal will constrain steel production. Suppose that the capacity of the steel industry grows at 5% but that the capacity of coal industry grows at 2%. As long as the necessary technology and the amount of coal needed to produce a set amount of steel remain the same, steel output will not be able to grow at more than 2%. The steel industry cannot use its extra capacity due to the bottleneck in the coal industry. If some of the resources used to increase steel capacity had been used to increase coal-mining capacity, economic growth would be higher than 2%.

Unbalanced growth. The primary argument for unbalanced growth, put forward by Albert Hirschmann, is that if government policy focuses on and assists in the development of one key sector, there will be positive externalities through intersectoral linkages and pressure for other sectors to grow as a result.[10] The concept of **intersectoral linkage** refers to the effects of conditions in one sector on other related sectors. There are two types of intersectoral linkages: **backward linkages**, effects on upstream sectors that play the role of

---

[9]Among other achievements, von Neumann made major contributions to computer science and invented game theory.

[10]Albert O. Hirschmann, *The Strategy of Economic Development* (Boulder, CO: Westview Press, 1988).

suppliers for a given sector, and **forward linkages**, effects on downstream sectors that are clients of a given sector.

Japan is an example that illustrates these intersectoral linkages. In the 1960s, the Japanese government wanted to focus on developing the country's car industry and was willing to contribute resources and implement a combination of tax incentives and subsidies in order to stimulate its growth. The developing car industry needed parts from sectors that were located upstream (steel, glass, tires, engines, etc.), which increased the demand for these parts and subsequently encouraged the development of the sectors that produced them. Entrepreneurs saw the demand for these sectors as lucrative business opportunities and established new businesses to serve the developing car industry. The increased demand for capital also helped to develop capital markets. Banks lending to the car industry tried to attract more deposits and competed to offer customers attractive incentives, which led to growth in the banking sector. These backward linkages helped strengthen the sectors that supported the car industry, both in manufacturing and capital markets. Downstream sectors that needed cars could now purchase domestic Japanese models that were cheaper than foreign models and more adaptable to local conditions. More cars on the country's highways encouraged road construction and the expansion of the transportation infrastructure. The increase in infrastructure reduced transportation costs and had positive effects for the Japanese economy as a whole.

Balanced versus unbalanced. From a purely theoretical point of view, the argument for balanced growth appears to be more sensible and have a more solid foundation in economics. It is, however, based on the premise that a government has the administrative capacity to help each sector equally, or to assist in such a way as to achieve equal growth in all sectors. Despite the best intentions, the administrative capacity of a government might be too deficient to attain this goal. Government economic policy usually focuses on one priority at a time and is often unable to pay equal attention to all sectors of the economy at the same time. If that is the case, a simultaneous focus on a few sectors, in a strategy of unbalanced growth, may help develop other sectors by means of intersectoral linkages and subsequently help the entire economy to grow.

To summarize, balanced growth is the theoretical ideal. In practice, however, unbalanced growth is more likely to succeed because it requires less administrative government capabilities and intersectoral linkages will correct the imbalances created by government policy.

Big Push Theories

Theories that promote the idea that development can only be successful when a government makes efforts to expand, simultaneously, various sectors on a very large scale are referred to as **big push theories**. These theories appeal to the **complementarities** between economic sectors. Complementarities between two objects exist when the objects must be combined in certain proportions in order to be effective. A car needs four wheels and a body, otherwise it cannot transport passengers; therefore, the body of the car and the wheels are complementary. Certain sectors require a combination of labor and capital, such as construction workers and bulldozers in the building industry. A good example of complementarity between economic sectors is that which occurs between the government infrastructure sector and the private sector. Without private investment by industrial firms to utilize the different types of infrastructure (roads, railroads, ports, airports, and telecommunication centers) available to move products to market, a government may view the money spent on that infrastructure as wasted. On the other hand, private investment can only be profitable if adequate infrastructure is already in place. Private investors need to be able to transport goods between different places; they do not want to invest in areas that have no roads or rails.

Although there are complementarities between various sectors, there may also be **coordination problems** that occur when each sector makes independent decisions but one sector's decision depends on another sector's decision. In our infrastructure investment and private investment example, there is a coordination problem between those responsible for infrastructure, a developing country's government on one hand and private investors on the other hand. If the government believes that private investors will not invest, then the government will see infrastructure investment, such as the building of a freight rail, as unprofitable and will not invest in it. If the government does not build the rail, then private investors will decide not to invest as well, due to the lack of transportation infrastructure. As a result, neither party makes an investment. The country then remains undeveloped in an inferior coordination equilibrium.[11] A "big push" by the government to finance a modern transportation infrastructure in a developing country, while simultaneously implementing policies to encourage private investment, may attract private investors and make the investment in infrastructure worthwhile. Such coordination on a superior equilibrium is advantageous for development.

The East Asian Miracle

A 1993 report by the World Bank examined the reasons for the success of East Asian economies such as those in Japan, South Korea, Taiwan, Hong Kong, and Singapore.[12] Economists have attributed this success in part to the efficient coordination abilities of East Asian governments to gather industry leaders from different sectors, explain the government's industrial strategy to those leaders, and create communication channels among firms to share information. In other words, the Asian Tigers are an example of successful coordination in the spirit of big push theories.

One example of coordination occurred between the export and financial sectors. East Asian governments created **development banks** that specialized in giving long-term loans for development purposes that would support the growth of export-oriented industrial firms. Government regulations also kept interest rates low in order to encourage private investment.

(Continued)

---

[11]We will be discussing coordination problems further in Chapter 7.

[12]*The East Asian Miracle: Economic Growth and Public Policy*, World Bank Policy Research Reports (New York: Oxford University Press, 1993).

East Asian governments have also invested heavily in infrastructure, be it in the development of road networks, railroads, airports, telecommunications, or water management. Once these forms of infrastructure were in place, domestic and international private investors were encouraged to invest heavily in new plants to make use of newly accessible markets.

Beyond infrastructure, governments also strengthened the education sector to ensure a high level of human capital. East Asian countries developed an advanced network of primary and secondary schools and this is how the South Korean secondary education system became one of the best in the world.

The Japanese economy's rapid post–World War II growth was due in large part to the government's active role in coordinating the investments of the large private firms across industrial sectors. The Japanese government avoided the buildup of excess capacity and price wars among the large export firms through industrial licensing, requiring firms to receive government approval for large-scale investments. In reviewing proposals and issuing approvals, the government also received information about the firms' investment projects. Whenever competing firms put similar investment projects forward, the government often asked these firms to cooperate. In the 1960s and 1970s, the South Korean government followed the Japanese model and coordinated the investments of large private firms, such as in the microchip production sector. East Asian governments have used a broad spectrum of government intervention, not only industrial licensing but also government procurement, export obligations, and subsidies to encourage firms to achieve economies of scale.

Development Strategies: Import Substitution versus Export Promotion

While linkages and coordination between sectors are important components of development strategies, how do we know on which sectors governments should focus? In this context, two important, and opposite, strategies have emerged in the last 50 years: import substitution and export promotion. **Import substitution strategies** focus on the development of a country's domestic industry with the objective of a gradual decline in imports of industrial products while the domestic sectors develop. **Export promotion strategies** focus on developing competitive sectors for the successful export of products to the world market.

After World War II, development economists encouraged developing countries to create their own manufacturing base in the hope that they would follow the path of industrialized nations such as Britain, the United States, and Europe. In the 1950s and 1960s, these import substitution strategies were very popular in theory because they appealed to the spirit of independence that arose in many countries during the years of decolonization, but they never delivered any major development successes. Instead, East Asian countries, such as Japan, Taiwan, South Korea, Hong Kong, and Singapore experienced strong and successful growth due to an entirely different strategy, one based on exporting goods efficiently. Due to the East Asian growth miracle, economists now consider export promotion to be the more successful of the two strategies, though they do not necessarily agree on the causes of its success. More recently, countries like China and Vietnam have also realized success in export promotion. India relied on import substitution for many decades after its independence in 1947, but it abandoned the strategy around the turn of the century and has since tried to focus on export promotion instead. In the next section, we look at the rationales behind each of these strategies as well as why import substitution failed whereas export promotion succeeded.

Import Substitution and the Prebisch-Singer Hypothesis

Data from the first half of the 20th century showed that the **terms of trade** for developing countries, the ratio of the export price index to the import price index, tended to decline. Declining terms of trade occur when a country's export prices grow more slowly than its import prices. In that case, a country must always export more goods in order to be able to afford the same basket of imports. This declining trend in terms of trade for developing economies created the impression that it would continue. The **Prebisch-Singer hypothesis** states that countries specializing in exports of **primary commodities** (raw materials, agricultural products) are doomed to experience a decline in their terms of trade. This hypothesis is based on the idea that as the world economy develops, demand for primary commodities will fall behind the demand for manufactured goods. The idea is rooted in the basics of consumer demand: as household income increases, demand for basic goods does not grow as fast as the demand for consumer durables and other manufactured goods.

While economists thought that the decline in terms of trade in developing countries would be permanent, it was, in fact, only temporary. The Prebisch-Singer hypothesis was popular from the 1950s to the 1970s, but it did not pass the test of time, specifically, the oil shocks of the 1970s when the terms of trade became very favorable for oil-exporting countries. Figure 5.6 shows that since 1980, the trend in terms of trade for developing countries has been virtually flat. Even for OPEC countries, a trend is not easily discernible. Many developing countries have benefited periodically from large commodity price increases in their favor for the commodities they export, be it oil, gas, gold, copper, etc. However, as the global economy has developed and more nations have turned to manufacturing, the supply of oil and raw materials has become increasingly scarce. In addition, productivity and competition have kept the prices of manufactured goods down.

There is no discernible trend in the terms of trade for developing countries, as we can see in Figure 5.6. Note, however, that OPEC countries have had large fluctuations in their terms of trade that were associated with movements in oil prices. After the oil shocks of the 1970s that led to high oil prices, the relative price of oil declined but then rose again around the turn of the millennium. Terms of trade are more volatile for countries that specialize in the export of a particular natural resource such as oil, coffee, cocoa, or copper because the world prices of these goods fluctuate significantly over time.

FIGURE 5.6   The Evolution of the Terms of Trade for Developing
Countries and OPEC Nations

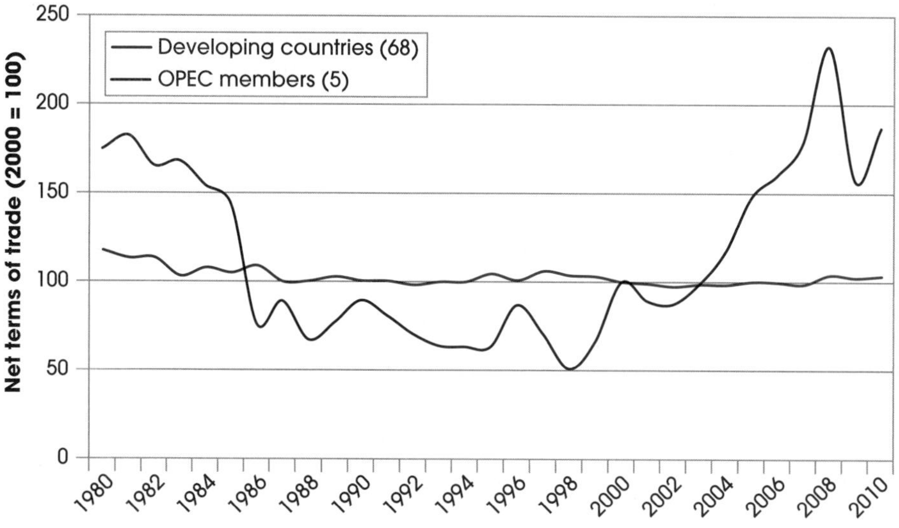

The percentage ratio of the export price index to the corresponding import price index
is measured relative to the base year 2000. The terms of trade for developing countries
have remained very flat. They have been quite volatile for OPEC countries as a result of
movements in world oil prices.

Source: The World Bank, World Development Indicators: Series net barter terms of trade, using
annual median per continent and/or group of countries. The sample of developing countries
consists of 68 countries for which complete data series for 1980–2010 is available. The OPEC
sample includes five countries: Algeria, Angola, Ecuador, Nigeria, and Venezuela.

Industrialization and the Protection of Infant Industries

In line with the Prebisch-Singer hypothesis, in the 1950s and 1960s many development economists felt that participation in international trade on the basis
of specialization in raw materials and natural resources would deliver limited
benefits for developing countries and would not deliver strong growth. They
advised those countries to follow the path of industrialization that Europe
and the United States had taken 150 years earlier. Implementing this strategy
meant that domestic industry and manufacturing would replace imports from
advanced industrialized countries, a strategy called **import substitution**. For
example, instead of exchanging coffee for steel, developing countries would
establish their own steel industries and would not be dependent on the export
of coffee to fulfill their need for steel. Because it worked in Europe and the
United States in the past, development economists thought that Brazil, India,
and other emerging economies should implement this strategy as well. By
investing in the industrial sector, there would always be strong demand for
industrial goods because these industrial goods had a higher **income-elasticity
of demand** than basic commodities. Income elasticity of demand is the growth
rate of demand as income grows by 1%. Industrial goods have a higher income-
elasticity than basic commodities. Therefore, shifting away from specialization

in basic commodities to focus on industrial goods would, in theory, be a winning development strategy.

As a result, **infant industries,** newly established firms that did not have a foothold in the global marketplace or the experience and knowledge of long-established industries, began to form in developing countries and their governments sought strategies for protecting those infant industries against competition from advanced industrialized economies. This was not the first time the issue of infant industries had arisen. When Germany began to industrialize in the 19th century, German economist Friedrich List (1789–1846) argued that while they were developing, infant industries needed temporary protection from more mature industries.[13] The German government had great success instituting protectionist policies such as import tariffs that shielded the emerging industries. Similar to Germany, the less-experienced, newly formed industries in modern-day developing countries were not as efficient as more established firms in advanced economies. Without protection, they would never have the chance to develop and become efficient enough to compete in the global marketplace. In principle, this protection would only be temporary because once the new industries had completed the learning curve, they would be able to compete on equal terms with the more advanced industries.

Because infant industry protection was successful in Germany, the argument was quite popular and uncontroversial with respect to modern-day developing countries. Supporters of import substitution readily acknowledged that developing countries needed temporary protection, and agreed to implement import tariffs for that purpose. Unfortunately, the import substitution strategies were disappointing in virtually every developing country that implemented them. While the protection from the competition of foreign goods worked, the new domestic industries had no incentive to become competitive in the world market. Time did not lead to large improvements in productivity or a reduction in costs. Because the new domestic industries did not become competitive, they asked for more protection; as a result, they continued to lack the incentive to stand on their own and a vicious circle set in; repeated calls for protection dulled the incentive to become competitive. Eventually, the protection became permanent and instead of improving economic performance, industrial leaders became representatives of vested interests, blocking reforms that would have opened up the economy. Toward the end of the 1970s, import substitution policies had become widely discredited as a development strategy.

Export Promotion and the Asian Miracle

While the strategy of import substitution was losing momentum, many Asian economies were implementing **export promotion** with great success. By employing policies that included preferential credit for exportation firms, easy access to imports, and even government subsidies to help firms offer competitive prices, governments in Japan, South Korea, Taiwan, Singapore, Hong Kong, and China encouraged industries to develop and export competitive products on world markets.

---

[13]Friedrich List, *The National System of Political Economy* (Kitchener, ON: Batoche, 2001): 412.

The Indian Experience of Import Substitution

In the decades that followed its independence in 1942, India based much of its development strategy on import substitution. In an effort to implement that strategy, the Indian government instituted a variety of economic measures:

- the creation of tariffs to discourage imports;
- the implementation of 5-year plans with goals for the development of various sectors such as steel and automobiles;
- the creation of a system of industrial licensing that established government control over the development of industry;
- government review of large private-sector investment decisions to ensure that private firms would be able to fulfill the goals of their licensing plans;
- the establishment of government-owned firms in key sectors such as steel, ship-building, coal, aircraft production, and telecommunications; and
- the development of an extensive system of price controls in industry to ensure low prices for inputs in sectors deemed a priority in the industrialization process.

Overall, economists deemed the Indian experience a failure. The industries developed under the auspices of import substitution remained protected and were not able to export successfully on world markets. Technological innovation in these sectors was very slow. The automobile sector remained stagnant, producing the same models for decades while consumers had to wait years before actually receiving the car they had purchased. The government-protected domestic industries suffered frequent losses and became accustomed to government bailouts.

The Indian government eventually realized the failure of the import substitution strategy. Since the early 1990s, it has implemented reforms in an effort to open the economy to international trade. Among these reforms, the government has

- liberalized foreign trade;
- lowered or abolished import tariffs on many goods;
- dismantled parts of the licensing system;
- abolished some forms of labor regulation; and
- sold shares in government-owned companies to the private sector and enacted financial reforms, for example allowing state-owned banks to raise funds on the markets by issuing shares.

India still bears the marks of the decades of the import substitution strategy. Labor unions and bloated, entrenched incumbent management continue to be vested interest groups, opposing full liberalization and modernization. Labor regulations have remained very pervasive despite early reforms, and in many sectors and regions of India, the government's role in industry has not disappeared.

In recent years, the emerging service, software, and telecommunications sectors have been the most successful, and they have grown without the negative impacts of the government's industrialization policy. Successful entrepreneurs are beginning to enter more traditional sectors and change the appearance of the industrial landscape. Some Indian multinational firms like TATA, which owns Jaguar and Land Rover among other automotive firms, are becoming global players on the world market.

Japan's Ministry of International Trade and Industry, the famous MITI, played an important role in supporting export firms. MITI was in charge of Japan's industrial policy and provided guidance to large firms that wanted to compete in the international market. Industry leaders and top MITI officials

The Success of Honda Motors' Exports

Japanese entrepreneur Soichiro Honda had a lifelong fascination with motorized vehicles. After working in and owning auto repair shops, he created Honda Motors in 1948. Initially, the company produced only cheap motorcycles for the Japanese market. Their low price, comfortable design, ease of use, and fuel efficiency made them very popular, and they soon began to conquer the world market.

Honda's entry into the U.S. market is a good illustration of the firm's progress as an exporter. In 1959, the Japanese company established the American Honda Motor Company and began to sell motorcycles in the United States. Funds from the Japanese government helped Honda re-engineer its models for American motorcyclists who rode at higher speeds than Japanese riders. Initially, Honda motorcycles tended to break down frequently, but careful re-engineering quickly made them very reliable. By the end of 1964, Honda motorcycles had 62% of the market share in the United States and Honda quickly became the world's largest motorcycle company.

The company did not want to stay confined to the motorcycle market. Its objective was to become a major player in the world's automobile industry. When the Honda Motor Company launched its first cars on the world market in 1962, consumers worldwide initially dismissed them as low-quality vehicles. Even MITI, which wanted to promote the Japanese automobile sector, sought to limit the number of exporting car companies to only Toyota and Nissan. In spite of this, Honda persevered; because of its low prices, Honda gained access to global markets as its models improved in quality. In 1973, when oil shocks led to sharp increases in gas prices, the fuel-efficient Honda Civic became a huge success. Over the years, the company continued to develop its models, making its cars a symbol of high quality and reliability, and Honda's production methods became the model for automakers worldwide. Today, Hondas are among the most popular cars worldwide.

were in very close contact and shared ideas on how to develop Japanese exports. MITI helped firms acquire access to foreign technologies and to foreign currency, and played a role in encouraging and coordinating investments in export-oriented sectors. Successful competition on world markets and assistance from the Japanese government have genuinely helped Japanese firms to climb the technology ladder.

Export promotion and protectionism. Even when a developing country has the governmental capabilities to implement successful export promotion, it can sometimes be the victim of its own success. One danger successful developing countries face is protectionism that originates in industrialized countries. Protectionist forces within the United States and the European Union have been lobbying to obtain restrictive measures against exports from Japan, China, India, Vietnam, and other successful exporting economies. While these forces have not always had the upper hand, the more successful the export promotion strategies, the stronger these protectionist forces will be.

Why did export promotion in East Asia work? Export promotion has been the most popular strategy for development in the last 3 decades. Economists do not always agree on the reasons for its success, however. One interpretation, called the neoclassical explanation and favored by famous economists such as Jagdish Bhagwati and Anne Krueger, is that export promotion worked primarily because of its market-friendly philosophy: instead of protecting their industries, countries participated in trade liberalization and encouraged the production of exports for the world market.[14] While governments did intervene to encourage export promotion, their focus was on competition in world markets, not on policies that would distort domestic prices. Moreover, governments kept the macroeconomic fundamentals right, balanced their budgets, placed a strong emphasis on education to foster capital accumulation, maintained low inflation, and kept government intervention to a minimum. However, other economists emphasize the central role played by governments in coordinating investments between firms and in helping particular sectors and firms. They see such government intervention as beneficial in promoting growth.[15]

Institutions and export promotion. Despite these controversies, given its success in practice, why has the strategy of export promotion not been implemented everywhere? Why have most countries in Latin America and Africa not implemented similar strategies that follow the Asian example?

It seems that the most convincing answer lies in the varying strengths of institutions across countries. A developing country needs a government that is strong enough to be able to organize competition between firms, to set the rules for competition, and to uphold those rules. In other words, there has to be a skilled government bureaucracy in place that is able to understand all aspects of business projects, including technology, management, and marketing. Moreover, the government bureaucracy has to be strong enough to resist the pressure and influence exerted by firms that want to bend the rules in their favor.

It is not surprising that the export promotion strategy has, for the most part, only worked in Asia, where countries tend to have strong governmental institutions and highly skilled people working in government administration.

---

[14]Jagdish Bhagwati, "The Miracle That Did Happen: Understanding East Asia in Comparative Perspective," in *Taiwan's Development Experience: Lessons on Role of Government and Markets,* Eric Thorbecke and Henry Wan, eds. (Boston: Kluwer Academic Publishers, 1999) 21–39; and Anne O. Krueger, "Why Is Trade Liberalisation Good for Growth?" *The Economic Journal* 108, no. 450 (September 1998): 1513–1522.

[15]Robert Wade, *Governing the Market: Economic Theory and the Role of Government in East Asian Industrialization* (Princeton: Princeton University Press, 1992); Alice H. Amsden, "Why Isn't the Whole World Experimenting with the East Asian Miracle to Develop?: Review of the East Asian Miracle," *World Development* 22, no. 4 (1994): 627–633; and Dani Rodrik, "Getting Interventions Right: How South Korea and Taiwan Grew Rich," *Economic Policy* 20 (1995): 53–107.

The Strength of Chinese Institutions

China is a good example of a country with strong governmental institutions. China retained its basic authoritarian political structure when it opted to transition to a market economy and chose to follow export promotion strategies. While the initial government emphasis on the creation of markets for the domestic economy was effective, the mobilization of the bureaucracy played a very large role in encouraging growth.

The government told provincial leaders that they would get faster promotions within the bureaucracy if they were able to obtain higher economic growth in their province as compared to other provinces. In effect, the Chinese introduced **yardstick competition**, a contest for the top-ranking economic performance within the Chinese bureaucracy and a policy the government used to rank provincial leaders according to the growth rates of their provinces. The leaders of the provinces that had the fastest growth were quickly promoted to higher levels of government. Given the fact that the Chinese generally find it a desirable goal in life to reach top levels of government administration, this yardstick competition gave leaders a very strong incentive to maximize growth in their provinces. Because the provinces enjoyed sufficient fiscal autonomy, being residual claimants of extra fiscal revenues they raised, provincial leaders had the instruments necessary to encourage economic development and growth.

The Foreign Aid Controversy

We will now turn to a discussion of the role of foreign aid in development strategies and consider how large should it be as well as how effective it can be. In the optimistic 1960s and 1970s, the dominant view among economists was that more foreign aid would help countries to invest, modernize, and achieve the necessary structural changes while on the road to prosperity. The governments of rich countries have always been criticized for spending too little on foreign aid. Scandinavian countries, which are the most generous donors among Western governments, have, for example, given 3 to 10 times more than the United States on a per capita basis for development aid. Non-governmental organizations and advocates for poor countries continuously lobby for more development aid. Jeffrey Sachs (see page 142), a professor of economics and Director of the Earth Institute at Columbia University, has in recent years championed the cause of more generous foreign aid.

On the other hand, a more pessimistic and cynical view has emerged that suggests a great part, if not most, of foreign aid has been wasted. The argument is that foreign aid is often diverted by corrupt officials or used inefficiently and therefore has no significant economic effects. William Easterly, an economist who worked at the World Bank for many years and is now a professor at New York University, has been one of the most vocal and competent proponents of this view. In the following sections, we look closely at the main aspects of the foreign aid controversy.

Sachs and the Argument for Foreign Aid

Jeffrey Sachs has described in a very eloquent way how foreign aid can help developing countries rise out of poverty.[16] The starting point of his analysis is that poor countries find themselves in a **poverty trap**. Similar to a household, if a country is very poor, it cannot afford to save because it must allocate all its income to consumption with no resources left for investment. The country is then trapped in a vicious circle: poverty prevents investment and that results in more poverty. However, a country that is able to reach a certain threshold of income can afford to save. There will thus be a positive cycle: investment creates growth that generates more income resulting in more investment. Sachs's basic idea is that if a country is given enough foreign aid to afford the investments necessary to get out of the poverty trap, it will find itself on a positive growth cycle. All that is necessary is a large, one-shot injection of foreign aid to achieve this objective.

Critical to this approach is that the amount of foreign aid must be sufficiently large enough for it to pull a country out of the poverty trap. Sachs argues that foreign aid should simultaneously target education, infrastructure, the environment, and government administration, because the effect of investment in one area of the economy reinforces the effect of investment in another area. For example, more investment in education will create a more skilled labor force that will contribute more to the economy as it takes advantage of the new opportunities created by an advanced telecommunications infrastructure. In other words, there are complementarities between these various investments. This is, in essence, a big-push strategy.

Sachs estimates that in order to meet the millennium development goal of halving extreme poverty, that percentage of the population living on less than 1 dollar a day, a global investment of 150 billion dollars would be needed, which is 50 billion above existing worldwide aid commitments. This objective can be achieved if rich countries commit to giving 0.7% of their GNP for foreign aid. Currently, aid from the United States represents about 0.15% of its GNP.[17]

Easterly and the Skeptics' View

William Easterly worked for the World Bank for 16 years as a research economist trying to find the best policies to help countries grow out of poverty. He strongly disagrees with Sachs's views on foreign aid.[18] Easterly states that all the foreign aid given to developing countries has little to show in terms of increased growth. Between 1965 and 2000, Africa received $568 billion (in today's dollars) but had virtually no growth during that period. There is even a negative correlation between aid and growth in Africa—aid to Africa increased while growth tended to decline during the last decades of the 20th century.

---

[16]Jeffrey D. Sachs, *The End of Poverty: Economic Possibilities for Our Time* (New York: Penguin Press, 2005).

[17]As a comparison, the annual U.S. military budget represents between 4 and 7% of GNP, depending on the estimates, and is at least 30 times higher than U.S. foreign aid.

Moreover, in terms of the size of the economies of recipient countries, foreign aid has been substantial. The aid given to the top quarter of receiving countries has been on average equal to 17% of their annual GDP, but with no effect on their growth. On the other hand, the East Asian countries that did have high economic growth, such as China and India, received very little aid compared to all other developing countries. In addition, there is significant evidence that increased aid led to increased consumption, but not to increased investment.

Easterly notes that not only was a large part of the aid diverted by corrupt officials, but that if a government received aid, it was less accountable for what happened to the funds because it did not have to secure that money by raising taxes from its population. It was accountable only to the donors who did not monitor closely the use of funds. Even with their noble motives to help developing countries, NGOs also had a vested interest in continuing the existing aid programs in which they were involved, and they were more concerned with renewing existing aid programs than evaluating them. It is only in recent years that various NGOs have taken seriously the need to evaluate the effectiveness of aid programs.

Easterly also argues that there is no good empirical evidence for poverty traps in development. The poorest countries 50 years ago did not have the lowest growth rates in subsequent years, a prediction one would expect from the poverty trap argument.

What Conclusions Should We Draw about Foreign Aid?

A first conclusion we must consider is that governments and NGOs should be cautious about what foreign aid can realistically achieve. If it has not achieved much in the past decades in terms of growth, skepticism is called for when considering what continued aid can achieve without further research into its effectiveness.

A second conclusion is that a bottom-up approach is more likely to work better than a top-down approach. It is crucial to find honest people who are ready to spend time and effort on projects that make a difference for the lives of local people.

A third conclusion is that in order to avoid wasting aid money, it is very important to have accurate evaluations of development projects that use the best scientific tools available. Much of the resurgence of development economics since the beginning of the 21st century is due to the introduction of randomized controlled trials that use the same scientific approach as in randomized medical experiments. The less we know about what works and what does not work to help local communities develop, the more we need to develop experiments that will help us gain these insights. The Poverty Action Lab at MIT in Cambridge, MA, and the Center for Evaluation of Global Action at UC Berkeley are examples of research centers in top universities that specialize in formulating tools for the evaluation of development projects. More and more governments and NGOs see the need for such fresh approaches to determining the efficacy of foreign aid.

---

[18]Easterly, W. R. (2008). *Reinventing Foreign Aid*. Cambridge, Mass., MIT Press.

Chapter Summary

Structural Change

The process of economic development implies a shift in employment and economic activity from agriculture to industry. As economies continue to develop, another shift occurs from the industry sector to that of services. During the process of development, some sectors expand while others shrink.

The Lewis Model of Structural Change

The Lewis model examines how labor can be transferred from the traditional agricultural sector to a profitable modern industrial sector, inducing capital accumulation in the latter and economic development in the country as a whole. The quality of institutions in different countries is a major reason why the predictions of the Lewis model fail to materialize. Weak institutions are the reason for a large and inefficient informal sector, for private investors' preference to invest capital abroad rather than in the domestic economy, and for the presence of large inefficiencies in government-sponsored industrial sectors.

The Harris-Todaro Model of Rural to Urban Migration

The Harris-Todaro model analyzes the motivations for migration from the countryside to the cities on the basis of the expected lifetime income in rural versus urban areas. People may expect a high income when moving to a city, but in reality they might become unemployed. If there is a fixed minimum wage level in the modern urban sector that is higher than the wage in the traditional agricultural sector, the Harris-Todaro model predicts that there will be excess migration to the cities, thus generating urban unemployment. Rural inhabitants with more education will be more tempted to migrate than those with less education. Government programs to create jobs for the urban unemployed may end up increasing unemployment, as they will tend to increase rural to urban migration.

Development Strategies: Sectoral Growth

Theories promoting balanced growth call for equal growth rates across sectors, while theories in favor of unbalanced growth rates call for higher growth in priority sectors. Strategies for balanced growth should theoretically lead to faster growth, but governments may not have the administrative capabilities to manage balanced growth and may have to focus on priority sectors. In that case, it is best to focus on the development of sectors whose expansion might have the most positive effects on upstream and downstream sectors.

Big-push theories state that governments should encourage the simultaneous development of different sectors on a scale large enough to benefit the whole economy. This is especially true for sectors that are complementary to each other, i.e., where the development of one sector makes the development of the other sector more attractive. Such government coordination may increase the attractiveness of private investment and pull countries out of poverty.

Development Strategies: Import Substitution versus Export Promotion

Import substitution strategies aim at relying less on the import of industrial goods and more on developing a country's domestic industrial base. One of the primary rationales for these policies was the fear that the prices of industrial goods would increase more than the prices of raw materials, a deterioration of the terms of trade for developing countries. However, since the 1970s this fear has proved largely unfounded. In order to create a new industrial basis as a substitution for imports, the need to temporarily protect infant industries against competition from established industrial countries has increased. Unfortunately, protected industries often lack the incentives to become more competitive and protection then tends to become permanent.

The success of Asian economies in recent decades is based on export promotion, a strategy of encouraging certain sectors to compete and gain important market shares on the world market. Government has played a significant role in helping export firms to expand their global market shares. However, many governments in developing countries do not have the administrative capabilities to fulfill such a role.

The Foreign Aid Controversy

Jeffrey Sachs and other proponents of increased foreign aid argue that the poorest countries are stuck in a poverty trap with too few resources to invest in developing their economies and that more foreign aid could create a big push. Skeptics such as William Easterly argue that foreign aid in previous decades has not led to successful growth even though some countries may have benefited from large sums. A significant problem is caused by large portions of foreign aid that have been diverted by corrupt officials. A more bottom-up approach is needed to identify valuable aid projects, while a more rigorous evaluation of aid projects is needed to improve the use of resources.

Key Terms

backward linkages
balanced growth
big push theories
capital flight
complementarities
coordination problems
development banks
export promotion
export promotion strategies
forward linkages
Harris-Todaro model
hukou
import substitution
import substitution strategies

income-elasticity of demand
infant industries
informal sector
intersectoral linkage
patronage
poverty trap
Prebisch-Singer hypothesis
primary commodities
sectoral composition
sectoral growth
structural change
terms of trade
unbalanced growth
yardstick competition

Review Questions

1. Modify the Lewis model and assume that there is a strictly positive marginal product of labor in the traditional sector. Use figures with production functions in the traditional and the modern sectors to show what the equilibrium is when no one wants to move away from agriculture. What assumptions do you have to make about production functions to arrive at the conclusion that fewer people will end up in agriculture?

2. Use the same starting point as in the previous question. Derive the demand for labor in the traditional and in the modern sectors. Show graphically what the characteristics of the equilibrium would look like when no one wants to change sectors.

3. Take the Lewis model and discuss what the effect of a declining trend in the terms of trade would be for the modern sector in a developing country on the country's growth path and on the rural to urban migration.

4. What is the main difference in prediction between the Lewis model and the Harris-Todaro model on rural to urban migration?

5. Given the validity of the Harris-Todaro model, what would you tell a government that wanted to eliminate urban unemployment by creating government-subsidized jobs in its cities?

6. What lessons would you draw from the Harris-Todaro model in terms of immigration policies in the United States? What are the

commonalities and differences between rural to urban migration and migration from poor to rich countries?

7. Define balanced and unbalanced growth. What are the advantages and disadvantages of each strategy? Give examples for both strategies. For which strategy is it more difficult to find examples?

8. Read the article by Oded Stark, Manash Ranjan Gupta, and David Levhari, "Equilibrium urban unemployment in developing countries: Is migration the culprit?" *Economics Letters* 37, no. 4 (1991) 1991: 477–482. How does this article contradict the Harris-Todaro model? Why? What explanation does it give for urban unemployment in developing countries?

9. Research the history of the Toyota company and its success in becoming a major car-exporting firm. What help did it receive from the Japanese government and how effective was this help?

10. Go on the FAO (Food and Agricultural Organization) website, http://faostat.fao.org, and construct figures for the share of agricultural labor in Brazil and Mexico between 1980 and 2000. Which country has had the fastest decline in the share of the agricultural labor force? Find articles about development in Mexico and Brazil to explain the different evolutions in both countries.

International Trade and Exchange Rates

6

The mainstream media have, in recent years, paid increasing attention to the phenomenon of globalization; its prominence as a buzzword reflects the fact that we live in a world that has become more open economically. Many stores in the United States offer fruits, vegetables, clothing, and consumer electronics from all over the globe. From the coffee we drink in the morning to the television we watch in the evening, from the cars we drive to the clothes we wear, many of these items were produced abroad and imported for our consumption. Similarly, many developing countries import products from overseas such as cars from North America, Japan, and Europe, consumer electronics from China, Japan, and Korea, and even junk food from the Unites States and Europe.

Not everyone benefits from globalization. Manufacturers in the United States complain about the low wages paid to Chinese workers, which make it possible to produce goods in China at a cheap price that threatens the jobs of higher paid American workers. Street vendors and local restaurants in Latin America blame bad business on the competition from McDonalds. Outside the United States, Disney's global presence overshadows local entertainment industries and raises the concern that local cultures might be disappearing in a deluge of American programming.

How did this level of global trade develop? Has it helped developing countries or has it hindered their progress? What have they been trading and why? In this chapter, we will see how trade has evolved over the past few decades. We will then take a closer look at the theories economists have used to explain trade patterns across the world. We will also examine political reactions, both in developing and developed countries, to the increase in global trade, and we will discuss how the World Trade Organization prevents countries from erecting trade barriers. Finally, we will look at how international trade affects the financial flows of developing countries and their exchange rates, and what the best exchange rate arrangements are for developing countries in a globalized world.

World Trade Evolution and Developing Countries

There are three basic trends of international trade in recent decades that we must consider. First, the share of exports in GDP has trended up for developed countries but even more so for developing countries. Second, this trend hides a large heterogeneity among developing countries; while exports of East Asian countries have gone up spectacularly, exports from Africa and the Middle East have grown more slowly than the rest of the world. Third, the pattern of export specialization by developing countries is changing over time.

The Increased Openness of Developed and Developing Economies

Trade openness is usually measured as the share of exports to GDP. An increasing share of exports over GDP is interpreted as increasing openness because it means that exports grow faster than GDP. Figure 6.1 shows the evolution of the share of exports in GDP since 1960 for the group of developing countries as a whole (low- and middle-income countries as defined by the World Bank) and for high-income OECD countries.[1] Note the upward trend over the last decades, which reflects the globalization process that has taken place during that period.

We see that in the last decades, especially since the 1990s, openness has increased in both developed and developing economies, although it has increased even more for developing than for developed countries. Until 2008, before the world economic crisis, that share was slightly above 25% for OECD countries, whereas it was close to 40% for developing countries.

FIGURE 6.1 Export Shares of GDP (Total Exports over GDP, Both in Constant 2000 dollars)

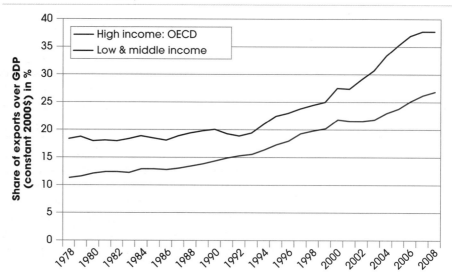

Exports as a share of GDP have gone up in developing and developed countries, but since the late 1990s, the increase has been higher for developing countries.

Source: The World Bank, World Development Indicators, http://databank.worldbank.org, series: Exports of goods and services (% of GDP) for developing countries (low- and middle-income countries in the World Bank classification) and high-income OECD countries.

---

[1]OECD stands for Organization for Economic Cooperation and Development. It was created in 1948 and counts as members 30 high-income countries who have signed its convention. Broadly speaking, they are high-income countries that are democratic and have free markets.

A Diverse Trade Performance across Regions

Figure 6.2 shows a regional decomposition of **trade shares** beginning in 1960 and continuing up to the world economic crisis of 2008. The trade share of a region represents the share of that region's exports as a percentage of total world exports. A region's increasing trade share means that it has had faster export growth than that of the rest of the world.

The first striking fact we notice in Figure 6.2 is the increasing trade share of East Asia, despite a blip around 1997 when the region experienced a significant economic crisis. East Asian exports have been growing much faster than those of most other regions whose shares have been declining. Sub-Saharan Africa's share of world exports has roughly halved since 1960. Latin America's shares have been declining less sharply; they decreased between 1960 and 1990, and have remained more or less constant since then. The shares of the Middle East and North Africa went up dramatically after the first oil shock in 1973, but declined after that. South Asia's (India and its neighbors) share had been dropping until 1990 but has since started to rise. Shares for Eastern Europe and Central Asia have also increased in recent years. As we can see, there is regional heterogeneity in the growth of exports of developing countries, with East Asia doing substantially better than the other regions.

FIGURE 6.2   World Trade Shares of Developing Regions (as a Percentage of World Exports).

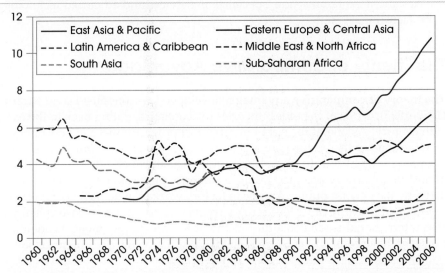

A region's trade shares are the aggregate exports of a developing region as a percentage of world exports. East Asia's share of world trade has gone up sharply while the shares of sub-Saharan Africa, the Middle East and North Africa have gone down.

Source: The World Bank, World Development Indicators, http://databank.worldbank.org, series: Exports of goods and services (current US$) for six regions of the world.

The Evolution of Trade Specialization in Developing Countries

As we look at the composition and evolution of exports from developing countries, we must consider two important facts. First, most developing countries have traditionally specialized in exports of primary commodities, goods that have not yet undergone industrial processing, such as raw materials and agricultural products. Second, in recent years, developing countries have expanded their exports from raw materials to manufactured products; for example, East and South Asia have become the most important manufacturing hubs of the world.

In Figure 6.3, we see the composition of exports for different regions in the developing world and its evolution. In 1980, food exports were the most important category for the majority of the developing regions. Exceptions to this were the Middle East and North African (MENA) region, where petroleum products were the primary export, and South Asia, where manufacturing exports were dominant.[2] But only 20 years later, we observe a large and striking increase in the share of manufacturing exports in all but the MENA region.[3] In South Asia, the share of manufacturing exports rose from less than 60% to more than 80%. In sub-Saharan Africa, however, the share of manufacturing exports has been rising at a slower pace.

In Figure 6.3, we can see that export specialization has emerged in developing regions. Roughly speaking, Asia specializes in manufacturing exports, the Middle East in petroleum exports, and Africa in food and agricultural exports, while Latin America represents a mix of manufacturing and raw materials exports.[4] This evolution in specialization reflects the fact that manufacturing has moved from the United States and Europe to Asia and parts of Latin America. Advanced economies now specialize in services and advanced technology manufacturing.

The Theory of Comparative Advantage

The **theory of comparative advantage**, developed by economist David Ricardo (1772–1823), is one of the oldest theories in economics, dating back to the early 19th century. As one of the simplest and most powerful ideas in economics, it provides one of the best explanations for which patterns of trade will emerge between different countries. It also provides a justification for free trade that is almost unanimously accepted by the economics profession, though not necessarily by the general public. American factory workers who have lost their jobs to low-paid Mexican or Chinese counterparts will, for obvious reasons, tell you that international trade constitutes a threat to U.S. employment. Economists, however, have come to the conclusion that international trade is a major source

---

[2]Historically, textiles have been one of South Asia's important exports, primarily due to British colonization.

[3]There, the share of petroleum exports has continued to increase.

[4]In the case of Latin America, we must not forget that countries such as Argentina and Chile are quite developed when compared to other Latin American countries.

FIGURE 6.3   The Composition of Developing Countries' Exports
in 1980 and 2000

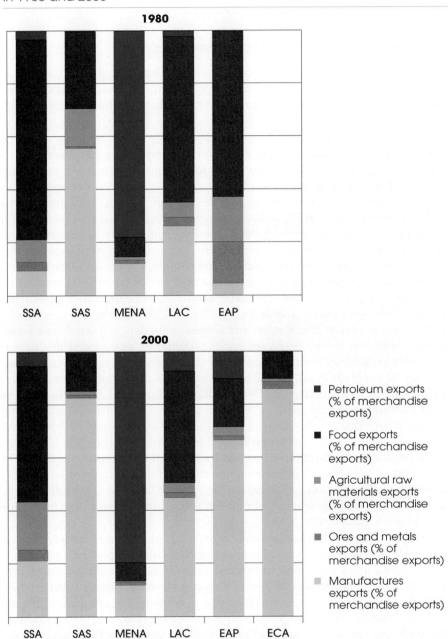

The composition of exports is calculated as the 3-year average of the median country export shares. (SSA) sub-Saharan Africa, (SAS) South Asia, (MENA) Middle East & North Africa, (LAC) Latin America & Caribbean, (EAP) East Asia & Pacific, (ECA) Eastern Europe & Central Asia. In 1980, developing countries specialized in food exports, with the exception of the Middle East, which specialized in petroleum exports, and South Asia, which specialized in manufacturing. By 2000, with the exception of sub-Saharan Africa, the Middle East, and parts of Latin America, most regions specialized in manufacturing goods.

Source: The World Bank, World Development Indicators: http://databank.worldbank.org, series for different categories of exports as a percentage of merchandise exports.

of prosperity. Free trade leads to specialization and greater efficiency, increasing the welfare of all countries involved in that trade. The economists' view is based on the theory of comparative advantage.

The Benefits of Exchange and Specialization

Two important ideas form the theory of comparative advantage. First, exchange is beneficial to all parties in the exchange. Second, there are advantages to **specialization**. These fundamental concepts are valid beyond the realm of international trade.

Exchange benefits all. Imagine a Peruvian farmer and a shepherd. Let us call them Ramon and Carlos, respectively. Ramon grows corn and Carlos rears lambs, and they both want to trade with each other. Ramon is not prepared to pay more than 1,000 pounds of corn for one lamb and Carlos is not prepared to sell his lamb for less than 200 pounds of corn. In other words, at a rate of 1,000 pounds of corn for one lamb, Ramon is indifferent to making the exchange. At a rate of 200 pounds of corn for the lamb, Carlos is indifferent to selling his lamb. As one can see, between 200 and 1,000 pounds, both benefit from making the exchange. If they for example agree on a price of 500 pounds of corn for one lamb, they will both be better off making the trade, since this rate is acceptable to both. Exchange thus benefits both.

How can we know that Ramon and Carlos are better off if we do not know their preferences? If they exchange goods voluntarily, as opposed to stealing, each of them must necessarily be better off trading than not trading; otherwise, they would not trade at all. Now Ramon might be a very poor farmer and Carlos a very rich ranch owner. A destitute Ramon might feel forced to trade in order to feed his family, while a prosperous Carlos may have stronger bargaining power due to his wealth. In this case, Carlos may use his bargaining power to get Ramon to give him 900 pounds of corn instead of 500. Nevertheless, Ramon still has the choice of not selling his corn if he feels the trade would make him and his family worse off. Even though Ramon may not have much bargaining power, as long as he trades his corn for lamb on a voluntary basis, he is better off. He may still be poor after trading, but he might be even poorer if he does not trade at all.

What do Ramon and Carlos have to do with international trade? Imagine now that the two traders are from different countries: Ramon sells corn from Mexico and Carlos sells lamb from Peru. Once transport costs are taken into account, it might still be advantageous to trade Mexican corn against Peruvian lamb. The economic principle that exchange is advantageous to those who participate is just as relevant to international trade as it is to local trade. The idea that trade enhances economic welfare is the first component of the economic theory of international trade.

The advantage of specialization. There is an economic advantage to specialization both for individuals and countries. Individuals tend to specialize in a particular job using the skills at which they excel. The same idea applies to international trade. The theory of international trade says that countries should specialize in those areas in which they have a **comparative advantage** relative to other nations. By comparative advantage, we mean that if two countries have different cost structures in different sectors, each country should specialize in the sector for which the **opportunity cost** of production, i.e., the cost of producing one good, and not producing other goods, is lower compared to other countries. This idea is more subtle than that which states exchange benefits all. It may even seem counterintuitive when we spell out its implications. In the following section, we will explain in a clear and simple way the meaning of comparative advantage in the context of international trade.

Japanese DVD Players and Chinese Shirts: Comparative Advantage in Action

In Table 6.1, consider the hypothetical example of the production of DVD players and shirts in Japan and China. Taking into account all the direct and indirect costs of producing a DVD player, let us assume that it takes 30 hours in Japan and 60 hours in China to manufacture one DVD player. It also takes 5 hours in Japan and 6 hours in China to produce one shirt. To keep things simple, we will assess total costs in terms of hours of production rather than monetary value.

Looking at Table 6.1, we can see that in Japan, it takes less time to produce both a DVD player and a shirt than it does in China. Japan thus has an absolute advantage in both sectors. Intuitively, one would think that Japan will never trade with China because China is less efficient than Japan at producing both DVD players and shirts. This is not what the theory of comparative advantage tells us. Let us now look at the opportunity cost (as opposed to the absolute cost) of the production of a DVD player and a shirt. In Japan, it takes 6 times more hours (30/5) to produce a DVD than a shirt, whereas in China it takes 10 times more hours. The opportunity cost of producing a DVD in terms of shirts is thus lower in Japan than in China. Japan has a comparative advantage in producing DVD players. Similarly, China has a comparative advantage in producing shirts because the shirt takes only one-tenth of the time necessary to produce a DVD, whereas in Japan it takes one-sixth of the time. The theory of comparative advantage says that it is in a country's best interest to operate in the sector in which it has the comparative advantage. Japan should thus specialize in producing DVD players and China should specialize in producing shirts.

In order to see why Japan should focus only on DVD players and China only on shirts, we need to compare **price ratios**, in this case the ratio of the

TABLE 6.1 Production of DVD Players and Shirts in Japan and China (in Hours)

	Japan	China
DVD player	30	60
Shirt	5	6

This simple table gives the total number of hours needed to produce a DVD player and a shirt in Japan and China.

price of a DVD to the price of a shirt (and the converse ratio) within each country before and after specialization and trade take place. If prices are equal to the cost in terms of hours, then the DVD/shirt price ratio in Japan is equal to the opportunity cost $30/5 = 6$. Similarly, in China it is $60/6 = 10$. As a result, DVD players are relatively more expensive in China than in Japan. Conversely, shirts are relatively more expensive in Japan than in China.

Keeping these domestic price ratios in mind, assume that the two countries open up to international trade and that transport costs across countries are equal to zero. It is then advantageous to trade Chinese shirts against Japanese DVD players and not against Chinese DVD players because six shirts are traded for one DVD player in Japan compared to 10 shirts for one DVD player in China. Similarly, in Japan, it is advantageous to trade a DVD player for Chinese shirts instead of Japanese shirts because we can get 10 shirts for a DVD player instead of 6. Therefore, with international trade, people in China and Japan will all want Japanese DVD players and Chinese shirts, and there will be no demand for Chinese DVD players and Japanese shirts.

Factor Endowments and Comparative Advantage

The example above begs the question: what determines a country's comparative advantage? The theory of international trade states that **relative factor endowments** are a key determinant of how a country chooses its specialization. Factor endowments are the capacities of a country in terms of its main production factors: capital and labor. Richer countries have relatively more capital than poorer countries because they have accumulated more wealth. In contrast, in developing countries, capital is relatively scarce, and thus labor is relatively more abundant than in industrialized countries. Because rich countries have relatively more capital and developing countries have relatively more labor, international trade theory predicts that rich countries should have a comparative advantage in capital-intensive sectors, using more capital in production, while developing countries should have a comparative advantage in labor-intensive sectors, using more labor in production.

Ricardo's theory of comparative advantage was based on the differences in labor costs in different sectors across countries. In the 20th century, the Heckscher-Ohlin, or neoclassical, theory of international trade was created to incorporate factor endowments as the basis of comparative advantage. An important difference between the Ricardo model and the neoclassical model is in the determination of prices. In the Ricardo model, prices are only a function of the total labor costs of a product. In the neoclassical model, prices are determined by preferences and by scarcities.

Figure 6.4 represents the example of Japan and China from the point of view of the neoclassical theory of comparative advantage. We assume the same preferences in Japan and China as indicated by the indifference curves of consumers between DVD players and shirts. The major difference between the two countries relates to the **production possibility frontier**, i.e., the maximum that can be produced of one good for a given quantity produced of the other good. As we can see, the production possibility frontier in Japan makes it possible to produce relatively more DVD players than shirts, whereas in China the opposite is true. This is because Japan has more capital than China and

FIGURE 6.4 Factor Endowments and Comparative Advantage

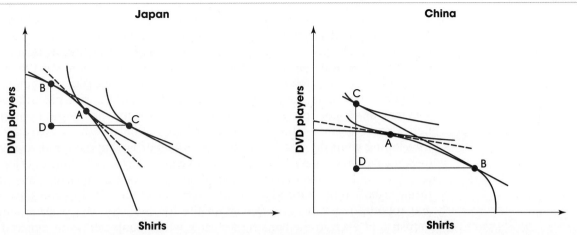

China and Japan have different production possibility frontiers. The opportunity cost of producing a DVD in terms of shirts is higher in China than in Japan. Point A is the production under autarky in each country, where the dotted line represents the price ratio under autarky in each country. Point B is the production under international trade in each country, where the solid line represents the price ratio on the international market. Point C is the new consumption point in each country bringing a higher utility than point A. The line between points B and D represents exports and the line between points C and D represents imports. Japan exports DVDs and China exports shirts.

the production of DVD players is assumed to be more capital intensive than the production of shirts. The opportunity cost of producing DVDs in terms of shirts is thus higher in China than in Japan. Therefore, China has a "flatter" production possibility frontier compared to Japan. Under autarky, without international trade, production is determined at the tangency point between the production possibility frontier and the indifference curve. This is point A for each country. The autarky solution has relatively more DVD players in Japan and relatively more shirts in China. The price ratio, the common slope of the indifference curve and the production possibility frontier at that tangency point (the dashed line), is also flatter in China so that more shirts must be exchanged to obtain a DVD player in China compared to Japan.

Now we introduce international trade with a price ratio that is somewhere between the price ratios under autarky. The international price ratio is represented by the line joining points B and C in both figures. Production will now be at point B at the intersection between the production possibility frontier and that price ratio. There is now more production of DVD players in Japan and more production of shirts in China. Consumption in each country will be at point C, on the same price line as point B, but at the intersection with the indifference curve. Note that point C is located beyond the production possibility frontier and on a higher indifference curve than under autarky. Trade can thus increase total consumption and consumer welfare. Since B and C are different points, production and consumption of DVDs and shirts in each country will not be the same. Each country will thus export and import goods. The export line is given by BD and the import line is given by CD. We thus see from Figure 6.4 that Japan exports DVD players and imports shirts whereas China exports shirts and imports DVD players.

Comparative Advantage and Patterns of Trade

The theory of comparative advantage explains some of the main patterns of international trade, in particular the specialization in labor-intensive production in developing countries and capital-intensive production in developed countries. The initial specialization of developing countries toward primary commodities reflects the relative scarcity of capital and the relative abundance of labor. Whether in the coffee plantations of Brazil, the rice plantations of Vietnam, or the gold mines in South Africa, labor is the main input in production. However, labor-intensive enterprises are not only in the primary sector. Developing countries such as China, where labor is abundant and relatively inexpensive, are engaging in labor-intensive manufacturing. While developing countries find that their comparative advantage is in a labor-driven manufacturing sector, industrialized countries have moved toward highly mechanized and robotized production, such as in the car industry, the pharmaceutical industry, or even in the banking industry where bank clerks are replaced by ATM machines and online banking.

We can explain the export patterns of successful developing countries using the theory of comparative advantage. Asian countries such as South Korea, Taiwan, or China began participating in international trade by producing labor-intensive manufactured goods that were relatively unsophisticated. As success in exports made these countries richer, they started manufacturing products that were more capital-intensive. In the 1950s, South Korea began exporting agricultural products, and also fish products and wood. During the 1960s and 1970s, it moved on to export more complex manufactured products, such as textile goods, using labor-intensive techniques. As capital accumulated in the Korean economy, manufacturing then shifted toward very sophisticated goods such as electronics and the products of heavy industry such as ships, cars, and complex machines. Today, countries similar to China and Vietnam tend to play the same role as South Korea did several decades ago and have engaged in labor-intensive manufacturing enterprises. As an economy grows, exported manufactured goods become more sophisticated; in recent years, Chinese firms have become quite specialized in the assembly of more advanced electronic products, such as computers and smart phones. The parts are imported from other countries and assembled in China, a strategy that takes advantage of the low salaries of Chinese workers.

Trade Specialization and Export Price Risk

Specialization based on comparative advantage not only has advantages, but it can also possess certain risks—especially for developing countries. Take the example of Colombia, one of the world's largest coffee exporters, putting an average 1.4 billion pounds of coffee per year on world markets. Coffee prices can fluctuate between 60 cents and $1.50 per pound. Assuming a constant volume of exports, this price fluctuation means that exports can total anywhere between $840 million to $2.1 billion a year. If the world price for coffee dips, as it did in 2001, then Colombia's income will also drop considerably. This dip in revenue is the risk Colombia takes when it practices strong specialization. In the 1950s, coffee exports accounted for 75% of the country's export revenues. While comparative advantage suggests that specialization in coffee is beneficial for the Colombian economy, it does not take into account the risks involved. In recent decades, Colombia has decided to diversify its exports because of these high risks and coffee's share of export revenues has significantly declined from its peak in the 1950s. In the 1980s, coffee still accounted for more than 50% of Colombian export revenues, but it has fallen below 10% since 2000.

Developing countries are more prone to export price risks than rich countries are for two reasons. First, while advanced countries specialize in manufactured goods, developing countries specialize in primary commodities, which have always been subject to stronger price fluctuations than have manufactured goods.[5] Second, developing countries' export portfolios tend to be less diversified. This is because richer economies produce a higher diversity of goods than do poor countries. Even if an advanced industrialized country specializes in cars, for example, it will still have a larger array of total exports. If the price of cars drops on the global market, that country can fall back on its remaining exports. Just as in finance, the best way to reduce the risk of investment is to hold a diversified portfolio. Price increases for some commodities offset price decreases for other commodities. The more diversified a country's export portfolio, the less that country will be subject to risk. A developing country that exports only coffee will not have the export "safety net" that developed countries have and will feel a drop in revenue more acutely.

The export risk does not imply that countries should not specialize in the direction of their comparative advantage. The Asian tigers understood that growth and industrialization were priorities, and despite the risks involved, they specialized by following their comparative advantage and were eventually able to diversify their exports and obtain more export security. As economic growth permitted more capital accumulation, investment was allocated to diversify the export sectors over time. The lesson is that countries should not be content to specialize and participate in the world economy only by following their comparative advantage. They should be able to grow and diversify their exports over time.

How important are the risks of specialization for developing countries? The best way to find out how is to look at the evolution of the terms of trade for developing countries. A country's terms of trade measure the evolution of the prices of its exports relative to the prices of its imports. When terms of trade are volatile, it is a sign that countries face significant export price risk in world markets. A high export price risk means volatile export revenues and thus a high export revenue risk.

Figure 6.5 shows the evolution of the terms of trade for various regions of the developing world before the 2008 economic crisis. We do see clear volatility in terms of trade. On the positive side, we see that the volatility in terms of trade has been decreasing over time. This reflects some diversification in export composition. Countries seem to have undergone a process similar to Colombia's, which moved from specialization in its exports to diversification. This diversification seems to have taken place as countries have developed stronger manufacturing exports while they have reduced the share of primary commodities in their exports.

---

[5]See David S. Jacks, Kevin H. O'Rourke, and Jeffrey D. Williamson, "Commodity Price Volatility and World Market Integration since 1700," *The Review of Economics and Statistics* 93, no. 3 (2011): 800–813.

FIGURE 6.5   Terms of Trade

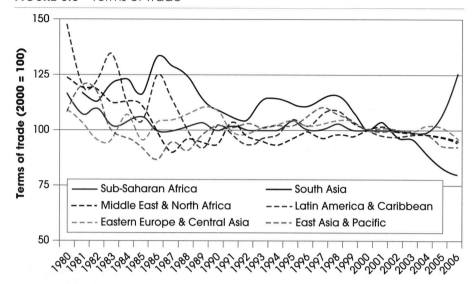

The percentage ratio of the export price index to the corresponding import price index is measured relative to the base year. The sample for sub-Saharan Africa consists of 31 countries for which a complete data series for 1980–2005 is available. The samples for South Asia, the Middle East, and North Africa as well as East Asia and the Pacific consist of 5 countries in each region. The sample for Latin America is 19 countries, while the sample for Eastern Europe and Central Asia is 3 countries.

Source: The World Bank, World Development Indicators, http://databank.worldbank.org.

The Politics of Trade

While economists generally accept the economic theory of international trade, politicians rarely follow the economists' advice. Protectionist ideas abound in the popular press and politicians, in both developed and developing countries, openly defend these ideas. The stark difference between the consensus of the economics profession on free trade and the defense of protectionism by politicians often puzzles economists. The answer to this puzzle lies in the **political economy of trade liberalization**, which analyzes the conflicts between sectors and firms that become winners and losers as a result of trade liberalization policies.

Winners and Losers in International Trade

Even though an economy's aggregate gains from trade liberalization are largely positive, there are still losers, not just winners. Export sectors that exploit a country's comparative advantage are clear winners, but sectors that must compete with imports are hurt. China, for example, has a comparative advantage in labor-intensive manufacturing sectors. Chinese manufacturers export goods that the world market is keen to absorb and these sectors gain from trade liberalization. On the other hand, China does not have a comparative advantage in service sectors such as banking. Trade liberalization hurts the banking industry because of the entry and competition from more efficient foreign banks. Those working in the export sector support trade liberalization because they benefit from it, but those in the banking sector who are afraid to lose market shares to foreign banking firms will oppose it.

The United States has a comparative advantage in sectors such as banking, which rely on human capital and high technology. Those working in the U.S. banking sector welcome trade liberalization because trade opens up the Chinese market to their sector. On the other hand, those working in low-tech U.S. manufacturing firms are at a disadvantage because imports from China will replace domestically manufactured goods.

In both countries, the import sector would suffer under trade liberalization, the export sector would benefit, and consumers would stand to gain. American consumers would have access to much cheaper manufactured goods and Chinese consumers would have access to more efficient banking services.

In the next section, we will examine how, and to what extent, governments take into account the interests of winners and losers from trade liberalization when making policy decisions.

Collective Action Failure

Battles over trade policy are driven by the push and pull between import-sector lobbies and export-sector lobbies. Consumers, who collectively gain the most from trade liberalization, are usually not active in these political debates and it is very difficult to organize this large group in the political arena. The cost to any single consumer who tries to organize other consumers is much larger than the individual gain from free trade. If other consumers organize a lobbying effort, then an individual consumer can benefit from those efforts without contributing any effort. Individual consumers therefore have no incentive to incur lobbying costs and remain disorganized. This is a **collective action failure**: a situation in which individuals fail to take an action that would be in their interest because they can free-ride on the actions taken by others. Consumers thus tend to remain disorganized and inactive during debates on trade policy. In contrast, import and export sectors suffer less from the collective action problem for two reasons. First, the benefits to these sectors from lobbying are much larger than for consumers. Second, it is easier for them to organize because they are fewer in number compared to consumers. Because consumers are not organized, politicians react only to pressure from export and import lobbies that support and resist trade liberalization, respectively.

"Give and Take"

Politicians tend to view trade liberalization as a series of "give and take" interactions between lobbying groups. For example, the United States will allow more exports from China if China lets the U.S. banking industry enter the Chinese banking market. Newspapers often depict these negotiations as reasonable trade-offs, but this "give and take" philosophy is not always the most efficient from an economic point of view. Even if China is unwilling to allow the U.S. banking industry to cross its borders, it might still be in the best interests of the U.S. economy to open its borders to Chinese manufactured goods. Such a unilateral move will benefit all the U.S. consumers of those goods. Consumers will be able to buy goods at lower prices and retailers will lower their costs of inputs, regardless of whether or not the United States is allowed to expand its banking sector in China. The reason the U.S. government would not consider such a unilateral move is that it does not take into account the interests of disorganized consumers, but only the potential losses of the organized U.S. manufacturers. Therefore, unilateral trade liberalization does not take place for political reasons even when it has the potential to increase overall economic welfare in a country.

The Costs of Trade Barriers

We now turn our attention to the specific ways that trade barriers can affect a country's economic welfare when politicians fail to liberalize trade policies. As we will see, trade barriers inflict losses on the economy where they are introduced.

Protectionism and Tariffs

Protectionism occurs when a country puts in place barriers to international trade in order to protect its domestic industries. These barriers aim at reducing the volume of imports as a means to guarantee those industries large shares of domestic markets. One of the most common forms of protectionism is **import tariffs**, taxes on imports. To illustrate the effects of tariffs, let us return to our initial example of Japanese producers of DVD players and Chinese shirt manufacturers. Imagine that the Chinese government wants to prevent Chinese consumers from buying Japanese DVD players and to encourage them to buy the more expensive Chinese DVD players. It can do this by imposing an import tariff on Japanese DVD players, so that an imported Japanese DVD player will cost the import price plus the tariff price.

Figure 6.6 shows the market for DVD players in China. The supply line for DVD players is S, which represents the marginal costs of different producers ranked in order of increasing marginal cost. Suppose that the price of Japanese DVD players for Chinese consumers is $100.[6] We see that at that price, demand by Chinese consumers (point B) is higher than what Chinese companies are able to supply at a marginal cost lower than $100 (point A). As a result, the excess demand for Japanese DVD players by Chinese consumers is reflected by the distance between Q^d and Q^s.

The tariff, assumed to be $20, has two effects. First, it reduces demand for Japanese DVD players because consumers pay a higher price. Demand is now at $Q^{d'}$ at point D. The tariff also makes it possible for Chinese producers, with a marginal cost higher than $100 and lower than $120, to enter the market. The supply of Chinese DVD players will increase to $Q^{s'}$ at point C. These are the intended consequences of the tariff: protect domestic industry, encourage (inefficient) domestic producers, and discourage demand for cheaper foreign goods.

While producers of Chinese DVD players may benefit from these tariffs, consumers buying the DVD players will be hurt. They will pay an additional sum for DVD players equal to rectangle HDGF in Figure 6.6, which represents

[6]We use a dollar measure to keep things simple.

FIGURE 6.6 Economic Losses Due to a Tariff Barrier

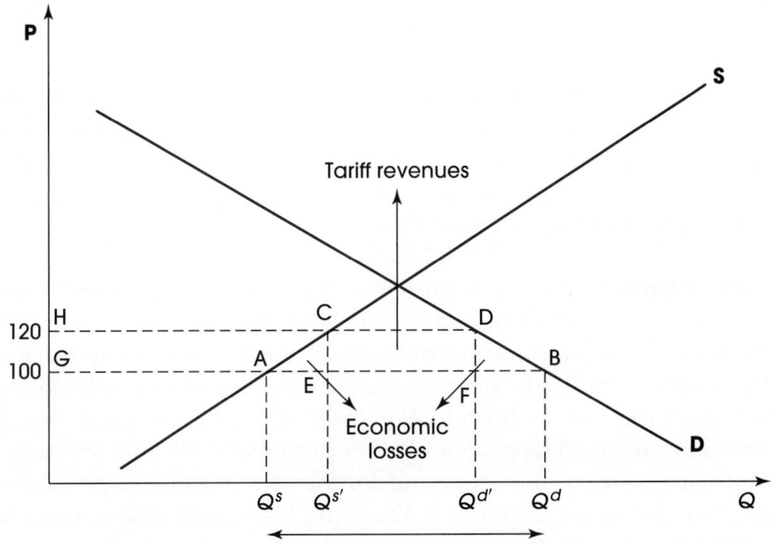

A tariff that increases the price of a DVD player from $100 to $120 creates an efficiency loss ACE because of the entry of inefficient producers and a loss in consumer surplus DBF.

the height of the tariff ($20) times the new demand $Q^{d'}$. This sum is not a complete loss for the Chinese economy because the government collects tariff revenues CDEF, which are available to fund public expenditures by the Chinese government. In addition, Chinese firms earn **rents** (i.e., extra profits) from selling at a higher price (equal to trapezoid HCGA). On balance, there are, nevertheless, clear welfare losses:

Welfare loss 1. The triangle ACE denotes the loss from the entry of inefficient firms with a marginal cost higher than $100. Instead of letting consumers buy Japanese DVD players at a price of $100, Chinese firms are producing them at a cost higher than $100.

Welfare loss 2. Triangle DBF represents the loss in consumer surplus. Without a tariff and with demand equal to Q^d, consumers who are ready to pay more than $100 enjoy a consumer surplus, the difference between what they would be willing to pay and what they are paying. When demand goes down to $Q^{d'}$ after the tariff is introduced, there is a loss of consumer surplus of DBF on top of the loss of HGDF mentioned above.

Nontariff Barriers

There are many other forms of protectionism that are often more insidious than tariffs because they are less visible but equally harmful. In this section, we review the most important types of nontariff barriers and their economic effects.

Import quotas. Many countries choose to implement **import quotas** instead of tariffs to protect domestic industries against imports because these quotas limit the total volume of imports to a country at a given moment in time.

A government can implement them through the allocation of the licenses required to import goods from abroad. By limiting the number of licenses, a government keeps the price of imports high, which protects domestic industries.

Voluntary export restraints. A government may decide to limit exports to a certain country out of fear of being hit by import quotas from that country to which its goods are exported. In the 1980s for example, Japan agreed to limit its exports of cars to the United States. The WTO has severely limited the use of **voluntary export restraints** in recent years.

Regulatory barriers. This is a form of protectionism that has been used more frequently over time and it can be difficult to detect. Governments issue domestic regulations that have the effect of limiting imports. For example, specifications for product standards are deliberately established or modified to favor domestic producers or to hurt foreign producers. Protectionist regulations may sometimes relate to labeling and other product details that are completely irrelevant to consumers, but are set up for the sole purpose of prohibiting the imports of foreign goods. Some U.S. Food and Drug Administration detention rules call for the examination of certain imported goods to determine whether they meet U.S. standards. During the time required for that examination, no imports of those goods are allowed. These detention rules have been used repeatedly to slow down imports of food products from Asia to the United States. Traditional Chinese medicines cannot be imported to the United States because they would be labeled as toxic. American catfish producers have managed to secure the imposition of a regulation that states only American catfish can be called catfish, denying the appellation to catfish from other countries. This regulation has been particularly damaging to Vietnamese catfish exports to the United States.

In general, it is not easy to detect these **regulatory barriers.** Countries have the right to regulate the safety of products offered to consumers. For example, many countries prohibit the importation of genetically modified agricultural products because of fears that genetically modified organisms (GMOs) endanger the environment, but U.S. exporters of GMOs see these prohibitions as regulatory barriers.

Cotton: An Example of U.S. Protectionism

America's cotton industry provides a good example of a developed country using protectionism as a trade barrier against developing countries. After China, the United States is the world's second-largest cotton producer and the world's largest exporter of cotton. Between 40 to 60% of U.S. cotton is exported and those exports represent roughly half of the world's cotton exports. The federal government hands out about $4 billion of production subsidies each year to only 25,000 U.S. cotton farmers. Nearly 80% of those subsidies go to the richest 2,000 producers. These subsidies have helped the United States export its cotton at prices that are roughly 30% below production costs. Given the large market share of U.S. cotton exports, these price subsidies have not only helped protect U.S. producers, but have also depressed world cotton prices.

The removal of U.S. cotton subsidies would be very beneficial to cotton farmers in the developing world; in sub-Saharan Africa alone, there are about 10 million cotton farmers.

In 2002, Brazil complained to the World Trade Organization (WTO) about these U.S. cotton subsidies. In 2005, the WTO ruled that the cotton subsidies were illegal and called on the United States to suspend them. The United States promised to comply, but the Brazilian government requested a panel to verify U.S. compliance. The panel found that the compliance was not as promised. The United States then asked for arbitration in this conflict with Brazil and in August 2009, the arbitration report concluded that the U.S. government was continuing to subsidize its cotton producers and had largely ignored the 2005 ruling. The WTO gave Brazil the right to retaliate by using countermeasures (such as subsidizing Brazilian cotton producers) and suspending its property rights obligations to the U.S. In 2010, an agreement was reached between Brazil and the United States in which Brazil agreed to a provisional suspension of countermeasures in exchange for annual payments of $147.3 million by the United States to a fund to support Brazilian cotton farmers. These payments were supposed to continue until the U.S. Congress voted on a new farm bill in 2012 that would reduce cotton subsidies, but Congress never voted on the bill and, as a result, the story of U.S. cotton protectionism is far from having been resolved.

Trade Institutions: Bilateral versus Multilateral

In global trade negotiations, countries practice either **bilateral trade negotiations** held between two countries, **multilateral trade negotiations** held between multiple countries, or a combination of both. Multilateral trade negotiations have been an important feature of international trade since World War II. They started in 1947 with the General Agreement on Trade and Tariffs (GATT);[7] multiple rounds of multilateral negotiations have regularly taken place since then.[8] Each of these rounds has led to agreements in which all the countries involved reduced their import tariffs. The World Trade Organization (WTO) replaced GATT on January 1, 1995.

Multilateral Trade Avoids Trade Diversion

From an economic point of view, multilateral trade liberalization is always preferable to bilateral trade liberalization. We can see why by expanding on our example of Chinese manufactured goods and the U.S. banking sector.

Assume that China and the United States agree to liberalize trade for Chinese manufactured goods and American banking services. Also assume that Japan and Vietnam would like to trade in these sectors as well. Vietnam is more

---

[7]The countries that participated in GATT included Australia, Belgium, Brazil, Burma, Canada, Ceylon, Chile, China, Cuba, the Czechoslovak Republic, France, India, Lebanon, Luxembourg, Netherlands, New Zealand, Norway, Pakistan, Southern Rhodesia, Syria, South Africa, the United Kingdom, and the United States.

[8]The last GATT negotiations were the Kennedy Round (1964–1967), the Tokyo Round (1973–1979), and the Uruguay Round (1986–1993).

efficient than China at producing manufactured goods and food products such as rice and catfish. Japan's commercial banking sector is more efficient than the United States', but the higher-level U.S. investment-banking sector is stronger than Japan's investment banks. What are the effects of bilateral liberalization between only the United States and China?

1. There might be an excess presence of U.S. banking firms in China compared to multilateral liberalization, in which there would be more efficient Japanese commercial banks in China along with U.S. investment banks.
2. There might be excess exports of Chinese rice and catfish to the United States compared to multilateral liberalization, where there would have been exports of cheaper Vietnamese catfish and rice to the United States.

It is very possible that bilateral liberalization can have distortionary effects called **trade diversion**, which is defined as trade flows that would not take place under full multilateral liberalization. While some American commercial banks offer their services in China, it would be more efficient if Japanese commercial banks were present instead because they have the comparative advantage in that sector. Similarly, Chinese exports of rice and catfish to the United States would be less efficient compared to similar Vietnamese exports.

Trade diversion is usually associated with bilateral trade agreements and/or **regional trade agreements** between a subset of countries.[9] For example, in Latin America, MERCOSUR is an economic and political agreement that establishes a common market between Argentina, Brazil, Paraguay, Uruguay, and Venezuela. Bolivia, Chile, Ecuador, Peru, and Colombia are associate members of MERCOSUR. In Asia, the Association of Southeast Asian Nations (ASEAN) is comprised of 10 countries: Indonesia, Malaysia, Philippines, Singapore, Brunei, Thailand, Vietnam, Laos, Myanmar and Cambodia. In Africa, the Common Market for Eastern and Southern Africa (COMESA) stretches from Libya to Zimbabwe. Other regional trade agreements include the North American Free Trade Agreement (NAFTA) between the United States, Canada, and Mexico, and the European Union (EU), which includes most European countries.

Multilateral Trade Agreements Are Politically Easier to Achieve

Multilateralism also has an advantage from the political economy point of view: enlarging the set of possible exchanges (more export concessions versus more import concessions) makes it easier to establish trade agreements between various governments. The idea behind multilateralism is similar to the advantage of market exchange in general: when only two people trade, both must want to trade with each other, whereas if there are many people on the marketplace, trades are easier to arrange. Say trader A has textiles and trader B has steel. For bilateral exchange to take place, B has to be willing to trade steel against textiles and A has to be willing to engage in the opposite

---

[9]See, for example, Jagdish Bhagwati, "Regionalism versus Multilateralism," *The World Economy* 15, no. 5 (1992): 535–556.

exchange. However, if this is not the case, bilateral trade will not take place. Suppose now that C has rubber and wants steel, and that A wants rubber. B can thus trade steel against rubber and trade the rubber with A against textiles. Exchanges can now take place. The more participants there are, the easier it is to arrange for such multilateral exchanges.

The same thing is true for multilateral trade liberalization. Suppose that A, B, and C are countries and that India has a comparative advantage in textiles, Russia in steel, and Indonesia in rubber. Bilateral liberalization between India and Russia may, for example, not take place because after liberalization, Russia will not export much more steel to India where domestic demand for steel is weak. However, if India, Russia, and Indonesia jointly agree to liberalize trade on rubber, steel, and textiles, there is more scope for exchanges in the spirit of the "give and take" that characterizes the political economy of trade. Multilateralism will not necessarily always work; the Doha Round organized by the WTO has been stalled for nearly a decade. Nevertheless, the point to remember is that multilateral trade liberalization works better than bilateral trade liberalization.

The World Trade Organization

Founded in 1995 to succeed GATT, the World Trade Organization (WTO) has 153 member nations. Its main role is to facilitate multilateral negotiations over free trade agreements, but over time it has also taken on other roles. In particular, it oversees the implementation of international trade agreements, settles trade disputes between countries, and has an important responsibility for the enforcement of trade agreements. It also provides rules for trade liberalization between countries.

WTO Rules for Trade Liberalization

Two basic principles are at the heart of WTO rules for trade liberalization. First is the principle of **nondiscrimination** between countries. This means that if a country grants a favor to another country in terms of trade, it must extend that favor to all other countries. This is called the **most favored nation clause**. Also, once an imported good is on a domestic market, it must be treated in the same way as domestic products. This is called the **national treatment clause** and it is designed to prevent nontariff barriers, for example the technical specifications for products, such as specific labeling, that are designed to protect domestic goods from competition by foreign goods.

A second principle is that of **reciprocity**. This means that if a country reduces its trade barriers, other countries must reciprocate. In other words, concessions from one country must be matched by concessions from others.

Ralph Ossa has proposed a simple but insightful theory to explain the usefulness of both rules.[10] Consider trade relations between three countries A, B, and C. To keep things easy, we assume that A trades with B and C, but B and C do not trade with each other. This allows us to

---

[10]Ralph Ossa, "A New Trade Theory of GATT/WTO Negotiations," *The Journal of Political Economy* 119, no. 1 (2011): 122–152.

focus on the behavior of A and the analysis can be done as shown in Figure 6.7. If A puts a tariff on imports from B, denoted t_{BA}, imported goods from B will be more expensive. This enables firms located in A to make more profits, while exporting firms in B incur losses. As a consequence of the higher profits in A, capital will flow from B to A. Also, the additional entry of firms in A will reduce domestic prices in A, which is good for welfare. Nevertheless, this comes at the expense of B, which suffers from the capital flight to A. However, if B also puts a tariff t_{AB} on imports from A, this capital relocation effect is undone. Indeed, both countries establish tariffs that impose costs on each other. The higher tariffs create higher prices for imported goods, which is bad for consumers. The principle of reciprocity eliminates the incentive to set tariffs unilaterally. It leads A and B to reduce or remove their tariffs because the principle of reciprocity requires that a reduction in tariffs by B must be followed by a reduction in tariffs by A.

However, this is not the whole story. If A and B reduce their tariffs on the basis of reciprocity, exports from C to A will be hurt if tariffs for imports from C remain unchanged at t_{CA}. The reason is that following the tariff reduction, prices in A will be lower, making it harder for exporting firms from C to compete on A's market. The principle of nondiscrimination solves this problem because if A reduces its tariffs on imports from B, it must also reduce its tariffs on C. To summarize, the reciprocity rule solves the incentive to raise tariffs in order to attract capital to a country. The nondiscrimination rule prevents reductions in tariffs remaining only bilateral.

FIGURE 6.7   Effects of Reciprocity and Nondiscrimination

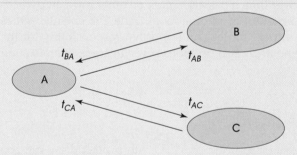

The principle of reciprocity forces A to reduces its tariffs t_{BA} on imports from B if B reduces its tariffs t_{AB} on imports from A. The principle of nondiscrimination further forces A to reduce its tariffs t_{CA} on imports from C. Again, because of reciprocity, tariffs t_{AC} in C on imports from A must be reduced in turn.

Despite its goals of serving free trade on the planet, the WTO has been the subject of many criticisms, one of which, endorsed by Nobel Prize–winning economist Joseph Stiglitz, is that the interests of rich countries have dominated the WTO's agenda, ignoring the interests of developing countries.[11] He accuses politicians from developed countries of protecting their agricultural sectors

[11]Joseph E. Stiglitz, *Globalization and Its Discontents* (New York: W.W. Norton & Company, 2002).

against the imports from developing countries, while still insisting on freely exporting their products to developing countries.

For example, U.S. cotton production is government-subsidized. As we have discussed, roughly 4 billion dollars a year go to about 25,000 rich farmers to help them compete against cotton production in developing countries. The European Union keeps subsidizing its dairy farmers with its Common Agricultural Policy; the average subsidy per cow received by a farmer in the European Union is higher than $2 a day, which is more than what the billion poorest people on the planet live on per day.

Liberalizing trade unilaterally in developing countries does result in benefits, but they would be more effective if trade liberalization focused on helping developing countries. The Doha Round of trade talks was stalled in Cancun in September 2003 and the same thing happened at the WTO meeting in Geneva in July 2008 when developing and developed countries had conflicting agendas and were not willing to compromise. Poor countries such as Brazil, India, and China are making their voices heard inside the WTO and have insisted that the priority in trade liberalization should be a far-reaching policy in the United States and Europe to ease restrictions on agricultural exports from developing countries. Brazil, India, and China also accuse developed countries of asking for sweeping liberalization of the services they export to developing countries in exchange for minor trade concessions to poorer nations on their exports to wealthy countries. At the close of the Uruguay Round in 1994, rich countries promised developing nations that the future Doha Round's results would be more in their favor, but no major concessions were ever made.

Another example of the WTO's bias toward the rich is the insistence by the WTO on the international enforcement of intellectual property rights. Advocates of developing countries criticize the Trade-Related Intellectual Property (TRIPS) agreement, signed in 1994 after the completion of the Uruguay Round, for unilaterally favoring rich countries. Access to intellectual property is very beneficial for developing countries because it helps them acquire needed technical knowledge from rich countries.

Exchange-Rate Policies in Developing Countries

Because international trade takes place through the purchase and sale of commodities on the world market, we will now turn to a discussion of the exchange-rate policies of developing countries. Different countries have different currencies, so international trade transactions involve currency exchange. A Chinese firm exporting shirts to Japan is paid in Japanese yen. These yen are exchanged back into yuan, the Chinese currency with which the firm can pay its workers, its suppliers, and its creditors. A Chinese firm importing DVD players from Japan must pay for them in yen, so it must exchange Chinese yuan against Japanese yen in order to make this payment.

In some situations, the exchange rate between the currencies of two countries affects trade between them. If the yen is high relative to the yuan (one yen is worth multiple yuan), Chinese exports priced in yen will seem cheap to Japanese consumers and there will be higher demand for Chinese products.

Conversely, Japanese goods will seem expensive to Chinese consumers and there will be lower demand for them in China.

In addition, exchange rates can adjust to trade imbalances between countries. If a country has a trade deficit and imports more than it exports, a reduction in the value of its currency will help boost exports by making them cheaper and reduce imports by making them more expensive. In the next section, we first cover the different degrees of convertibility a currency can have and then discuss the different options for exchange-rate regimes faced by developing countries.

Degrees of Convertibility

Until recent decades, the currencies of many developing countries were not convertible: the purchase and sale of units of these national currencies were restricted. If Americans went on vacation to a country with a nonconvertible currency, they had to register at the customs desk how many dollars they had exchanged for the local currency, and then had to sell back all the local currency they still held before leaving the country. Due to policies that liberalized exchange-rate regimes over the past few decades, nonconvertible currencies have become rare.

Trade convertibility. There are two types of currency **convertibility** (the freedom to convert the currency into another currency): trade convertibility and financial convertibility. **Trade convertibility**, also called current account convertibility, means that importers and exporters are free from restrictions on exchanging the proceeds of trade from one currency into another. For example, if a Chinese firm sells goods in the United States in dollars, it can convert those dollars back into yuan without restriction. However, it is possible to have trade convertibility but no financial convertibility.

Under Communist regimes, trade convertibility was generally absent. It is still the case with Cuba and North Korea today. If the United States wanted to sell goods to the Soviet Union before 1991, there had to be an equivalent dollar amount of imports from the Soviet Union and the clearing of exchanges between the two countries had to be organized by their respective trade authorities. When there is no trade convertibility, there can be no trade deficit. The value of imports and the value of exports between countries must be matched.

Financial convertibility, also called **capital account convertibility**, means that flows of capital in and out of a country are unrestricted. In other words, anyone can buy and sell any amount of the domestic currency against foreign currencies without restriction. Currently, most countries have capital account convertibility, but a number of countries, such as China, Malaysia, and India, have trade convertibility but no financial convertibility.

There is complete consensus among economists on the need for trade convertibility, but there is no consensus on the need for, or on the net benefits of, capital account convertibility for developing economies. Policymakers in the International Monetary Fund (IMF) and the World Bank as well as many economists hold that full financial convertibility is good for an economy because capital can move in and out of countries in search of the best financial return. The implicit assumption behind the IMF orthodoxy is that capital markets are efficient markets and the international forces of competition will yield the best possible allocation of capital across the world. If governments do not allow their capital to be mobile, then there can be **financial repression** when governments make domestic returns to capital artificially low. Banks can exploit financial repression by offering very low returns on deposits. Under financial repression, there will be underdevelopment of the financial sector because low returns on capital discourage its development. This is the case in China today where households cannot exchange their savings against foreign currency and foreign financial assets. Most Chinese households have no alternative other than to put their savings in domestic banks where the rate of return is unattractively low relative to the rate of return on international financial markets.

Those who are opposed to financial convertibility for developing countries point to the potentially devastating effects of large capital movements, many of which are of a speculative nature. Under full financial convertibility, speculators are in search of opportunities with high returns. This often leads to large inflows of purely speculative capital into a country. Large capital inflows that lead to the appreciation of a country's currency are potentially destabilizing. They can result in an appreciation of the price of the country's exports and can negatively affect a country's competitiveness. Large capital outflows are even more destabilizing. They lead to a dramatic depreciation of a country's currency and to a large decline in its terms of trade, forcing it to export much more than previously in order to afford the same basket of imports.

The East Asian Crisis

In 1997, after decades of capital inflows due to successful growth and development, there was an abrupt flight of capital away from East Asia. This capital flight was so severe that it led to a strong regional decline in GDP: the 1997 East Asian crisis. The triggering point of the crisis was the Thai foreign debt. Investors were apparently losing confidence in the ability of the Thai government to repay its foreign debt. There ensued a capital flight from Thailand, which led to a dramatic decline of its currency, the baht. However, the crisis spread quickly to other East Asian currencies, triggering a massive capital flight away from the region. Incorrect macroeconomic advice from the IMF, which told countries to increase interest rates and reduce government spending, only compounded the crisis. The IMF reasoned that increased interest rates would stop the capital flight, but the increase had the effect of drastically reducing economic activity. Most Asian governments did not have budget deficits and the IMF's advice to cut spending also led to macroeconomic contraction and GDP per capita fell drastically. Between 1997 and 2005, Indonesia's GDP per capita dropped by roughly 20%; in Thailand, GDP per capita fell by 6%; and in Malaysia it fell by 6.5%.

The East Asian crisis did not affect China because it never had financial convertibility. Indeed, the absence of financial convertibility made speculation against the Chinese currency impossible, whereas Taiwan, South Korea, the Philippines, and Indonesia suffered from major speculative attacks against their currencies. The only fallout for China was the indirect effects of its declining exports to neighboring countries. The Chinese authorities who, prior to 1997, had been pressured by the IMF to engage in financial liberalization, were validated in their cautious approach.

A financial crisis in a country is often triggered by macroeconomic mismanagement and the crisis forces the country to deal with that problem immediately. Capital mobility enforces discipline as it punishes bad macroeconomic management. On the other hand, the consequences of a financial crisis can be unnecessarily severe. In 2001, Argentina had high macroeconomic imbalances. Suddenly, there was a large capital flight caused by these deteriorating trends. People panicked and ran to the banks to change their pesos into dollars. This led to a **bank run**, a situation in which a bank's customers make massive withdrawals of their deposits, usually causing the bank to close because it cannot satisfy these demands for deposit withdrawal. As a result, Argentina's government decided to freeze bank accounts and only allow citizens to withdraw minor amounts. The government suspended convertibility of the currency, and the savings accounts of millions of household were destroyed in this crisis.

While the 1980s saw significant movement toward financial liberalization, episodes such as the East Asian crisis have generated more widespread skepticism about the benefits of liberalizing a country's capital account. Countries have not responded to the crisis by eliminating financial convertibility where it already existed, but instead have accumulated large amounts of foreign reserves in order to protect themselves against potential speculative attacks. This accumulation of dollars, euros, and yen may have destabilizing effects in the future if these large amounts of foreign reserves are abruptly thrown into international financial markets to defend a country's currency against a speculative attack.

Fixed and Floating Exchange-Rate Regimes

Countries can adopt two basic types of exchange-rate regimes: fixed exchange rates or floating exchange rates.

Fixed exchange rates. In a **fixed exchange-rate regime**, the price of a country's currency in terms of other currencies remains fixed. Because the country's currency is convertible and because the price of the currency is not allowed to move, the supply and demand for the country's currency will rarely be equal.

The Chinese currency, the renminbi or yuan, has been fixed for many years. For a while, the exchange rate between the dollar and the yuan was 1:10. With a fixed exchange rate, the supply of yuan may be lower than the demand for yuan. What causes supply–demand imbalances on the exchange-rate market? Excess demand for the yuan, for example, at the going exchange rate may be due to the fact that Chinese exports to the United States are very competitive. Because of the competitive rate, the dollars earned in the export market translate into high demand for yuan as export revenues are repatriated. In order to avoid confusion, remember that export revenues for Chinese firms translate into demand for yuan in the yuan–dollar market. It might also be the case that imports from the United States appear expensive and the volume of imports from the United States might not be very high. This low volume results in a low supply of yuan on the yuan–dollar foreign exchange market. If the exchange rate is high (a high yuan price for the dollar), the supply of yuan may thus be lower than the demand.

If there is excess demand for the yuan on the foreign exchange market, the People's Bank of China (PBOC), the Chinese central bank, must supply the missing yuan if it wants to maintain the existing exchange rate. It must also hold the dollars that have been exchanged against the yuan. In other words, the central bank must increase its holding of dollar reserves.

If the exchange rate were lower, the situation would be the opposite: the supply of yuan would be higher than the demand for yuan. In this case, the central bank would have to intervene and sell dollars from its reserves to absorb the excess supply of yuan.

Under fixed exchange rates, a central bank like the PBOC must constantly intervene on exchange-rate markets to maintain the exchange rate by buying and selling reserves of foreign currency.

Floating exchange rates. A **floating exchange-rate regime** occurs when the exchange rate for a currency varies on a daily basis, in line with the supply and demand for that currency. The exchange rate is then a market price. If there is excess demand for yuan, then the price of the yuan must adjust upward and appreciate. In other words, the exchange rate, or the price of the dollar, would go down automatically following market forces. Conversely, if there were a net supply of yuan on the foreign exchange market, then the price of the yuan would have to fall and depreciate, and the exchange rate would have to go up.

In reality, however, these movements are more complicated because the foreign exchange market is not simply between two currencies. The demand and supply for yuan is derived not only from exports and imports with the United States, but also with the whole world. Nevertheless, the basic principle remains that under floating exchange rates, the price of a currency appreciates when there is net demand (and depreciates when there is net supply) for that currency on the foreign exchange market.

Developing countries and pegging. Developing countries face various trade-offs when they must choose between a fixed or a floating exchange-rate regime. For a very long time, countries were told by economists and the IMF that it was best for them to have a fixed exchange-rate regime and to **peg** their currency to a major currency such as the dollar, meaning that the fixed exchange rate a developing country chooses is linked to a particular currency. If a country pegs its currency to the dollar, and the dollar falls relative to the euro and the yen, the currency of that country will also depreciate relative to those currencies.

The Hong Kong dollar has always been pegged to the U.S. dollar and it depreciated as the dollar fell in the first decade of the 21st century. Some countries, such as Saudi Arabia and other Gulf states, peg to a basket of currencies because they want to avoid being subject to the variations of a particular major currency.

Pegging creates stability in price expectations; if the currency stays stable, then import prices and export prices will remain relatively stable; if a currency is subject to a lot of volatility, import prices may rise abruptly when the currency suddenly depreciates, or exports might become suddenly less competitive when the currency unexpectedly appreciates. If flexible exchange rates lead to large exchange-rate volatility, then this volatility might create disturbances for the domestic economy of a developing country and generate damaging volatility for prices and output.

Fixed versus floating in developing countries. Fixed exchange rates also have drawbacks. They are not as efficient as floating exchange rates for dealing with external economic shocks. Suppose that oil prices drastically rise in a short period of time; everything else being equal, this rise makes imports more expensive. Import expenditures will rise and create a current account deficit. It is likely that a current account deficit triggered by an oil shock would last for several years. Fixed exchange rates are not flexible enough to deal with such a shock; persistent current account deficits could ensue. With flexible exchange rates, the currency depreciates immediately in order to bring the current account back to balance.

Flexible exchange rates also help to deal with internal economic shocks. Suppose that there is an inflation shock in an economy due to wage pressures. Under a fixed exchange rate, the inflationary shock would lead to a loss of competitiveness that will last unless inflation is brought down again, which might take a long time. Under a flexible exchange rate, the currency depreciates, preventing a loss of competitiveness.

Fixed exchange rates can, however, serve as a commitment device to fight inflation. Because inflation will have negative consequences and lead to a loss of competitiveness under fixed exchange rates, it is therefore more likely to be opposed by policymakers. The more difficult it is to devalue the currency to adjust to an inflationary shock, the stronger the anti-inflationary credibility of fixed exchange rates.

An extreme example of such a fixed exchange-rate regime is a **currency board**, a system that existed in Argentina until the crisis of 2001 and still exists in countries like Bulgaria, Estonia, and Lithuania. A currency board allows a country's central bank to print the local currency only in proportion to the amount of foreign reserves that come in. The Argentinean peso was linked to the dollar in a 1:1 ratio; additional pesos could be printed only if there were an inflow of U.S. dollars.

Economists have recognized the merit of currency boards in terms of credibility. A currency board is a way for a country's government to commit completely to not printing more money to finance government expenditures and the country effectively renounces a monetary policy of its own. Since economic agents know the government has its hands tied, their inflationary expectations are accordingly lower, which has positive anti-inflationary effects. However, if the government cannot control inflation or deal effectively with inflationary shocks due, for example, to an abrupt increase in aggregate demand or a decrease in aggregate supply, the currency board is a recipe for disaster. The country will gradually lose export competitiveness because of higher domestic inflation. As a result, the economy will slow down without much hope of a recovery and the country in question will have to abandon the currency board system in the midst of economic chaos, as Argentina did in 2001.

A big disadvantage of fixed exchange-rate regimes is that they do not work well when the capital account of a country is fully convertible under financial convertibility. Under this regime, a country is indeed susceptible to devastating speculative attacks. Suppose that the government of a country with fixed exchange rates is expected to announce a **devaluation**, a change in the exchange rate that makes foreign exchange more expensive. People with enough capital can, in anticipation of such a decision, transfer large sums of money overnight to another currency in the expectation that after the devaluation, they will have made a lot of money. Suppose that the Hong Kong dollar, which has been pegged to the U.S. dollar, is expected to devalue by 10%. Also suppose that the Hong Kong dollar is worth US$0.1. After the devaluation, the Hong Kong dollar will be worth US$0.09. A Hong Kong investor can convert 10 million Hong Kong dollars into 1 million U.S. dollars. Suppose the devaluation takes place. The 1 million U.S. dollars will now be worth 1 million $\times$ 1/0.09 = 11.1 million Hong Kong dollars, a gain of 1.1 million Hong Kong dollars overnight! Such overnight speculative movements do not carry any risk for the speculator. If the expected devaluation does not take place, then he or she will not have lost much, whereas if it does take place, the investor can make a very large return in a few days. These speculative movements can be completely destabilizing for a country and force a much larger devaluation than was really needed on purely economic grounds. In our example, the speculative capital flight away from the Hong Kong currency may cause a devaluation of 20% instead of the 10% that was initially planned.

The East Asian crisis was caused to a large degree by such speculative movements. Sudden capital flight from the East Asian economies led to huge devaluations of their domestic currencies. The Thai baht lost more than half its value and went from 25 baht per $US to 56 baht per $US. The Indonesian rupiah went from 2,000 rupiah per $US to 18,000 rupiah per $US during the crisis. The South Korean currency went from 800 won per $US to 1700 won per $US. The Philippine peso went from 26 pesos per $US to 54 pesos per $US.

Floating exchange rates, on the other hand, create higher costs for speculators. Suppose investors believe a currency will depreciate. By the time they sell, it will be too late, as other sellers will have already made the currency depreciate. If the currency appreciates at the time they want to repatriate their capital, they will have lost money. Speculative capital movements are more risky under floating exchange rates.

In light of all these arguments, the case for floating exchange rates seems, on the whole, stronger. Most advanced economies have now adopted a regime of floating exchange rates and would not consider going back to a system of fixed exchange rates. The advantages of moving toward floating exchange rates are not as great for developing countries as they are for developed countries. Financial markets in developing countries are generally underdeveloped, which means that small variations in the inflow and outflow of foreign currency in a developing country may result in large variations in the equilibrium exchange rate. The poorer the country and the more underdeveloped its capital markets, the more severe this problem is. As we have seen, pegging with financial convertibility also invites speculation. Countries that choose to peg should not have capital account convertibility, but should limit themselves to current account convertibility.

Chapter Summary

World Trade Evolution and Developing Countries
Both developed and developing economies have become more open in recent decades as exports grew, on average, faster than GDP. Regional shares in world trade reflect their economic importance. Asia's share has been growing very strongly in recent decades, while the sub-Saharan African share has been declining. Although developing countries traditionally have specialized in the export of raw materials and food products, they are undergoing increased specialization in the export of manufacturing goods.

The Theory of Comparative Advantage
Comparative advantage, a lower opportunity cost of producing some goods in terms of other goods, is the basis for specialization in international trade for some countries. Developing countries have a comparative advantage for labor-intensive activities, but as they become richer and accumulate more capital, that comparative advantage shifts to more capital-intensive activities. The flip side of the comparative advantage is that specialization increases export revenue risk, especially for poor countries: their export revenues can experience wild swings due to the volatility of world market prices for oil, coffee, cocoa, etc.

The Politics of Trade
Politicians generally do not respond to unorganized consumers who may gain or lose from free trade. They only respond to organized groups such as exporters who want free trade and domestic producers who compete with foreign imports and demand protection. This gives politicians a bias toward protectionism. Politicians see trade negotiations as exchanges: you open your markets to my exporters and I will do the same for yours.

The Costs of Trade Barriers
Protectionism, the erection of trade barriers to protect domestic industry, has significant economic costs in terms of losses in consumer welfare and inefficiencies in production.

Trade Institutions: Bilateral versus Multilateral
Multilateral agreements provide the full benefits of free trade, while bilateral arrangements can create trade diversion, i.e., inefficient trade flows between countries. The WTO is the international organization responsible for multilateral trade negotiations and the enforcement of free-trade agreements. The WTO rules work reasonably well in sustaining and enforcing multilateral trade agreements, but it has, however, been criticized for favoring the interests of rich countries.

Exchange-Rate Policies in Developing Countries
Developing countries face an uneasy choice between fixed exchange-rate regimes with no capital account convertibility, or capital account convertibility with floating exchange rates. Capital account convertibility with fixed exchange rates is a recipe for disaster because it invites speculation that destabilizes currencies and leads to financial crises.

Key Terms

bank run
bilateral trade negotiations
capital account convertibility
collective action failure
comparative advantage
convertibility
currency board
devaluation
financial convertibility
financial repression
fixed exchange-rate regime
floating exchange-rate regime

import quotas
import tariffs
most favored nation clause
multilateral trade negotiations
national treatment clause
nondiscrimination
opportunity cost
peg (currency peg)
political economy of trade liberalization
price ratios
production possibility frontier
protectionism

reciprocity
regional trade agreements
regulatory barriers
relative factor endowments
rents
theory of comparative advantage

trade convertibility
trade diversion
trade openness
trade shares
voluntary export restraints

Review Questions

1. What is the difference between Ricardo's theory of comparative advantage and the Heckscher-Ohlin theory of comparative advantage? Do they lead to different conclusions? Explain.

2. Find information about NAFTA, the North American Free Trade Agreement, online. Can NAFTA be accused of trade diversion? If so, construct an example of possible trade diversion created by NAFTA.

3. Politicians view trade agreements as a series of exchanges. Which interests are politicians forgetting when conducting their trade policy? Explain why. How could these interests be better represented?

4. Read the following article: Alexander Keck and Simon Schropp, "Indisputably Essential: The Economics of Dispute Settlement Institutions in Trade Agreements," World Trade Organization: http://www.wto.org/english/res_e/reser_e/ersd200702_e.pdf.
   What does this article say about trade dispute settlement in the WTO? How do the ideas in this article relate to the ideas in this chapter?

5. Go to the World Trade Organization's website   http://stat.wto.org/StatisticalProgram/WSDBStatProgramHome.aspx?Language=E, and click "selection." For Subject, add "Total merchandise trade" to the selected indicators. For Reporter, select the group "All individual reporters (Incl. world)," then add Mexico and the United States to the selected reporters. For Partner, add "World" to the selected partners. For Trade Flow, add "Exports" and "Imports" to the selected trade flows. For Year, add all years since 1960 to the selected years. Click Download to download the results. Download in Excel data base format. Then compare the series for exports for Mexico and for the United States. To draw figures, it is easier to recalculate the data. Divide the whole series by the number for 1960, so that export and import indices for both countries are equal to 100 in 1960 and then take a logarithmic transformation of that series. What do you observe when you compare the times series properties of exports and imports for Mexico and the United States? In particular, what can you say about the growth trends and volatility of foreign trade for both countries? Can you relate your observations to the content of the chapter? Explain.

6. Consider the market for oranges in Israel. Assume the supply and demand lines take the following form: $S = 20 + 20P$, $D = 200 - 10P$, where P is the price for oranges. Assume that the world price is equal to $2. Assume that a 50% tariff is imposed on imported oranges. Calculate the welfare loss. In order to do that, it is useful to make a drawing similar to Figure 6.6.

7. What are the advantages and disadvantages of pegging the currency of a developing country to a major currency such as the U.S. dollar? List the specific conditions that are incompatible with pegging.

8. Find the main export specializations of Angola, Bangladesh, Belize, Bermuda, Bhutan, Ethiopia, Grenada, Guinea Bissau, Iraq, Kuwait, Mali, Mongolia, Nepal, Nigeria, Rwanda, and Sierra Leone. The UNCTAD (United Nations Conference on Trade and Development) has handbooks where you can find these data. What recurring patterns do you detect from these observations?

9. Assume that the price and volume index for Pakistani exports and imports are at 100 in year t. Assume that the Pakistani rupee devalues by 10% relative to the U.S. dollar. Assume

that the elasticity of Pakistani exports is equal to 2.5 and its elasticity of imports is equal to 2. What will be the growth (positive or negative) in exports and imports from Pakistan (traded in dollars)? What effect will this have on Pakistan's balance of trade? You can answer this question without knowing what the effective current balance of trade is.

10. Return to the World Trade Organization webpage (http://stat.wto.org/StatisticalProgram/WSDBStatProgramHome.aspx?Language=E) and click "selection." For Subject, add "Merchandise trade indices" to the selected indicators. For Reporter, select the group "All individual reporters (Incl. world)," then add Pakistan and the United States to the selected reporters. For partners, add "World" to selected partners. For Trade Flow, add "Exports" to the selected trade flows. For Unit, add "unit value index -Prev. year = 100". For Year, add all years since 1981 to the selected years. Click Download to download the results. Download in Excel-Database format. Then compare the series for exports for Pakistan and for the United States. Use those data to calculate annual growth rates of export prices. Calculate the standard deviation of the growth rate for each country. How do you interpret the result?

Institutions and Economic Development

7

Compare a simple transaction in a developed and a developing economy—the purchase of land by a farmer. In a developed country, land ownership is protected by law, real estate transactions and land surveys are thoroughly recorded, and a dispute over a deed can be resolved in court. A registered title to land can be used as collateral to obtain a loan to finance improvements to the land. In a developing economy, however, this simple transaction can be fraught with many problems. There may be no system to track ownership titles and no surveys of a property's exact boundaries, so it can be difficult for a poor and often uneducated farmer to defend himself against encroachment by neighbors, who may destroy his crops or dig trenches within the borders of his newly purchased land. Local authorities may evict the farmer without adequate compensation in order to build roads or housing projects. This lack of legal protection tends to support rich and influential landowners and government officials. When a farmer cannot document ownership of his land, a large investment in seed, fertilizer, livestock, or equipment is a risky venture. The farmer will thus be less likely to contribute to the economic development of his country.

This simple example illustrates the importance of institutions that facilitate economic transactions and, thus, economic development. Although we have mentioned various institutions in previous chapters, we have not yet explored them in detail and what effect they can have on economic performance and development.

The economic concept of **institution** is defined as the constraints placed by law and *social norms* on human behavior. These constraints help reduce **transaction costs**, the costs associated to simple transactions such as buying or selling merchandise, borrowing money, or investing in a business. Every day, there are millions of transactions by consumers and producers within an economy. Just as tiny streams converge to form a great river, transaction costs contribute to a powerful effect on the aggregate performance of an economy and its growth rate. This chapter examines transaction costs in detail and how they are affected by institutions.

We begin our discussion of institutions by defining precisely what they are. We then discuss what institutions can do to reduce transaction costs. We compare institutional development in advanced economies and in developing economies, and get a better understanding for why a lack of more advanced institutions makes transaction costs higher in less-developed countries and creates serious obstacles to their economic development.

What Are Institutions?

Following the example of Douglass North, Nobel Prize–winning economist, we define institutions as constraints on behavior imposed by societal rules: "Institutions include any form of constraint that human beings devise to shape human interaction."[1] This broad definition includes all constraints imposed on individuals and groups by a society's system of beliefs and values.

People who live in the advanced economies of the world often take institutions for granted. Even mainstream economics has long ignored them; it explains *how* the price mechanism helps balance supply and demand, but says very little about the institutions underlying efficiently functioning markets. A simple transaction such as a purchase of a commodity can be fraught with uncertainty without an adequate institutional environment. A commodity purchase requires the transfer of that commodity from the seller to the buyer and the transfer of payment from the buyer to the seller. If the two operations are not synchronized, there may be problems, depending on who moves first. If the buyer makes the payment first, the seller may never show up to deliver the goods, but if the seller transfers the goods first, the buyer may never bring the payment. Even if the operations in a transaction are synchronized, cheating is possible. The buyer may write a check that will bounce or the seller may hide important information from the buyer about the product sold.

The more sophisticated the transaction, the more opportunities there are for cheating and predatory behavior. Without adequate institutions, transactions are much more costly and the volume of transactions will then be much lower and less economic development will take place.

Formal Institutions

In some societies, **formal institutions** are codified in writing and are generally more precise than unwritten rules. Speed limits that specify how fast we can drive and electoral laws that incorporate the procedures for translating votes in an election into seats in a legislature are examples of formal institutions. Authorities can enforce formal rules with established statutes, which are also officially recorded. When talking about a country's formal institutions, it is useful to distinguish between *political* and *legal* institutions.

Political institutions. Political institutions are the set of rules that define the powers of the major political bodies and players (chief executive, legislators, etc.), and how they are selected. Political institutions determine the differences between political regimes, such as democracies and dictatorships. Democratic institutions make it possible to oust politicians who have misbehaved or change leaders when ideological preferences among the electorate have shifted, options that are not possible under a dictatorship. Usually, democracies incorporate separation of powers, whereas dictators hold all the power in

---

[1] Douglass North, *Institutions, Institutional Change, and Economic Performance* (New York: Cambridge University Press, 1990): 3.

a government. Therefore, the rule of law is usually better enforced in democracies than in dictatorships. This is not always the case, however; there can be imperfect democracies as well as beneficial dictatorships. For example, in several Asian countries, such as Singapore, there are political regimes that are not democratic, but they still uphold the rule of law. We will study political institutions in more detail in Chapter 9.

Legal institutions. Non-political institutions codified by laws, legal institutions across the globe differ in many ways, and these differences can have important economic effects. Some legal institutions are strongly rooted in religion as is the case in certain Islamic countries where Sharia law, expressed in the Qur'an, is both religious law and moral code, and in Israel, where the Talmud is the foundation of many laws. Ancient cultures such as the Chinese or the Hindu civilizations have developed their own legal traditions based on customs that date back thousands of years.

Legal institutions not derived from religious traditions fall into two main categories: the common law and the civil-law systems. The **common-law system**, developed in England and other Anglo-Saxon countries (Canada, Australia, and New Zealand for example), is based on customary Saxon law, the law that existed in England before the Norman invasion of 1066. Legal arguments in the common-law system rely heavily on legal precedents, decisions made in past court cases. **Civil-law systems** rely mostly on recorded legal statutes and have developed from Roman civil law. Legal arguments in the civil-law system are made on the basis of the consistency or inconsistency of a decision with the principles laid down in statutory law.

These different legal systems are important to economic development because the legal systems in many developing countries were inherited from former colonizers. British colonies inherited the common-law system, while Spanish and French colonies inherited the civil-law system. In Chapter 10, we will examine legal institutions.

Informal Institutions

Informal institutions are those that are not legally codified; they are based on **social norms** (or **conventions**), accepted and expected standards of behavior. They are enforced in an informal way using peer pressure, feelings of guilt, and moral obligations. Even when a country is ruled by formal institutions, informal institutions still play a large role in terms of politeness and civility, hospitality, courtship, traditions, holiday celebrations, and rites of passage. Even in a country where formal laws exist, disputes between citizens are often solved first by referring to mutually understood and accepted social norms. When informal institutions cannot solve a problem, people turn to formal institutions.

Informal institutions are based on a country's **culture**, the set of beliefs and values passed down from generation to generation. Beliefs concern nature, interactions between humans and nature, and interactions among humans in a society. **Values**, the intrinsic worth a culture or society places on certain behaviors and beliefs, determine the set of social norms in a society. Religion is a fundamental part of culture and encompasses most of the beliefs, values, and social norms in many societies. We will talk more about culture in Chapter 11.

Interactions between Institutions

There are complex interactions between formal and informal institutions. First, laws often evolve with culture and social norms. The death penalty, for example, was a popular method of punishment until many countries did away with it as a result of rising popular opposition.

Second, it is very difficult to impose formal laws or formal institutions that are not in accordance with existing social norms; conflict between formal institutions and social norms can create conflict in developing countries. For example, international borders established in Africa after decolonization did not correspond to existing ethnic subdivisions. Tribes were separated across formal borders, but (informal) tribal and ethnic loyalties took precedence over (formal) national loyalties. As a result, politics polarized along ethnic lines, resulting in violence. Legal systems inherited from former colonial powers conflicted with social norms associated with tribalism. Even though there were formal rules prohibiting nepotism, politicians favored their families and friends because this favoritism was seen as the fulfillment of long-established moral obligations to fellow tribe members. Similarly, in a country where social norms are based on religion, it is very difficult to impose laws that appear to violate religious obligations, prohibitions, or constraints. A case in point is the prohibition of the Islamic veil in schools and public places in certain countries, which is seen by practicing Muslims as violating their religious norms.

Third, formal institutions often strengthen the effects of informal institutions. The social norm of honesty is supported by a legal system punishing a dishonest trader and makes that norm easier to enforce throughout the society. Similarly, informal institutions often complement and reinforce formal institutions; legal codes may be incomplete and social norms can help to supplement them and make them more effective. In some legal systems, citizens are obligated by law to help someone who has had an accident or whose life is in jeopardy. Even when the law does not specify in detail when this legal obligation applies, social norms provide the moral obligation to help a person in danger.

Formal and informal institutions tend to be complementary and to have increased effectiveness in a society or culture when they are based on the same fundamental set of beliefs. If they are in conflict, formal institutions do not work as well as established social norms.

What Do Institutions Do?

As we discuss the economic role of institutions, we will examine five important problems that occur in basic economic transactions and show how institutions can help to solve these problems: informational problems, hold-up problems, commitment problems, cooperation problems, and coordination problems. The solutions to these problems have significant economic effects on the development of commerce, entrepreneurship, trade, innovation, and investment.

Efficient institutional solutions provide critical reductions in transaction costs and contribute to economic development.

Informational Problems

A simple transaction often involves informational problems, as one party is bound to have more information about a product's quality than the other party does, a situation that economists call **asymmetric information**. For example, food distributors may ship food products that were not stored under proper conditions, a used car salesman might sell cars with hidden mechanical problems, a software company may sell an operating system that has programming flaws, or a real estate agent may sell a house that has hidden structural defects. In most cases, the buyer may not have the information necessary to decide whether or not to purchase an item and/or it might be very costly or outright impossible to acquire all the relevant information prior to making a purchase. These informational problems are present in all economies, both developed and less developed. Lack of information about a product and a possible lack of trust in the seller may prevent the buyer from completing the transaction. Because of asymmetric information, many transactions, even legitimate ones, might not take place at all.

Asymmetric information is also detrimental to transactions that do not involve the exchange of goods. This is the case for credit contracts, where there is usually an informational asymmetry between the lender and the borrower. The lender does not know the **creditworthiness** of the borrower, his or her willingness or ability to fulfill a debt contract. Because of asymmetric information, a creditor may refrain from lending even to a very creditworthy individual. Entrepreneurs who have good ideas for the productive use of capital may not be able to realize those ideas because they might be unable to obtain loans to start their businesses. This is a very serious problem in developing economies.

Adverse selection. Informational problems may lead to **adverse selection**, a situation caused by informational asymmetries in which reputable lenders and sellers leave the market to disreputable players, resulting in a possible market collapse. George Akerlof received the Nobel Prize in Economics for his article "The Market for Lemons," in which he showed how informational asymmetries and adverse selection can cause the disappearance of markets or even severe market failure.[2] He described second-hand car markets in which the seller has information about the quality of the car but the buyer does not. Assume that there are good second-hand cars that cost the seller $10,000 (purchase plus repairs) and are worth $12,000 to consumers. Also assume that there are bad second-hand cars that cost the seller $5,000 but are worth only $4,000 to the buyer. If there are no informational asymmetries, good cars would sell and deliver a profit of $2,000 to the seller and bad cars would not sell because they would deliver a loss of $1,000. Assume now that there is informational asymmetry and that 50% of the cars are good and 50% are bad. A buyer now faces a 50% chance of buying a car that is worth $12,000 and a 50% chance of buying a

---

[2]George A. Akerlof, "The Market for 'Lemons': Quality Uncertainty and the Market Mechanism," *The Quarterly Journal of Economics* 84, no. 3 (1970): 488–500.

car that is worth $4,000. A buyer who is **risk neutral**, who values upside and downside payoffs equally and weighs them according to their probability, would not be ready to pay more than the expected value ($(0.5 \times 12,000) + (0.5 \times 4,000) = \$8,000$) for a car. In other words, a risk-neutral agent looks at the **expected payoff** of a decision: the downside payoff ($4,000) times its probability (.5) plus the upside payoff ($12,000) times its probability (.5). A **risk-averse** buyer, who puts less weight on the upside payoff than on the downside payoff for given probabilities, would pay even less or would possibly not even be ready to pay more than $4,000 to buy the car.

In this situation, the seller of a bad car would make a profit of $8,000, but the seller of a good car would suffer a loss. Compared to a situation of perfect information, asymmetric information would tend to drive out the reputable sellers from the market and attract the disreputable sellers. If the honest sellers withdraw because they cannot make a profit, buyers will soon realize that only bad cars are available for which they are only willing to pay $4,000, and the market will disappear.

Adverse selection also occurs in the credit market. Suppose that there are two types of borrowers, good and bad. The good borrower is creditworthy and needs financing for a project that will earn a 10% return. The bad borrower does not intend to repay the loan at all. The bank must pay depositors an interest rate of 6%, otherwise they will withdraw their deposits and put their money elsewhere. Note that the return on the project for the good borrower (10%) is higher than the market return for depositors (6%). Assume that among the population of potential borrowers there is a 50% chance that a potential borrower is good and a 50% chance that he or she is bad. Without asymmetric information, the bank would not lend to the bad types and would lend only to the good types, making a profit because it could charge the borrowers up to 10% interest. Under asymmetric information, however, the bank cannot discriminate between good and bad borrowers and would have to charge the same interest rate to all borrowers. In order to pay back its depositors, the bank must charge an interest rate of at least 12% (6% divided by 50%, the probability that a loan is paid back). This interest rate will be too high for the good borrowers, who will decide not to apply for a loan, but the bad borrowers would not be discouraged by the high interest rate, because they do not intend to pay back the loan. Good borrowers are thus driven out of the market by the excessively high interest rate.

Note that because of adverse selection, the price of credit, the interest rate, cannot serve as an efficient mechanism to adjust supply and demand in credit markets. If there is an excess demand for credit and if banks decide to adjust the interest rate upward to reduce that demand and attract more depositors, the effect is likely to be a decline in the quality of the credit pool, as some good borrowers whose projects have a somewhat lower profitability become discouraged by the higher interest rate while bad borrowers remain undeterred. The bank might reduce its profits by increasing interest rates because of the deterioration of the quality of the credit pool. For that reason, banks prefer not to increase the interest rate to market clearing rates and instead decide to ration credit (**credit rationing**). This means that only some applicants receive a loan and many other applicants are turned down. Obviously, banks try to gather as much information as they can on potential borrowers and use this information to decide to whom they allocate credit. While this information search helps to alleviate informational asymmetries, it is usually only a partial solution to the problem: many creditworthy borrowers are still denied loans while untrustworthy borrowers are approved for credit.

Moral hazard. Another problem that arises from asymmetric information is **moral hazard**, the possibility of unobservable actions one of the contracting parties can take that will hurt the interest of the other contracting party. A typical example of moral hazard arises in the relationship between a landlord and a wage laboring farmer. If the landlord pays the farmer an hourly wage to work the land, the farmer may not work as hard as he would if the land were his own because the landlord cannot observe how hard he works and he receives the same wage whether he works hard or not.

The difference between moral hazard and adverse selection is not always clear. Moral hazard involves asymmetric information as well as unobservable actions. Adverse selection involves only asymmetric information. Take the example of the automobile insurance market. Assume a situation in which there are good and bad drivers, but all drivers do their best to avoid accidents. This is a case of adverse selection. Drivers differ only in their abilities and insurance companies cannot, without prior investigation, distinguish between good and bad drivers when offering an insurance contract. Now assume a situation in which all drivers are equally good but they may decide to drive less carefully because they know they are insured. This is a case of moral hazard in which the action taken is how carefully to drive.

In the case of a credit relationship, the difference between adverse selection and moral hazard is blurred. Adverse selection occurs if the quality of the loan is independent of actions taken by the borrower, as is the case if the borrower is intrinsically dishonest or incompetent. On the other hand, there is a moral hazard problem when the quality of the loan depends on the actions of the borrower. The borrower can deliberately choose a riskier project or fail to take the necessary actions to make the project profitable. In reality, a combination of both moral hazard and adverse selection exists, but it is important to keep in mind the conceptual difference between them.

Institutional solutions to informational problems. The obligation by one or more parties to a transaction to disclose information relevant to the transaction is referred to as **disclosure rules**, legal solutions to informational problems such as in the case of the sale of a house or a company that is listed publicly. The seller of a house must, for example, disclose information on past repairs or damages to the house. Executives of a company listed for sale must reveal information about their business dealings and about their governance. In many professions, there is **regulation of access or entry**, rules that govern entry into and the practice of a profession, and require a candidate to earn a qualified diploma or pass an exam as a means to screen out unqualified people. This is the case for doctors; without rules for entering the medical profession, consumers would have no formal way to distinguish between qualified and unqualified doctors. As a result, most countries strictly regulate the qualifications of medical professionals. This issue seems obvious, but in India, for example, many doctors (sometimes a majority of the practicing physicians in certain areas) do not have a medical degree. These "doctors" are often completely incompetent: they are unable to make correct diagnoses and tend to prescribe unnecessary medicines.[3]

Other solutions to informational problems are the result of actions taken by firms that are sometimes backed by legal institutions. An obvious example is the association of a **warranty** (the obligation by a seller to guarantee the quality of a product) with a sales contract. Warranties take different forms, such as a guarantee to repair goods for free within a specified amount of time after the purchase of a good or after the replacement of a deficient component of that good. **Return policies** allow the buyer to bring purchased goods back to the seller within a specified time after their purchase. Warranties and return policies make it possible for the seller to give credible information about the product. If consumers can learn quickly about the quality or usefulness of a product, a return policy signals to a buyer that the seller is confident in the quality of the product. If it requires long-term use of a product to determine its quality, a warranty is a better way to signal quality to a consumer by shifting any repair risk onto the seller.

Sellers also use brand names to indicate quality. **Signaling** is an economic term that means taking certain actions to provide other parties in a transaction with credible information. In the case of a sales contract, it means giving credible information to consumers about the quality of a product. Consumers consider a well-known brand name with a reputation for good quality to be reliable, and they will trust products from that brand. The company that has established a brand name has an interest in keeping its reputation because it is the basis for consumer trust in its products.

Entering a franchise contract allows an entrepreneur to benefit from the reputation of a brand, which makes it possible to attract customers more easily. Franchising allows businesses to expand very easily, but firms need to monitor their franchisees, as loss of brand reputation can be quite damaging. In China, the developing world's largest economy, there has been an expansion of franchised fast-food chains in recent years with KFC and McDonalds from the United States, Ajisen Ramen or Saizeriya from Japan, or even Chinese fast-food chains such as Da Niang Dumpling and Ji Xiang Wanton. According to the marketing research firm A. C. Nielsen, food hygiene security is cited as the top reason for the popularity of fast-food chains in China, as opposed to restaurants. This concern is understandable; cases of food poisoning in Chinese restaurants have increased in recent years. For example, the Xinhua News Agency reported that in 2007, 258 people died from food poisoning in China, an increase of 32% over 2006. Some fast-food chains in China have failed precisely because they were not able to build a reputation for safe food. This was the case for Rong Hua Chicken, which tried to compete directly with KFC. The chain was started in 1994, but had closed by 2000 because it was unable to enforce strict rules on the quality of raw and processed foods, leading to safety concerns.

Chain stores also rely on the logic of brand recognition. We know familiar names such as CVS, Best Buy, or Walmart in the United States, but there are

---

[3]See, for example, Jishnu Das and Jeffrey Hammer, "Which Doctor? Combining Vignettes and Item Response to Measure Clinical Competence," *The Journal of Development Economics* 78, no. 2 (2005): 348–383.

also famous chain stores in developing countries—Marayana in Indonesia or Sanborns in Mexico. Brand-name chain stores sell hundreds of different types of products and unreliable merchandise could hurt their reputations. Chain stores are not only sales intermediaries between brand-name firms and consumers; they are also **informational intermediaries** because they gather information about the products they sell before offering them in their stores.

Rating agencies also specialize in gathering information that is relevant for consumers or companies. Credit reporting companies, for example, gather information on borrowers and rate their creditworthiness. However, even in advanced market economies this reporting system is far from perfect. Larger credit rating agencies such as Moody's, Standard & Poor's, and Fitch, which rate the creditworthiness of large firms and securities, were accused of serious inaccuracies in the years preceding the global financial crisis of 2008–2009. They were heavily criticized for giving good ratings to mortgage-backed securities based on subprime mortgages and for severely understating the risks associated with those securities. This huge failure in the financial sector has highlighted the need for more stringent regulation of credit-rating companies.

Another example of a rating system is eBay's transaction feedback. When eBay started to expand its online sales in the late 1990s, users reported many cases of fraud. Because of the risk consumers take when purchasing an item online, eBay devised a rating system in which buyers and sellers review a transaction after its completion. These ratings help members evaluate buyers' and sellers' reputations for good faith and honesty.

It is not a coincidence that many of the examples of contractual solutions to informational problems are from advanced economies rather than developing economies. These solutions only work well with the support of efficiently functioning formal institutions. In a country where the legal system is inadequate, where law enforcement is inconsistent, and where the court system is inefficient or corrupt, warranties give less protection than they do in a country where there are strong legal institutions. A dishonest seller can use a warranty to attract customers but then break his promise to provide a quality product. If disgruntled customers cannot use the court system effectively to protect their rights, then warranties are meaningless.

Informal solutions to informational problems. When formal institutions are deficient, which is most often the case in developing economies, informal institutions emerge to deal with informational asymmetries. If courts are not effective, repeated interactions and reputations are the main instruments buyers and sellers can rely on to overcome informational asymmetries.

When informational asymmetries exist with no formal institutions to help overcome them, market competition becomes less effective even when there are many buyers and sellers. As a result, buyers and sellers will enter into long-term relationships with a network of trusted personal contacts. This is called **relational contracting**. Buyers will have fewer incentives to search for sellers offering lower prices or even to do business with them because the buyers will not know whether a product is of lower quality than what they can obtain from their usual suppliers. Similarly, sellers will not have the incentive to search for buyers who are willing to pay a higher price because they do not know whether alternative buyers will uphold their promise to pay. For example, in Madagascar's agricultural markets, the largest trading firms always do business with the same suppliers and customers.[4] Having a large number of these time-tested relationships is seen by the traders as the biggest determinant of success in business. These business contacts are not only used to exchange information, but also to share risks and to borrow or lend money when necessary. In the 1990s, during the turbulent period of transition in Russia's market economy, legal institutions were very weak; as a result, firms developed repeated business relationships with a fixed set of suppliers and clients and were reluctant to enter into new business relationships.[5]

In a situation of relational contracting, breach of trust can be fatal to the relationship. If a partner deviates from honest behavior, his or her counterpart could end the relationship immediately, forcing the now-unreliable partner to face the uncertainty of the market environment. Because the prospect of finding another reliable trading partner in the market is fraught with informational asymmetries, the threat of terminating the relationship can serve as a deterrent to opportunistic behavior.

Less competition for new partners, and buyers and sellers stuck in unprofitable relationships creates an environment that will hinder market growth. The expansion of markets is stronger when formal institutions work to enforce contractual solutions to informational asymmetries.

Reputation also plays a role when formal institutions are deficient. Economic agents who build a reputation of honesty, reliability, and efficiency will benefit because their reputations will make them desirable business partners. Reputable buyers and sellers have fewer incentives to indulge in opportunistic behavior due to the significant investments of time and effort necessary to acquire their good reputations.

However, in order for reputations to be effective when formal institutions are deficient, there has to be an adequate and efficient circulation of information. Without this movement, information about reputations does not move through the marketplace. In the modern world, communicating this information is easy because it is available instantaneously on the Internet, whether through e-mail, blogs, or social media. Unfortunately, poor countries are at a disadvantage because information technology is not well developed in them. In many of these countries, the primary means of disseminating information is still by word of mouth. Because of inefficient communication between buyers and sellers, the incentives to build a reputation are weaker and the incentives to behave opportunistically are stronger. Developing countries are more likely to have "fly-by-night" traders and itinerant swindlers. For instance, in Nigeria there are many small retail outlets or vendor booths that rotate through a region's local markets, selling shoddy electronic goods. Consumers often spend a large part of their household budgets on faulty electronic products that break down after a couple of weeks. These products are sold without warranties and consumers have no hope of receiving a refund. There are countless

---

[4]Marcel Fafchamps and Bart Minten, "Relationships and Traders in Madagascar," *The Journal of Development Studies* 35, no. 6 (1999): 1–35.

[5]Kathryn Hendley, Peter Murrell, and Randi Ryterman, "Law, Relationships, and Private Enforcement: Transactional Strategies of Russian Enterprises," *Europe-Asia Studies* 52, no. 4 (2000): 627–656.

similar examples of opportunistic sellers on markets in developing countries who contribute to consumers' lack of trust and slow the development of reliable markets, putting poor countries at a double disadvantage. Not only are developing countries more likely to have weaker formal institutions, but the informal institution of reputation is less effective without the support of formal institutions and without good circulation of information.

The Hold-Up Problem

A widespread problem in business contracts, the **hold-up problem**, refers to a situation in which a business partnership requires an investment from one of the parties that is specific to the transaction in question. Once the investment has been made, however, the other partner "holds up" the party that made the investment in order to renegotiate the deal.

For example, suppose a truck manufacturer in India agrees to subcontract the production of axles to another party. An investment of $10,000 is needed to produce the axles and it costs $20 to produce each axle, including the cost of capital. The truck manufacturer contracts an order of 1,000 axles and promises a price of $30 per axle. At that price, the transaction, based on the order of 1,000 axles, makes it possible for the axle subcontractor to break even, since he will be able to recover both the investment cost and the production costs. Indeed, the cost will be $10,000 + ($20 × 1,000) = 30,000 and sales will be $30,000.

Once the axle company has made the investment in the machines to produce axles, however, the truck manufacturer tells the subcontractor that he is now ready to pay only $25 for an axle. What does the subcontractor do? He has the choice of either producing the axles at the lower price of $25 or not producing at all. If he does not produce, he loses $10,000, but if he goes ahead with production, he will only lose $5,000 (his operating profit will be $25 × 1,000 − ($20 × 1,000) − $10,000 = −$5,000); as a result, the subcontractor will prefer to produce the axles. Because the investment cost is already sunk (**sunk cost**), the only thing that matters in deciding whether or not to produce the axles is the difference between sales ($25 × 1,000) and operating costs ($20 × 1,000), which is $5,000.[6]

Because the subcontractor will decide to produce, even though he will incur a loss, the truck manufacturer can take advantage of the subcontractor's situation when proposing the lower price. The truck manufacturer is holding up the subcontractor, taking advantage of the subcontractor's weaker bargaining position after he has made the investment. If the subcontractor had known the truck manufacturer was going to behave in this manner, then he would not have invested in the first place. A profitable investment opportunity can thus be lost because of the hold-up problem. In general, hold-up problems cause underinvestment, which is economically damaging in particular in developing countries.

Hold-ups are not confined to specific industries. Suppose the representative of a food company convinced a farmer to change crops and produce cocoa,

---

[6]Remember the notion of sunk cost. Once a cost has been incurred and cannot be recovered, it should not count in economic calculations of future choices. We apply this principle here.

promising a high price once the crop was mature. The farmer changes crops, and for the first year, harvests cacao beans from which cocoa is produced. If the food company comes back and offers a lower price for the crop, the farmer is still forced to sell to the food company or face the loss of an entire year's income.

Another example occurs in the rental market. If a farmer who is leasing land from a landlord has made significant efforts to improve the productivity of the land by building irrigation systems using his own money and effort, he may be evicted by the landlord, who can charge a higher price to other farmers because of the improvements, or can threaten to evict the farmer unless he agrees to an increase in the rental price.

The hold-up problem is more acute the more **relationship specific** the investment is. In the axle example, the investment to produce axles only has value when the subcontractor sells the axles to the specific truck manufacturing company. When an investment only has value in the context of a specific partnership with another firm, this relationship specificity is also called **asset specificity**. If the axle producer can sell the same axles to another truck company, the hold-up problem is solved because there are alternative uses for the investment. If the truck manufacturer knows this, he may refrain from trying to lower the price after the investment is made. Even if the axles are specific to a particular contract, the hold-up problem might still be mitigated if the prior investment can be restructured at a relatively low cost for alternative uses. Suppose that the subcontractor producing the axles can restructure his facility to produce metal parts for the construction industry; he might opt to do that instead of submitting to the demands of the truck manufacturer to lower the price of the axles.

Note that the hold-up problem is not related to informational asymmetries. The axle producer knows that the truck manufacturer will have an interest in holding it up. The hold-up problem is related to asset-specificity, the sunk cost of investment and opportunistic behavior.

Institutional solutions to the hold-up problem. Binding and legally enforceable contracts are the primary solution to the hold-up problem. If the buyer is contractually obligated to buy products from the subcontractor at a specified price, the problem should disappear. Countries with strong legal institutions have an advantage over countries with weak institutions in terms of the hold-up problem.

However, legal institutions do not always provide full protection against hold-ups. Because contracts are often incomplete and lack specific details, it is often possible for a buyer to invoke a contingency that was not built into the initial contract and lay the blame on the seller. One tactic is to claim that certain characteristics of a product that were not actually specified in the contract are not as initially agreed upon. Many of these claims are often not very credible, but it can be costly to mount a defense against them in court. The truck manufacturer can threaten the axle subcontractor with legal proceedings unless the axles' price is renegotiated downward, and the subcontractor may not have the resources to defend himself. Between the costs of a lower axle price and the cost of a lawsuit, the subcontractor may choose the lower axle price. The less detailed the contract, the more possibilities there are for hold-up.

Informal solutions to the hold-up problem. If legal protections against the hold-up problem are insufficient, then a widespread solution is **vertical integration**, a situation in which two firms working together as supplier and client merge into a single firm. In the hold-up example above, vertical integration means that axle and truck production would be part of the same firm. The truck company would produce the axles it needs because the axle subcontractor does not trust the truck manufacturer enough to be ready to make an investment in a joint business deal. This solution might be inefficient and the cost of producing the axles inside the truck firm might be higher than using a subcontractor.

Because there are fewer legal protections in developing countries, firms should have more incentives to engage in vertical integration. Unfortunately, the obstacles to achieving vertical integration are also higher because it requires a high level of capital to operate properly. In a poor country, this level of capital is more difficult to achieve due to less pre-existing wealth and underdeveloped capital markets.

Most multinational corporations that operate in developing countries are vertically integrated and control the complete manufacturing process from raw materials to the final product. They do not face the severe capital constraints that confront domestic firms in developing countries because they are able to raise funds on international capital markets. Operating as vertically integrated units in developing countries is therefore less of a problem for multinational corporations than for domestic firms.

Social norms might also work to mitigate the hold-up problem by reducing the amount of opportunistic behavior, but it is debatable by how much. Economists are skeptical of the effectiveness of social norms to eliminate this behavior because they tend to think that economic agents pursue their own self-interest. Social norms work well only to the extent that there are credible punishment mechanisms for those who deviate from them.

The Commitment Problem

In all types of behavior, when one party reneges on prior commitments made to another party in the course of joint transactions, it is referred to as the **commitment problem**. This widespread problem occurs in all kinds of transactions but is potentially present in all **sequential transactions** that do not take place at the same time but rather in a certain order. Take the simple transaction of purchasing a bicycle. The transaction is simultaneous if the buyer delivers the money at the same time that the seller transfers ownership of the bike. The same transaction is sequential if ownership precedes the money transfer or vice-versa. In any sequential transaction, a commitment problem can occur; if the buyer is to pay after delivery of the bike, she may take it but fail to pay for it. Similarly, if delivery occurs after payment, the seller may renege on his promise to deliver the bicycle after he receives the buyer's money.

The commitment problem is very general and does not require any investment or sunk cost. Commitment problems arise because the optimal choice for one of the contracting parties at one point in time is no longer optimal at a later stage. Economists call this difference in the optimality of decisions at different periods in time **time inconsistency**. In our bicycle example, it is optimal to promise to pay for the bicycle before its delivery, but it may no longer be optimal to pay once the delivery has occurred, especially if the buyer can renege with no consequences.

Consequences of the lack of commitment. The inability to commit hurts both parties in a transaction and is, in many cases, an impediment to transactions. There are also situations in which one party's inability to commit weakens its bargaining power and renders its threats not credible to the other party. For example, a government could commit to a non-negotiation policy with terrorists or pirates who take hostages, but might be unable to resist the pressure to negotiate once such a hostage situation occurs. This wavering of resolve weakens the government's bargaining power and invites further hostage-taking actions.

Credibility, a party's ability to uphold the commitments it makes, plays an important role in monetary and fiscal policy. A government might promise not to run fiscal deficits, but before an election, it could abandon that commitment by raising expenditures to garner votes. Lack of credibility in this case means that agents will expect fiscal deficits and behave accordingly. In particular, a central bank may want to announce a tight monetary policy, but may later engage in unexpected monetary expansion to stimulate the economy. The central bank's lack of credibility will lead agents to expect inflation to be higher than the targets announced by the central bank. A monopoly may be unable to commit to maintain current prices once it has sold to the customers with the highest willingness to pay, as has often been the case with new types of computers, DVD players, and with flat-screen TVs. Initially, these televisions were quite expensive and many consumers preferred to wait for the price to fall, secure in their knowledge that the manufacturers would drop their prices as soon as demand declined, regardless of announcements made to the contrary. In this case, if the monopoly could make credible commitments not to lower prices, consumers would not wait for the price to fall before making a purchase.

Institutional solutions to the commitment problem. When formal institutions are reliable, contract enforcement plays a crucial role in solving commitment problems. The parties draw up a contract that makes commitment legally binding and possibly provides specific penalties for breach of contract. If one party reneges on a commitment, the other can go to court to punish the guilty party. This "third-party enforcement" serves as a powerful instrument to solve commitment problems. Legally enforceable contracts thus help to "tie one's hands," which is usually beneficial for both parties.

Solving the commitment problem by legally binding contracts does not necessarily imply rigidity. A contract may specify actions that are no longer optimal for both parties. For example, two companies may have a delivery contract for a certain good over a certain period of time. If the producer comes up with a new product that is both less costly to produce and gives more utility to the buyer, the two parties can agree to void the existing contract or to draw up a new agreement. However, the existing contract still protects each party to the contract. If the two agree to void a contract, it must indeed be the case that both are made better off, and no one suffers from the decision.

The weakness of formal institutions in developing economies tends to make the commitment problem more prevalent than in developed economies.

Informal solutions to the commitment problem. In traditional societies, witnesses were usually present when promises were made between two parties in a trade agreement or other type of contract. Witnesses to a marriage commitment are an important institution in many societies throughout the world; today's "best man" and "maid (or matron) of honor" are participating in an ancient tradition of witnessing a binding contract.

Parties to agreements have often devised ingenious informal mechanisms to create credible commitments. This is the case in all spheres of life: trade, crime, and arms sales, as well as societal commitments such as marriage. For example, army generals have often signaled their commitment to fight on, regardless of the consequences, by burning bridges behind their troops so that the soldiers had nowhere to retreat. These actions have rarely failed to impress the enemy. In the business world, a company might undertake a very large investment that can only be recouped if the product becomes the "next great thing" with booming sales. The company undertakes the investment to show its commitment to challenge other market competitors. On a darker note, in Japan many businesses hire the *yakuza*, organized crime syndicates, as debt collection agencies. Yakuza agents who threaten a recalcitrant debtor will go so far as to cut off their own finger in front of the debtor to emphasize their commitment to recovering the debt.

Because formal contract enforcement is so important in solving commitment problems, developing countries with deficient formal law enforcement must often use informal enforcement agencies.

As is the case with hold-up problems, informal institutions are much less effective than formal ones when it comes to solving the commitment problem.

The Russian Mob in a Market Economy

Informal enforcement methods were widespread in Russia during the 1990s, when the country started its transition to a market economy, and they often involved criminal organizations or firms that had close links to organized crime. These connections were efficient at using the threat of violence to enforce commitments made by private agents in a variety of contractual situations. Obviously, there was a downside to the use of criminal organizations as enforcement agencies: their methods turned quickly into abuse as contracting parties increasingly turned to the threat of violence as a means to renegotiate agreements. The criminal agencies engaged in racketeering by extorting money or favors from the firms that had hired them in the first place. Competition among criminal agencies led to a deepening spiral of violence and terror. When formal institutions in developing nations cannot enforce both criminal and civil laws, businesses may be forced to use criminal agencies to protect themselves and their business interests.

The Cooperation Problem

In a situation where individuals follow their self-interest in making their choices and where the outcomes of these choices are less than optimal for all parties, a **cooperation problem** arises. This means that if individuals cooperated to find a solution that would be better for all parties involved, they could achieve a better payoff.

The prisoner's dilemma. Economists represent the cooperation problem with the prisoner's dilemma, an important example of **game theory**, which studies decisions of agents with payoffs that depend on the actions of other agents.

In the **prisoner's dilemma**, two suspects have been arrested by the police and are interrogated in the attempt to extract confessions to a joint crime. Each prisoner is in a separate cell and cannot communicate with the other. As Table 7.1 shows, if neither confesses, they will both serve a maximum of 6 months in jail. If they both confess, they will each serve 2 years. However, if one confesses and the other does not, the one who confesses will be set free immediately while the other will spend 10 years in jail. What will happen? Game theory tells us that the **Nash equilibrium**, a situation in which each agent has chosen an action that is optimal given the action of the other, is the scenario in which both confess. A Nash equilibrium also occurs when one player does not want to deviate from his or her actions given the actions of the other.

Let us examine the strategies presented by the prisoner's dilemma. Suppose B confesses. It is then in A's best interest to confess also. If A does not confess, he will get 10 years, and if he does confess he will get 2 years. If B decides not to confess, it is again in A's best interest to confess. Indeed, if A does not confess, he will get 6 months, but if he does confess, he walks free. We see that whether B decides to confess or not, it is always in A's best interest to confess. This is called a **dominant strategy**, a situation in which the same action is optimal and independent of what the other player chooses. It is a dominant strategy for Prisoner A to confess. Since Prisoner B's reasoning is the same as Prisoner A's, Prisoner B will also decide to confess. Therefore, they will both serve 2 years.

They would both be better off if they had decided not to confess. In that case, they would each only get 6 months. However, this is not a Nash equilibrium. Suppose that they each decided not to confess. In that case, each would gain individually by changing his mind and confessing in order to walk free.

TABLE 7.1   The Prisoner's Dilemma

	B stays silent.	B confesses.
A stays silent.	Both serve 6 months.	Prisoner A serves 10 years. Prisoner B goes free.
A confesses.	Prisoner A goes free. Prisoner B serves 10 years.	Both serve 2 years.

Prisoners A and B decide individually whether to confess to a crime. It would be in their joint interest for both to stay silent, but if they follow their self-interest, they will both choose to confess ... and end up staying in jail longer.

Note that the commitment problem comes into play here. If both could precommit never to confess and were able to enforce such commitment, they would both be better off. However, if there is no mechanism to implement such precommitment, then it is in their self-interest to confess and the outcome is suboptimal. We can understand all cooperation problems in terms of the logical structure of the prisoner's dilemma.

The inefficiency of pure self-interest maximization. The prisoner's dilemma is often called a cooperation problem because it is a typical representation of a scenario in which each agent follows only his or her self-interest and where the outcome is suboptimal for everyone. If cooperation could be enforced (in this case, a precommitment not to confess), then it would be better for both parties. The prisoner's dilemma is often invoked as a symbol of the inefficiency of a pure laissez-faire system, in which individuals only follow their self-interest. This view is usually contrasted with traditional visions of laissez-faire, where following self-interest is best for society as a whole.

There are many relevant examples of the cooperation problem, such as protecting the environment. It is costly for any single country to take measures to prevent climate change; reducing carbon dioxide emissions means introducing new car models that run on low-carbon or carbon-free fuels, investing in public transport, and developing energy-saving technologies. If all countries took these measures simultaneously, then they could achieve tangible results. However, countries also face the prisoner's dilemma: if all other countries take measures to preserve the environment, then it is possible for a single country to benefit from the investment of the others without incurring the costs.[7] If all other countries decide not to invest in averting climate change, then it is not in the interest of a single country to incur the necessary costs because these investments will not yield benefits if other countries fail to reduce their carbon emissions. It is thus a dominant strategy not to invest in reducing carbon dioxide emissions. This lack of cooperation can be a tragedy in the long run. As most environmental issues reflect the prisoner's dilemma, institutional solutions are needed to solve them.

One such solution came in the form of the **Kyoto Protocol**, a modest first step toward international cooperation to prevent climate change. The Kyoto Protocol required 36 developed countries to reduce their greenhouse gas emissions by 5% relative to their 1990 levels. This was considered by climatologists to be too modest a target. However, even that first step was far more than some countries were willing to take, and led by the Bush administration, the United States refused to sign the agreement. In December 2009, the United Nations' **Copenhagen Accord** failed to reach an agreement with binding commitments by participating countries to reduce their carbon emissions. This failure illustrates the cooperation problem and the difficulties of finding solutions to complex problems when the parties involved follow their own self-interests.

---

[7]This is not true for a very large country. The United States alone is responsible for about a third of carbon dioxide emissions in the world, so it would not benefit that much from free-riding on the environmental efforts of others since a U.S. failure to curb emissions would directly affect climate change, and thus hurt the U.S., too.

The Tragedy of the Commons

Cooperation problems have always been present in human societies. One example is that of the tragedy of the commons. In English villages before the 16th century, parcels of land, called the commons, that belonged to a collection of individual farmers were accessible to the whole village. While all villagers could let their sheep graze on the commons, individual villagers had an incentive to let their sheep overgraze there without feeling responsible for the potential damage to the land. No matter what the other villagers decided to do, an individual's maximum self-interest lay in letting his sheep graze as much as possible on the commons so that each villager would have to secure less feed for his sheep. Of course, this self-interest led to serious overgrazing.

In the 16th and 17th centuries, there was an "enclosure" movement launched by the British landed aristocracy to keep the commons away from those who did not have property claims, usually the poor peasants. This movement had major social effects on the English countryside and resulted in large numbers of peasants becoming severely impoverished and leaving their villages for the cities.

We do not know exactly how much overgrazing there was in England at the time, but the tragedy of the commons is an illustration of a more general phenomenon that has occurred over and over in history, the overexploitation of arable land and the depletion of natural resources. The "fertile crescent" in the Middle East, around the Nile, Jordan, Tigris, and Euphrates rivers, was one of the most arable and productive areas of the ancient world. Overexploitation has eroded the quality of the soil and led to desertification. Similar problems have occurred in other regions due to deforestation; the population of Easter Island nearly became extinct following its complete exploitation of the island's native tree species.[8] Deforestation of the Amazon rain forest in South America, the major producer of oxygen on the planet, is occurring at a phenomenal speed; the annual loss of rain forest in the Amazon region is roughly 10,000 square miles, nearly the size of Massachusetts.

The collective-action problem. Another important example of the prisoner's dilemma is the **collective-action problem**, when people fail to undertake a collective action even though it is in their joint interest to do so. Imagine an Indian municipality's decision to authorize the construction of a chemical factory that will pollute the town's air and water, and suppose that the residents are opposed to the decision. To defeat the project, the population needs to be organized, but doing so is costly. Assume that if at least half the population shows up at a demonstration to protest the decision, the project will be abandoned. If, instead, less than half of the population shows up, the project will go forward. Demonstrating is costly and inconvenient, however, and much of the population would rather spend their free time elsewhere. Just as in the prisoner's dilemma, if very few demonstrate, participation will not be effective and it will not be optimal for anyone to demonstrate. However, if at least half of the population goes to the demonstration, any resident can **free ride** and benefit from the

---

[8]See, for example, James A. Brander and M. Scott Taylor, "The Simple Economics of Easter Island: A Ricardo-Malthus Model of Renewable Resource Use," *The American Economic Review* 88, no. 1 (March 1998): 119–138.

actions of the others while not incurring any of the costs of taking action. Thus, it is a dominant strategy for an individual not to demonstrate and the result is that no one demonstrates and the project is implemented, an outcome that is suboptimal for the residents. Everyone wants the demonstration to happen, but no one wants to participate individually, leading to collective-action failure.

Collective-action failures are fundamental to understanding human societies. They help to explain why inefficient institutions persist in developing countries. We frequently read in the press of African dictators who loot their countries' resources and put the proceeds, sometimes billions of dollars, in Swiss banks. Why do such situations continually occur? It is precisely because the collective-action problem prevents people from overthrowing corrupt leaders or dictatorial regimes.

Institutional solutions to the cooperation problem. Institutions are necessary to solve cooperation problems. Historically, labor unions in many countries have helped workers organize collective actions in order to obtain better working conditions and higher wages. Professional organizations such as associations of farmers, fishermen, construction workers, and doctors defend the interests of their professions in both the legislative process and the media. Political parties serve as organizations that promote competing political platforms via the elections of party members and the passage of legislative bills.

International institutions can also solve the cooperation problem. The United Nations (UN) was founded after World War II to prevent similar global conflicts from ever occurring again. Unfortunately, the UN was not given much power by the sovereign countries that make up its membership. This has prevented the organization from becoming an effective and powerful international institution able to intervene effectively in various world conflicts. The European Union (EU) is a more successful institution than the UN. European nations have been at war with each other for most of the last 1,000 years, but the creation of the EU was seen by Europeans as an institutional solution to cooperation problems in the region. Institutional solutions to the environmental problems of the planet will require new forms of international cooperation in which world leaders meet and jointly agree on solutions, and then commit to their implementation.

Economists do not completely understand how the myriad associations and organizations that we observe in the world are able to overcome collective-action problems. People are not only organized into political parties, trade unions, and professional associations at the national level, but they also organize to cooperate at the international level. There are many small-scale examples of spontaneous collective action as well, such as villagers organizing to rebuild their homes after a fire or a flood. According to standard game theory, these associations and organizations should not emerge spontaneously because of the collective-action problem. It takes very dedicated individuals to incur the heavy cost of spending time and money to set up these cooperative efforts. The members of nongovernmental organizations (NGOs) often feel passionately about the causes for which they fight, whether it is the environment, the eradication of poverty, or advancements in world health, in contrast to people who take a more passive approach to these problems and do not choose to spend time, energy, or money to organize and participate in new problem-solving associations.

Elinor Ostrom and Institutional Solutions to the Preservation of Common Resources

In 2009, Elinor Ostrom was the first woman to receive the Nobel Prize in Economics, which was jointly awarded to Oliver Williamson, one of the most famous researchers working on institutions. Ostrom's best-known work focuses on the emergence of institutions to solve tragedy-of-the-commons situations, in particular the management of common resources. Examples include water supplies, fish stocks, forests, and grazing lands. Economists automatically tend to think of two basic solutions to manage common resources: privatize them by selling rights to access them or let a central government regulate access to them. Ostrom found that in many of these situations, structures emerge from local governments that prevent overexploitation of common resources. Local communities establish rules to regulate access and put in place conflict-resolution mechanisms to enforce the rules and monitor resource use. For example, farmers would take turns to graze cows or utilize scarce water. People in the community would create boundaries where wood cutting was allowed, etc. These local structures also enforce sanctions for violation of the rules. The governance structures generally work well when they are based on democratic decision-making processes and are most effective in smaller communities where people know and trust each other, and interact regularly. It is also easier in smaller communities to enforce collective sanctions on individuals who break the rules.

Democracy and the collective-action problem. Political institutions can either help to overcome collective action problems or can exacerbate them. In dictatorships, the leaders usually ban political parties and associations; as a result, the opposition must organize secretly. Punishment for establishing or participating in opposition groups may mean death or lengthy jail time.

In democracies, freedom of association is a fundamental right. Professional associations and NGOs even receive assistance from the government in the form of grants and subsidies, even though they are associated with the government. In other words, democracy allows and even encourages the establishment of associations to overcome collective-action problems. Moreover, elections, the primary institution of democracy, provide a way to overcome one of the most fundamental collective-action problems faced by societies, replacing corrupt or inefficient leaders with better leaders. In a democracy, people come to the polls and can vote out incumbent leaders who no longer represent voters' interests or who have abused their powers.

Informal solutions to the cooperation problem. Most solutions to the cooperation problem tend to be formalized in some way. For example, trade unions, professional associations, and NGOs have their own rules and organizational structures that ensure the groups' proper functioning. This does not mean that there are no informal solutions to the cooperation problem. For example, spontaneous riots can break out in a developing country that can potentially lead to political change. Mine workers might engage in a spontaneous strike without consulting trade-union leaders. In 1989, Protestant activists started small demonstrations against the East German Communist regime in Leipzig. Within a few weeks, these demonstrations were joined by tens of thousands of East German citizens who had never before demonstrated. Two years previously, a similar uprising occurred, protesting the dictatorship in South Korea. The country had been living under various forms of dictatorship since the end of the Korean War. Student organizations began actively fighting for democracy and, in 1987, nationwide protests erupted, eventually leading to the downfall of the dictatorship.

Large-scale riots are usually spontaneous and the result of some dramatic event such as a hike in food prices or the political assassination of an opposition leader. These forms of collective action are usually unpredictable and not well understood by social scientists. Because they are spontaneous and not backed by a formal organization, these collective actions are also fragile and their momentum is often difficult to sustain. Participants may demobilize very rapidly and the mass movement may die out without having achieved any precise goal. Sometimes, these mass movements are however more powerful and sustained than expected and lead to revolutionary change, like in the case of the Arab Spring.

The Coordination Problem

Game theorists define a coordination problem as a situation in which agents can all coordinate on a specific action and the action an individual chooses depends on what others do. There are **multiple equilibria** possible in coordination problems, different possible sets of actions on which individuals coordinate. Imagine a situation in which there are no motor vehicle statutes and individuals must decide on their own whether to drive on the right or on the left. All individuals would quickly unite to drive on one side or the other. However, we do not know on which side they would choose to drive. In terms of game theory, these choices are both Nash equilibria. If an individual sees everyone else driving on the right, he has an incentive to drive on the right as well, but if he sees all others driving on the left, he will have an equally strong incentive to drive on the left. Once everyone drives either on the left or on the right, no one will have an incentive to deviate because that would be dangerous. The only thing we can predict is that people will decide to adopt a single rule addressing on which side to drive.

The difference between coordination and cooperation problems. The difference between these problems lies in the fact that in a coordination problem, what is optimal for an individual depends on what the others do. This is why there are multiple equilibria. There is no longer a dominant strategy as in the prisoner's dilemma where there is only one possible equilibrium, the inefficient one. In the case of the driving rule, none of the two equilibria (everybody driving to the left or everybody driving to the right) seems better or worse than the other, assuming that steering wheel can be adjusted to the prevailing equilibrium. There are many coordination problems in which all equilibria give the same payoffs to agents. In some countries, when people decide to meet at the train station, the meeting place is below the main clock. In others, it is at the main exit, by the cab station or on the platform.

There are also coordination games with equilibria that are not all equally efficient. Imagine the very relevant situation in developing countries where people can either decide to be law-abiding citizens or to engage in illegal activities. They would choose to be law-abiding citizens if there were a significant chance that they would be caught in the commission of a crime, but would engage in illegal activities if there were a low chance of being apprehended. The police have limited resources to fight crime, so the probability of being caught depends on the number of people engaged in illegal activities. If few people break the law, then the probability of being caught is high and it is preferable to be honest, but if many break the law, the probability is lower and there are more incentives to engage in illegal activities. We have two equilibria: one in which people are honest under the rule of law and one in which people engage in illegal activities with no adequate law enforcement, and thus no rule of law. If the rule of law is a condition for productive investment to take place, which is crucial for growth, then the rule of law equilibrium will be better for citizens in the long run. Here again, an individual's choice depends on the choice of others.

Understanding coordination problems is important in the context of development for a variety of reasons. First, the social norms that have emerged in various countries are quite diverse. Norms of politeness vary greatly among countries and a lack of knowledge of these norms can easily lead to social misunderstandings. In some Asian countries, for example, entering a house or even a restaurant without taking off your shoes is extremely impolite. Norms of conversation in parts of East Africa require repeating what the previous speaker said before expressing one's own opinion.

Second, we can observe in many countries coordination on a suboptimal equilibrium with a low level of law abidance, high levels of tax evasion, a large informal sector, and a high level of acceptance for corruption. Reforms that help a country shift from one equilibrium to the other are very difficult to design and implement because they require a collective effort that, as seen above, can be difficult to achieve. Diagnosing the problem is often easier than finding an effective and practical solution.

Coordination and "big push" strategies. We can look at the "big push" strategies of structural change discussed in Chapter 5 from the perspective of coordination problems. If there is little infrastructure (ports, roads, or electricity), private investors will be reluctant to invest in a country because their investment will not be very productive without infrastructure. A government, in turn, will not want to spend money on infrastructure if it thinks that there will be little private investment. This results in a coordination equilibrium, where there is minimal infrastructure and minimal private investment.

We can interpret the "big push" idea as an attempt to move from that low investment equilibrium to one in which there are high levels of both infrastructure and private investment. If there is a well-established infrastructure, private firms will be more willing to invest in the country and the government will be more willing to invest in the infrastructure if it thinks there will be significant private investment. The "big push" strategy consists of providing aid for infrastructure investment while simultaneously developing policies to encourage private investment.

The Stag Hunt Game

The stag hunt game is a coordination problem that was first formulated by the 18th-century French philosopher, Jean Jacques Rousseau (1712–1778). Economists and social scientists often use it as the prototype for all the coordination problems faced by societies and other groups in the real world. The following table illustrates the stag hunt game.

	A: Stag	A: Hare
B: Stag	4, 4	0, 3
B: Hare	3, 0	3, 3

Two hunters, A and B, are stalking game in a forest. Each can either choose to hunt a hare or a stag. A stag is more valuable than a hare but will only be caught if A and B hunt together. In this case, they both get a payoff of 4. If a player chooses to hunt a hare, he will get a payoff of 3. However, a player who chooses to hunt a stag while the other hunts a hare will not be successful and will have a payoff of 0. This table shows the benefits of hunting together because the payoff for hunting a stag together is higher than hunting for a hare individually. This is a coordination game, since it has multiple equilibria (both hunt a stag and both hunt a hare) and there is no dominant strategy: if one player hunts a stag, then the other will choose to do the same, but if one player hunts a hare, then the other player will also hunt a hare.

We can easily use the structure of the stag hunt game to examine issues that are relevant to developing countries, such as high or low levels of coordination in terms of law abidance or tax evasion.

Institutional solutions to coordination problems. In developing countries, formal laws help individuals and groups select one coordination equilibrium over another. This is the case for the traffic law example. The regulation of standards is another important solution to the coordination problem; railroads, for example, have different track widths in different countries, but most nations have implemented the international standard track width of 56.5 inches (1,435 mm). India and Pakistan instead inherited a broader gauge of 66 inches (1,676 mm) from the British colonial period, while Russia and the other nations of the former Soviet Union, as well as Mongolia, adopted a gauge of 59.84 inches (1,520 mm). Differences in gauge across countries tend to persist because of the costs of standardization. This requires passengers to change trains at international borders or await an axle adjustment, both of which are costly.

Informal solutions to coordination problems. Conventions, a type of social norm, are enforced informally by peer pressure and experience, and do not require legal enforcement. For example, when a telephone conversation is interrupted, the caller is usually the one to recall. Otherwise, each caller would be calling or no one at all would be calling back.

In 2005, Thomas Schelling received the Nobel Prize in Economics for his studies of coordination problems. He put forward the concept of **focal point** to understand how people can coordinate their actions. A focal point is a solution to a coordination problem that most people will find without having to communicate. For example, if two people decide to meet in a big city like Rio de Janeiro, but forget to specify where and do not have the opportunity to call each other again before their appointment, it is likely that both will go to the Central Station. This is an example of a focal point.

Conventions are usually well understood within a country or a particular culture, but not always across countries. In many cultures, a nod of the head up and down means "yes," while a movement of the head back and forth from left to right means "no." When greeting someone, Americans shake hands, but the Japanese bow. The exchange of business cards is fundamental to business etiquette in most of Asia, but not in many other countries. In the Middle East, showing the sole of your shoe to somebody else is considered an insult. Similar body movements or actions can have different interpretations in different societies. There are hundreds, probably thousands of social cues that differ across cultures and can make cross-cultural communication difficult, even when the language barrier is not significant. It is always respectful in a foreign country to show the locals that you have some knowledge of their local customs and conventions.

Many social norms are not necessarily fundamental for economic development. Some norms may, however, play a very important role: norms of honesty and trust, norms of conflict resolution (peaceful or violent), norms of equality between men and women, norms related to individual savings behavior, or norms related to effort. We will discuss many of these issues in Chapter 11 when we discuss the effect of culture on development.

The Persistence of Inefficient Institutions

We have seen how institutions help solve economic problems that stem from lack of information, commitment, and cooperation or coordination problems. While developed countries have institutions to solve these problems, developing countries are often not as fortunate. The lack of formal institutions impedes economic growth by raising the costs of transactions and slowing the flow of capital into a developing country. If improving institutions is crucial for successful development, we should ask why it is not happening. Reforming institutions is not as simple as signing a contract between two individuals. Inefficient institutions can even persist for a very long time and for a variety of complex reasons.

The Functionalist Fallacy

In this chapter, we have seen what institutions do, but not why institutions are in place. Understanding the functions that institutions perform is one thing; understanding why they emerge is another.

Institutions, just like technical innovations, are often the unintended consequences of actions designed to solve other problems. We know what microwave ovens do; they have become indispensable household appliances to warm or defrost food quickly. The microwave oven can warm a meal much faster than a traditional oven but that was not the purpose its inventor had in mind. It was an accidental byproduct of research to make better radar systems. Dr. Percy Spencer, an engineer working for the Raytheon Corporation, was testing a vacuum tube called a magnetron while researching improvements to conventional radar when he noticed that a candy bar in his pocket had melted. He put an egg and some corn kernels near the tube and found that those foods cooked quickly when exposed to microwaves. Thus, there can be a significant difference between the original purpose of an invention and its ultimate practical function, which in the case of the microwave, was quite accidental. This is also the case for many inventions such as silicon, saccharin, and the cardiac pacemaker among many others.

A similar process has occurred for many institutions. Settlers who came to North America or Australia did not have in mind the goal of creating institutions for successful economic development. They were primarily focused on preventing the creation of a monarchy such as the one they had left in England. Freedom from tyranny was their objective. They had no idea that the institutions they created would lead to phenomenal economic success.

This discussion illustrates the idea that function does not constitute an explanation for existence. There is the danger of the **functionalist fallacy**, which mistakes an object's function for the cause of its existence. Why is this distinction important? If we did not pay attention to this problem, we would tend to adhere to the view that institutions are always efficient. Indeed, if institutions solve certain problems, we would tend to believe that once a problem emerges, an institution will automatically appear to solve it. If this were the case, institutions would always be efficient. In fact, many institutions are typically inefficient, and inefficient institutions can persist for a very long time. Bringing about change to institutions requires overcoming the collective-action problem. This is very difficult to do in developing countries, especially if democratic institutions are absent or imperfect.

We will take a closer look at inefficient institutions throughout this book. Corruption is rife in many developing economies, with inefficient courts, dictatorial regimes, little protection for property rights, and a lack of formal titling systems. Inefficient formal institutions are very hard to overcome, especially when they aim to prevent agents from organizing to change them. Until considerable individual courage and group mobilization can overcome inefficient institutions, they may persist for a very long time.

Leaders in Institutionalism

The expansion of institutionalism that has taken place in economic theory is a revival of sorts. Economists developed contract theory and principal agent theory to analyze problems with individual transactions between agents who are in a contractual relationship. Game theory provides the tools to consider such problems analytically. Nevertheless, before game theory was developed, many economists already took institutions very seriously even though they were not part of mainstream theory. Throughout the 20th century, quite a few famous economists tried to understand the role of institutions and how they develop. We mention some of these prominent economists below.

Thorstein Veblen (1857–1929), in a famous book called *The Theory of the Leisure Class* (1899), coined the concept of **conspicuous consumption**, explaining that consumption among the rich was dictated more by a desire to show one's wealth and status rather than by the useful characteristics of the good consumed. He also believed that

(Continued)

much of human behavior was influenced by cultural and social norms.

John R. Commons (1862–1945) believed that transactions were the basis of any economic activity. He was interested in the legal and institutional aspects of transactions, and defined an institution as a collective action. He was one of the first economists to use the concepts of bounded rationality, incomplete contracts, and property rights, which became very prominent in institutionalist thinking.

Ronald Coase (1910–) is a British economist who spent his career at the University of Chicago. His research centered on the notion of transaction costs, which he considered to be the reason why firms exist and why we observe many transactions taking place within a firm rather than across legal entities. His 1937 article, "The Nature of the Firm," is one of the most influential writings in economics. His 1960 article, "The Problem of Social Cost," in which he developed the famous Coase theorem, states that private contracts can efficiently deal with externalities as long as there are well-defined property rights in place. He strongly encouraged the development of research at the intersection between Law and Economics and received the Nobel Prize in Economics in 1991.

Oliver Williamson (1932–) developed transaction-cost economics and his ideas gained wide acceptance among mainstream economists. He also developed the idea of the hold-up problem and of asset-specific investments, as well as many other related concepts. He received the Nobel Prize in Economics in 2009.

Douglass North (1920–) is an economic historian who emphasized the role of institutions in securing property rights and in explaining economic success over the long term. He received the Nobel Prize in Economics in 1993.

Mancur Olson (1932–1998) was the first economist to put forward the collective-action problem and to explain that individuals could free ride on the efforts of others. He developed the idea that collective action is like a public good and will be underprovided by only private efforts. He predicted that large groups with a minimal stake in public action will tend to suffer more from the collective-action problem than will small groups with a very large stake in public action. His work was seminal in understanding why inefficient institutions may persist.

Chapter Summary

What Are Institutions?

We have introduced the concept of institutions and shown that institutions matter for economic development. We have defined institutions as constraints on human behavior imposed by societal rules. Formal institutions, such as legal and political institutions, are written rules with codified statutes of enforcement verified by courts. Informal institutions are social norms or patterns of behavior dictated by cultural or religious beliefs. Informal rules are enforced in an informal way by peer pressure, a sense of moral obligation, or by informal enforcement agencies.

What Do Institutions Do?

Institutions play a role in solving problems inherent to economic and social transactions: informational problems, commitment problems including the hold-up problem, cooperation, and coordination problems.

Informational problems arise most often when one of the parties to a transaction has information about the object of the transaction that the other party does not have. Informational problems are an impediment to efficient market transactions. Institutional solutions to informational problems are, for example, disclosure rules, warranties, return policies, or the emergence of informational intermediaries such as rating agencies and chain stores. Informal institutional solutions to informational problems involve the reputation of economic agents and the circulation of information about their reputations.

Commitment problems arise when a party in a transaction has an incentive to renege on a promise made to the other party. Formal institutions solve the commitment problem by enforcing legal contracts. Informal enforcement of commitments is more difficult and sometimes requires the use of criminal organizations.

Cooperation problems arise because agents must incur individual costs when participating in any form of joint action, but can benefit from the effort of others even when they do not participate in the action. As a result, collective action occurs less often than is necessary. Formal institutional solutions to collective action include political and civil associations. Democracy is an important solution to collective action by means of elections, which allow voters to make collective choices for leaders and policies. Informal solutions include riots, spontaneous strikes, and other actions that occur in special circumstances.

Coordination problems arise when the actions of some agents affect the actions of others and when agents coordinate on positive behaviors (behaving honestly, trusting others, paying taxes) or negative behaviors (behaving dishonestly, not trusting others, evading taxes). Formal solutions to coordination problems involve laws and standards; informal solutions involve social norms and conventions.

The Persistence of Inefficient Institutions

Inefficient institutions have negative long-term effects on the economy. They may, however, persist for a very long time precisely because reforming institutions requires overcoming cooperation and collective-action problems.

Key Terms

adverse selection
asset specificity
asymmetric information
civil-law systems
collective-action problem
commitment problem
common-law system
conspicuous consumption
cooperation problem
Copenhagen Accord
credibility
credit rationing
creditworthiness
culture
disclosure rules
dominant strategy
expected payoff
focal point
formal institutions
free ride
functionalist fallacy
game theory
hold-up problem
informal institutions

informational intermediaries
institution
Kyoto Protocol
moral hazard
multiple equilibria
Nash equilibrium
prisoner's dilemma
rating agencies
regulation of access or entry
relational contracting
relationship specific
return policies
risk averse
risk neutral
sequential transactions
signaling
social norms (conventions)
sunk cost
time inconsistency
transaction costs
values
vertical integration
warranty

Review Questions

1. Give an example (different from those discussed in the chapter) of an economic transaction that is more difficult to complete in developing countries than it would be in developed countries.

2. Many solutions to informational problems emerge spontaneously as contractual innovations. Is there a role for the formal institution of law with respect to these contractual innovations, and if so, why?

3. Reputation is important for contract enforcement when formal institutions are weak. Explain. What conditions in the economic environment make reputation work more or less efficiently? Why?

4. Give examples of formal and informal institutions as solutions for the cooperation problem that we have not discussed in the chapter. Explain your choices.

5. Why is the coordination problem important in the context of development?

6. Write down the problem of cooperation for two countries, A and B, in the fight against climate change and use a payoff matrix as in the case of the prisoner's dilemma. Payoffs are $y_A(x_A, x_B)$ and $y_B(x_A, x_B)$, where x_A and x_B can take two values: 1) if measures are taken in the country against climate change and 2) if no measures are taken. What are the conditions of the payoffs in each cell for each player so that there is a unique Nash equilibrium in which no country takes any action against climate change?

7. Assume a coordination problem related to honest business practices, based on the following payoff matrix:

	B is honest.	B is dishonest.
A is honest.	a, a	d, b
A is dishonest.	b, d	c, c

What are the conditions on the payoff matrix so that both A and B being honest and dishonest are both equilibria? How would you have to change the payoffs so that both A and B being dishonest is the only equilibrium? What change would that represent in the problem analyzed?

8. Assume that an Indian firm is contacted by a multinational car company to produce brake systems. This requires an initial investment of I from the Indian subcontractor and a variable cost c per braking system. The car company plans to buy n brake systems from the subcontractor. What is the price p at which the Indian subcontractor would break even? At what price p' can the car company still convince the subcontractor to produce the systems once it has made the investment?

9. Look up the following article by Simon Brinsmead: "Oil Concession Contracts and the Problem of Hold-Up," downloadable at http://www.dundee.ac.uk/cepmlp/journal/html/Vol17/Vol17_11.pdf. How do the ideas in this article relate to this chapter's discussion? Assume you were advising the government of a developing country with oil reserves. What kind of contract would you recommend to the government? Explain.

10. Download the governance indicators from the World Bank (click on Download full dataset) in either excel or stata format: http://info.worldbank.org/governance/wgi/index.asp

    Look at the Rule of Law index ranking of countries in 2010 and in 1996. What observations do you make when comparing these two rankings?

Markets and Hierarchies

8

At the end of the Korean War in 1953, the Korean peninsula was separated into two countries: the Democratic People's Republic of North Korea (DPRK), known as North Korea, and the Republic of Korea (ROK), or South Korea. By the war's end, the population on the peninsula was impoverished and in great need of economic development. North Korea embraced a socialist economic system based on central planning and government ownership of resources. South Korea opted for a market economy based on private ownership.

Before the division, North Korea was slightly wealthier than South Korea because most industries were located in the north, which was richer in natural resources. Nevertheless, the result of economic development in both countries is quite shocking. In 2009, North Korean GDP per capita in purchasing power parity was estimated at $1,800 and was probably even lower, comparable to poor countries such as Chad, Kenya, or Senegal. That same year, South Korean GDP per capita was above $28,000, comparable to Israel or New Zealand. Because both nations share the same history, culture, and general geographical conditions, the stark contrast in economic development can be traced to the differences in their economic systems and institutions. Why did central planning fail so badly, both in North Korea and in other communist countries?

The difference between the performance of North and South Korea underlines a basic question in economics: how should nations coordinate economic activity? Markets and hierarchies are two fundamental institutions that coordinate this activity. Markets are the pillar of the capitalist system. Hierarchies are no less important in modern economies composed of very large business organizations whose total sales often far exceed the gross national product of many small countries.

In the development context, during much of the 20th century, there was a common belief that the coordination of economic activity through hierarchies would be more effective than coordination through markets. The idea was that an entire economy could be transformed into a single hierarchy, called a centrally planned economy. The history of both Koreas underscores the contrast between the failure of central planning and the success of market-based and export-led growth. Despite the demise of central planning, there are many people who argue today that the governments of developing countries should play a bigger role in coordinating economic activity. In particular, this is the case in Russia since Vladimir Putin's rise to power or in Venezuela after Hugo Chavez became president. Since the Great Recession of 2008, socialist ideas of central planning have become fashionable again among young people all over the world. It is therefore important to examine why central planning failed so as not to repeat past mistakes.

Although most economists now recognize that central planning is flawed, the problem of coordination using markets or hierarchies is still relevant. Although the recent success of Asian economies, particularly that of China, is a result of export-led growth and competition on world markets, governments have played a fundamental role in coordinating the strategy of export-led growth. Moreover, much of the success in these economies is a consequence of the expansion of large firms with quite efficient hierarchies. Therefore, it is important in the development context to better understand the respective role of markets and hierarchies in coordinating economic activity.

Despite a trend in the 1980s to privatize most economic activities and to let market forces determine all economic activities, it remains the case that all over the world, fire departments, armies, police squads are usually coordinated through a hierarchy, not through the market. Why? This question has been the subject of debates not only about how to structure public services in municipalities, but also about how to organize governmental administration. This chapter examines the theory of coordination, which provides answers to the question of markets versus hierarchies as fundamental methods of coordination.

Finally, this chapter discusses a related question, that of "the boundaries of the firm": when do transactions take place inside the firm and when do they take place outside the firm with other firms? In some countries, firms rely primarily on suppliers for raw materials and parts, and have contracts with outside firms to deliver those supplies or to provide specialized services. In other countries, firms rely less on outside entities and produce these parts and services themselves. These boundaries can have important economic effects.

The Central Planning Debate

In the 19th and 20th centuries, economists debated whether markets or hierarchies should be the primary method for economic coordination. Economists influenced by Karl Marx, or who tended to lean toward socialist economic theory, thought that central planning should take precedence. This resulted in the so-called "central planning" debate that had a prominent place in economic and political circles during the first half of the 20th century. This debate had a worldwide intellectual influence outside academia. Countries with an established Communist regime, such as the Soviet Union, China, and most of Central Europe after World War II, embraced central planning wholeheartedly. In developing economies such as India's, which had then barely gained their independence from colonial powers, this debate was taken seriously. Central planning played a crucial role in the Indian economy in the first decades after the country achieved independence from England in 1947, just as it did for Algeria after its war of independence against France and in many other developing countries such as Vietnam or Cuba.

Now, at the beginning of the 21st century, central-planning debates are once again relevant as socialist-leaning governments emerge in Venezuela, Bolivia, and Nicaragua. The dire economic situation of millions of people in the former Soviet Union following the collapse of Communism in the early 1990s and the worldwide recession of 2008–2009 is revitalizing these debates. Even in China, which has embraced transition to the market economy, the 2008–2009 recession

The Fathers of Central Planning

During in the 19th century, socialist thinker and economist Karl Marx witnessed England's extraordinary industrial revolution that subsequently spread throughout Europe. Technological change was altering landscapes and everyday life. Ample supplies of coal and steel made large-scale industrial mechanization possible, and that led to modern manufacturing techniques for a broad range of goods such as the mechanized production of textiles. With these huge technological advancements came promises of widespread affluence (and the utter neglect of environmental concerns) and the hope of a better life for millions. At the same time, industrialization was moving millions of people from the countryside into cities. These workers earned low wages and faced the risk of unemployment, poverty, and starvation; no mechanisms for the protection of laborers existed. These conflicting impressions of industrialization led Marx to theorize that if society, which was largely composed of workers, controlled the big industries, it would improve living conditions for the working class much faster and create material abundance. The fruits of that increase in productivity would go directly to the workers. Similarly, by coordinating economic activity at the central level, society could prevent economic depressions. His ideas about how such coordination would be achieved were extremely vague, but the general ideas were quite popular among the working class and left-leaning intellectuals. In contrast to early critics of industrialization, Marx was an enthusiastic proponent of technical progress and the economic and social changes that resulted from it. He thought that if the ownership of factories were simply taken away from capitalists, technological change could be put to use in the service of all members of society.

Vladimir Lenin, the Russian revolutionary, had views similar to those of Marx. He admired the German post office system that could quickly channel thousands of letters among individuals and companies every day. At that time (the early 20th century), it was considered throughout the world as a model of efficient organization. When explaining the benefits of having a socialist economy, Lenin often said that an entire economy would be run like a giant post office.

has strengthened the position of those within the Communist leadership who are hostile to market reforms. The minority of socialist economists who favor a return to central planning has become increasingly vocal.

The Theoretical Argument against Central Planning

While revolutionary leaders such as Marx and Lenin recommended replacing the market economy with the centrally planned economy, academic economists in the early 20th century developed theoretical arguments against central planning. Enrico Barone, an Italian economist, and Ludwig von Mises, a famous Austrian economist, criticized the central planning project and claimed that a socialist economy could never be as efficient as a market economy because of the absence of the price system.[1] Their argument was that if central

---

[1] Enrico Barone, (1908) "Il Ministro della Produzione nello Stato Collettivista," *Giornale degli Economisti* 2 (Sept./Oct. 1908): 267–293, trans. as "The Ministry of Production in the Collectivist State" in F. A. Hayek, ed., *Collectivist Economic Planning* (London: George Routledge & Sons 1935): 245–290; and Ludwig von Mises, "Die Wirtschaftsrechnung im sozialistischen Gemeinwesen," trans. as "Economic Calculation in the Economic Commonwealth" in F. A. Hayek, *Collectivist Economic Planning* (London: George Routledge & Sons, 1935): 87–130.

planning were to replace markets, there would be no prices to indicate scarcities in the economy, as is the case in the market economy. For example, if oil becomes scarce in the market economy, then its prices will increase to reflect this scarcity, encouraging consumers to reduce their demand and firms to look for alternative technologies that would be more cost effective. If the whole economy were coordinated as in a single enterprise, such scarcity signals would not appear and agents would not be aware of them. As a result, agents would not have incentives to reduce the use of scarce resources or to employ more cost-effective technologies.

Lange's Rebuttal

Oskar Lange, a famous Polish economist, vigorously challenged this view.[2] He claimed that Barone and von Mises' argument was wrong because the existence of markets is not necessary to generate signals of scarcity. He argued that in computing a plan for the economy, it was perfectly possible to calculate scarcity signals that had the same function as prices. He maintained that a planning problem could be represented as a mathematical problem of optimization under constraints, where the constraints represent the scarcities of resources available for an economy. Moreover, claimed Lange, the centrally planned economy would have the big advantage that it will reach economic equilibrium right away rather than going through the economic fluctuations of business cycles typical of a market economy. Lange's reasoning, based on the then-blossoming developments in mathematical economics, convincingly refuted the claims of the conservative economists.

At the time these debates were taking place, the public mood favored central planning. While the Great Depression of the 1930s threw millions of people in the United States and Europe into unemployment and misery, the Soviet Union was launching a vigorous industrialization campaign to wake the rural Russian economy from its torpor that was achieving very impressive growth rates. Economic growth in the USSR at the time seemed as impressive as China's growth at the turn of the 21st century. Many intellectuals impressed by the Soviets' economic performance during the 1930s started to believe that a centrally planned economy could prove superior to a market economy. Another contributing factor to strengthening this belief was the development of large corporations like Ford and GM whose innovations in technology and organization resulted in significant increases in productivity. While things seemed chaotic and anarchic outside the firm, economic progress seemed to thrive inside large business organizations.

During World War II, progress in the mathematical theory of planning (the discovery of linear programming by George B. Dantzig and Philip Wolfe, invented years earlier by Soviet economist Leonid Kantorovich, who would receive the Nobel Prize in Economics in 1975) played a considerable role in organizing the U.S. effort in the Pacific war. After the end of World War II and

---

[2]Oskar Lange, "On the Economic Theory of Socialism," *The Review of Economic Studies Ltd.*, part I, vol. 4, no. 1; part II, vol. 4, no. 2, 1936.

the spread of Communism in Central Europe and China, the world seemed to move in only one direction: toward socialism. Joseph Schumpeter, the famous economist who had no sympathies for socialism, saw the "bureaucratization of the world" as inevitable. Central planning bureaus were being established in France and the Netherlands, among other countries. In the decades following World War II, economists were thoroughly engaged in research on the mathematical theory of planning.

Hayek's Fundamental Criticism

While the world seemed to move in the direction of central planning, an Austrian-born economist, Friedrich August Hayek, delivered a damning critique of central planning.[3] Hayek did not dispute that Lange's reasoning had been theoretically correct in his debate with von Mises, but Hayek claimed that the Achilles' heel of the centrally planned economy lay in the practical impossibility of computing a balanced central plan (where demands and supplies are equalized) because of the complexities of a modern economy. The beauty of a market economy, according to Hayek, is that there is no need for a central information repository. Millions of people constantly make economic decisions based on limited information, following what they perceive to be their economic interest. To coordinate this activity through a central plan, it would be necessary to gather all that information in a single place and use it productively. Given the size and complexity of modern economies, such a task would be impossible, claimed Hayek. It would never be feasible to centralize all information with the same ease and efficiency as the market could.

At the time, Hayek's view was met with skepticism. The prevailing view was that with the advent of modern computers, this centralization of information would become increasingly accessible. However, as economies progress, the amount of information that circulates in them grows exponentially, possibly much faster than any progress in computer technologies. Hayek's claim was not logical or even scientifically proven, but it was practical, based on judgment and deep observation of modern economies. His view would turn out to be prophetic. The complexities associated with computing central plans invariably made it impossible to calculate plans at a level of itemization below very aggregate categories in the Soviet economy. When the transition process toward a market economy started in that economy after 1989, there were about 12 million different products in the economy, and balanced plans could only be computed for about 200 broad product categories. To calculate balanced plans for 12 million different products, assuming all information had been stored correctly, would have taken the most modern computers over 300 billion years of computing time![4] Such is the complexity of a modern economy.

---

[3]Friedrich A. Hayek, "The Use of Knowledge in Society," *The American Economic Review* 35, no. 4 (1945): 519–530.

[4]Gérard Roland, "Complexity, Bounded Rationality, and Equilibrium: The Soviet-Type Case," *Journal of Comparative Economics* 14, no. 3 (1990): 401–424.

Taken at face value, this conclusion presents us with a very serious question: if calculating a balanced plan was too complex a task, how were economies that replaced the market system with central planning able to function in reality? Why was there not total chaos?

The Central Planning Experiment

For many decades, entire economies, such as those in the Soviet Union, Central Europe, and China, were subject to the biggest economic experiment of the 20th century: central planning. Algeria and India, among others, also introduced central planning, but never in quite as comprehensive a way as did the countries with Communist regimes.

The primary goal of central planning was to accelerate economic development. For decades, development economics did not include the study of centrally planned economies, which was a field of economics in itself called *comparative economics* or *economic systems analysis.* Now, former Soviet-bloc countries are poor or middle-income nations and there is no reason to exclude them from the study of development. If we want a clear understanding of how central planning worked, it is best to look at the Soviet Union, not China or India.

Managerial Incentives under Central Planning

Under central planning, a firm's manager did not decide from whom to buy inputs. Managers were told by the planning office where to buy their inputs and how much they were allowed to purchase. Managers also received output quotas that they were expected to fulfill, and they were told to which firms to deliver that output. We might think that managers were similar to train dispatchers receiving inputs, transforming them into outputs, and sending them on their way. But they were not that passive. It was sometimes said that managers did not have enough incentives under central planning. This, too, was inaccurate. They faced strong incentives, but ones inherent to the centrally planned economy. These incentives explain many of the negative results of central planning, in particular the inferior quality of products, which was one of the core reasons for the dismal economic performance of central planning.

The plan-fulfillment bonus system. Firm managers faced a basic task: fulfilling their production plan. Firms were assigned annual output plans that were often divided into quarterly or monthly targets. Managers were given strong incentives to meet those goals. Figure 8.1 illustrates the basic plan-fulfillment bonus scheme. If plan fulfillment was below 100%, managers would receive a flat payment, their basic salary. This salary was the same, whether plan fulfillment was 95% or 99%. However, as soon as plan fulfillment reached 100%, managers received a bonus. This is the discontinuity shown in Figure 8.1 at 100%. The bonus for plan fulfillment was the main incentive payment for managers. Above 100%, managers would receive an additional bonus for plan over-fulfillment that was proportional to the percentage of over-fulfillment, but bonuses for over-fulfillment were generally small compared to the bonus for plan fulfillment.

FIGURE 8.1   The Basic Plan-Fulfillment Bonus

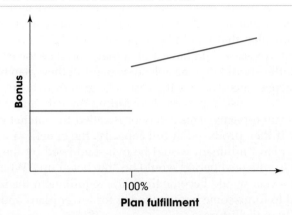

A manager's pay was flat below 100% of plan fulfillment. By fulfilling a plan, the manager would receive a large lump sum bonus with linear increases to that bonus for fulfillment above 100%.

Given this bonus scheme, the big difference for managers was the one between 100% and 100% − ϵ plan fulfillment. Managers thus had a strong incentive to make sure they exceeded the 100% plan fulfillment threshold even if this meant introducing some distortions in the quality or composition of output. This problem was called the success indicator problem.

The success indicator problem. The output plans that managers had to fulfill were expressed in some unit of measure, indicating either volume or value of output. Output volume could be expressed in various kinds of units. For example, electricity output plans were in terms of kw/hour. Electricity is one of the most homogeneous goods and it is impossible to manipulate its quality. However, this is not the case for most other products. For example, steel output was planned in tons and managers, for the sake of plan fulfillment, tended to produce steel that was too heavy. Different measures of output each led to different quality distortions. For example, the production of Soviet glass was initially planned in tons and, not surprisingly, the glass tended to be too heavy. In this case, planners decided that tons were not the right measurement unit and decided to plan glass output in square meters. Managers responded: suddenly glass became too light and frequently broke.

The success indicator problem is a universal economic problem. It occurs whenever a success indicator is an imperfect measure of performance, which is nearly always the case. If, as a condition for a loan, the IMF (International Monetary Fund) requires a country to bring its inflation level or budget deficit below a certain percentage, then that country's government is likely to make distortionary decisions to fulfill that requirement. For example, price controls on a select number of goods will artificially depress the inflation rate without solving the underlying problem of excess demand. Cuts in infrastructure investment will keep the deficit down while jeopardizing future economic growth. Businesses and bureaucracies in all economic systems, including in market economies, offer many other examples of the success indicator problem.

The ratchet effect. Although the output plans received by centrally planned firms were not balanced, they were rarely over-fulfilled by a large margin. Given unbalanced plans, we should expect some enterprises would have an overly ambitious plan that would be impossible to fulfill, but we should also expect other enterprises would have a plan that would be too easy to fulfill. In principle, the latter should then be able to over-fulfill their plan by a large margin. But in practice, this was not the case. Margins of over-fulfillment rarely exceeded 2 or 3% because managers were hiding capacity and deliberately did not produce at full capacity. This behavior is called the **ratchet effect**. Managers feared that if they produced at full capacity, the benefit of a higher bonus for, say, 120% plan fulfillment would be overshadowed by the disadvantage that their plan for the next period would be "ratcheted up." What was 120% of the plan for this year would become the 100% requirement the following year. They preferred to forgo some bonuses today for lower plans and the benefit of slack in capacity in the future.

The ratchet effect exists beyond the socialist economy and central planning, and is a frequent phenomenon within organizations in general. Highly skilled secretaries try not to work at full capacity for fear of being given even more work. Similarly, divisions in firms or in government bureaucracies feverishly spend their budgets at the end of the year to make sure that next year's budget will not be cut.

Illustrating the Ratchet Effect

Table 8.1 illustrates the ratchet effect as a general incentive phenomenon within organizations.

Assume two workers, with one more productive than the other. We will call the more-productive worker the "high type" and the less-productive worker the "low type." With low effort, the low type can produce 90, but with high effort he can produce 100. The high type can produce 100 with low effort and 110 with high effort. If the employer knows the workers' types, she will compensate them for their effort, which, for both types, is assumed to be 0 for low effort and 5 for high effort. Assume now that there is asymmetric information and that the employer can make the payment conditional only on the output level but not on the type. In that case, paying 5 for an output of 100 will compensate the low type for his effort but give the high type a rent of 5 (a payment of 5 minus an effort cost of 0). It will no longer be possible to pay 5 for an output of 110 because the net benefit to the high type will be 0. The high type is better off exerting low effort. To give an incentive to the high type to produce 110, the manager must provide a rent of at least 5. Because the cost of effort is 5, the payment

TABLE 8.1 The Ratchet Effect

	110	100	90
Effort of high type	5	0	—
Effort of low type	—	5	0

The high type can produce 100 with no effort and 110 with an effort of 5, whereas the low type can produce 90 with no effort and 100 with an effort of 5.

must then equal 10. It is, however, still optimal for the employer to pay 10 for an output of 110 because the net benefit to the employer is 110 − 10 = 100, whereas for an output of 100, the net benefit is 100 − 5 = 95. This is a general result from the theory of incentives and contracts using asymmetric information: the more productive worker must be given a rent to have an incentive to perform optimally.

What is the link with the ratchet effect? Assume again that a payment of 10 is offered for a production of 110 and a payment of 5 for a production of 100. However, assume now that production is repeated during two periods. In this case, the one-period incentive scheme will not work as planned. If the high type produces 110 in period 1 and receives a payment of 10 (thus with a rent of 5), the employer will have found out the workers' types. In that case, there is no longer asymmetric information, and in period 2 the employer can propose an incentive scheme based on information about the workers' types. In other words, the high type will receive 5 for 110 and 0 for 100, whereas the low type will receive 5 for 100 and 0 for 90. The high type will end up with total rents of 5 over the two periods. It is therefore in the interest of

the high type to "hide" in the first period and to produce 100 instead of 110. In that case, both the high and the low types will have produced 100 and have received a payment of 5, and the high type will still have a rent of 5. Moreover, because the high type only produced 100 instead of 110, his type has not been revealed. Asymmetric information has been maintained and the high type can earn rents in the future. Because the manager has not learned the workers' types, she will still have to use an incentive scheme based on output; that is, the same as the one-period incentive scheme described above (a payment of 10 for 110, of 5 for 100, and 0 for 90). The high type will thus be able to earn a rent of 5 in period 2 by producing 110 and receiving 10. It is in the interest of the high type not to produce at full capacity in the first period so as to be able to hide his type and continue earning rents in the second period. This is the ratchet effect. As a result, the only way to provide an incentive to the high type to produce 110 in period 1 is to give him as many rents as he would get if he hides, that is, a total of 10. In other words, the employer would have to pay 15 to induce the high type to produce 110 in the first period.

The ratchet effect is an incentive problem that appears 1) when a principal (here, the employer) and an agent (here, the worker) are in a repeated relationship; 2) when there is asymmetric information about how productive the agent can be; and 3) when the principal cannot commit to a preestablished incentive scheme. In this case, the principal cannot commit not to exploit the information learned after the first period about the agent's type. This absence of commitment is not good because it induces the worker to hide capacity.

The soft-budget constraint. Another important incentive problem in a centrally planned economy is that of the **soft-budget constraint**. This is a term that Janos Kornai coined in his theory of the socialist system.[5] Firms in socialist

---

[5]János Kornai, *Economics of Shortage* (Amsterdam: North-Holland Publishing Company, 1980). For the most comprehensive examination of the socialist system, see János Kornai, *The Socialist System* (Oxford: Oxford University Press, 1992).

economies had soft-budget constraints in the sense that if they incurred losses, they never feared the government would close them down. The general expectation was that in case of financial distress, the government would bail out these firms. Because a firm's main goal was to fulfill its production plan, this often came at the expense of financial discipline. Cost overruns were frequently the flipside of managerial efforts to fulfill the plan.

Soft-budget constraints were, however, not limited to socialist firms. They have been observed universally, not only in state-owned enterprises worldwide, but also in large firms and in the financial sector. The U.S. government bailed out Chrysler in the early 1980s as well as a number of banks during the savings and loans scandal. The East Asian crisis revealed widespread soft-budget constraints in the banking sector of many economies as well as in many large enterprises and conglomerates in the region. During the Great Recession in 2008, large U.S. banks received huge bailouts to prevent them from closing down. In the U.S. automobile industry, the federal government bailed out GM and Chrysler during the same period. In the European sovereign debt crisis that followed the Great Recession, the European Union bailed out Greece and Spain. Such episodes of large bailouts are likely to reoccur in the future.

To understand the soft-budget constraint problem, assume a contractor receives a budget of 100 to construct a new apartment building. After a certain point, the contractor has spent that initial budget of 100, but the building is only half-finished. The market value of the unfinished building is very low, and no apartments are available to rent. The contractor asks for an additional 50 to finish the project and agrees to be closely monitored until he has completed the construction. It is estimated that the finished building will have a return of 120. What does the investor do: terminate the project or agree to refinance?

In both cases, this project will incur a loss. If the investor terminates it, 100 will have been lost. If he agrees to refinance it, the total costs will be 150 and the return will only be 120. However, the losses end up being smaller if the project is refinanced. Once a decision has to be made on termination or refinancing, the initial 100 will have already been lost. It is a sunk cost; the investor cannot go back and recover the 100. The only question that remains is whether it is better to refinance or to terminate. If the investor refinances the project, he incurs an outlay of 50 but realizes a return of 120. The net return from refinancing is thus $120 - 50 = 70$. On the other hand, the net return from termination is 0. It is thus better to refinance than to terminate. The investor bails out the project. Once the initial 100 is sunk, refinancing is a better option than termination. This is at the heart of the soft-budget constraint problem. It can make economic sense to bail out a project once it has begun even if it ultimately incurs a loss. It may appear preferable not to have started the project in the first place, but the investor did not know that the project would end up being unprofitable. The project might have become profitable if the investor could have refused to refinance; perhaps the contractor knew that it would be in the investor's interest to refinance. This might have led him to be inefficient and to incur cost overruns. Perhaps he would have been more careful with costs if he had known that the project would be terminated automatically in case of overruns. We can see that soft-budget constraints occur when an agent expects to be bailed out in case of losses and adapts his behavior accordingly, possibly by being less watchful of costs or by choosing a riskier project.

Similar to the ratchet effect, the soft-budget constraint is an incentive problem that arises from a commitment problem. The investor would like to be able to commit to not refinancing the project because that would lead the contractor to remain within the specified budget. But if the investor cannot do so, he will prefer to refinance once cost overruns occur.

The reasons to bail out a project might be numerous. They might be financial, as in the example above, or they might also be political. If a municipal authority builds a bridge that ends up costing much more than expected, it might prefer to finish the bridge in order to cover up its mistake. While the costs of a bridge can be determined, the economic benefits cannot. Voters might thus be unhappy to see that their tax money has financed an unfinished bridge rather than a costly completed structure. There are other political reasons for possible bailouts. The government might bail out a large enterprise to prevent massive layoffs that would also adversely impact politicians seeking reelection. In all cases, however, a commitment problem lies at the heart of the soft-budget constraint.

Soft-budget constraints are a recurring economic problem. They are more frequent in state-owned enterprises but can occur in large enterprises in sectors where little economic competition exists. This is a reason why they were more frequent in socialist economies and why they were a big problem during the transition from socialism to capitalism. They are, nevertheless, a general problem and, to various degrees, plagued large state-owned enterprises in developing economies.

Central Planning and Shortage

The consequence of the managerial incentives in the centrally planned economy was **shortage** a situation in which demand exceeds supply. We will now examine how this situation relates to managerial incentives and their outcomes.

Mismatch between demand and supply. First, note that in order to fulfill output plans, managerial incentives distorted the output mix, which led to a mismatch between supply and demand. Production decisions were geared toward satisfying a plan's targets at the expense of satisfying clients' demand. This mismatch took various forms.

Poor-quality products were the first and principal form of mismatch, as a higher quantity of output to satisfy the plan usually came at the expense of quality. Products of inferior quality were infamous in centrally planned economies. Cars were unreliable and often broke down, televisions imploded, furniture broke, fabrics tore, and so on. Poor quality did not only affect consumer goods but also raw materials, investment goods, such as machines and buildings, and industrial products in general. Poor quality was not only detrimental to consumer welfare and confidence, it was also detrimental to industrial innovation; for example, new machines that were made from inferior components adversely affected productivity. There were only a few exceptions to the generally substandard quality of products and these were mostly in military and space programs where the state was the direct consumer and closely monitored quality.

A limited assortment of products was another form of output mismatch. For example, a wide range of screw widths was a rarity; narrow screws were often difficult to find and firms adapted the screws they received to fit their needs. Inadequate assortment was not related to bad quality, but it nevertheless resulted in inefficiency and dissatisfaction on the demand side. These different forms of mismatch were a source of waste and inefficiency. It should have been possible, at little cost, to provide a more complete assortment of products and thereby substantially increase consumer satisfaction.

Shortage was cumulative, overproduction was not. Shortage was a major consequence of the mismatch between supply and demand. However, we might think that output mismatch would also create an excess supply of many goods, in particular all those products that were unsold or of poor quality. This was, however, not the case. Excess demand was much more frequent than excess supply. Overproduction occurred for some categories of consumer goods, and unwanted consumer goods remained unsold on the shelves. However, in the industrial sector, excess supply was nowhere to be seen. In fact, it was never the case that an enterprise could not sell its goods. Why?

In the central planning system, shortage was cumulative, whereas overproduction was not. If an enterprise fulfilled only 90% of its planned output, it was not able to deliver all its planned supplies to the downstream enterprises. These firms would then be in a difficult position, unable to fulfill their delivery plans. Shortage at one point of the industrial chain would flow downstream to the rest of the economy. On the other hand, if an enterprise over-fulfilled its production plan, it would never have difficulty selling the excess production. Downstream enterprises would, as a rule, be happy to buy extra supplies for at least two reasons. First, this would allow them to over-fulfill their own production plan or give them some slack. Second, buying extra supplies would satisfy a hoarding motive. Due to the widespread occurrence of shortages, enterprises were happy to hoard supplies because they expected future shortages. Soft-budget constraints ensured that purchasing additional supplies would never be an issue.

The cumulative character of shortage stands in stark contrast to the market economy, where excess supply is cumulative. If a firm cannot sell its output, it will reduce its demand on the upstream side leading other enterprises to face a demand shortfall, which results in further upstream cuts in demand. Excess supply thus tends to spread in the economy. It is rarely a problem in the market economy, as any excess demand is absorbed by price increases, which will quickly reduce demand.

The theory of shortage explained above is based on distortions on the supply side that are related to managerial incentives under the central-planning system. Another explanation for the widespread presence of shortage in the socialist economy is Kornai's theory of the soft-budget constraint, which is based on demand behavior. The idea is that enterprises with soft-budget constraints will have a higher demand level than enterprises with hard-budget constraints. In the absence of hard-budget constraints, enterprises will not be financially constrained when determining their demand. For the same reason, demand will be less sensitive to price variations. As production and supply are limited, soft-budget constraints naturally lead to excess demand.

Both explanations of shortage, the supply side (output distortions) and the demand side (soft-budget constraints), can be seen as complementary. In any case, shortage was pervasive in the centrally planned economy and can be seen as the main characteristic of the socialist economy. Its widespread presence had important effects on the behavior of economic agents.

Economic Behavior under Shortage

Shortage creates uncertainty of supply, both in terms of quantity and quality. In the centrally planned economy, firm managers were never sure whether they would receive their planned supplies and they were also never sure about the quality of those deliveries because of the distorted managerial incentives of upstream firms.

At any point in time, firms could experience both excess supply and shortage. Some inputs were available in excess relative to what was needed to fulfill the plan, but other necessary inputs were short. To managers, only the "shortage" goods were of value because more of those goods could help increase production and fulfill the production plan. This was not the case for the excess inputs. Dealing with shortages was a critical challenge for managers, both on a day-to-day basis and over the long term. Firms had to adjust to short-, medium-, and long-term shortages. In the short term, a firm's plan is assumed to be a given. In the medium term, the plan of the enterprise can vary, but the capacity of the firm is a given. In the long term, the capacity can vary. We will now examine these different adjustments.

Short-term adjustment to shortage. In the short term, firms had several ways of adjusting to shortages. The first was **forced substitution**. A firm would substitute shortage goods for excess but available inputs. If light steel was not available, heavy steel would be used. If short screws were not available, long screws would be used. It was part of the day-to-day life of a business to operate with all sorts of forced substitutions to keep production running. This reinforced the incentives for "statistical" plan fulfillment. Making forced substitutions caused managers to feel less anxiety and be more cynical about producing low-quality products or distorting their output mix, and that in turn made managers of downstream enterprises undertake their own forced substitutions.

The second form of short-term adjustment to shortage was the proliferation of activities to influence upstream firms in an effort to ensure priority supply in case of shortage. If the upstream firm was not able to fulfill its production and delivery plan, its downstream clients would face rationing. Each firm thus made a significant investment in developing and maintaining good relations with its suppliers to ensure that it would be treated well in case of rationing. Each firm had its professional "pushers" whose main activity was to make sure the enterprise was well-treated by its suppliers. Their role was to keep good relations with upstream firms and lobby to secure priority supply of inputs. If, for example, the upstream firm could only fulfill 90% of its plan, the downstream firms all tried to make sure that they would still be receiving their planned supplies or that they would receive at least 90% of their allotment. These influence activities were, of course, a zero-sum game; any additional supplies that would go to one firm would mean fewer supplies for another firm. The influence activities were wasteful in terms of the time invested, but individual firms still had an incentive to engage in them. If one of them neglected relations with its upstream suppliers, it would risk falling to the end of the rationing queue. This courting of suppliers contrasts with the activity of firms in market economies, where efforts focus instead on downstream activity to ensure sales, but it is not surprising; excess demand was the main form of disequilibrium in the centrally planned economy, whereas excess supply is the main form of disequilibrium in the market economy.

The third form of short-term adjustment to shortage was barter and the use of gray markets. Under socialism, market exchanges between state-owned enterprises were outlawed. All sales and purchases had to go through the planning system. Nevertheless, firm managers often undertook these prohibited market transactions in order to deal with shortages. Barter was quite common; companies sought to exchange inputs that were in excess supply for goods that were in short supply. Regardless of official prohibitions on barter, the central planners generally tolerated it. As is always the case, barter requires a "double coincidence of wants": each of the traders must want to acquire what the other is offering. Managers also resorted to illegal purchases of inputs on the "gray market," which were called **gray-market transactions** because their purpose was to help fulfill the plan even though they were illegal, and firms had slush funds that they used for these transactions.

Black-market transactions, in contrast, were illegal transactions for the purpose of private profit and they withdrew resources from the planned economy. All socialist economies had a substantial black-market sector, the size of which was estimated at between 5% of GDP in some countries to roughly 25% in others. Depending on the extent to which managers had invested in information about activities taking place outside the sphere of the plan, the temptation to switch from gray-market to black-market activities could be quite strong. Toward the end of the Soviet system, there were thriving export markets for all sorts of products, from aluminum rejects to ancient Russian religious icons. Black-market activities were present in all spheres of the economy, and high-standing members from the *nomenklatura*, the Communist bureaucratic elite, also participated. This sowed the seeds for some of the corruption that would be prevalent in the transition process, in particular in privatization reforms.

Medium-term adjustment to shortage. This adjustment occurred over a longer period and involved changes in the firm's plan as well as actions by the planning hierarchy. The key players were the powerful sectoral ministries responsible for specific areas of the economy such as steel, coal, cars, or textiles. We saw that the plan-fulfillment bonus system encouraged enterprises to do everything they could to reach statistical plan fulfillment. However, this system had another consequence: managers were indifferent between reaching 90% and 95% plan fulfillment because in both cases they would not receive the plan-fulfillment bonus. If, for example, they were experiencing acute shortages and it became impossible to fulfill the plan, managers would become discouraged and forsake any effort to increase production. However, the economic ministers and the bureaucracy supervising the firm's activities were rewarded according to the total output of the companies under their supervision. Unlike the individual managers, they were not indifferent between 90% versus 95% plan fulfillment in one of the companies they supervised. If, for example, a firm could only reach 95% plan fulfillment with extreme effort, the ministry would lower the firm's next plan to 95% of its pre-existing plan. This would give the manager a goal that could be reached, and the plan-fulfillment bonus provided a strong-enough incentive to achieve it.

However, given that the ministry's plan was composed of the sum of all the plans of all the firms under its jurisdiction, a reduction in one plan had to be compensated by an increase in another. This is one of the reasons why the ratchet effect was quite prevalent in the socialist economy. Ministries were constantly on the lookout for excess capacity in the enterprises under their jurisdiction. To be able to manage changes in plans, ministries needed to control their firms' supplies. However, supplies were also centrally planned and as a result, ministries constantly fought to gain control over the supplies of the firms they supervised.

Because managers expected shortages to continue in the future, when the moment came to establish next year's plan, they generally tried to bargain for lower plans. They purposely underestimated their capacity and came up with all sorts of reasons why they should receive a low plan or, at the very least, why their plan should not be increased. On the other hand, the planners would generally not believe the managers and would set higher plans for their firms. This could result in mistakes; some firms received plans higher than their output capacity, while others received plans lower than what they could actually produce. However, on average there would not necessarily be systematic mistakes. Ministry officials had moved up through the ranks of the Soviet governing hierarchy and generally had reasonably accurate knowledge of the companies in their sectors, so they were not regularly deceived. Nevertheless, the absence of incentives for managers to reveal their true production capacity did lead to a mix of plans that were either too ambitious or too easy.

Another medium-term consequence of shortage, which expectations of shortage lead to, is **hoarding demand**. If a manager expects goods to be in short supply in the future, he will increase today's demands relative to a situation in which he expects no shortages.

Hoarding Demand and Shortage

Hoarding demand by itself can create shortage. Imagine a situation in which a firm needs an annual input quantity of 100. Assume that total supplies available for the year are also equal to 100. Over the course of the year, demand and supply are thus balanced. Assume now that deliveries take place 10 times a year and that holding inventories is costly: to hold one unit of inventory entails a cost c. If demand and supply are balanced, then the optimal strategy is to order a quantity of 10 units 10 times per year. The average cost of inventories will then be $5c$ (10/2 because on average, 5 units will be held). To see this, assume that there are 10 periods and one unit is used in each period. At the beginning of the first period, there are 10, and at the end of the 10th period there are none. On average, there are 5. Take the beginning of the second period and the end of the ninth period and the average will be $(9 + 1)/2$. Repeat with the beginning of the third period and the end of the eighth period and so on. The

(Continued)

result will always be 5. If, on the other hand, the firm decided to order 100 units once per year, the average cost would be 50c, which is higher. Therefore, it is generally preferable to order 10 units 10 times per year than to order 100 units once per year.

However, when there is large uncertainty of supply, if the manager orders 10 units each period, the firm is more likely to face shortages at some later period during the year. In that case, the production shortfall may be irreversible. On the other hand, by ordering more than 10 each period, the manager attempts to ensure against future shortages. Building a security buffer, in case of future shortages, can avoid a production shortfall. However, this hoarding demand increases demand and can actually create shortages. The expectation of shortages will then be self-fulfilling. Hoarding demand will then be repeated period after period.

The example given in the box shows that the hoarding motive not only reinforces existing shortages and shortage expectations, but it can even rapidly create shortages. The existence of soft-budget constraints reduces the cost of hoarding because the firm's manager will not fear the extra costs. Therefore, when there are shortages, the benefits of hoarding necessarily outweigh its costs. Shortages thus lead to hoarding demand, which can itself aggravate shortage.

Long-term adjustment to shortage. In the long term, shortage had consequences on a firm's investment demand. A first consequence was a tendency toward vertical integration. Companies tried to reduce the uncertainty of supplies by producing the supplies they needed and managers tried to obtain investment allocation approval for that purpose. Some large firms had whole units with workshops that produced supplies, spare parts, and other inputs. As a rule, productivity was lower and costs higher than if these inputs had been produced by the relevant specialized suppliers. However, if firms had soft-budget constraints, reducing the uncertainty of supply was quite valuable because it helped mitigate the uncertainty of plan fulfillment, and thus the uncertainty of plan-fulfillment bonuses. In addition, because it was in their interest to reduce the uncertainty of supply, ministries helped their firms achieve this goal of vertical integration.

Firms were also trying to increase the size of their production capacity. Being at the head of a larger firm did not only deliver higher social status, but it also helped when faced with rationing. Smaller firms generally had lower rationing priority.

Also related to long-term adjustment to shortages was the fact that investment was mostly for expansion rather than for modernization. In other words, investment was primarily targeted at increasing existing capacity rather than at increasing productivity. There are two reasons for this. First is the ratchet effect at the ministerial level. Ministries, like companies, also received production plans that aimed for constant growth. Therefore, shutting down existing facilities to modernize them was a risky proposition. Investment duration was uncertain because of shortage and a modernization investment risked temporarily reducing current output, which could jeopardize the annual plan. Ministers would be blamed for output shortfalls even if they had a good excuse. As a result, they preferred to use investment to increase total capacity rather than to modernize.

A second reason for the bias toward investment for expansion rather than modernization is that the latter increased the volatility of production, an arithmetic effect of increased productivity. Call x the output level, call r the level of inputs received, and call a the number of inputs necessary to produce one unit of output. The productivity is then $1/a$, that is, the quantity of output that can be produced per unit of input. We thus have $x = \dfrac{1}{a} r$. We then see that the variance of output is $\text{var}(x) = \dfrac{1}{a^2} \text{var}(r)$. An increase in productivity, that is, an increase in $1/a$, will lead to an increase in the variance of output. Intuitively, if productivity is higher, the availability of one more unit of input will lead to an increased level of output, but the availability of one less unit of input will lead to a higher decrease in output. This would be fine if the firm's plan would not be increased because a modernization investment increases its capacity (for a given level of output). However, this would not be the case. Modernization investment would lead to a corresponding increase in the firm's output plan. The only effect of modernization for the manager would be higher output volatility and thus a higher risk of not fulfilling the plan. Incentives to modernize were therefore absent at the plant level and any modernization investment had to be initiated from the ministry level. This lack of incentives to modernize was a significant drawback of central planning.

Finally, just as input demand was bloated because of the hoarding motive, shortage and soft-budget constraints led to a strong demand for investment. This hunger for investment, whether for expansion motives or for vertical integration motives, was nearly insatiable. Demands for new investment projects tended to underestimate the costs in order to try to obtain approval from the higher authorities. The central planning officials knew this and tended to revise estimates of investment costs upward. Nevertheless, because of this lack of transparency, mistakes happened and many investment projects turned out to be more costly than anticipated, even when correcting for underestimated costs. As a result, excess investment demand often led to a diversion of resources from other sectors, in particular from the consumer goods sector. Because resources were limited, excess investment demand tended to increase shortages in the whole economy.

These shortages led to an investment cycle in the planned economy: as increased signals of shortage arrived at the central planning offices, planners would decide to cut down on future investment projects and to complete those that were still unfinished first. Cuts in investment tended to alleviate shortages. However, central planners subsequently eased their vigilance and began to approve more investment projects, which, in turn, led to new increases in shortage levels until investment was cut again, and so on. This investment cycle was paradoxical in the socialist economy. Planning was supposed to eliminate the business cycle inherent to the market economy. Nevertheless, the centrally planned system could not avoid investment cycles although they did not have a very large amplitude compared to the business cycles in market economies.

Worker Behavior

Just as managers tried to hoard inputs in expectation of future shortages, they also tried to hoard labor. This was a direct consequence of shortage. Hoarding labor was useful because of the irregular rhythm of production; at the beginning of the month it was calmer, but it became quite hectic at the end of the month when firms had to achieve their monthly plan targets. Suppose that three-quarters of monthly production was done in the second half of the month. Therefore, compared to regular production, the need for labor was $0.75/.5 = 1.5$, that is, 150% or 50% more than the amount of labor that would be needed under a regular production rhythm. As a result, at the end of the month, demand for labor was strong and there was a shortage of labor as well as for inputs.

A seller's market for workers. Labor shortages had various consequences for both workers and businesses. They gave workers, in particular, a strong bargaining power. Markets with excess demand are sometimes called **sellers' markets** because sellers have all the bargaining power. Buyers have to beg sellers to serve them, knowing that they are competing with other buyers. For example, going to the butcher was an ordeal under socialism. Not only were there shortages for all kinds of meat, but the shop clerks also treated the customers badly. As consumers forced to participate in sellers' markets, the citizens of socialist economies were miserable, but they knew better than to complain. However, as workers they were on the good side of the market because companies were always competing for scarce labor. Unemployment was not a concern. Being fired was not a disaster because a worker could easily find another job elsewhere. Because of labor shortages, managers were also reluctant to fire their workers. One myth about the socialist economy is that unemployment was "hidden" and that firms were forced to hire excess labor so that the Communist leaders could advertise to the world that the fear of unemployment, typical for capitalist economies, was absent in the Soviet utopia. In reality, firms were not forced to hire labor. Their demand for labor was high because of the demands of plan fulfillment and because of soft-budget constraints. There were shortages in labor markets just as there were in most other markets. Worker mobility was generally voluntary; for every worker who was fired, two left their jobs voluntarily in search of others.

One of the consequences of labor shortages and the strong bargaining power of workers was minimal labor discipline. Absenteeism was quite high; management was not concerned about workers taking sick leave as long as they showed up at critical moments when it was time to fulfill the monthly production plan. It was better to have a worker on the payroll, even a lazy one, as long as that worker contributed to the plan fulfillment. Management also tried to prevent workers from leaving the firm. Although they could not increase workers' wages, which were set by central planning, managers found all sorts of schemes to attract and keep workers. They offered benefits in kind such as daycare centers, vacations, and better apartments. Shops were set up inside firms so that workers could buy food before leaving for home. Managers made sure that their shops were better supplied than the regular establishments consumers patronized, which was a big advantage for the workers.

Managers also used fake promotions as a way to increase workers' salaries. Secretaries were registered on the payroll as middle managers, and regular workers were registered as skilled engineers. Higher wages, however, had negative economic externalities. Assume a given supply of consumer goods. Higher wages given to some workers would result in increased demand for those goods and would increase shortages. Higher shortages tend to dull worker incentives and result in a reduction in their productivity, which then would lead to a lower supply of goods and, in turn increases in shortages. This is called the **supply multiplier**. One way of expressing this vicious circle was the motto of workers under socialism: "They pretend to pay us and we pretend to work."

Centralized wage setting. Because wage increases could adversely affect shortages and production, the central planners always maintained their wage-setting authority. Centralized wage setting was a crucial institution of socialism. Reforms—such as those in Yugoslavia in 1965, Hungary in 1968, Poland in 1980, and the Soviet Union in 1987—were introduced with the objective of giving firms more autonomy to set their workers' wages. A form of wage inflation quickly followed. Because there was a shortage of labor and firms had soft-budget constraints, they used their increased autonomy to compete for labor by bidding up wages. This wage inflation had different effects in different countries. In the Soviet Union, for example, where prices were fixed, the result was increased shortages, which, by the supply multiplier, led to lower output. In Yugoslavia and Poland, where firms also had some autonomy in setting price levels, the result was price inflation, which tended to increase yearly as inflation expectations continued to accelerate.

Egalitarian wage drift. Although central planners viewed wage inequality as healthy for incentives, socialism ultimately produced the unintended consequence of wage equality. The trend toward equal wages is related to the "paradox of the laziest worker." Labor discipline was low and managers tolerated it as long as all workers participated in the necessary extra efforts to fulfill the monthly production plan. The laziest workers with the lowest discipline were brought in at the last moment. However—and this is the paradox—the laziest workers also had the largest marginal labor product, as the marginal product of those workers made all the difference for plan fulfillment. Large bonuses for managers depended on that difference and managers were ready to entice those lazy workers by offering them the maximum salary possible. In contrast, engineers and other dependable, skilled workers whose constant presence was critical for the plants' long-term functioning showed up for work every day. The most skilled labor was used first, and lazy workers were only used toward the end.

Under classical socialism, firm managers had no autonomy over wages. However, the demands for short-term plan fulfillment led to pressures to revise the centralized wage schedules toward greater equality of actual official wages, across all skill levels. Under Stalin, wage schedules were quite unequal, a situation that tended to decrease progressively under subsequent regimes. Toward the end of socialism, groups of illegal workers (working outside the plan) in the Soviet Union, called *shabashniki*, would offer their services to various enterprises that were experiencing labor shortages, as a means to guarantee the fulfillment of production quotas. The market wages these workers received were two to three times higher than officially set wages. This illustrates the importance of plan fulfillment and the resulting marginal-quality products that made the difference between plan fulfillment and nonfulfillment. It also illustrates the short-term focus that characterized firm management under socialism: wages of marginal workers were more important to managers than those of engineers who could improve overall productivity.

Ineffective labor-discipline campaigns. In the Soviet Union and other centrally planned economies, there were several attempts to introduce labor discipline from above. For example, in the 1930s, Stalin introduced drastic laws stipulating that the third time a worker showed up late for work, he or she would be sent to a Siberian labor camp. These laws were very unpopular, not only with workers but also with managers who did not want to lose their workers, even the less disciplined ones. As a result, managers made sure the laws were not enforced by not reporting worker absenteeism. In 1983, then-general secretary Yuri Andropov launched an important campaign to reinstate labor discipline. During working hours, police checked the identification papers of workers coming out of movie theaters and shops to see if they were supposed to be at work. However, the effects of this campaign were short-lived: workers realized that it was impossible to place policemen at each street corner and expected correctly this kind of campaign to be short-lived. Managers continued to tolerate low labor discipline because it was in their best interests not to alienate their workers.

Complexity, Coordination, and the Slow Demise of Central Planning

In an economy without free markets and where it was impossible to compute balanced plans except at the most aggregate level, why was there not absolute chaos? Why were managers able to fulfill plans year after year and why did production keep growing, albeit at a slower pace each decade?

Planning from the achieved level. A primary reason for the balance between supply and demand for the millions of goods in a centrally planned economy is called **planning from the achieved level**. Firms' fulfillment plans were usually computed by taking the previous year's output as the initial level of production and then adding some growth rate to it. The idea was that what a firm could produce last year it could presumably still produce this year unless the overall economy had lost capacity. There was no guarantee that the assigned growth rates could be achieved, but this is where all the improvisation, shortage management, and output distortions could play a role. This is another paradox of central planning. Ideally, central planning was supposed to have a significant advantage over the market system because it should have been able to accommodate large structural shifts in the economy that would present difficulties for the market system, which was capable only of smoother and more gradual shifts. However, because it was impossible to compute balanced plans, the centrally planned economy experienced significant inertia and had a hard time making those large structural shifts. This became even clearer as the economy became more complex and managing shortage became ever more difficult.

The role of sectoral ministries. A second form of supply and demand adjustment was that made by the large sectoral ministries. As we have discussed, the ministries tended to revise the fulfillment plans of their firms in response to shortage signals. Because the ministries managed the production of homogeneous types of products, many of these products were close substitutes. It was easier to substitute one form of steel for another than to substitute steel for glass. Ministries made adjustments within the firms under their jurisdiction with the objective of fulfilling the aggregate ministerial fulfillment plan. They thus tended to make substitutions that would further a higher overall output level. This was the case, for example, when a ministry would lower the plan of a low-productivity firm to raise the plan of a high-producing enterprise. Because the sectoral ministries were seen as the backbone of central planning, their day-to-day management of shortages and operating substitutions as a means to fulfill their own ministerial plans played a key function in stabilizing the economy.

Parallel activities. A third form of supply and demand adjustment was via the parallel activities of the gray market. These parallel activities tended to increase over time and were quite well developed in economies such as Hungary, Poland, and Yugoslavia, which had undergone some reforms in the direction of a market economy. A semiprivate sector developed and operated illegally in those countries, but was largely tolerated by the Communist authorities.

Quality adjustment. A fourth form of supply and demand adjustment occurred in the quality of products. Managers typically chose to lower the quality of their products to meet their targets, but there were drawbacks to this approach. If a mild deterioration in quality meant an increase in the quantity produced, then lower quality would help alleviate shortages. If, however, quality was already so bad that an additional decrease would make products useless, increased shortages would be the result.

These forms of supply and demand adjustment can explain why there was no economic chaos and why plans were fulfilled yearly. They also explain some of the chronic deficiencies of central planning such as inferior quality, shortages, and the short time horizon of firms. As the socialist economy grew more complex, central planning became increasingly less able to manage it. Planning became more rigid, innovation more difficult to initiate from above, and the consequences of poor product quality became more detrimental. As we can see in Table 8.2, the growth of the Soviet economy, which had been impressive in its first decades, experienced a continuing decline. It is doubtful whether the economy was still actually growing in the 1980s, the last decade of central planning.

The centrally planned economy probably could have survived for several more decades, but increasing frustration and dissatisfaction with the system, even among its leaders, reached a tipping point. In 1985, when Mikhail Gorbachev was selected as general secretary of the Soviet Union, he initiated a number of reforms that would destabilize the Soviet political and economic systems and ultimately lead to the collapse of the Berlin Wall and to the implosion of the Communist-bloc regimes, events that no one would have predicted even a few years before. This heralded the transition from socialism to capitalism. Presently, only Cuba and North Korea have kept the old socialist economic and political systems.

TABLE 8.2   Comparative Average Growth Rates (%) of the Soviet Union and the USA

	USA			USSR
1929–1950	2.5	1928–1940	5.4
1950–1960	3.3	1950–1960	6.0
1970–1984	3.0	1970–1980	3.7
		1980–1984	2.0

In its first decades, the Soviet economy had higher growth rates than the U.S. economy, but they declined substantially in later decades.

Source: Paul R. Gregory and Robert C. Stuart, *Russian and Soviet Economic Performance and Structure* (Boston: Prentice Hall, 2001).

Prices versus Quantities

Even though the centrally planned economy failed as a viable system, many areas of economic activity are still coordinated inside large organizations, under a form of central planning. While market coordination happens as a result of **price signals**, coordination within hierarchies happens mainly through **quantity signals**. Understanding when it is more advantageous to use price or quantity coordination is especially important in the context of developing economies. When is market coordination better and when is quantity coordination better?

Coordination Mistakes Using Price and Quantity Signals

Economist Martin Weitzman, in a famous article entitled "Prices versus Quantities," studied the tradeoffs between coordinating economic activity using price versus quantity signals.[6] Figure 8.2 illustrates these tradeoffs. To aid in the analysis, first assume we are dealing with an environmental problem, for example, the degree of water pollution in a large urban area such as Mexico City. In this case, the quantity axis, which is the horizontal axis in Figure 8.2, represents the degree of water purity. A higher level of q on the horizontal axis means cleaner water.

Now assume a situation with perfect coordination, in which there is no uncertainty and all information processed by various economic agents is correct. The optimal decision is to equate the marginal benefit and the marginal cost of cleaning the water. We assume that the marginal benefit MB decreases as the water becomes cleaner (if the water is very pure, increasing that purity does not add much utility to consumers) and that the marginal cost MC increases with the degree of purity. In other words, if the water is already very clean, it is more costly to make it cleaner than if it were quite polluted. These assumptions are standard in the economic analysis of such problems.

---

[6]Martin L. Weitzman, "Prices versus Quantities," *The Review of Economic Studies* 41, no. 4 (1974): 477–491.

FIGURE 8.2   Coordination through Prices versus Quantity Signals

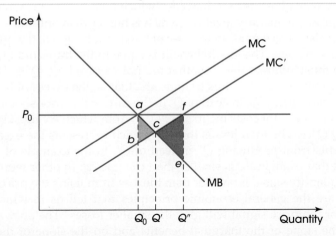

If the marginal benefit schedule is estimated at MB and the marginal cost schedule is estimated at MC, the optimal quantity is Q_0 and the optimal price is P_0 at point a. If the true marginal cost is, however, at MC', the optimum should be at point c, but point a will be chosen instead using quantity coordination and point f using price coordination. Using quantity coordination, the welfare loss is therefore triangle acb and using price coordination, the welfare loss is equal to triangle cef.

The optimum is then Q_0 where marginal benefit and marginal cost are equal. This is point a in Figure 8.2. As long as the marginal benefit is higher than the marginal cost, there is a gain from further purifying the water. Beyond that point, it makes no sense to continue to clean the water if the marginal benefit from doing so is smaller than the marginal cost to society.

The two coordination mechanisms at work. How do the different coordination mechanisms work? If quantity signals are used to coordinate, then quantity target Q_0 will be given by the city government to the organization or agency in charge of purifying the water. On the other hand, if price signals are used, the planner working for the city government will compute the price corresponding to the optimum, which is price P_0. The agency in charge of cleaning the water will then be given the price P_0 per unit of clean water and it will then maximize profits. This means that it will equate its marginal cost to price P_0. As we see from Figure 8.2, coordination through quantity signals and through price signals will yield the same result if perfect information exists about both marginal costs and marginal benefits.

Results are, however, different once we allow for mistakes. Suppose that the true marginal cost schedule is not MC but instead MC' in Figure 8.2. The firm knows its costs and thus has an advantage over the planner in that it can always adjust the quantity it produces to equate the price it is given to its real cost schedule. The optimum should now be point c and quantity Q' where the true marginal cost schedule MC' crosses the marginal benefit schedule MB. Because the planner is mistaken about the true marginal cost schedule, he will make mistakes either when coordinating by the quantity signal or by the price signal. In the former case, he will order the agency to produce Q_0 instead of Q'. In the latter case, he will communicate to the agency price P_0, which is no longer appropriate and is in fact higher than what the optimal price should be. The agency will adjust its marginal cost (which it knows) to the wrong price. It will then produce quantity level Q'', which is higher than optimal.

Which mistake is worse? In the case of the quantity signal, the quantity produced is insufficient. The loss in benefit is equal to the trapezoid $Q_0 Q'ac$ from which we must subtract the costs that are not incurred, $Q_0 Q'bc$. The net loss from the quantity signal is thus triangle *abc*, that is, the excess of benefits over costs from producing Q_0. instead of Q' In the case of the price signal, the loss is equivalent to the extra costs incurred $Q'Q''cf$, from which we must subtract the benefits $Q'Q''ce$. The total loss is thus *cef*, which represents the excess of costs over benefits from producing Q'' instead of Q'. In the example of Figure 8.2, it appears that triangle *abc* is smaller than triangle *cef*. In other words, the loss from the quantity signal is smaller than the loss from using the price signal.

What are the general economic principles that tell us in which case the quantity or the price signal will give the smaller losses? The answer depends on both the slope of the marginal benefits and on the slope of the marginal costs. The general principle is: the steeper the marginal benefit and the flatter the marginal cost, the better coordination is using quantities; the flatter the marginal benefit and the steeper the marginal cost, the better coordination is using prices. Why is that?

If the slope of marginal costs is very steep, then making a mistake on costs will significantly increase them. Price signals are more sensitive to marginal costs and thus the mistake in costs will tend to be lower than with quantity signals. If the slope of marginal costs is relatively flat, then a mistake will not lead to much higher costs. Conversely, if the slope of marginal benefits is very steep, then getting the quantity wrong will lead to a large loss in utility. If, however, the slope of marginal benefits is relatively flat, then the utility loss of a mistake in the quantity signal will be relatively small.

Coordination by quantity signals will thus be better if it is more important to get the quantity right, which will be the case when the slope of marginal benefits is high, whereas coordination by price signals will be better if it is more important to get the costs right, which will be the case when the slope of marginal costs is high.

A case in which quantity coordination is better. Figure 8.3 illustrates a case with a steep marginal benefit and a flat marginal cost. The figure shows that the loss from using the price signal is worse than the loss from using the quantity signal. Triangle *cef* in Figure 8.3 is much larger than triangle *abc*.

If the marginal benefit schedule is very steep, then it is important that the quantity not deviate too much from the optimal marginal benefit as this would entail important utility or benefit losses. This will be achieved with coordination by quantity.

The downside to coordination by quantity is that we can be less attentive to minimizing costs. However, If the marginal cost schedule is relatively flat, making a mistake on costs is not that important because the marginal cost will not vary that much. Therefore, we do not lose that much relative to coordination by prices if the marginal cost schedule is flat.

With steep marginal benefits and flat marginal costs, coordination by quantities thus dominates coordination by prices. Consider the example of a fire brigade. If we think of quantity as measuring the speed of its arrival at a fire,

FIGURE 8.3   A Case in Which Quantity Coordination Is Better

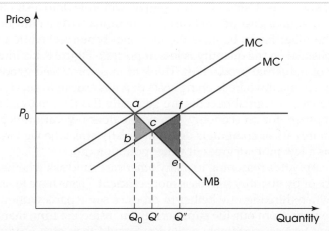

The loss using quantity coordination *acb* is smaller than the loss using price coordination *cef* with steep MB and flat MC.

it is clear that speed matters more than costs. Putting out the fire is the brigade's first order of business. If there is some waste in costs, it appears to be of secondary importance. A similar reasoning can be made with ambulances and emergency-room services. In the case of many environmental issues, the same would probably also hold. There are thresholds of pollution beyond which public health hazards become very serious. In all these cases, the costs of achieving the desired objectives seem to be of secondary importance.

A case in which price coordination is better. Figure 8.4 illustrates the opposite case of that shown in Figure 8.3, with a flat marginal benefit and a steep marginal cost. In this case, we see clearly that the loss *acb* from quantity coordination is larger than the loss *cef* from price coordination.

FIGURE 8.4   A Case in Which Price Coordination Is Better

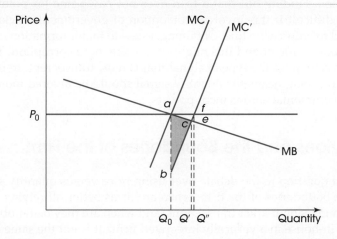

The loss using price coordination *cef* is smaller than the loss using quantity coordination *acb* with flat MB and steep MC.

In this case, because marginal costs are very steep, price signals do a better job of adjusting costs. Using quantity signals would lead to a significant error in terms of marginal cost (in this case, the marginal cost would be much too low). On the other hand, because the marginal benefit schedule is quite flat, making a mistake on the quantity is less important. Figure 8.4 is illustrative for most cases of industrial production. Think of mass-produced goods in a competitive environment where keeping costs down is crucial to surviving competition. Moreover, marginal benefits are generally flat. The marginal benefit of cars or computers for an economy as a whole does not vary much. Having a thousand more cars or computers does not greatly affect the welfare of a country, whereas a few more degrees of water pollution can.

We can apply this reasoning to many other cases and ask whether coordination by price or by quantity signals is more efficient. Firms have to answer these questions when thinking of whether to produce some parts within the firm or to purchase them from outside suppliers. Even inside the firm, managers must think of how best to coordinate activities. Should they give production units production quotas, or should they give them production autonomy and prices for their output, and ask them to adjust their production to maximize profits?

Can we identify any particular feature of developing economies that strengthens the case for price versus quantity coordination? An important issue relates to weaker governmental enforcement powers, which in turn relates to the quality of a country's institutions. Many governments in developing countries have relatively weak enforcement powers. How does that, in turn, affect the relative advantage of using price versus quantity signals?

Let us look at the example of a polluting chemical factory in China. Assume that the quantity signal is a threshold for the level of pollution and that the price signal is a fine levied above a certain level of pollution. In case there is absolutely no enforcement of either, we cannot say much because the private firm will pollute as much as it wants irrespective of the signal it receives. Suppose instead that enforcement is weak. In case of the quantity signal, we may expect that it would be easier for journalists or environmental associations to discover that the pollution threshold is ignored. Knowing that a pollution threshold exists, it might be possible to come up with independent measures of pollution. Finding out that a firm does not pay a fine for pollution might be more difficult if this involves corruption of government officials who are supposed to enforce the fine. Obtaining access to that information might therefore be more difficult and this might encourage more corruption. The general principle is to favor the type of signal that is most transparent. In this particular example, that means the quantity signal should be favored more in case of weak governmental enforcement powers.

Institutions and the Boundaries of the Firm

A related question to the debate over using price versus quantity signals concerns the boundaries of the firm: when are firms better off relying on subcontractors and using market transactions, and when are they better off producing supplies in-house in a vertically integrated firm? It is not the same question as the one we discussed on price and quantity coordination because it asks about ownership rather than about coordination. It is, however, closely related to the markets and hierarchies theme of this chapter because independent firms contract on markets, whereas vertically integrated units operate within a firm's own hierarchy. The question of the firm's boundaries is related to the hold-up question discussed in Chapter 7. It was first raised by Ronald Coase in a famous 1937 article entitled "The Nature of the Firm" and has been studied by many economists since its publication.[7]

The Trade-Off between Efficiency and Holdup

In many cases, a firm would benefit from using independent subcontractors who could specialize in specific parts. Such an arrangement could be more efficient than producing the parts within the company, possibly at a higher cost. However, for this arrangement to work, the subcontractor would have to make investments that are specific to the relationship. For example, think of a Brazilian company producing tractors and needing wheels. Instead of producing its own wheels, the manufacturer might be better off contracting with a company that specializes in producing wheels and selling them to companies that manufacture tractors as well as to firms that make trucks or cars. The company that produces the wheels would still need to make specific investments and install new machines or retool existing equipment in order to produce the larger tractor wheels. This is where the hold-up problem kicks in.

Once the wheel company has made the specific investments to produce the larger wheels, the tractor company may want to renegotiate its contract with the wheel company. To the extent that the investment was specific, because it is a sunk cost, the investment is only of value to the wheel company for producing wheels for the tractor company. The latter can try to hold up the wheel company in order to buy wheels at a lower price than initially contracted. As long as the price exceeds its marginal cost, the wheel company would agree to do so, but the price might not be high enough to allow it to recoup its investment. The wheel producer might incur a loss otherwise. Because of the hold-up problem, the tractor company may not be able to find a subcontractor that would agree to produce wheels at a lower price. Any potential subcontractors might reasonably worry that once they have made the necessary investment, they would be victims of the hold-up problem, too. If the tractor company is unable to find a wheel subcontractor, it might be forced to produce the wheels for its tractors, albeit under less efficient conditions. In other words, the tractor company would vertically integrate the production of tractors and wheels.

Less Vertical Integration with Better Institutions

Good legal institutions can mitigate the hold-up problem. With solid contracts and the possibility of using the court system, subcontractors will be more willing to invest knowing that the law protects them to a certain extent against the

---

[7]Ronald H. Coase, "The Nature of the Firm," *Economica* 4, no. 16 (1937): 386–405; see, for example, Oliver E. Williamson, *Markets and Hierarchies. Analysis and Anti-Trust Implications* (New York: Free Press, 1975); and Oliver Hart, *Firms, Contracts, and Financial Structure* (Oxford: Oxford University Press, 1995).

hold-up problem. This is also in the interest of the tractor company that can commit contractually not to hold up the subcontractor and therefore be in a position to buy wheels for its tractors at a lower price. However, the quality of legal institutions will play a crucial role here. If they are weak, then the hold-up problem is likely to be more pervasive and there will probably be more vertical integration in the economy. Everything else being equal, countries with weaker legal institutions are likely to have more vertical integration, while countries with more advanced and efficiently functioning legal institutions are likely to have less vertical integration. The quality of institutions therefore affects firms' boundaries.

Chapter Summary

The Central Planning Debate
Socialists such as Karl Marx thought that central planning could provide better economic coordination and prevent economic depressions. The big advantage of the market economy over a centrally planned economy, however, is that it does not require centralization of all the information necessary to coordinate economic activity. Such coordination is far too complex, as Hayek correctly argued 4 decades before the inferiority of central planning was recognized.

The Central Planning Experiment
Central planning was initially thought to be a good path for fast economic development and was introduced in many poor countries. However, managers responded to the incentives of plan fulfillment and not to consumer demand. These managerial incentives led to mismatches between supply and demand, creating shortages that spread through the economy. Economic agents adjusted to shortage in the short, medium, and long term. Different mechanisms made adjustments to imbalances possible despite the absence of detailed central plans. As the economy became more complex, coordination problems became more severe and inefficiencies grew.

Prices versus Quantities
Coordination by price signals refers to firms receiving price information and maximizing their profits. Coordination by quantity signals involves giving production orders. Price coordination mistakes can be huge when the marginal benefits are steep and the marginal costs are flat. Quantity coordination mistakes are significant when marginal costs are steep and marginal benefits are relatively flat.

Institutions and the Boundaries of the Firm
The economic boundaries of the firm are determined by the relative advantages of coordination inside the firm compared to market transactions with outside suppliers. Vertical integration reduces the hold-up problem but at the cost of lower efficiency. Weak institutions provide an advantage to coordination within the firm and thus to stronger vertical integration.

Key Terms

black-market transactions
forced substitution
gray-market transactions
hoarding demand
planning from the achieved level
price signals

quantity signals
ratchet effect
sellers' markets
shortage
soft-budget constraint
supply multiplier

Review Questions

1. Central planning failed because managers did not have enough incentives. Discuss.

2. Why was there no unemployment under central planning?

3. Many multinational firms are larger than former centrally planned economies. Nevertheless, they manage to be efficient and produce high-quality goods, whereas centrally planned economies failed to do so. How do you explain these differences?

4. Imagine that the whole world had lived under central planning. Do you think central planning would have lasted longer than it did? Discuss.

5. Use the Internet to find data for GDP in North Korea and South Korea, going back as far as possible. Look at the trends and interpret them in terms of the comparison between central planning and the market economy. Carefully document your sources.

6. The Cuban socialist economy was once praised for its advanced education and health care systems. However, it relied heavily on Soviet subsidies that ended in 1991. Do some research and find what effects the termination of these subsidies had on the Cuban economy. How did the Cuban authorities react to this loss of subsidies?

7. Download the following article that advocates a socialist economic system: http://socialistworker.org/2006-1/573/573_12_Planning.shtml. Based on the discussions in this chapter, what fallacies can you identify in this article? Explain.

8. If there were no coordination mistakes, coordination by quantities would be superior. Do you agree? Discuss.

9. What effect should institutions have on vertical integration? What does this mean in the context of developing countries?

10. Assume that the estimated marginal cost of a technology to purify water has the following form: $MC = 2 + 2q$. Assume that the estimated marginal benefit of 1 degree of cleaner water takes the following form: $MB = 14 - 2q$. Calculate the optimal number of units of cleaner water for a population. Calculate the optimal price to be paid for one degree of cleaner water. Assume that the true marginal cost is $8 + 2q$ and calculate the optimum quantity under the true marginal cost as well as the welfare loss under quantity and price coordination.

9

Political Institutions

When tropical cyclone Nargis hit the Asian nation of Myanmar (formerly Burma) in May 2008, the country experienced its worst-ever natural disaster. Large areas of the low-lying nation were flooded by torrential rains and storm surge, and landslides occurred in many places as a result of unstable water-logged hillsides. As many as 138,000 people may have been killed. What was particularly devastating about the catastrophe is that many lives could have been saved if Myanmar's military government had allowed international aid to enter the country. Food and medical supplies came from all over the world in reaction to the news of the Myanmar floods, as did doctors, nurses, and aid workers who volunteered to fly in to rescue the thousands of people whose lives were threatened. But the Myanmar military dictatorship denied entry visas to those aid workers and refused to let the aid supplies into the country. The international community was shocked at the regime's lack of compassion toward its own people, which may have caused tens of thousands of unnecessary deaths.

Compare this to the government reaction to the 1984 industrial disaster in Bhopal, India, one of the world's largest to date. A Union Carbide pesticide plant accidentally released an estimated 42 tons of toxic methyl isocyanate (MIC) gas, exposing more than 500,000 people to MIC and other potentially harmful chemicals. The international community had very little knowledge of how to cope with such a major environmental disaster and given the lack of experience with accidents of this type, the Indian government's response, both at the central and local levels, was less than optimal. Nevertheless, the solidarity of the response within India and across the world was immediate. The medical and scientific communities mobilized rapidly. Hospitals and medical and social services were quickly established at the scene. An international medical commission was empowered to investigate all aspects of the disaster; ultimately, its recommendations for reform were communicated to the Indian government, its citizens, and to the surviving victims. If a similar disaster had happened in Myanmar, the scope of the catastrophe could have been many times greater and thousands more lives could have been lost.

Political institutions are very important for economic development. The difference in disaster responses mentioned above illustrates only one of the differences between autocracy (or dictatorship) in Myanmar versus India's democracy. Although there are many kinds of democracies, there are even more types of autocracies—all of which can have very different effects on economic development. For example, the nondemocratic regime of Singapore, where the rule of law is respected and the market economy thrives, and the North Korean Communist dictatorship, where there is no rule of law and the state prohibits private business, have very little in common. It is therefore important to make clear distinctions between the different kinds of both democracies and autocracies.

Political institutions play a key role in society because they determine the allocation of political power between different groups of citizens. The allocation of power affects how laws are made and whose interests they serve. Political institutions have potentially important economic consequences and can affect both the dynamic performance of an economy, that is, how efficiently wealth is created, as well as how wealth is distributed in the society. If all power is concentrated in the hands of a narrow minority, then the political system will likely serve that minority's interests. If, on the other hand, power is distributed more equally, then political decisions will have to be more inclusive and take into account the interests of many different groups.

Because of the way political institutions allocate political power, they are critical to understanding a country's success or failure in terms of economic development. Different institutions can have conflicting interests in an economy's development. Some will benefit from growth, while others will promote barriers to market entry and development.

In this chapter, we explain the principal differences between the various types of democracies and autocracies, and discuss their effects on economic development. We also discuss the processes of democratization, or how countries come to overthrow an autocratic regime and establish a democracy in its place, and what are the difficulties presented by these processes.

Political Regimes

The two main types of political regimes are *democracies* and dictatorships or autocracies. The word *autocracy* is preferable to the word dictatorship because it includes the different types of nondemocratic regimes. Although **autocracy** is defined as a government in which all power resides in a single person such as a dictator, monarch, or supreme religious leader. In this book, we use it to refer to any nondemocratic regime.

The word **democracy** comes from ancient Greek and means "power of the people." Today, democracies are representative governments with political leaders who are selected through free, fair, and competitive elections in which all adult citizens have the right to vote and all political parties have the right to participate in elections and governance. Democracy is founded on the premise that all citizens enjoy fundamental rights such as freedom of expression, freedom of association, and freedom of movement. Freedom House, headquartered in Washington, DC, is a nongovernmental organization that publishes an annual report on the status of freedom and democracy around the world. Freedom House lists a number of conditions that a country must satisfy to be called an "electoral democracy":

- a competitive multiparty electoral system;
- universal adult suffrage;
- regularly conducted elections with ballot secrecy, ballot security, and absence of fraud; and
- for political parties, significant public access to the electorate through the media and through open political campaigning.

Figure 9.1 shows Freedom House's world map of electoral democracies in 2008. Countries in blue satisfy the criteria for democracy, while those in gray do not. The Americas, Western Europe, and Oceania (Australia, New Zealand, and surrounding Pacific islands) all have electoral democracies. The picture is more mixed in Africa and Asia. The countries of the Middle East and North Africa, as well as many sub-Saharan nations, do not qualify.[1] China, Vietnam, and North Korea are not democracies, nor are some other Asian countries such as Myanmar and Pakistan. Russia and many of the former Soviet republics also do not qualify.

The Polity IV is a relevant database that provides indicators of democracy and autocracy for all countries since 1800 or independence. The democracy index ranges from 0 to 10 and takes into account the competitiveness of political participation, constraints on the executive, and openness and competitiveness in the recruitment of candidates for the executive. The autocracy index is constructed in a similar fashion, but measures the degree to which competitiveness of participation is repressed, participation is regulated, authority is concentrated in the executive, and executive recruitment is closed. The polity composite index shows the difference between the democracy and the autocracy index. A full democracy will have a polity index of 10, whereas a full autocracy will have an index of -10. The polity score has an advantage over the Freedom House index because it identifies not only which countries are democratic or autocratic, but it also gives scores for how advanced a democracy is

FIGURE 9.1   Freedom House Electoral Democracies in 2008

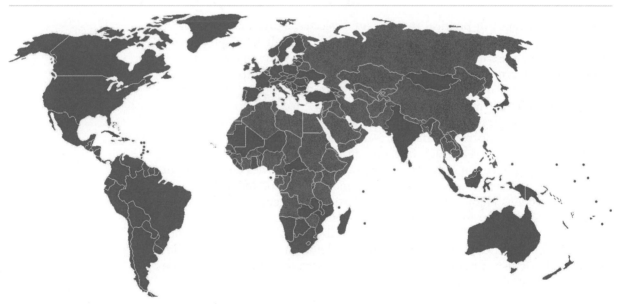

Countries in blue are considered electoral democracies while countries in gray are not.

Source: Freedom in the World 2011, Freedom House, January 2011.

---

[1]Note, however, that since the Arab Spring in 2011, several authoritarian regimes in the Middle East were overthrown and fragile democracies were already established in Tunisia and Egypt, with others possibly to follow.

FIGURE 9.2   The 2010 Polity IV Index of World Democracy

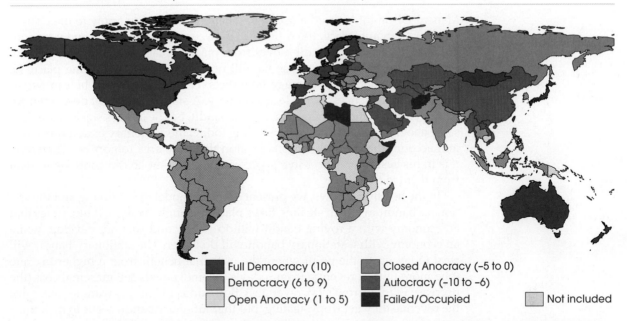

■ Full Democracy (10)	■ Closed Anocracy (–5 to 0)
■ Democracy (6 to 9)	■ Autocracy (–10 to –6)
■ Open Anocracy (1 to 5)	■ Failed/Occupied ■ Not included

The Polity IV score provides a nuanced view of political regimes. Between full democracies (with a score of 10), partial democracies (a score of 6 to 9) and autocracies (a score of –10 to –6), many countries have a hybrid regime between democracy and autocracy, the anocracy (a score of 5 to –5).

Source: Global Report 2011. *Conflict, Governance and State Fragility* by Monty G. Marshall and Benjamin R. Cole, Report by Center for Systemic Peace, p. 11. www.systemicpeace.org. Reprinted by permission.

or, conversely, for how authoritarian an autocracy is. As Figure 9.2 illustrates, the Polity IV index provides a more nuanced picture than the Freedom House index. Most Latin American countries, for example, while satisfying the Freedom House criteria for democracy, have a total polity score that is lower than that of the United States or the European democracies. A similar situation exists for Turkey, India, and Indonesia as well as some African democracies. Countries with a score between –5 and 5 have regimes that are neither a true democracy nor a true autocracy. They are labeled as anocracies in Figure 9.2. This is not a specific form of governance but a hybrid regime with elements of both autocracy and democracy. Russia, Venezuela, Algeria, and many African countries fall in this category. Some of these countries are likely to become stabilized democracies in the future, but others might not.

Economic Effects of an Autocracy versus a Democracy

A simple way to think about the effects an autocracy versus a democracy has on an economy is to start by assuming that those who hold political power will tend to use it and abuse it in their own interests. In other words, we apply to politicians the utility maximization hypothesis of economics.

The Theory of Autocracy

Mancur Olson introduced a useful distinction that we can apply to the characteristics of an autocracy: the difference between a roving bandit and a stationary bandit.[2] A roving bandit moves from place to place and plunders what he can wherever he goes. Because he will not come back to the same place, he does not care about the damage he inflicts. He will steal what he can, whatever the consequences for the local economy. A stationary bandit does not have higher ethical standards than the roving bandit, but he always steals within the same geographical entity. When stealing today, the stationary bandit must take into account that he still needs to steal in the same area tomorrow. Therefore, it is in his best interest to leave people enough so that he can continue to steal from them in the future.

In the box that follows, we present a simple model of the roving and the stationary bandit in which stealing takes places through taxation. It illustrates that an economy with a roving bandit will do poorly and will not develop, while an economy with a stationary bandit will do better. The stationary bandit will steal today up to the point where the marginal benefit from a higher tax rate (one more unit of revenue from today's income) equals the marginal cost (the decrease in tomorrow's tax revenues). Both kinds of bandits want to maximize the revenue they get from stealing, but the stationary bandit seeks to maximize not only current revenue but revenue over time.

A Model of the Roving and Stationary Bandits

To better understand the roving and stationary bandits, we study a two-period model. In the first period, the economy yields output y_1. A proportion t of y_1 is plundered. In the second period, output is a function of the remaining output:

$$y_2 = f[(1 - t)y_1]$$

where f is a concave function of $(1 - t)y_1$. It is assumed that the derivative of that function estimated at zero $f'(0) = \infty$. Note that if $t = 0, y_2 = f(y_1)$, and if $t = 1$, then it is assumed that $f(0) = 0$. At the end of the second period, all the output can be plundered.

Calling β the discount rate, that is, the rate at which the future is discounted relative to the present, the roving bandit who stays only in period 1 will be interested in maximizing ty_1,

whereas the stationary bandit who will be there for both periods plunders part of the output in period 1 and gets to plunder all the output in period 2. In other words, the stationary bandit will be interested in maximizing

$$ty_1 + \beta y_2 = ty_1 + \beta f[(1 - t)y_1].$$

The roving bandit, then, will choose $t = 1$. To find the preferred tax rate of the stationary bandit, we take the derivative of the objective function with respect to t and set it equal to zero:

$$y_1 - \beta y_1 f'[(1 - t)y_1] = 0 \text{ or } \beta f'[(1 - t)y_1] = 1,$$

which will always lead to an optimal choice of $t < 1$ because $f'(0) = \infty$. Figure 9.3 shows the maximization problem of the stationary bandit and the optimal solution. The plundering rate t is on the horizontal axis, and the curve depicts

[2]Mancur Olson, "Dictatorship, Democracy, and Development," *American Political Science Review* 87, no. 3 (1993): 567–576.

FIGURE 9.3   The Stationary Bandit's Optimization Problem

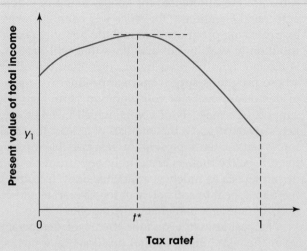

Present value of total income for the stationary bandit first increases as the period 1 tax rate increases, but it decreases once it has reached t^*. This is because once the tax rate becomes high enough, higher period 1 tax revenues are more than offset by lower period 2 revenues.

the objective function of the stationary bandit: $ty_1 + \beta f[(1-t)y_1]$. If $t = 0$, the objective function is $f(y_1)$ assumed larger than y_1. If $t = 1$, the objective function is y_1. The optimum is reached when the slope of the curve is equal to zero, that is, for t^* which is strictly <1.

Note that a reduction in the discount rate β, implying a higher impatience, leads to a higher t^* because we value even more the present relative to the future. Also, an upward shift of the function f that transforms today's net income into net future income leads to a lower t^*.

How does this theory relate to different kinds of autocracies? A dictator expecting to be in power for a long time will behave like a stationary bandit, whereas dictators whose power is unstable will behave more like roving bandits.

If we assume that the dictator sets taxes not only to finance his private consumption but also to finance public services, what level of services would a dictator provide by behaving like a stationary bandit? From the point of view of the dictator's own interests, he should provide public services only to the extent that it will lead to a future increase in taxable revenues that will be higher than the revenue that is lost today. The dictator will not take into account the public's preferences for those services. Nevertheless, the dictator's interests might be partially aligned with those of the population. The Egyptian pharaohs and the Chinese emperors not only spent a large part of tax revenues on their palaces, pyramids, mausoleums, armies, and court administrations, but also on irrigation and water management systems that helped increase agricultural productivity. They did this because higher agricultural output would yield higher tax revenues.

The Theory of Democracy

What are the differences for people living in a democracy as compared to an autocracy? Candidates for office will compete for votes among the population by promising programs that include not only taxes, public services, and redistribution of wealth, but also laws that will protect the populace. The winner is the one who receives more votes than the other candidates and therefore whose programs appear more appealing to a majority of voters. Two aspects of democracy warrant consideration here. First, elected candidates have the support of a majority of voters, which means that government policy will by necessity encompass the interests of at least that majority. Second, competition forces candidates to present the best possible mix of policies to potential voters. Even if policy makers are purely opportunistic and would like to serve their own interests as much as a dictator does, free and competitive elections force them to appeal to a majority of the electorate and create a strong link between majority interests and government policy.

The best-known economic theory of democracy is the so-called "median voter theorem." Imagine that positions on a line, as shown in Figure 9.4, can represent a population's policy preferences. Say that the line represents the left–right ideological dimension, with preferences going from left to right, with *L* and *R* representing the preferred policies, respectively, of the extreme left and the extreme right. More moderate preferences will thus be in the middle.

The median voter *M* is the voter whose policy preferences are such that 50% of voters are to her left, and 50% of voters are to her right. If a politician can appeal either to all voters to the left (or to the right) of *M* and also to the median voter, then he will have gained a majority plus one vote, that of the median. To understand the logic of the median voter theorem, let us look at the first line on Figure 9.4. Here, politician *A* has a platform that is halfway between the most extreme left position and the median voter's preferred policy platform. The same holds for politician *B* who is on the right side of the political spectrum. If these were the platforms presented by these politicians, a clear competition would exist between left-wing candidate *A* and right-wing candidate *B*. Each would obtain 50% of the votes because all those to the left of *A* would vote for *A* and all those between *A* and the median voter would also vote for *A*. Similarly, those to the right of *B* and those between the median *M* and *B* would vote for *B*. Median voter *M* would be indifferent between those two platforms and would toss a coin in an election. This cannot be a political

FIGURE 9.4   The Median Voter Theorem

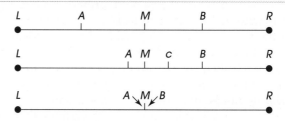

Electoral competition pushes parties *A* and *B* to propose policy platforms that are located at the median voter's preferred position.

equilibrium, that is, a situation in which no candidate has an incentive to move away from his platform given the platform presented by the competitor. Both politicians will indeed have strong incentives to move toward the center until their platform is the one the median voter prefers.

Look now at the second line on Figure 9.4. Here, candidate A has moved more toward the center while candidate A has not. A then gets the votes of all those who are to the left of A and of all those who are to the left of half the distance between A and B, that is, all those between A and c. As point c is to the right of the median, A will get more than 50% of the votes, and B will get less than 50% and will be defeated. B will then be far better off moving toward the median voter in order to react to A's move and attract more votes. Candidates A and B will only stop moving once both propose a platform that corresponds exactly to the preferences of the median voter as in the third line in Figure 9.4. They then each get exactly all the votes to the left and to the right, respectively, of the median. The median voter is indifferent between both and will toss a coin. Each party thus has exactly a 50% chance of winning the election, but both are offering the same platform, that preferred by the median voter. Once they compete at the median, neither has an incentive to move away. A political equilibrium has been reached.

The main focus of political disagreement in democracies is the left–right conflict. We can interpret this as preferences for income redistribution, with voters on the left the most in favor of redistribution and those on the right the least in favor. Preferences for redistribution are often strongly correlated with income levels. Because poorer individuals pay fewer taxes, they will prefer higher taxes on wealthy individuals to redistribute income from the rich to the poor. Those with higher incomes will prefer lower taxes and those with the highest incomes will prefer no redistribution at all. Preferences for taxation and redistribution are thus inversely related to income. What does the median voter theorem tell us in this context? The median voter will be the one with median income, that is, the voter whose income is exactly higher than the 50% poorest in the population and exactly lower than the 50% richest. The more unequal the income distribution, the lower the income of the median voter will be and the stronger his or her preference for redistribution. This implies that in a democracy, high income inequality will lead to a high level of redistribution. The box on page 241 illustrates this idea.

The median voter model relies on a number of very specific assumptions. It assumes that only one dimension of political conflict exists. In many countries, however, left–right conflicts over income redistribution are only one political dimension, while others such as ethnic, religious, or territorial divisions as well as attitudes about abortion, gay marriage, and other social issues also exist. The median voter model is unable to deliver predictions if there is more than one dimension. Also, it unrealistically assumes that politicians know voter preferences perfectly and it assumes that there are only two parties. If there are more than two parties, the situation becomes more complicated. The model further assumes that citizens vote sincerely, in the sense that they vote for the party closest to their preferences. If there are more than two parties, voters may vote strategically and sometimes vote for a larger party farther from their preferences because the party they prefer has no hope of winning the election or of influencing government policy. Despite these limitations, the median voter model is very useful for characterizing political conflicts over income redistribution in a democracy. It is also the most popular model researchers use to examine policy choices in a democracy.

The Median Voter Theorem and Redistribution

To better understand the median voter theorem and its effects on income redistribution policies in a democracy, we present a political model of taxation. Call y_i the income of individual i and call y average income in the economy. Call t the tax rate on income that will be determined in the democracy. Call f the lump-sum redistributive transfer received by each voter in the economy and financed from tax revenues. The budget constraint (on a per capita basis) is such that average tax revenues (or the tax revenue on average income) finance the per capita lump-sum transfer. We assume a distortionary loss from taxation that is a convex function of the tax rate. For simplicity, we assume that this loss is quadratic and takes the following form: $\frac{1}{2}t^2 y$. This loss must thus be deducted from the tax revenues. The budget constraint of government can thus be written:

$$(t - \tfrac{1}{2}t^2)y = f$$

The net income of an individual (after tax and redistribution) is therefore:

$$(1 - t)y_i + f$$

Given the budget constraint, we can replace f in the expression for net individual income and get:

$$(1 - t)y_i + (t - \tfrac{1}{2}t^2)y$$

The preferred tax rate maximizes this objective function. The derivative of this function with respect to t will be equal to zero at the maximum:

$$-y_i + y - ty = 0 => t = 1 - \frac{y_i}{y}$$

The preferred tax rate of an individual is thus higher the lower that individual's income y_i is relative to average income y. Individuals with a higher-than-average income would prefer a negative tax rate, which is not possible. They are thus opposed to redistributing income from rich to poor. In a political equilibrium, the tax rate will be that preferred by the median voter:

$$t_m = 1 - \frac{y_m}{y}$$

The lower the income of the median voter relative to average income, the higher the tax rate and thus the level of redistribution. The median voter model predicts, therefore, that more income inequality should lead to more income redistribution through the political process. In effect, the principle of "one person, one vote" gives poor people the same weight as rich people in elections. In this way, elections give the majority of poor the possibility to correct an unequal income distribution.

Autocracy and Democracy Compared

Let us now compare the economic effects of democracy and autocracy. A democracy redistributes some income from the rich to the poor. This redistribution is accomplished through the principle of "one man, one vote," which we should call "one person, one vote." In contrast, an autocracy does not usually redistribute from the rich to the poor.[3] It might engage in redistributive programs, but the only motivation would be fear of a popular uprising that could overthrow the regime. Such uprisings are, however, rare.

Democracies and autocracies also differ in terms of the provision of public services. An autocratic regime will only fund public services to the extent that the investment brings in more tax revenues to the dictator than direct taxation would. In contrast, a democracy is much more dependable in terms of providing public services, as political decisions take into account the interests of at least a majority of voters. Before the advent of democracy, the primary public expenditures of autocratic regimes were for the military and the police, as well as those funds directed to the construction of palaces and statues that benefited those in power. Democracy offers basic public services, such as education and health, which benefit the population at large and redistribute wealth from the rich to the poor.

A democracy and an autocracy also often differ in a number of other critical aspects related to economic development. In autocratic countries, a small group of elites usually controls a large part of the country's wealth and productive assets. The elite will tend to use the political regime to perpetuate its economic control and privileges by discouraging both the entry of new firms into the economy and market competition, favoring instead to erect barriers to market entry via laws and regulations. In contrast, in a democracy, while special interests and political lobbies generally favor established firms, there are also countervailing tendencies as consumers favor market competition and low prices, and small and medium enterprises favor low costs of entry into the economy.

The two forms of government also often differ in terms of social mobility. The elite in autocratic regimes want to perpetuate themselves by securing positions within the ruling elite for their offspring, therefore restricting access to those positions by anyone else. The elite favors erecting barriers to social mobility that often take subtle forms and are based on prejudice. Sometimes social barriers to mobility can represent outright discrimination, denying certain ethnic or social groups access to specific professions.

Another significant contrast between democracy and autocracy lies in the accountability of the executive and other elected representatives, one of the most important principles of a democracy. Elected leaders may make mistakes (sometimes serious), they may appear incompetent or corrupt once in power, or they may deviate from their electoral promises and abuse their powers. However, elections provide voters the opportunity to replace incompetent, dishonest or disappointing leaders. Accountability is fundamental to democracy; it keeps politicians on their toes if they want to be reelected; as a result, they must make an effort to please voters. In an autocracy, accountability is absent. The only way for the populace to oust a dictator is by means of a popular uprising. This is not only more costly in terms of economic disruption and the potential for lives lost, but is also a typical case of a collective-action problem.

---

[3]Communist regimes were the exception as they fully expropriated the assets of the rich and nationalized all wealth. Their motivation was ideological and not based on economic interest.

The beauty of democracy is that elections provide an institutional solution to this collective-action problem.

One often overlooked difference between democracy and autocracy is the issue of secession. Autocracies tend to expand their borders, while democracies tend to experience regional secessions. Shortly after India became independent and democratic in 1947, Pakistan seceded from it and Bangladesh later seceded from Pakistan in 1971. Secession occurred in many other countries after decolonization—Eritrea, Rwanda, and Burundi are just a few examples. When Communism collapsed and democracy was introduced in Eastern Europe, former Soviet republics such as Latvia, Lithuania, and Ukraine seceded, while some Soviet-bloc countries such as Yugoslavia and Czechoslovakia were broken into smaller countries.

Dictators tend to expand their territories because the greater the area over which they have control, the more taxable revenues they can appropriate. Why do democracies tend to experience secession? In a democracy, there are costs and benefits to secession, which voters usually understand equally as well as they recognize the advantage of voting for one candidate over the other. The main advantages of secession are that it a) limits the amount of income redistribution across geographical units, and b) reduces heterogeneity or diversity in voter preferences. If a country has both rich and poor regions, income redistribution will tend to be seen as redistribution from richer to poorer regions. By seceding, citizens in a rich region stop the flow of redistribution toward poorer regions. The poorer regions do not benefit from secession, but they usually cannot prevent a rich region from seceding unless they are able to mount a credible threat of violence.

Different preferences for redistribution are simply a manifestation of heterogeneity in voter preferences. Suppose a country with two regions inhabited by groups that differ either in their ethnicity, religion, or income. If one region is larger than the other in terms of population, it is likely that region will dominate politically. The minority region would get a large political benefit from seceding because in the new country, it would be a majority with policies more aligned to its preferences. Even if the two regions are more or less equal in size, the country would be hard to govern and political compromises would constantly have to be found. These compromises would not be accepted in either region, and a majority in each region might decide that they are better off seceding.

Democracy is often imperfect at protecting the rights of minorities. However, if minorities are concentrated in well-defined geographical areas, they can escape oppression by seceding. They could attempt this in an autocracy, but they would be virtually guaranteed to be met with significant and sometimes forceful opposition by the established regime. For example, a majority in Tibet would likely want to secede from China, but the Chinese government would immediately send in its troops to prevent such a secession. In a democracy, if secession is organized peacefully after a popular referendum, opposition is less likely, though not impossible. However, secession also has costs. First, retaliation by the original country is possible. It could be a military response or it could take more subtle forms such as barriers to trade or to free movement of people across borders. A second possible cost is the loss

CHAPTER NINE Political Institutions

of economies of scale in the provision of public services. After secession, the government in the newly seceded state will provide services on a smaller scale and economies of scale may be lost, making the provision of those services more costly. Loss of economies of scale may not be important in the case of a seceding region with a language different from that of the official language of the united country. Indeed, countries with multiple official languages need to face the difficulties of administering the provision of public services using several languages.

A final difference between a democracy and an autocracy is commitment. In Chapter 7, we saw that institutions solve a variety of commitment issues. The problem of commitment between government and private citizens is more difficult to solve than the commitment problem between private parties. In the latter case, commitment is obtained by enforcing contracts, and the legal system acts as the third party enforcing the contract. If the government is one of the contracting parties, however, it faces a commitment problem because there is no third party that can enforce commitment between a government and its citizens. The reason is that the government has a monopoly over violence, making it non-credible for any third party to threaten the government if it reneges on its commitments. Autocracies usually lack any commitment obligation to honor promises made to their citizens—for example, to not expropriate the property of private investors. The only way to obtain commitment in an autocracy is by reputation. If a dictator manages to establish a reputation for being strongly pro-business, that reputation can act as a long-term commitment device for repeated interactions between the government and the private sector. A good example would be Singapore, which has scored very well on indicators of the rule of law and protection of property rights even though it has a nondemocratic government.

In a democracy, the principles of the rule of law and the separation of powers between the different branches of government help to mitigate the commitment problem. Most democratic countries have constitutions that include a bill of rights for citizens as well as established rules for the functioning of government. Constitutional guarantees protect citizens from a government encroaching on their rights and abusing its power. Constitutional articles describe the extent and limits of the powers of different branches of government. Constitutionally established courts uphold citizens' rights and the executive branch is obligated to yield to the courts' decisions. This represents a commitment device because the executive branch, which controls the potentially repressive apparatus of government, is bound by the constitution and the limits it imposes on government powers. Constitutions are usually very difficult to change; amending a constitution typically requires supermajorities, often two-thirds or more of a legislature's votes. The requirement of a supermajority to amend a constitution also serves as a commitment device because it makes it impossible for the executive branch to abuse its powers through a constitutional change approved by just a simple legislative majority. The supermajority guarantees a near consensus among democratically elected representatives on the proposed constitutional amendments, which means that the changes are seen as benefiting nearly all represented interests.

Separation of Powers in a Democracy

The three major branches of government in a democracy are:

- The *executive branch*, responsible for the day-to-day operation of government and the execution of the laws passed by its legislative branch. The executive controls the military and the national police force as well as various ministries and government agencies. It has very limited powers in terms of enacting laws, and the extent of its powers is constrained by constitutional law. The head of the executive branch is usually directly elected by universal suffrage in a presidential democracy, or by the legislative branch in a parliamentary democracy.
- The *legislative branch*, directly elected by citizens, is responsible for making laws. It has no executive powers and limited investigative powers.

- The *judicial branch* is composed of professional career judges and is usually not elected. Its role is to interpret and uphold the laws passed by the legislative branch, to ensure that those accused of a crime have a fair trial, and to punish those who are convicted of violating the law.

The advantage of separation of powers is that the executive cannot enact laws on its own, which could result in an increase in, and abuse of, its powers. Similarly, executive actions must comply with the rule of the law as laid out in the constitution, and the judicial branch is empowered to punish any deviation from the law by the executive or the legislative branch. Because legislators are democratically elected, the laws they enact usually express the interests of a majority of the population.

Political Institutions in a Democracy

When comparing democracies, the two principal features to analyze are political regimes and electoral rules. Political regimes vary in how the different branches of government function and interact. Electoral rules differ in how the executive and legislators are elected.

Presidential and Parliamentary Democracies

The two main types of democratic regimes are presidential and parliamentary systems. In a **presidential regime**, the president, who heads the executive branch, is usually directly elected by voters. In a **parliamentary regime**, the executive branch is appointed by a parliamentary majority. In a presidential regime, the executive branch derives its power from a source independent of the legislative branch, the electorate. In a parliamentary system, it is the opposite: the legislative branch of government decides on who will head the executive branch. In a presidential system, the legislative branch does not have the power to dismiss the executive for political reasons. Procedures to impeach the president are rarely initiated and only in case of gross ethical misconduct, not because of political disagreement. In a parliamentary regime, by contrast, the legislative branch can routinely vote down an executive for political reasons through a vote of no confidence. This is the case, for example, if a coalition party decides to leave the majority, provoking a government crisis.

It is thus very rare in a parliamentary government to have an executive that does not have a majority support in the legislative branch. When it happens, it is called a minority government. In a presidential system, however, because both the president and the legislature are elected independently, it can happen that the president does not have the political support of a legislative majority. The president can be a member of one party, while another party controls the legislature. This is called **divided government**. Figure 9.5 shows a map of the distribution of presidential and parliamentary democracies in the world.

Presidential regimes are most often found in North and South America as well as in some of the countries of the former Soviet Union, in particular Russia. In the Americas, after countries gained their independence from the British and the Spanish monarchies, they established presidential systems. Parliamentary regimes are more the norm in Western Europe. They can also be found in former British colonies such as India.

Electoral Rules

Legislators can be elected by a variety of methods. One common electoral rule is the **majoritarian rule**, often also called "first past the post," "plurality rule," or "single-member district." In the majoritarian rule, only one

FIGURE 9.5 Presidential and Parliamentary Democracies

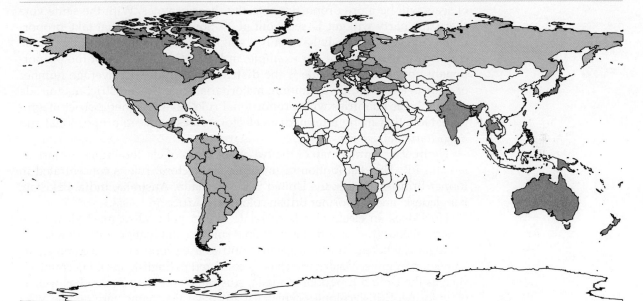

Presidential   Parliamentary

Countries in blue have presidential democracies while countries in gray have parliamentary democracies. The data are based on Freedom House research on political and civil liberties from 1990–1998. All other countries are not democratic. Note that the set of democratic countries is not exactly the same as that shown in Figure 9.1 as the criteria for democracy are somewhat weaker in Figure 9.2 and the time span covered is not the same.

Source: Torsten Persson and Guido Tabellini, *The Economic Effect of Constitutions* (Cambridge: MIT Press, 2003).

representative—the candidate with the most votes—is elected per legislative district. The term "majoritarian rule" is not well chosen because it is not necessary to have a majority of votes to win an election with this method. All that a candidate needs is to have more votes than the other candidates. For example, a candidate who garners 20% of the votes while 8 others only receive 10% of the votes wins under this plurality rule. Theoretically, a party could get 100% of the seats in a legislature with only 20% of the votes if the candidates in all districts received the same distribution of votes. This is an extreme example, but it is possible for a party to gain a majority of seats without having a majority of votes.

The other common electoral rule, one that stands in contrast to the majoritarian rule, is the **proportional rule**, often called PR. In its purest form, the proportional rule allocates the share of seats for the different parties proportionally to the number of votes each party receives. This is not always exactly possible, as the number of representatives is a whole number. For example, in a parliament of 100, if a party gets 13.5% of the votes, it does not get a half seat and will win either 13 or 14 seats depending on the particulars of the electoral rule. An electoral rule is more proportional if the size of the electoral district is very large. If, for example, there are only three seats in a district, the proportion of seats will tend to deviate from the share of votes. If a party gets 56% of the votes, it will get 2 seats out of 3, the closest integer number to 56% out of 3. However, if the district has 30 seats, the allocation of seats will be more proportional to the share of votes. With the same vote share, the party will get 17 seats out of 30. Some countries that take proportional rule very seriously have only a single legislative district for the whole country. This is the case, for example, in Israel. One measure of the proportionality of an electoral rule is the **district magnitude**, the average number of seats in a district. By definition, majoritarian rule has a district magnitude of 1, whereas countries with proportional rule have a higher district magnitude. Note that many intermediate electoral rules between proportional and majoritarian also exist.

Figure 9.6 shows a map of the two main types of electoral rules, majoritarian and PR. The distribution of majoritarian electoral rule is concentrated in former British colonies: the United States, Canada, Australia, India, Pakistan, Bangladesh, and the former British colonies in Africa and Asia.

How does an electoral rule correlate with a political regime? Most Latin American countries use the proportional rule in combination with a presidential regime, whereas most European countries use proportional rule and a parliamentary regime. Majoritarian rule is restricted to English-speaking countries such as the United Kingdom, Canada, Australia, and New Zealand as well as other former British colonies, which usually have a parliamentary regime, with the exception of the United States.

The Economic Effects of Democratic Institutions

Do institutional differences between the various types of democracy matter for economic performance? It turns out they do. Table 9.1 shows data relative to the outcomes of fiscal policy in democracies with presidential and parliamentary regimes, and in those with majoritarian and electoral rule.

FIGURE 9.6   The Distribution of Electoral Systems

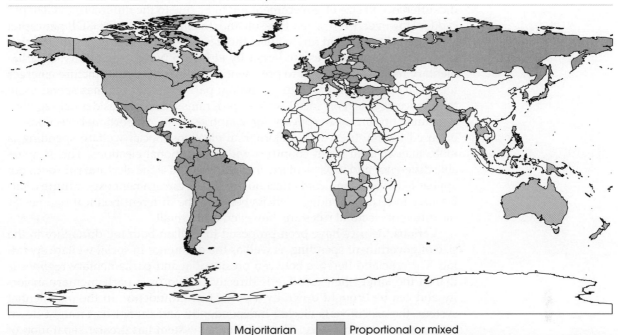

| Majoritarian | Proportional or mixed |

Countries in blue have majoritarian electoral rule while those in gray have proportional (or mixed—partly proportional, partly majoritarian) electoral rule. All other countries are not democratic. The criteria used to measure democracies are the same as in Figure 9.5.

Source: Persson and Tabellini, *The Economic Effect of Constitutions*, 2003.

Government expenditures are smaller in presidential regimes as compared to parliamentary regimes by more than 10 percentage points—a big difference. Only a one-percentage-point difference separates countries with majoritarian and proportional electoral rules. We should be cautious in jumping to conclusions because many other variables besides political regimes might affect this difference. We can, for example, argue that presidential countries are generally

TABLE 9.1   Political Institutions and Fiscal Policy Outcomes

	Presidential Regimes	Parliamentary regimes	Majoritarian elections	Proportional elections
Size of government expenditures	18.7	30.1	25.4	26.5
Social security and welfare spending	4.4	9	5	8.8
Budget deficit	2.4	3.3	2.5	3.3

Presidential democracies have smaller government expenditures (all data expressed as a % of GDP). Countries with majoritarian rule spend less on social security and welfare.

Source: Persson and Tabellini, *The Economic Effect of Constitutions*, 2003.

poorer than parliamentary countries because most are in Latin America and the difference in size of government might be due to the difference in GDP per capita. However, even when Persson and Tabellini control for GDP per capita and other variables that might affect the size of government, they still find that government expenditures are larger by at least 5 percentage points in parliamentary regimes compared to presidential regimes. A similar picture emerges for social security and welfare spending; parliamentary regimes spend more than twice as much on social welfare programs than do presidential regimes. A similar finding also appears for countries with proportional elections as opposed to countries with majoritarian elections. Social welfare spending is more than 60% larger in countries with proportional elections. This is a sizable difference and is particularly intriguing because the electoral rule does not appear to have a significant effect on the size of government expenditures. Differences in terms of budget deficits between the different political regimes or the different electoral rules are, however, quite small.

Various theories have been proposed to explain both the difference in the size of government spending as well as the difference in social welfare spending. The crucial difference between presidential and parliamentary regimes is that in the latter, the executive is directly chosen by a parliamentary majority and can be brought down by a vote of no confidence. In the presidential system, the executive is elected independently and cannot be brought down by a vote of no confidence. The presidential system has greater separation of powers between the executive and legislative branches. (This is not true for all presidential systems; in some cases, significant power is concentrated in the executive branch while the legislative branch has few powers.) Where it does exist, separation of powers makes it possible to a divided government with a legislative majority that can even be hostile to the policies favored by the president. This situation can have two potential results: a) legislative gridlock, in which the legislature blocks policies the president proposes or the president vetoes laws the legislature enacts; or b) healthy checks and balances between the legislative and executive branches that can prevent collusion between politicians who make decisions that are not in the voters' interests (such as diverting money for their own use or for that of their party or their cronies). In both cases, separation of powers should lead to fewer government expenditures.

In the parliamentary system, there is less separation of powers between the two branches of government. The parties who control a majority in parliament also control the executive. This can lead to less legislative gridlock, but it also results in fewer checks and balances. Stronger separation of powers in the presidential system can thus explain that system's smaller government expenditures.[4]

Why do countries with proportional elections have more social welfare spending than those with majoritarian elections? In a majoritarian system, to win a majority of seats, a party needs to win a plurality of votes in a majority of districts. This means that the party will concentrate its efforts on winning the marginal districts, that is, the districts in which there is the closest competition

---

[4]For more on this subject, see Torsten Persson, Gérard Roland, and Guido Tabellini, "Comparative Politics and Public Finance," *Journal of Political Economy* 108, no. 6 (2000): 1121–1161.

and which make the difference between having a majority versus a minority of seats. In the extreme, the party might put all its effort into winning the one district that could deliver a majority of seats. Trying to please voters in districts that will deliver safe seats would not make sense, as this would deliver more votes but not more seats. Similarly, it does not make political sense to spend resources in districts sure to be won by other parties.

Political incentives are different in the case of proportional elections. As the share of seats is proportional to the share of votes, a party will try to please as many voters as possible. It makes no sense to concentrate only on certain categories of voters, as it is possible to gain more seats by appealing to a broader share of the electorate. The incentives of politicians are thus different under the two different electoral rules. What does this difference in incentives mean in terms of fiscal policy? Under majoritarian elections, politicians will pay more attention to local public services that benefit only the voters in the districts that are relevant to winning an election. Under proportional elections, they will pay more attention to services that benefit the largest possible number of voters. As a result, social welfare spending will be greater in the latter category. Politicians in majoritarian systems have fewer incentives to spend on social welfare programs that are not targeted to a specific electoral district. Spending one more dollar per person is more costly for social welfare or pensions because more people will benefit from it in the majoritarian system. The results are greater and less costly when spending higher sums on the swing voters in the marginal districts. This may explain why countries with proportional elections spend more on social welfare than countries with majoritarian elections.

Political Institutions in an Autocracy

Turning to nondemocratic regimes, or autocracies, which currently exist only in developing countries, their various types are distinguished by the interests they represent, the ideology they defend, and among other characteristics, their rules for the succession of leadership.

Communist Regimes

In 1917, a Communist regime came to power in Russia; after World War II, similar regimes appeared in Eastern Europe, China, and parts of Asia (Mongolia, North Vietnam, and North Korea). Cuba established a Communist regime shortly after Fidel Castro's revolutionaries overthrew the right-wing dictator Fulgencio Batista in 1959. Communist regimes are characterized by the one-party rule, suppression of democratic freedoms, and an economic system with central planning and government ownership of economic assets. These systems were founded on Communist ideology, which claimed that central planning and redirecting a society's focus on individualism toward collectivism would lead to larger economic prosperity than would capitalism. Political repression was considered necessary to fight attempts by capitalist regimes to destroy Communism. With their intense ideology, Communist regimes became **totalitarian** in the sense that they sought to influence and control all aspects of citizens' lives. Children were encouraged to denounce their parents if they heard any "counterrevolutionary" thoughts expressed at home.

The Cultural Revolution in China

A significant example of totalitarianism was China's Cultural Revolution during the second half of the 1960s. It was a massive social and political campaign that indoctrinated young people, organized into "Red Guard" paramilitary units, to purge the country of all traces of its cultural and historic past. Intellectuals were sent to the countryside to "reform their own view of the world" by laboring in the fields with peasants. Millions of people died from persecution, the country's cultural inheritance (temples, statues, books, and art), accumulated over thousands of years was destroyed, and the Chinese economy was in shambles for over a decade thereafter.

The centrally planned socialist economic system introduced in Communist countries ultimately proved to be inferior to capitalism. Communist ideology has virtually vanished from the world as most of the regimes based on it eventually failed and collapsed.

Nazism and Fascism

As a political and economic system, **Nazism** was more short-lived than Communism. In Germany, the Nazi regime began in 1933 under Adolph Hitler's leadership, and was predicated on power centralized in a totalitarian dictatorship, the superiority of the Germanic races, and the supremacy of the *Führer*, the leader. It lasted until 1945, when the combined Soviet and Western Allied forces defeated the Nazis at the end of World War II. In Italy, Benito Mussolini set up a similar regime in 1922 that was called **Fascist** and exalted similar values: nationalism, corporatism, the cult of violence and of the supreme leader, the *Duce*. It lasted until the Allied forces began the liberation of Italy in 1943. Similar right-wing dictatorships were established in Spain by General Francisco Franco at the end of the Spanish Civil War (1939) and in Portugal after a military coup in 1926 that was followed by António de Oliveira Salazar's dictatorship (1932–1968). Many leaders in developing countries were inspired by these regimes, as was the case for Juan Peron, president of Argentina between 1946 and 1955.

Despite the brutality of their dictatorships, the Fascist governments of Italy, Spain, and Portugal were not as barbaric and totalitarian as Hitler's Nazi regime, which systematically exterminated 6 million Jews and at least 5 million others (gypsies, the disabled, psychiatric patients, homosexuals, political opponents, and other racial minorities and non-Germanic peoples). Nazism was based on a nationalist ideology that claimed Germans were members of a superior Aryan race and that all other races were inferior, often deemed not worthy of continued existence. It venerated a cult of violence and physical strength. Economically, Nazism as well as the various forms of Fascism did not favor central planning or government ownership but advocated what was at the time called **corporatism**, that is, an economic system in which access to markets and competition are severely restricted so as to favor established industries and the financial status quo. Nazism and Fascism virtually disappeared after World War II and are currently supported only by small fringe groups across the world.

Right-wing dictatorships. During the Cold War (1945–1989), when the principal geopolitical tensions in the world were between Communist and capitalist countries, a number of right-wing dictatorships emerged in developing countries, primarily in Latin America and Africa. These regimes were not ideologically driven; they had no blueprints for remaking society. They usually relied on repression and U.S. subsidies to stay in power. In the strange logic of the Cold War, the U.S. government supported all right-wing military dictatorships that were staunchly anti-Communist and could prove that they were able to repress left-wing rebellions in their countries.

In the 1970s, most Latin American countries were headed by military dictators such as General Augusto Pinochet in Chili, who violently toppled the left-wing government of Salvador Allende in 1973, and General Jorge Rafael Videla in Argentina, who was extremely repressive and routinely killed his left-wing opponents. In Brazil, a military dictatorship was in power between 1964 and 1985. Paraguay was governed by the dictatorship of General Alfredo Stroessner between 1954 and 1989. Military dictators ruled Bolivia between 1964 and 1978, Uruguay between 1973 and 1985, Honduras between 1972 and 1982, and Peru between 1968 and 1980.

In Africa, the Mobutu Sese Seko regime in the Democratic Republic of the Congo (then Zaire) was known both for its longevity (1965–1997) and for its widespread corruption and inept governance. However, Mobutu was a staunch ally of the United States against Soviet influence on the continent and probably the most loyal ally the United States had in Africa. From 1967 to 1998, Indonesia was ruled by the dictatorship of General Suharto. He came to power by staging a military coup followed by a repressive campaign in which at least 500,000 opponents were slaughtered. Virtually all of these military dictatorships disappeared after the end of the Cold War, which underscores how critical U.S. support was for their survival. Many if not most of these regimes were utterly corrupt. In the economic sector, the regimes would protect the interests of the families and friends of those in power, favoring established firms and opposing competition and transparency.

A number of right-wing dictatorships in the post–World War II period, such as Singapore, Taiwan, and South Korea, were characterized by aggressive pro-business policies. Following the example of Japan, these regimes encouraged export-led growth in Asia that resulted in significant economic success, several decades before China embarked on its impressive path toward economic growth. They were typically less corrupt than many other right-wing dictatorships and placed great value on reaching high rates of development. They actually score better than most other countries on international indicators of the quality of the rule of law.

Waves of Democratization

Democratization is very much a 20th-century phenomenon. Samuel Huntington has observed that the world has experienced three waves of democratization.[5] Table 9.2 regroups countries by their last wave of democratization and the year in which it occurred (not counting invasions by foreign countries).

---

[5]Samuel P. Huntington, *The Third Wave: Democratization in the Late Twentieth Century* (Oklahoma City, OK: University of Oklahoma Press, 1991).

The first wave of democratization took place before and around World War I, mostly in Europe as the working class movement was developing and fighting for universal suffrage. Democracy was introduced very early in the United States and the United Kingdom, as well as in Costa Rica, Switzerland, Belgium, Canada, and Luxembourg. By today's standards, these were very imperfect

TABLE 9.2   Year of Last Wave of Democratization

First wave		Second wave		Third wave	
United States	1800	Iceland	1944	Greece	1975
United Kingdom	1837	Austria	1945	Papua New Guinea	1975
Costa Rica	1841	Italy	1945	Senegal	1975
Switzerland	1848	France	1946	Portugal	1976
Belgium	1853	Israel	1948	Dominican Republic	1978
Canada	1867	Sri Lanka	1948	Spain	1978
Luxembourg	1879	Germany	1949	Ecuador	1979
Norway	1898	India	1950	Peru	1979
Australia	1901	Japan	1952	Belize	1981
New Zealand	1906	Colombia	1957	Bolivia	1982
South Africa	1910	Malaysia	1957	Honduras	1982
Denmark	1915	Venezuela	1958	Turkey	1982
Finland	1917	Jamaica	1959	Argentina	1983
Netherlands	1917	Cyprus (G)	1960	El Salvador	1984
Sweden	1917	Trinidad & Tobago	1962	Brazil	1985
Ireland	1921	Malta	1964	Guatemala	1985
		Gambia	1965	Uruguay	1985
		Singapore	1965	Philippines	1987
		Barbados	1966	Pakistan	1988
		Botswana	1966	South Korea	1988
		Mauritius	1968	Chile	1989
		Bahamas	1973	Paraguay	1989
				Poland	1989
				Romania	1989
				Zimbabwe	1989
				Bulgaria	1990
				Czech Republic	1990
				Fiji	1990
				Hungary	1990
				Namibia	1990
				Nepal	1990
				Nicaragua	1990

(*Continued*)

First wave	Second wave	Third wave	
		Bangladesh	1991
		Belarus	1991
		Estonia	1991
		Latvia	1991
		Ukraine	1991
		Zambia	1991
		Ghana	1992
		Russia	1992
		Taiwan	1992
		Thailand	1992
		Slovak Republic	1993
		Malawi	1994
		Mexico	1994
		Uganda	1994

The first wave of democratization occurred around World War I, the second after World War II, and the third around the end of the Cold War.

Source: Persson and Tabellini, *The Economic Effect of Constitutions*, 2003: 83–87.

democracies because large segments of the population did not have voting rights (for example, women and those men who did not own property), but there were, nevertheless, competitive elections. Note that the first wave does not include any developing country other than Costa Rica, which is not among the poorest developing countries.

The second wave took place after World War II. It affected some European countries in which democracy had been introduced but subsequently abolished, as in Germany under Hitler or in Italy under Mussolini. This second wave also included developing countries that became independent after World War II at the beginning of the decolonization process, such as India, Sri Lanka, and Malaysia.

The third wave took place around the end of the Cold War. It included former Communist countries that transitioned to democratic regimes, as well as many Latin American countries that had been democratic, but instituted dictatorships during the Cold War and then reverted to democracy. The same is true for some European countries such as Greece, Spain, and Portugal, where democracy had once preceded right-wing dictatorships. The third wave is by far the largest but democracy is not yet firmly established in some of these countries.

To understand why certain countries democratized earlier than others, why some countries have had regime changes between democracy and dictatorship, and why some countries have failed to democratize at all, we now turn to theories of democratization.

Theories of Democratization

Researchers have put forward many theories of democratization. This section examines only those theories that emphasize a few key variables as determinants of democracy. In other words, we will use the usual economics method of trying to isolate a few important variables while ignoring the rest. Reality is complex and it is better to have theories that are incomplete but that capture the most important variables and their effects.

Income and Democracy

Political scientist Seymour Lipset has proposed one of the oldest and most famous theories of democratization.[6] He noticed a correlation between income and democracy and suggested that as countries become richer, they tend to adopt a democratic system. Figure 9.7 plots the log of income per worker in 2000 on the horizontal axis and the Polity IV index of democracy on the vertical axis. It shows that a positive correlation exists. Countries that have a higher income per capita tend to be more democratic, while poorer countries tend to be less democratic. As Figure 9.7 illustrates, there are also a few exceptions: Singapore, Libya, and the oil-exporting Persian Gulf states (Saudi Arabia, Kuwait, Bahrain, Oman, and the United Arab Emirates) have a high level of income per capita and a low democracy score. This strong international correlation between income per capita and democracy has been the basis for one of the best-known theories in the social sciences that posits a causal relationship between development and democracy.

Lipset's argument is that as a society modernizes and develops economically, its urbanization rate increases, the level of education rises, and the complexity of social processes increases. As a consequence of these modernization processes, the demand for democracy on the part of the educated masses increases. More economically developed countries should, therefore, have a greater demand for democracy and, on average, should be more democratic. This theory has found significant support among economists, including the famous macro-economist Robert Barro.[7]

Political scientist Adam Przeworski and his co-authors claim that the positive correlation between income and democracy is mainly driven by the fact that richer countries remain democratic, whereas poorer countries have more fragile democracies and, as a result, have experienced military coups and reversals of democracy.[8] These reversals have also been taking place in countries with a less extensive history of democracy; that is, in countries that belong to the second wave of democratization.

---

[6]Seymour M. Lipset, "Some Social Requisites of Democracy: Economic Development and Political Legitimacy," *American Political Science Review* 53, no. 1 (1959): 69–105.

[7]Robert J. Barro, "Determinants of Democracy," *Journal of Political Economy*, 107, no. 6 (1999): 158–183.

[8]Adam Przeworski, Michael E. Alvarez, Jose Antonio Cheibub, and Fernando Limongi, *Democracy and Development: Political Institutions and Well-Being in the World, 1950–1990* (Cambridge: Cambridge University Press, 2000).

FIGURE 9.7   Log Income Per Capita and Democracy

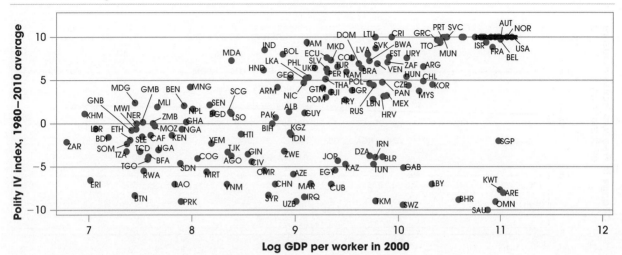

Countries with a higher income per capita tend to have a higher democracy score, but that is not the case for all countries, especially for the oil-exporting countries of the Persian Gulf.

Source: Polity IV data (http://www.systemicpeace.org/inscr/inscr.htm) and Penn World Tables (http://pwt.econ.upenn.edu/).

The problem with the international correlation between income and democracy is that it does not prove any causality between the two. It only shows that richer countries are generally more democratic than poorer countries. It could be the case that an underlying variable, such as culture or religion, affects both the political institutions and economic development. For example, Max Weber, in his famous book *The Protestant Ethic and the Spirit of Capitalism*,[9] argued that Protestantism was behind both democracy and economic development.

In contrast, economists Daron Acemoglu, Simon Johnson, James Robinson, and Pierre Yared show that there is no good evidence that as a country gets richer, it becomes more democratic.[10] Figure 9.8 shows the correlation between the change in income from 1970 to 1995 on the horizontal axis and the change in the Polity IV measure of democracy during the same period. There is no correlation. The relation appears to be flat. In other words, richer countries are more democratic, but there is no good evidence that as a country becomes richer, it becomes more democratic.

Education and Democracy

Another version of the modernization theory identifies education as the key condition that leads to democracy. It suggests that a minimum level of

[9]Daron Acemoglu, Simon Johnson, James A. Robinson, and Pierre Yared, "*Income and Democracy,*" *The American Economic Review* 98, no. 3 (2008): 808–842.

[10]Max Weber, *The Protestant Ethic and the Spirit of Capitalism,* (New York: Penguin Books 2002).

FIGURE 9.8   Change in Income and in Democracy, 1970–1995

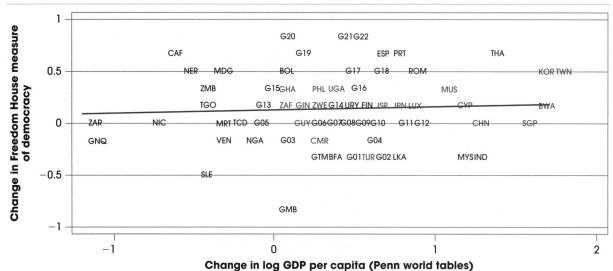

The relationship between a change in income from 1970 to 1995 and a change in the democracy score is flat.

Source: Daron Acemoglu, Simon Johnson, James A. Robinson, and Pierre Yared, "Income and Democracy," *The American Economic Review* 98, no. 3 (2008): 811. Printed with permission of American Economics Association.

education is a prerequisite for democracy. If people are illiterate, they are not able to follow or participate in political campaigns and will likely have a hard time at the ballot box recognizing the names of candidates. Also, when people are more educated, they are better able to communicate with each other and, as a result they are more able to organize on a larger scale and fight for democracy. Figure 9.9 shows a positive correlation between education, measured by the total average years of schooling and the Polity IV index.

However, just as in the relationship between income and democracy, there is not evidence of a causal relationship between education and democracy. It is possible the causality might run the other way—the introduction of democracy might lead to significant improvements in education. Moreover, a third variable, such as culture, might also contribute to more education and to democracy. The data only tell us that countries with better education are more democratic. Here, again, if we try to determine whether countries that experience an improvement in their educational systems also experience an improvement in democracy, we do not find any positive relationship. Figure 9.10, taken from another paper by Acemoglu et al., shows the relationship between changes in education in the 1970–1995 period and the change in the Freedom House Political Rights Index over the same period.[11] Just as in the case of changes in income and in democracy, the relationship is flat.

---

[11]Daron Acemoglu, Simon Johnson, James A. Robinson, and Pierre Yared, "From Education to Democracy?" *The American Economic Review* 95, no. 2, papers and proceedings of the 117th annual meeting of the American Economic Association, Philadelphia, PA, January 7–9, 2005: 44–49.

FIGURE 9.9   Education and Democracy

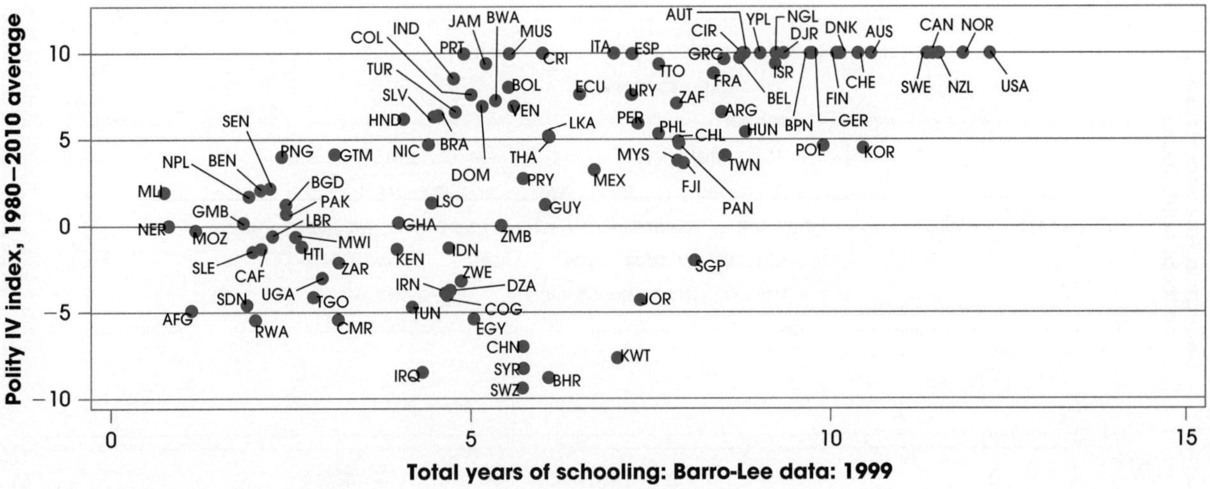

A higher level of education is correlated with a higher democracy score.

Source: For the Polity IV data, see http://www.systemicpeace.org/inscr/inscr.htm; for education data, see the Barro-Lee data set, http://www.barrolee.com.

Inequality, Social Conflict, and Democracy

Other theories of democratization link it to income inequality. The median voter theory of democracy tells us that a more inegalitarian society will have more wealth redistribution compared to a less inegalitarian society. In the more inegalitarian society, the rich have therefore more to lose from the introduction of democracy because there would be more redistribution. Because they have more to lose, the rich in the more inegalitarian society would resist the introduction of democracy more. Why, then, might the rich accept democracy in a less inegalitarian society when they would also lose from redistributive policies? Acemoglu and Robinson have formulated a theory of democratization that answers this question.[12]

Take as starting point a nondemocratic regime. Imagine that its citizens have organized and are able to overthrow the existing elite and expropriate their assets through a revolution. Historically, these revolutionary movements have mobilized millions of people to demonstrate in the streets and demand fundamental changes, as was the case with the Arab Spring in 2011. These events are usually not predictable and usually do not last very long. How can the elite react to a revolutionary threat? They can be passive and allow the complete expropriation of their wealth, or they can promise redistribution of income to the poor and to public welfare programs such as government-funded education and health services that benefit the poor. The problem is that

---

[12]Daron Acemoglu and James A. Robinson, *Economic Origins of Dictatorship and Democracy* (Cambridge: Cambridge University Press, 2006).

FIGURE 9.10   Changes in Education and Changes in Democracy (1970–1995)

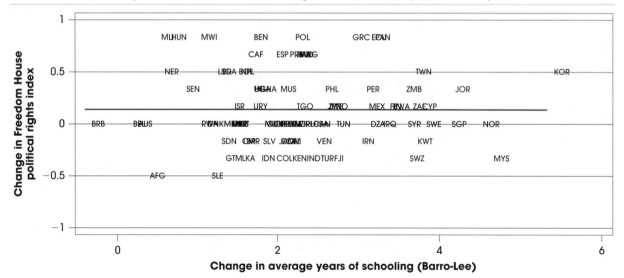

The relationship between change in average years of schooling from 1970 to 1995 and change over the same period of the democracy score is flat.

Source: Daron Acemoglu, Simon Johnson, James A. Robinson, and Pierre Yared, "From Education to Democracy?" *The American Economic Review* 95, no. 2, papers and proceedings of the 117th annual meeting of the American Economic Association, Philadelphia, PA, January 7–9, 2005: 44–49. Printed with permission of American Economics Association.

these promises may not be credible. In most cases, revolutionary threats do not last very long. People cannot demonstrate and strike indefinitely. Once the mobilization cools down and people return to their ordinary activities, the elite may renege on their promises to redistribute income or may cease to keep their promises and curtail the redistributive programs they implemented under a revolutionary threat. It would be in their best interests to do so because such policies are very costly. There would be a very good chance that the elite could get away with this breach of commitment because it is unlikely that citizens could remobilize quickly and revive a revolutionary threat. Promises of redistribution would therefore not be enough to calm the revolutionary fervor and protect the assets of the elite from expropriation. It is here that democracy plays a key role.

Democracy as a commitment to redistribution. The introduction of democracy presents a credible way to promise redistribution while simultaneously preventing a revolution. Democracy gives formal political power to citizens. Even after the revolutionary mobilization has subsided, elections make it possible to vote for redistributive programs without the necessity of solving the multiple collective-action problems associated with organizing a revolutionary movement. Because expropriating the assets of the elite through a revolution is costly for the populace because it prevents capital accumulation and growth, democracy offers as a practical solution that benefits both the elite and the citizens in the event of a revolutionary threat. Democracy is preferable to revolution for both the elite and the citizens, and it is a credible way of promising redistribution from the elite to the citizens. Democratic institutions guarantee redistribution because of the formal political powers given to the people. Democracy thus solves an important commitment problem.

Revolutionary threats. In developing countries, decolonization and democratization were often introduced simultaneously. Much of the developing world in Africa and Asia was still under colonial rule by the end of World War II. Anticolonial movements had developed and were gaining strength. In India, one of the most populated countries in the world, the anticolonial movement had grown quite powerful under the leadership of the Congress Party and its leader, Jawaharlal Nehru. Britain, similar to other European colonial powers, feared that the anticolonial movements would seek the support of the Soviet Union, which had by then become a considerable military and political presence after taking control of Central and Eastern Europe and supporting a Communist revolution in China. The British government, fearing a radicalization of the Indian populace in the face of the Congress Party's dedication to independence and democracy, granted independence to India in 1947 and it has been a democracy ever since.

Historical Evidence of the Introduction of Democracy in Response to Revolutionary Threats

There is consistent historical evidence that democracy was usually introduced as a response to revolutionary threats. In Great Britain, one of the first countries in which democracy was introduced, it was the fear of a revolutionary movement that prompted the Reform Act of 1832, which extended the franchise from 492,700 to 806,000 voters. In 1830, revolutionary movements had destabilized many European countries and the British aristocracy wanted to make limited concessions to calm social disturbances. However, these concessions were not enough to quell the unrest.

The Chartist movement developed to represent working class interests in Victorian England in the nineteenth century and to demand universal suffrage. During a recession in the late 1860s and after alarming riots in London's Hyde Park in 1866, a second Reform Act was passed in 1867, which further expanded the electorate to 2.48 million. Another Reform Act followed in 1884. By that time, 60% of adult males had the right to

vote, and the working class could finally exercise political power. After World War I, all adult men and women over the age of 21 were granted voting rights. It was then that the Labour Party became powerful enough to participate in the government. As in many European countries, the radical extension of suffrage in Britain was seen as a way of avoiding a revolution, such as the one that wracked Russia, in the aftermath of the war's carnage that had killed millions of young working-class men across Europe.

The waning months of World War I were indeed a turning point in many European countries. The revolutionary threat had never been greater. Communists had seized power in Russia in late 1917, while in Germany, revolutionary uprisings were taking place in many large cities such as Munich, where the Marxist Spartacists were becoming increasingly powerful. Soldiers, fed up with the war, were ready to use their weapons against their officers and the empire of

(*Continued*)

Kaiser Wilhelm II rather than against the French and English. The threat of revolution played a major role in the political upheaval that subsequently took place in Germany. Kaiser Wilhelm abdicated, the Weimar Republic was established, and the war ended for Germany. Workers were given voting rights, while the leaders of the Spartacist movement, Rosa Luxemburg and Karl Liebknecht, were assassinated in the streets of Berlin by a group of veterans who were members of a paramilitary unit.

In Europe, the spirit of the times after World War I was such that the elite were terrified by the prospect of the Communist revolution expanding worldwide, a goal that the Russian Marxists were actively supporting. In other countries such as Belgium, Finland, the Netherlands, and Sweden, voting rights were dramatically extended to make concessions to the working class and prevent a revolution that would expropriate the assets and privileges of their elites.

In other countries, decolonization also took place as a response to the development of radical anticolonial revolutionary movements that threatened to expropriate colonial interests. But decolonization did not necessarily result in democratization. In Algeria, for example, a nationalist one-party rule was instituted after the French left the country in the aftermath of a very bloody colonial war.

Democratization and income inequality. While we know that the elite may accept democratization and even propose it in response to revolutionary threats, we still have not addressed why there should be more democratization when income inequality is lower. Acemoglu and Robinson's theory also provides an answer to that question. We have seen that democracy was overthrown in some countries. Many military coups d'état have abolished democracy and introduced a military dictatorship that favors the interests of the elite. But coups do not happen overnight; just as revolutionary threats do not arise every day, the political and military conditions necessary for mounting a successful coup must be present and a sufficiently large number of the elite must be in favor of it. Moreover, coups are very costly. They may fail, in which case the result could be disastrous for the elite. Those who organized the failed attempt might lose their lives or land in prison. The reaction to an attempted overthrow of the existing government would almost surely lead to retaliatory measures against the elite, leading to expropriation of their assets and privileges. Even when a coup is successful, it is costly to consolidate and maintain, as very strong repression measures must be put in place. Given the fact that coups are costly, they occur more often in those cases where the benefits of staging them are larger. In societies where inequality is significant and where democracy may lead to severe redistributive outcomes, the elite may benefit more from a coup to prevent or undo those outcomes. In more egalitarian societies, the costs of organizing a coup might outweigh the benefits. Therefore, coups and reversals of democracy are more likely to occur in societies where inequality is greater. The elite in countries where inequality is significant might also resist democratization more. Instead of making concessions, they might gamble on repression in the hope that revolutionary movements would be thwarted. While this is not always the case, revolutions are more likely in countries with greater inequality.

While democracy provides a credible commitment to income redistribution, its success can prove more fragile in societies with higher income inequality because a coup could bring down a nascent democracy. Acemoglu and Robinson's theory of democratization enables us to make several predictions.

First, an improved level of **civil society development** should lead to earlier democratization with fewer reversals. Better civil society development means that the citizens are more organized in various associations, political parties, unions, etc. In other words, citizens increase their ability to overcome collective-action problems. As a result, the bargaining power of citizens with the elite is stronger and the elite are more inclined to make concessions to avert a revolutionary threat. For similar reasons, the costs of staging a coup when civil society is well developed are much higher. Early democratization and a stable democracy are therefore more likely in countries where civil society is more developed.

Second, there is an increased likelihood that democratization will occur in times of crisis, such as economic recession, bad harvests, financial emergencies, etc. Typically, these are events that not only result in revolutionary movements but in the democratization that is likely to occur as a response. Crises are also situations that lend themselves to coups d'état. The elite might be more easily convinced to unite behind a dictator, because national crises might justify the necessity of drastic policies to restore stability.

Third, in countries where the wealth of the elite derives primarily from land ownership rather than from industrial capital, democratization is less likely to occur. If it does, it is less likely to be stable. There are several reasons for this. First, land is easier to tax than physical or human capital. Landowners have more to fear from redistributive taxation because they cannot hide their land assets. Second, repression and social turbulence are more costly for industrial and human capital than for landowners. Repression is never very efficient as a method to compel people to work, but it is even less efficient for skilled human capital. Agricultural laborers can be forced to work the land, but talented and skilled workers cannot be made to work efficiently under the threat of force. Similar to the captive scientists in spy movies, skilled workers can always make a minimum effort more easily than unskilled workers. Third, while angry mobs can destroy physical capital, they cannot actually destroy land. The costs of social conflict are thus smaller for the landed elite than for the industrial and urban elite. Therefore, democratization is more likely in societies where the assets of the elite are mostly industrial rather than agrarian. Because the agrarian elite have fewer incentives to make concessions, revolutions are more likely to occur in countries in which they control the wealth. This was the case in Russia, China, Vietnam, Cuba, and Nicaragua. For the same reasons, coups are less costly in countries with an agrarian elite, and thus democracy is less likely to be stable.

A fourth prediction suggests that democratization is less likely with either very low or very high levels of inequality. In very equal societies, the elite might be more willing to make concessions, but citizens will have less reason to revolt. In very unequal societies, citizens will have ample reasons to revolt, but the elite will have a lot to lose and are thus more likely to resist democratization. It is in societies where inequality is intermediate that we are more likely to witness democratization followed by a stable democratic government.

A fifth and related prediction is that the presence of an established middle class is a factor in democratization. The middle class can act as a buffer between the elite and the poor. It will not support policies of excessive redistribution under democracy. Because the middle class plays a pivotal role in elections, redistributive policies will be less extreme under democracy and democratization will appear less threatening to the elite. When there is no middle class or it is very fragile, democracy becomes more threatening to the elite, as the pivotal voters will belong to the poor and not to the middle class.

Finally, globalization may positively affect democratization and the stabilization of democracy. It makes capital more mobile and thus more difficult to tax. The elite then have less to fear from taxation under democracy. Moreover, integration in the world economy will increase the costs of economic and social disruption. Periods of revolutionary upheaval or repression will prove to have significant economic costs. Further, repressive policies in nondemocratic countries can lead to international sanctions, such as trade boycotts, from democratic countries.

Chapter Summary

Political Regimes

The two main types of political regimes are democracy, which spreads political power broadly across society, and autocracy, which concentrates power in the hands of a dictator or a small elite.

Economic Effects of an Autocracy versus a Democracy

The theory of democracy emphasizes that political competition to gain a majority of votes leads to the enactment of policies preferred by the median voter. The theory of autocracy emphasizes that more stable autocracies tend to be less predatory on their populations in terms of extracting tax revenues. Autocracy, in contrast to democracy, does not redistribute income to the poor and it erects barriers to market entry for new businesses as well as barriers to social mobility. It lacks accountability to its citizens and often promotes policies of territorial expansion.

Political Institutions in a Democracy

Presidential democracies have smaller governments than do parliamentary democracies because they have more separation of powers. Countries with proportional electoral rules spend more on welfare than countries with majoritarian electoral rules.

Political Institutions in an Autocracy

Autocracies can differ greatly. Recent history has seen Communist dictatorships, Nazi and Fascist dictatorships, and right-wing dictatorships established during the Cold War.

Waves of Democratization

The world has experienced three waves of democratization: before and after World War I, after World War II, and toward the end of the Cold War. Democratization in developing countries was more concentrated in the third wave. Many developing countries also experienced a reversal of democracy, while some developing countries have never became democratic.

Theories of Democratization

Theories of modernization emphasize that as countries become richer and more educated, they tend to become more democratic. While countries with higher income per capita are more democratic, an increase in income and education does not correlate with an improvement in democracy. Another theory of democratization sees it as a commitment device by the elite to redistribute wealth to the poor as a means to prevent a revolution. In countries where income inequality is very high, democratization is very costly for the rich, who prefer to take the risk of repressing political parties that represent the poor.

Key Terms

autocracy
civil society development
corporatism
democracy
district magnitude
divided government

Fascist
majoritarian rule
Nazism
parliamentary regime
presidential regime
proportional rule

Review Questions

1. To what extent do Mancur Olson's ideas of the roving and stationary bandit explain differences among dictatorships in developing countries?

2. What are the differences between autocracies and democracies in terms of the provision of public services? Explain.

3. How is the commitment problem for government solved in a democracy and in an autocracy?

4. Explain the difference between proportional and majoritarian electoral rule. Give five examples of developing countries with presidential and parliamentary regimes based on either rule.

5. Is it possible in a majoritarian electoral system that a party can win more than 50% of the seats without having 50% of the votes? Explain.

6. Download the latest Freedom House Index of political rights (http://www.freedomhouse.org) and the latest World Bank rule of law index (http://info.worldbank.org/governance/wgi/index.asp) for Brazil, Colombia, Nigeria, Uganda, Singapore, and Hong Kong. Compare the scores on both indices for these countries. What are your findings? How can you explain them in the light of this chapter's theories?

7. Take the median voter model, in which the net income of an individual (after tax and redistribution) is $(1 - t)y_i + f$, where y_i is the income of individual i, t is the tax rate, and f is a lump-sum transfer financed by taxation. Assume that the distortionary cost of taxation is $b\frac{1}{2} t^2 y$, where y is average income. The government budget constraint is thus $(t - b\frac{1}{2} t^2)y = f$. Assume average income is equal to 20 and median income is equal to 15. Calculate the equilibrium tax rate under democracy as a function of b. What is the equilibrium tax rate if $b = 1, b = 1.5, b = 2, b = .5$? Explain your results. How does the equilibrium tax rate vary as b increases? Why?

8. Assume an autocratically led country. The autocrat lives for 2 periods. In period 1, he can choose to tax income $y_1 = 100$ at rate t. In period 2, income that has not been taxed away yields period 2 income equal to $2[(1 - t)y_1]^{0.5}$. Assume no discount rate, but assume that there is a 20% chance that the autocrat will be toppled after period 1. Calculate the optimal period 1 tax rate for the autocrat, assuming that he will want to tax away all income in period 2. What is the optimal period 1 tax rate if there is a 60% chance that he will be toppled after period 1? What is the connection between the probability of losing power in period 2 and the period 1 tax rate?

9. Read Larry J. Diamond and Marc F. Plattner's article, "Hong Kong, Singapore, and 'Asian values,'" *Journal of Democracy* 8, no. 2 (1997): 9–10. What do you conclude about the effects of Confucianist thought on how a political system should be run? What is your view on these ideas?

10. Do an online and library search on India and Pakistan. What political institutions emerged from the decolonization process? How would you explain the differences in the political evolution of the two countries?

10

Legal and Fiscal Institutions

No one likes to receive a check that later bounces. How long it takes, however, to collect on a bounced check varies significantly across countries. If you have to file a claim and then go to court to collect the money, the length of the process is roughly 54 days in the United States. In Sri Lanka, it is 440 days. Sri Lanka is a poor country and it is not surprising that its legal system is not as efficient as that of the United States. However, the quality of a country's legal institutions also matters in terms of how those institutions affect transaction costs in the economy and thus the process of development. In Ghana, also a poor country, the whole process would last only 90 days, nearly 5 times faster than in Sri Lanka. In this chapter, we will examine the role of legal institutions in economic development.

The quality of the fiscal system in a developing country is also a critical consideration. Basic public services such as health, education, and infrastructure require a stable tax base. These services are important both for social welfare and economic growth in developing countries. Raising taxes in a developing country to pay for these services is, however, a challenge, given the large size of the informal sector that pays no taxes. In the Democratic Republic of the Congo, until recently, even government officials' income taxes were not paid at the source. How do poor countries collect taxes and what problems do they face in doing so? Why do some developing countries collect taxes more effectively than others? This chapter will also consider fiscal institutions in developing countries.

Legal Institutions

Quite broadly, the legal institutions of a country are the set of laws and the controlling authorities (the police and the justice system) that enforce those laws. In democratic societies, laws stipulate the rights of individuals and corporations and prohibit or control actions and behaviors that could infringe on those rights. In nondemocratic societies, laws may have other purposes such as enforcing religious prescriptions or the edicts of a monarch. Laws exist in all spheres of society. In the economic sphere, commercial law is generally comprised of rules related to trade and exchange transactions. Financial and securities laws relate to financial markets, and labor laws relate to labor markets. Administrative law, procurement law, and constitutional law control the actions of government.

In recent years, an important body of research has compared the economic effects of different legal systems. The two most important legal systems in the world are the common-law legal system, which prevails in countries of Anglo-Saxon descent (the United Kingdom, the United States, Canada, New Zealand, Australia) and former British colonies, and the civil-law system, which predominates in continental Europe, Latin America, all former Spanish and French colonies, and many Asian countries. Both legal systems generally meet modern standards of fairness and rely on the presumption of innocence and the necessity of bringing hard evidence to convict a party accused of violating a law.

Differences between the Common-Law and Civil-Law Systems

The main distinction between the common-law and the civil-law systems is that the common-law system relies mostly on precedent, that is, on previous judgments, whereas the civil-law system relies on a written code of civil law. Common-law countries have written legal codes, but the justice system, legal arguments, and judicial decisions are mainly based on case law and jurisprudence, i.e., legal precedents. In civil-law countries, precedent also plays a role, but arguments based on precedent are primarily used when the written law is not precise enough and can be subject to multiple interpretations. This important distinction gives a different role to judges, who have a narrower role in civil-law systems. Their task is to apply the written law to all cases brought to them. **Bright-line rules** are precise descriptions of prohibited actions. Civil codes typically contain many bright-line rules that give judges little or no leeway for interpretation. If the law prohibits driving above 55 miles per hour, it is a bright-line rule. In contrast, only a legal standard that states, for example, that fast driving is against the law would provide room for interpretation. Judges in common-law systems have more power in the sense that they must base their judgments on precedents, which leaves more room for interpretation. If different judges have ruled differently on very similar cases, judges in future cases have significant leeway in their decisions.

Common-law systems rely greatly on oral argument and evidence. This is an inheritance from the tradition of customary law. Among ancient Anglo-Saxon tribes, whenever there was a dispute between individuals, an assembly of villagers or of wise elders would hear the different parties and make a decision, relying on long-standing traditions and precedent. This is the origin of trial by jury, whereby citizens are chosen to adjudicate a legal case. It is, in essence, a decentralized system of justice that requires citizen participation. Historically, because jurors were generally illiterate, evidence had to be provided orally. In contrast, the modern version of civil law that was developed in the Napoleonic code and subsequently formed the basis for the legal system in many countries, relies on written evidence. Adjudication is by appointed judges whose task is to implement the law. In the civil-law system, justice is typically rendered by a panel of judges, whereas in a common-law system it is rendered by the jury assisted usually by a single judge.

Civil law is a more centralized system designed to render justice in a more uniform way. There is a judicial hierarchy that provides a comprehensive system of legal review; judges in the upper levels of the hierarchy use the written evidence in a case to help them monitor decisions by judges at lower levels. Legal decisions can be appealed and reconsidered based not only on legal arguments, but also on how the facts of the case were presented. This allows the detection of incompetence or poor judicial conduct by lower-level judges. In contrast, in the common-law system, appeals are much rarer and are not based on the determinations of fact but only on the basis of legal arguments related to the conduct of judicial proceedings

Another major difference between both systems is that common-law systems are adversarial, while civil-law systems are inquisitorial. In the **adversarial system**, each party brings evidence to court. The prosecution presents evidence against the defendant, and the defense offers evidence in favor of the defendant. In the **inquisitorial system**, an investigative judge who is in charge of instructing the case before the trial opens collects all the evidence for both parties. A case can be made that in the adversarial system, each party has stronger incentives to collect evidence, because it can make a significant difference in the outcome. On the other hand, if the investigative judge in the civil-law system finds either more evidence for or against the defendant, or little information for or against, it does not make much of a difference for the outcome; more evidence on both sides will tend to "cancel out" in terms of the final adjudication. There are thus fewer incentives to look for more evidence. Table 10.1 summarizes the main differences between the two systems.

Why do these differences between civil law and common law matter? Economist Friedrich Hayek argued that the common-law system has two major advantages over the civil-law system.[1] First, it gives greater political independence to the judiciary branch of government. Second, it has the property of flexibility and adaptability in terms of a changing societal environment. Let us explore these points in turn.

Several elements contribute to less judicial independence in the civil-law system compared to the common-law system. First, the civil-law system relies more on judges appointed by the executive branch of government, which makes them less independent than juries. Second, the civil-law system, with its hierarchy of judges and emphasis on written documents, allows better monitoring of low-level judges by their superiors, making the system quite dependent on the judicial hierarchy. Third, in the civil-law system, a judge has less power because his or her role is limited to implementing the laws that the legislative branch has passed. Finally, add to these restrictions the specific judicial parameters described in bright-line rules. In contrast, common-law judges must interpret legal precedents in reaching their decisions. As a result, legislative statutes

TABLE 10.1   Differences between Common-Law and Civil-Law Systems

Common law	Civil law
• Primarily based on non-statutory law: precedent (jurisprudence) • Emphasis on oral argument and evidence • Generalized use of juries • Accusatorial method • Less higher appeal	• Primarily based on statutory law: code and bright-line rules • Emphasis on written record of evidence • Adjudication mostly by appointed judges presiding as a panel • Inquisitorial method • Frequent higher appeal

---

[1] Friedrich A. Hayek, *The Constitution of Liberty* (Chicago: University of Chicago Press, 1960).

Historical Origins of Civil and Common Law

The civil-law system dates back to Roman law as codified in the Justinian code. Justinian was emperor of Byzantium, the Eastern Roman empire, from 527 to 565 CE. Monks and priests studied the code during the Middle Ages and the Catholic Church chose to use the Roman law as the basis for its code of ecclesiastical laws, known as canon law. The Church also adopted the inquisitorial system, collegial adjudication by judges, and presumption of innocence. The civil-law system was formally introduced in France during the reigns of Philip Augustus (1165–1223) and Louis IX (1215–1270). It was studied and taught in the first European universities and was thus widely disseminated and eventually adopted everywhere in Europe, except in England. For the most part, modern civil law was influenced by the Napoleonic code, which, in the 19th century, was intended to replace feudal laws with a modern written legal code in accordance with the principles of the French Revolution and its declaration of human rights. The Napoleonic Code had an important influence on Latin American countries that eventually adopted versions of it after independence. It also significantly influenced Scandinavian law. Civil-law systems existed in Prussia, Bavaria, and Austria, and Germany adopted one after its unification in 1871. Japan copied parts of the German system during the Meiji restoration period (1868–1912) when it began to import Western institutions in its drive for modernization.

Common law originated in the customary laws practiced by the ancient Saxon, Celtic, and Germanic tribes. Today's common-law system, however, developed under England's King Henry II (1133–1189). He decreed that the country's various ecclesiastical and civil law systems should be unified into a single legal code and he instituted the use of jury trials. Juries were initially composed of local notables who, under oath, gave traveling judges all available local knowledge relative to potential suspects. Initially, the role of juries was only one of information-gathering. The unification of the legal system by Henry II nevertheless challenged the powerful canonical courts of the Church and was heavily criticized by the Catholic Archbishop of Canterbury, Thomas Becket, who was later murdered by the king's henchmen. The role of juries strengthened over time and was expanded to include a determination of guilt or innocence. Juries were seen as protectors of the wrongfully accused because they would tend to mitigate very harsh criminal laws. The Magna Carta (1215), a charter of liberties and rights that English nobles forced King John (Henry II's son) to sign, included the right to "lawful judgment of peers," which Parliament interpreted centuries later as the right to a jury trial.

carry less weight when compared to civil-law systems in which legislation is the source of law. The origins of modern civil-law systems under Napoleon and Bismarck were part of a process of state-building and consolidation of power in the central government with the explicit intention to have less judicial independence. As a result, property rights are potentially less secure against government expropriation in civil-law systems compared to common-law systems.

It can be argued that the common-law system is more flexible and adaptable because of the greater discretion given to judges. If the social and cultural environment changes and existing laws become inefficient, they can be challenged and gradually amended or replaced. While the consideration of precedent can result in some inertia in terms of the evolution of laws, it can also give momentum to new approaches to the adjudication of certain types of cases. In contrast, in the civil-law system, judges persist in implementing inequitable or outdated laws as long as the legislative branch does not change them.

The Economic Effects of Different Legal Systems

With various coauthors, Andrei Shleifer, a Harvard economics professor, has done extensive research on the economic effects of the differences between legal systems. The researchers have found these differences primarily affect the comparative development of financial markets, believed to be an important ingredient for economic development. Central to the operation of financial markets is the issue of protecting the rights of shareholders and creditors in common-law versus civil-law countries.[2]

Shareholder protection. Table 10.2 presents data on shareholder rights. Countries are identified according to their legal systems and their level of economic development.

TABLE 10.2   Shareholder Rights in Common-Law and Civil-Law Countries (in % of Countries)

Indicators of shareholder rights	Common-law countries (developed)	Common-law countries (developing)	Civil-law countries (developed)	Civil-law countries (developing)	Average
One share–one vote	11	22	14	36	21
Proxy by mail allowed	67	11	14	00	23
Shares not blocked before meeting	100	100	14	79	73
Cumulative voting/proportional representation	22	33	14	36	26
Oppressed minority	100	89	14	36	60
Preemptive right to new issues	44	44	86	50	56
Percentage of share capital to call an extraordinary shareholders' meeting	08	10	11	17	11
Sum of shareholder rights	352	309	167	254	270

The last row sums all the shareholder rights. These rights are more extensive in common-law countries than in civil-law countries in both developed and developing economies. The common-law countries in the sample include Australia, Canada, Ireland, Hong Kong, Israel, New Zealand, Singapore, the United Kingdom, and the United States for developed countries; and India, Kenya, Malaysia, Nigeria, Pakistan, South Africa, Sri Lanka, Thailand, and Zimbabwe for developing countries. For the civil-law countries, Belgium, France, Greece, Italy, the Netherlands, Portugal, and Spain are the developed countries; and the developing countries include Argentina, Brazil, Chili, Colombia, Ecuador, Egypt, Indonesia, Jordan, Mexico, Peru, the Philippines, Turkey, Uruguay, and Venezuela.[3]

Source: Rafael La Porta, Florencio Lopez-de-Silanes, Andrei Shleifer, and Robert W. Vishny, "Law and Finance," *Journal of Political Economy* 106, no. 6 (1998): 1130.

---

[2]Rafael La Porta, Florencio Lopez-de-Silanes, Andrei Shleifer, and Robert W. Vishny, "Law and Finance," *Journal of Political Economy* 106, no. 6 (1998): 1113–1155.

[3]The sample only includes countries that have adopted a version of the French civil-law system because countries that adopted either the German or Scandinavian forms of civil law are all developed countries.

Let us discuss the indicators in Table 10.2. For each of the variables of shareholder protection listed, the number in the table gives us the proportion of countries in a particular category that features the particular shareholder protection. For example, only 11% of common-law developed countries have the one share–one vote rule, which implies that nonvoting shares are prohibited or that there is no limit on the number of votes per shareholder. This rule can be broken in many ways; for example, shares of the company founders can carry more votes, shares held for a longer time period may carry more votes, and some shares may carry no votes at all. Very few countries have the one share–one vote provision. Interestingly, it tends to be more prevalent in developing countries and it is highest in the civil-law developing countries.

A second variable, proxy by mail, protects small shareholders who may not be able to attend meetings. Here, common-law countries do better. The third variable, shares not blocked before meeting, prohibits firms from requiring that shareholders deposit their shares prior to a shareholders meeting, so as to prevent them from selling the shares. These requirements discourage small shareholders from attending a meeting by making it more costly to do so. All common-law countries have this provision, but it is less prevalent in civil-law countries.

The fourth variable relates to the protection of minority shareholders. Cumulative voting means that a shareholder can cast all of his or her votes for one candidate for the board of directors; proportional representation means that the law allows minority interests to be proportionally represented on the board. The fifth variable, the oppressed minority, refers to a) whether company law gives minority shareholders a judicial venue to challenge management decisions or decisions of the shareholders assembly, and b) whether minority shareholders can force the company to buy their shares if they object to fundamental changes such as mergers. Common-law countries do better here. All developed common-law countries have an oppressed minority mechanism as do 89% of the developing common-law countries. Less than 50% of civil-law countries have this mechanism.

The sixth variable, preemptive rights to new issues, refers to the shareholder right to buy new issues of company stock. This protects shareholders from dilution of their shares, a tactic that management often uses to weaken certain groups of shareholders. No major differences between groups of countries exist for this variable, except that developed civil-law countries score higher. Finally, a lower percentage of shares to call an extraordinary shareholders meeting favors small shareholders as it makes it easier for them to organize. It is somewhat lower in common-law countries and is higher in developing civil-law countries.

The shareholder rights index is the summation of the seven variables listed. Minority shareholder rights are, in general, better protected in common-law countries compared to civil-law countries. Developed common-law countries do better than developing common-law countries. For civil-law countries, it is the opposite.

Protection of creditor rights. We now look at the protection of creditor rights in the same groups of countries. These are the rights that creditors have when debtors default on their payments. Table 10.3 shows the key variables. As in

TABLE 10.3   Creditor Rights in Common-Law and Civil-Law Countries (in % of Countries)

Indicators of creditor rights	Common-law countries (developed)	Common-law countries (developing)	Civil-law countries (developed)	Civil-law countries (developing)	Average
No automatic stay on assets	56	89	29	25	50
Secured creditors paid first	89	89	71	62	78
Restrictions for going into reorganization	56	89	29	50	56
Management does not stay in reorganization	56	100	14	33	51
Sum of creditor rights	257	367	143	167	235

In both developed and developing nations, creditor rights are more extensive in common-law countries than in civil-law countries.

Source: La Porta et al., "Law and Finance," 1998: 1133.

Table 10.2, the numbers give us the percentage of countries in a particular country category for the particular creditor right listed.

There are two ways to deal with a firm when it defaults: liquidation and reorganization. Creditor rights are important in both cases. In some countries, reorganization imposes an **automatic stay on the assets**; that is, assets of the firm cannot be claimed by creditors. This prevents automatic liquidation and protects current management. "No automatic stay" can thus be seen as a protection of creditor rights. This is more prevalent in common-law than civil-law countries (with the important exception of the United States) and by a significant margin. Note that the developing common-law countries score even better than the developed common-law countries for this variable.

The second variable refers to seniority rules in bankruptcy. Secured creditors, those creditors with collateral rights, are usually paid before other classes of creditors in bankruptcy proceedings. However, this is not the case in all countries. Common-law countries score better here, too.

Third, in some countries, management can seek protection from creditors by filing for reorganization. Restrictions on these strategies exist when the consent of creditors (who are generally opposed to reorganization) is required. Here again, common-law countries score better. Finally, in some countries management is automatically removed from its responsibilities when reorganization is implemented, while that is not the case in other countries. The requirements in this category are more rigorous in common-law countries than in civil-law countries. Note that the United States, which is a common-law country, does not score well with these variables, but it is a clear exception within common-law countries.

The creditor rights index sums up the four variables discussed. Its value ranges from 0 (weakest) to 400 (strongest). We can see that common-law countries offer better protection of creditor rights than do civil-law countries. Interestingly, the developing countries generally score better than the developed countries within each legal category.

Quality of law enforcement. Tables 10.2 and 10.3 compare measures of existing shareholder and creditor rights. However, the quality of law enforcement is even more important for protecting those rights. Table 10.4 presents a series of variables that attempt to measure law-enforcement quality.

The indicator of efficiency of the judicial system is a score from 0 to 10 taken from Business International Corporation, which rates the risks associated with investing in a particular country. It represents investors' assessments of the "efficiency and integrity of the legal environment as it affects business, particularly foreign firms." It has a higher value for common-law than for civil-law countries, but the biggest difference occurs between developed and developing countries: scores for the former are clearly higher than for the latter. A similar pattern holds for the indicator of the rule of law, which is from another rating agency, the International Country Risk Guide. Here, no difference exists between common-law and civil-law countries. The only difference occurs between developed and developing countries, illustrating once again the importance of institutions to development. We can draw a similar conclusion from the next three indicators, corruption, risk of appropriation, and risk of contract repudiation, also taken from the International Country Risk Guide: common-law and civil-law countries do not differ substantially in terms of law-enforcement quality. The main difference is again between developed and developing countries. We can thus conclude that while the differences in the legal protections for shareholders and creditors between common-law and civil-law systems are relevant, the common-law and civil-law distinction in developing countries is of second-order importance relative to the issue of the quality of law enforcement, which fundamentally affects the security of property rights. Laws, however imperfect, protect property rights. Weak law

TABLE 10.4 Law-Enforcement Quality in Common-Law and Civil-Law Countries

Indicators of law enforcement	Common-law countries (developed)	Common-law countries (developing)	Civil-law countries (developed)	Civil-law countries (developing)	Average
Efficiency of the judicial system	9.78	6.53	7.57	6.05	7.48
Rule of law	8.66	4.26	8.57	4.79	6.57
Corruption	8.87	5.26	8.00	4.76	6.72
Risk of expropriation	9.31	6.51	9.16	6.61	7.90
Risk of contract repudiation	8.86	5.95	8.68	5.91	7.35

In both common-law and civil-law countries, law-enforcement indicators are lower in developing countries compared to developed countries.

Source: La Porta et al., "Law and Finance," 1998: 1142.

enforcement implies weak property-rights protection. This correlation is thus quite important in assessing the effects of differences in legal systems.

Let us now look at the effects of these differences on measures of financial market development.[4] Table 10.5 reports three measures of financial market development: 1) stock market capitalization as a percentage of GNP, a rough measure of the importance of share ownership in the economy; 2) the total number of listed firms per million inhabitants, also a measure of the depth of financial markets; and 3) total private sector debt as a percentage of GNP, which measures the extent of the debt market in the economy. For all three measures, common-law countries do better than civil-law countries. However, for development of debt, no real difference exists between common-law countries and developed civil-law countries. Only the developing civil-law countries lag behind. Also, when we look at the number of listed domestic firms, the main difference is between developed common-law countries and all the others, although the developed civil-law countries do somewhat better than the developing countries. Nevertheless, the general message is that financial markets are more developed in common-law countries.

Controversies over the Importance of Common and Civil Law

The research of Shleifer et al., on the comparison between legal systems has been quite influential, but it has also generated controversy. Their evidence on the better performance of common-law systems may seem less impressive when we look at measures of financial development over time. This is precisely what Raghuram Rajan and Luigi Zingales have done.[5] They report two surprising

TABLE 10.5 Financial Market Development in Common-Law and Civil-Law Countries

	Common-law countries (developed)	Common-law countries (developing)	Civil-law countries (developed)	Civil-law countries (developing)	Average
Stock market capitalization as share of GNP (%)	62	56.8	18.9	22	39.9
Number of listed domestic firms relative to population (in millions)	61.7	9.24	14.2	7.3	23.1
Private sector debt as share of GNP (%)	75	59	65.6	32.3	58.0

Different measures of financial development show that common-law countries tend to have more developed financial markets than do civil-law countries.

Source: Based on Rafael La Porta, Florencio Lopez-de-Silanes, Andrei Shleifer, and Robert W. Vishny, "Legal Determinants of External Finance," *Journal of Finance* 52, no. 3 (1997): 108.

---

[4]Rafael La Porta, Florencio Lopez-de-Silanes, Andrei Shleifer, and Robert W. Vishny, "Legal Determinants of External Finance," *Journal of Finance* 52, no. 3 (1997): 99–118.
[5]Raghuram G. Rajan and Luigi Zingales, "The Great Reversals: The Politics of Financial Development in the Twentieth Century," *Journal of Financial Economics* 69, no. 1 (2003): 5–50.

findings: 1) there was a very large variation in the development of world financial markets throughout the 20th century; and 2) financial markets were more
developed in 1913 than in 1980 and have only recently surpassed the 1913 level.
Figure 10.1 illustrates the evolution of three measures of financial development.

The first two variables in Figure 10.1 are similar to those listed in Table 10.5:
stock market capitalization as a share of GDP and the number of listed domestic companies per million inhabitants. The third variable measures equity
issues by domestic corporations as a share of gross fixed capital formation, that
is, gross investment. It gives us an idea of what percentage of the economy's
investment is financed by issuing shares. Even though the three measures vary
over time, common patterns nevertheless exist. First, from 1913 until the stock
market crash of 1929, stock market development was stronger than in much of
the rest of the 20th century, at least until the 1990s. Second, stock market development declined from the period of the Great Depression (the 1930s) until at
least the late 1980s. Third, there was rapid financial market development in the
1990s, the period we now identify with globalization. These data remind us
that globalization had already begun in the early 20th century.

If financial market development has varied so much over time, what are
we to make of the distinction between common-law and civil-law countries in
terms of this measure? Figure 10.2 shows the evolution of stock market capitalization as a share of GDP over time for these categories of countries. Note that
the sample of developing countries is much smaller here. Only India and South
Africa are in the sample for common-law developing countries, while Argentina,
Brazil, Chile, and Egypt represent the sample for civil-law developing countries.

FIGURE 10.1   Financial Market Development in the 20th Century

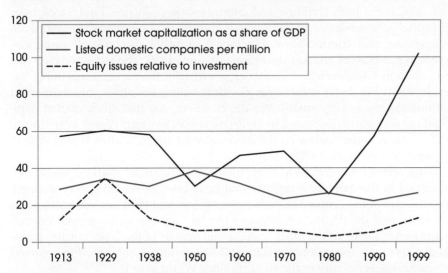

Financial market development has varied greatly in the 20th century. Financial markets
were generally more developed in 1913 than in 1980. Only in the last few decades have
they experienced significant expansion.

Source: Raghuram G. Rajan and Luigi Zingales, "The Great Reversals: The Politics of Financial
Development in the Twentieth Century," *Journal of Financial Economics* 69, no. 1 (2003): 13.

FIGURE 10.2   Dynamics of Stock Market Capitalization in Common-Law and Civil-Law Countries

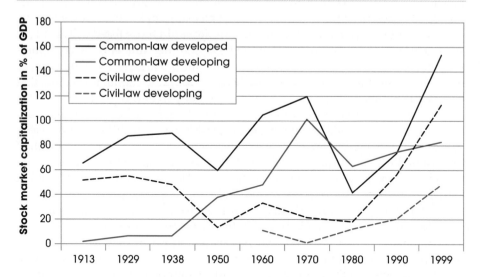

Common-law and civil-law countries have experienced similar dynamics in terms of financial market development over time.

Source: Rajan and Zingales, "The Great Reversals: The Politics of Financial Development in the Twentieth Century," 2003: 14.

Figure 10.2 demonstrates that the dynamics throughout the 20th century were similar for both civil-law and common-law countries. First, stock market capitalization relative to GDP was higher in 1913 compared to 1980, both for civil-law and common-law developed countries. Second, all categories have had rapid stock market development since 1980. The slope for civil-law and common-law developed countries is virtually the same; if anything, the development has been weaker for the developing countries (but remember that our sample is very small). We do, however, see that stock market capitalization was quite depressed in civil-law countries from World War II until 1980, whereas common-law countries developed strongly after World War II, despite a decline in the 1970s.

What should we conclude from all this? If financial markets were well developed in the early 20th century and have been developing very strongly since the end of the century in both common-law and civil-law countries, does that mean that the distinction between the two legal systems is not very relevant? Perhaps, but on the other hand, in the middle of the 20th century, financial markets were more depressed in civil-law countries compared to common law-countries, especially in the 40 years since World War II.

Rajan and Zingales suggest why we may see this pattern. The evolution of civil law is more dependent on the actions of the legislature, that is, the laws politicians enact. Firms lobby to obtain or maintain favorable monopoly positions, rents, and legal arrangements. This is called **rent-seeking**. Rajan and Zingales argue that the incentives for interest groups to lobby against financial development were different in a world where both trade and capital flows were open (as in the early and late 20th century) as compared to a more closed world such as that between the Great Depression and the 1980s. Openness to trade increases competition and thus the need for firms to raise funds to invest and stay competitive. Without financial openness, firms could lobby the government for subsidies and privileged loans, which was the case in many countries after World War II. However, if trade openness is combined with financial openness, that is, free capital mobility, the government's ability to intervene in favor of certain firms will decrease as it faces the possibility of capital flight out of the country. Capital flight will punish government subsidization of established dinosaur firms and imprudent macroeconomic behavior (running large deficits). Capital mobility thus works as a device to discipline the government. This, in turn, reduces the benefits of lobbying to obtain rents and privileges. Because civil law is more sensitive to decisions in the legislature, Rajan and Zingales argue that the countries with this system were more vulnerable to rent-seeking that prevented financial development in the period between the Great Depression and 1980, when there was less financial and/or trade openness in the world economy. However, in an open world, demand for financial development will be strong and civil-law countries will ultimately pass better legislation for financial development. Thus, the distinction between common-law and civil-law systems may matter more in periods when there is less trade and financial openness than in periods of global trade and increased international capital mobility.

Fiscal Institutions

Fiscal institutions are the rules and means by which government assures adequate revenue. Fiscal institutions are important because they determine the extent to which the governments of poorer countries can finance public services as well as the extent of **tax distortions** associated with tax collection. Developing countries desperately need basic public services such as health, education, and infrastructure. These services are crucial not only for social welfare, but also for economic development. On the other hand, poorer countries have fewer means available to support an efficient tax administration apparatus. In less-developed economies, it is also much more difficult to collect information about economic transactions. In many developing economies, transactions are in cash and only a minority of households and firms use banks. Because of these difficulties, developing countries face severe tax collection challenges. Therefore, a much smaller portion of tax revenues come from income taxes on households. Foreign trade taxes are still an important source of revenues. Because of the significant costs of tax collection, governments are often tempted to finance their expenditures by printing money. As a result, inflation is also a serious problem in many developing economies.

Taxation in Developing Countries

Let us start our examination of fiscal institutions by comparing the importance of government revenues and tax revenues in developing and advanced economies. Figure 10.3 presents data from the IMF's Government Financial

FIGURE 10.3 Tax and Government Revenues as a Percent of Gross National Income in Different Countries

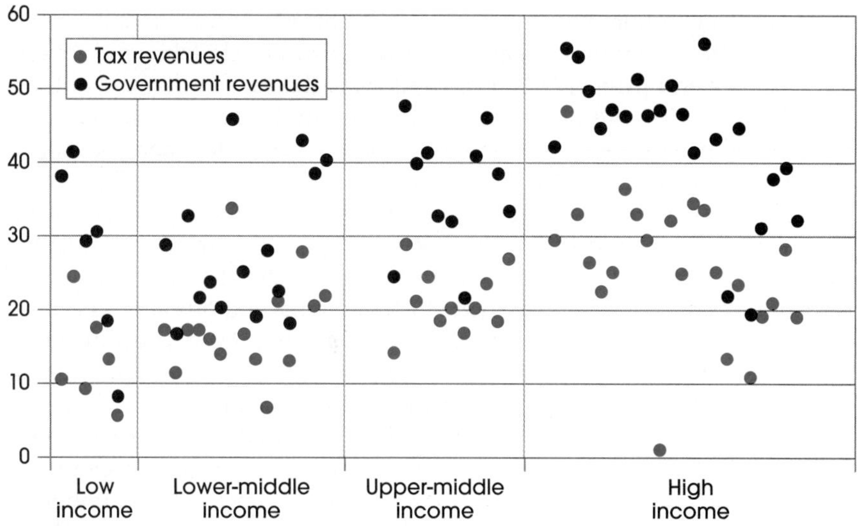

Tax and government revenues as a percentage of gross national income are higher in countries with greater income per capita.

Source: International Monetary Fund, Government Financial Statistics (GFS) dataset, 2007.

Statistics to show the importance of total government revenues and tax revenues as a percentage of gross national income.[6] Tax revenues and government revenues are not necessarily the same because not all government revenues come from taxes. For example, in Kuwait, tax revenues are only 1.2% of national income, whereas total government revenues represent 47% of national income. The difference is due to oil revenues. Figure 10.3 presents data for roughly four income categories: low income, lower-middle income, upper-middle income, and high-income countries.

Figure 10.3 shows that total government revenues are greater in the higher income countries (43.1% of gross national income compared to 29% in the low-income countries). In a large country such as India, for example, government revenues are only 8.2% of gross national income, whereas even in the United States, where the size of government is smaller than in most European countries, government revenues are above 30% of gross national income. In addition, tax revenues as a percentage of gross national income are also higher in developed countries. Even though tax revenues are only 19.1% of gross

---

[6]These are data from before the 2008 Great Recession. They provide a better picture of long-term trends than do data from more recent but more turbulent years in the world economy.

national income in the United States (much lower than the average of 25.9% for high-income countries), average tax revenues represent only 15.7% of gross national income in low-income countries. In India, tax revenues constitute only 5.8% of gross national income.

This lower share of tax revenues in poor countries means that developing countries are less successful at raising taxes to finance public services. Note also that in these countries, there is a greater discrepancy between government revenues and tax revenues. In low-income countries, tax revenues are barely above 50% of total government revenues. In other countries, tax revenues constitute at least 60% of total government revenues. The difference between tax revenues and total government revenues is either related to income from natural resources such as oil and gas or to income from government-owned industries and services. We have already discussed the example of Kuwait, but there are many more. In the Democratic Republic of the Congo, tax revenues are only 10.6% of gross national income, whereas government revenues constitute 38.1% of gross national income due to the returns from natural resources such as copper. The lower share of taxes in government revenues generally indicates the difficulty of raising tax revenues in these poorer countries.

Tables 10.6a and 10.6b compare the composition of taxes between developing and developed countries. Note that the share of income taxes in total government revenues is very low in poor countries—only 14.2%. In contrast, income taxes represent roughly 30% of government revenues in high-income countries—slightly more than double their share in poor countries. Middle-income countries also have a lower share of income taxes.

Another difference between developing and developed countries is that corporate income taxes constitute about half or more of all income taxes in poor countries, whereas in rich countries income taxes are mainly paid by individuals. In high-income countries, corporate income taxes constitute roughly a quarter of all income taxes. In lower-middle-income countries, they constitute roughly two-thirds of income taxes.

Now consider indirect taxes, the share of which in government revenues is at 30.5% in low-income countries and 24.4% in high-income countries. Poor countries thus rely more on indirect taxation than on direct taxation. By contrast, in developed economies direct taxation is somewhat more important than indirect taxation. Note that middle-income countries also rely quite heavily on indirect taxes.

Another notable difference between developed and developing countries concerns taxes on foreign trade, that is, tariffs and export duties. Slightly more than 10% of government revenues in low-income countries are raised through foreign trade. While this source of revenue is smaller than that from direct taxes, it is nevertheless roughly two-thirds as important. In high-income countries, less than .5% of government revenues are raised from foreign trade taxes, making them completely negligible as a revenue source. Finally, consider social security contributions: they are insignificant in low-income countries, but they constitute between 15 and 25% of government revenues in developed countries.

TABLE 10.6a   Composition of Taxes in Developing Countries (in % of Government Revenue)

	Total taxes	Income taxes	Corporate income taxes	Domestic indirect taxes	Foreign trade taxes	Social security
Lower-income countries						
Congo, Dem. Rep.	27.8	4.0	0.0	16.3	6.6	4.2
India	71.1	18.9	7.3	41.6	6.2	17.1
Bhutan	33.1	16.5	12.2	13.9	1.4	0.0
Lesotho	78.6	21.7	5.4	14.9	41.7	0.0
Moldova	57.7	12.4	6.0	39.0	4.8	21.7
Mongolia	59.0	16.3	11.5	35.0	5.4	15.1
Tajikistan	72.4	9.3	3.1	52.8	8.8	9.7
Average	**57.1**	**14.2**	**6.5**	**30.5**	**10.7**	**9.7**
Lower-middle-income countries						
Bolivia	59.9	6.4	6.4	38.3	3.6	7.6
Albania	67.3	13.6	9.6	43.9	8.7	16.3
Belarus	73.5	14.5	7.4	42.1	5.2	23.3
Armenia	70.2	11.9	6.8	36.0	3.0	13.2
Bulgaria	54.5	16.0	7.2	34.2	1.6	25.6
Colombia	66.5	17.6	17.6	20.3	4.7	5.8
El Salvador	68.2	20.3	9.7	39.3	7.0	14.3
Georgia	71.1	18.9	7.3	41.6	6.2	17.1
Iran, Islamic Rep.	24.7	9.0	6.0	4.3	6.7	11.9
Kazakhstan	94.9	36.4	6.4	33.0	4.6	0.0
Peru	72.7	20.4	26.8	49.4	7.0	9.4
Romania	53.5	16.1	12.4	33.2	2.1	33.5
Serbia and Montenegro	65.1	13.7	7.3	37.4	5.8	25.4
Thailand	80.8	28.1	1.0	42.0	8.4	3.8
Ukraine	53.8	26.0	19.0	22.0	3.9	27.6
Average	**65.1**	**17.9**	**12.5**	**34.5**	**5.5**	**15.1**

Source: International Monetary Fund, Government Financial Statistics (GFS) dataset, 2007.

Overall, tax revenues tend to be lower in developing countries because of difficulties associated with raising taxes. Income taxes and social security contributions also constitute a much smaller portion of revenues in these countries, while tariffs and foreign trade taxes represent a higher portion compared to that of developed countries.

TABLE 10.6b   Composition of Taxes in Developed Countries (in % of Government Revenue)

	Total taxes	Income taxes	Corporate income taxes	Domestic indirect taxes	Foreign trade taxes	Social security
Upper-middle-income countries						
Costa Rica	58.6	13.7	n.a.	37.8	4.3	25.1
Croatia	61.0	13.1	4.7	44.4	2.3	30.7
Czech Republic	53.8	23.9	11.5	27.5	1.0	39.1
Hungary	59.1	22.8	5.4	31.5	1.8	29.2
Latvia	57.5	22.4	5.2	31.3	0.8	27.5
Lithuania	63.4	24.5	3.1	36.5	0.8	27.3
Mauritius	78.7	12.1	6.5	40.8	20.1	3.6
Poland	49.4	15.4	4.8	29.0	1.1	35.2
Russian Federation	52.1	17.6	9.6	23.8	7.3	22.3
Slovak Republic	48.0	16.4	6.7	29.6	0.6	35.2
South Africa	80.5	43.3	15.1	27.6	2.4	1.6
Average	**60.2**	**20.5**	**7.2**	**32.7**	**3.9**	**25.2**
High-income countries						
Canada	69.8	37.4	7.4	21.1	0.6	13.1
Denmark	84.7	52.1	5.2	28.9	0.0	2.3
Finland	61.1	33.4	7.2	25.7	0.0	22.7
France	53.3	20.7	4.7	22.0	0.0	32.7
Germany	50.5	25.5	1.5	23.3	0.0	38.7
Greece	53.3	20.0	6.9	29.4	0.0	24.7
Iceland	78.6	35.7	2.9	34.4	0.9	6.7
Israel	64.4	26.8	5.0	26.9	0.6	12.9
Italy	63.8	31.1	6.0	28.4	0.0	26.9
Kuwait	2.5	0.4	0.4	0.0	1.9	0.0
Luxembourg	63.8	33.1	18.0	27.1	0.0	25.3
Netherlands	53.6	22.2	7.0	26.6	0.5	30.9
New Zealand	83.1	48.8	10.7	26.9	2.7	0.0
Norway	59.7	33.6	14.4	24.1	0.2	17.7
Portugal	58.3	23.4	9.1	31.9	0.0	26.0
Singapore	62.0	30.3	n.a.	21.6	1.0	0.0
Slovenia	52.7	17.2	3.6	29.8	1.3	35.6
Spain	56.6	25.3	8.1	24.8	0.0	31.5
Sweden	61.7	32.9	4.9	21.4	0.0	24.8
Switzerland	56.4	32.4	n.a.	16.6	0.6	23.7
United Kingdom	71.8	33.3	7.7	32.9	0.0	17.8
United States	59.7	35.4	5.9	14.0	0.6	22.1
Average	**60.1**	**29.6**	**6.8**	**24.4**	**0.5**	**19.8**

Compared to higher income countries, lower income countries have a higher share of corporate taxes, taxes on foreign trade, and indirect taxes as well as a lower share of income taxes contributing to tax revenues.

Source: International Monetary Fund, Government Financial Statistics (GFS) dataset, 2007.

The Value-Added Tax

One indirect tax that has worked quite well in developing economies is the **value-added tax**, more commonly called the **VAT**. It has several advantages. First, it avoids a taxation cascade that occurs with sales taxes in many countries. Consider a chain of supply and production, from raw materials to final sales. A sales tax increases the cost of production and thus the sales price at each stage of production. This increases the relative price of final goods and thus creates a larger distortion for those goods than for unfinished goods. The VAT avoids that, as the tax is only levied on the value added. In other words, at each stage in production, the value of the purchased inputs is deducted from the sales figure. The tax is thus solely levied on the value that has been added at that stage and taxation cascade is avoided.[7]

A numerical example clearly shows the difference between the value-added tax and a sales tax. Consider two goods, cloth and shirts. Cloth is used to produce shirts. Assume that the price of cloth to produce a shirt is 10 and the price of a shirt is equal to the price of cloth plus 40. Without taxes, the price of a shirt is 50. Then consider a sales tax of 20%. The cloth will then sell at 12, and the shirt will sell at $(12 + 40) \times 1.2 = 62.4$. Note that the shirt is 24.8% more expensive as a result of the tax. This is because of the cascade of the sales tax. The shirt buyer pays both the tax on the shirt and the tax on the cloth. How will things look with a value-added tax of 20%? The cloth will still sell at 12, but the tax on the shirt will now be 20% of 40 (the value added when producing the shirt), that is, 8. The shirt will thus sell at 60 and the tax cascade is avoided.

A second advantage of the VAT is that it is more difficult to avoid than other forms of indirect taxation. When paying a value-added tax, a business owner deducts the costs of inputs from a product's sales so that the tax is only on the value added. One person's sales are another person's purchases. The cloth producer would like to "under-invoice" in order to declare fewer sales. However, the cloth purchaser (the shirt producer) has the opposite incentive. If he decides to declare fewer purchases, he will pay a higher value-added tax. To hide the VAT, multiple sellers and buyers must participate in a chain of collusion, which is much more difficult than in a transaction that involves only two parties. The VAT thus has a built-in mechanism to prevent tax evasion.

Brazil introduced the VAT in 1967, and since then more than 60 developing countries have adopted it. For example, Mexico, Turkey, Colombia, and Indonesia introduced the VAT when they implemented fiscal modernization and the results have generally been quite successful.

Determinants of Tax Structure

To understand the difference between the tax structures in developing and developed countries, it is useful to review what economic theory has to say about the determinants of tax structure.

First, remember that taxation is **distortionary**, that is, it modifies the economic decisions of economic agents. Let us start with the examples illustrated in Figures 10.4a and 10.4b.

---

[7]Note that the United States has only a retail sales tax, not a VAT, and thus avoids cascade effects.

FIGURE 10.4a   Tax Distortion on Labor Supply

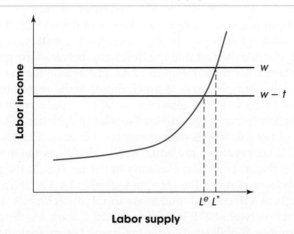

FIGURE 10.4b   A Larger Distortion with More Elastic Labor Supply

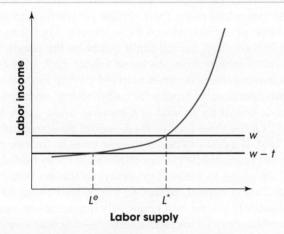

Taxation of wages distorts labor supply downward from L^* to L^e. The more elastic the labor supply is, the greater the distortion.

Concentrate first on Figure 10.4a. The curve shows the labor supply behavior of an individual as a function of the wage paid to him or her. The wage is on the vertical axis and the quantity of labor supplied is on the horizontal axis. The individual will want to equate the marginal benefit of one more hour of work, the wage, with the marginal cost, that is, the disutility of labor. Each point on the labor supply curve represents the optimal labor supply as a function of the wage rate. The supply curve becomes steeper, indicating that the marginal disutility of labor is higher with every extra hour worked. If the equilibrium market wage rate is w, then the optimal labor supply of the individual will be at level L^*. This is the optimal labor supply decision without taxation.

Now introduce taxation and assume a tax t on the hourly wage. The hourly after-tax wage becomes $w - t$ instead of w. The effect of taxation will be to reduce the labor supply to L^e instead of L^*. The reduction in the labor supply $(L^* - L^e)$ represents the distortion introduced by taxation.

How important is the tax distortion? This will depend on the elasticity of the tax base. Look now at Figure 10.4b. There, the tax distortion is higher than in Figure 10.4a, despite the fact that the difference between the gross wage and after-tax wage is smaller than in Figure 10.4a. The reason for the higher distortion is that the labor supply curve is much flatter in the region between w and $w - t$. This has to do with the elasticity of labor supply with respect to the wage rate: a slightly lower wage will lead to a large decrease in labor supply.

The extent of tax distortions also affects the tax base. The **tax base** is what is being taxed. If tax revenues are equal to tL, where L is the amount of labor supply, then L is the tax base. The **elasticity of the tax base** is the percentage by which the tax base declines if the tax rate increases by 1%. If a 1% increase in the tax rate leads to a decline of total labor supply by 0.5%, we determine that the tax base is not very elastic. If it declines by 10%, then it is very elastic.

What determines the elasticity of a tax base? Let us look first at production factors: capital, labor, and land. Here, **factor mobility** is the key element in determining the elasticity of the tax base. Capital is a very mobile factor. In today's global world, capital can move halfway across the world with the click of a mouse. Investors place their capital where they expect the highest returns, but taxation of capital reduces those returns. Therefore, in response to capital taxation in a country, capital flight might be the result. Labor is much less mobile. We occasionally hear stories of French rock singers and Swedish movie directors leaving their countries to avoid paying income taxes, but these situations are rare. Because of labor's lack of mobility, an increase in taxation on labor income is less likely to lead to a massive brain drain. Finally, land is not at all mobile.[8] Of the three factors, then, capital is significantly more mobile than labor and land. If a country needs to raise taxes to finance public services, it will be better to tax immobile factors rather than those that are mobile. Taxing the land is not going to make it go away, so the tax base is almost completely inelastic. Taxing capital, however, might lead to capital flight, which might make the country poorer and negatively impact tax revenues.

Mobility is not the only factor that determines the elasticity of the tax base. As we saw in the example of labor supply in Figures 10.4a and 10.4b, taxation of labor income might reduce labor supply. However, labor supply is, in general, not very elastic. People need to earn a living; in some cases, an increase in taxation on labor income might even cause people to increase rather than decrease their labor supply because they have a target income amount. Capital, on the other hand, is a cumulative factor, that is, capital increases with the amount of investment made in the economy. Because people have a choice between investing and consuming, taxing capital might cause economic agents to substitute consumption for investment. Eventually, this would lead to less capital accumulation. Capital is thus quite elastic with respect to the tax rate and it is better to tax consumption rather than investment and savings so as to encourage people to invest more.

In terms of taxes on specific commodities, tax elasticity should, in principle, be equivalent to price elasticity, at least when consumers are perfectly informed

---

[8]Land taxation may nevertheless still discourage land improvement.

about the tax and the price of a commodity. Indeed, the tax raises the price on a good and is thus equivalent to a price increase. Therefore, it makes better economic sense to increase the tax on those goods that have low price elasticity rather than on those that have high price elasticity. Taxing goods with high elasticity will lead to a significant reduction in demand, whereas this will not be the case for goods with relatively low elasticity. The price elasticity of specific goods depends primarily on how easily consumers can substitute other goods for them. Taxing grain and not potatoes, for example, will not make much sense because they are acceptable substitutes for each other. Luxury goods, in contrast, are usually quite inelastic.

Tax elasticity is not the only consideration to take into account when deciding on a tax structure. Equity also plays a role. A low tax rate on capital income and a high tax rate on labor income will tend to favor the rich and burden the poor. On the other hand, taxation of land makes economic sense and it is redistributive, especially if there is significant inequality in land ownership.

Economic considerations also help to explain the tax structure in advanced economies. Income taxes, which are mostly taxes on labor income, as well as direct taxation on labor, such as social security contributions, are an important source of government revenue. Low corporate income taxes and significant indirect taxes demonstrate that taxes on consumption are also an important source of government revenue. How, then, can we explain the differences in tax structures in developing countries, in particular 1) the lower share of income taxes (but higher share of corporate income taxes); 2) the higher share of indirect taxes; and 3) the higher share of foreign trade taxes? Also, how do we explain the lower level of taxation in developing countries?

Why Does Taxation Differ between Developed and Developing Countries?

Several explanations are possible for the differences in taxation between developed and developing countries. First, administrative constraints may affect the tax structure. Second, the political economy may account for these differences. Third, disparities in the financial sector's development might play a role. Fourth, the size of the informal economy may have an important effect.

Administrative constraints. One possible reason why the tax structure is different in developing economies is that the government's ability to collect taxes is limited. Tax collection requires relatively skilled labor. In addition, the government needs taxpayer registries, information on taxation sources, and methods for cross-checking tax returns. An enforcement apparatus to ensure that taxes are collected is also necessary. Given these requirements, developing economies are at a disadvantage because of the scarcity of advanced administrative skills. They have fewer financial resources to develop an efficient tax administration. Tax inspectors are often not motivated to identify and prosecute tax evaders because in many cases, the tax inspectors are bribed to look the other way. Lower literacy rates in developing countries mean that it is not only more difficult to find good administrators, but it is also more difficult for households and small businesses to file accurate tax returns.

Administrative constraints on tax collection are compounded by the fact that it is easier to evade taxes in a developing economy. In largely rural settings, it is difficult for the government to identify and trace income. Because most of the income from farm plots is consumed directly by the farmers' households, it is challenging to trace and tax. Transactions between farmers and merchants are also difficult to track. In cities, many small businesses are nothing more than stands in open-air markets. Moreover, a large part of the small-business sector is not officially registered with the taxing authority and operates in the informal sector. Tracking down small-business owners is thus very costly and the tax yield from this source suffers.

Because of these administrative constraints, developing countries are only able to tax effectively a small proportion of the income generated. Because much of rural and small-business income is out of reach for tax collectors, it is more cost-effective to concentrate on collecting taxes from corporate income and the labor income of large firms. This means that the effective tax base for income tax collection is generally much smaller in developing economies. Tax revenues tend to be lower, and they tend to be generated from the most modern sector in the economy. This results in a significant dilemma: the temptation can be strong to tax the modern sector more to compensate for a shallow tax base, but this may hinder the modern sector's development.

Another consequence of administrative constraints is that foreign trade taxes are among the easiest to levy. Imported and exported goods transit through international customs where they can be identified and taxed. Levying these duties is easier than levying sales taxes on small grocery shops. This is certainly why foreign trade taxes are still substantially higher in developing economies despite the general global trend toward abolishing tariffs.

Political economy constraints. There are important political economy constraints on changing the tax structure in developing economies. In other words, there can be powerful interests blocking reforms that move a country toward a more efficient tax structure. The most obvious case is that of land taxation. Taxing land makes good economic sense and land is the most important source of income for many developing countries. However, in some countries, the concentration of land ownership is critical. In many Latin American countries, the landed elite not only have title to most of the land but they also wield enormous political power, which they have used to prevent increases in land taxes. For example, legislative attempts to introduce a tax on land in Colombia in 1973 and in Argentina in 1986 failed to pass. In some countries, protected industries that stand to lose from more foreign competition have also successfully blocked efforts to reduce import tariffs.

Underdevelopment of the financial sector. According to Roger Gordon and Wei Li, the underdevelopment of the financial sector can offer a convincing explanation for the tax structures often observed in developing countries.[9] When firms use the banking sector for transactions, banks usually

---

[9]Roger Gordon and Wei Li, "Tax Structures in Developing Countries: Many Puzzles and a Possible Explanation," *Journal of Public Economics* 93, nos. 7–8 (2009): 855–866.

keep track of those transactions. The government can then use its leverage with the banks to obtain that information. Many banks in developing countries are under government ownership, but even when the banks are privately owned, governments are usually strong enough to pressure them into providing information on their clients' transactions. When, however, firms do not use the banking sector and rely on cash transactions, it is nearly impossible to obtain transaction information and thus to tax the income of those firms appropriately.

As a result, the firms face a trade-off between the benefits of using banks and the costs of paying income taxes. Banks offer clear benefits. Money in the form of bank deposits is more secure, making bank transactions easier and less costly. Banks also provide loans and pay interest on term deposits. More capital-intensive firms that need capital will tend to benefit more from the banking system and will thus pay more taxes. Smaller and less capital-intensive firms will remain hidden from government scrutiny. Following this logic, the more efficient the banking system, the stronger the incentives are for firms to use it and thus to pay more taxes. The extent of the tax base will thus depend on the financial sector's development. However, the reasons behind a firm's decision whether or not to enter the formal sector are more complex. These decisions are as much related to the costs of entry as to the benefits from using banks. The costs of remaining in the informal sector are also more complex than just the motivation to avoid taxation.

The hidden economy. If we take the size of the informal sector as a given due to more general institutional factors in the economy (and not simply the degree of development of the financial sector), then there is a more direct link between the quality of institutions and the size of the formal sector, and thus between the quality of institutions and the size of the tax base. The size of the informal economy varies greatly in developing economies. The median size of the informal sector is around 40% of GDP in developing economies, compared to roughly 15% in OECD countries. It reaches 71% of GDP in Thailand and 76% in Nigeria. A vicious circle is at play here. If a country has weak institutions, it is likely to have a large informal sector. This creates a narrow tax base, which makes it difficult to raise funds to improve existing institutions. Lack of institutional improvements in turn leads to the persistence of a large informal economy. Finding a way out of this conundrum can be very complicated.

Chapter Summary

Legal Institutions

Legal institutions are critical for economic development because they affect both property rights and the rights of individuals. The two principal legal systems in the world are the common-law system, present in countries of Anglo-Saxon descent and in former English colonies, and the civil-law system, present in Europe, and in former Spanish and French colonies. The common-law system relies primarily on legal precedent, while the civil-law system relies primarily on a written code of law enacted by the legislative branch of government. Common-law countries provide better protection of shareholder and creditor rights, and therefore have more developed financial markets. Law enforcement is, however, weaker in developing countries, both in common-law and civil-law countries. The development of financial markets varies much more over time than across countries, so the differences between legal systems is less important than it may seem for financial development.

Fiscal Institutions

Fiscal institutions determine the ability of governments in developing countries to raise taxes to finance the provision of public services. Governments in developing countries are less able to raise taxes than are those in developed countries. Developing nations rely more on indirect taxes and taxes on foreign trade, and less on direct taxes.

Taxes are distortionary. The degree of distortion depends on the elasticity of the tax base to taxation. Capital is very elastic, whereas labor and land are less so. Developing countries have limited administrative capabilities. There are political constraints on the taxation of land in countries where landowners are politically powerful and the financial sector is less developed, which makes monitoring transactions more difficult. Moreover, the size of the informal economy is huge in many countries, which makes tracking income and levying more taxes costly.

Key Terms

adversarial system
automatic stay on the assets
bright-line rules
distortionary
elasticity of the tax base
factor mobility

fiscal institutions
inquisitorial system
rent-seeking
tax base
tax distortion
value-added tax (VAT)

Review Questions

1. What are the main differences between common-law and civil-law systems? How do these differences relate to the evolution of these legal systems?

2. Which aspects of shareholder and creditor rights differ most between common-law and civil-law countries? How do these rights vary between developed and developing countries?

3. Using the data collected by La Porta et al., cited in this chapter, compare shareholder and creditor rights in India and in Brazil. Interpret the differences you observe.

4. Give two reasons why we might be skeptical that the difference between common-law and civil-law systems may be important for economic development.

5. Search the Internet and find those countries in which financial markets are governed by Islamic law. Which countries have the strictest interpretation of the Qur'an, and which

countries have a more open interpretation? What common patterns do you find in countries governed by Islamic law as compared to other legal systems?

6. Why do developing countries collect fewer taxes as a percentage of national income than do developed countries?

7. Assume that labor supply follows the following equation $L^s = 2 + w^{1.8}$. Assume that the wage is equal to 3 without taxes and that the after-tax wage is 2.4. What is labor supply with and without taxes? Calculate the elasticity of labor supply to wages.

8. Using the Internet, find the latest data on government revenues and expenditures in India and in the United Kingdom. What differences do you find in terms of the composition of revenues and expenditures in the two countries?

9. Research the tax reforms implemented in Tanzania around the turn of the 21st century.

What was the situation before these reforms were put in place? What were the principal changes resulting from the reforms and what were the economic effects of those changes? Choose another country that implemented tax reforms after 1990 and perform the same analysis.

10. On the World Bank's "Doing Business in the World" site, go to the page devoted to taxation: http://www.doingbusiness.org/ ExploreTopics/PayingTaxes/. The information on countries concerns not only their tax rates but also the time it takes a business to prepare and pay taxes. How do the tax rates and the time to pay taxes correlate? Which countries have the most demanding requirements on business in each of these categories? How do you think your results relate to other institutions (legal, political, cultural) in these countries and how do tax rates correlate with these other institutions?

Culture

From an early age, Chinese children are taught to save money. In Chinese cities, even children from poor families have savings accounts. Even though their family income is much smaller than that of an average American family, many Chinese children have more money in their savings accounts than do most American children. To encourage children not to spend their savings, parents sometimes promise to increase their children's pocket money by 50%. The culture of thrift taught to children from an early age plays a potentially important role in explaining why China has one of the highest savings rates in the world. This is just one example of the importance of culture to economic development.

Culture, understood as a people's values and beliefs about the world and the social norms derived from those beliefs, has traditionally been absent from economic theory. Economists have been reluctant to embrace cultural explanations as a means to understand questions about development and economics in general. They believed that culture was a topic best left to anthropologists or sociologists. One reason economists have shied away from including the consideration of culture in economic theory is that culture is not easy to define and even more difficult to measure. We can measure wealth and most of the variables used in economic theories, but how do we measure culture?

Nevertheless, it is difficult to defend the claim that economists, especially those interested in economic development, should not be interested in culture's economic effects. In addition to influencing attitudes about thrift, cultural values also affect people's attitudes about work and effort, the role of women in society, and social and religious tolerance, among others. These values arguably have economic effects that are possibly quite significant to development.

Culture plays a fundamental role in other social science theories. Max Weber (1864–1920), the famous German sociologist, considered culture to be a primary force of economic change. In his famous book *The Protestant Ethic and the Spirit of Capitalism,* he argues that the Protestant ethic of Calvinism was a powerful force behind the early development of capitalism. Calvinism emphasized the virtues of hard work, asceticism, and frugal life. According to Calvinism's doctrine of predestination, God selected only certain people for salvation; everyone else faced damnation. Calvinists believed that their hard work and accumulation of wealth proved they were among God's chosen. Unlike the Catholic Church, Calvinism did not condemn usury, the lending of money with exorbitant interest rates, and it was critical of charity, which it believed encouraged the poor to be lazy and depraved, behaviors that proved they had not been chosen for salvation. Weber argued that Protestantism's stronger emphasis on thrift and hard work compared to Catholicism's path to salvation through sacraments and obedience to clerical authority were fundamental reasons why Protestant countries such as the United Kingdom and the Netherlands industrialized earlier than Catholic countries such as France or Spain.

How does culture relate to institutions? We discussed in Chapter 7 that we can define institutions as constraints imposed on human behavior. Institutions can be formal or informal. Culture imposes constraints in the sense that its moral values and social norms influence individuals' behavior. Think of the constraints religion imposes. Most of the Ten Commandments are specific constraints on undesirable human behavior—for example, "Thou shalt not steal." Even those commandments that are not negative, such as the duty to honor one's parents, are constraints in the sense that they exclude behavior that violates the commandment. Because the social norms imposed by a culture create clear constraints on individual behavior, we can see that culture is an example of informal institutions.

This chapter provides a brief overview of issues related to culture in the context of economic development. Because it is a topic that economists have traditionally been reluctant to explore, much research has yet to be done on culture in economics and on its effects in terms of development. However, research in this area is expanding rapidly. We will first survey the different measures of culture that research has used and discuss their advantages and disadvantages. We will next look at some of the historical evidence for culture's effects on economic performance. We will then review some of the research that considers cultural influences on development.

Measuring Culture

People use the word *culture* in many contexts. Sometimes it can mean cultural expression such as literature, movies, art, music, etc. However, this is not the meaning we will use in this chapter. Nor will we use culture to reference culinary habits, ethnic costumes and architecture, and so forth. Instead, we define culture as the set of values and beliefs people have about how the world (both nature and society) works and the behavioral norms derived from that set of values. According to that definition, culture and religion are closely related. Most world religions are quite comprehensive; they include beliefs about how the world works and they promote specific behavioral norms. However, it would be misguided to equate religion and culture. While religions profoundly affect a society's culture, we should appreciate culture as a more inclusive concept. The culture of Christians, Muslims, and Buddhists in the 20th century is not the same as it was 8 centuries ago. Beliefs evolve and they can be influenced by events such as wars, social change, technological advancements, or other factors that we do not yet understand.

It is challenging to identify measures of culture because culture encompasses many different kinds of beliefs. In recent years, researchers have nevertheless proposed various methods to make meaningful comparisons of cultures across the world.

The World Values Survey

The most popular database economists use to try to understand cultural differences is the World Values Survey (WVS). It was developed by Ronald Inglehart, a political science professor at the University of Michigan. Since 1981, in a series of 4 multi-year waves (1981–1984; 1989–1993; 1994–1999; 1999–2004), his research team has conducted extensive worldwide surveys of cultural values on a number of issues. The most recent wave started being carried out in 2010–2012. The original wave included 20 countries, primarily in European or Anglophone nations. Since this initial wave, some 90 countries have been surveyed, some in multiple waves for a total of nearly 200 surveys. In each country, a baseline questionnaire is adapted and administered to a representative national sample. Over 250,000 respondents worldwide have provided responses to nearly 1,000 questions that focus on personal attitudes about life, family, and society; the environment; work; the importance of tradition; gender roles; democracy and government; health; education; religion, spirituality, and morality; and honesty. To identify any particular value, respondents may be asked to rate their attitudes on scales of 1–5 or 1–10. Many questions are open-ended, while others force the respondent to choose from a specific list of answers.

Figures 11.1– 11.3 plot regional averages for selected responses from the WVS 1999–2004 survey grouped under the headings 1) Economic Interventionism, 2) Corruption and Trust, and 3) Attitudes toward Thrift/Work. The first question in Figure 11.1 concerns attitudes about income inequality. In particular, people were asked whether they thought incomes should be made more equal or, in contrast,

FIGURE 11.1   Economic Interventionism

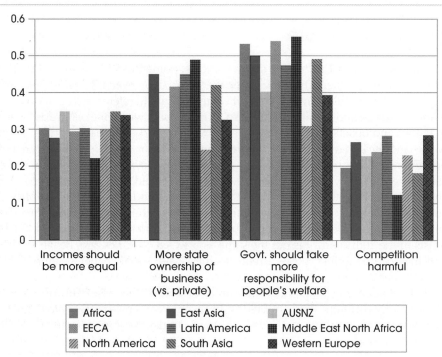

Cultures favoring more economic interventionism want more income equality, government ownership of business, and government involvement in people's welfare, and these cultures also consider competition harmful. Cultures that place greater value on economic freedom want less interventionism. Note that regions that are pro-interventionism in some categories are not necessarily so in all categories.

Source: World Values Survey, 1999–2004 wave: http://www.worldvaluessurvey.org/.

whether large income differences were necessary to provide incentives for individual effort. A higher score means a preference for more income equality while a lower score represents a stronger preference for income inequality. The variation across the world is not extremely large. Note that South Asia, Western Europe, and Australia and New Zealand favor income equality, while the Middle East and North Africa, East Asia, North America, Eastern Europe, and Central Asia prefer income inequality. The second question asks about support for private versus state ownership of business and its answers show more variation. Support for state ownership is the strongest in the MENA (Middle East and North Africa) region and in East and South Asia. Support for private ownership is the strongest in North America, Australia and New Zealand, and Western Europe.

The next question asks whether government or individuals should be responsible for a person's well-being. Support for more government intervention in welfare is strongest in the MENA region, Eastern Europe and Central Asia, Africa, and South Asia. Support is weaker in North America, Western Europe, and Australia and New Zealand. The answers to the last question show that competition is seen as harmful primarily in Western Europe, Latin America, and East Asia, while it is seen as more helpful in the MENA region, Africa, and South Asia. Note the low overall scores for this question, which reflect the view that competition is, in general, less harmful than it is good for society.

Figure 11.2 shows attitudes related to corruption and trust. The first question on the left asks people whether they think that tax cheating is justifiable.

FIGURE 11.2 Corruption and Trust

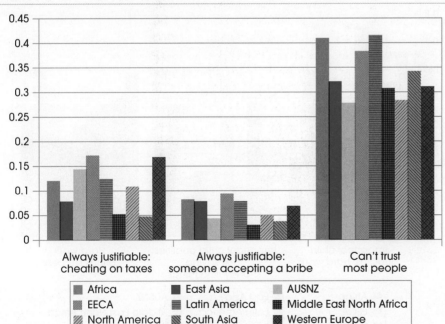

Responses differ across regions of the world on whether tax cheating and accepting bribes is always justifiable. Responses also differ on whether most people are trustworthy.

Source: World Values Survey, 1999–2004 wave: http://www.worldvaluessurvey.org/.

The highest number of positive responses is in Western Europe, Eastern Europe, and Central Asia. People in the MENA region, South Asia, and East Asia are least in favor of tax cheating. The next question asks whether receiving a bribe is always justifiable. The positive responses are very low, but the highest positive response rate is in Eastern Europe and Central Asia, Latin America, Africa, and East Asia, while the lowest positive response rates are in the MENA region, South Asia, and Australia and New Zealand. The last question asks, "Generally speaking, would you say that most people cannot be trusted?" Higher scores in Figure 11.2 represent less trust. This is an important question; less trust means that people will have a less cooperative attitude in interactions with others. The highest levels of distrust are in Latin America, Africa, Eastern Europe, and Central Asia. The highest levels of trust are in Australia and New Zealand, North America, and the MENA region.

Figure 11.3 displays response rates relative to the values of thrift and hard work. The first chart on the left shows positive responses to the importance of hard work as an aspiration for a child. The highest scores are in Eastern Europe and Central Asia, Africa, South Asia, and East Asia. The lowest scores are in Australia and New Zealand, Western Europe, and Latin America. The second chart reports the positive responses to the importance of educating children to be thrifty. The highest scores are in East and South Asia, Eastern Europe, and Central Asia, and the lowest scores are in Australia and New Zealand, Africa,

FIGURE 11.3 Thrift and Hard Work

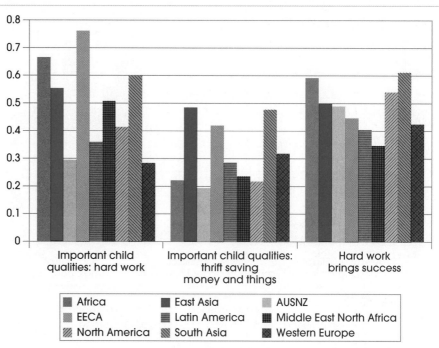

The value of hard work and thrift varies across the world.

Source: World Values Survey, 1999–2004 wave: http://www.worldvaluessurvey.org/.

and North America. The chart on the right shows the positive responses to the statement, "In the long run, hard work brings a better life." The highest scores are for South Asia and Africa, and the lowest for the MENA region, Latin America, and Western Europe.

Schwartz's Cultural Mappings

While economists and social scientists increasingly rely on the World Values Survey, its methodology has been subject to a variety of criticisms. First, the same words may mean different things in different cultures. The meaning of "hard work" may be very different in North America than it is in the former Soviet Union. Furthermore, depending on the question asked, an individual's frame of reference could distort the data interpretation. For example, in countries with a weak social safety net, such as the United States, greater government responsibility for individual welfare may be desirable, whereas in those countries with a relatively strong safety net, less government support may be preferred. In that case, a country's local conditions may affect answers to these kinds of questions, and values expressed might not be easily comparable across countries.

Shalom Schwartz is an Israeli cross-cultural psychologist who has developed a core set of values that have common meanings across cultures and can provide a basis for the comparison of cultures across countries. Between 1998 and 2000, Schwartz gathered survey responses from K–12 schoolteachers and college students, for a total of 195 samples drawn from 67 nations and 70 cultural groups. Each sample generally includes 180–280 respondents, for a total of over 75,000 surveys. Schwartz's value survey consists of 56–57 value items that ask respondents to indicate the importance of each as "a guiding principle in my life."

From the data generated by those surveys, he has constructed a "cultural map," shown in Figure 11.4, which displays seven important cultural dimensions. In the upper right, embeddedness of the individual in the traditional community emphasizes a high degree of respect for tradition and security. At its opposite are autonomy, both intellectual and affective. Intellectual autonomy emphasizes self-direction, whereas affective autonomy emphasizes mostly hedonism and stimulation. Hierarchy is valued in societies where stability of the social order is paramount. It emphasizes power, tradition, and conformity. At its opposite is egalitarianism, which emphasizes benevolence and universalism. Mastery is about self-assertion and is based on the values of achievement. Harmony is its opposite and fosters the values of universalism. Figure 11.4 also shows the position of different countries along the map's axes. The countries with high scores for the value of embeddedness are mostly from Africa and the Middle East. They also have high scores for hierarchy. Asian countries have elevated hierarchy scores, with China being the farthest along on that axis. Northern European countries score high on egalitarianism and autonomy, and English-speaking countries score high on affective autonomy and mastery. Harmony scores are the highest in some Eastern European countries. Latin American and Eastern European countries (including Turkey) are more in the middle of the map and seem to be at the intersection of the primary cultural types.

FIGURE 11.4   Schwartz's Cultural Map

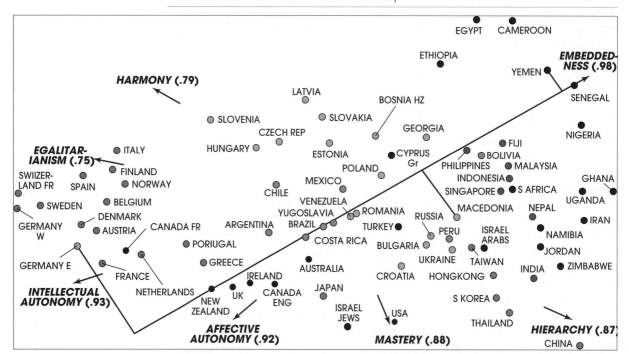

Cultures of various countries are mapped along different axes. Countries in the South–West quadrant value intellectual and affective autonomy, whereas those in the North–East quadrant value embeddedness and tradition. Countries in the North–West quadrant score high on egalitarianism, whereas those in the South–East quadrant score high on hierarchy.

Source: Shalom Schwartz, "Mapping and Interpreting Cultural Differences around the World," in *Comparing Cultures: Dimensions of Culture in a Comparative Perspective,* ed. Henk Vinken, Joseph Soeters, and Peter Ester (Leiden, the Netherlands: Brill Academic Publishers, 2004): 55.

Even though his approach is based on psychology, economists have used Schwartz's data and methodology in their research.[1] The data's comparability across countries is viewed as an important advantage despite the more abstract psychological concepts used, which are not easy for economists to grasp.

Hofstede's Index of Individualism and Collectivism

Dutch social psychologist Geert Hofstede has compiled another database on culture.[2] His data are based on a worldwide survey done among 116,000 employees of IBM, the multinational technology and consulting company, in 79 countries between 1967 and 1980. The idea was to survey people with equiv-alent jobs in the same company in different countries so as to measure cultural

[1]See Amir N. Licht, Chanan Goldschmidt, and Shalom H. Schwartz, "Culture, Law, and Corporate Governance," *International Review of Law and Economics* 25, no. 2 (2005): 229–255; and Amir N. Licht, Chanan Goldschmidt, and Shalom H. Schwartz, "Culture Rules: The Foundations of the Rule of Law and Other Norms of Governance," *Journal of Comparative Economics* 35, no. 4 (2007): 659–688.

[2]Geert Hofstede, *Culture's Consequences: Comparing Values, Behaviors, and Organizations across Nations,* 2nd ed. (Thousand Oaks, CA: Sage Publications, 2001).

differences among individuals with comparable professional positions. Hofstede's surveys therefore focused on people who worked in IBM's marketing department, the only department present in all countries. (The Schwartz data were collected in a similar manner, as that survey was done only among schoolteachers and students.) To avoid cultural biases in the way questions were framed, the translation of the survey into local languages was done by a team of both English and local native-language speakers. The questionnaire contained 60 questions on employees' personal goals and beliefs as well as their perception of their work environment. On the basis of the surveys' answers, Hofstede constructed four basic cultural indicators: individualism, power distance, masculinity, and uncertainty avoidance.[3]

The individualism score is the first and most important component in Hofstede's factor analysis. It measures the extent to which people believe that individuals are supposed to take care of themselves as opposed to being strongly integrated in and loyal to a cohesive group, which is characteristic of collectivism. Hofstede's individualism index is positively correlated to survey answers that put a high value on individual freedom, opportunity, achievement, advancement, and recognition. It is negatively correlated with answers that put a high value on harmony, cooperation, and good relations with superiors. In other words, individuals in countries with a high individualism score value personal freedom and individual status, while individuals in countries with a low level for that indicator value harmony and conformity.

The power distance indicator measures the extent to which the less powerful members of organizations and institutions (both social and familial) accept and expect that power is distributed unequally. A higher value of the indicator means a greater acceptance by the less powerful of inequality in the distribution of power.

The index of masculinity refers to the dominance of men over women and to the dominance of "male" values, such as assertiveness and competitiveness, versus the "female" values of caring and modesty.

The uncertainty avoidance index measures a society's tolerance for uncertainty and the extent to which members of society feel either comfortable or uncomfortable in situations that are novel, unknown, surprising, or unusual. Cultures that avoid uncertainty try to minimize the possibility of such situations by strict laws and proscriptions, as well as with safety and security measures. They are less tolerant and reject diversity within their societies.

Among these four cultural dimensions, cross-cultural psychologists who have worked a lot with the Hofstede data find that the individualism–collectivism cleavage appears to be the most important and the most relevant to understand cross-cultural differences.[4] In terms of the main axes in Schwartz's cultural mappings, Hofstede's individualism index has a significant

[3]The technique used to construct these indicators is called factor analysis. It reduces a large number of variables (60 in this case) to a small number of variables that are a) a function of the initial variables, and 2) statistically independent of each other. Thus, from 60 variables (the answers to the questions), Hofstede constructed four variables or indicators that are not correlated with each other.

[4]See, for example, Steven J. Heine, *Cultural Psychology* (New York: W. W. Norton & Company, 2008); and Daphna Oyserman, Heather M. Coon, and Markus Kemmelmeier, "Rethinking Individualism and Collectivism: Evaluation of Theoretical Assumptions and Meta-Analyses," *Psychological Bulletin* 128, no. 1 (2002): 3–72.

positive correlation with Schwartz's cultural variables of affective and intellectual autonomy, and it is negatively correlated with his embeddedness variable. As a result, we can see that a major cultural difference across countries is their degree of individualism or collectivism.

Hofstede's data have several advantages over other databases that measure cultural differences across countries. First, the individualism–collectivism cleavage is easy to grasp. Second, it corresponds to the main cultural cleavage established by other cross-cultural psychologists in various theoretical and empirical studies. Third, and probably most important, more than 60 other studies done on other professionals, such as airline pilots, lawyers, academics, artists, labor leaders, or corporate managers, have validated Hofstede's individualism index and found a ranking nearly identical to the one he proposed. For example, across various studies and measures, the United Kingdom, the United States, and the Netherlands are consistently among the most individualist countries, while Pakistan, Nigeria, and Peru are among the most collectivist.

Figure 11.5 shows a world map based on the Hofstede individualism index.[5] We can make several observations. First, countries of Anglo-Saxon descent (the United Kingdom, the United States, Australia, Canada, and New Zealand) and Western European countries (the Netherlands, Italy, Belgium, France, and the Scandinavian countries) are among the most individualist. Other countries tend to have lower individualism scores, particularly in Asia and in northern and western Latin America (Ecuador, Colombia, Venezuela, Peru). Among the 20 countries with the lowest individualism score, nine are in

FIGURE 11.5 Hofstede's Individualism Index (2001)

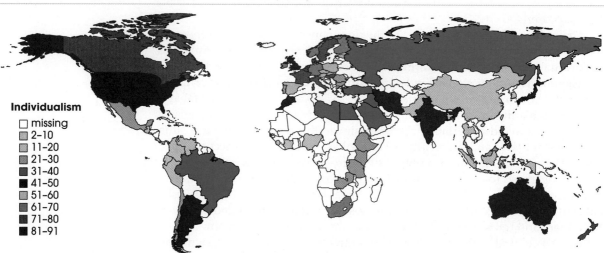

Anglo-Saxon and West European countries have more individualistic values, whereas Asian and Latin American countries have more collectivist values. The individualism score also varies within continents.

Source: Based on http://www.geert-hofstede.com/.

[5]The most current version of the data is available at http://www.geert-hofstede.com/dimension-data-matrix.

Latin America and eight are in Asia. Note, however, that there is also sufficient variation within continents. In Africa, the more individualistic countries are South Africa, Morocco, and Libya, and the more collectivist countries are Ghana, Sierra Leone, and Nigeria. In Latin America, the more individualistic countries are Argentina and Brazil, who are in the middle range of the individualism score, and the most collectivist countries are Guatemala and Ecuador. In Asia, the most individualistic country is India and the most collectivist countries are Indonesia and Pakistan. In Europe, Portugal has a low individualism score, in the same range as Kenya or Zambia, as do Bulgaria and Romania with individualism scores close to that of Mexico.

While Hofstede's data have been widely used in the social sciences, economists are starting to use them to analyze the effect of individualism on entrepreneurship, technical diffusion, growth and development, and institutions.[6]

Culture's Effect on Institutions

What is the relationship between culture on one hand and political and legal institutions on the other? In this section, we provide some clear evidence that a strong culture of democracy is correlated with more efficient provision of public services and improved functioning of government institutions. We also demonstrate that culture, because it evolves more slowly than do formal institutions, has a causal effect on these institutions of governance.

Culture and the Quality of Democracy

In an influential book, political scientist Robert Putnam and his research colleagues put forward the idea that there is a strong link between the development of **civil society**, that is, the presence of a network of diverse voluntary associations, and the success of democratic institutions.[7] The development of civil society is associated with a culture of democratic participation in which citizens believe that they must be actively involved in civil associations. In other words, for democracy to work well, citizens need to participate actively in social life through a complex associative network.

Putnam's research is based on data gathered in Italy. Although Italy is not a developing economy, economically, southern Italy has always lagged behind

---

[6]For the effects of individualism on entrepreneurship, see Michael H. Morris, Duane L. Davis, and Jeffrey W. Allen. "Fostering Corporate Entrepreneurship: Cross-Cultural Comparisons of the Importance of Individualism versus Collectivism," *Journal of International Business Studies* 25, no. 1 (1994): 65–89; for its effects on technical diffusion, see Alessandra Fogli and Laura Veldkamp, "Germs, Social Networks and Growth," working paper New York University, 2012; for its effects on growth and development, see Yuriy Gorodnichenko and Gérard Roland, "Culture, Institutions, and the Wealth of Nations," NBER Working Paper no. 16368 2010; for its effects on institutions, see Mariko J. Klasing, "Cultural Dimensions, Collective Values, and Their Importance for Institutions," *Journal of Comparative Economics* 41, no. 2 (2013): 447–467.

[7]Robert Putnam, Roberto Leonardi, and Rafaella Y. Nanetti, *Making Democracy Work: Civic Traditions in Modern Italy* (Princeton: Princeton University Press, 1994).

northern Italy. While the northern regions of Italy are among the richest in the world, the southern Mezzogiorno region has a GDP per capita closer to that of Argentina, Mauritius, or Poland. Italy is an interesting case to consider in terms of the functions of formal and informal institutions. The same formal political and legal institutions exist in both the north and the south. However, the efficiency of government institutions in the southern regions is much lower than for those in the north. Putnam constructed a number of indicators to measure this difference in performance. He concluded that the Mezzogiorno had much higher instability (i.e., turnover) of regional governments, more delay in budget approval by local governments, a worse statistical apparatus, a lower quality of legislation, and a lower provision of public services.

Let us examine more closely the issue of an inferior provision of public services. In 1977, the central government made funding available to set up daycare centers throughout the country. By 1983, Emilia Romagna (the Bologna region) in the north had set up a daycare center for every 400 children, whereas Campania (the Naples region) in the south had only one center for every 12,560 children. Because there was no funding inequality between the regions, this contrast is a clear indicator of the differences in quality for the provision of public services. A similar situation existed for the 1974 establishment of family clinics. By 1978, Umbria in the north had a family clinic for every 15,000 residents, whereas Puglia in the south only had a single family clinic for its 3,850,000 total inhabitants. On many other measures, Putnam found that government institutions in the south were performing much less efficiently than those in Italy's northern and central regions.

Putnam's research indicated that these differences in the performance of government institutions operating within the same formal legal framework could be traced back to variations in the level of civil-society development. The idea is that citizens who have a culture of civic engagement and active participation in various associations will be more involved citizens. They will demand more from their political representatives, including greater attention to the quality of public policy and public services. In other words, civil-society development is a measure of the degree to which citizens are able to overcome their collective-action problems. Cultural attitudes play an important role here, as social norms of solidarity, reciprocity, and trust create an active citizenry. In contrast, if citizens are passive and solely focused on maximizing self-interest, then they will face many collective-action and free-riding problems that corrupt or incompetent politicians can exploit.

Putnam measures of civil-society development by looking at participation both in different associations and in elections, newspaper readership, voting for general issues, and patronage voting for candidates who give jobs and favors to their local constituencies. Figure 11.6 shows, on the left, a map of institutional performance in Italy's various regions, where the darker colors represent better performance of regional governance and lighter colors represent worse performance, with white being the worst. The right-hand map in Figure 11.6 shows civic society in Italy, where again darker colors indicate higher levels of civil-society development, and lighter colors lower levels. The correlation between both maps, while imperfect, is nevertheless striking. The performance of regional government is closely related to measures of civil-society development.

FIGURE 11.6 Italy's Institutional Performance and Civil-Society Development by Region

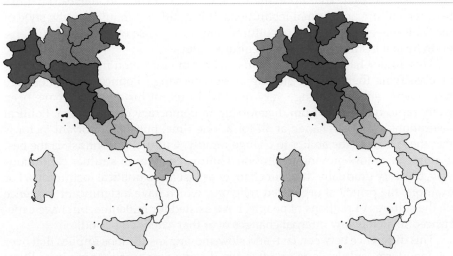

The map on the left represents institutional performance across Italy, with darker colors representing regions with better performance and lighter colors representing those with weaker performance. The map on the right gives measures of civil society for the same regions, with darker colors indicating a higher level of civil-society development. Better development of civil society correlates with better institutional performance.

Source: Robert Putnam, Roberto Leonardi, and Rafaella Y. Nanetti, *Making Democracy Work: Civic Traditions in Modern Italy* (Princeton: Princeton University Press, 1994).

How can we explain these variations in Italian civil-society development? They originate in the different histories of the northern and southern regions. For more than 1,000 years, the south experienced a feudal autocratic rule by aristocratic landlords, with little development of independent cities. In contrast, the towns of northern Italy developed in the late middle Ages and early Renaissance period into vigorous, self-governed city-states. Although they were not democracies in the modern sense of the word, there was very strong political participation by the elite merchants and a broad class of notables in the northern regions. Skilled craftsmen and other professionals developed various associations, similar to the guilds, and these groups became very influential. Interestingly, in the 12th century, there was not yet much of a development or wealth gap between the north and the south. The north became richer only after the development of the city-states and their vigorous culture and trade.

Putnam's research reveals a complementarity between formal political institutions and culture. The famous French writer Alexis de Tocqueville noted the same connection when he described the vigor of American democracy in the 19th century. De Tocqueville was struck by how well the local networks of social and civic life supported and reinforced American democratic institutions, which were usually based on the social norms dictated by religion, in particular the multiple denominations of Protestantism. For both Putnam and de Tocqueville, a culture of civic participation and engagement reinforced formal democratic political institutions.

Culture and Norms of Governance

We must consider an important question that relates to the causal links between culture and formal institutions. It is a difficult inquiry, in the style of the "chicken–egg" puzzle: are cultural values the cause of formal institutions, or do formal institutions generate cultural values?

This author has argued for a causal effect of culture on formal institutions by classifying them as fast-moving or slow-moving.[8] Political institutions are fast-moving and can change very quickly. In recent history, there have been many rapid transitions from dictatorship to democracy or vice-versa. Political institutions may not change at all for a long time, but the important factor is that they do have the ability to change rapidly. Culture, in contrast, is the best example of a slow-moving institution. Culture changes in a rather continuous way, but very gradually. It never changes as fast as do political institutions. For example, the principal organized religions, which have a significant influence on the cultures of millions of people, have existed for millennia, but have experienced relatively few internal changes over that extended period.

This difference between fast- and slow-moving institutions implies that over the long term, culture is more often the driving force for changes in political and legal institutions. Culture is therefore likely to have a causal effect on formal institutions—for example, the culture of the Renaissance and the Enlightenment that led to the structure of our modern legal and political institutions. On the other hand, the exogenous imposition of formal institutions that are in opposition to the local culture will not make these institutions as effective as when they are in sync. This was one of the lessons of Putnam's work.

However, can we empirically prove a causal effect of culture on institutions? Licht, Goldschmidt, and Schwartz have established a causal link between culture and formal institutions, more precisely as measures of good governance.[9] They have developed an original empirical strategy by exploiting a link between language and culture. One of the important variables Schwartz emphasized in his initial work, cited above, is the opposition between embeddedness and autonomy. Embeddedness emphasizes tradition, security, and the traditional order, whereas autonomy emphasizes individual freedom. It turns out that there is a linguistic difference that relates to the opposition between embeddedness and autonomy, that is, whether grammar permits a pronoun to be dropped in a sentence. In English, unlike some other languages, we cannot drop the "I" or "you" as subjects in a sentence. The license to drop the pronoun indicates that the social context is more important than the specific person who speaks. Language and grammar function here as a vehicle for cultural transmission, a fact that linguistics scholars have long emphasized. Licht, Goldschmidt, and Schwartz construct a "pronoun drop" variable, taking a value of 1 if the language allows for a pronoun drop and a 0 otherwise. They find that the pronoun drop variable correlates well with the Schwartz measure of embeddedness and autonomy.

---

[8]Gérard Roland, "Understanding Institutional Change: Fast-Moving and Slow-Moving Institutions," *Studies in Comparative International Development* 38, no. 4 (2004): 109–131.

[9]Amir N. Licht, Chanan Goldschmidt, and Shalom H. Schwartz, "Culture, Law, and Corporate Governance," 2005.

While a correlation exists between grammar and culture, grammar arguably has no direct effect on norms of governance. This means that it is possible to use instrumental variable regression to investigate the causal effect of culture on institutions (see the Econometrics appendix on instrumental variable regression on page 562). Because grammar has no effect on institutions, by regressing culture on grammar, we estimate the variation in cultures across the world that is explained by the variation in grammar. Governance thus cannot cause the variation in culture predicted by the variation in grammar. We can then regress governance on the instrumented cultural variable. In other words, we estimate the part of the variation in governance that is explained by the variation in culture explained by the variation in grammar. This then gives an estimate of the causal effect of culture on governance.

When instrumented in this way by the grammatical variable, Licht et al., find that a high score on the embeddedness variable leads to lower scores in terms of the various measures of governance that the World Bank has constructed: 1) the rule of law, which measures the respect for property rights and the enforceability of contracts; 2) "non-corruption," which measures subjective perceptions of integrity among public officials; and 3) democratic accountability, which measures civil liberties, political rights, and the presence of mechanisms for democratic accountability. We obtain similar results when using corruption indices by Transparency International and rule of law indices by the International Country Risk Guide. Conversely, high scores on the cultural variable of autonomy, also instrumented by the grammatical variable, lead to high scores in terms of rule of law, non-corruption, and democratic accountability. The relation holds when controlling for other variables such as income per capita, inequality, ethno-linguistic fractionalization, and British colonial heritage. The work of Licht et al., thus represents one of the first empirical studies to show culture's effect on formal institutions.

Culture and Contract Enforcement

Using an innovative approach, economic historian Avner Greif has shown the effect of different cultures on mechanisms of contract enforcement.[10] He compares these mechanisms between two groups of traders in the late medieval period (12th to 14th century): the Genovese traders from the city-state of Genoa, and the Maghribi, a group of Jewish traders from Northwest Africa. Both groups traded and shipped goods across the Mediterranean Sea, and faced the same environment with the same available technologies. Because they had to ship goods by sea, these traders needed to hire agents throughout the region to manage the transport and sale of the merchandise for them. Both groups had to solve an important agency problem: how to make sure the agents hired would be honest and not steal the goods they were carrying.

Greif studied how the differences in cultural beliefs between these two groups led to differences in the contract enforcement mechanism. Under the collectivist beliefs of the Maghribi, if one agent was caught stealing, all merchants would refrain from hiring that agent in the future. Under the individualist values that

---

[10]Avner Greif, *Institutions and the Path to the Modern Economy: Lessons from Medieval Trade* (Cambridge, MA: MIT Press, 2006).

prevailed among the Genovese merchants, if an agent were caught stealing, he would be fired. But there was no solidarity between the merchants and an agent who had cheated one merchant could be hired by another. At first glance, the collectivist beliefs of the Maghribi seem more effective as a contract enforcement mechanism. The punishment for cheating was harsher under collectivist beliefs. Therefore, the wage that would convince an agent not to cheat was lower under the collectivist enforcement system. However, in the long run, collectivist beliefs proved to be less effective as they work well only in a closed and tightly knit community. Genovese traders could take up new trade opportunities in new markets when they became available by hiring foreign agents while the Maghribi failed to do so because they were limited to hiring only members of their own community.

Let us examine this in a bit more detail. Think of the decision problem of an agent who considers whether to cheat or to be honest. The choice is between a) stealing today and reaping a large sum, but being banned from working in the future and then receiving very little income; and b) being honest and receiving a steady flow of wage income today and in the future. The wage necessary to convince an agent to be honest was lower under the collectivist system because cheating once made it impossible to get a job ever again as no merchant wanted to hire that agent. Under the individualist enforcement system, an agent who cheated and was caught could still expect to find work in the future. That agent therefore had to be promised a higher wage to dissuade him from cheating, compared to the collectivist enforcement system. Under collectivist enforcement, then, the cost of keeping agents honest was lower than under the individualist system.

Greif also found that other differences resulted from these variations in cultural beliefs. For collectivist enforcement to be effective, strong information flows between the merchants were necessary. This was not the case under the individualist enforcement system. Information flows between traders were quite strong in the Maghribi world, but there is no evidence that they occurred among the Genovese merchants. On the contrary, these merchants tended not to share information with others. The collectivist beliefs also led to more horizontal contractual relationships, whereas the individualist beliefs led to more vertical contractual relationships. It was not uncommon for Maghribi traders to act as agents for other agents, whereas in Genoa there was a strict social stratification: merchants worked as merchants only and agents as agents only. This is because it was more advantageous to hire a trader as an agent under the collectivist enforcement system because if that trader cheated, he could no longer count on the solidarity of the other traders in the future. In other words, if he cheated, he could not be sure that other traders would not hire agents who had previously cheated on him. A cheating trader would thus become vulnerable to the dishonest behavior of other agents. This represents another harsh punishment for cheating and it created a strong incentive for a trader to behave honestly when working as an agent for another trader. Nothing similar existed in the case of individualist beliefs. It was more expensive to hire a merchant rather than an agent under the system of individualist beliefs because merchants were richer to start with and had better outside options. Indeed, being richer, they could enjoy themselves more when not working, making the opportunity cost of working higher. Keeping them honest as agents would thus have required higher payments than when hiring an ordinary agent.

However, the collectivist enforcement system had one weakness that in the long run proved immensely disadvantageous. The collectivist system works well only within a tight and closed community. The strength of the collective punishment mechanism is critically dependent on enforcement within the strict boundaries of the community. It was not in the interest of the Maghribi to hire agents from outside communities if these agents could, after cheating on a Maghribi trader, find work outside the Maghribi community. Under the Genovese enforcement system, hiring an outside agent was not a problem. When opportunities for trade increased, the Genovese merchants were able to seize these opportunities and vastly expand their trade networks, while the Maghribi were unable to take advantage of them. In the end, the Genovese merchants prospered vastly more than the Maghribi traders.

This difference in collectivist and individualist beliefs in contract enforcement in the late Middle Ages gives us a glimpse of the link between the individualist culture and the later development of the rule of law. In an individualist culture, anonymous exchange and trade between people who are unknown to each other can take place. Economic agents benefit greatly from a rule-of-law system with established courts in which a third party can resolve conflicts. Individuals who do not necessarily know each other can sign contracts with the confidence that they can be enforced without the need to rely solely on the other party's reputation within the community. On the other hand, under collectivist beliefs, the community polices itself effectively. A formal system of law and courts is less of a necessity. However, a cost results because transactions remain restricted to pairs of individuals who have information on each other's reputation. An even bigger cost results because there will be less demand for the development of formal institutions and long-term economic development suffers as a consequence.

While Greif's research relates to the Middle Ages, it is very important in the context of current economic development, as some cultures are more collectivist while others are more individualistic. Greif's research demonstrates how cultural beliefs influence the way contracts are enforced in different cultures. There is no doubt that the quality of contract enforcement is fundamental to economic development.

Cultural Obstacles to Economic Development

In addition to the relationship between culture and formal institutions, direct links exist between culture and economic development. Egalitarian norms that have prevailed historically in tribal societies discourage and even punish wealth accumulation by individuals. Many religious interdictions have also directly affected economic behavior. Catholicism, for example, created obstacles to economic development, in particular because of its long-standing prohibition on charging interest rates. Historically, Islam has been the source of similar religious and cultural obstacles to economic progress, particularly with regard to inheritance laws.

Egalitarian Norms and Development

In many tribal societies, particularly in Africa, strict egalitarian and collectivist norms prevail that prohibit members of a society from aspiring to individual achievement, behaving differently from established norms, or becoming prosperous.[11] These social norms are transmitted from generation to generation and have a significant effect on individual behavior. Exceptionally productive individuals are viewed with suspicion and are pressured into sharing their surplus with the community. Collective punishments exist to penalize the rich; they take the form of social ostracism, loss of status, or even violence. One form of social ostracism is to boycott the funerals for relatives of richer farmers. Communities have also frequently used accusations of witchcraft to punish greed and acquisitiveness as well as attempts to move away from the community. Poisoning the cattle of more affluent individuals has even been used as both punishment and threat in various African communities.

Motivating this repression of any kind of economic or social differentiation is the fear that individuals will start to compete and the community's cohesiveness will be undermined as a result. There is also a concern that an individual who proves more successful will leave the village or will not redistribute any surplus harvest or other production. Finally, poor villagers believe that if they borrow money from richer individuals they are under no ethical obligation to repay, a norm that acts as an obstacle to the development of credit inside these traditional communities.

Such norms are likely to have a negative effect on economic development because they tend to prevent individuals from excelling in productivity or innovation. They tend to repress the entrepreneurial spirit and incentives to modernize, which perpetuate poverty and stagnation. On the other hand, in a case of significant resource scarcity, such collectivist norms will lead to an egalitarian distribution of food, leading in turn to survival for a larger number of community members. These norms were no doubt quite effective in ancient times and the tribes in which they prevailed had, in all likelihood, a higher survival rate than tribes with less collectivist norms.

Religious Taboos on Interest

For centuries, the Catholic Church has prohibited its members from charging interest on a loan. This was called the **sin of usury** and many of the Church's prominent theologians, such as Saint Thomas Aquinas, wrote against it. For centuries, Catholics considered it immoral because they believed the interest was not the result of effort or labor. Some scholars have argued that this religious prohibition created an obstacle to the development of financial markets. Historian Raymond de Roover, who studied financial development in medieval Europe, argued that the ban on usury increased transaction costs.[12] In Italy, for example, merchants who wanted to avoid the accusation of usury had to draw up complex contracts. For example, if a merchant needed a loan to buy some merchandise, he entered into a contract with a bank wherein the bank, rather than the merchant, would pay in

---

[11]See Jean-Philippe Platteau, *Institutions, Social Norms, and Economic Development* (Newark, NJ: Harwood Academic Publishers, 2000).

[12]Raymond De Roover, *The Rise and Decline of the Medici Bank, 1397–1494* (Cambridge, MA: Harvard University Press, 1963). See also Mark Koyama, "Evading the 'Taint of Usury' Complex Contracts and Segmented Capital Markets," working paper no. 412, Department of Economics, Oxford University, November 2008.

advance for the merchandise and would resell it to the merchant later at a higher price. This was the equivalent of charging interest on a loan. Other loan contracts were written in such a way that a borrower would repay a loan in foreign currency. These loan contracts were acceptable to the Church because they involved foreign exchange risk and the Church accepted that this risk should be rewarded. The increasing complexity of contracts designed to avoid the accusation of usury represented growing costs for both transactions and for entry into business. Gradually, the Church allowed exceptions to the prohibition of usury as it came to accept that any labor in the management of loans could be rewarded. In contrast to Europe, in late medieval Japan, where the economy was at a stage of development similar to that of European economies, there was no prohibition of interest; the use of simple loan contracts against interest payments was universal.[13]

Today, Islam still prohibits charging interest on loans. In Pakistan, for example, it is a violation of national law. Islamic banks write contracts that are in strict accordance with Islamic law; if an individual wants to buy a car on credit, the bank will buy it for the consumer and allow the consumer to repay in installments, but for a higher total price. We might argue that these methods of circumventing religious laws undo their economic harm, but we can also make the case that these laws act as a brake on financial innovation in general.

Islam and Inheritance Laws

Timur Kuran, an economic historian, has researched the reasons why Islam was once a highly advanced civilization but failed to innovate and modernize during the Renaissance. He argues that a critical reason for this is related to certain aspects of Islamic inheritance laws.[14] Neither Judaism nor Christianity have specific prescriptions when it comes to inheritance. In contrast, the Qur'an spells out in great detail the principles of Islamic inheritance law. Based on Qur'anic precepts, *Sharia* law requires that two-thirds of any estate is reserved for the deceased's children and family. A daughter only receives half as much as a son. Because these laws are explicitly set out in the Qur'an and are believed to be sacred religious edicts, they cannot be repealed or amended and, as a result, Islamic countries have abided by them for centuries.

The disadvantage of these rules is that they tend to fragment property and this has negatively affected the development of partnerships in the economies of Islamic countries. The standard Islamic partnership, the *Mudaraba*, typically involved only two parties even though there were no legal limits on the number of partners. There were also no limits on the length of a partnership, but in practice the duration tended to be short. The explanation for why partnerships were small and of short duration lies in the inheritance law, which required that when a partner died, his business could only be divided among his heirs. A partnership, then, would usually not outlast the life of its founders because when one of them

---

[13]See Suzanne Gay, *The Moneylenders of Late Medieval Kyoto* (Honolulu: University of Hawaii Press, 2001).

[14]Timur Kuran, "The Islamic Commercial Crisis: Institutional Roots of Economic Underdevelopment in the Middle East," *The Journal of Economic History* 63, no. 2 (2003): 414–446.

died, his heirs inherited his business interests, making the partnership more difficult to maintain because the heirs might have had neither the skills nor the interest to pursue their father's business interests. For the same reason, there was no purpose in building large partnerships; as soon as a partner died, the partnership faced fragmentation. As a result, these inheritance laws represented an ongoing obstacle to the development of large and durable partnerships.

By contrast, such inheritance laws did not exist in the Italian city-states, where large business organizations were expanding rapidly. Because there were no religious prescriptions regarding inheritance, there was institutional experimentation. For example, the institution of **primogeniture**, whereby the oldest son inherits the business (or land) of his father, was soon seen to be economically advantageous, even though highly unequal within the family. It allowed business organizations to develop in size and duration rather than being dispersed among a group of heirs, and that led to specialization, division of labor, and organizational innovations. It would be difficult to imagine the modern industrial firm without the historical experience of the large business organizations that had their historic origins in the Italian city-states.

Islamic inheritance law provides an example of a specific religious edict with long-term economic consequences. Note that in general, Islamic culture was not, and is not, opposed to commerce. Islam was more sympathetic to merchants than was Catholicism. Nor was Islam generally opposed to innovations in commerce, science, and technology as significant innovations in these fields took place in the Islamic world during the Middle Ages. Economic development in the Islamic world might have been much different if the Qur'an had not explicitly addressed inheritance rules.

On the other hand, the inheritance rules were not the only impediment to economic development. Another Islamic institution is the *waqf*, a religious duty to establish an unincorporated trust under *Sharia* law for charitable purposes, which would be overseen by a judge in the *Sharia* court.[15] A pious Muslim would establish a *waqf* to provide a service allowed under Islamic law, be it the construction of a mosque, a water well, a park, a road, or a school. An important stipulation is that it had to be provided in perpetuity in the same way its founder had defined. Many public services were provided by this method in Islamic countries, in particular under the Ottoman Empire. In a way, this religious obligation can be seen as a way to overcome the collective-action or free-riding problem and provide public services. It thus served a useful purpose, creating a tradition of providing private charitable works.

While the Qur'an does not specifically mention the *waqf*, its pious purpose gave it a sacred character, justifying the perpetuity of the service as defined by its founder. This, however, created an important rigidity: resources were allocated inefficiently when modernization or technical improvements became necessary. Schools could not update their curricula, water wells could not be incorporated into modern water delivery systems, etc. In the 19th and 20th centuries, to improve the provision of local public services, reformers tried to dismantle the *waqf* system and introduce the modern municipality system, but, due to the weight of tradition, the *waqf* system remains quite influential.

---

[15]Timor Kuran, "The Logic of Financial Westernization in the Middle East," *Journal of Economic Behavior & Organization* 56, no. 4 (2005): 593–615.

The Effects of Culture

We next turn to culture's effects in the contemporary world. Does culture influence economic growth or the propensity to save? Does culture affect the willingness to trust people from other countries or communities? Research in these areas is only very recent and fragmentary, but its conclusions are of great interest to our discussion.

Religiosity and Growth

Economists Robert Barro and Rachel McCleary have analyzed religion's effect on economic growth.[16] While religious beliefs are clearly a very important part of culture, Barro and McCleary do not analyze the specific effects of different religions, but rather examine whether countries with higher levels of religiosity grow faster than do more secular nations. This kind of analysis is tricky to do because the relationship between religiosity and growth could go both ways— religiosity might affect growth, but growth might also affect religiosity. Indeed, the **secularization hypothesis** initially formulated by Max Weber and reformulated by many social scientists states that as countries become richer, the influence of religion in society should decline.[17]

As measures of religiosity, Barro and McCleary use statistics on church attendance and the frequency of beliefs in heaven and hell. Because the relationship between religiosity and growth could go both ways, Barro and McCleary perform an instrumental variable estimation of religiosity's effects on growth. They use as instruments for religiosity 1) the presence of state religion, assumed to affect religiosity in a positive way; 2) regulation of state religion, assumed to have a negative effect on religiosity because it reduces competition between religions; and 3) religious pluralism, assumed to have a positive effect on religiosity because competition for religious attendance should improve the quality of religious services. The economists then regress growth rates of per capita GDP on the instrumented religious variables, controlling for other determinants of growth such as initial levels of GDP per capita, education, demographic variables, investment rate, openness, and the proportion of specific religions in a country, among others.

Barro and McCleary's primary finding is that a greater belief in heaven and hell among the population is associated with higher growth, whereas increased church attendance is associated with lower growth. Despite the use of instrumental variables, it is not clear that the instruments are unrelated to growth. The presence of state religion might, for example, directly affect economic growth, which would make it an invalid instrument. The results should, then, be interpreted with caution.

However, what reasonable interpretation of these findings can we make? People who believe in heaven or hell may have a longer time horizon and thus

---

[16]Robert J. Barro and Rachel M. McCleary, "Religion and Economic Growth across Countries," *American Sociological Review* 68, no. 5 (2003): 760–781.

[17]Max Weber, *The Protestant Ethic and the Spirit of Capitalism* (New York: Scribner and Sons, 1958).

be more willing to save, which could lead to higher growth via larger investment. The fear of hell might also positively impact individuals in terms of making them more virtuous. These channels are, however, not directly tested. In other words, regressions of beliefs in heaven and hell on savings or some measure of virtue are not performed. Greater church attendance might reflect a religion's stronger influence on social and political life, which might negatively affect growth. Again, the channel has not been investigated. These are just preliminary results on religion's effect on growth, and they only look at a few aspects of religion, but this topic is likely to become important in the future. It is indeed not clear that the secularization hypothesis is valid in the long run; different societies, even very affluent ones, experience periods of religious revival as well as periods of increased secularization.

Religious Beliefs and Trust

Trust is important for development in many ways. When people trust each other, business transactions are made easier. Law enforcement is less costly as most people are trustworthy. This means the controls to ensure that citizens abide by the law will be less costly. Politicians and bureaucrats will also be more accountable as high standards of honesty will be expected of them. Deviations from these standards are likely to be punished harshly. Moreover, because generalized trust is usually associated with a civic culture, people will participate more in collective activities and will tend to free-ride less. Is there a relationship between people's religious beliefs and their willingness to trust others? This is a question that Luigi Guiso, Paolo Sapienza, and Luigi Zingales have investigated using the World Values Survey.[18] The dependent variable is the question on generalized trust, coded as 1 if an individual agrees with the statement, "Most people can be trusted." The independent variable is religion, with controls for gender, age, health, education, social class, income, and country and year effects. Figure 11.7 shows the results.

As Figure 11.7 shows, being religious increases trust in others by nearly 20%. Being raised religiously increases the propensity to trust others by 2.6%. As with Barro and McCleary, the fact of being religious has effects on people's beliefs, in this case their propensity to trust others. The effect of different religions on trust is, however, not the same. As we can also see in Figure 11.7, Protestants have an increased propensity to trust by nearly 10% and for Catholics trust increases by nearly 5%. There is no significant effect for Jews, Muslims, and Buddhists, while Hindus are less inclined to trust than are other religions (−5.1). To understand the information in Figure 11.7 correctly, on average a practicing Hindu will still have a higher propensity to trust than a nonreligious person, by plus 19.6% minus 5.1% (equal to 14.5%).

Culture and Thrift

Guiso, Sapienza, and Zingales also examine the link between religion and preferences for thrift. The dependent variable is the response rate to the question of how important it is for a child to aspire to the qualities of thrift and saving.

---

[18]Luigi Guiso, Paolo Sapienza, and Luigi Zingales, "Does Culture Affect Economic Outcomes?" *The Journal of Economic Perspectives* 20, no. 2 (2006): 23–48.

FIGURE 11.7   The Effect of Religion on Trust

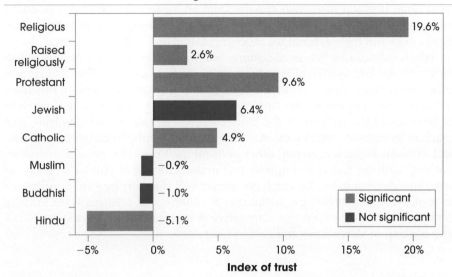

Religious people trust others more. The effect is stronger for Protestants and Catholics but weaker for Hindus.

Source: Luigi Guiso, Paolo Sapienza, and Luigi Zingales, "Does Culture Affect Economic Outcomes?" *The Journal of Economic Perspectives* 20, no. 2 (2006): 23–48. Printed with permission of American Economics Association.

Using the same controls for gender, age, health, education, social class, income, and country and year effects, the researchers found that, compared to nonreligious people, Catholics are 3.8% more likely and Protestants 2.7% more likely to view thrift as an important value. Buddhists and Hindus are 7.2% more likely than nonreligious people to place a high value on thrift. For Jews, there is no significant effect; some value thriftiness very highly but others do not. In addition, a high value on thrift significantly affects national savings rates—an increase of one standard deviation in the share of people who value thrift as an element of children's education leads to a 1.8 percentage point increase in the national savings rate, the ratio of savings to GDP. This suggests that culture might affect national savings rates as we saw in the example that opens this chapter.

Pitfalls to Avoid in Research on Culture

Does an emphasis on the importance of culture and its inertia effects for development mean that we should develop a fatalistic attitude toward development? Does the fact that certain countries have inherited cultural beliefs that make them less prepared for economic development mean that those countries are doomed to remain underdeveloped? Not necessarily. Understanding the inertia of culture certainly means that we should be cautious in thinking that people's values and beliefs can change overnight. We must recognize that these values and beliefs are very stable and do not change quickly. We also must be wary of expectations that cultural change can be influenced in a predictable way. We still do not understand very well the origins of culture or how and why it evolves and changes. The diversity of cultures in the world means that different countries must often develop their own specific legal and political institutions or adapt imported institutions to reflect their local cultures. "One size fits all" institutions do not exist, but there is room for experimentation and cultural exchange.

When considering issues of culture, we must be especially cautious not to rank cultures and apply value judgments to them. Even if we find that certain cultures are more suited for economic development as we know it, this does not mean that "superior" and "inferior" cultures exist. There is surely much to criticize about the cultures of the more economically advanced countries, and much to learn from other cultures in terms of philosophy, well-being, wisdom, and virtuous behavior, among other cultural qualities. This should, however, not stop us from trying to improve our understanding of culture's effects on economic development. Research on culture will certainly be seen as offensive to some, just as psychology, sociology, or other social sciences were initially considered to be offensive. It is imperative that researchers take care not to fall into the trap of stereotypes and cultural imperialism.

Chapter Summary

Measuring Culture

Culture may seem impossible to measure, but several gauges of culture have developed in the social sciences. Since 1981, the World Values Survey has collected survey answers from people around the world on their basic values and beliefs. Psychologist Shalom Schwartz has run alternative surveys on values based on questions that have universal meaning and are similarly understood in different countries. Dutch sociologist Geert Hofstede has developed a well-known database on individualism and collectivism and other cultural dimensions.

Culture's Effect on Institutions

Robert Putnam's research on northern and southern Italy shows that, given identical formal institutions, differences in the culture of civil participation affect the quality of institutions. Empirical research has also found that culture causally affects both corruption and the quality of governance. Different cultural beliefs also lead to different methods of contract enforcement, as Avner Greif has shown in his study of contract enforcement in the individualist values system of Genoa and in the collectivist values system of the Maghribi traders.

Cultural Obstacles to Economic Development

Collectivist and egalitarian norms in tribal societies have been an obstacle to wealth accumulation and to individuals aspiring to prominence or success in their communities. Another cultural obstacle was the centuries-long prohibition against interest payments condemned by both Islam and Catholicism as a sin of usury. This led to higher transaction costs in financial markets, as agents tried to circumvent this interdiction. Islamic inheritance law derives from the Qur'an and is thus sacred and not subject to change. It has resulted in fragmented inheritance and has been an obstacle to the formation of modern corporations.

The Effects of Culture

Research findings tend to show that societies in which people believe more in heaven and hell have faster economic growth and that societies with more church attendance have lower growth. Religious people are found to tend to trust others more. Buddhists, Hindus, Protestants, and Catholics appear to place a higher value on thrift than do nonreligious people. Research on the economic effects of culture is still in its infancy and we must be careful in interpreting its findings, and even more cautious before drawing any policy conclusions.

Key Terms

civil society
primogeniture

secularization hypothesis
sin of usury

Review Questions

1. Research and explain the difference between the views of Karl Marx and Max Weber on the role of culture in economic development. What is your view?

2. What has Putnam's research shown in terms of the interaction between culture and democracy? Explain.

3. Culture affects political institutions, but political institutions could affect culture. Licht, Goldschmidt, and Schwartz have proposed instrumental variable regression as an efficient way to measure culture's effect on political institutions. Explain how this regression helps to measure such a causal effect. Explain what instrument the researchers chose. Why is it a good instrument?

4. Greif has compared contract enforcement methods among Genovese merchants and Maghribi traders during the late Middle Ages. What was the main difference in their contract enforcement systems? How does that difference relate to culture? Explain the implications of these different contract enforcement methods.

5. Choose a continent in the developing world. Research the dominant (or one of the dominant) culture(s) on that continent. When and how did it emerge? What are its main components? How did it spread? Which components of this culture do you think favor economic development? Which favor economic development less? Explain.

6. Download the data from the Hofstede website on scores of individualism (http://www

.geerthofstede.com/dimension-data-matrix). Compare these scores with the Schwartz cultural map (see Figure 11.4). Which of the dimensions on the map seem the closest to the Hofstede individualism scores?

7. Choose one developing country from Asia and one from Latin America. Go to the World Values Survey website and download its data (http://www.worldvaluessurvey.org/). Compare the survey answers for those two countries. Which answers are the most similar? Which answers differ the most between these two countries?

8. Download the article "Culture and Economics" from Raquel Fernandez's website (http://sites.google.com/site/raquelfernandezsite/research). What does she mean by the epidemiological approach to culture? What are the main insights from her research?

9. Data from the United States are often used to understand culture in developing countries. Why? In what ways are the data interesting to understand culture and why can they lead to econometrically convincing results? Do an online search for relevant examples of studies using data from the United States that were not cited in this chapter.

10. Download a conversation with Amy Chua, Yale professor of law and author of *World on Fire: How Exporting Free Market Democracy Breeds Ethnic Hatred and Global Instability* (http://globetrotter.berkeley.edu/people4/Chua/chua-con0.html). How do Chua's ideas relate to the ideas in this chapter?

12

Rural Land Rights and Contracts

For centuries, and perhaps for millennia, rice has been a vital and traditional crop in India's northern province of Uttar Pradesh, but rice productivity, in tons per hectare (10,000 square meters), varies enormously within the province. A typical sharecropping household cultivating a modern rice variety on 0.8 hectares of irrigated land will typically achieve a yield of 1.9 tons per hectare. Between 33% and 40% of the crop goes to the landlord and, in some cases, it is as much as 50%. Contrast this harvest with that of Shri Shukla, a small private farmer who owns land in the village Gopalpur in the Faizabad district of Uttar Pradesh. He was convinced to try a new variety of hybrid rice (called Narendra Sankar Dhan-2) and managed to harvest 11 tons of it on his 1-hectare farm. Not all farmers are as successful as Shri, but his harvest still represents a significant improvement in rice productivity for farmers across the province. Can it be that private ownership of land gives more incentives to farmers to innovate and work hard than does sharecropping or other forms of renting or leasing land? This is one of the main questions we will be investigating in this chapter.

Humans have been working the land ever since the first nomadic tribes became sedentary. Farming is physically demanding. More or less effort exerted by a farmer for fundamental tasks such as plowing, sowing, and harvesting make a big impact on his crops. If he does not plow deeply enough, does not sow carefully, or fails to harvest at the right time, the farmer will realize lower returns than his neighbor who invests more effort in the tasks at hand. Moreover, effort does not always carry immediate rewards. Some farming investments take years before generating substantial income. For example, fruit trees must grow for years before they will bear a crop. Long-term investments will only be worthwhile if the farmer can be sure to benefit fully from their returns. Farming also bears risks. Bad weather such as drought or floods will adversely affect a harvest, while market volatility will affect income. Decisions to try a new fertilizer or a new crop may result in a large increase in income, but might also lead to significant income losses if unexpected contingencies occur: the new crop might not be adapted to the existing soil conditions, its market price may fall, or the fertilizer could create health hazards for the farmer's family. Effort, in the short and long term, as well as risk, are thus essential parts of farming. Existing institutional arrangements for working the land create incentives or disincentives for effort and affect risk management, and therefore impact agricultural productivity.

In poorer countries, especially in many rural areas in Africa, the village clan still owns and manages the land. This kind of communal property has adverse effects on investment in the land's quality and productivity. Even where private ownership of land is predominant, various sorts of contractual arrangements for use of the land still exist. The most important arrangements are sharecropping, land rental, use of wage labor, and small privately owned farms. As we will see, while these farms are, in general, the most efficient means of raising crops and livestock, this does not make them the dominant form of land ownership in developing countries. Worldwide, variations in institutional environments can account for the large differences in the types and patterns of land ownership. Inequality in land ownership is very high in some regions of the world, such as in Latin America, where Spanish colonization has left a deep mark on rural areas: wage labor on large plantations or land rentals to small farmers is prevalent and there is little private ownership of small farms. In other regions, such as East Asia, land is distributed very equally because land reforms have redistributed land from the rich to the poor.

Land reform appears to be fundamentally important for the economic development of agriculture in those countries where existing land ownership arrangements result in low productive efficiency, that is, low output per hectare. How do land reforms redistribute arable land from large estates to peasant families? When do such distributions occur? What are the obstacles to such reforms, and what are their economic effects? These are some of the questions we will address in this chapter.

Worldwide Land Distribution and Land Contracts

What types of land contracts and forms of ownership are the most prevalent in different regions of the world, particularly in developing countries? Table 12.1 shows some basic facts about inequality in land ownership. These data are not collected very often, so some are old and do not come from comparable years. However, the data are useful because land inequality does not change very much over time. The Gini coefficient is a summary measure of inequality discussed in Chapter 2; in Table 12.1, it represents values between 0 and 100. A higher Gini coefficient means higher inequality of land ownership. Higher inequality of land ownership means that a small number of landowners control large tracts of land, while many small farmers work on modest plots. Table 12.1 highlights differences among regions of the world in terms of land inequality. Latin America tends to have the highest land Ginis, while Asia has the lowest.

These differences in land inequality raise several questions. Can disparities in agricultural technologies explain the variation across countries in the distribution of land ownership? In other words, is high ownership inequality more efficient in Latin America while high ownership equality is more efficient in Asia? If this is the case, what are the technological differences that may explain this? If the variation across countries is not explained by technologies that promote efficiency, then what arrangement is more efficient: a higher or a lower inequality in land ownership?

Table 12.2 displays the distribution of farms and farmland according to ownership and contract status worldwide. Africa, the world's poorest continent, has the smallest average farm size, at 1.5 hectares. Only 5% of farms are cultivated by their owners. There is, however, also very little tenancy, that is, farmers renting the land they work on from landlords. Nearly 60% of African farmland falls outside the categories of ownership or tenancy. Instead, land is held by means of various forms of communal tenure. In this case, the tribal chief usually has authority to regulate land use by different households and

TABLE 12.1   Land Ginis across the World

Sub-Saharan Africa			South Asia		
Burkina Faso	1993	39.1	Bangladesh	1977	41.7
Cameroon	1972	40.7	India	1986	57.9
Central African Rep.	1974	33.8	Nepal	1971	54.2
Congo, Dem. Rep.	1970	53.2	Pakistan	1989	55
Cote d'Ivoire	1974	41.5	Sri Lanka	1961	62.3
Ethiopia	1977	42.4			
Gabon	1974	40.2	**East Asia & Pacific**		
Ghana	1970	53	China	1997	43.8
Guinea	1989	45.2	Indonesia	1993	45.4
Kenya	1974	63.1	Korea, Rep.	1990	37.2
Lesotho	1990	41.1	Laos	1998	38.2
Liberia	1971	68.1	Malaysia	1960	68
Mozambique	1999	36.8	Myanmar	1993	46.3
Niger	1980	31.2	Philippines	1991	54.7
Senegal	1998	47.8	Singapore	1973	29.1
Sierra Leone	1970	42.4	Taiwan	1960	39
South Africa	1960	64.3	Thailand	1993	44.7
Swaziland	1971	83.5	Vietnam	1994	47.4
Togo	1970	51			
Uganda	1991	57.4	**Middle East & North Africa**		
Zambia	1971	69.9	Algeria	1973	63.5
			Egypt	1961	63.3
			Iran	1988	67.7
			Iraq	1958	82
			Jordan	1983	64.3
			Kuwait	1970	72.5
			Morocco	1962	57.7
			Saudi Arabia	1972	74.2
			Syria	1971	64.3
			Tunisia	1961	61.6

Latin America & Caribbean			Developed Countries		
Argentina	1988	81.4	Australia	1971	80.5
Barbados	1989	84.8	Austria	1990	61.2
Brazil	1985	80.2	Belgium	1970	57.8
Chile	1997	84.1	Canada	1961	52.6
Colombia	1988	74.3	Czechoslovakia	1921	63.3
Costa Rica	1963	73.9	Denmark	1989	42.8
Dominican Republic	1960	74.5	Finland	1959	33.8

(Continued)

Latin American & Caribbean			Developed Countries		
Ecuador	1974	77.2	France	1988	54.6
El Salvador	1961	78.3	Germany	1971	49.4
Guatemala	1964	77	Greece	1993	53.9
Guyana	1989	63.9	Ireland	1960	57.5
Haiti	1971	46.2	Israel	1970	69.8
Honduras	1993	65.3	Italy	1990	73.3
Jamaica	1961	75.7	Japan	1995	51.1
Mexico	1960	69.4[a]	Netherlands	1959	55.7
Nicaragua	1963	75.9	New Zealand	1972	71.2
Panama	1990	82.2	Norway	1959	36.2
Paraguay	1991	84.9	Portugal	1989	73.5
Peru	1994	81.1	Spain	1989	80.2
Puerto Rico	1987	73.4	Sweden	1961	48.8
Trinidad and Tobago	1963	69.1	Switzerland	1969	50.4
Uruguay	1960	79.1	United Kingdom	1993	64.4
Venezuela	1961	85.7	United States	1987	71.9

A high land Gini means that the distribution of land ownership is very unequal, with a small percentage of rich landowners possessing large tracts of land. A low land Gini means that there is a more equal distribution of land.

Source: Ewout Frankema, "The Colonial Origins of Inequality: Exploring the Causes and Consequences of Land Distribution" (working paper presented at the International Economic History Association Congress, Helsinki, September 2006), http://www.helsinki.fi/iehc2006/papers3/Frankema.pdf.

tribal members. Land investment is also often regulated at the communal level. Property rights to land are therefore not well defined in Africa in the modern sense of individual ownership rights.

Forms of land ownership in Asia are very different from those in Africa: 92% of farms and 80% of farmland are owner cultivated, while tenants cultivate only 12% of farmland. Though larger than in Africa, the average Asian farm size (1.7 hectares) is distinctly smaller than the world average (10.9 hectares). In Latin America, the average farm size is 67.3 hectares, 40 times larger than in Asia! Only 69% of Latin American farms are cultivated by their owners. Latin America has a high level of tenancy—21%—relative to the rest of the world. However, tenants cultivate only 5% of total farmland in Latin America, indicating that farms managed by tenants are relatively small. Given the large size of farms in Latin America, we might expect a larger role for tenancy, but large farms typically use wage labor instead of renting out farms to tenants. Note also that only 16.1% of land worked by tenants involves contracts with share tenancy, that is, sharecropping. Tenant farmers usually pay a fixed rent in Latin America. By contrast, the overwhelming majority (84.5%) of tenant contracts in Asia are subject to sharecropping.

TABLE 12.2 Forms of Land Ownership across the World

	Asia	Africa	Latin America	Europe	North and Central America	World
Number of countries enumerated	14	20	7	20	16	90
Number of farms (million)	169.8	24.3	9.9	15.3	7.5	227.2
Average operational farm size (hectares)	1.7	1.5	67.3	22.3	86.9	10.9
Distribution of farms (%):						
Owner cultivation	92	5*	69	83	57	89
Pure tenancy	2	2*	4	3	11	3
Other single forms of tenure	1	7*	17	5	6	2
Under more than one form of tenure	4	86*	7	8	27	7
Distribution of farmland (%):						
Owner cultivation	80	35	88	51	83	85
Pure tenancy	12	8	5	49	15	11
Other	8	57	7	1	1	5
Percentage of shared tenancy in tenanted land	84.5*	0*	16.1*	12.5*	31.5*	36.1*

Different continents vary significantly in terms of the average size of farms, the percentage of owner-cultivated farms, and the share of tenancy.

Source: United Nations Food and Agriculture Organization (1981), (1990).
*Data taken from 1980 and 1990 World Census of Agriculture. In 1990, data are only available for Congo (called Zaire at the time), Egypt, Guinea, Guinea Bissau, Reunion Island, and Uganda.
Countries enumerated are:
Asia—Cyprus, India, Indonesia, Iran, Israel, Japan, Korea, Myanmar, Nepal, Pakistan, Philippines, Thailand, Turkey, Vietnam
Africa—Benin, Botswana, Burkina Faso, Cape Verde, Congo, Djibouti, Egypt, Ethiopia, Guinea, Guinea Bissau, Lesotho, Libya, Malawi, Namibia, Reunion Island, Sao Tome and Principe, Swaziland, Tanzania, Uganda, Zambia
Latin America—Argentina, Brazil, Colombia, French Guiana, Paraguay, Peru, Uruguay
Europe—Albania, Austria, Belgium, Czechoslovakia, Denmark, Finland, France, Germany, Greece, Ireland, Italy, Luxembourg, Netherlands, Norway, Poland, Portugal, Slovenia, Spain, Switzerland, United Kingdom
North and Central America—Bahamas, Barbados, Canada, Dominica, Grenada, Guadeloupe, Honduras, Martinique, Mexico, Panama, Puerto Rico, Saint Lucia, St. Kitts and Nevis, St. Vincent, United States, Virgin Islands
World—Oceania in addition to the above cited countries

These data raise several questions: Why do tenant contracts in Latin America primarily take the form of rental contracts, and why is there very little sharecropping? Why is there more sharecropping in Asia compared to other regions of the world? What differences do these contracts imply for the tenant and for the landlord? What difference do they make in terms of efficiency?

Properties of Land Contracts

Let us examine the economic properties of the five basic forms of ownership and tenancy contracts. These include farmer ownership, communal ownership, fixed land rental, sharecropping, and labor contracts. We can use the first, the privately owned farm, as a benchmark to discuss the effect of land contracts on four important dimensions of farming: 1) effort, 2) investment, 3) risk, and 4) farm size.

Farmer Ownership

When a farmer owns the land he works, he receives the full residual returns of his labor investment. Because of this he will put in exactly the optimal amount of labor (time and effort); that is, the amount that equalizes the marginal benefit and the marginal cost of labor. The farmer also has the optimal incentives to invest in the land. Many investments in agriculture take time to mature, and a farmer will only undertake these investments if he can be sure to reap their returns.

The disadvantage of ownership is that the farmer-owner bears all the risks. If bad weather such as a drought or flood destroys a crop, the farmer bears all the associated income losses. However much a farmer works, he cannot avoid the hazards of nature. Agricultural productivity depends very much on the quality of the land: the quality of the soil, its mineral content, its exposure to sun and wind, the degree of land erosion, etc. Technological progress can improve land quality through irrigation systems, levees, and modern cultivating practices, and fertilizers also help to improve soil quality. However, no technology can protect a farm from the consequences of a drought, flood, or tornado. Insurance contracts can also help, but insurance markets are imperfect and companies will in most countries not insure a farmer against natural disasters. In developing countries, where technology is less available and where insurance markets are more imperfect, farmers must bear even more risk.

Apart from the risks that nature presents, there are also economic risks. The prices of various crops can vary greatly over time. Price volatility can be quite high, as is the case for coffee or cacao trees, from which cocoa is made. There are usually no insurance markets that minimize the risk of price volatility for farmers. They exist only for the wholesale traders who can hedge prices by signing contracts on futures markets that guarantee the traders established sales prices. The poor Colombian coffee grower cannot access futures markets and cannot therefore insure himself against price risk. However, if access to insurance markets is unavailable, farmers can minimize price risk by diversifying their crops, especially those whose prices are negatively correlated with each other. In that case, if the price of one crop goes down, it can be compensated for by the increase in the price of the other crop. However, crop diversification is not often possible for poor farmers in developing countries, especially if they own only a small plot of land on which, due to size constraints, they can grow only one type of crop. The principle of decreasing marginal utility tells us that poorer farmers are more risk averse and are most in need of insurance, but in reality they have little or no access to it.

Given the limits on the total labor investment of the farmer and his household, there is a limit to the amount of land that they can optimally cultivate. This limit is directly dependent on the degree of agricultural mechanization. A greater degree of mechanization increases the optimal amount of land that a single farm family can manage. If the farm's basic operations can be accomplished with machines, then it is possible for a single farmer to hold a larger amount of land. However, machinery is not the only requirement; the farmer must also have modern crop storage capacity as well as modern transportation infrastructure to move crops to markets efficiently. In other words, there are complementarities between infrastructure and mechanization: the returns earned through mechanization are higher when a modern infrastructure is also available.

As we have discussed previously, the availability of modern infrastructure depends on a country's general level of development. The average size of a farm is larger in the United States than in Europe, where farm size is, in turn, larger than in Asia. Note that in Europe, as well as in various Asian countries, the size of farms is artificially lower than what market forces could support because farms receive heavy subsidies that allow smaller farms to stay alive. Finally, not all farming operations are easily mechanized and some farming activities, such as growing grapes or coffee, are more labor intensive than growing corn or wheat.

To summarize our discussion, with individual ownership, the farmer who owns the land has the right incentives in terms of effort and investment. However, he also bears all the risks. The amount of land that a single farmer can operate is limited. This limit varies with the degree of economic development and with characteristics of particular crops.

Communal Ownership

Communal ownership is a form of landholding by a village or a clan. Currently, it is still quite common in Africa, but was, historically, widespread in various regions of the world.

Communal ownership might create incentives, but only on a short-term basis. If a farmer is sure to receive the fruits of his labor in an agricultural cycle, that is, in the short term, he will put in an optimal amount of effort. However, he will fail to invest in the land because it will almost surely be handed over to another member of the community who will then reap the benefits of his efforts. The higher the probability of handover to someone else, the greater is the disincentive to invest in the land. This disincentive effect is important: progress in agricultural productivity is crucial to creating a surplus so that farm labor can be freed to move to manufacturing and the provision of services. This disincentive can thus have very negative consequences for growth and development. However, one possible advantage of communal ownership is that it can serve as a useful insurance policy inside the community. If different plots have different potentials for productivity, then a turnover may benefit farmers who receive an inferior plot because they will receive a superior plot later on. Because there are strong disincentives for technical progress in areas with communal ownership of land, small landholdings and few innovations in agricultural practices are typical of this type of farming.

Fixed Land Rental

A fixed land rental is a contract in which a farmer pays a fixed rent to the landlord who owns the land. Farmers who cannot afford to buy land often have no other option than to rent a piece of land. This kind of contract is widespread in Latin America. The tenant in this type of contract does not receive the full returns of his labor because part of the farm income must go to the landlord in the form of rent payment. But the tenant does get the **residual return** on his labor. In other words, the farmer will receive any extra income earned beyond his rent obligation through additional work on the land.[1] Say that the farm usually produces 100 and pays a rent of 50. The farmer's net income is 50. If he works more or introduces a new technology that improves his harvest, and gets 120 as a result, the additional 20 in income will belong to him. In that sense, the incentives for the tenant to provide additional effort are the same as for a farmer who owns the land.

What about the incentive to invest in the land? This is directly dependent on the actual length of the rental contract. If the contract must be renewed every year and the tenant farmer might be evicted at the time of renewal, then the incentives to invest in the land are poor or nonexistent. The return on the investment might go to someone else. If, on the other hand, the rental contract is long term, then the incentive to invest would be nearly identical to outright ownership. For example, when Chinese agriculture was decollectivized in 1978, the Communist leaders were not yet ready, for ideological reasons, to give land ownership to peasants; instead, they gave farmers 15-year leases, which were reasonably long-term contracts. This had a tremendous incentive effect on Chinese agriculture. Output doubled within 10 years after these long-term leases were introduced. However, while the long-term lease may be nearly identical to ownership, it is not the formal length of the rental contract that is important. Rather, it is its actual—and thus also its expected—length. If a landlord can evict a tenant by threat or intimidation, and the tenant is not legally protected, then the tenant has, in effect, a precarious contract that will negatively affect his incentives to invest.

What about risk? With a fixed rental contract, the landlord always receives a fixed income, in good or bad times. The landlord bears no risk, and all the risk is borne by the tenant. But that is also the case when the farmer owns the land. Are ownership and land rental equivalent in terms of risk? No—a tenancy contract is riskier than ownership. Let us take the example from above in which average farming income is 100 and rent is 50. Suppose that income is risky and fluctuates with weather conditions, markets, etc. Say that farming income will be good with 50% probability and yield an income of 125; it will be bad with 50% probability and a yield of 75. The owner thus has a risk (upside and downside) of 25% of his average income, which is significant.

What about the tenant? Because he must pay 50 in good and bad times to the landlord, his net income will be 75 with 50% probability and 25 with 50% probability. This represents a risk of 50% relative to an average income of 50. The risk is therefore higher relative to income than it would be if he owned the land. It has doubled as a share of income. The tenant is poorer than the owner, but the absolute risk he faces is the same and thus represents a larger proportion of his income. An income risk of 50% is quite substantial, especially for a poor tenant. This example does not capture an additional element of risk for the tenant: the rent might be sufficiently high that if the harvest turns out to be bad, the farmer will not be able to pay the rent. In that case, the farmer faces the risk of eviction.

What about the size of rented farms? They are not likely to be higher than family-owned farms for the same reason that a family can only work so much land. The actual size is likely to be smaller because tenants are poorer than farmer-owners and can thus rely less on machinery.

---

[1]The residual return is different from the marginal return. The marginal return is the return from the last hour worked. The residual return is all the return left after all the costs, including rental costs, have been paid. Obviously, the marginal return is included in the residual return.

Sharecropping

In a sharecropping contract, the tenant gives the landlord a certain portion of the crop. If the crop is good, the landlord receives more. If it is bad, he receives less. Sharecropping is a form of rental contract that amounts to paying a lower rent in bad times and a higher rent in good times. Consider our numerical example. Suppose that by contract the landlord receives 50% of the crop. On average, he will receive 50 from the tenant. However, in good times, he will receive 62.5, and in bad times he will receive 37.5. Compared to a fixed rental contract, the landlord shares part of the risk. As a consequence, compared to a pure rental contract, the tenant will face less risk. In good times, his income will be 62.5 (half of 125) instead of 75. In bad times, it will be 37.5 (half of 75) instead of 25. Because average income still is 50, the risk now represents 25% of the tenant's income. As a result, sharecropping reduces the farmer's income volatility as compared to a fixed rental contract. Note also that the farmer can never be insolvent relative to the landlord because he delivers a given proportion of the crop. Sharecropping thus eliminates the risk of eviction that exists with rental contracts and it reduces the overall risks a tenant faces compared to a fixed rental contract.

However, sharecropping also has its disadvantages. The principal drawback is that incentives are weaker than they would be with ownership or a fixed rental contract. Now the tenant is only a residual claimant to a share of the crop, not to all of it. Why is this bad for incentives? When deciding how much effort to put into raising a crop, the tenant equates the marginal benefit to the marginal cost of his labor. When the sharecropper considers whether or not to work one hour more, he understands that he must share the marginal benefit from that hour of work. Because labor costs time and effort, and because the marginal benefit of labor is decreasing, the sharecropper will prefer to work less so as to equate his marginal cost of effort with his share of his labor's marginal benefit. The farmer-owner, however, is ready to work longer hours because when he contemplates the benefit of an additional costly hour, he instead gets the whole marginal benefit. Sharecropping thus dilutes the incentives to invest effort into the farming operation. Sharecropping contracts reduce the risk for a tenant but they also reduce the incentives for effort.

The distortionary effects of sharecropping can be partially offset if the landlord tells the tenant that he will compensate him for a portion of his labor. In that way, the landlord shares not only the benefits but also the costs. Now the tenant will equate his share of the marginal benefit with his share of the marginal cost. If these shares are equal, then the incentives will be equivalent to those present with ownership or a fixed rental. It is easy to share the costs of inputs such as fertilizers that are easily observed. However, effort exerted in a farming operation is typically not observed, which results in asymmetric information. In that case, there is no easy way to share the cost of effort. The sharecropper's incentive will thus still be lower than with ownership or a fixed rental.

Labor Contracts

Not all farmers are owners or tenants. Many agricultural workers are laborers who work for a wage. For now, we will discuss the case of a **fixed wage**, that is, a wage paid by the hour. Many wage laborers are seasonal workers, as extra hands are always needed at harvest time, even in the most advanced economies. But many other farm laborers work all year for a fixed wage.

The wage contract is at the other extreme of the fixed rental in terms of both risks and incentives. The worker bears no farm output risk because he receives a fixed wage. Whether the harvest is plentiful or meager, the wage remains the same. It is a fixed payment from the owner to the worker, just as the rent discussed above is a fixed payment from the tenant to the landlord. However, there are no incentives at all to work harder in a fixed-wage contract. Whether the worker sleeps in the field or works hard all day does not make a difference to his wage. Therefore, wage laborers require supervision. If it is effective, supervision forces laborers to work hard during their paid hours, but the more imperfect the supervision, the more serious the incentive problem.

Wage labor has, however, one big advantage when combined with effective supervision of labor: there are few limits to the size of the farming operation on the landowner's property. This means that it is possible to obtain economies of scale through labor specialization; the various harvesting tasks can be separated into efficient operations that certain groups of workers can perform quickly, just as is the case for labor specialization within industry or services.

When wage labor is supervised efficiently, it is possible to cultivate much larger tracts of land than those a single farmer could manage on his own or with just his household. The wage-labor system is common on large plantations and other farming operations. Supervision is easier when many laborers work together in defined areas. It requires, however, a large pool of cheap labor. Plantations in the southern United States were operated with slave labor until the 1860s. In Latin America, the Spanish colonizers created the *encomienda* system, which forced local Indian populations to work for Spanish landlords and subjected them to highly exploitative feudal conditions. Landowners had the power of life and death over their Indian workers. In both the American South and Latin America, plantation owners took advantage of an abundant labor force that was in virtual servitude on the land. When the *encomienda* system was gradually abolished, already several decades after its establishment, the large *haciendas* (estates) that replaced it continued to impose quasi-feudal relations on the peasants who worked the land.

Incentive Effects with Land Ownership, Rental Contracts, and Sharecropping

Let us look more closely at the incentive effects of different types of land contracts: individual ownership, fixed rental contracts, and sharecropping. We abstract from the other aspects discussed, namely the risk aspects as well as the effects on optimal farm size.

Assume that farm output Y is a function of total labor input, which includes hours worked as well as the intensity of labor effort. Call this function $F(L)$. Assume a diminishing marginal product of labor, so that $F'(L)$ declines as L increases. In other words, assume that $F(L)$ is

(Continued)

a positive and concave function of L. Assume also that $F(0) = 0$, that is, output equals zero if labor equals zero. Assume finally that the cost of labor is simply L itself. This is a simplification, as there are additional cost elements other than labor. Also, the disutility of labor might be a (convex) function of labor effort, but we abstract from that. The individual farmer's choice of how much labor effort to invest will be the result of the profit maximization with

$$\Pi = F(L) - L$$

The maximum profit is attained when the derivative of Π with respect to L is equal to zero, which gives us $F'(L) = 1$. In other words, the farmer will work the land up to the point where the marginal product of his labor equals 1. This optimal level of effort is L^*, shown in Figure 12.1.

In a fixed rental contract with rent R, the tenant will maximize:

$$\Pi - R = F(L) - L - R$$

Because R is fixed and does not vary with L, $\Pi - R$ is also maximized when $F'(L) = 1$.

Figure 12.1 also shows the solution: the tenant will work just as hard as the individual owner, but his income will be lower.

In a typical sharecropping contract, the tenant is allowed to keep a share s ($0 < s < 1$) of output and must give the rest to the landlord. The tenant will thus maximize:

$$sF(L) - L$$

This objective function is maximized when $sF'(L) = 1$ and will lead to a choice of effort L^s that is lower than L^*. Figure 12.2 shows this solution: sharecropping thus reduces the tenant's incentive relative to ownership and a fixed rental, and the optimum can only be restored if the landlord is ready to pay a share s of the cost of effort. In that case, the tenant maximizes:

$$sF(L) - sL$$

This expression is maximized if $sF'(L) = s$, which thus gives $F'(L) = 1$, the same condition as in an ownership or fixed rental contract.

FIGURE 12.1   Incentives with Ownership and Fixed Rental Contracts

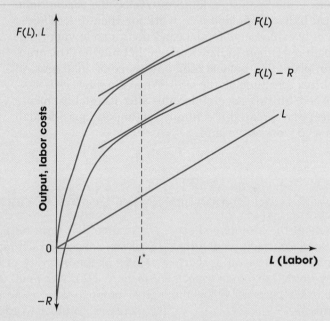

The farmer equates the marginal benefit of his labor to its cost, yielding the optimal amount of labor L^*. The optimum is the same with farm ownership or with a rental contract because in the latter case, the incentives at the margin are the same.

FIGURE 12.2 Incentives with Land Ownership and Different Forms of Sharecropping

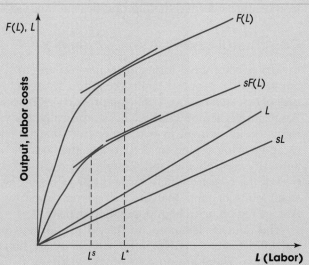

With a sharecropping contract in which the farmer only receives a portion s of output, incentives are lower and the farmer equates marginal benefit and marginal cost of labor at L^s. To restore incentives to the same level as in ownership, the landlord must make the farmer pay only for a portion s of his labor costs.

TABLE 12.3 The Properties of Land Contracts

	Effort	Investment	Risk	Size
Private ownership	First best	First best	High	Limited; varies with technology
Communal ownership	First best	Low due to plot turnover	Lower due to plot turnover	Limited
Fixed rental contracts	First best	Low; higher if long-term	Very high	Limited
Sharecropping	Lower	Low	Lower	Limited
Labor contract (fixed wage)	Lowest unless directly supervised	None	Lowest	Potentially large

This table summarizes the properties of the various types of land contracts in terms of effort, investment, risk, and size of land holding.

Table 12.3 summarizes the discussion on the effects of various kinds of land contracts on the key economic variables discussed: effort, investment in productivity improvements, risk, and size of the farm.

Economic Effects of Land Contracts

We have looked at five different forms of ownership or contractual arrangement in agriculture: farmer ownership, communal ownership, fixed land rental, sharecropping, and labor contracts on large plantations or estates. We have also discussed the economic properties of these different contractual arrangements. In this section, we will examine whether empirical research on land contracts verifies these properties and their economic outcomes.

Communal and Private Ownership

In Africa, communal forms of ownership are, to some extent, still dominant, but individual property rights are gradually becoming more common. A great deal of research has been done on property rights and their evolution in Africa. For example, Timothy Besley has empirically analyzed the effects of property rights on investment in two regions of Ghana.[2] The first region, Wassa, is a cacao-growing region in the west of the country where, traditionally, tribal authority controls the land. The second region is Anloga in the southeastern part of the country where farmers specialize in the production of shallots on small plots of land that are passed on primarily through inheritance. The Anloga region has a high population density.

The data Besley used are based on surveys of 217 households operating 1,074 fields in Wassa, and surveys of 117 households owning 494 fields in Anloga. There are no data on the value of investments made in the land, but researchers did ask the farmers specific questions about their investment decisions. In Wassa, they asked whether the farmers had planted new cacao trees. In Anloga, they asked about different forms of investment: continuous manuring of the land, ditching for drainage and irrigation, construction of shallot beds, and mulching the beds. The measure of investment was whether the farmer had made one of those decisions in the last year. Researchers also asked farmers about the rights they had to the land. Six specific rights were considered: the right to sell, rent, mortgage, pledge, bequeath, or donate the land. Researchers also asked the farmers whether they needed approval from the lineage (the elders in the extended family) to exercise those rights. This is an important distinction: If farmers needed approval from the lineage, it indicated strong communal ownership. In contrast, if farmers could exercise their land rights without lineage approval, this indicated established individual property rights.

Besley found that, controlling for a number of variables (the average age of the household; the value of durables and livestock owned; the number of years of education for the head of the household; the number of males and females in the household; the number of rooms in the house; the number of fields owned; field area; the distance of the fields from the house; past investment decisions; and village effects (taking the value of 1 if the data were from that village and 0 otherwise) to take into account omitted variables that are specific to particular villages and do not vary over time, an additional right to the land in Wassa caused an increase in the probability of planting new trees by 11 to 12%. Besley also analyzed the effect of a variation in ownership rights on different fields owned by the same household. Investment would increase by 28% if there were an additional right without approval, which is a very strong effect. The findings were significant as they demonstrated how the protection

---

[2]Timothy Besley, "Property Rights and Investment Incentives: Theory and Evidence from Ghana," *Journal of Political Economy* 103, no. 5 (1995): 903–937.

of individual property rights increased investment. They also suggested that property rights matter primarily as protection against expropriation.

An alternative effect of property rights on investment might occur through the credit market. More individual property rights increased the collateral value of land (the value a creditor could recover by selling the land in case of default on a loan), which would help a farmer to fund necessary investment. If the farmer did not have those rights, he would not be able to use the land as collateral. If this collateral value were the main determinant for the effect of property rights on investment, we should not observe any difference between field-specific rights. A household could use the stronger property rights it held on a given field to secure credit for another field for which the rights were less secure The specific rights attached to different fields of the same household should not matter for the purpose of securing credit because the creditor could take any plot belonging to the household in the event of default. It is only the average rights of the different fields that should matter. Besley's finding of field-specific effects suggests that the collateral value explanation was not present and that it was protection against expropriation that was the source of a higher investment level when individual property rights were present.

In Anloga, the shallot-growing region, Besley found no significant effect of individual property rights on investment. His overall findings, then, are mixed. It is interesting to note that the effects of property rights were significant in the Wassa region, where communal ownership of land has traditionally been more important, and it is likely that the transition to individual property rights in this region represented a more significant break with custom.

Markus Goldstein and Christopher Udry performed similar research.[3] They conducted a two-year survey in the Akwapim South District of eastern Ghana, a region in which farmers grow mostly maize and cassava. The primary method to improve land productivity was **fallowing**, leaving a field idle during a growing season to let the soil retain nutrients and moisture for future crops. This method can thus be seen as a form of investment in the land. However, because of the communal ownership system, the lineage leadership could reallocate a farmer's fallow land to other members of the lineage. (Note that the kinship system in this region was matrilineal, that is, kinship is identified through a family's maternal line.) This absence of individual ownership rights may have been a disincentive to investment; a farmer might have been less willing to leave land fallow because he would bear the costs of not harvesting a crop from it, but somebody else might get the benefit if the fallow land were reallocated.

Goldstein and Udry were able to estimate the effect of property rights on incentives by incorporating in their research the fact that some individuals in a village were more powerful than others and therefore had stronger property rights. Individuals with more connections to those with political power in the village were more confident in their rights over land than those who have fewer connections and they tended to fallow their land more. Those who fallowed less thus had smaller yields on their crops. The inefficiency that was the

---

[3]Markus Goldstein and Christopher Udry, "The Profits of Power: Land Rights and Agricultural Investment in Ghana," *Journal of Political Economy* 116, no. 6 (2008): 981–1022.

result of fallowing less was estimated at one-third of a plot's output and it represented a sizeable effect on incentives. The researchers also found that when farmers obtained plots through commercial transactions (through rental and sharecropping contracts), the plots were fallowed for more than 6 months longer than plots allocated through the lineage. This also indicated the advantage of individual over communal ownership.

Rohini Pande and Christopher Udry analyzed the evolution of the property rights system in the same regions of Ghana.[4] The communal system evolved in a time of land abundance, when there was always enough land for everyone and land could be left fallow for longer periods without resulting in a loss of income. However, as population density increased and land became less abundant, the efficiency losses associated with insecure property rights took effect, and fallow periods became considerably shorter. However, as land became scarcer, pressures for more secure property rights grew. Areas with higher population density tended to have a higher proportion of cultivated land secured through commercial contracts.

Sharecropping Compared to Privately Owned Farms

Some studies have compared the efficiency of sharecropping to private ownership. Radwan Ali Shaban, using data from India, has shown that productivity is lower with sharecropping than with land ownership.[5] Shaban's research was quite influential as the effect on productivity is, in general, not easy to estimate econometrically because a lower productivity on sharecropped land may be due to factors other than incentives alone. Farmers who were owners may for example have been more entrepreneurial, energetic, and less risk averse than sharecroppers. Shaban was able to estimate the effects on productivity of sharecropping versus private ownership because he was able to control for land quality, but the most ingenious part of his research design was that he was able to exploit the fact that the same farmer quite often worked some land that he sharecropped simultaneously with other land that he owned.

The data Shaban used in his study came from a previous village-level study done in India by ICRISAT (the International Crops Research Institute for the Semi-Arid Tropics). Researchers selected three different agro-climatic zones from the three provinces of Andhra Pradesh, Maharashtra, and Gujarat. They selected two representative villages in specific districts of these provinces. In each village, they randomly chose households and followed them between 1975 and either 1979 or 1982. What is quite unique about these data was that many individuals cultivated both their own plots and plots that they rented with a sharecropping contract. Any difference in productivity on owned versus sharecropped land should therefore not be related to differences in the individual characteristics of farmers (risk attitude, ability, strength, etc.). Using the ICRISAT data, Shaban

---

[4]Rohini Pande and Christopher Udry, "Institutions and Development: A View from Below," in *Advances in Economics and Econometrics,* ed. Richard Blundell, Whitney K. Newey, and Torsten Persson (Ninth World Congress of the Econometric Society, 2006): 2: 349–411.

[5]Radwan Ali Shaban, "Testing between Competing Models of Sharecropping," *Journal of Political Economy* 95, no. 5 (1987): 893–920.

found that a farmer's productivity was lower on plots that he sharecropped compared to plots that he owned, controlling for possible differences in the quality of land (plot value, soil type, and area irrigated). On the whole, he found that output per acre on owned land was 16.3% higher on average compared to sharecropped plots. He also showed that there was less input intensity (fertilizer, seeds, and other improvements) on sharecropped land. Looking only at sorghum plots, output per acre was nearly 30% higher on owned plots.

Sharecropping Compared to Fixed Rental Contracts

In a Tunisian study, Jean-Jaques Laffont and Mohamed Salah Matoussi compared sharecropping with fixed rental contracts and also estimated the effect of the length of tenancy contracts.[6] They used data from a 1986 survey in a rural area called El Oulja, 40 miles west of Tunis. Researchers interviewed 100 families and gathered information about their wealth and income, and the number of days each year they worked in agriculture. The researchers also gathered information about each plot of land, which included the plot's size, the type of crop grown on it, the type of contract (fixed rental or sharecropping) that secured its use, output levels, and information on labor and other inputs to the land. Their principal finding, in line with economic theory, was that output was 50% higher under a fixed rental contract compared to a sharecropping contract. Also, a 3-year sharecropping contract increased production by 38% compared to a 1-year contract.

Plantations and Slave Labor

Beyond its ethical issues, the standard economic view on slavery has always been that it was extremely inefficient given the absence of incentives for slaves. It therefore had to rely only on supervision, which was often brutal, but also necessarily imperfect since it is very difficult to monitor closely, and all day long, how hard somebody works on the land. Economic historians Fogel and Engerman have, however, argued that productivity on slave plantations in the southern United States was higher than on free farms both in the South and in the North.[7] Using historical data, they computed an index of farm productivity that was a geometrical average of labor productivity, capital productivity, and land productivity. They found that slave-labor farms were 40% more productive than farms owned or worked by freemen in the North and 28% more productive than freemen farms in the South. They argued that this was primarily due to the ability to organize the slaves in work gangs in which there was an extreme division of labor, with several slaves performing the same task who were required to move in rhythm. For example, to harvest cotton, rows of

---

[6]Jean-Jaques Laffont and Mohamed Salah Matoussi, "Moral Hazard, Financial Constraints and Sharecropping in El Oulja," *The Review of Economic Studies* 62, no. 3 (1995): 381–399.

[7]Robert W. Fogel and Stanley L. Engerman, *Time on the Cross: The Economics of American Negro Slavery* (Boston: Little, Brown and Company, 1974); and Robert W. Fogel and Stanley L. Engerman, "Explaining the Relative Efficiency of Slave Agriculture in the Antebellum South," *The American Economic Review* 67, no. 3 (1977): 275–296.

slaves were ordered to pick lines of plants and overseers could determine who moved the fastest and the slowest. They could also check to see whether the picking had been thorough. The fastest and most productive slaves were rewarded and this generated a kind of yardstick competition, that is, a rivalry to perform better than other slaves in the same row, which had the effect of achieving a very fast hourly production rate.

Fogel and Engerman's productivity figures have been subject to many controversies and debates. On the basis of the theory of division of labor discussed above, we could argue that economies of scale may give a productive edge to plantations, especially if labor practices include monitoring. However, plantations were mostly based on slave labor or quasi-slave labor. Although owning slaves had a cost, it was lower than that of labor by freemen. When slavery was abolished in the South and in other countries such as Brazil or the Caribbean nations, the organization of agriculture changed. In the southern United States, former slaves usually did not become wage laborers but instead became sharecroppers on small plots owned by large landholders. Large plantations were, however, maintained in many South American countries in conditions such that if the indigenous populations were not actually enslaved, at best they faced quasi-feudal conditions in which they had no other options than to work on the plantations. This suggests that the economies of scale on large plantations were only possible because the labor used on the land was virtually, if not literally, enslaved. If plantations had been run more efficiently using the labor of freemen, land owners would have been happy to pay the former slaves a wage that was higher than the income they would have received as sharecroppers or small farmers. All parties would then have benefited from the greater efficiency of plantations. As this was not the case, we have good reason to doubt the efficiency of large plantations in the absence of slave labor.

Plantations and Privately Owned Family Farms

In general, evidence suggests that large plantations are less productive than small family farms. Measuring farm productivity is not easy as there are different production factors to consider (land, capital, and labor). Due to issues of data availability, studies usually focus only on land productivity, which measures output per hectare of land. A classic study is that by Robert Berry and William Cline, who collected a large amount of data on farm size and productivity, and documented an inverse relationship between the two.[8]

Table 12.4 shows that smaller farms are always more productive than are the largest farms, whether they are in Brazil, Pakistan, or Malaysia. The productivity difference is the strongest in Brazil (more than 5 times, or a 400% difference!), where the size differential is the largest. The difference is least in Malaysia (48% larger), where the size differential is the smallest. Other studies have reached similar conclusions.[9]

---

[8]Robert A. Berry and William R. Cline, *Agrarian Structure and Productivity in Developing Countries: A Study Prepared for the International Labour Office within the Framework of the World Employment Programme* (Baltimore: Johns Hopkins University Press, 1979).

[9]See, for example, Alain de Janvry, *The Agrarian Question and Reformism in Latin America* (Baltimore, MD: Johns Hopkins University Press, 1981).

TABLE 12.4 The Inverse Relation between Farm Size and Productivity

Farm size	Northeast Brazil	Punjab, Pakistan	Muda, Malaysia
Small farm (hectares)	563 (10–49.9)	274 (5.1–10.1)	148 (0.7–1)
Largest farm (hectares)	100 (over 500)	100 (over 20)	100 (5.7–11.3)

The productivity of the largest farm, measured as output per hectare of land, is normalized to 100. Note that the small farms were not picked in the smallest size range, but in a somewhat higher size range. This was done in order to avoid data outliers. The size of the small farms is thus slightly overestimated.

Source: Agrarian structure and productivity in developing countries, Copyright © International Labour Organization, 1979.

A more recent study by Mark Rosenzweig and Hans Binswanger using the ICRISAT data on rural India, which contains information on the total wealth of farmers, also confirms an inverse relationship between farm size and productivity.[10] They find a systematically higher level of profit per unit of inherited wealth for small farmers than for wealthier farmers. Note that in this rural context, wealth and land size are almost perfectly correlated. However, they also find that smaller farmers face more risk as measured by the volatility of the onset of the **monsoon** (measured by its standard deviation), the rainy season. As the volatility of the monsoon increases, the profit of small farmers falls much faster than that of wealthier farmers even though the profit of the former remains higher than that of the latter.

While it is possible to argue that larger farms can benefit from economies of scale, the empirical evidence shows that incentives for those who work the land are the most important determinant of farm productivity. The evidence to date suggests that individual ownership is the most efficient form of agricultural organization because of the strong incentives associated with it.

Institutions and Patterns of Land Inequality and Land Contracts

Both theory and evidence strongly suggest that individual and family farming are more efficient than other contractual land arrangements. The size of family farms should, in theory, be a function of technological progress. However, it would seem that no difference in the natural endowments of land or in climate conditions (which may have different effects on farm work conditions across the world) can explain the large variation in the distribution pattern of contractual arrangements. This is an important point: if variations in land quality and in climate offer no convincing explanation for differences in land ownership and land contracts around the world, then variations in institutions would appear to play a major role in explaining these differences in land ownership.

---

[10]Mark R. Rosenzweig and Hans P. Binswanger. "Wealth, Weather Risk, and the Composition and Profitability of Agricultural Investments," *The Economic Journal* 103, no. 416 (1993): 56–78.

It may be that institutional constraints have prevented efficient land ownership arrangements from emerging in various parts of the world.

Variations in institutions are themselves a result of history. Communal ownership in Africa derives from custom and traditional social arrangements. We can trace the high inequality in land ownership and significant prevalence of rental contracts and sharecropping in Latin America back to colonial times and, in particular, the legacy of the *encomienda* system. In fact, the colonial period had a long-standing influence on patterns of inequality in landholdings throughout the world.

Hans Binswanger, Klaus Deininger, and Gershon Feder have argued that an important determinant of land distribution and contracts was the ruling elites' use of coercion and distortions to make large landholdings competitive with small family farms.[11] They identify four types of distortions that ruling elites used: 1) allocation of unoccupied lands only to members of the ruling class, allowing free peasants to cultivate only the less fertile lands in remote areas for their own crops; 2) discrimination in taxation, imposing high taxes on small family farmers and giving tax exemptions to large landowners; 3) restriction of market access to small farmers by arranging exclusive contracts between monopolistic buyers and large farms; and 4) influencing public decisions in favor of rich farmers by directing the provision of rural public services such as roads and waterways toward the large farms as well as through regulations to prevent the mobility of workers or tenants.

These distortions have been present on all continents at some point in time. They were present in European colonies as well as in the Ottoman Empire, India, Africa, and Asia, regardless of the diverse cultural backgrounds of the colonies. In other words, inequality in land ownership used to be the norm due to the power of the landed elites, who were able to use both the threat of violence and its actual use to subjugate the peasants. How can we explain why some countries have instituted land reforms to redistribute land from the rich to the poor, while other countries have not? We will address this question in the next section.

Land Reform

While it can have various meanings, in the last century **land reform** has primarily referred to the redistribution of land from large landholders to small farmers. This is the meaning we will use in our discussion.

The Experience of Land Reform

While many large-scale land reforms in the 20th century redistributed land from ruling elites to family farmers, they had mixed results. Both the Russian Revolution of 1917 and the Chinese Revolution of 1949 confiscated land from landlords and initially redistributed it to the peasants. However, because

---

[11]Hans Binswanger, Klaus Deininger, and Gershon Feder, "Agricultural Land Relations in the Developing World," *American Journal of Agricultural Economics* 75, no. 5 (1993): 1242–1248.

communist ideology was the motivating force behind these revolutions, the Russian Bolshevik Party and the Chinese Communist Party soon nationalized the land and organized agriculture into collective farms under centralized government control. Stalin instituted land collectivization in 1929 through a brutal process in which harvests were confiscated from the peasants, who were forced to work under police supervision to provide grain to Russian cities. Millions of Ukrainian peasants died from starvation during this process. In China, a collectivization process was launched in 1955 that organized farmers into communes. Incentives were virtually nonexistent under collectivized farming because the peasants worked as wage laborers and, as a result, land productivity plummeted. The Chinese commune system lasted until the agricultural reforms of 1978 under Deng Xiaoping.

In Africa, countries such as Ghana under Kwame Nkrumah, Guinea under Ahmed Sékou Touré, and Tanzania under Julius Nyerere, introduced land reforms aimed at collectivizing farms. In Tanzania, these were called the *ujamaa* villages. However, the conditions in Africa that preceded these efforts were vastly different from those in Russia or China before the introduction of collective farming. The attempts to transition from Africa's traditional communal subsistence farming to more modern collectivist farming failed. No incentives were put in place to increase productivity, and forced collectivization violated local communal traditions.

Land reform was one of the primary motivating factors of the Mexican Revolution, which lasted from 1910 to 1921. A radical program was launched under the presidency of Alvaro Obregon to confiscate the landholdings of large domestic and foreign landowners, and redistribute it to peasants. Politically, this was possible because the landlords who owned the large estates, or **haciendas**, lost their hold on power during the revolution. Interestingly, many peasants saw the reforms as an end to the rule of the Spanish colonial landlords and a return to the communal land ownership of the *ejido* system that had existed during the Aztec Empire in the 15th and 16th centuries. Under this system, peasants collectively owned an *ejido,* an area of communal farmland that they could work but could not sell.

The revolution nationalized the land and gave it to the peasants to work and a state-owned bank provided them with credit. Initially, the implementation of land reforms was slow; by 1928, less than 10% of landholdings had been redistributed as *ejidos.* However, between 1934 and 1940, President Lázaro Cárdenas accelerated land reforms and redistributed close to half of the land in the form of *ejidos.* Further reforms were undertaken in the 1970s under President Luis Echeverria, when large foreign-owned plantations were turned into *ejidos.*

The typical size of the *ejido* was usually too small, however, to be profitable using modern farming technology. Moreover, because farmers could not resell the land, there could be no market for the *ejidos* and they could not be used as collateral, so credit was not available to farmers. Under President Carlos Salinas (1988–1994), sale of *ejido* land, as well as its use as collateral, was finally permitted. One of the reasons for this reform was NAFTA (the North American Free Trade agreement), signed by the United States, Canada, and Mexico in 1994. After it became law, U.S. corporations wanted to buy land in Mexico to set up manufacturing facilities. Wealthy Mexicans bought up *ejido* land to build tourist resorts and factories, and the peasants who sold their *ejidos* became even more vulnerable economically as a result.

In Japan, South Korea, and Taiwan, important land reforms introduced after World War II drastically redistributed farmland from the wealthy land-lords to small farmers, often the landlords' former tenants. These reforms were comprehensive and egalitarian in their design. In Japan and South Korea, the U.S. occupation forces implemented the reforms. Traditionally, Japanese tenant farmers had to give roughly half of their rice crop to the landlord. Because the land-lords had supported Japan's military regime during the war, one of the objec-tives of land reform was to break their traditional power and dismantle the country's feudal social and political systems, particularly in the countryside.

In South Korea, much of the reforms consisted of confiscation of land that had been held before and during World War II by the Japanese occupation government, Japanese companies, and individual Japanese citizens. Wealthy Korean landowners were also obliged to divest most of their land. Because American occupation forces were concerned about a Communist takeover on the Korean peninsula, they decided to take a radical approach and give the land to the peasant farmers in order to prevent the Communists from gain-ing support in the countryside. As a result, a new class of independent family farmers was created in both Japan and South Korea. Note that in both coun-tries, reforms were the result of a foreign occupation power with a specific interest in making the reforms happen. In Taiwan, land reform was introduced by the Chinese nationalist regime after the end of World War II, with the help of the U.S. government. It was targeted, to a large extent, at lands held by for-mer Japanese owners who had fled Taiwan after Japan's defeat. Taiwanese landowners whose properties were expropriated were compensated through the sale of properties seized from the Japanese.

While other countries in East Asia, including the Philippines, Malaysia, Thailand, and Indonesia, did not undergo radical land reform as in Japan, South Korea or Taiwan, important land reforms did take place in India after decolonization. The 1949 Indian constitution stipulated that Indian states had the power to institute land reforms. Four types of reforms took place in the decades following independence. The first type was tenancy reforms, which were aimed at securing the rights of tenant sharecroppers and making their eviction more difficult. Provided the tenant paid his share of the harvest to the landlord (which could not exceed 25% of the crop) and did not leave the land fallow, his rights to work the land were secure. In some cases, tenancy reforms even involved attempts to transfer ownership rights to tenants. The second type of reform aimed at abolishing the intermediaries, the **zamindari**, who col-lected tax revenues for the British and extracted large rents from tenants. The third type of reform provided limits on the amount of land an individual could own with a view toward redistributing it from the wealthy to the landless. The fourth type of reform consolidated disparate landholdings by organizing an exchange or trade of land so that individual owners could work on contigu-ous plots. Consolidation laws were implemented vigorously in some states but halfheartedly elsewhere. Later in this chapter, we will discuss the effects of these four types of land reform.

In South Africa, starting in 1994, the government bought large landholdings from white owners and redistributed it to poor black farmers. The objective was to have black farmers run 30% of commercial farmland by 2014, but only a third of the objective had been met by 2012. Zimbabwe at first implemented a program similar to South Africa's; initially, only voluntary transactions were envisioned, but in 1998, the Zimbabwean government launched an expropriation program, taking land from white farmers and redistributing it to veterans of the country's Liberation War. In 2000, a constitutional referendum to give the government the right to expropriate land without compensation was defeated, but armed bands of veterans subsequently seized white-owned farmland. While agricultural output used to be quite impressive in Zimbabwe, it has fallen dramatically as a consequence of the reforms. Despite the dismal results of Zimbabwe's land expropriation, pressure has also been building in South Africa to implement a program that would expropriate white-owned farmland. In 2012, the African National Congress Youth League for example called for land expropriation without compensation, but no actions were taken so far.

The history of land reforms in the 20th century reveals that as a rule, they were not the result of a benevolent government's decision to increase agricultural efficiency. Land reforms usually took place in the aftermath of political turmoil such as a revolution, a foreign occupation, or decolonization. These turbulent events usually represented shifts in political power and land reforms generally reflected the interests of whatever party was currently in power. The Mexican revolution ended the domination of the large hacienda owners as did the Russian and the Chinese revolutions. The U.S. occupation of Japan and Korea deposed the militarists who had been supported by the large landlords. In the case of decolonization, the lands of former colonizers were confiscated and redistributed. Shifts in political power lead to shifts in property distribution. In the case of Russia and China as well as many former colonies, ideology also played a role in land reform. In those cases, newly powerful ideologues tried to exert direct control over farmers in accordance with a partisan blueprint.

Obstacles to Land Reform

Not surprisingly, in countries where there were no revolutions or large shifts in power, obstacles to land reform have been quite formidable. Binswanger, Deininger, and Feder argued that land reform met the most obstacles in countries where land ownership was very concentrated in the large *haciendas*. For the most part, laborers rather than tenants worked the land in those countries, and large landowners fiercely resisted reforms.[12] Compared to other continents, Latin America had the least favorable conditions for land reform.

In Brazil, 1.6% of the landowners controlled roughly half (46.8%) of the land on which crops could be grown. Only 3% of the population owned two-thirds of all arable land. Much of the large landowners' holdings were left uncultivated and unproductive. Nevertheless, these landowners, who had always held great political power and influence, vigorously opposed any attempt at

---

[12]Binswanger, Deininger, and Feder, "Agricultural Land Relations in the Developing World," 1993.

land reform. Instead of asking for radical land redistribution, peasants fought hard for the more modest goal of redistributing the uncultivated land.

For decades, Brazil had a "landless worker movement," the MST (in Portuguese, *Movimento dos Trabalhadores Rurais Sem Terra*). The MST was estimated to be the largest social movement in Latin America, with approximately 1.5 million landless members organized in 23 out of Brazil's 26 states. Beginning in late 1980 and early 1981, over 6,000 landless families established a squatters' encampment on a portion of land located between three unproductive estates in Brazil's southernmost state of Rio Grande do Sul. With the support of many associations and organizations, including many progressive Catholic clergy, the families eventually pressured the military government into expropriating nearby uncultivated land for the purposes of agrarian reform.[13] In 2005, the MST organized a popular march to demand that left-wing president Luiz Inácio Lula Da Silva implement promises to allocate unused land to landless farmers. The large landowners have strongly resisted even these limited reforms and their private militias have routinely gunned down peasant activists fighting for land redistribution.

Bolivia adopted an important land reform law after universal suffrage was introduced after the 1952 revolution by the left-wing nationalist revolutionary movement in power. However, due to the weakness of successive governments and the fragility of Bolivia's democracy, the law's implementation was very slow. By 1970, only 45% of peasant families had received title to land. When he took office in 2006, the new socialist president, Juan Evo Morales, a member of the Aymara tribe, restarted land reform. In 2006, Bolivia's senate passed a bill authorizing the government to redistribute land among the nation's impoverished, and mostly indigenous, peasants. Politicians representing the landlords, however, expressed adamant opposition to the bill. They pledged to reverse the reforms but have, so far, been unsuccessful.

In Chile, no significant land reform took place before the 1960s. Under Marxist President Salvador Allende (1970–1973), a radical land reform program was undertaken, and farms of more than 198 acres (80 hectares) were expropriated. However, when General Augusto Pinochet overthrew Allende in a military coup in 1973 with the support of the U.S. Central Intelligence Agency, the process was halted and partially reversed. Because Pinochet represented the interests of the large landholders, expropriated land was either returned to its previous owners or auctioned off to the highest bidder.

Guatemala's recent history has been characterized by intense violence, due in part to issues of land reform. In 1954, a coup orchestrated by the C.I.A., with the support of a coalition of landowners and right-wing paramilitary organizations, overthrew President Jacobo Árbenz after he expropriated large tracts of land exploited by the United Fruit Company to grow bananas. Between the 1970s and the 1990s, the Guatemalan army actively repressed and even massacred Indian peasants while rural guerillas fought for land redistribution. The army destroyed 450 Mayan villages and one million peasants became homeless. The army was accused by international public opinion of orchestrating

---

[13]Gabriel A. Ondetti, *Land, Protest, and Politics: The Landless Movement and the Struggle for Agrarian Reform in Brazil* (University Park, PA: The Pennsylvania State University Press, 2008): 67–69.

genocide against Guatemala's indigenous peoples. In 1992, the Nobel Peace Prize was awarded to Rigoberta Menchú for her efforts to bring international attention to the government-sponsored genocide of the indigenous population. In 1996, a peace accord was signed between the guerillas and the government. Land reform is still a contentious policy issue in Guatemala where less than 1% of landowners hold 75% of the best agricultural land.

In Venezuela, after Hugo Chavez came to power in 1999, a program called Plan Zamora (named for Eziquiel Zamora, a 19th-century peasant leader) was adopted in 2001 to redistribute government land and unused private land to poor peasants. Conservative forces strongly opposed the reforms and when they staged a coup against Chavez in 2002, they soon cancelled the program. However, the coup ultimately failed, Chavez came back to power, and since then thousands of peasant households have received land titles as a result of Plan Zamora. However, significant opposition to the plan has occurred in the countryside, where large landlords are still politically powerful. The Chavez government has had little influence in many rural areas and, since 2001, a number of activist leaders have been assassinated.

Effects of Land Reform

What effects does land reform have on poverty or on land productivity? In order to answer this question, we must look at the experience of specific countries and compare land productivity and other economic variables before and after the institution of reforms. Unfortunately, land reforms are rare events and studies of their effects are scarce. The sections that follow describe some recent studies.

Effects on poverty and growth. Timothy Besley and Robin Burgess examined the effect of land reforms in India.[14] Their data covered reforms from the following Indian states: Bihar, Gujarat, Haryana, Jammu and Kashmir, Karnataka, Kerala, Madhya Pradesh, Maharashtra, Orissa, Punjab, Rajasthan, Tamil Nadu, Uttar Pradesh, and West Bengal. The researchers counted the number of reforms in the four main categories of Indian land reform mentioned earlier in this chapter: 1) making eviction of tenants more difficult; 2) abolishing the *zamindari* intermediary system; 3) placing limits on total landholdings; and 4) consolidating disparate landholdings. Using a count of reforms is not precise because some laws may be more important than others, but it is not easy to develop better alternative measures. Besley and Burgess found that tenancy reform and abolition of the intermediary system reduced poverty, but that the two other reforms (ceilings on landholdings and land consolidation) did not. This suggests that the latter reforms were ineffective. Most rich landowners were able to circumvent the laws on limits to landholdings by distributing land to immediate family members, cousins, and friends. Consolidation laws were implemented halfheartedly in many states where the political influence of wealthy landlords was strong.

Besley and Burgess also found that land reforms positively affected the wages of agricultural workers. They also determined that tenancy reform had

---

[14]Timothy Besley and Robin Burgess, "Land Reform, Poverty Reduction, and Growth: Evidence from India," *The Quarterly Journal of Economics* 115, no. 2 (2000): 389–430.

a negative effect on state agricultural income, while land consolidation legislation had a positive effect. The other two types of reforms had no effects.

Land consolidation thus did not affect poverty, but it positively affected output. In other words, it had positive efficiency effects but no significant redistributive effect, which suggests that the richest peasants probably were able to use land consolidation laws to their advantage by buying land adjacent to their properties and selling land further away from their main holdings. As for tenancy reform, it had an important effect on poverty reduction but a negative effect on output. One interpretation of these results is that tenancy reform increased the bargaining power of tenants, which reduced poverty because they could negotiate better tenancy contracts, but the same reform also made it more difficult to evict less productive tenants and tenants who shirked, i.e., did not work much. This latter effect negatively impacted output.

Effect of long-term tenure. In another study, Abhijit Banerjee, Paul Gertler, and Maitreesh Ghatak found evidence for a positive output effect of tenancy reform in West Bengal.[15] Their argument was that even though protection from eviction can lead to more shirking, there is another effect that is related to tenants' stronger bargaining power: When tenants had more power to negotiate terms, the landlord gave them a more favorable contract that granted them a higher share of output. This created incentives to work harder and it offset the negative effects of improved security. The researchers based their evidence on West Bengal, where, in 1977, a new government passed a reform act that made it harder for landlords to evict tenants. The government also launched Operation Barga, a well-publicized campaign in villages to inform tenants of their rights and to encourage them to register as tenants so that their rights could also be registered. This operation was a success and by 1993, more than 65% of sharecropper tenants in West Bengal had registered.

To assess the effect of the reforms, the researchers compared the records of rice yields in West Bengal to those in neighboring Bangladesh, where no reforms took place. Rice is the main agricultural product on both sides of the border, covering more than 70% of agricultural land. Before Operation Barga, rice yields were not noticeably different in West Bengal and Bangladesh. However, after the program's introduction (1984–1993), rice yields were significantly higher in West Bengal by 5 to 18%, leading to a possible increase of yields on sharecropped land of about 42%.

The researchers also tried to estimate the effect of the reforms by using another empirical strategy: the registration rate of sharecroppers per district as a measure of the success of Operation Barga. They then regressed rice yields on sharecropper registration with a 1-year lag, controlling for district and for year effects. The success of the reform is thus the effect of a change in registration on rice yields multiplied by the change in the registration rate. At 60%, this strategy provided even higher estimates of the increase in rice yields.

Overall, the existing evidence shows that land reform has clear positive effects in terms of reducing poverty. The studies also show that reforms to

---

[15]Abhijit V. Banerjee, Paul J. Gertler, and Maitreesh Ghatak, "Empowerment and Efficiency: Tenancy Reform in West Bengal," *Journal of Political Economy* 110, no. 2 (2002): 239–280.

improve the security of tenants may have either positive or negative effects on output. However, on the basis of the theoretical discussion earlier in this chapter, we have good reasons to believe that more radical reforms giving full ownership rights to tenants would have positive effects on output.

Persistence of past institutional arrangements. If individually owned farms are more efficient than sharecropping contracts, do differences in efficiency related to differences in institutional arrangements persist over time after land reforms, possibly decades old, have changed the property right arrangements? Ahbijit Banerjee and Lakshmi Iyer found that this was the case in India.[16] When the British colonized India, they instituted two different systems for collecting land revenue. In certain regions such as Bengal and Bihar, land revenue collection was assigned to landlords, the *zamindari*. During the Mughal Empire, these landlords had been state officials, but over time, they became the de facto owners of large tracts of land. In this landlord-based system, a *zamindar* was responsible for collecting revenue from the peasants under his jurisdiction. These revenue-collecting rights could be bequeathed to heirs and could also be bought and sold. Sharecropping was quite widespread in the *zamindari* areas. On the other hand, in regions such as Gujarat, Karnataka, or Andhra Pradesh, land revenue was collected by the British rulers directly from the individual farmers; the British did not encourage a landlord-based system. Early on, these areas also developed a detailed system of titling and land records through a cadastral system that recorded a parcel's owner, its size, and its value for the purpose of computing land taxes.

The land revenue system has historic roots. In the early period of British rule, the landlord system was favored because it required less British administration. Areas colonized after 1820 were more likely to have the direct revenue collection system partly because individual administrators such as Sir Thomas Munro, governor of Madras, or Lord Elphinstone, governor of Bombay, favored the private ownership system. James Mill, the father of John Stuart Mill, wrote extensively on British administration in India; he also favored private ownership over landlord-based systems and was quite influential in the East India Company, England's monopolistic trading company in South Asia. Landlord-based systems were responsible for great inequality in land distribution and wealth, while private ownership systems had a more egalitarian distribution. This distinction between these two systems ceased after Indian independence in 1947. Since then, there have been many land redistribution reforms, but intriguingly, this early institutional difference has had long-run consequences.

To document this persistence of past institutional arrangements Banerjee and Iyer regressed variables that measure agricultural investments (irrigation, fertilizer, and high-yield grain varieties) and agricultural productivity on a variety of geographical controls. These controls include altitude, latitude, mean annual rainfall, soil type, coastal versus inland regions, and the proportion of villages, estates, or other tracts of land in a district that was not under landlord

---

[16] Abhijit Banerjee and Lakshmi Iyer, "History, Institutions, and Economic Performance: The Legacy of Colonial Land Tenure Systems in India," *The American Economic Review* 95, no. 4 (2005): 1190–1213.

control during British rule. The data cover the period from 1956 to 1987. The researchers found that in nonlandlord districts, on average 6.5% of additional land was subject to irrigation. Given that roughly 28% of land was irrigated, that represents an improvement of 24% over the average proportion of land irrigated. They also found that in nonlandlord districts there was greater use of fertilizer and of high yield-varieties of rice, wheat, and other cereal grains, which resulted in higher yields in those districts.

How can we explain this persistence of historical differences in institutional arrangements? Banerjee and Iyer argue that the best explanation is the difference between the political environments found in former landlord versus nonlandlord districts. One important difference is the provision of public services. Since the 1960s, former landlord districts have spent nearly 50% less on rural development per capita than the former nonlandlord districts. This period also has seen significant technological change in agriculture in the nonlandlord districts. Nonlandlord districts also invested more in health and education, achieving higher literacy rates and lower infant mortality rates. These differences in public expenditures can arguably be attributed to an atmosphere of class conflict and class resentment in the former landlord districts.

Chapter Summary

Worldwide Land Distribution and Land Contracts

Land is distributed equally in Asia and very unequally in Latin America. While small private farming is predominant in Asia, communal farming on small plots is the predominant type of land distribution in Africa. Latin America typically has large plantations, while in South Asia, sharecropping predominates.

Properties of Land Contracts

Individual privately owned farms are more efficient because they provide optimal incentives for effort and investment, but farmers bear all the risks. Farm size depends on the availability of technology.

Economic Effects of Land Contracts

Empirical studies confirm the theoretical predictions for the effects of different land arrangements.

Patterns of land ownership and farm size are explained less convincingly by efficiency measures than by historical and institutional legacies.

Land Reform

Land reform is the redistribution to small farmers of large tracts of land owned by landlords. Land reform most often occurred after important shifts in political power such as revolutions, foreign occupations, or decolonization. Large and politically powerful landowners resisted both radical land reform and more modest reforms such as the redistribution of idle land to landless peasants. Land reform has had positive effects in terms of both poverty reduction and output. In India, reforms that provide more security to tenants have had both positive and negative effects on productivity.

Key Terms

ejido
encomienda
fallowing
fixed wage
haciendas

land reform
monsoon
residual return
zamindari

Review Questions

1. What is the main determinant of land size for individual farm ownership? Why?

2. Does communal ownership become more inefficient when population density is higher? Explain.

3. What empirical evidence do we have about the different effects of sharecropping and individual farm ownership? What are the empirical problems in trying to measure such a difference and how did Shaban (1987) overcome those problems?

4. What evidence is available about the relationship between land size and productivity? What is the relation between risk and those two variables?

5. Read the following article about land tenure issues in South East Asia: http://www.fao.org/docrep/009/a0306t/A0306T04.htm#ch3. What connections can you draw between the discussion in this chapter on land contracts and property rights, and the issues in this article? What issues related to property rights does this article cover that the chapter does not?

6. Pick a developing country of your choice that has undergone land reform. Find information regarding land reform in that country. When did it happen, what form did it take, and what results did it have? Describe any possible flaws in the reforms in that country and provide an explanation for what caused those flaws.

7. Compare the situation of two farmers, one who owns his land and the other who rents it from a landlord. In good times (which happen with probability $\frac{1}{2}$), the owner-farmer earns an income of 125. In bad times (also with probability $\frac{1}{2}$), he earns an income of 75. The tenant works on a farm that is twice as large and earns an income of 250 in good times and 150 in bad times (both with probability of $\frac{1}{2}$). However, he must pay a rent of 100. Calculate the expected net income of both farmers. Assume that their utility function takes the following form: $U = y^{\frac{1}{2}}$, where y stands for the farmer's net income. Calculate the expected utility of both. Compare this result to the calculation on expected income. What do you conclude in terms of the different risks that both farmers face?

8. Consider a sharecropping arrangement where farmers earn a share s of output $F(L)$, where L denotes their hours of labor. Consider two farmers, where one is more productive than the other. The more productive farmer has costs aL ($a < 1$). The less productive farmer has costs L. This reflects the fact that the more productive farmer can get more work done in an hour. Calculate the optimal amount of labor for each farmer. Which farmer will work more? Assume that the landlord does not know which farmer is more productive. Assume he is willing to share labor costs so that each farmer only incurs a share s of his labor costs. Which of the two farmers will work more, and how close will effort of the latter be to that in a privately owned farm? What if the farmers are made to incur only a share sa of the cost? Explain the reason for these results.

9. A private farmer hesitates in considering buying new machines to work on his land. The cost of the new machines is K. Without new machines, the output on his land is Ta, where T stands for land. With new machines, output will be bTa, where $b > 1$. Calculate the amount T above which it is profitable to use the new technology.

10. Download the following article: "Land Institutions and Land Markets," by Klaus Deininger and Gershon Feder, http://papers.ssrn.com/sol3/papers.cfm?abstract_id=636211. What connections do these authors make between land rights and the development of markets for the sale of land?

13 Property Rights and Efficiency in Urban Areas

The Nairobi neighborhood of Ntumba cannot be found on city maps. It is a dense gathering of 800 shacks on less than 15 acres. On official maps, the area is a habitat for giraffes and rhinos because it borders Nairobi National Park. Ntumba is one of the thousands of city neighborhoods in developing countries where inhabitants live in houses built on land to which they have no title. If the meager property they possess is stolen, residents cannot complain to the police because they live outside the formal, legally recognized sector of the economy.

In Mexico City, around the Zocalo, the city's huge main square, as soon as it starts to rain, hundreds of women and children show up to sell umbrellas to tourists and pedestrians. If it does not rain, they sell school pens, jewelry, or chewing gum. Their income is not much above the poverty line (roughly $5 US per day) and their businesses are everywhere and nowhere. They do not own registered businesses nor do they have business licenses. A large part of the urban economy in developing countries operates in this informal sector. Those who run these businesses do not pay taxes and they operate under the radar of local and national officials. They are therefore condemned to minimal productivity. Why is there such a large informal sector in developing countries and how does the size of the informal sector in the economy affect the growth and development of these nations? This chapter analyzes property rights and contracts in urban contexts and their effect on economic efficiency.

Because formal institutions are nonexistent for millions of families and business owners in developing economies, this chapter will also examine the significant potential for positive economic effects of reforms aimed at securing a valid title to a property and bringing households and businesses into the formal economic sector. We will examine why, in countries with weak property rights protection, market infrastructure develops more slowly, competition is less efficient, and investment incentives are much weaker.

While small businesses often operate outside the formal sector in developing countries, large firms are traditionally state-owned. State ownership was widespread not only in countries with centrally planned economies such as China and the Soviet Union, but also in India, Latin America, and other parts of the world. A large state sector was a legacy of the development policies from the 1950s and 1960s, which saw capital concentration in state-owned industries as a way to accelerate economic development.[1] In the 1980s and 1990s, however, countries around the world initiated privatization reforms because

---

[1] See the discussions in Chapters 5 and 8 on earlier policies favoring the development of state-owned enterprises.

of disillusionment with those strategies. As we will see, while privatization turned out to improve efficiency more modestly than initially hoped, it also had negative redistributive effects. For example, it has badly hurt poor people by substantially increasing prices for basic necessities such as food and water. Why have these negative effects occurred, can they be avoided, and if so, how? This chapter will address these questions as it examines the effects of privatization policies in developing countries.

Property Rights and the Informal Sector

A major theme Hernando de Soto forcefully expresses in his popular book is that a large part of the economy in developing countries stays hidden in the informal sector.[2] These economic activities are not declared and therefore not taxed, the businesses are not registered, and they operate in buildings that are without legal title. This is also true for a great deal of urban real estate; millions of people in developing countries build their dwellings illegally on land for which they do not have an official title. De Soto estimated that in the Philippines, 57% of city dwellers and 67% of people in the countryside live in extralegal dwellings. In Peru, the corresponding figures are 53% and 81%. In Egypt, at least 92% of city dwellers and 83% of people in the countryside live in extralegal housing. The market price of these dwellings is very low compared to the value of a house in a working class neighborhood in the United States or Europe. For example, an untitled nice bungalow with a garage outside Lima, Peru, is priced at about $20,000, while an untitled Haitian shanty will not be worth more than $500. However, because there are so many illegal dwellings, their total value is huge.

De Soto estimates the value of untitled urban and rural real estate holdings in Haiti at about $5.2 billion. This represents 4 times the value of all of the assets of all legally operating companies in Haiti, 9 times the value of the country's government-owned assets, and 158 times the value of all foreign direct investment in Haiti since 1995. In Peru, the value of the informal real estate holdings is estimated at $74 billion, or 5 times the total valuation of the Lima stock exchange before the 1998 economic slump. In the Philippines, untitled real estate is estimated at $133 billion—4 times the Philippine stock exchange and 7 times the total deposits in the country's commercial banks. It is very difficult to estimate these values accurately. Whatever their true value, De Soto correctly points out that the value of untitled real estate in developing countries is enormous, certainly much larger than the total value of assets listed on the stock markets of emerging market economies.

The fact that there is so much hidden wealth in developing economies might be seen as encouraging: perhaps those countries are not as poor as the official economic statistics make them appear because so much of the economy operates outside the formal sector. However, the fact that such a large share of real estate and small business in developing economies operates in the informal sector represents a serious obstacle to development. There are

[2]Hernando de Soto, *The Mystery of Capital: Why Capitalism Triumphs in the West and Fails Everywhere Else* (New York: Basic Books, 2000).

many important costs associated with the informal sector. Property rights to informal holdings cannot be secured legally. The lack of a title that would secure property rights to a business or real estate holding results in many transaction costs that have negative economic consequences. We will review each of them in turn.

The High Transaction Costs in the Informal Sector

There are nine principal types of transaction costs associated with the informal sector.

1. Without legal property rights, an individual cannot use a property as collateral to obtain a loan to start or expand a business. In a developed economy such as the United States, it is common to use your house as collateral to obtain a loan to start a small business. Many people even start businesses using only a credit card. These options do not exist for most citizens in developing economies. If they could obtain legal title to their real estate holdings, even at the existing low prices, the collateral value would already be high enough to start many new legal businesses.
2. Many basic services, such as sewage, telephone, water, and electricity, cannot be obtained without legal title.
3. The absence of legal title makes it difficult to trade assets. Because of asymmetric information, buyers of nontitled dwellings cannot go to court if they feel they have been cheated in a transaction. As a result, most buyers are wary of purchasing unregistered property.
4. Property owners cannot obtain insurance contracts in the informal sector, whether for a business or a residence. The absence of legal title thus strongly reduces the ability to minimize risk. Because people without legal title to their dwellings or their businesses are usually poorer, they would benefit most from access to insurance.
5. Attracting capital in the informal sector can be very difficult. The absence of legal title makes it difficult to expand a business by attracting other owners who could bring additional capital. Because informal sector businesses are not legal, there is no mechanism for solving potential conflicts among joint owners. As a result, investors who have capital may prefer to make more secure investments in the formal sector.
6. The informal sector makes people vulnerable to the predatory behavior of bureaucrats and officials who demand bribes by arbitrarily threatening legal action against an illegal business. It is possible that the sum of bribes paid to various officials through this kind of blackmail could be higher than the taxes a property or business owner would pay in the formal sector. In addition, the vulnerability to abuse by corrupt officials increases as formal legal institutions become weaker. In contrast, taxation policies are bound by written rules and the law protects taxpayers against potential abuse by tax collectors.
7. Informal businesses cannot use the courts to enforce contracts with clients or other business partners. Property disputes between neighbors also cannot be solved in courts. Thus, people must rely on informal contract

enforcement mechanisms that are not as efficient as those offered by formal institutions, as discussed in Chapter 7.[3]

8. Informal businesses are restricted in their scope. People who work in the informal sector can only do business with those they trust (and only people who trust them will be ready to do business with them) because they cannot rely on formal institutions to protect their rights in a transaction. Informal businesses also cannot openly advertise the way formal businesses routinely do. Limiting factors such as these restrict the potential scope of business. In contrast, legally registered businesses can take advantage of every opportunity to extend their scope, which results in market expansion.

9. Informal businesses cannot exploit economies of scale as can formal businesses. Because they need to stay beneath a government's radar, they will operate several small concealed workshops rather than a large factory that would be vulnerable to official inspections and blackmail. There are more subtle but no less important reasons why informal businesses cannot achieve economies of scale. Without secure property rights, farmers must take their pigs to the market and sell them one at a time, but where property rights systems are well developed, there is no need to transport the real pigs each time a trade takes place. In advanced commodities exchanges, commodities are not traded directly, but rather rights to commodities are bought and sold. Commodities such as pigs only move after trades have been arranged and their transport to the marketplace can be grouped together so as to economize on transport costs.

Institutional Obstacles to Entry in the Formal Sector

Given the large costs associated with operating in the informal sector, why do businesses and households not enter the formal sector? Typically, the main reason offered is that individuals and firms want to avoid paying taxes. However, considering the huge transaction costs associated with the informal sector, it is doubtful that this is the most accurate explanation. A more likely reason is that the high costs of entry imposed by the inefficient legal systems of developing countries are prohibitive for most poor people. Moreover, the poor quality of formal legal institutions (dysfunctional court systems, corruption, etc.) significantly reduces the benefits of entering the formal sector.

In 1980, De Soto and his team wanted to test how difficult it was to register a small business by obeying the letter of the law; they opened up a small garment workshop in the outskirts of Lima. The whole application process (filling forms, standing in line, collecting required certifications) was extremely time consuming. The researchers were eventually able to register the business

---

[3]These informal enforcement mechanisms rely either on repeated interaction in business transactions (the cheating party will lose a regular business partner) or on reputation (loss of reputation leads to loss of business opportunities). Relying on repeated interaction leads to loss of new business opportunities, while incentives to maintain a good reputation only work well when information about that reputation circulates efficiently, which is often not the case in developing countries.

The Tunisian Fruit Vendor and the Arab Spring

Mohammed Bouazizi was a street vendor in the rural Tunisian town of Sidi Bouzid, selling fruit from his wheelbarrow. He had applied for a job in the army but had been rejected. Other job applications were also declined. With his meager income (roughly $140 per month), he supported his mother, his uncle, and his younger siblings. Policemen regularly harassed him because he did not have a vendor permit, demanding he pay them bribes to avoid harassment. On December 16, 2010, he borrowed $200 to buy the fruit he was going to sell the next day; he was again harassed by the police that next day, but refused to pay a bribe. His electronic scales were confiscated and his wheelbarrow was thrown aside. Bouazizi ran to the governor's office to ask that the police return his scales, but the governor refused to see him. Later, he came back to the front of the governor's office building and, in the middle of the street, doused himself with a can of gasoline and ignited the fuel to protest his treatment. He later died from his burns.

Because the case of Bouazizi symbolized the plight of small vendors mistreated by police and government officials, his death triggered national protests in Tunisia, which sparked the beginning of the **Arab Spring**, protests all over the Middle East and North Africa, ultimately leading to regime change in Tunisia, Egypt, Libya, and Yemen, political changes in Morocco, and civil war in Syria.

298 days after they started the process (in the United States, it would have taken 5 days). Even though the workshop was supposed to operate with only one worker, the legal registration costs amounted to $1,231, which represents 31 times the monthly minimum wage. In a similar case, 207 administrative steps in 52 government offices in Lima were required to build a house on state-owned land. The process took nearly 7 years!

Informal businesses in other developing countries face similar hurdles. In Egypt, to acquire and obtain a legal title to a lot on state-owned desert land, an individual must go through 77 procedures at 31 agencies. The process can take between 5 and 14 years. Building a legal dwelling on land formerly used for agriculture takes between 6 to 11 years of bureaucratic procedures. In Haiti, before settling legally on government land, a citizen must first lease the land for 5 years, but it takes 65 bureaucratic steps requiring roughly 2 years before obtaining that lease.

The World Bank has launched an important initiative, the Doing Business project. The goal is to monitor the cost of doing business in different countries across the world, and encourage them to reduce these costs. The plan targets many issues, such as the start-up costs for a business, the difficulty of obtaining credit, labor regulations, rules of bankruptcy, etc. Table 13.1 lists start-up costs in different regions of the world. Measures used are the average number of procedures necessary to start a business, the average number of days the procedures take, and the cost as a percentage of gross national income per capita. We can see that the poorest regions of the world (sub-Saharan Africa and Latin America, in particular) have higher start-up costs than do richer regions. For the categories listed, all regions in the developing world underperform compared to OECD countries. Note that among developing regions,

TABLE 13.1   Business Start-Up Costs in Different Regions of the World

Region	Procedures (number)	Duration (days)	Cost (% Gross National Income per capita)
East Asia and Pacific	8.6	44.2	32.3
Eastern Europe and Central Asia	7.7	22.6	8.6
Latin America and Caribbean	9.7	64.5	39.1
Middle East and North Africa	8.4	23.5	41
OECD	5.8	13.4	4.9
South Asia	7.4	32.5	31.9
Sub-Saharan Africa	10.2	47.8	111.2

Due to the larger number of procedures, their longer duration, and higher costs compared to OECD countries, business start-up costs in poorer regions are higher than in developed regions.

Source: The World Bank, Doing Business Report 2011.

Eastern Europe and Central Asia do best, especially in terms of start-up costs. This is most likely the result of the transition policies implemented since the early 1990s to encourage the growth of private enterprises in that region.

The Economic Effects of Titling

In developing countries, what are the effects of institutional reforms that provide legal titles to real estate? Erica Field has analyzed the effect of a land-titling program in Peru.[4] In 1996, the Peruvian government engaged in a large-scale effort to register informal real estate holdings. Due to the prohibitive cost of registering a property title, a quarter of Peru's urban population had no legal title to their dwellings. The titling program gave residents a claim on their dwellings if they had been built on eligible public property. The only condition was verification of residence. An interesting feature of the program is that titles were to be distributed to all residents in a qualifying neighborhood, not just to those who applied for one. Because the project did not reach all neighborhoods at the same time, Field was thus able to compare the behavior of households protected by a legal title with those that remained unprotected.

Figure 13.1 shows the percentage of housing renovations done by households that benefited from the program in 1996 (vertical dotted line) compared to those undertaken by households who had not benefited from the program as of 1999. Before 1996, the two lines are nearly identical. After 1996, the renovation trend grows increasingly steeper for households that benefited from the titling program. Overall, Field estimated that land titling led to a 68% increase in the number of housing renovations. Titling property thus had a positive incentive effect on investment in residential dwellings.

---

[4]Erica Field, "Property Rights and Investment in Urban Slums," *Journal of the European Economic Association* 3, nos. 2–3 (2005): 279–290.

FIGURE 13.1 Percent of Housing Renovations in Titled and Untitled Peruvian Dwellings

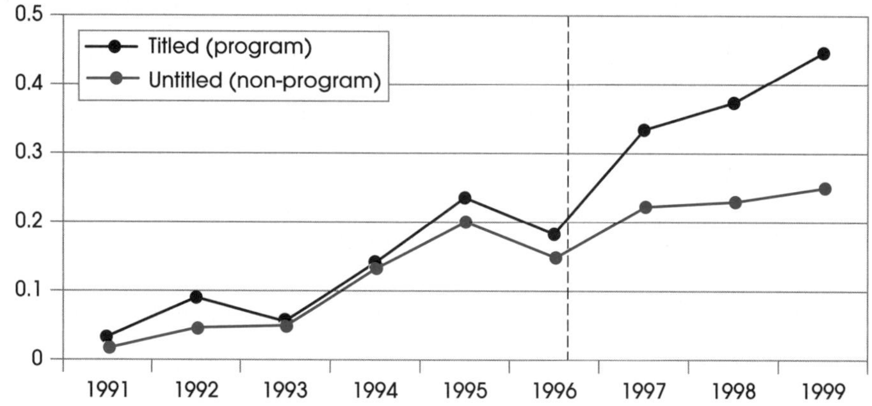

Peruvian households that received a title to their properties in 1996 engaged in significantly more housing renovations than did those without a title.

Source: Erica Field, "Property Rights and Investment in Urban Slums," *Journal of the European Economic Association* 3, nos. 2–3 (2005): 284.

To these incentive effects we must add another advantage of titling: the possibility of using a residence as collateral to obtain credit. In the Peruvian study, titling positively affected both the demand for credit and its allocation. Even though over 60% of households that received a formal title did not ask for credit to fund renovations, requests for credit for the purpose of home renovation still increased by 100% as a consequence of the titling program. However, credit received only increased by roughly half that amount, indicating that the banks' credit supply did not match the increase in credit demand from households. Overall, Field found that the increase in the number of renovations was as high among households that borrowed as among households that did not borrow.

She also found that the property titling program positively affected the supply of labor and a willingness to work outside the home.[5] When property was not protected by a title, households tended to protect it themselves. Field found that in Peru, households with no claim to property spent an average of 13.4 hours per week to maintain security of their dwelling. When property was titled, this incentive disappeared and households participated more in the labor market. She estimated that the effect of titling on the average labor supply of a household was 23 hours per week, a nearly 25% increase. Moreover, households with no secure title over their dwellings were also 28% more likely to have members that worked at home. Once households received legal title to their dwellings, the overall labor supply thus tended to increase. Titling reduced home business activity by nearly 28%.

---

[5]Erica Field, "Entitled to Work: Urban Property Rights and Labor Supply in Peru," *The Quarterly Journal of Economics* 122, no. 4 (2007): 1561–1602.

Institutions and Property Rights Protection: Lessons from Transition Economies

The transition countries in Central and Eastern Europe provide a unique opportunity for understanding the effects of institutions on property rights security and its economic consequences. These countries went through massive institutional changes after the collapse of their Communist regimes. Some were successful, while others developed many of the symptoms of the weak institutional environments frequently observed in developing countries. The differences between institutional environments in these transition countries affected the strength of their market development, competition, and investment, and these differences thus markedly affected their economic performance.

The Informal Sector and Institutional Quality

The size of the informal economy in developing countries is an indicator of the inefficiency of the country's institutions. Figure 13.2 gives an overview of the estimated evolution of the unofficial economy in transition countries.

The economic transition started in 1990. The blue bar represents an estimate of the size of a country's unofficial economy in 1989 before the transition. The estimate of the size of the unofficial economy is based on data for electricity consumption in the economy, which is not easy to hide because it was recorded

FIGURE 13.2 The Evolution of the Unofficial Economy as a Share of GDP in Selected Transition Countries between 1989 and 1995

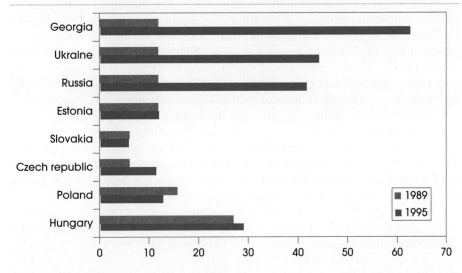

The size of the unofficial economy increased significantly during the transition process in certain countries but not in others.

Source: Simon Johnson, Daniel Kaufmann, and Andrei Shleifer, "The Unofficial Economy in Transition," Brookings Papers on Economic Activity, no. 2, 1997: 159–239.

quite accurately in those countries at the time. Because there is a stable relationship, in the short term at least, between electricity consumption and GDP, we can use data on electricity consumption to estimate the real level of GDP in a given year, albeit with a potentially large measurement error. The difference between estimated GDP and measured GDP then gives an estimate of the size of the unofficial economy. Note that Hungary and Poland have the highest share of the unofficial economy because those countries experienced more pro-market reforms under socialism than did other countries. In fact, the governments in those countries tolerated the development of a private sector but did not allow it to be officially recognized. In the other countries, the unofficial private economy was ruthlessly repressed and its share was much smaller.[6]

What is particularly striking in Figure 13.2 is that in 1995 (the red bar), the share of the unofficial economy had hardly moved in Poland and Hungary. It had slightly increased in Hungary but slightly decreased in Poland, but given the estimates' lack of precision, we can conclude that it has not moved significantly. Note also that the former Czechoslovakia always had a very small unofficial economy; the informal sector was not tolerated because of a repressive regime established after the 1968 Soviet invasion. Following transition, the informal sector either remained stable, as in Slovakia, or increased, as in the Czech Republic. However, it remained at a relatively low level compared to other countries. In contrast, the size of the unofficial economy in countries of the former Soviet Union increased drastically. It went from 12% to 41.6% in Russia, to 44.2% in the Ukraine, and to a stunning 62.6% in Georgia. This represents an enormous increase and indicates a deep problem with the economic institutions that were established as a result of the transition. Note that not all countries from the former Soviet Union went through this evolution. In Estonia, there was virtually no increase in the share of the unofficial economy.

We now take a closer look at the differences in institutional quality across various transition countries. In the following discussions, Tables 13.2– 13.4 are not based on aggregate estimates but on surveys of small- and medium-size private firms from three Central European (Poland, Slovakia, and Romania) countries that subsequently joined the EU, and from two of the largest countries of the former Soviet Union (Russia and the Ukraine). These countries represent the key variations in institutional environments in transition economies.

The first row in Table 13.2 attempts to estimate the size of the unofficial economy. Firm managers were asked what percentage of sales goes unreported in their economic sector. Although the table cannot accurately estimate the size of the unofficial sector, the differences in responses are illuminating. In the Central European countries, the response was always below 10%, in Russia it was nearly 30%, and in the Ukraine it was over 40%.

The next question asked firms whether they thought other firms in their sector paid bribes for government services. This was a polite way to inquire about corruption because firms would likely not have responded truthfully

---

[6]There is only one estimate for the size of the unofficial economy in 1989 for the Soviet Union, at 12%. However, the size of the unofficial sector varied across the different Soviet republics. The size of the unofficial sector in Georgia, for example, was certainly larger than 12%.

TABLE 13.2 Corruption, the Legal System, and the Size
of the Unofficial Sector

	Poland	Slovakia	Romania	Russia	Ukraine
Percentage of sales not reported	5.4	7.4	5.7	28.9	41.2
Percent of firms that believe other firms make extralegal payments for government services	20	38	20	91	87
Percent of firms that believe other firms pay for protection from organized crime	8	14.9	0.6	92.9	88.8
Percent of firms that believe courts can enforce an agreement	72.9	67.9	86.9	58.4	54.7

The data show that the unofficial sector makes up a significant portion of the Russian and Ukrainian economies, with large-scale corruption and organized crime racketeering, and less efficient courts than are found in Poland, Slovakia, or Romania.

Source: Simon Johnson, Daniel Kaufmann, John McMillan, and Christopher Woodruff, "Why Do Firms Hide? Bribes and Unofficial Activity after Communism," *Journal of Public Economics* 76, no. 3 (2000): 495–520.

to a more direct question such as "Do you pay bribes?" Here, the difference between countries was also striking. Positive responses were about 90% in Russia and the Ukraine, and only 20% in Poland and Romania. Corruption appeared to be much more prevalent in Russia and the Ukraine compared to Central Europe, and widespread corruption is one indicator of the absence of rule of law. Firms' property rights are made insecure as a result of the predatory behavior of corrupt bureaucrats who extract bribes. In countries where property rights are not protected, entrepreneurs are also subject to the predatory behavior of organized crime. When asked whether other firms paid criminal organizations for protection, roughly 90% responded positively in Russia and the Ukraine, while in Central Europe about 10% responded positively.

The final question asked about the quality of courts. In response to whether courts could be used to enforce a contract, 70–80% of Central European firms responded positively compared to just over 50% in Russia and the Ukraine.

Property Rights, Investment, and Market Development

We have seen that institutions for protecting property rights are much weaker in Russia and the Ukraine than in Central Europe; now, we will look at some of the economic consequences of this disparity. Table 13.3 shows some interesting facts about investment behavior and the development of market infrastructure. The first question asked firm managers whether or not they would invest $100 to receive $200 in 2 years, correcting for inflation.[7] This is a large return,

---

[7]In other words, if there were an inflation rate of 50% in two years, the $200 would become $300.

TABLE 13.3 Development of Property Rights and Market Infrastructure

	Poland	Slovakia	Romania	Russia	Ukraine
Percentage of managers who would not invest $100 now to receive $200 in 2 years	22.1	24.6	16.2	98.9	99.3
Percentage of a firm's sales through a wholesale intermediary	26	19	7	5	4
Percentage of firm's sales going to different cities or countries	64.7	67.6	53.8	23.3	30.5
Percentage of a firm's sales not going to SOEs or spinoffs	61.3	55.5	67.7	38.1	36.3

In Russia and the Ukraine, managers were not willing to make a profitable investment inside their country. Markets were also less developed according to indicators such as transactions through wholesale intermediaries, percentage of sales going outside the firm's city, and percentage of sales not going to state-owned enterprises or to a firm's spinoffs.

Source: Simon Johnson, John McMillan, and Christopher Woodruff, "Property Rights and Finance," *The American Economic Review* 92, no. 5 (2002): 1335–1356. Printed with permission of American Economics Association.

roughly 26% per year. To refuse such an investment, a manager must be facing large risks. The refusal percentage can therefore be seen as an indicator of investment risk due, in particular, to insecure property rights. Nearly 100% of respondents in Russia and the Ukraine responded that they would not invest, whereas only about 20% of managers in Central Europe responded that they would not invest.

The next questions concerned the development of market infrastructure. The more secure property rights are, the easier it is to conduct business that is not restricted to transactions with people one knows. In other words, the more developed the market infrastructure is, the larger the scope of markets will be. When asked what percentage of the firms' sales went through a wholesale intermediary, the response was higher in Poland and Slovakia than in Russia, the Ukraine, and Romania.

The third row also provides an indicator of market development. Roughly two-thirds of sales in Poland and Slovakia went to different cities or countries than the city in which the firm was located. For Romania, the response was somewhat lower, but in Russia and the Ukraine it was significantly lower (23.3% and 30.5%, respectively). Weak institutions prevent firms from selling very far from where they are located because they cannot trust business partners who are too far away and with whom they have no personal relations.[8]

The responses to the last question in Table 13.3 went in the same direction. More than 60% of firms in Poland and Romania (55.5% in Romania) did not sell to state-owned enterprises (SOEs) or spinoffs of SOEs, whereas the percentage was much lower in Russia and the Ukraine. In an environment where

---

[8]There are other determinants of market development that we will discuss in more detail in Chapter 14.

property rights are insecure, it is safer to sell to SOEs because governments are less likely to default on their payment obligations.

Weak property rights institutions have additional consequences, as shown in Table 13.4. Because courts cannot always be trusted and businesses cannot depend on the legal system to enforce contracts, firms need to collect more information on potential business partners. However, in this situation, a firm's reputation becomes crucial to attracting potential business partners. In the first question, firm managers were asked if they participated in trade associations that provided information on suppliers and customers. Only about 20% of firms in Poland and Slovakia responded positively. The percentage in Russia and the Ukraine was 3 times as large, and in Romania it was twice as large. Firms in Vietnam were also surveyed in this research, and that country's percentage was closer to those of Poland and Slovakia. Including Vietnam is interesting because it is a poorer country from a different continent. It is also still a Communist country. We might thus expect Vietnam to have done worse than the countries from Central and Eastern Europe.

Another consequence of weak property rights institutions is that firms will prefer to do business with acquaintances. The percentage responding that they had a customer firm managed by family or a friend was higher in Russia and the Ukraine compared to Poland and Slovakia, and even to Vietnam, but it was even higher in Romania. When institutions are weak, firms tend not to trust businesses they do not know well, preferring to maintain trusted existing business relationships. This is called **relational contracting**. Firms develop long-term business relationships with a limited number of firms that they trust. As a result, these firms also know that they have nothing to gain by cheating on each other because the loss of the relationship would be more costly than the gain from cheating. However, relational contracting has significant negative consequences for competition and market efficiency: firms are reluctant

TABLE 13.4   Trust and Relational Contracting

	Poland	Slovakia	Romania	Russia	Ukraine	Vietnam
Percentage participating in trade associations that provide information on suppliers and customers	20.8	23.4	44.2	60	64.1	26
Percentage doing business with customer firm managed by family or friend	6.4	13.4	30.5	22.2	18.7	14.6
Percentage that would buy from new supplier at price 10% lower than current supplier	42.5	48.4	62.5	1.4	7.9	29

In Russia and the Ukraine, there was less trust and more relational contracting. Russian and Ukrainian managers participated more in trade associations to gather information about other businesses. As a result, they did more business with family and friends and were less willing to switch to cheaper but unfamiliar suppliers.

Source: John McMillan and Christopher Woodruff, "Interfirm Relationships and Informal Credit in Vietnam," *The Quarterly Journal of Economics* 114, no. 4 (1999): 1285–1320; and Simon Johnson, John McMillan, and Christopher Woodruff, "Courts and Relational Contracting," *The Journal of Law, Economics and Organization* 18, no. 1 (2002): 221–277.

to switch business partners and do business with a more competitive partner offering lower prices.

In the survey, firms were asked whether they would be willing to buy from a new supplier at a price 10% lower than their current supplier offered. Nearly 50% said yes in Poland and Slovakia, and nearly two-thirds said yes in Romania. However, only 1.4% in Russia and 7.9% in the Ukraine said yes. In Vietnam, the number was significantly higher than in the former Soviet Union countries but lower than in Central Europe. Weak institutions are thus detrimental to market competition and efficiency.

Privatization

The transfer of firm ownership from the state sector to the private sector is referred to as **privatization**. Just as better institutions that protect private property rights should encourage entrepreneurs to operate in the formal sector, privatization policies aim at increasing the share of the economy that is based on private property rights. A large wave of privatization swept the world in the last 2 decades of the 20th century and stood in stark contrast to the wave of nationalization that took place in many countries after World War II.

From Nationalization to Privatization

After the Great Depression and World War II, there was widespread skepticism about the market economy's ability to bring about comprehensive growth and prosperity, and prevailing political trends moved toward central planning.[9] While advanced industrialized countries such as the United States and the European nations suffered from the economic devastation of the 1930s, the Soviet Union, which had adopted central planning, was experiencing high economic growth rates.

Because of these developments, in many developing economies central planning and government ownership to achieve economic growth were very popular economic policies after World War II. Following the defeat of the Japanese Army and a civil war between the nationalist Kuomintang and Mao Zedong's guerrilla forces, mainland China adopted a Communist regime similar to that of the Soviet Union and introduced central planning. In contrast, after independence from the British in 1947 India became a democracy. Nevertheless, the leaders of the new Indian democracy favored the development of a large state-owned industrial sector. After its independence in 1962, Algeria opted for similar policies. Most other developing countries that did not adopt a Communist regime did not go as far as India or Algeria in terms of state-owned industries, but most nevertheless favored some form of state intervention in the economy.

As a result of this widespread enthusiasm for economic central planning, many large firms in developing countries came under government ownership, but by the 1960s and 1970s, the performance of state-owned enterprises had proved to be disappointing. No economic miracle occurred in the countries

---

[9]For more on central planning, see Chapter 8.

that had depended on central planning; in contrast, the countries that experienced high growth during that period were the "Asian tigers," including South Korea, Taiwan, Hong Kong, and Singapore. They had followed in the footsteps of Japan's post–World War II economic success, which was not based on central planning and state-ownership of firms, but rather on the active promotion of exporting firms in the private sector that were able to compete successfully in world markets.[10] Compared to the competitive and efficient exporting firms of the Asian tigers, the state-owned firms in other developing countries were bloated with excess labor and crippled by rigid regulations. Their productivity was too dismal to enable these firms to compete in world markets.

Chile and Malaysia were among the first developing countries to embrace privatization of state-owned enterprises in the 1970s and 1980s respectively. In Chile, military dictator Augusto Pinochet was a strong supporter of free markets. After the successful military coup against President Salvador Allende in 1973, Chile engaged in ambitious liberalization programs that included the privatization of Chile's state-owned enterprise sector. Chile even went so far as to privatize its social security system. In Malaysia, the government of President Mahathir Mohamad launched a large-scale privatization program in 1983 after it became clear that expansion of the state sector had not succeeded in developing his country. In developed countries, the privatization wave accelerated in the 1980s mostly in the United Kingdom, under the conservative government of Margaret Thatcher.

When the Berlin Wall fell in 1989, the largest privatization movement in modern history took place in the nations of Central and Eastern Europe. The transition from socialism to capitalism required the privatization of most large state-owned enterprises in former Communist countries. In less than 10 years, the majority of large state-owned enterprises in the region were transferred to private ownership by means of the various privatization policies implemented by the different countries.

Privatization Goals and Problems

The obvious goal of privatization is to enhance the economic efficiency of state-owned firms. A basic premise of economic theory is that firms operating in a market environment strive to maximize profits. In a competitive environment without externalities, profit maximization is socially optimal because the marginal benefit to society of producing one more unit of a good equals the marginal cost to society, a situation that is socially optimal. Maximization of government revenue is also a goal of privatization because the transfer of state assets to the private sector should provide government with sufficient fiscal revenues.

The objectives of state-owned firms are, in general, not as clear. State ownership can be justified in case of a **natural monopoly**, a market with economies of scale that are so large there is only space for one firm. In that case, because the monopolists do not face a competitive environment, they will tend to under-produce to obtain monopoly profits. State ownership of a natural monopoly may then be able to achieve the socially optimum production level, provided that this exact optimum level is known. Note, however, that the existence of a natural monopoly need not imply state ownership. Another solution

---

[10]See Chapter 5 on export promotion strategies in Asia.

adopted in the United States, among other countries, is the regulation of private monopolies. In theory, just as a state enterprise can have a production target that achieves the socially optimum production level, the government can impose a minimum production quota on a regulated monopoly to achieve the same optimum level.[11]

In reality, many, if not most, of the firms nationalized after World War II were not in the category of a natural monopoly. In general, state-owned enterprises were not asked to maximize profits or to pursue a socially optimum production level. Instead, they pursued a mix of objectives: minimum production targets, sales at subsidized prices to achieve redistributive goals, and adequate hires to absorb unemployment or fulfill promises resulting from political patronage practices. Their efficiency was usually low and technological innovation was minimal. As a result, many nationalized firms in developing countries were not able to compete in world markets.

Getting the incentives right. Given the low efficiency of state-owned enterprises in most countries, much was expected of privatization. However, similar to the illusions about central planning in the mid-20th century, there were somewhat naïve views about what to expect from privatization by the end of that century. The widespread assumption held that the transfer of state-owned enterprises into private hands would automatically translate into higher efficiency. There is little doubt that the small private entrepreneur works to maximize profits, but state-owned enterprises that are privatized are usually large enterprises in which there is **separation of ownership and control**. This occurs when the owners are not directly overseeing the firm and use professional managers to do so. How well the owners are able to monitor management depends on the firm's **corporate governance**. If there is little monitoring due to bad corporate governance, managers may engage in activities that go against the interests of shareholders, such as giving themselves perks or even diverting money into private accounts.

Another problem is that of **dispersed ownership**, in which shares in a privatized enterprise are sold or distributed to a very large number of shareholders with no single shareholder holding a significant number of shares. In this situation, the small shareholders face a problem of **collective action**, as discussed in Chapter 7. Because monitoring management is both valuable and costly, in a case of dispersed ownership, the small individual shareholders have incentives to free ride on the monitoring of management, in which case very little or no monitoring at all will take place. Therefore, management will tend to pursue its own interests instead of those of the shareholders. One solution is to have **large blockholders**, shareholders who own a sufficiently large number of shares so as to have strong incentives to monitor the firm. In privatization, this can be achieved, for example, by auctioning off blocks of shares jointly as one packet.

Selecting the right owners. Getting the incentives right in a large private firm so that management's actions are aligned with those of shareholders is, however, not enough to achieve efficiency. Even when the largest owners play an active role in supervising management, when privatizing a firm it is also important to sell it

---

[11]There are other instruments of regulation that governments can use to achieve social objectives such as price ceilings, quality norms, or universal service obligations.

to the "right owners," that is, owners who will have the best and most efficient plans to maximize the firm's value. Some owners may want to pursue a certain strategy, say fresh produce for the Latin American markets, while others favor another strategy, say fresh produce for the Asian markets. Suppose that the Latin American strategy is the better option given the firm's assets and specialization. In that case, it is important that the privatization method ensure the selection of the best owner for the firm undergoing the transition.

While this objective is straightforward, it is less obvious how to achieve it. In principle, auctions that sell assets to buyers who are most willing to pay should achieve this objective. However, many potential buyers in developing countries may not have enough wealth to compete in privatization bids. Firms might be sold to buyers who have the money but who are not necessarily the best potential owners.

Problems arising from privatization policies. Because state-owned enterprises have often been used to redistribute resources, privatization can generate popular protests because of a regressive redistributive effect, whereby the rich benefit at the expense of the poor. For example, privatization of utilities is frequently associated with the introduction of unsubsidized user fees. If state utilities delivered water at subsidized prices to the poor and privatization policies then eliminate those subsidies, privatization may bring about higher efficiency in water provision, but poor people will likely be subject to higher prices. The protests that can result from privatization's regressive redistributive effects can ultimately lead to political instability.

Institutional weaknesses can also cause problems in privatization programs. When a country has a very weak rule of law, it is unrealistic to expect that privatization of large enterprises will happen in a fair, transparent, and efficient way. Corruption is particularly problematic in a privatization process; government officials may be bribed into accepting a lower price than the firm's actual value, and they may be bribed into selling the firm to less qualified owners. Corruption in the privatization process can have significant negative impacts on a government's revenue and on market efficiency.

Another issue involving corruption is **regulatory capture**, which occurs when the regulators, who are supposed to monitor a private firm in the public interest, are "captured" by that firm. In other words, instead of becoming advocates for the public interest in regulating the firm, they become the firm's advocates within the government. Regulatory capture leads to regulations that favor the firm over social welfare. Regulatory capture is often the result of corruption or it may simply be the consequence of **influence activities**, biased information supplied by interest groups to policy makers in order to influence them in the interest group's favor. Take the example of environmental regulation. A firm may give a regulator information that understates the extent of environmental damage from the firm's products and overstates the effects of environmental regulations on its production costs.

Regulatory capture is a problem in all countries, but developing countries are particularly prone to it because regulators are usually somewhat less informed than interest groups and have fewer resources for gathering information independently. They are also more predisposed to corruption when the local culture tolerates dishonesty.

Methods of Privatization in Developing Countries

One method to privatize a firm is through a **public offering**, when shares of the firm are floated (sold) on the stock market. This is the primary method used in the United Kingdom and in many European countries that have had a significant experience with privatization, but it is rarely used in developing countries where stock markets are nearly nonexistent. Public offerings also require sufficient legal protection for minority shareholders, who would not place their savings in risky shares without being protected against scandals or mismanagement. Finally, in countries that are too poor to have a sufficiently large middle class to purchase shares of large enterprises, public offerings do not make much sense.

A second privatization method is **direct sales** of firms by the government to interested parties. It is a simple method but is also fraught with problems. First, the sale price is likely to be too low because the government generally does not know the buyer's willingness to pay and the problem of asymmetric information arises. The buyer is thus likely to propose a much lower price than what it would actually be willing to pay. The government can set a minimum sale price, but it is never going to get more than that price under a direct sale. Second, the government does not know if a prospective buyer is the most qualified to run the firm and whether there may be more competent buyers. These two problems can potentially result in fewer revenues for the government and inefficient owner selection. The direct sales method is also likely to be less transparent and subject to corruption. The buyer may, for example, bribe the government agency to obtain a favorable deal.

A third privatization method is an auction, which does not have the disadvantages of direct sales. Encouraging multiple buyers to attend an auction and compete to purchase a state-owned firm solves both of the problems of less revenue and inefficient selection. If the auction is run effectively, say by the English auction method, then revenues will be higher and owner selection will be better.[12] A potential qualified buyer will always prefer to bid up the price as long as there are competing bids. The revenue generated will thus invariably be at least as high as the readiness to pay of the second most willing buyer (the one who dropped out last). Moreover, the remaining bidder is the one with the highest readiness to pay and, in principle, the most able buyer among those who competed.

A potential problem when conducting a standard auction is that all the qualified buyers may not have the ability to compete because of insufficient funds. A domestic entrepreneur in a developing country may have a great idea about how to run a firm, but lacks liquidity and may not be able to compete with a multinational company with less knowledge of the local conditions but with ample funds to bid up the price. In that case, the domestic buyer might be the most qualified owner, but he will be outbid. The government could mitigate this problem if it could provide credit to potential buyers, but this creates another problem as there may now be buyers willing to make large bids because they have no intention of paying back the government loan. The

---

[12]The English auction is the typical method used, for example, in art sales: interested buyers show up and bid up the price until only one buyer is left.

problem will be even more severe if there is only mild punishment for this strategic default.

Auctions can present another problem; sometimes buyers engage in collusion instead of competing with each other. Imagine a situation in which there are five multinational telecom firms and five or more countries of equal size privatizing their telecommunications sectors. The telecom firms may secretly agree to share the markets, deciding to submit low bids and agreeing on who will place the (slightly) higher bid in each country. National antitrust agencies may have a hard time proving collusion and they may be bribed to look the other way.

A fourth privatization method is giveaway of assets. This method was used primarily in former socialist economies and is obviously not designed for generating revenues. It also does not generally result in an efficient allocation of ownership because any form of giveaway must involve some chance. Giving a firm's assets to its current managers is risky because they may not be the most competent, but dispersing shares to the general population does not encourage strong block-holder ownership. Giveaway methods will, in theory, lead to efficient allocation only if financial markets work well enough to allow the ownership of the initially distributed shares to change hands. This assumes efficient financial markets, which is usually not the case in developing countries.

Privatization Outcomes

It is useful to review privatization outcomes by continent. There are geographical similarities not only in terms of the policies implemented, but also in terms of the problems encountered.

Privatization in Latin America. In 1976, Chile was one of the first countries to start a large-scale privatization program. In the late 1980s and 1990s, many other Latin American countries also embarked on extensive privatization policies. Particularly prominent were the programs launched in Mexico under President Carlos Salinas and in Argentina under President Carlos Menem. Although Bolivia, Peru, Brazil, and El Salvador also engaged in ambitious privatization programs, not all Latin American countries have been swept up by the privatization wave. Uruguay, Paraguay, Costa Rica, Honduras, Ecuador, and many of the small Caribbean countries did not undertake significant privatization programs.

Privatization in Latin America is generally considered to have been an effective tool for generating revenues. In the 1980s, many Latin American countries had a high level of foreign debt. When interest rates increased worldwide in the early 1980s as a result of the monetary policies of then–U.S. Federal Reserve chairman Paul Volcker who significantly tightened money supply, many countries were unable to service their debt by paying the interest and principal on schedule. As a result, the debt of many Latin American countries had to be restructured, with part of the debt forgiven and debt payments on the remainder rescheduled. With the acute need for government revenues, privatization was thus seen as a major source of revenues these countries could use to pay back their foreign debt.

Another positive outcome of privatization has been the generally strong flow of investment into the privatized firms, which has helped them improve their profitability and productivity. Privatization is also often thought to have had a positive impact on the quality of goods and services. For example, privatization of water utilities in Argentina led to improvements in water quality. Researchers have found that child mortality fell by 8% in areas where water utilities were privatized.[13] These improvements were initially welcomed by the population and generated some political support for privatization.

However, political support for privatization in Latin America has waned since the end of the 1990s for two reasons. First, privatization in many cases has not ended subsidies or government investment in the targeted sectors. Ending subsidies was one of the expected privatization outcomes and although privatization has generated a onetime flow of revenues, it has often not reduced the annual flow of government expenditures into the privatized sectors, doing very little to solve the problem of chronic government deficits caused by subsidies. Indeed, there have been accusations that the new owners of privatized firms were able to convince incumbent governments to continue granting them subsidies.

While restructuring in many privatized firms has also led to significant job losses and criticism of the policy, a second and more politically important reason for waning support relates to the redistribution of the gains from privatization. Privatization has typically generated large profits for the new owners, but these rents have not been shared with the general public.

Water Privatization in Bolivia

Bolivia's Cochabamba water concession is a good example of the poorer segments of a population facing price increases for water after privatization has taken place. In Cochabamba, 70% of the people live below the poverty line. The price of water tripled in January 2000 after government subsidies to the concession's private operator, International Water, were reduced. The local peasants (primarily Quechua Indians) had previously used the water free of charge and were now charged market prices like other urban dwellers. This price hike ignited large popular protests. The private operator explained that the price increases in Cochabamba were due to the expense of a US$300 million project involving the construction of a dam, a tunnel, and several water purification plants that would increase water supplies to the Cochabamba area. Whether or not the private operator had engaged in regulatory capture and convinced the regulators to pass on the cost of the large investment to the population, this example demonstrates how privatization can lead to regressive redistributive effects. In this particular case, soon after the protests, the private operator pulled out of Bolivia, and the government repealed its water privatization legislation.[14]

---

[13]Sebastian Galiani, Paul J. Gertler, and Ernesto Schargrodsky (2005) "Water for Life: The Impact of Privatization of Water Services on Child Mortality," *Journal of Political Economy* 113, no. 1 (2005): 83–120.

[14]For more information, see Antonio Estache and Lourdes Trujillo, "Privatization in Latin America: The Good, the Ugly, and the Unfair," in *Privatization: Successes and Failures,* ed. Gérard Roland (New York: Columbia University Press, 2008): 136–169.

Despite the role of competitive auctions in the privatization process, in practice there has often been little competition between bidders. This might be due to collusion between private firms. In some markets, there can be an extreme concentration of certain international firms that are the only potential buyers in a position to place bids in many different countries at the same time. For example, in the international sanitation business (water, sanitation, and solid waste), only five large companies have been involved in all privatization deals worldwide for that sector.

Another problem has occurred in Latin American countries when many firms have been able to renegotiate their privatization deals some time after signing the initial contract with the governments involved, leading to higher prices and more profits to private owners. One in three privatization deals in the infrastructure sector was renegotiated in this way, and one out of two in the transport sector. These renegotiations took place less than 3 years after the award of the contracts and two out of three requests for renegotiation came from the operators, not from the governments.[15] This is another illustration of governmental weakness in developing countries when bargaining with powerful multinational private firms.

Privatization in Asia. Not only have privatization outcomes been quite diverse in Asia, but the intensity of privatization has also varied considerably. Although Malaysia has been a pioneer in privatization, its neighbor Indonesia has not experienced significant privatization, even after the 1997 crisis that seriously impacted the country's public finances. China still maintains a large state sector, but made efforts, especially in the 1990s, to privatize many of its state-owned enterprises. It began by privatizing smaller state-owned enterprises and then gradually privatized larger firms. In 2006, the Industrial and Commercial Bank of China (ICBC) raised private funds through what the financial press celebrated as the world's largest initial public offering (an IPO, a first-time sale of a firm's shares on the stock market). This was the third large Chinese bank to float shares publicly. However, in all these cases, privatization was only partial, and the state kept majority ownership, China continues to maintain a large state sector.

Privatization in South Asia has been relatively modest. Despite its large state sector, India has not been swept up in the global privatization wave. Most privatizations in India were partial and involved the divestiture of only a minority of shares in public enterprises so that the state kept a controlling stake in the firms. Nevertheless, it would be a mistake to dismiss partial privatization. The case of India is not unique. In many other parts of the world, including Western and Central Europe, governments have also kept controlling stakes in firms. Economist Nandini Gupta has shown that, in India, partial privatization has had positive effects because offering shares on the country's stock market has improved the monitoring of management.[16] Indeed, the private partners

---

[15]See Estache and Trujillo, "Privatization in Latin America: The Good, the Ugly and the Unfair," 161.

[16]Nandini Gupta, "Partial Privatization and Firm Performance," *The Journal of Finance* 60, no. 2 (2005): 987–1015.

who have acquired shares in India's state-owned enterprises have actively monitored their managers and encouraged them to adopt more modern management techniques.

The fact that jobs in India's state-owned enterprises are used for political patronage accounts for the reluctance of its politicians to privatize these firms. Gupta finds that privatization tends to be slower in those Indian provinces where incumbents face sharp political competition because they are more reluctant to abandon this traditional source of patronage.

Privatization in Africa. African governments have not favored privatization of state-owned firms and very few of those firms have been privatized. Other than in South Africa, Ghana, Nigeria, Zambia, and the Ivory Coast, minimal privatization has occurred, and across Africa, very little privatization has taken place in the large infrastructure sector. Similar to Asia and other parts of the world, when privatization does take place, the government involved usually keeps a significant ownership share. There is no systematic empirical evidence of privatization's effects in Africa, and the scarce available evidence is mixed at best.[17] Privatization in Cote d'Ivoire seems to have had positive effects on firm performance, and a similar picture emerges from Ghana. However, researchers have only observed positive effects when privatization was associated with enhanced competition and efficient regulation so that it is difficult to disentangle the effect of privatization from the effect of those other policies.

Unfortunately, the researchers also found evidence of rent-seeking and regulatory capture in Africa, strong indications of corruption, reduction in the affordability of public services, and job losses—phenomena that have also been observed in Latin America. These negative factors feed popular resentment and reinforce African governments' reluctance to privatize further. There is also widespread skepticism that African countries have the institutional foundations necessary to support successful and transparent privatization programs.

Privatization in Central and Eastern Europe. The most spectacular examples of privatization are undoubtedly the transitions from socialism to capitalism that took place in the nations of Central and Eastern Europe during the first half of the 1990s. In those countries, privatization was generally considered a key component of the transition, though priorities were quite different across countries. For example, Russia and Czechoslovakia prioritized privatization of their large state-owned enterprises, while countries such as Hungary, Slovenia, and Poland, focused on the development of their new private sectors, built from the ground up by entrepreneurs.

Economists were deeply divided about privatization methods in transition countries. One group, the most prominent members being Andrei Shleifer and Jeffrey Sachs, advocated a rapid privatization that relied on giveaway schemes, also called **mass privatization**. The other group advocated a

---

[17]See John Nellis, "Privatization in Africa: What Has Happened? What Is to Be Done?" in *Privatization: Successes and Failures,* ed. Gérard Roland (New York: Columbia University Press, 2008): 109–135.

more cautious approach based on gradual sales of state assets. This was the position taken by Janos Kornai, John McMillan, and this author, among others. The literature abounds with various proposals for implementing these two approaches. Russia, the Ukraine, the Czech Republic, Lithuania, and, to a certain extent, Slovakia adopted forms of mass privatization programs, while Hungary, Poland, Slovenia, and Estonia adopted the gradual sales approach.

The most ambitious mass privatization program was implemented in Czechoslovakia in 1992 under then–Prime Minister Václav Klaus and continued in 1993 in the Czech Republic after Czechoslovakia was partitioned. All adult citizens had the right to purchase, at a very low price, vouchers with which they could bid for shares of firms in the privatization program. These shares would thus be priced in terms of numbers of vouchers. At the time, some economists criticized the plan for leading to dispersed share ownership; because each citizen was given the right to buy an equal number of vouchers, even in the unlikely event that citizens would use all their vouchers to purchase one firm, share ownership would still be significantly dispersed. As a consequence, shareholders could not efficiently monitor the existing management. Replacing those managers was an important objective of privatization because many of them were former socialist managers who would likely have difficulties adapting to the market economy.

In practice, the corporate governance that resulted from privatization was even more complicated. Government-owned banks were supposed to be privatized along with most other large firms. However, these banks set up investment funds and encouraged Czech citizens to invest their vouchers in them. The banks' managers then used the investment funds to participate in voucher trading and buy up majority shares in the banks. In other words, the voucher program enabled bank managers to acquire controlling shares of the banks through the voucher program. It is not surprising that minimal restructuring took place in the banking sector thereafter because no real transfer of control had occurred. After major bank failures in the late 1990s, the Czech banks were gradually sold to foreign entities such as Belgium's KBC bank or Japan's Nomura Group.

Disreputable individuals were also associated with investment funds in the Czech Republic. The most famous of them was Czech financier, Viktor Kozeny, who set up a fund called Harvard Capital and Consulting (no connection with Harvard University) that used vouchers of Czech citizens to acquire control over various firms. Once in control, Kozeny engaged in what was called "tunneling," or finding ways to siphon off the firms' wealth. One such technique involved establishing a company in which the founder has 100% of shares and uses control over the privatized company to sell its products at a very low price to the new enterprise, which the founder controls entirely, or even to sell off the firm's machines and buildings at a very low price, thereby cheating the small shareholders of the privatized enterprise. Kozeny later fled the Czech Republic and, in 2003 the Manhattan district attorney, Robert Morgenthau, brought charges against him for other fraudulent deals in which he cheated U.S. citizens.

While many other scandals tarnished Czech mass privatization, some privatization deals involving foreign investors had very positive effects.

Skoda Auto, which had been infamous for the poor quality of its products, was taken over by Volkswagen and went on to be quite successful at producing inexpensive cars of decent quality, gaining significant European market shares.[18]

Russia's privatization program was quite different from the Czech experience. Firm managers and workers were given the option to buy back the firm at a very low price. Jointly with the mass privatization plan, a more limited voucher program was established that allowed private citizens to buy minority shares in businesses. The Russian plan was criticized at the time for favoring the current managers because it gave them direct ownership stakes. The hope was that workers would sell their shares to serious potential owners to buy consumer goods or even that the new owners would sell at a high price on the market to new and more able owners. These hopes did not materialize. First, managers in many cases kept control of workers' shares; the workers were then afraid to sell for fear of losing their jobs. Second, managers rarely agreed to sell to potential new outside owners. However, because managers generally retained ownership, privatized enterprises were not able to borrow to finance restructuring activities since the managers did not have capital of their own and they were not creditworthy given their lack of experience with the market economy. Many of them formed so-called **financial industrial groups**, together with banks and other enterprises. These were large conglomerates that were able to finance their activities internally and work together.

It was during this period of rapid privatization that the so-called Russian **oligarchs** emerged. These were individuals who became immensely rich in a short period of time by gaining control over a large number of enterprises either through financial industrial groups or via other schemes that enabled them to gain control over large enterprises without spending much money. For example through the "loans for shares" program (1995–1996), shares of large enterprises were auctioned off against promises of loans to the Russian government. Participation in the auctions was most often restricted to people who had close connection to the Kremlin and the family of president Yeltsin. They thus acquired control over large enterprises against promises of relatively small loans. The oligarchs indeed gained enormous political influence in the 1990s when Boris Yeltsin was president, but the power of many oligarchs was later weakened when Vladimir Putin came to power.

Overall, the studies that looked at the effects of privatization on firm performance in Central and Eastern Europe revealed astonishingly diverse results. Many studies were made very shortly after privatization. Others relied on rather general measures of ownership, such as the public-private dichotomy, and could not measure differences in ownership structure and corporate governance. More importantly, many studies suffered from a potential selection bias. They compared the performance of privatized firms to state-owned firms. Most studies of that type found that the performance

---

[18]A joke in the 1980s went as follows: What is the difference between a Skoda car and a traveling salesman? Answer: One can close the door on a traveling salesman but not on a Skoda.

of privatized firms, whether in terms of increased sales or productivity, was generally higher than that of state-owned enterprises. These studies suffered from a **selection bias**, i.e., firms selected for privatization did not have similar characteristics to firms not selected for privatization. The particular selection bias in this case would be that the better performing enterprises were privatized first. Because of this selection bias, these studies then did not necessarily identify the effect of privatization, but also picked up the effect that the enterprises initially selected for privatization performed better from the start. In other words, if the more profitable firms were privatized first, their superior performance could not be the result of privatization. Nandini Gupta, John Ham, and Jan Svejnar found this to be the case in Czechoslovakia, where firms that were privatized initially tended to perform better.[19] The studies that correct for the selection bias generally found that privatization had more modest effects. The strongest effects seem to have been reached in cases of privatization that resulted in foreign owners. Employee and manager ownership were rarely found to have a significant positive effect on firm performance, whether it was total factor productivity, labor productivity, or profitability.

We can draw a number of important conclusions from our discussion of privatization. First, its efficiency effects are generally mixed but rarely negative. This is true even though many empirical studies tend to overestimate these effects due to sample selection bias. While privatization appears uncontroversial in competitive sectors (even though its effects may be small relative to the incentive effects of competition), it is more complex in sectors with higher monopolistic trends, where good regulation is a necessary and crucial factor. Calls for better regulation would require a major institutional overhaul that requires a long time horizon.

Second, the privatization policies of particular countries at best may have had second-order effects on growth. Countries such as China, India, and Vietnam that have experienced impressive growth in recent years have not had an impressive privatization policy. Rather, they have been able to unleash the productive energies of millions of small entrepreneurs, creating a vibrant and thriving sector of small and medium businesses that serve both the domestic and the export market.

Third, the partial privatization practiced primarily in Asia seems to have more positive effects than initially predicted. Two effects have been noticed: 1) The sale of shares of state-owned enterprises on stock markets provided a monitoring device for these enterprises. Any act of mismanagement could be punished by a fall in share prices. This has been something of a disciplining device as a fall in share prices may lead to public scrutiny, media coverage, and small-shareholder dissatisfaction, which may be costly for the incumbent government. 2) The active participation of private sector managers on the board of state-owned enterprises can play a positive role in improving management and introducing more modern management techniques.

---

[19]Nandini Gupta, John C. Ham, and Jan Svejnar, "Priorities and Sequencing in Privatization: Evidence from Czech Firm Panel Data," *European Economic Review* 52, no. 2 (2008): 183–208.

Chapter Summary

Property Rights and the Informal Sector

A large portion of the economy in developing countries functions outside the formal sector and institutional inefficiencies are barriers to formal-sector entry. Remaining in the informal sector entails many transaction costs that could be avoided with better legal and titling systems. Titling programs have demonstrated that moving into the formal sector has positive economic effects, particularly in terms of increased investments.

Institutions and Property Rights Protection: Lessons From Transition Economies

Countries that have experienced a limited transition to privatization have developed symptoms of weak institutions typical of developing economies: a large informal sector, corruption, organized crime racketeering, and inefficient legal systems. There are substantial negative consequences for these institutional weaknesses: lack of competition, underinvestment, underdevelopment of market infrastructure, and inefficient market networks.

Privatization

Privatization transfers ownership of state-owned firms to the private sector. After World War II, many firms were nationalized in the hope that a strong government sector would result in growth, but poor economic performance by state-owned enterprises led to an increase in privatization programs. The goals of privatization were to increase firms' efficiency and generate revenues. The results of privatization on firm performance were more modest than initially expected but were, nevertheless, positive. Outcomes were better when privatization was combined with policies that encouraged competition and regulatory reform, but this was out of reach for many countries with weak institutions. Privatization may be susceptible to corruption and privatized firms may be in a position to capture and influence regulators.

Key Terms

Arab Spring
collective action
corporate governance
direct sales
dispersed ownership
financial industrial groups
influence activities
large blockholders
mass privatization

natural monopoly
oligarchs
privatization
public offering
regulatory capture
relational contracting
selection bias
separation of ownership and control

Review Questions

1. Explain the transaction costs incurred by an informal business.
2. In terms of its objectives, explain why privatization through auction sales is better than privatization by direct sales.
3. Discuss the possible links between the size of the informal sector in developing economies and rural-urban migration trends.
4. Go to the website of the World Bank Governance Indicators (http://info.worldbank.org/governance/wgi/index.asp) and examine the indicators for Asian countries. From the information you find there, in which country would you be most willing to invest, and in which would you be least willing to invest? Why?

5. Download the article by J. David Brown and John S. Earle, "Does Privatization Raise Productivity? Evidence from Comprehensive Panel Data on Manufacturing Firms in Hungary, Romania, Russia, and the Ukraine" at (http://papers .ssrn.com/sol3/papers.cfm?abstract_id=694401). Compare this article's findings with those in the article by Nandini Gupta, John Ham, and Jan Svejnar discussed in this chapter (http://papers .ssrn.com/sol3/papers.cfm?abstract_id=294541). Discuss the possible problems in interpreting the results of the Brown and Earle study in the light of the findings of Gupta, Ham and Svejnar.

6. Go on the "Doing Business" website of the World Bank (http://www.doingbusiness.org/). Download the data on rankings for starting a business and resolving insolvency. Are these rankings correlated? If so, why might this be?

7. Read "The Informal Sector in Developing Countries: Output, Assets and Employment" by Sangeeta Pratap and Erwan Quintin, 2006 (http://www.wider.unu.edu/publications/ working-papers/research-papers/2006/en_GB/ rp2006-130/). What methods do the authors discuss for measuring the size of the informal sector? What general conclusions do they draw about the causes and effects of the informal sector?

8. Relational contracting develops between firms when institutions are weak. Compare the efficiency of these informal institutions with formal institutions using the material discussed in this chapter and in Chapter 8.

9. Do an online search to find out about privatization policies in Argentina. What methods were used, which sectors were most involved, and what did you learn about the effects?

10. Read the following article on the informal urban sector in Nigeria: "The Urban Informal Sector in Nigeria: Towards Economic Development, Environmental Health, and Social Harmony" by Geoffrey I. Nwaka (http://www.globalurban .org/Issue1PIMag05/NWAKA%20article.htm). What topics from this article are also covered in this chapter? What additional topics does the article cover that are not covered in this chapter?

14 Market Development

Farmers from a local cooperative in Kenya saw their lives change when the Environment Liaison Centre International (ELCI) in Nairobi provided them with Internet access. Using e-mail, the farmers were able to establish a relationship with the U.S.-based *EarthMarketplace* service to sell their produce directly to North American consumers. The Internet helped these farmers to bypass the traditional middlemen who would purchase their produce at a much lower price and sell at a higher price. As a result, these farmers' revenues were significantly increased. Similarly, a British supermarket is planning to use e-mail to conduct "just-in-time" purchases of chili peppers from a Kenyan farm by flying them overnight directly to the supermarket as soon as they are harvested. In Niger, Tuareg craftspeople are also using the Internet to sell their products worldwide. Their crafts appear alongside many other African cultural products in a "cybermall" hosted on a Canadian website.

These examples demonstrate how the Internet can contribute to the growth of markets in developing economies. Poor producers who were in contact with only a single buyer and able to supply only a limited market with their crops or crafts, are now negotiating for good prices with buyers worldwide. As a result, they can invest in their operations and expand their production. But while innovations such as the Internet and cellular phones have expanded market opportunities and reduced telecommunication costs, they do not by themselves provide sufficient conditions for markets to develop. Other factors are necessary, as we will discuss in this chapter by analyzing the emergence and expansion of markets in developing countries.

Market development, as discussed in Chapters 12 and 13, is significantly related to issues of property rights. Weaker government institutions and property rights laws make market expansion more difficult, while better enforcement of property rights has been demonstrated to facilitate market development. For vigorous markets to develop, strong governmental and legal systems are necessary.

Not only is market development subject to the standard transaction costs we have identified beginning with Chapter 7 (adverse selection, moral hazard, commitment and hold-up problems, etc.), but there are specific problems related to market development in poor countries that we will discuss in this chapter. For example, we will demonstrate that, when a conflict arises between the parties involved in a transaction, it is more costly to use the courts in developing countries even if they operate efficiently. The relative absence of modern communication technologies and insufficient transport infrastructure also presents problems for the creation and expansion of markets in developing countries. In addition, market participants are continually involved in a search process that enables buyers and sellers to find each other. We will examine how this process is facilitated or hindered in different developing countries.

Transition economies offer a unique historical opportunity to understand how markets emerge. Under socialism, free markets were generally prohibited and did not play an important role in resource allocation. The goal of the transition from socialism to capitalism was to build market economies on the ashes of central planning. However, in those countries making the transition, when prices were liberalized precisely for the purpose of creating markets, there generally was a huge fall in production. Why did this occur and how can we explain it? What does it teach us about market development in general and why specifically was China able to avoid such an output fall?

Rural **monopsonies** (single buyers on a market) are not uncommon in developing countries. Farmers may indeed only have access to a single buyer who offers them extremely low prices for their crops. How this affects farmers' incentives and how farmers can avoid monopsonists are also questions we will examine in this chapter.

We will explore to what extent markets for similar goods are integrated over large geographical areas in developing countries and we will discuss how to measure market integration and discuss what are the biggest obstacles to it in developing countries. In addition, the role of transport and communication infrastructures, and regulatory barriers to market integration will be part of our discussion.

Last but not least, a critical topic in the discussion of market development and market integration is famine. When do famines occur and what is the role that market imperfections play in extreme food shortages? Famines can usually be prevented, but they often occur as the result of entitlement or institutional failures. Those members of society who are socially and economically most marginalized are the first to be deprived of sufficient food when shortages occur. We will discuss the role political systems appear to play in famines; some of the most terrible famines of the 20th century have occurred under Communist regimes such as North Korea, while a famine has never happened in a democracy. Finally, we will discuss the topic of the food crisis that occurred in 2008 as rising food and oil prices impacted the poorest people on the planet.

Institutions and Market Development

In this section, we will examine the link between institutions and market development. We start by drawing on material covered previously (Chapters 7, 11, and 12) to see how institutions contribute to market development. We will then analyze specific problems affecting market development in poor countries: higher transaction costs, higher costs of court proceedings, and issues with transportation and communication infrastructure. We will then look at the role of business networks in market development.

Taking Markets for Granted

Standard economics takes markets for granted. In the context of market development, this can be a huge mistake; it was made by policy makers in Central and Eastern Europe as these regions transitioned from socialism to capitalism. Under socialism, there were no markets and prices were fixed. Policy makers and most economists concerned with this transition process thought that once prices were allowed to move freely, markets would emerge spontaneously, creating vigorous economic activity. Instead, they experienced a nasty surprise: when governments in these regions liberalized prices and abandoned central planning, all these countries experienced a huge fall in output. This drop was not only unexpected, but it also took many years before economists could explain what had happened. We will return later in the chapter to this particular episode, but it makes clear that we cannot take markets for granted.

When markets develop, the forces of supply and demand ensure that if there is an unsatisfied demand or an expected purchase of goods, it will be matched with unsatisfied supply or expected sales. Once all demands and supplies are matched, if there is still unsatisfied demand, the market price of a commodity will rise, encouraging added supply and discouraging demand until the market is in equilibrium and there is no excess demand or excess supply. Conversely, if there is excess supply, prices will fall until the market has absorbed all the excess. However, the markets described in modern economics textbooks do not emerge that smoothly in the real world. Matching potential sellers with potential buyers can be difficult and information about potential buyers and sellers must be available. Moreover, the market does not readily reach the single equilibrium price. Different sellers may be demanding various prices and different buyers may be offering to pay various prices, all for identical commodities. If information about prices cannot circulate efficiently, identical goods may be sold at different prices. This can result in arbitrage opportunities in which some agents can buy the same good at a lower price and sell it at a higher price than that good would demand elsewhere in the market. It is thus necessary for information about offers, demands, and prices to circulate among buyers and sellers in order for the market to settle on a single price for the same good as represented by the textbook model. Moreover, as we saw in Chapter 7, even single transactions between one buyer and one seller face various problems such as informational asymmetries about the quality of goods, the honesty of agents, commitment problems, etc.

For markets to develop, the formal institutions that deal with informational and commitment issues in simple transactions must be in place. When these formal institutions are weak, informal institutions must take their place. However, by themselves these institutions are not enough for markets to develop. Goods must be brought to markets and transportation costs in developing countries, where distances between cities can be considerable, are often very high. Similarly, search costs that bring buyers and sellers together can be quite substantial. To all the general institutional problems related to market development, we must add the specific problems related to poor countries.

Specific Problems of Market Development in Poor Countries

Even if we were to assume that emerging nations had the same formal institutions in place as are found in advanced countries, the low level of economic development in those emerging nations makes market expansion more difficult. There are various reasons why this is the case.

First, because smaller amounts of commodities are traded in the markets of poorer as compared to richer countries, it is less worthwhile going to court to settle a conflict over a business transaction. There are economies of scale involved in using the court system. A conflict over 1 ton of rice would likely be just as costly to resolve in court as would a conflict over 2,000 tons of rice. Because there are smaller returns with smaller transactions, a court system and its associated costs will be a less attractive option for conflict resolution. As we saw in Chapter 7, an efficient court system is an important institutional condition that reduces transaction costs, encourages business, and thus makes market expansion possible.

Second, fines imposed by a court are not effective if the guilty party is unable to pay them. Those who can pay fines are hurt by them, but those who cannot pay fines have nothing to lose. Jail can be a substitute for fines, but incarcerating someone for a minor conflict over a transaction is costly, especially for developing countries with scarce government revenues, and particularly if that person does not represent a danger to society. The incentives provided by the court system not to cheat in business transactions are thus weaker because of this minimal effectiveness of fines.

Third, a court system will require proof, such as a signed contract, that a trader promised to pay a certain price for a ton of rice and that the payment was less than the agreed-upon amount; only then is it likely that the court will impose a judicial decision on that trader. However, when there is no contractual agreement, the court must rely on the testimony of witnesses, a more difficult and costly procedure, though one that has been used widely throughout history.

Fourth, in poorer countries market development is made more difficult because of the higher costs of gathering and circulating market information about prices and supply and demand, especially without modern communication infrastructure. This lack of market information can depress competition and have a negative impact on incentives for farmers to expand operations and sales further from home. As we have previously mentioned and will discuss further, cell phones and Internet access are very efficient tools for market integration.

Fifth, given the low population density and the large size of many emerging nations, transportation costs are a critical element in market development. Without a reliable transportation infrastructure, it can be difficult to transport goods from farms to cities, and this can also contribute to suppressing competition and producer incentives. For example, based on research by Fafchamps and Gabre-Madhin, the chart in Figure 14.1 shows the factors contributing to marketing costs in the country of Benin in West Africa.[1] As we can see, transportation represents by far the largest cost and constitutes 45% of traders' total marketing expenses. Marcel Fafchamps and Eleni Gabre-Madhin also document a similar situation in Malawi and several other African countries.

---

[1]Marcel Fafchamps and Eleni Gabre-Madhin, "Agricultural Markets in Benin and Malawi," *The African Journal of Agricultural and Resource Economics* 1, no. 1 (2006): 67–94.

FIGURE 14.1   Breakdown of Traders' Marketing Costs in Benin

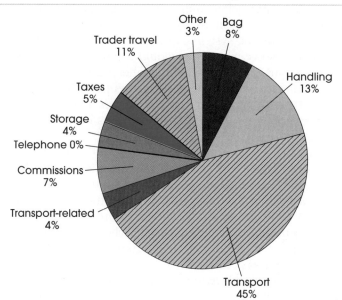

Transportation costs are by far the largest marketing expense for traders in Benin and in other African nations.

Source: Marcel Fafchamps and Eleni Gabre-Madhin, "Agricultural Markets in Benin and Malawi," *The African Journal of Agricultural and Resource Economics* 1, no. 1 (2006): 76. Printed with permission.

Sixth, in many developing nations, there are no standardized systems of weights and measures, and traders customarily use a wide variety of plastic and burlap bags as units of sale rather than uniform containers representing regulated weights such as kilograms or pounds.

Overall, weak or nonexistent institutions combined with poverty, limited access to technology, and high transportation costs are specific contributing factors that must be taken into account when discussing market development in emerging nations. Historically, these factors have had a negative influence on market development and will likely continue to do so.

Business Networks in Development

As discussed in Chapter 13, relational contracting is the norm for trade when formal institutions are weak. Buyers and sellers invest in long-term relationships with business partners they have learned to trust and for whom the continuation of that long-term partnership is advantageous.

Marcel Fafchamps has extensively studied business networks in sub-Saharan Africa and has found that most African manufacturers and their suppliers have, on average, a long-term relationship of over 7 years.[2] Manufacturing

---

[2]Marcel Fafchamps, *Networks, Communities, and Markets in Sub-Saharan Africa: Implications for Firm Growth and Investment* (Oxford: University of Oxford, Institute of Economics and Statistics, Centre for the Study of African Economies, 1999).

firms typically use only one supplier for a specific input and have a continuing business relationship with that supplier even when the firms can choose among many different suppliers.

How is information about the reputation of particular businesspeople circulated in emerging nations? Typically, because businesspeople try to economize on the costs of information gathering and transmission, personal recommendations play a very important role in business relationships. Rather than trying to gather information about individuals' past business dealings, their honesty, reliability, etc., African businesspeople generally will only deal with someone if that person has been recommended by other businesspeople they trust, and they will typically do little business outside the market networks to which they belong.

In some emerging nations, ethnic and religious affiliations play an important role in terms of creating communities of people who trust each other sufficiently enough to do business together. This results in parallel business networks with ethnic or religious affiliations. For example, Jean Ensminger showed that being a Muslim helped an individual enter numerous Islamic-dominant business networks in Kenya and other East African nations. Muslim businesspeople were more likely to trust others of their faith and, as a result, many people converted to Islam in order to be able to participate in these predominantly Muslim business networks.[3] James E. Rauch and Vitor Trindade showed that Chinese ethnic communities in Asian nations played a crucial role in facilitating international trade between countries.[4] Chinese businesspeople formed trade associations that provided information about distributors and suppliers to producers. These associations also helped to match buyers and sellers, and they provided referral services and information on the reputation of particular businesspeople.

However, there is, generally, significant diversity in the nature and composition of business networks in emerging nations. In Ghana for example, there is no strong ethnic or religious homogeneity in the business networks that have formed. In contrast, the manufacturing sector in Kenya is dominated by entrepreneurs from India and other South Asian nations; as a result, it is very difficult for entrepreneurs from other groups to enter business networks in that sector. In Zimbabwe, while manufacturing has been controlled by Europeans and Asians, small businesses are overwhelmingly controlled by native Zimbabweans. There is a historical legacy at play; Zimbabwe was formerly Rhodesia, an unrecognized state in the United Kingdom controlled by British settlers. However, even after white rule ended in 1980, networks of white businesspeople have continued to dominate Zimbabwe's large firms, leaving firms of smaller size to non-white groups.

The Emergence of Markets in Transition Countries

An example of emerging markets is the experience of the transition countries in Central and Eastern Europe and in Asia during the period when market economies replaced central planning. Because there were no markets under

---

[3]Jean Ensminger, *Making a Market* (Cambridge: Cambridge University Press, 1992).

[4]James E. Rauch and Vitor Trindade, "Ethnic Chinese Networks in International Trade," *Review of Economics and Statistics* 84, no. 10 (2002): 116–130.

central planning, their emergence and subsequent development were key parts of the transition process. Analyzing this process can provide unique insights into nascent markets and their expansion in developing economies.

The Output Fall in Central and Eastern Europe

Most economists thought that when prices were liberalized in the formerly socialist economies of Europe, market forces would immediately kick in and bring marked improvements in the allocation of resources. Economists were quite surprised at the unexpected result: in all the countries of Central and Eastern Europe, price liberalization led to a large fall in output. Table 14.1 provides some figures for growth before and after the transition process began in these nations. Price liberalization took place in 1990 in Poland; in 1991 in Czechoslovakia (now the Czech Republic and Slovakia), Bulgaria, Romania, and Hungary; in 1992 in Russia; and in 1994 in the Ukraine. Looking at Table 14.1, we see that these nations experienced significant output falls during those years. Initially, economists had a hard time even believing the numbers and thought there might be some statistical mistake or artifact influencing them. It was difficult to accept that output could fall in countries where the economy was so far from its production possibility frontier. In other words, when there was so much room for efficiency improvements, why did output fall?

The reason economists were surprised by the figures is that they evaluated the economies of these nations in terms of traditional price theory; that is, the theory of supply and demand. They could not arrive at an explanation that made sense using that model. Why? In supply and demand theory, output cannot fall unless there is an exogenous fall in demand (a downward shift in the demand schedule) or a large increase in costs (an upward shift in the supply schedule). Some of these factors were observed in certain transition countries

TABLE 14.1   The Output Fall: Real GDP Growth Rates in Central and Eastern Europe

	1989	1990	1991	1992	1993	1994
Poland	0.2	−11.6	−7.6	2.6	3.8	5.0
Hungary	0.7	−3.5	−11.9	−3.0	−0.9	2
Czech Republic	1.4	−0.4	−14.2	−6.4	−0.9	2.6
Slovakia	1.4	−0.4	−14.5	−7.0	−4.1	4.8
Russia	n.a.	n.a.	−13	−19	−12	−15
Ukraine	4	−3	−12	−17	−17	−23
Bulgaria	0.5	−9.1	−11.7	−7.3	−2.4	1.4
Romania	−5.8	−5.6	−12.9	−10.0	1.3	3.4

Output fell not only in the year prices were liberalized in transition countries, but in subsequent years as well.

Source: European Bank for Reconstruction and Development, Various Annual Reports.

but not in all of them. Supply and demand theory teaches that if the initial market situation is one of disequilibrium because prices are not allowed to vary, then reaching equilibrium will lead to a higher level of quantity exchanged on the market. The output fall thus presented a real puzzle in terms of the traditional supply and demand theory.

It took quite a while for economists to figure out what had happened. Olivier J. Blanchard and Michael Kremer, as well as Thierry Verdier and this author, found answers that were not based on price theory, but on the theory of contracts and institutions.[5] Under central planning, firms were linked to each other; each firm had designated suppliers and clients, and did not have a choice of either. Price liberalization meant not only that prices could freely move in response to market forces, but also that firms had the freedom to do business with whomever they wanted and, as a consequence, the freedom to stop doing business with the suppliers and clients they were forced to work with under central planning. If a firm breaks off its relations with other firms, it is likely it will do so only if it expects to increase its profits.

Blanchard and Kremer made the following argument for how a fall in output trumped established economic theory: If a firm breaks its contract with another firm in hopes of making more profits, it can disrupt the existing production chain. Take the example of car production. Assume that a key supplier of tires breaks its supply contracts in order to sell its products to a foreign firm. In that case, the existing production chain for manufacturing cars breaks down because the supply of tires is no longer available. In principle, with efficient bargaining, the firms in the existing production chain would be willing to contribute to pay the tire producer a higher price for its product in order to discourage it from doing business elsewhere and breaking the supply chain. This should always be the case if the value of the existing production chain is higher than the value of the new production chain with which the supplier wants to work.

However, in order to make an offer to the tire producer, the firms need to know how much it will receive from the new foreign customer. Otherwise, the tire producer may be tempted to exaggerate the size of the foreign offer. In a country with weak institutions, the court system will likely be unable to verify that the outside offer received by the tire supplier is real and is not inflated. Without such a verification process, any firm can claim to have higher outside offers than it actually has and thus hold the other members in the production chain hostage. If legal verification is not possible, then the firms in the existing production chain will not be willing to compensate the tire producer for what they might perceive as a fake outside offer. If the offer is real, the production chain will still break down and it will be too late for bargaining and compensation to avert an output fall. Blanchard and Kremer explained the output fall in Central and Eastern Europe as the result of a multitude of breakdowns in bargaining due to weak institutions that lead to a disruption of production chains. To the extent that the loss in output from this disruption was larger than the

---

[5]Olivier Blanchard and Michael Kremer, "Disorganization, *The Quarterly Journal of Economics* 112, no. 4 (1997): 1091–1126; and Gérard Roland and Thierry Verdier, "Transition and the Output Fall," *Economics of Transition* 7, no. 1 (1999): 1–28.

output gain from the formation of new business partnerships, there was an output fall in the economy as a whole.

Verdier and this author's argument is slightly different. They also view price liberalization as an opportunity to break existing production partnerships and form new ones. However, the output fall is due to a combination of two factors: **search frictions** and **investment specificity**. After price liberalization, existing firms search for new profitable partners, but in the absence of pre-existing markets, this search takes time. This is what we mean by search frictions. Also, while firms are searching for new partners, they will not invest with existing partners. The idea is that investments are specific to a given production relationship. This is what is meant by investment specificity. If a firm expects to discontinue its current relationship with existing partners, it will not invest in it. It will only invest once it has found a new long-term partner. The combination of search frictions and investment specificity will lead to an output fall because of two factors: first, there will be little investment while the economy-wide search takes place and this will depress output. Second, once a firm has found another partner, there is, as Blanchard and Kremer's argument describes, a disruption of the existing production chain.

The output fall in Central and Eastern Europe forced economists to take a fresh look at how markets emerge. It is not just a story of supply and demand, forces that work well when markets preexist, that is, when search frictions are not too significant and when there are strong formal institutions to enforce contracts and help resolve business conflicts. Supply and demand are thus only one part of the story. But analyzing markets only through the lens of supply and demand can result in misleading conclusions.

China and the Dual-Track System

Contrary to what economists observed in Central and Eastern Europe, there was no output fall in China when prices there were liberalized. The primary explanation for this is related to the specific method of price liberalization used in China, called **dual-track liberalization**. Under dual-track liberalization, only part of a firm's output is liberalized: one part is produced on the **plan track**, following plan orders of output, planned supplies and deliveries set in previous years, while all extra production is sold freely at free market prices on the **market track**. Figure 14.2 illustrates what dual-track liberalization does, in contrast to normal liberalization. We first use a simple supply and demand diagram because, despite its limitations described above, it easily explains the dual-track method. However, further on, when discussing why there was no output fall in China, we will depart from the supply and demand framework.

Consider a situation in which prices are not liberalized. Assume that the price is at P_P, below the equilibrium market price P_E. The quantity being sold is Q_P. With normal price liberalization, the quantity will be Q_E at price P_E. Note that this quantity is higher than Q_P. Then, consider the case of dual-track price liberalization in which there is a plan track that corresponds to existing plan contracts and obligations. Firms are, however, told that once they have fulfilled their plan obligations, they can then contract freely. In other words, quantity Q_P must still be delivered at price P_P, but beyond Q_P prices are allowed to freely move in response to supply and demand forces. Note then that the equilibrium

FIGURE 14.2   An Illustration of Dual-Track Price Liberalization

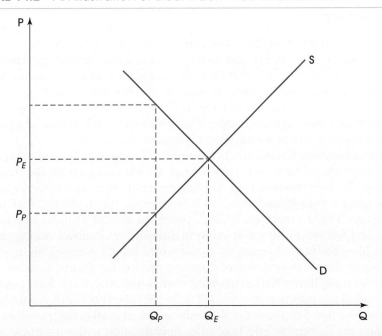

With the dual-track system, the plan track Q_P is delivered at price P_P and $(Q_E - Q_P)$ is delivered on the market track at the equilibrium market price P_E.

price and the quantities will be exactly the same as under normal price liberalization, except that now only the quantity $(Q_E - Q_P)$ is sold at price P_E. This is the dual track that results in the planned price and the planned quantity, and the market price and the market quantity.

The dual-track system was implemented in China beginning in 1984 in all sectors of the economy. Results were as predicted by theory; firms continued to respect previous contractual arrangements of the plan while they also seized opportunities to provide additional output on the market track. Over time, the plan track became increasingly less important while the market track continued to expand. Price liberalization thus took place in the context of 10% annual GDP growth rates and no output fall was ever observed.

The dual track implemented in China is especially interesting because it prevented the output fall observed in Central and Eastern Europe. In fact, because the planned quantity Q_P must continue to be delivered, there cannot be any output fall if planned obligations are fulfilled. There can only be an increase in output on the market track. The logic is very simple but also very powerful.

Note that the reasoning does not rely at all on the supply and demand framework that we used only to simplify the exposition. Because of this logic, there was thus no output fall in China under the dual-track method. Over time, the market track continued to increase relative to the plan track, which was eventually abolished. The dual-track method thus proved to be a very useful tool to prevent the kind of production chain disruption that was observed in Central and Eastern Europe.

Lessons from the Effects of Transition on Market Development

The lessons learned from the transition process on market development are quite important. The supply and demand framework familiar to economists assumes that markets exist, that there is information available about supply and demand, and that institutions exist to enforce transactions using legal precedents. However, the output fall in Central and Eastern Europe taught economists that making these standard assumptions in the context of emerging market economies can be a humbling experience.

Are these lessons historically unique or do they have a more general application? They are, in fact, more general and are relevant beyond the transition experience for two reasons. First, they demonstrate that we cannot view markets as simple supply and demand adjustments. Solid institutional underpinnings are vital to markets. Second, problems similar to those observed in Central and Eastern Europe may occur in developing countries during periods of trade liberalization. Opening up to the world economy may lead to an inefficient disruption or destruction of domestic production chains. To what extent episodes of trade liberalization have led to an initial output fall that could have been avoided is a question that has yet to be the subject of much research.

These new insights about the slow emergence of markets in transition economies and the disruptive effects of price liberalization without sufficient market development imply that developing countries may have to prepare themselves more thoroughly to absorb the shocks of trade liberalization. One way to accomplish this is to establish free-trade zones first and allow them to develop while simultaneously preparing the domestic economy for trade liberalization. As shown by Dani Rodrik, the island nation of Mauritius, in the Indian Ocean off the eastern coast of Madagascar, owes a large part of its economic success to the 1970 creation of an export-processing zone that specialized in garments exported primarily to Europe.[6] While Mauritius was establishing this export-processing zone, its domestic economy remained protected until the mid-1980s. As a result, the creation of the zone led to an economic expansion without domestic disruption. In particular, labor markets remained segmented, with different wage levels in the export-processing zone compared to the domestic economy. Mauritius has managed to implement a form of dual-track liberalization similar to what was done in China with domestic price liberalization: protecting the domestic economy while expanding the export-processing zone.

Rural Markets and the Monopsony Problem

Rural markets suffer from all the problems we have identified so far in this chapter: weak institutions, poverty, lack of communications technology, long distances, and high transportation costs. One particular problem that arises in

---

[6]Dani Rodrik, "The New Global Economy and Developing Countries: Making Openness Work" (policy paper, Overseas Development Council, distributed by Johns Hopkins University Press, Washington, DC, 1999).

many rural markets is the monopsony problem. This is a word that you certainly have heard less than the word "monopoly." While monopoly refers to a commodity controlled by a single producer, a monopsony occurs when a given market is controlled by a single buyer. Monopsonies are rarer than monopolies, but they are frequently found in the markets of developing countries. In regions where farmers are poor and work on small plots of land far from city markets, how do they sell their farm output? In many cases, the simple answer is that they do not. Much of the farming that takes place in Africa is subsistence farming. In other words, farmers work small land holdings to feed themselves and their families but do not commercialize the extra output produced because of the expense, or are unable to because of the size limitations of their lands. What does this have to do with the monopsony problem? When farmers do want to grow beyond subsistence farming, increase the size and productivity of their land, and make sufficient money to improve the economic situation of their families, they are faced with the difficult problem of how to sell their agricultural output. It is often too costly for individual farmers to go to a city market, sometimes hundreds of miles away, to sell their crops without a means of transport, such as a small truck. At best, they can only sell to a trader who will come to them. Rarely will more than one trader make an offer on their crops and provide them with the opportunity to sell to the highest bidder. These farmers will thus face a monopsonist, a single buyer who controls the market for their output. Because the trader will propose to buy a farmer's output at a very low price, the single low offer is enough to discourage farmers from making any investment that would increase the productivity of their land. Let us see why.

Monopsony and the Hold-Up Problem

In order to understand the monopsony problem better, we can work with a numeric example. Imagine an individual farmer who can choose between two technologies: a low-level technology with costs only for labor, and a new, more productive technology requiring a fixed investment. Suppose the farmer can produce 100 pounds of rice at a cost of 5 pesos per pound with the old, low-level technology. Assume that the cost per pound represents the total manual labor put into working the land and harvesting the crop. This is how the farmer has always worked. Suppose that with the new technology, the farmer can produce 150 pounds of rice at a cost of 2 pesos per pound, but only after having made an investment that costs 400 pesos on an annual basis for fertilizer, modern seeds, an irrigation system, tools, and a harvesting machine.

Suppose that the farmer sells his rice to a merchant who is a monopsonist, the only person who ever shows up in the village and offers to buy agricultural products. Because all other markets are distant, it is very costly for the farmer to sell the rice himself so he is pleased to get at least some income from selling his surplus rice without having to solve the difficult and time-consuming problem of transporting it to another market. However, the monopsony can be an obstacle to investing in the new technology. Suppose that the initial price the farmer can get from the monopsonist is 6 pesos. Under the old technology, the farmer makes a profit of $6 \times 100 - 5 \times 100 = 100$ pesos. At the price of 6 pesos, would the farmer prefer to invest in the new technology? If the farmer does make the investment in the new technology, he would make a profit of $6 \times 150 - 400 - 2 \times 150 = 200$ pesos, which is a higher return. Recall that we assume under the new technology that the farmer can produce 150 pounds at a unit cost of 2 pesos and a fixed cost of 400 pesos. This sounds like good news—at the price of 6 pesos, the farmer makes a profit of 100 pesos under the old technology and a profit of 200 pesos under the new technology. The farmer will thus have an interest in investing in the new technology at that price.

Does the farmer need to worry about a possible price change? Yes, he certainly does. Suppose that after the farmer has invested in the new technology, the merchant tells him that now he is only willing to pay a price of 3 pesos per unit of rice. Does this remind you of something? It is exactly the hold-up problem we discussed in Chapter 7. The merchant will try to force the farmer to accept the lower price by exploiting the fact that he has already made the technology investment. The farmer will still want to produce if the price is 3 pesos; because the investment is a sunk cost—it no longer enters his calculations. At a price of 3 pesos, the farmer thus makes an operating profit of $3 \times 150 - 2 \times 150 = 150$ pesos. Note that at the price of 3 pesos under the old technology, the farmer would have incurred losses and thus would not have invested in the new technology. The merchant is tempted to lower the price from 6 to 3 pesos once the farmer has made the investment in the new technology because he knows the farmer will agree to sell at a price of 3 pesos.

The possibility of the hold-up problem is, however, the cause of a very serious economic disincentive. Before making the investment in the new technology, the farmer will consider the possibility that the merchant may hold him up at a later stage. If the merchant cannot commit to not lowering the price, the farmer will prefer to stick to the old technology and not take the risk of investing in the new technology and be worse off because of the hold-up problem. Indeed, the total operating profit of 150 when the price is 3 pesos would not compensate for the investment of 400.

Note that monopsony is at the heart of the hold-up problem here. If the farmer had the possibility of selling his rice to another competing merchant, he could sell it at a higher price and enjoy the benefits of his investment, but the existence of the monopsony makes that impossible. Therefore, it is not profitable to invest in new technology and improve the land's productivity, and this creates a very serious problem for developing economies.

Monopsonies in Developing Countries

Monopsonies are common in many regions of Africa where the distances between producers and markets are large and population density is low. They are also present in other continents such as Asia, for example, where rice is often purchased by owners of rice mills who act as local monopsonists. Many vegetable markets in Indonesia are ruled by monopsonies that in many cases have even been encouraged by the government. In South America, the Honduran government tried to create a large agro-food industry by investing in large processing plants and encouraging farmers to switch to crops for exports. However, the firms buying the crops were monopsonists and, as a result, the farmers failed to make the investments expected from them because of the low prices that were an effect of the monopsony problem.[7] For example, in the case of palm oil, an edible vegetable oil, the Honduran government placed all oil-crushing mills in the control of one firm, Coapalma, that was able to earn enormous profits by paying monopsony prices for palm fruit. These were hold-up prices that only compensated growers for their yearly production costs and not for the investment cost of planting new trees, which discouraged farmers from planting new palm trees and expanding their oil-producing operations.

Possible Solutions to the Monopsony Problem

In developing economies, solving the monopsony problem is a key factor in improving productivity in agriculture, and its solution can also help to expand markets because increased productivity will lead to increased supply and multiple buyers, which in turn will lead to more competition and increased demand. What are some solutions to the monopsony problem?

Long-term relationships. The first possible solution to the monopsony problem is the establishment of long-term business relationships between the farmer and the buyer. It does not completely solve the monopsony problem, but it does alleviate the bad behavior that is related to monopsony power. In fact, a buyer can also suffer from his own hold-up behavior if he has a long-term relationship with the farmer. He would be better off refraining from offering a lower price after the farmer has invested in productivity enhancements on his land because he stands to benefit in the long run from the higher output volume and sales—and the lower costs—that result from technological improvements introduced by the farmer once he knows he will not be subject to the holdup.

It is, however, not clear that the buyer necessarily has an interest in the development of long-term relationships. He might be better off going from farmer to farmer offering to buy their products at a very low price. For example, if there is a weak institutional environment characterized by conflict, like a civil war, or weak legal and law enforcement institutions, then it might be difficult to sustain long-term relationships. When there is conflict or the threat of bandits, merchants might also be unable to depend on the regular use of roads between farms and markets.

Competition. A second, more obvious solution to the monopsony problem would be to introduce competition. If a farmer were able to attract more than one buyer, he could use that competition to bid prices up and could then always sell to the highest bidder without confronting the hold-up problem. However, this is easier said than done. There might be various reasons that would make competition difficult to sustain. In particular, competition might not be feasible if it is not profitable for two buyers to go to the same village.

Our numerical example can also illustrate the issues that affect competition. Assume that the buyer can sell the rice for 10 pesos per pound on the market. Recall that his purchase price was 6 pesos per pound. But also assume that he

---

[7]Catherine de Fontenay, *Institutions, Market Power, and the Big Push: The Case of Agro-Exports in Northern Honduras* (Kensington, New South Wales: University of New South Wales, School of Economics, 1999).

has a transport cost of 400 pesos. At a purchase price of 6 pesos and an output of 100, the merchant makes 400 pesos in operating profit but will barely break even because of the transport cost of 400 pesos. Assuming that two buyers have a 50% chance of purchasing the rice crop if they offer the same price to the farmer, each merchant would still have to make a profit of 400 pesos on the sale in order to break even. With a production level of 150, each merchant would have to make an operating profit of $5\frac{1}{3}$ pesos per unit of rice. Indeed, $0.5 \times 150 \times 5\frac{1}{3} = 400$. As a result, each merchant could not afford to pay more than 10 pesos minus $5\frac{1}{3}$ pesos, which gives a maximum price of $4\frac{2}{3}$ pesos per unit of rice to the farmer. The farmer cannot make a profit with the new technology at that price. Indeed, taking the investment into account, his net profit is $150 \times 4\frac{2}{3} - 150 \times 2 - 400 = -100$ pesos. At a production level of 100 with the old technology, each trader would have to make a profit of 8 pesos; that is, the traders could not afford to buy rice at more than the price of 2 pesos, which is clearly not profitable. Moreover, each buyer would have an incentive to undercut the other. In the long run, encouraging competition would seem to be the obvious way to solve the monopsony problem, but because only one buyer would remain to negotiate with the farmer, there would still be a stable monopsony as it would not be profitable to have more than one buyer make the trip to do business with the farmer.

Marketing cooperatives. A third solution that can provide an alternative to the monopsony problem is to establish marketing cooperatives for farmers. There are numerous examples of these cooperatives in developing countries, from wool producers in Kyrgyzstan, to dairy farmers in South Asia and the Middle East, to beekeepers in Turkey. Marketing cooperatives exist for virtually every kind of agricultural product.

For the purpose of our discussion, assume that if a farmer markets his own product, he has to pay the transport cost (400 pesos) himself, but he also loses time working on the farm because of the time spent in transporting his product. To make things simple, assume (unrealistically) that the farmer loses all his output if he has to make a trip to the market. Then, assume that the farmers in the area form a cooperative and take turns bringing all their output to market. How many farmers does it take to make adoption of the marketing cooperative profitable?

If a single farmer's output is sold directly on the market at the price of 10, the net profit to the farmer is $10 \times 150 - 400 - 2 \times 150 = 800$. The cost to one farmer to sell on the market is lost profit (800) plus the transport cost $400 = 1200$. In this example, it is too costly for a single farmer to market his product directly, but just two farmers working together would be enough to support a marketing cooperative. The total production profit per year would be 800 because one of the two farmers would forgo all his individual profits when transporting the output to the market. Even though the transport cost of 400 would have to be deducted from this total profit, each farmer would get half of the total profit $(800 - 400 = 400)$, or 200. With more farmers belonging to the cooperative, the profit per farmer would increase.

If a marketing cooperative can be profitable with just a few participating farmers, it seems as if it would be relatively easy to set one up. However, if larger numbers of participating farmers are needed, they may fail to establish the cooperative because of the collective-action failure discussed in Chapter 7.

They would all be better off if, as a group, they shared the costs of establishing the cooperative, but each individual farmer would be even better off if all participated except for him. The collective-action failure can thus be a very serious obstacle to the establishment of cooperatives and can present a significant obstacle to agricultural and economic progress in developing countries.

A problem that often arises with marketing cooperatives is that those individuals who take a leadership position can hijack the cooperative and make it work for their own benefit. Cooperative leaders can keep a large part of the cooperative's profits for themselves by diverting funds away from other members. Sometimes cooperatives are even transformed into the monopsonies that they were supposed to replace, paying a low price to members for their crops and selling them at a high price. In other words, an agency problem emerges within the cooperative when those who are supposed to serve the interests of all members instead serve only themselves. Agency problems are ubiquitous in any collective organization; they are inherent even in modern democracies when elected politicians abuse their power and serve themselves instead of their constituents. Addressing agency problems necessitates the establishment of rules within the cooperative that make the leadership accountable to the members and that enable members to replace leaders who violate those rules. This is often easier said than done.

Because the collective-action problem often prevents the establishment of cooperatives, governments in various countries have implemented policies that encourage their creation. This has been the case in India for many decades. But while government support for cooperatives can help farmers, it can also create problems of its own. Cooperatives may spend time lobbying for subsidies or neglect the efficient management of their operating costs, with the expectation that in a worst-case scenario, they will be bailed out by government money. In other words, they may suffer from the problems of soft-budget constraints discussed in Chapter 8.

Many marketing cooperatives also play the role of credit cooperatives because they can rarely abstain from providing credit to their members. They not only help farmers market their output but also pool member resources to finance the purchase of supplies, or equipment by their members. Issues of credit in the rural areas will be discussed in Chapter 15.

Market Integration

When analyzing markets, whether in developing or advanced countries, economists try to measure the degree of **market integration**. What do we mean by this term? Say that there is shortage of rice in region A but not in region B. If markets are only local and are not integrated, then there will be an increase in the price of rice in region A but not in region B. If markets are integrated, however, rice will be transported from region B to region A in order to satisfy demand. This means that the price will increase by a smaller amount in region A due to the additional supply, but it also means that the price will increase in region B. In general, when markets are perfectly integrated, assuming no transportation costs, the price for a product should be the same everywhere. If the price is higher in one region, then merchants will immediately rush there to supply additional quantities at the higher price until prices are equalized.

Now, if we allow for transportation costs, prices will not necessarily be the same everywhere because these costs vary from region to region; however, price variations will be the same. Indeed, look again at the example of the two regions. Suppose there is a shortage of rice in region A but not in region B. Traders will move rice from region B to region A up to the point where the advantage of selling in region B or transporting rice to region A and incurring the transport costs are equal. The point here is that prices in region B will increase following the price increase in region A; as rice moves out of region B to region A, the supply of rice in region B is reduced, thereby leading to an equivalent increase in price in region B as well.

Measures of market integration that economic researchers have devised aim precisely at capturing to what extent prices for the same goods move in the same direction at the same time. If this simultaneous movement is present, we can say that markets are integrated. If, on the other hand, prices in different regions do not move in the same direction at a specific moment in time, this can be seen as evidence that markets are not integrated. The methods researchers use to measure this integration are quite technical and we will not analyze them in depth. However, the general principle is to test whether prices of the same or similar goods are moving in the same direction at the same time across different regions.

Lack of integration or insufficient integration may be due to several different factors. For example, lack of communication and transportation infrastructures can impact market integration. Without adequate communication technologies, traders in region B may not be aware of shortages in region A; as a result, there will be no market reaction to those shortages and merchants will not take advantage of the arbitrage opportunities that emerge. Transportation difficulties can also affect integration if it is very difficult to move goods between regions, either because of geographical factors (distance, terrain, etc.) or lack of infrastructure (roads, bridges, trains). There may, however, also be obstacles to integration that are the result of government regulations. We will look at these different obstacles in turn.

Communication Obstacles to Market Integration

In modern markets, communication is a key factor in integration. In financial markets, trades are made continuously on a 24-hour cycle. Any information on world events (an earthquake in Asia, poor returns for a global enterprise, a war that flares within or between nations) is instantaneously transmitted to the world's financial markets where this information is then reflected in prices. Global markets for commodities function in a similar way. Physically, most of these markets are located in the wealthiest cities in the world: New York, Chicago, London, Paris, Frankfurt, and Tokyo. In the poorest regions of the world, however, communication is much slower, with the result that markets do not respond as quickly to changing conditions as they do in the developed world.

A good example of the effects of communication technologies is a study done by Jenny Aker on integration in Niger's grain market before and after the introduction of cell phones.[8] Niger, in West Africa, is one of the poorest nations in the world, with 85% of the population living on less than US$2 per day. Grain, primarily millet and sorghum, accounts for over 75% of the country's food consumption. In a country that is roughly 3 times the size of California, grain is transported from remote farms to consumers by means of a complex system of grain markets that take place only once per week. Traditionally, traders had to travel long distances between farms and markets in order to obtain information on supply, demand, and current prices. Therefore, the communication of market information was quite slow. Between 2001 and 2006, however, cell phone service was phased in throughout Niger, providing grain traders and other market participants a fast, inexpensive technology for disseminating market information. The use of cell phones has improved communication speed and has led to a reduction in price dispersion as traders can now quickly learn local market conditions and then exploit arbitrage opportunities by transporting goods to those markets with the highest prices.

Because cell phone service was established incrementally, it has been possible to estimate the effects of rapid communication on market integration. Price dispersion should be lower between markets for which cell phone service was established. Indeed, Aker found that the availability of cell phone service reduced grain price dispersion across markets by a minimum of 6.4% and reduced intra-annual price variation by 10%. Because traders no longer need to travel to gather information, cell phones have had a greater impact on price dispersion between any two markets that are remote from each other, as well as for markets with poor transportation infrastructure.

It is worth noting that improved communications can have significant positive impacts on the welfare of a developing nation's population. In 2005, there was a localized food crisis in Niger, with acute grain shortages in certain regions. In areas where grain was in short supply, prices were 20% higher than in those regions with adequate supplies. At the time of the food crisis, only 24% of the markets in regions facing the possibility of famine had cell phone coverage, as compared to 83% of the markets in regions not facing famine. Cell phone coverage, by providing arbitrage opportunities for market traders, enabled the rapid transport of grain to many of those areas in crisis.

Better market integration means that there are fewer instances of excess supply in some regions and excess demand in others. As market information circulates more rapidly, goods travel to those areas where there is more demand and prices are highest. Better market integration also leads to more price stability in individual regions because the movement of goods from low-price to high-price markets tends to stabilize prices. All this is particularly important when there are localized food shortages.

---

[8]Jenny C. Aker, "Information from Markets Near and Far: Mobile Phones and Agricultural Markets in Niger" *American Economic Journal: Applied Economics* 2, no. 3 (2010): 46–59.

Transportation Obstacles to Market Integration

We know that better communication enhances market integration as information circulates faster and more efficiently. However, improved information circulation is offset when goods cannot be transported easily between different regional markets. What effect can better transportation infrastructure have on market integration?

An interesting study by Zhigang Li analyzed the effect on market integration of a large investment in railroad infrastructure improvements in China.[9] Before 1994, transportation between China's western Xinjiang province and its eastern provinces depended on a one-track railroad between the city of Lanzhou (LAN in Figure 14.3), the capital of Gansu province, and the city of

FIGURE 14.3   Map of China and the Lanzhou–Xinjiang Railroad

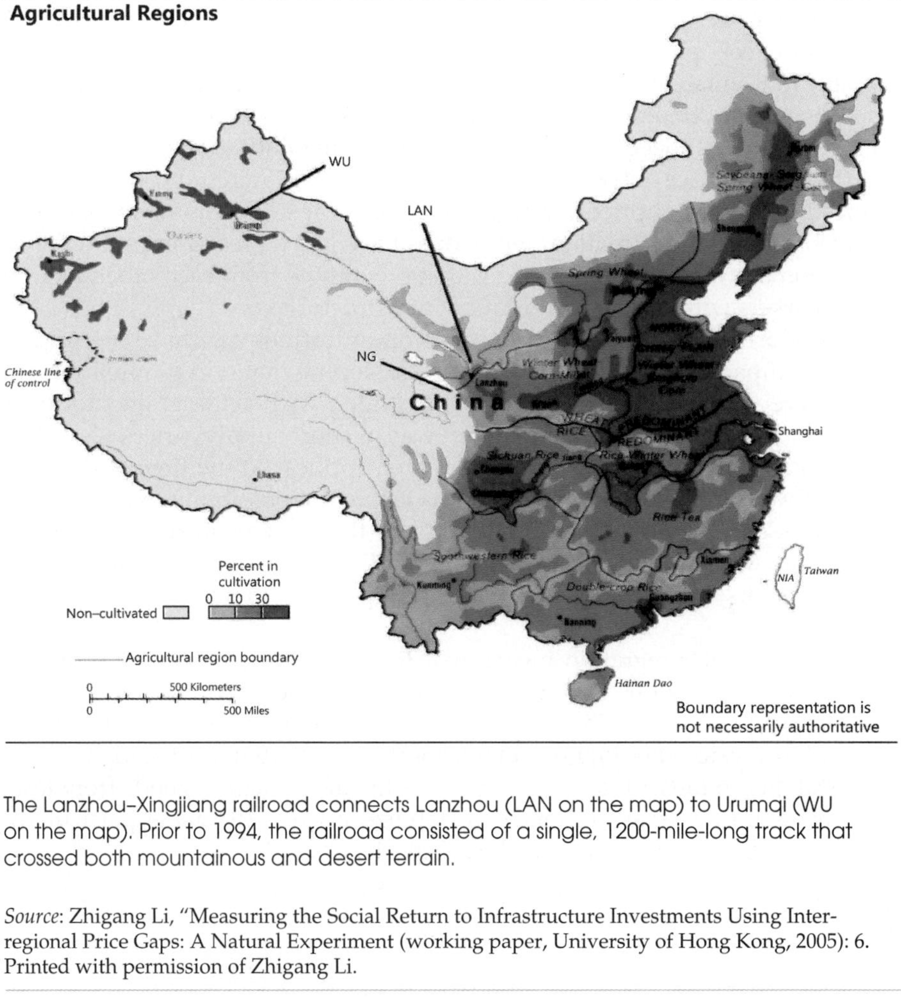

The Lanzhou–Xingjiang railroad connects Lanzhou (LAN on the map) to Urumqi (WU on the map). Prior to 1994, the railroad consisted of a single, 1200-mile-long track that crossed both mountainous and desert terrain.

Source: Zhigang Li, "Measuring the Social Return to Infrastructure Investments Using Interregional Price Gaps: A Natural Experiment (working paper, University of Hong Kong, 2005): 6. Printed with permission of Zhigang Li.

---

[9]Zhigang Li, "Measuring the Social Return to Infrastructure Investments Using Interregional Price Gaps: A Natural Experiment (working paper, University of Hong Kong, 2005).

Urumqi (WU in Figure 14.3), the capital of Xinjiang province. Figure 14.3 shows the 1200-mile LAN–WU railroad, also called the Lanzhou–Xingjiang railroad, that connected the two cities. Roughly 95% of transportation between Xinjiang and China's other provinces relies on this railroad as distances between them are long, roads are poor, and the mountainous and desert terrains are challenging. Until 1994, because there was just a single track, only one train at a time could travel on this 1200-mile stretch, severely restricting the transportation of goods. Since 1994, with the addition of a second track, there has been a substantial increase in transportation capacity.

Figure 14.4 analyzes the price gap for four types of commodities shipped from Urumqi to Lanzhou: gasoline, diesel, and cold- and hot-rolled thin sheet steel. As is evident in the figure, after 1994 and the completion of the second track, there is a significant drop in the price gap for all four goods.

These figures by themselves do not prove that the transportation investment had a major effect on reducing the price differential. Other factors might

FIGURE 14.4   Evolution of the Price Gap between Urumqi and Lanzhou

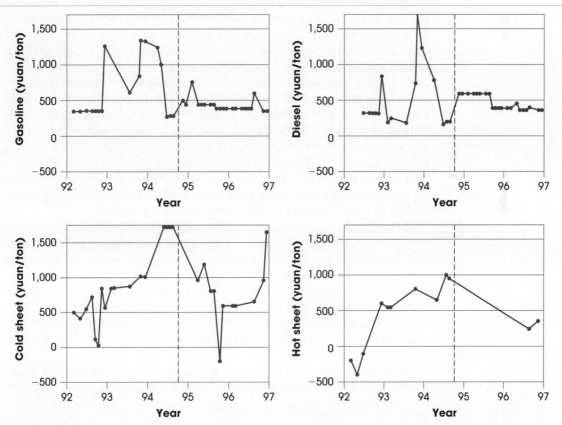

The price gap for four commodities transported between Lanzhou and Urumqi dropped after 1994 when a second railroad track was built between these two cities.

Source: Li, "Measuring the Social Return to Infrastructure Investments Using Interregional Price Gaps: A Natural Experiment: 9. Printed with permission of Zhigang Li.

also have been at work, such as a reduction in government regulations or variations in economic conditions that had nothing to do with the investment. However, Li shows that for similar goods transported between other regions of China, there was no such reduction in the price gap. The doubling of the railroad track thus had the effect of substantially reducing the price gap between Xinjiang and the rest of China, and the study demonstrates that transportation investment contributed both to an increased and more rapid flow of goods between different geographical regions, and to the reduction of price differentials across those regions.

Regulatory Obstacles to Market Integration

During the mid-1980s, some Chinese provinces liberalized their market prices earlier than others. Suppose that some provinces liberalized the price of grain while other provinces maintained price-control policies for grain to keep the price lower. Farmers who had the right to sell their grain freely would have wanted to export it to those provinces where the liberalized price was higher. However, the initial reaction of local authorities in the provinces with price controls was to erect trade barriers that prevented the export of grain to other regions. In fact, export barriers were established in various Chinese provinces for a variety of goods during the 1980s and even the early 1990s.[10] Later, however, officials removed these export barriers and made significant progress toward market integration across all of China.

Li looked systematically at price differentials for 50 industrial goods in 36 major cities between 1992 and 2005.[11] The goods he considered were generally homogeneous (i.e., not diversified) and thus comparable, such as aluminum, cement, coal, caustic soda, copper, lead, polystyrene, rubber, sodium carbonate, and zinc, and the prices for each good across regions can thus be considered comparable. Figure 14.5 illustrates the evolution of median price differentials for cement and aluminum. We can see a decline in the differential for cement prices and a stable price differential for aluminum. This suggests a decline in trade barriers for cement but not for aluminum.

Li found that the primary variable for price differentials was transportation costs, which is consistent with high market integration. When markets are very integrated, goods should have the same price, exclusive of transportation costs. These costs should explain any difference in prices. The study also suggested that local protectionism did not play a significant role in explaining price differentials across China. Overall, the evidence shows that China has experienced significant progress in market integration during recent decades and that local barriers to trade across regions have been significantly reduced or abolished.

India has had a long history of regulatory barriers to internal trade that have resulted in a negative effect on market integration. Different provincial

---

[10]Alwyn Young, "The Razor's Edge: Distortions and Incremental Reform in the People's Republic of China," *The Quarterly Journal of Economics* 115, no. 4 (2000): 1091–1135.

[11]Zhigang Li, "Determinants of Trade Barriers within China: Evidence from Price Differentials" (working paper, University of Hong Kong, 2007).

FIGURE 14.5   Median Price Differentials for Cement and Aluminum
in China

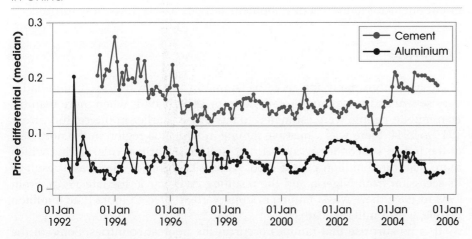

The price differential for cement declined while the price differential for aluminum remained stable when trade barriers between Chinese provinces were removed in the early 1990s.

Source: Zhigang Li, "Determinants of Trade Barriers within China: Evidence from Price Differentials" (working paper, University of Hong Kong, 2007): 10. Printed with permission of Zhigang Li.

standards for goods have actually prevented internal trade, while cumbersome systems of multiple licensing requirements have hindered market entry and integration. If merchants need a license in one state to purchase certain goods, they will need another license in another state to sell those same goods. An extremely inefficient and corrupt bureaucracy discourages entrepreneurs from obtaining the necessary licenses, while regulations establishing price controls also prevent market integration by deterring traders from selling their goods in those areas with price controls, encouraging them instead to sell their good in other regions where there are no price controls. Moreover, goods crossing borders between different Indian states are subject to taxation.

The reason that regulatory intervention frequently prevents market integration is not that governments are, *per se*, against it; rather, it has more to do with a government's response to internal pressures that, in turn, result in obstacles to market integration. Say that the price of rice increases in a developing country, as happened in many countries in 2008. The poorest people might then be on the brink of starvation, and if famine breaks out, the result could be food riots. In these situations, a government's response is often to establish price controls to avert the threat of famine and civil unrest. Because controlled prices tend to be lower than market prices, not only will there be excess demand, or shortages, but traders will try to move merchandise to those regions where prices are higher and where there are no price controls, and this will exacerbate the shortages. The government will then feel forced to intervene and prevent goods from moving away from areas of price control, thereby creating obstacles to market integration.

Does this mean that markets by themselves prevent famines? The issue of markets and famines, as well as the cause of famines in general, is a very important factor in market development and one to which we now turn.

Famines

There have been many instances of famine in modern history. China had a very severe and wide-ranging famine from 1959 to 1961, when more than fifteen million people were estimated to have died. Earlier in the century, from 1943 to 1944, there was a massive famine in Bengal, a region in the northeast of the Indian subcontinent, at that time still under British rule, during which more than three million people died. Famine occurred in Biafra as a result of its secession from Nigeria and the resulting civil war in the late 1960s. From 1983 to 1985, there was a famine in Ethiopia that affected more than 8 million people, with 1 million deaths.

It is no surprise that famines occur in the poorest countries. Some of the worst famines of the 20th century have, however, been associated with Communist regimes and with disastrous agricultural policies that resulted in millions of deaths. Consider, for example, the collectivization of agriculture in the Ukraine under Joseph Stalin in the early 1930s in combination with his policy of deporting thousands of Ukrainians to prison camps, and his deliberate starvation of those who remained; the dictator Pol Pot's mass deportation of Cambodia's urban population to the "killing fields" of the countryside from 1975 to 1979 where those who survived mass executions were left to starve to death; and China's "Great Leap Forward" in 1959, a disastrous attempt by Communist leaders to rapidly transform the country's ancient agrarian society into a modern industrial nation. Peasants were forced to produce steel in their backyards while agricultural production was neglected. The resulting fall in agricultural output led millions to starve to death. As we will see, there is a clear association between famines and the absence of democracy.

Famine occurs when there is a particularly high mortality risk that results from a significant reduction in food supplies for at least some groups of people in a geographic area. A famine does not have to be associated with a reduction in aggregate availability of food in a country or even in a region; rather, the criterion is whether some groups of people at some point in time lack access to food supplies in a way that threatens their lives. Groups that are at risk of suffering from famine are those that are politically and socially more vulnerable and weak.

Amartya Sen's Analysis of Famine

Born in Bengal in 1933, economist Amartya Sen experienced the 1943 Bengali famine firsthand when he was young. In 1981, he developed an innovative approach to the analysis of famine and was awarded the Nobel Memorial Prize in Economic Sciences in 1998. According to Sen, people die in famines not because there is not enough food for everybody, but because of the inequalities in the entitlements to food that are themselves related to a country's formal institutions. The central concept in Sen's analysis of famines is that of an individual's **entitlement set**, which is defined as all the goods that an individual can obtain with the resources he or she commands, given the laws of his or her society. According to Sen, starvation is the result of an entitlement failure that occurs when social norms and laws in a society are such that in the case of a food shortage, some individuals are "left out" to starve.

In situations of famine, there may be enough food to prevent any single individual from starving, but some categories of the population may witness a fall in income that does not allow them to acquire enough food to survive. If there is a food shortage, the distribution of food in poor families may be sufficiently unequal that the poorest members of the family (usually the elderly and female family members) starve while the other family members do not. Markets may be insufficiently integrated so that they cannot remedy negative shocks to a local food supply. Government emergency distribution funds may not work appropriately. While aggregate drops in food availability may trigger famines, they are neither a necessary nor a sufficient condition for famines to occur. Indeed, many famines occur without even a decline in aggregate food availability. Moreover, there are cases in which food availability declines substantially, but no one starves.

Figure 14.6, based on research by Martin Ravallion, shows the negative relationship between real wages and famine in the 1974–1975 Bangladesh famine in Matlab Thana, one of the country's administrative regions.[12] The vertical

FIGURE 14.6   Deaths per Month in Matlab Thana 1974–1976.

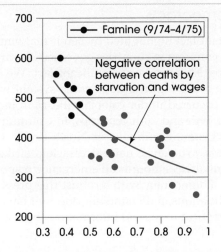

The vertical axis measures deaths per month and the horizontal axis measures monthly wages in *maunds* (25 pounds) of rice per 10 days across the time period. In times of famine, the number of deaths by starvation in Bangladesh is negatively correlated to wages.

Source: Martin Ravallion, "Famines and Economics" (policy research working paper no. 1693, The World Bank, Washington, DC, 1996): 16.

---

[12]Martin Ravallion, "Famines and Economics" (policy research working paper no. 1693, The World Bank, Washington, DC, 1996).

axis represents the monthly number of deaths and the horizontal axis represents the log of real wages expressed in terms of quantities of rice. A strong negative relationship is apparent: the higher the wage, the lower the number of deaths. Note, however, that this negative relationship only occurs during a famine period. It appears that the poorest people who are already economically marginalized are the first to suffer famine when there is an adverse shock in the economy such as reduced food availability or higher food prices. A small drop in food consumption for the poorest can thus lead to famine.

Even perfectly efficient markets cannot prevent famines if poor people do not have sufficient purchasing power to acquire enough food to survive. Simple expectations of future price increases for food may lead to hoarding behavior, the effect of which is actual price increases that leave the poor vulnerable to starvation. However, famines most often occur when markets are functioning imperfectly. Breakdowns in transportation systems prevent food from reaching the regions most threatened by starvation. High inventories of food in some areas can coincide with starvation in others, and lack of market integration due to the causes we have previously identified (poor communication and transportation infrastructures, regulatory barriers) may lead to famines that could otherwise be prevented if there were better market integration. As we see, famines are not necessarily only the results of droughts, floods or wars; they can occur due to economic marginalization of the most vulnerable and poor citizens and because of failures in market integration.

Famines and Democracy

Another very important fact highlighted by Sen is that famines do not occur in democracies, but are common in countries governed by various forms of autocracies or dictatorships. This is a very significant fact. We cannot find a single example of a famine occurring in a democratic system with a relatively free press. Famines have occurred under colonial rule, as in India or Ireland under British control in the 19th and 20th centuries, in Communist regimes such as in China, the Soviet Union, Cambodia, or North Korea. In a healthy democracy with a free press, whenever natural disasters strike or food shortages occur, the government always mounts an emergency response that manages to avoid famine. While a democracy with a robust free press forces its leaders to respond to famine situations, a dictatorship does not have a free press, and it often makes a greater effort to repress information about a famine.

The North Korean Famine

One of the most recent examples of famine occurring under a dictatorship happened in the late 1990s in North Korea, one of the world's last remaining Communist regimes. Under the autocratic rule of Kim Il Sung and that of his son, Kim Jong Il, the country consistently suffered from an inefficient centrally planned economy, but the economic situation became grave in the early 1990s. The regime had been heavily subsidized by the Soviet Union, but following the collapse of Communism and the breakup of the USSR in 1991, Russia suspended its assistance to North Korea.

Thereafter, the regime decided to reduce grain rations to the population. The government launched an "eat only two meals per day" campaign and, by 1993, there were rumors of food riots. In 1994, rations were further cut, officially to 400–450 grams of grain per person, but according to refugees, rations may have been as low as 150 grams per person. As rations steadily grew smaller, the government organized campaigns to seize grain in the countryside. Rural households responded by hoarding, reducing grain production on the land they farmed collectively, and intensifying production on their own private plots. As a result, the food supply became even scarcer. Fuel shortages and deficiencies in the country's transportation infrastructure exacerbated the crisis.

Famine began to occur in many regions, while others were unaffected. Food supplies, including international food aid, began to appear on black markets. Only those able to pay high prices could purchase the additional food necessary to prevent starvation. Following a series of floods in 1995 and then a drought in 1996 that brought the agricultural system to its knees, an extreme famine occurred from 1996 to 1999. As many as 600,000 people may have died from starvation. More than 3 million people may have been impacted in some way by the famine. While the North Korean regime has consistently denied the famine, it clearly is unable to feed its citizens and its reliance on external aid continues to increase.

North Korea's famine resulted from an aggregate drop in agricultural output caused by loss of aid from Russia and by a series of floods and drought. It was, however, exacerbated by other elements: (1) entitlement failures resulted in many citizens becoming too poor to afford the minimum level of food; (2) the failure of market integration, as food did not circulate freely to those areas where shortages were the most acute; and (3) a dictatorial and oppressive regime with no accountability to its citizens.

Chapter Summary

Institutions and Market Development
We have analyzed the interaction between institutions and market development. Markets develop as transaction costs decrease. Informational and commitment problems associated with transactions that we identified in Chapter 7 are important for market development. In poor countries, formal institutions provide little assistance to market development; market participants have fewer reasons to use courts to resolve contractual disputes because the monetary stakes in a transaction are usually lower than the cost of legal remedies and contracts are often verbal, making judicial verification more difficult. Moreover, there are significant problems related to transport and communication infrastructure. Given the weakness of formal institutions in developing nations, business networks play an important role in market development, and relational contracting that involves long-term business relationships is ubiquitous.

The Emergence of Markets in Transition Countries
When prices were liberalized in Central and Eastern Europe after the fall of Communism, economists thought that markets would develop smoothly. However, there was a large initial output fall after price liberalization because of the absence of pre-existing market institutions that could have compensated for the disruption of existing production chains. Only China managed to avoid the output fall because of its dual-track liberalization system, keeping existing production plans at a predetermined level and encouraging enterprises to market any output above the planned level.

Rural Markets and the Monopsony Problem
Given the paucity of market development in emerging nations, farmers who want to market their output often face monopsony, markets controlled by a single buyer who is only willing to pay extremely

low prices for agricultural products. Monopsonists can hold up farmers and discourage them from making investments that improve agricultural productivity. Competition is often not sustainable because farming communities are too dispersed to sustain competition between buyers. Farmers have the opportunity to bypass monopsonists by forming marketing cooperatives. However, they often face severe collective-action problems when undertaking the establishment of a cooperative.

Market Integration

Markets are said to be integrated when the prices for the same product in different geographical areas move together. While prices need not be the same because transportation costs must be taken into account, to what extent prices for the same goods move in the same direction at the same time is an important criterion for market integration. We have analyzed three types of obstacles to market integration: communication obstacles, transportation obstacles, and regulatory obstacles. Lack of communication means that information on supply and demand in different areas is not efficiently transmitted and market adjustments

cannot take place. Lack of adequate transportation infrastructure can significantly hamper market development, while infrastructure investment contributes to market integration. Regulatory obstacles can be diverse and government authorities may constrain the movement of goods across geographical areas or jurisdictions, all of which create formidable obstacles to market integration.

Famines

There is a relationship between market development and famines, which do not generally occur because of actual shortages in food availability resulting from floods or droughts, but rather because of entitlement failures. In a famine, the weakest members of a society are excluded from food allocation either because they are too poor to afford enough food to survive or because they are given low priority in food distribution in families and communities. Low market development exacerbates famines. Famines have never occurred in democratic countries, suggesting that political accountability and a free press work to prevent them.

Key Terms

dual-track liberalization
entitlement set
investment specificity
market integration

market track
monopsony
plan track
search frictions

Review Questions

1. In this exercise and the next, we formalize the discussion of monopsony. Assume that a farmer can produce Q_L of output at a per unit cost c_L under a traditional technology. Assume that using a modern technology with investment I, the farmer can produce Q_H of output at a per unit cost c_H. Calculate the break-even price for the farmer under both technologies, that is, the price at which the farmer makes zero profits. What price level will encourage the farmer to invest in the new technology rather than the traditional one? What price can the monopsonist charge the farmer under both

technologies? What effect does this have on the investment choice of the farmer? Explain.

2. In this exercise, we examine the conditions under which monopsony is inevitable. Call p_M the market price that a trader can realize on the market and call T the transportation cost for moving goods from the village to the market. If there are two traders, assume that the probability one of them buys the goods from the farmer is 50% (alternatively, assume that the trader can only buy half of the farmer's output) but both traders will incur

transportation costs to the village and back to the market, whether or not they succeed in contracting with the farmer. Consider the minimum price at which the farmer makes no profit under the traditional as well as the new technology. What are the conditions of transportation costs for which profits are positive for a monopsonist but negative if there are two or more traders?

3. In this exercise, we analyze the dual-track system of price liberalization that was implemented in China. Assume a market in which supply and demand follow, respectively, the following equations: $P = 2 + 4Q$, $P = 14 - 2Q$. What are the equilibrium price and quantity? Assume that a quantity of 1 must be delivered at the planned price of 5 on the plan track. Draw the supply and demand curve. Basing your computations on Figure 14.2, draw the consumer surplus under the plan track (assuming that those with the greatest willingness to pay are served first), and then draw the consumer and producer surplus under price liberalization, where the equilibrium quantity is traded at the equilibrium price. How will total consumer plus producer surpluses under the dual-track system compare with total surplus under full-price liberalization, that is, the standard market equilibrium?

4. Read the following article by Marcus Noland: "Famine and Reform in North Korea," *Asian Economic Papers* 3(2) 2004: 1–40. Was the famine in North Korea associated with an aggregate fall in agricultural output? What are the main economic causes of the famine? On the basis of the information in the article, discuss how lack of market development and dictatorship may have exacerbated the food crisis.

5. Read the following article by Deepthi Kolady, Sujana Krishnamoorthy, and Sudha Narayanan: "India—Marketing Cooperatives in a New Retail Context: A Case Study of HOPCOMS" (http://www.regoverningmarkets.org/en/filemanager/active?fid=1024). According to this article, what benefits did farmers receive from marketing cooperatives?

6. Why do formal institutions provide little assistance to market development in poor countries?

7. Why do increases in oil prices lead to increases in food prices? Describe the various factors affected by rising oil prices that, in turn, contribute to rising food prices.

8. Do some online research to find what the spontaneous reactions of governments were to the food crisis of 2008. What effect did government reactions have on food markets? What institutional failure is the source of these reactions? What solution would you suggest to avoid similar problems in the future? Explain.

9. Why was the output fall in Central and Eastern Europe a surprise to economists? Use a standard supply and demand framework, assuming that the planned price is below the market equilibrium price. What does the supply and demand framework predict in terms of variation in output after price liberalization? Discuss the reasons given in the chapter for the output fall.

10. Download the following article by Elizabeth Roebling on trade at the border between Haiti and the Dominican Republic: http://www.ipsnews.net/2009/04/dominican-republic-haiti-border-market-embodies-inequalities/. Which facts in this article illustrate the themes that we have been analyzing in this chapter?

15

The Role of Credit Markets in Development

The Netrakona district in Bangladesh, with a population of 1.9 million, is bordered on the north by India. It is one of the country's poorest districts and highly vulnerable to flooding, similar to many other regions in this flat nation. Agriculture is the main economic activity and there is limited potential for the development of industry or the service sectors. About half of households make a meager living from farming small plots (less than one hectare), for the most part growing only rice. They would gain by adding vegetable and fruit crops, but they have no access to the credit they need to diversify. Their situation reflects that of hundreds of millions of poor farmers in developing countries.

Many Indian farmers have suffered from a different problem than that of the Bangladeshi farmers. A wave of suicides has swept the Indian countryside. Between 1997 and 2007, as many as 150,000 Indian farmers committed suicide, and the major cause was reported to have been an unbearable debt burden. Because of the Green Revolution that took place from the 1960s to the 1980s, farmers were able to make significant improvements in land productivity thanks to investments in fertilizer, new, highly productive strains of rice and other crops, irrigation systems, and more modern farming technologies. Loans for these new investments were, however, usually financed by local moneylenders, the only source of credit for most farmers, who charged a very high interest rate for loans. The high interest rates imposed a significant financial burden on farmers and when poor harvests made it impossible to service their debts fully, farmers had to sell their land and their belongings, sometimes even forcing their wives into prostitution. When nothing else was left to sell, desperate farmers chose to commit suicide.

These examples from Bangladesh and India are illustrative of some of the problems of credit markets in developing countries. Financial systems tend to be underdeveloped, a condition that is detrimental to economic development and social welfare. Efficiently functioning and equitable credit markets are important for development because they improve the allocation of capital. In the past, many developing countries have suffered from misallocation of capital; scarce government money was often given to inefficient, large-scale projects while poor farmers and aspiring small-scale entrepreneurs did not have access even to modest loans to start a family business.

As discussed in Chapter 7, credit relationships are rife with transactions costs. Informational asymmetries are present when lenders do not know the reliability of borrowers. Commitment problems are also a problem; borrowers may default after obtaining a loan. Because of these problems, banks are generally unwilling to lend unless a borrower puts up collateral to secure the debt. However, acquiring collateral is much more difficult in developing economies than in wealthier economies, in part because most people in developing nations are poor and do not have property. Even if they are fortunate enough to own a house or small parcel of land, they often cannot use it as acceptable collateral because of the absence of property titling systems. When borrowers do not have collateral, creditors sometimes agree to lend if they can closely monitor the use of the loan, but because monitoring is costly, creditors then charge high interest rates for the loans. This makes repayment more difficult and often leads to situations similar to the farmer suicides in India.

Given the difficulties of accessing credit in developing countries, special institutions have evolved to provide credit to the poor. A particular institutional innovation is that of **microcredit**, small loans made available to poor households and villages. Microcredit does not require collateral, but instead uses peer pressure from the local community to enforce loan repayment. This saves on the costs of monitoring the loan and provides the poor with cheap access to credit. The founder of one of the most successful microcredit firms, Muhammad Yunus of the Grameen Bank in Bangladesh, received the Nobel Peace Prize for his efforts to make credit available to his country's poor. Microcredit, as developed in Bangladesh, is only one of the forms of microfinance available in developing countries. In this chapter, we discuss the development of different forms of microfinance and how these various types of credit contribute to alleviating the problems of informational asymmetry and commitment. As we will see, microfinance also has its problems and banks providing microcredit have had a hard time achieving financial sustainability.

The Demand for Credit in Developing Economies

What are the main sources of demand for credit in developing economies? In countries where agriculture is the main source of economic activity, credit is important because of the time lag between purchasing inputs and receiving revenues from harvested crops. Farmers need to buy seeds, fertilizers, equipment, and other supplies up to a year before they receive revenues from their crops. More affluent farmers may not need credit if they can use their savings to purchase agricultural inputs in advance, but poor farmers rarely have enough savings.

In nonagricultural sectors, most enterprises incur both fixed and variable costs from the first day of operations until revenues are received at some future date. Entrepreneurs need credit for fixed capital expenditures such as manufacturing equipment, trucks, and computers, and they also need credit for working capital to cover rental payments, utility bills, wages, and the purchase of various supplies and materials.

Demand for credit is related not only to production expenses, but also to various household expenditures. Credit is needed for children's educational expenses and for various consumer items. In many countries, households spend a large amount of money, often a multiple of their annual income, for weddings and even, at times, for funerals. With economic development, the demand for consumer credit increases as households purchase electronics such as radios, televisions, cell phones, and home computers.

Demand for credit may also be related to the various unexpected economic shocks that households can experience. These are income disruptions such as a job loss, the death of the household's wage earner, or a fall in crop prices. There can also be expense shocks in the form of a sudden health problem or paying for damages that are the result of a natural disaster such as a flood, hurricane, or earthquake. Households generally cannot buy insurance coverage for protection against these risks, so they must borrow the money necessary to weather these adverse events.

The Theory of Credit Markets in Development

In order to understand problems with credit markets, we need to focus on the transaction costs associated with credit. These costs are related to informational and commitment problems. We will examine informational problems in this section and discuss commitment issues in the next section. We also discuss why these problems tend to be more acute in developing countries compared to developed countries.

As mentioned in Chapter 7, adverse selection and moral hazard are pervasive in credit markets because of informational asymmetries. Banks do not know the quality of borrowers, nor do they know what choices borrowers may make and how those choices will affect the likelihood of loan repayment.

Financing an Entrepreneur in Mumbai

To help us more clearly understand credit problems that arise from informational asymmetries, let us start with a numerical example. Assume two investment projects, one safe and the other risky, both requiring an investment of 100. Take the example of an Indian tailor in a big city such as Mumbai. With the safe project, the tailor would purchase sewing equipment to start a tailoring workshop. With the risky project, the tailor would purchase a car to start a taxi business. Obviously, both projects involve some risk. We assume, however, that the tailor is quite knowledgeable about supply and demand conditions in the tailoring business, but is relatively ignorant about these factors in the taxi business. He is curious about the taxi business because he has heard stories of people from his native region who have become quite successful as taxi drivers.

The safe project, in this case the tailoring shop, is assumed to yield a return of 150 with probability 1. Not only is there a high return (50%), but there is also no risk: the return is always the same, under any circumstances. However, the risky project, purchasing a car, yields a return of 280 with 50% probability and a return of 0 with 50% probability.[1] Because we will use this example extensively in this chapter, we represent it in Table 15.1.

Which project should the tailor choose? Let us assume that the tailor is **risk neutral**; that is, he bases his decision only on the expected return without taking the risk into account. The safe project has an expected return of 150 and the risky project has an expected return of $0.5 \times 280 + 0.5 \times 0 = 140$. Indeed, the expected return is equal to the return in the good state (280) times its

---

[1]These numbers are somewhat extreme, but they make things simpler.

TABLE 15.1   Choosing between a Safe and a Risky Project

	Safe project	Risky project
Investment required	100	100
Probability of high return	100%	50%
Probability of low return	0%	50%
High return	150	280
Low return	Not relevant	0
Expected return	150	140

The safe project earns 150 with probability 1, whereas the risky project earns 280 with a probability of 50% and 0 with a probability of 50%.

probability plus the return in the bad state (zero) times its probability.[2] The safe project thus has a higher expected return. This is the project any rational risk-neutral investor would choose. If the tailor is **risk averse,** then he will prefer the safe project even more because it has no risk, whereas the other project is clearly risky. Risk-averse people put more value on what they could lose than on what they could win. Losing 100 entails more utility loss (more dissatisfaction) to a risk-averse investor than winning 100 gives that investor a utility gain (more satisfaction).[3]

Assume that the tailor has no capital and must borrow 100 from the bank to finance the initial investment. Also assume that he must pay back 110 to the bank out of the return on the chosen project. We know that if the tailor did not have to borrow, he would choose the safe project because it brings the highest expected return. But if he must borrow, will he still choose the safe project? We will now show that this is not the case and that the tailor prefers to choose the risky project when borrowing from the bank!

With the safe project, the expected net return to the tailor after paying back the loan with interest is $150 - 110 = 40$. With the risky project, the expected net return is $0.5(280 - 110) + 0.5(0) = 85$. Indeed, if the outcome is good, the tailor gets 280 and must pay back the loan with interest. There is thus a net return of 170 and this occurs with 50% probability. However, there is also a 50% probability that the project yields zero return. In that case, the tailor cannot pay the bank back and the bank then faces a "bad loan" situation.

Because the tailor will only pay back the loan if it generates a return, and this happens with only a 50% probability, he will now prefer the risky project to the safe project because the former has an expected net return of 85 while the latter has an expected net return of 40. This is because of the **limited liability** of the tailor: he cannot be made liable for a larger amount than the money that

---

[2]When there is risk involved, economists use the term "state of the world" to refer to particular contingencies. In this example, we assume two states of the world: a good state and a bad state.

[3]Another way of looking at this is to consider two wagers that have the same expected return (say, winning and losing 100 with 50-50 probabilities and winning and losing 200 with the same probabilities); the risk-averse person always prefers the wager with less risk (here, choosing the wager with 100 rather than the wager with 200).

remains in his firm. In case he cannot pay back the loan, limited liability makes it impossible to extract any payment from him. The bank cannot seize his private assets or force him to work extra to pay back the loan.[4] If the tailor does not pay back the loan in the bad state, this induces him to prefer the risky project over the safe one. The bank would obviously prefer the tailor to choose the safe project because he will then pay back the loan with 100% probability. From the point of view of society, or social welfare, it would also be better if the tailor were to choose the safe project because the total return to both the tailor and the bank is then higher. We thus conclude from this example that when an agent borrows and has limited liability, he may have an incentive to choose a risky project over a safe one and this may be bad from the point of view of social welfare.

This example also helps us to distinguish between adverse selection and moral hazard, concepts already introduced in Chapter 7. Adverse selection arises when a bank faces loan demands for both safe and risky projects, and has no information about the quality or risk of the individual projects. Adverse selection means that when interest rates rise, entrepreneurs with safe projects stop asking for loans so that the bank only faces risky projects. Moral hazard arises when the bank cannot observe the choices borrowers make between safe and risky projects. Moral hazard means that the borrower will likely choose the risky project with its possibility of higher returns, whereas the bank would prefer the borrower choose the safe project. Note that the example above is formulated as a case of moral hazard.

Moral hazard in the lending relationship does not mean that the borrower will always choose a risky project with a higher expected return over a safe project. The borrower may, for example, engage in an unobserved level of effort and this choice may affect the probability of the expected returns. If, in the example discussed above, the tailor chooses to put low effort into the risky project, it would yield 280 with 50% probability and zero with 50% probability. If, instead, he chooses a high level of effort, then the project would yield 280 with 80% probability and zero with 20% probability.

Adverse Selection and Credit Rationing

Let us first discuss the case of adverse selection. Assume that 50% of entrepreneurs have a risky project (280 return with 50% probability and zero return with 50% probability) and the other 50% have a safe project (150 with 100% probability). Assume that a bank knows the types of projects and their proportions, but does not know which borrower has a safe or a risky project. If the bank did have this information, it would only lend to those borrowers with safe projects. When the bank considers making a loan, a firm's project could thus be either risky (with 50% probability) or safe (with 50% probability). How much would the bank have to charge in interest so as not to lose money, that is, in order to realize a loan repayment of 100?

---

[4]Note that even when there are no limited liability laws in developing countries, small entrepreneurs in urban areas can find ways to run away from their obligations to a bank and reemerge elsewhere in a city and go on with their lives. By doing so, they shield themselves from the downside aspects of risky projects.

Call B the sum of the principal and the interest. The bank knows that 50% of projects are safe and they would pay back B. There are also 50% of projects that are risky and they would only pay back in 50% of the cases. In other words, the probability of the bank being paid back is only 50% plus 50% of 50%, or 75% in total. As a result, the bank recovers its money if the following equation holds:

$$0.75B = 100 \rightarrow B = 100/0.75 = 133.3.$$

Thus, due to lack of information about the quality of the given projects and a 25% delinquency rate, the bank would have to charge an minimum interest rate of 33.3% for all loans in order to get back 100% of its original investment.

Assume now that at an interest rate of 33.3%, there is excess demand for loans. In other words, the total demand for loans is higher than what the bank is able to lend. What happens if the lender charges a higher interest rate? We might think that this would increase the bank's profits as long as the total demand for loans is higher than the supply of loans. This is the standard lesson we learn from traditional supply and demand analysis. If I am selling raincoats, I am better off increasing my price as long as I can sell all the raincoats I have in stock. Not so for banking! Increasing the interest rate can decrease the bank's profits.

As soon as the interest rate becomes higher than 50%, the demand for loans to fund the safe projects disappears and only the demand for the risky loans remain. Indeed, at an interest rate above 50%, the safe project would yield 150, but the entrepreneur would have to pay back more than 150. The safe project becomes unprofitable. The demand for risky projects would, however, still be present. Referring to the example we have used so far, the risky project yields 280 with 50% probability, and because the borrower must pay back 150, the expected net return becomes (280 − 150) = 130 times 50%, or 65. Recall that with 50% probability, the project yields zero and the borrower cannot pay back the loan. We can thus see that at an interest rate of 50%, borrowing for a safe project becomes unprofitable, while borrowing for a risky project remains profitable. In this case, an increase in the interest rate above 50% leads to adverse selection: the demand for safe loans disappears while the demand for risky loans remains. This is called adverse selection because it is the opposite of what we would want the market to do, which is finance the safe projects and not the risky ones.

Increasing the interest rate above 50% decreases the expected profits of the bank. The bank would only be paid back half of the time instead of 75% of the time. In other words, the bank would now incur losses even though the interest rate is higher. An interest rate of 100% (= 200 × 0.5) would then be necessary in order for the bank to break even. In this case, it would be better, for example, to charge an interest rate of 40% instead of an interest rate of, for example, 60%. With an interest rate of 40%, the bank would receive a return of 140 × 0.75 = 105. It would also make a profit of 5. With an interest rate of 60%, the probability of a borrower paying back a loan is only 50% because the only loans in demand are for the risky projects. In this situation, the bank gets back 160 × 0.5 = 80. The bank then incurs a loss because it lends 100 and is only paid back 80.

Because low interest rates encourage a high demand for loans, a bank may decide to **ration credit**, that is, not satisfy all demand for credit if that demand is higher than what the bank is willing to supply. Credit rationing occurs every day. Potential borrowers are always anxious that a bank may not approve their loan applications. Indeed, loan applications are routinely refused by banks. In contrast, this rationing does not generally happen on markets for goods. When someone enters a shop to buy a raincoat, it is rare that the merchant will refuse to sell the merchandise; it only happens if the raincoats are out of stock. However, credit rationing is in the best interests of a bank and it is the corollary of setting an interest rate at which not all demand can be satisfied.

How broadly can we apply the reasoning we have used so far? Is it just a consequence of the particular numbers of our examples? The logic is, in fact, quite general. As soon as banks lack information about the quality of borrowers, the logic of our arguments will apply.

Moral Hazard and Collateral

Let us now turn to the case of moral hazard using the same example we discussed above. With adverse selection, some borrowers had safe projects and others had risky ones, but the bank had no information on who had which type of loan. With moral hazard, borrowers can choose between the safe and the risky project, and the bank cannot observe what choice they make.

We have seen that if an entrepreneur has to borrow 100 to finance a project, he or she has an incentive to choose the risky project because limited liability acts as an insurance against failure. Indeed, the loan will not be repaid if the entrepreneur does not have the funds to do so. If every borrower chooses the risky project, the failure rate of those projects would be 50%, the probability of failure. The bank would thus have to charge an interest of 100 in order to break even.

How can a bank mitigate moral hazard? The most obvious way is by taking **collateral** against the loan, assets that the borrower permits contractually to be seized in case the loan does not get repaid. If the borrower agrees to collateralize his or her assets to the full extent of the loan, it means that in case of failure, the bank has the right to seize the collateralized assets in order to recover the value of the loan, the interest on it, and any other possible fees that might be included. Take the case of an Indian farmer who can either invest in growing a safe or a risky type of crop. If his land is collateralized, the lender can seize the land in case of the farmer's default.

Collateral reduces the risk for the bank because it ensures that the loan will be paid back. It also changes the incentive of the borrower. Assume that the borrower has a collateral of 100 or more, say 110. With collateral, the borrower will prefer the safe project to the risky project. The safe project yields a net return of $150 - 110 = 40$ with an interest rate of 10%. With the same interest rate, the risky project yields $0.5(280 - 110) + 0.5(0 - 110) = 85 - 55 = 30$. The borrower now prefers to choose the safe project. Note that collateral aligns the interest of the borrower with that of social welfare: it induces the borrower to choose the project with the highest expected return.

The use of collateral reduces the risks of lending in two ways. First, it mitigates the risk of the borrower defaulting on the loan because collateral works like an insurance policy that protects the bank from that risk. Second, it eliminates the borrower's incentive to choose a risky project because of limited liability. Indeed, collateral presents a downside risk for the borrower that is absent under limited liability.

Note also that a bank can charge a lower interest rate to borrowers with collateral. Without collateral, the bank would have to charge an interest rate of 100 in order to break even because there would be a 50% chance that a loan will not be repaid because of moral hazard. With collateral, an interest rate of 0 is enough to break even.

Providing collateral is more difficult in developing countries than in wealthier nations because most people in emerging economies are too poor to have wealth they can use as collateral. There are additional obstacles for banks, as well. Take the example of the Indian tailor who borrows to establish a taxi business. In the case of default, the bank may seize the taxi. However, the tailor may instead disappear with the taxi and work in the informal economy in another city, making it nearly impossible for the bank to find him. Seizing land as collateral in a rural village is also less attractive for a bank. The land is only of value if the bank can resell it and in a poor village, there may be no one who has the money to buy the land. Moreover, villagers may protest the seizure of the land, resulting in a costly foreclosure operation for the bank. The bank may also decide that a poor farmer's land has little or no collateral value and will deny the farmer's loan application. At that point, credit rationing would occur, as discussed above.

Moral Hazard and Monitoring

Monitoring is another tool for preventing moral hazard that can be more useful in the context of the development of credit markets. A bank may closely monitor the use of a loan in order to obtain information about the borrower's choices. Monitoring may alleviate, or even eliminate, informational asymmetries, but it comes at a cost for the bank.

Let us continue to use the example we have discussed above. Assume that if the bank spends 40 on monitoring, it can make sure the borrower chooses the safe project instead of the risky one. In that case, the bank will lend only if it gets at least 140 back. If it charges 150 (with an interest rate of 50%), it only gets 10 back as interest. The disadvantage of monitoring is its cost, which drives up the interest rate. With monitoring, the bank would have to charge a higher interest rate to break even than it would charge for a loan secured with collateral. Even in a situation without collateral, monitoring still brings down the interest rate compared to a situation of unconditional lending and moral hazard. Indeed, with unconditional lending, the bank has to charge an interest rate of 100% to break even, whereas with monitoring, the minimum interest rate is only 40%. As long as the cost of monitoring is lower than the minimum interest rate under unconditional lending, monitoring is advantageous.

In general, monitoring works better for larger rather than smaller loans because regardless of the size of the loan, the costs of monitoring will often be comparable as those costs are frequently fixed. Imagine a project twice the size of the example we have been discussing so far. The project would thus cost 200 and bring a safe return of 300. If the cost of monitoring is still 40, the minimum charge to break even is 240, which represents an interest rate of 20% (40/200) instead of 40% for a project half the size. Loan monitoring tends to be more advantageous for large projects and less advantageous for small projects if there is a fixed cost of monitoring, independent of the project's size.

This presents a problem in developing countries because the size of the loans needed in these nations tends to be small due to the small scale of farming and entrepreneurial operations.

Thus, as tools to fight moral hazard, both collateral and monitoring tend to work less efficiently in the development context either because people are too poor to have acceptable collateral or because the loans they need are too small and involve monitoring costs that are high relative to the size of the loan.

Monitoring and Variation in Interest Rates

In developing countries, banks and other lenders can charge borrowers very different interest rates. People who deposit their money in a bank may also receive very different rates for those deposits. A large variation in interest rates is often observed within the same region, town, or village—or even within the same industrial or economic sector (textile, transport, catering, etc.). Loan contracts in India's rural sector may vary between 24% and 48% on an annual basis. Amil Dasgupta's *Report on Informal Credit Markets in India: Summary* reported that professional moneylenders in rural areas, who provide about three-quarters of the commercial loans outside the formal banking sector, were charging interest rates between 36% and 60% or more.[5] In other countries, similar findings emerge; lower interest rates are usually charged on larger loans, typically those made to wealthier borrowers, while higher interest rates are charged on smaller loans, often those made to less affluent individuals.

This variation in interest rates is consistent with the importance of loan monitoring. If the monitoring costs of a loan are primarily fixed, then it is relatively more costly to monitor smaller loans than larger ones. Therefore, it is reasonable to expect that higher interest rates are charged for smaller loans and lower interest rates are charged for larger loans. If those who apply for larger loans also have collateral, then they would likely be charged an even smaller interest rate. In any case, it is apparent that loan monitoring plays an important role in developing economies. Small loans and the resulting need for monitoring are thus important reasons for high interest rates.

An alternative explanation for variation in interest rates might be monopolistic lending. In advanced market economies, the difference between rates on loans and rates on deposits, called the **intermediation margin**, is usually taken as a measure of the level of competitiveness in the banking sector. The higher the margin, the less competitive the banking sector and vice versa. A high intermediation margin is often observed in developing countries, but it is not always a sign of monopolistic lending. Borrowers often have a choice between various lenders, even when they live in small villages.[6]

---

[5]Amil Dasgupta, *Report on Informal Credit Markets in India: Summary* (New Delhi: National Institute of Public Finance and Policy, 1989): 140.

[6]See, for example, Abhijit V. Banerjee, "Contracting Constraints, Credit Markets and Economic Development," (working paper, Massachusetts Institute of Technology, Cambridge, MA, 2001). Also see Mathias Dewatripont, Lars P. Hansen, and Stephen J. Turnovsky, eds., *Advances in Econometrics: Theory and Applications,* vol. 3, Eighth World Congress of the Econometric Society (Cambridge: Cambridge University Press, 2003): 1–46.

Dealing with Default

Default is a risk that banks face when they loan money. One reason for default might be that an economic project does not generate enough return to repay a loan. Another might be that the borrower decides not to pay back a loan. This is called **strategic default**, a situation in which the borrower is able to fulfill his debt obligations but decides not to. Think of the example of the taxi driver who decides to run away and not pay back his loan. His decision might be the consequence of not having enough money to repay the bank, but he might also choose to run away even though he could, in principle, service his loan.

Seen this way, default is a commitment problem. Imagine that the borrower has limited liability and that the value of the outstanding loan is higher than whatever assets the bank can seize from him. The borrower may choose to default out of self-interest. This is economic opportunism, but it is economically rational. After the 2008 collapse of housing prices in the United States, many households that were "underwater" with a mortgage higher than the market value of their homes, decided to walk away from their mortgages. This type of behavior can be observed in both developing and developed economies.

Default due to a commitment problem does not necessarily entail an informational problem, as is the case with adverse selection and moral hazard. The bank might have been monitoring the activities of the borrower and how he or she made use of the bank loan. The bank may be perfectly aware that the borrower is defaulting for strategic reasons, but may be unable to prove in court where the money has gone, or the cost of locating it might be too high to warrant the expense. The borrower may disappear or even simply hide the money and declare bankruptcy. As a result, the bank might not be able to get its money back, even though it knows that there has been a strategic default.

How can banks enforce loan repayment and avoid strategic defaults by borrowers? Monitoring is obviously not an adequate solution unless the bank knows exactly where the money is. Collateral is a possible instrument to protect against strategic default; if the bank can seize assets equivalent to what it is owed, there is a clear incentive for the borrower to repay the loan. In the absence of credible forms of collateral, the only instrument that may help is a borrower's reputation for honesty. If a borrower has a solid history of loan repayment, then the bank will likely lend to that person even in the absence of collateral. The debtor will not want to default because of a damaged reputation and the inability to borrow in the future. Unfortunately, reputation is no help for those who have not had the opportunity to build a history of reliable loan repayment.

Contrary to what we might expect, loan defaults are rather low in developing countries. A study by Irfan Aleem showed that the median rate of default in Pakistan was between 1% and 2%.[7] Most studies also tend to find that the costs of default are rather small in emerging economies. This suggests that the diversity of interest rates observed in developing countries cannot be

---

[7]Irfan Aleem, "Imperfect Information, Screening, and the Costs of Informal Lending: A Study of a Rural Credit Market in Pakistan," *The World Bank Economic Review* 4, no. 3 (1990): 329–349.

explained, or can be explained only partially, by the need of creditors to charge higher interest rates in order to cover losses from defaults.

Does that mean that default is not an issue in these nations? Not necessarily. It may be that the fear of default is an important reason why lenders refuse to make loans. Nevertheless, how can we explain the low observed default rate? The most probable explanation seems to be that borrowers value the reputation of being creditworthy that results from repeated applications for credit and subsequent loan repayments. Monitoring may also be at work to reduce the default rate.

Credit Constraints in Developing Countries

The discussion of the theory of credit markets suggests that credit constraints should be important in developing countries. But in reality, how significant are they? How much do they impede economic development?

A firm is credit constrained if it is unable to obtain all the credit it wants at the going interest rate. If a firm has a project that will generate a higher return than the market interest rate, it will want to invest in that project but may be prevented from doing so because of credit constraints. Credit-constrained firms will thus always have a marginal product of capital that is higher than the market interest rate. Remember that the marginal product of capital is the additional return from an additional unit of capital.

The Difficulty of Measuring Credit Constraints

It is difficult to identify empirically whether a firm is credit constrained. Information is needed on both the demand for credit by that firm and the supply of credit to the same firm in order to verify whether the demand for credit at the going interest rate exceeds the supply of credit. When demand is not satisfied, measuring demand is very challenging because it is not directly observed. How then do economists measure credit demand?

Many surveys ask firms about their credit demand to see whether they would want to borrow more than what a bank might offer. However, these types of questions generally deliver unreliable answers. Firms might say they would like to borrow more but do not really have the serious intention to do so, as answering positively costs nothing. Survey answers could thus overestimate the extent of credit constraints.

A survey might ask firms if they were turned down for credit and by how much. This seems to be a better way of gauging the seriousness of firms' credit demand intentions. However, many firms might decide not to submit a credit application because they expect to be turned down. In this case, using this type of question to measure the extent of credit constraints could underestimate the true extent of credit constraints.

Because using survey questions to measure credit constraints is not very reliable, researchers have developed other, more indirect methods. One procedure is to perform regressions of current investment on past profit. If the regression coefficient is positive and significant, this is seen as evidence of credit constraints and it means that, in the past, a firm wanted to invest, but was unable to do so because of credit constraints; only when profits increased could the firm finance some or all of its proposed investment by using retained earnings. This method of identifying credit constraints is based on the idea that there is, in general, no reason that investment should depend on past profits; rather, the desired investment of a firm should depend on its expectations of future profits. Therefore, if a firm is not credit constrained, its investment demand should not, in principle, be correlated to its past profits.

This reasoning does not address the fact that profits can often be **serially correlated**; that is, past, present, and future profits might be correlated. For example, assume that a firm works in a sector such as the production of cell phones where demand continues to expand. In the past, expanding demand has allowed the firm to make profits and it expects to increase those profits in the future. The firm would still make its investments on the basis of future expected profits. However, future expected profits are correlated with past profits because of demand expansion. An econometric analysis would thus find a positive correlation between investments and past profits. This correlation would not, however, necessarily be due to credit constraints, but rather to serial correlation of profits. Significant positive regression coefficients may thus significantly exaggerate the effect of credit constraints.

There are other ways to measure credit constraints indirectly. Say that someone unexpectedly inherits money and subsequently makes an investment. This would be indicative of credit constraints because the inheritance acts as a substitute for credit. If there had not been any credit constraint, there would be no reason that an investment should be linked to an unexpected inheritance. Another example might be a firm that experiences a "cash flow shock," a surprise inflow of cash as a result of many clients paying accounts receivable at the same time. In this case as well, if there is a correlation between positive cash flow shocks and investment, it would be indicative of credit constraints. However, the objection that profits can be serially correlated (i.e., correlated over time) may apply in this case, too. The surprise cash flow may be a signal of future profitability and lead the firm to invest. Here again, a correlation between cash flow shocks and investment may not be due only to credit constraints.

Exploiting the Indian Priority Lending Reform

For all the reasons just discussed, it is difficult to develop a reliable measure for the extent of credit constraints and researchers need a lot of ingenuity to come up with a convincing measure for them. One example is a study by Abhijit Banerjee and Esther Duflo that exploits a reform, implemented in 1998 in India, that was meant to improve access to subsidized credit.[8] Before 1998, India had a "priority lending" program in which banks, whether public or private, were

---

[8]Abhijit Banerjee and Esther Duflo, "Do Firms Want to Borrow More? Testing Credit Constraints Using a Directed Lending Program" (working paper, Massachusetts Institute of Technology, Cambridge, MA, 2004).

required to allocate at least 40% of their net credit to sectors of the economy designated by the government to have "priority" status. These included agriculture, agricultural processing, transportation, and small-scale industries. The interest rate on priority lending was typically lower than the market rate.

In January 1998, the government changed the definition of the small-scale industrial sector. Previously, only firms with a total investment in plant and machinery below 6.5 million rupees were included. The reform extended the definition to include firms with investment in plants and machinery up to 30 million rupees. In January 2000, the reform was then partially undone by a new change: firms with investment in plants and machinery above 10 million rupees were excluded from the priority sector. Thus, from 1998 onward, all firms with investment between 6.5 and 10 million rupees benefited from priority lending, while between 1998 and 2000, firms with investments between 10 and 30 million rupees also benefited from priority lending.

These changes provided an opportunity to measure the extent of credit constraints for Indian firms affected by the reform. If there were credit rationing, firms in the category between 10 and 30 million rupees should have benefited from the 1998 reforms and received loans to which they would not previously have had access. After the 2000 reform, they would have lost access to that credit. The additional credit received by these firms between 1998 and 2000 would thus be a good measure of the extent of their credit constraints. Because these were relatively large firms, because lending to large firms is relatively less costly than lending to small firms (see our discussion above on monitoring costs), and because banks needed to allocate 40% of their loans to priority lending, the banks would certainly have been willing to lend to those firms after the 1998 reform.

We need some initial theoretical analysis in order to interpret the evidence provided by Banerjee and Duflo correctly. Assume a firm must pay a fixed cost C to start production. Call k the level of investment necessary to produce output represented by $F(k)$. We now introduce two definitions: First, if a firm wanted to borrow more than a lender was willing to lend at a given interest r, we would say that a firm is **credit rationed**. Second, we would say that a firm is **credit constrained** if the borrower wanted to borrow more than *all possible* lenders were willing to lend at a given interest r. In order to make those two definitions operational, assume that there are only two lenders, a bank and the "market." The former lends at rate r_b and the latter at rate r_m, where $r_b < r_m$. This assumption reflects the fact that under the priority lending program, firms obtained loans at an interest rate that was lower than the market rate.

Figure 15.1 illustrates the case of a firm that is credit rationed but not credit constrained. The horizontal axis represents k, the amount of capital invested. The vertical axis measures the marginal product of capital $F'(k)$. The marginal product of capital is decreasing and therefore downward sloping: as the firm increases the size of its investment, the last unit of capital adds less to output than the previous unit of capital. Assume that, initially, at interest rate r_b, the supply of capital to the firm is limited to k_{b0} and that at interest r_m, the firm can borrow as much as it wants. The firm is thus credit rationed with the bank, but is not credit constrained because it can borrow as much as it wants on the market. Under those conditions, the firm's total demand for credit is

FIGURE 15.1   A Credit-Rationed Firm

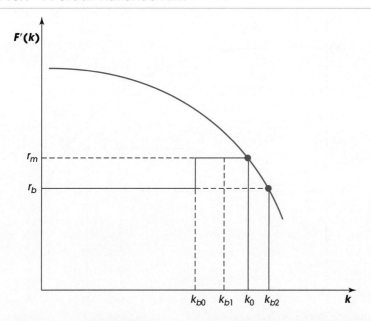

A firm can borrow k_{bo} from the bank at rate r_b and the difference up to k_0 at rate r_m. At k_0, the firm's total demand for credit is satisfied as the marginal product of capital is equal to r_m. The firm is credit rationed but not credit constrained. If the bank extends its credit to $k_{b1} > k_{b0}$, total credit demand by the firm remains at k_0.

k_0. Indeed, k_0 is the level of capital at which the marginal product of capital is equal to the market interest rate r_m. For a level of capital above k_0, the marginal product is lower than the interest rate, which means that the firm would lose money from investing above k_0. The firm would thus borrow k_{b0} at the lower rate r_b and the difference between k_0 and k_{b0} at rate r_m.

Now assume that the firm can borrow the higher amount k_{b1} from the bank, where $k_{b1} < k_0$. In this case, the firm will borrow k_{b1} at rate r_b and the difference between k_0 and k_{b1} at rate r_m. The firm's total demand for credit remains at k_0, but it now borrows more from the bank and less from the market. The total demand for credit by the firm stays the same. Because the firm simply reallocates its credit portfolio, the higher availability of credit from the bank does not have any effect on the firm's output. In other words, when a firm is credit rationed but not credit constrained, a lower rationing of credit does not have an effect on the total demand for credit and thus on the firm's output level.

Now consider the case of a firm that is credit-constrained, as illustrated in Figure 15.2. In contrast to the previous case, it is assumed that the firm is also rationed on the credit market. Initially, it can only borrow k_{b0} at rate r_b and it can only borrow up to k_0 at rate r_m on the market. At k_0, the marginal product of capital is higher than r_m. The firm would therefore like to borrow more but is not able to do so. It is not only credit rationed, it is also credit constrained. In this case, if the bank increases the supply of capital it is willing to lend to the

FIGURE 15.2   A Credit-Constrained Firm

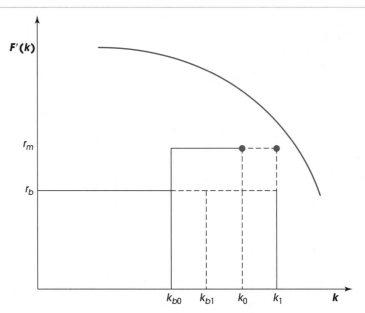

A firm can borrow k_{b0} from the bank at rate r_b and the difference up to k_0 at rate r_m. Its total demand for credit is not satisfied, as the marginal product of capital at k_0 is higher than r_m. The firm is credit rationed and credit constrained. If the bank extends its credit to $k_{b1} > k_{b0}$, total credit given to the firm increases from to k_0 to k_1.

firm from k_{b0} to k_{b1}, then the effect will be to increase the total investment of the firm from k_0 to k_1. This results in an effect on output because the total level of capital invested in the firm increases.

   To summarize the discussion, a firm that is only credit rationed but not credit constrained will take more credit at the subsidized rate, if offered, but it will not increase its total level of investment and output. On the other hand, a firm that is credit constrained will increase its investment and output when offered more credit at the subsidized rate.

   Banerjee and Duflo tested these predictions on a database that included 249 Indian firms with investments between 6.5 and 30 million rupees. These firms received increases in working capital after 1998, while those with capital between 10 and 30 million rupees were subject to a reduction in working capital after 2000. Between 1998 and 2000, firms did not experience a significant fall in interest rates. This means that the increase in working capital was not due to a fall in interest rates, but to the reform in the rules for priority lending. The most important finding is that the expansion of loans for larger firms was not associated with a significant fall in market lending. Increased lending was associated with an increase in output as measured by sales. These results suggest not only the existence of credit rationing for firms, but also the clear presence of credit constraints. Further studies are likely to show that credit constraints are pervasive in developing countries.

Microfinance

Microfinance is an institutional innovation that has emerged in developing economies in response to the pervasiveness of credit constraints faced by small firms and poor households. Microfinance was featured in the news in 2006, when the Nobel Peace Prize was awarded to Muhammad Yunus, founder of the Grameen Bank, a lending institution he created in Bangladeshi communities to provide microcredit, small loans to poor households and villages. Microcredit has been present for decades in many countries and has even spread to wealthy nations. There are many microcredit associations in the United States and globally, more than 10 million households benefit from microcredit. In 1976, while visiting the village of Jobra in Bangladesh, Yunus found that women who were producing bamboo furniture had to take out loans at very high interest rates to buy their bamboo. He then lent US$27 to 42 women in the village, a small sum, and was positively surprised to be repaid in time. In 1983, he founded the Grameen Bank with the purpose of providing small loans to the rural poor in Bangladeshi communities. The Grameen Bank in Bangladesh currently serves 5 million borrowers and it is interesting to note that the clients of the bank are primarily women. Microcredit is often seen as one of the success stories in development. It can finance the purchase of a cell phone, small tools, raw materials, seeds, livestock, and, more rarely, a car or a truck. The credit requested is often below $100, a relatively small sum for a loan.

Microcredit is a very promising institutional innovation because it provides solutions to two of the most common financial problems present in developing economies: the absence of collateral and the high costs of monitoring small loans.

How Does Microcredit Work?

There are many different types of credit contracts offered by microcredit institutions around the world. These contracts share many common features, but can also have unique characteristics. One very important feature is that no collateral is required of borrowers. This is critical because, as we have discussed, collateral is not readily available in developing countries to curb moral hazard and to facilitate lending at low interest rates.

A second and very important feature of microcredit is **group lending**. A bank approves a loan to a group of people in a village or neighborhood. The composition of the group is usually decided by the villagers or the residents of the neighborhood. The members of the group are then jointly responsible for paying back the loan. There are many variants of group lending; for example, one type provides specific loans only to certain people in a group, but all members of the group are liable for repayment. Say that 10 people have borrowed 100 each. If 1 of the 10 does not repay his or her loan, the nine others who have received loans have to pay an additional 100/9 each. This group responsibility imposes a discipline on the group and on each of its members, but for poor people the alternative to group lending is most often no loans at all. Group lending resolves both the lack of collateral and the monitoring problems. Group liability becomes a substitute for collateral. Even if individuals are poor, the community is usually able to come up with a sum to repay the bank in case of default by one person. In addition, monitoring is done by the people in the village or neighborhood who are jointly liable for the loan. They have an incentive to ensure that no members of the group default or make bad decisions because everyone would suffer the consequences. Local ties are thus used to monitor and discipline those who make use of the microcredit loans.

A third characteristic of microcredit is called **progressive lending**. A group may initially receive a rather small loan, but the size of the loan can increase over time as the group demonstrates its reliability as it pays back the original amount. The size of the loan can thus become progressively larger.

Finally, a fourth characteristic present in most microcredit contracts is a very strict and regular reimbursement schedule. As soon as a loan contract is signed, repayment begins immediately and payments are often made on a weekly basis.

Incentive Properties of Microcredit

In numerous publications, economists have analyzed the specific features of microcredit contracts. We will now discuss some of the most important incentive properties of these contracts.

A first incentive effect is that microcredit helps to prevent moral hazard. Recall that when discussing moral hazard, we assumed that the borrower could either choose a safe or a risky project. In the example used in this chapter, the borrower has an incentive to choose the risky project because limited liability artificially increases that project's expected return to the borrower, whereas in reality the safe project has a higher expected return. With group lending, members of the group are liable for the individual borrower's choices and thus have the incentive to do everything they can to pressure the borrower into choosing a safer project.

To illustrate the importance of incentives to microcredit lending, let us again consider the example previously discussed in this chapter. The safe project would yield 150 for an outlay of 100 and the risky project would yield 280 with 50% probability and zero with 50% probability. Assume that the interest rate is equal to 10%, so that 110 must be paid back after the return on the project has been realized. Remember that with limited liability, the net payoff to the borrower for the risky project would be $0.5(280 - 110) = 85$, while the net payoff for the safe project would be $150 - 110 = 40$. Now assume a group with two borrowers, A and B. Also assume that if one of them fails, the other must pay 100 as part of the joint liability contract. Say that A chooses the project and that B is liable (the converse reasoning will, of course, also hold). A gains $85 - 40 = 45$ from choosing the risky project over the safe project. However, B is expected to lose 50. As a result, B, who can observe A's choices, would thus be prepared to pay up to 50 in order to convince A to choose the safe project and could possibly do so by offering to pay A a sum above 45. Joint liability effectively creates incentives to choose the safe rather than the risky project and is thus good protection against moral hazard.

A second incentive effect is sorting borrowers into risk groups, with those individuals preferring less risk forming a group that will not accept potential borrowers inclined to take on riskier projects. Borrowers favoring more risk would then form their own group. Group lending takes advantage of the tendency of people to self-sort into homogeneous risk groups and provides good protection from adverse selection. But why do borrowers have this tendency to self-sort?

Assume that there are four borrowers, A, B, C, and D, and that A and B each have a safe project in which they want to invest. Let us change our example slightly and assume that the safe project would yield 210 with 85% probability and zero with 15% probability. We assume that C and D each have a risky project proposal that would yield, as in previous examples, 280 with 50% probability and zero with 50% probability. If we compare the two projects, we see that the risky one has a higher probability of failure but a higher payoff if it is successful. Note that the expected net return from both projects is the same and is equal to $0.85(210 - 110) = 0.5(280 - 110) = 85$. Will A and B with their safe projects join forces or will they each team with one of the borrowers with a risky project? Assume again that the interest rate is 10%. Assume also that there is a joint liability of 50. A has a safe project; by teaming with B, A would receive $0.85(210 - 110 - 0.15 \times 50) = 78.625$. However, if A wanted to team with C, A would only receive $0.85(210 - 110 - 0.5 \times 50) = 63.75$.

The clearest way to look at this is to consider A's expected cost of teaming with B or C. If A teams with B and is successful, which happens with 85% probability, there is still a 15% probability that B is not successful, in which case A is liable for B's failure. The expected cost of teaming with B is thus $0.85 \times 0.15 \times 50 = 6.375$. On the other hand, if A teams with C, in case of success for A, there is still a 50% probability that C fails. In that case, A is liable. The expected cost for A of teaming with C is thus $0.85 \times 0.5 \times 50 = 21.25$, which is considerably larger. It is then apparent that A would likely prefer to team with B rather than C. In other words, with group lending, borrowers with a safe project prefer to team with those who also have a safe project rather than with those who have a risky project.

It is also the case that those borrowers with a risky project may want to team with those with a safe project. However, it takes two to tango. Borrowers with a safe project will prefer the opportunity to team with those who also have a safe project. Now, couldn't those with a risky project pay those with a safe project to team up with them? Given the principle of group lending and the effect of sorting, we can demonstrate that this proposition would be too expensive (see the box on the next page on group lending and sorting). In effect, the sorting is done as a result of the pressures created by joint liability: the conservative borrower who teams with a risky borrower is more likely to be liable for any bad returns from the latter's project.

The progressive lending aspect of microcredit also has powerful incentive effects: it creates good incentives to avoid default, eliminates informational asymmetries over time, and reduces risk. Let us review these in turn. First of all, the cost of defaulting on a loan today is higher if you know you could be eligible in the future for a larger loan if you reliably make payments on your current loan. This dynamic incentive is quite strong; why default on $100 today if repayment means you could borrow $10,000 in the future? There are people who would prefer to default in the absence of progressive lending but who would avoid default with progressive lending. Reducing the incentive to default on a loan is a significant advantage of progressive lending.

Group Lending and Sorting

Algebra helps us to understand the logic of how group lending leads borrowers to self-sort into different risk groups. Assume two types of projects, one risky and the other safe. The safe project has a probability of success p_s, in which case there is a return R_s. In case of failure, the return is zero. The risky project has a probability of success p_r that is smaller than $p_s (p_r < p_s)$, but the return R_r is higher than $R_s (R_r > R_s)$. For simplicity, we assume that the expected return is the same in both cases: $p_s R_s = p_r R_r$. Agent A, with a safe project, teaming with agent B, also with a safe project, would have an expected return of $p_s[R_s - r - (1 - p_s)c]$, where r is the interest rate and c is the joint liability payment that would have to be paid to the bank if B's project fails. Note that A will pay c only in case he or she is successful and B is unsuccessful. If both are unsuccessful, they cannot pay back c.

Now, if agent A would team with agent C who has a risky project, A would have an expected return of $p_s[R_s - r - (1 - p_r)c]$. When we calculate the difference between both expressions, we find that the gain for A of teaming with a borrower with a safe project rather than with a borrower with a risky project is $p_s(p_s - p_r)c$. This expression is positive because $p_s > p_r$.

Let us now look at the gain for agent C with a risky project of teaming with a borrower with a safe project. Using the same logic as above, we find that this return is equal to $p_r[R_r - r - (1 - p_s)c]$. Similarly, the return to C from teaming with agent D's risky project is $p_r[R_r - r(1 - p_r)c]$. The gain from teaming with the safe project (the difference between the two expressions) is thus $p_r(p_s - p_r)c$. This expression is also positive. Note, however, that $p_r(p_s - p_r)c < p_s(p_s - p_r)c$, because $p_r < p_s$. In other words, the gain for agent C with a risky project to team with agent A with a safe project rather than with agent D with a risky project is smaller than the loss agent A would incur by teaming with agent C rather than with agent B. Because $p_r(p_s - p_r)c$ is the maximum agent C would be prepared to pay agent A to team together rather than to team with agent B, and because that sum is lower than $p_s(p_s - p_r)c$, which represents the sum that would be necessary to convince agent A to do so, the deal would not go through as the net gains are negative. Sorting by risk types is thus efficient because none of the agents can use gains from trade to convince the others to change their decisions.

Second, progressive lending eliminates informational asymmetries because borrowers and lenders develop long-term relationships. When a lender knows little or nothing about a borrower, the lender is less willing to risk providing the borrower with higher loan amounts. However, as the lender accumulates more information about the borrower's competence and reliability, the lender is more willing to provide funds to the borrower. Progressive lending also reduces risk. A default on a smaller loan is less risky than a default on a larger loan. As the lender acquires more information about the borrower, the lender may (or may not) be willing to take more risk.

Progressive lending's incentive properties are, however, independent from the properties of group lending. A borrower can have an individual loan, without joint liability features, that includes progressive lending. But because progressive lending only works when there is a long-term relationship between the borrower and the lender, problems can arise. What if there is competition between lenders with one lender willing to lend more upfront today than the others? This competition will not necessarily be good for incentives. In the absence of commitment, lenders may reasonably expect borrowers to leave the relationship at any moment in order to do business with the competition. In that case, the advantages of progressive lending will be undone and the only force working against default will be the incentive of the borrower to maintain a good reputation. If lenders circulate information among themselves about those borrowers who default, the lenders may agree never to lend to that person or that enterprise again. Reputation would thus reduce the incentive to default. Nevertheless, reputation requires efficient circulation of information, which can be a problem in poor countries.

It seems that, in practice, progressive lending works particularly well with women. They respond better to dynamic incentives for at least two reasons. First, they are less mobile. This means that if they default on a loan, they are less likely to run away. Women also have less opportunities to borrow. Microcredit provides a unique opportunity for women in developing countries and because it is more difficult for women to obtain loans from conventional lending institutions, progressive lending works better for them.

The very regular payment schedules associated with microcredit might seem counterintuitive. What is the point of borrowing if you have to start repaying the loan immediately? In practice, this feature has proved very useful for screening out undisciplined borrowers and sending early warning signals about problems with a loan or a borrower. It does, however, require borrowers to have some source of income and, when that income is seasonal, as is the case with farmers, meeting those regular payment schedules can be very difficult.

Other Forms of Microfinance

Microcredit that involves group lending is only one of the various forms of microfinance, methods to finance small loans or investments in developing countries. In one version of microfinance, loan approval is associated with the borrower's obligation to contribute to an "emergency fund" that serves as a substitute for collateral. A slightly different version found in other types of microfinance contracts is that of a "group tax," a form of mandatory saving that requires individuals to contribute on a regular basis to a joint fund from which money can only be withdrawn at a future date.

In Africa and Asia, a widespread form of microfinance is **rotating savings and credit associations (ROSCAs)**. No outside financial institution is involved with ROSCAs. In a village, a group of people, usually women, decide to save money together and then lend to the different group members on a rotating basis: one individual receives a loan from the group first; after repayment of the first loan, a second individual receives a loan, and so on. An individual's place in the rotation scheme is often chosen at random. The ROSCA system is less practical than microcredit because those individuals who can borrow from the savings of others early on in the lending rotation have an advantage as this works for them as an immediate loan, while those who borrow later in the rotation could likely have saved the money by themselves. Nevertheless, the ROSCA does serve as a significant commitment to savings. Because there are regular meetings, each member of the group commits to contributing a certain amount of savings to the association on a regular basis. This is not just a commitment device for members; many women also find that the ROSCA is a practical device for preventing the money saved by the household from being misspent on nonessential purchases such as alcohol.

To appreciate the diversity of different microfinance programs across the world, Table 15.2 describes the features of some of the most successful of these programs worldwide. The Grameen Bank is the most well-known microfinance institution. Its mode of operation has been copied by hundreds of microcredit associations across the globe, including a number in the United States. It has over 2 million members in Bangladesh, 95% of them women. In 1998, the average loan size was barely above $100. Loan duration is roughly a year. Group lending, group liability, and progressive lending are key features of its contracts. Groups form voluntarily and generally consist of five borrowers. Similar to a ROSCA, loans are given out on a rotating basis, initially to the first two members, then to the next two, and finally to the fifth. A group meets weekly with seven other groups and the bank's staff.

TABLE 15.2 Characteristics of Selected Leading Microfinance Programs

	Grameen Bank, Bangladesh	BancoSol, Bolivia	Bank Rakyat, Indonesia, Unit Desa	Badan Kredit Desa, Indonesia	FINCA Village Banks
Membership	2.4 million	81,503	2 million borrowers; 16 million depositors	765,586	89,986
Average loan balance	$134	$909	$1007	$71	$191
Typical loan term	1 year	4–12 months	3–24 months	3 months	4 months
Percent female members	95%	61%	23%	N/A	95%
Rural/urban	Rural	Urban	Mostly rural	Rural	Mostly rural
Group lending?	Yes	Yes	No	No	No
Collateral required?	No	No	Yes	No	No
Voluntary savings emphasized?	No	Yes	Yes	No	Yes
Progressive lending?	Yes	Yes	Yes	Yes	Yes
Regular repayment schedules	Weekly	Flexible	Flexible	Flexible	Weekly
Target clients for lending	Poor	Largely non-poor	Non-poor	Poor	Poor
Currently financially sustainable?	No	Yes	Yes	Yes	No
Nominal interest rate on loans (per year)	20%	47.5–50.5%	32–43%	55%	36–48%
Annual consumer price inflation, 1996	2.7%	12.4%	8.0%	8.0%	N/A

This is a comparison of some of the world's leading microfinance programs.

Source: Jonathan Morduch, "The Microfinance Promise," *Journal of Economic Literature* 37, no. 4 (1999): 1569–1615. Printed with permission of American Economics Association.

The BancoSol or Banco Solidario in Bolivia started a microfinance program by lending to groups and then later introduced individual loan contracts with group liability. It is a more urban bank, its borrowers are typically wealthier than the clients of the Grameen Bank, and its loans are generally larger, as well. The BancoSol has become an important player in Bolivia's banking system.

Bank Rakyat in Indonesia is a more traditional institution. It does not provide group lending and does require collateral. Its loans are roughly 10 times higher, on average, than those of the Grameen Bank. However, it operates primarily in rural areas and lends on a relatively small scale, while encouraging people in those areas to save. Progressive lending is a key formula for Bank Rakyat and its repayment rates have been very high, even higher than those for conventional commercial banks.

Bank Kredit Desa, which also operates in Indonesia, makes smaller loans to the poorest households. In 1996, the average loan size was even smaller than that for the Grameen Bank, and loan duration was rather short, 3 months on average. The system replicates some of the properties of group lending even though it does lend to individuals. The originality of the bank's approach is that it uses the rural authority structure to allocate loans and to enforce loan payments. Bank funds are allocated by village-level management commissions that are led by village leaders. Decisions are made locally using readily available information about the reliability and intent of borrowers, with the result that the worst credit risks are avoided. Using the local authority structure also works well in terms of enforcing loan repayment; default rates on these loans have been very low.

In Latin America, the Foundation for International Community Assistance (FINCA) set up a network of village banks in the mid-1980s. Its model has been replicated in other countries and continents, and it serves nearly 90,000 clients in Peru, Haiti, Malawi, Uganda, and Kyrgyzstan, and the United States. Under the program, nongovernmental organizations (NGOs) help FINCA set up village bank branches in partnership with local authorities or civil associations, allowing substantial local autonomy over loan decisions and management. As with the Grameen Bank, clients are mostly poor women in rural areas and the size of the loans is quite small. In the standard model, an initial loan is made to the village bank and its 30–50 members. The bank then lends to members of the program, starting with amounts of about $50 with a 4-month term. Subsequent loan sizes are tied to the amount that members have on deposit with the bank. The originality of the program is that it includes a savings component; the size of a loan cannot exceed 5 times the value of the savings deposit.

Is Microfinance Profitable?

Is microfinance simply a private innovation made by profit-maximizing entrepreneurs or is it more a form of development aid? Is microfinance profitable? Is it sustainable without subsidies and outside financial aid?

The answers to these questions depend on the bank in question. The general answer, though, is that profitability is not a general characteristic of microfinance institutions. Table 15.3 provides some figures that give an idea of profitability.

TABLE 15.3   Performance Indicators of Microfinance Programs

	Number of observations	Avg. loan balance ($)	Avg. loan as % of GNP per capita	Avg. operational sustainability	Avg. financial sustainability	Avg. return on equity	Avg. percent of portfolio at risk	Avg. percent female clients	Avg. number of active borrowers
Sustainability									
All microfinance institutions	72	415	34	105	83	−8.5	3.3	65	9,035
Fully sustainable	34	428	39	139	113	9.3	2.6	61	12,926
Lending method									
Individual lending	30	842	76	120	92	−5.0	3.1	53	15,226
Solidarity groups	20	451	35	103	89	−3.0	4.1	49	7,252
Village bank	22	94	11	91	69	−17.4	2.8	92	7,833
Target group									
Low end	37	133	13	88	72	−16.2	3.8	74	7,953
Broad	28	564	48	122	100	1.2	3.0	60	12,282
High end	7	2,971	359	121	76	−6.2	1.9	34	1,891
Age									
3–6 years	15	301	44	98	84	−6.8	2.2	71	9,921
7 or more years	40	374	27	123	98	−2.4	4.1	63	16,557

Village banks have a "B" data quality; all others are graded "A." Portfolio at risk is the amount in arrears for 90 days or more as a percentage of the loan portfolio. Averages exclude data for the top and bottom deciles. Many microfinance institutions can generally cover their operating costs with their revenues, but they do not generate enough revenue to cover the costs of capital, as their average return on equity tends to be negative.

Source: Jonathan Morduch, "The Microfinance Promise," 1999.

Operational sustainability is the ability of a financial institution to generate enough revenue to cover operating costs. As Table 15.3 shows, operational sustainability is generally achieved by microfinance programs except for village banks and those banks targeting the poorest borrowers. **Financial sustainability**, on the other hand, requires banks to be able to cover the cost of capital as well. Imagine that a bank has revenues of 105 and costs of 100, which would make it operationally sustainable. Imagine, however, that investing 100 would, on average, return 110 to the bank. Alternatively, assume that the costs of 100 would have to be borrowed at an interest rate of 10%. In that case, if we want to include the cost of capital, we must add 10 to the costs of 100. Total costs, including the cost of capital, are thus 110, which is larger than the revenues of 105. In this case, the bank would have operational sustainability but not financial sustainability.

Looking again at Table 15.3, we see that all microfinance programs generate only 83% of the required amount to reach financial sustainability. Village banks and banks targeting the poorest borrowers generate roughly 70% of the necessary revenue. Banks that target a broader economic spectrum of customers have a better performance, as is the case with BancoSol in Bolivia and Bank Rakyat in Indonesia. Returns to the equity invested in the programs give us the same picture. Even the fully sustainable microfinance institutions do not receive high returns to equity considering the risks involved. The Grameen Bank, which is the flagship institution for microcredit, does not make a profit; it charges an interest rate of 15.9%, whereas it should charge upward of 32% to be sustainable. Microfinance institutions are often subsidized by government agencies or NGOs. Many microcredit organizations do not aspire to financial sustainability, but even when they do, they are only successful in roughly half of the cases. The reason for their lack of financial sustainability is usually the same as it is for the Grameen Bank: the reluctance to charge higher interest rates to poor households. Subsidies from donors are used to cover the financial gap. Donors have been happy to give money to microcredit associations because of their positive effects on poverty alleviation. On the other hand, microcredit associations are often of the opinion that these subsidies should be temporary. In the long run, the question of the financial sustainability of microcredit associations remains open.

Achieving financial sustainability for microcredit associations is not easy. Increasing the interest rates charged to households does not appear to solve the problem. As seen in this chapter, higher interest rates often lead to adverse selection in the pool of borrowers and have the potential to increase losses from default rather than yield increased gains. Dean Karlan and Jonathan Zinman have done some research on the credit elasticity of poor households in South Africa, using randomized controlled trials.[9] **Credit elasticity** measures by what percent demand for credit drops when the interest rate increases by one percentage point. Their results show that at higher interest rates, demand for credit is much lower, as are repayment rates. The Grameen Bank policies could thus be justified by high credit elasticity and the negative effects of interest rates on repayment rates. While credit elasticity is high for poor households in South Africa and other developing countries, that is not the case everywhere. Microcredit associations in Latin America are less afraid to charge higher interest rates and have proved to be financially sustainable. Are these an exception to the high credit-elasticity story, or is credit elasticity less widespread than we might think? Further research is needed to answer that question.

A justification for subsidizing microfinance might be the following: if money is going to go to poverty alleviation anyway, it might be better spent

---

[9]Dean Karlan and Jonathan Zinman, "Expanding Credit Access: Using Randomized Supply Decisions to Estimate the Impacts," *Review of Financial Studies* 23, no. 1 (2010): 433–464.

subsidizing microcredit associations because the money loaned generates income and wealth that might not otherwise be the result of more traditional poverty alleviation programs. This is, of course, only an argument. Serious research is needed to measure the costs and benefits of using microcredit as a tool for poverty alleviation compared to other instruments.

Evaluating Microfinance

Despite microcredit's significant success in providing loans to the poor, few studies have tried to evaluate its effects on economic development systematically. However, Ahbijit Banerjee, Esther Duflo, Rachel Glennerster, and Cynthia Kinnan have put together one of the first randomized trials to evaluate the effects of microcredit.[10] In 2005, some 52 of the 104 neighborhoods in Hyderabad (India's fifth largest city and the capital of the state of Andhra Pradesh) were randomly selected as locations for branches of the Spandana Company, one of the fastest growing microfinance institutions in Andhra Pradesh. Microcredit would then be available to households in these "treated" areas but not to those in the other 52 neighborhoods in the "control" areas.

Similar to the Grameen Bank, Spandana provides group loans. A group includes 6–10 self-selected women who are jointly responsible for all loans made to the group's members. The size of a first loan is the equivalent of $1,000 at purchasing parity exchange rates. Loan duration is 50 weeks with a 24% annual percentage rate (APR). If all loans within a group are reimbursed, group members are eligible for a second loan of a somewhat larger size. Only women aged 18–59 are eligible, provided they have resided in the same neighborhood for at least 1 year and have valid identification and proof of residence. At least 80% of the women in a group must own their homes.

Fifteen to 18 months after the branches opened, the research team conducted a survey in about 6,850 households in all 104 neighborhoods (an average of 66 per neighborhood). Among households surveyed, 27% in the 52 treated neighborhoods had a loan from a microfinance institution against 18.7% in the 52 control neighborhoods. This confirms that microfinance leads to more borrowing by households. One out of five of these additional loans in the treated neighborhoods led to the creation of a new business. While households in the treated neighborhoods did not display higher household spending than in those in the control neighborhoods, they did spend more on durable goods (bicycles, cell phones, watches, televisions) and less on "temptation goods" such as cigarettes, alcohol, or gambling. This suggests that microcredit encourages households to be more disciplined and to invest more in durable goods that can be useful when starting a business.

According to the study, microcredit did not change the bargaining power within households; women in treated neighborhoods were no more likely to be the primary decision makers for household expenditures, financial choices, or children's education than those in the control neighborhoods. Moreover,

---

[10]Ahbijit Banerjee, Esther Duflo, Rachel Glennerster, and Cynthia Kinnan, "The Miracle of Microfinance? Evidence from a Randomized Evaluation" (working paper, Massachusetts Institute of Technology, Cambridge, MA, 2010).

households in treated neighborhoods did not spend more on health, as is usually observed in households where women have more bargaining power. Because the survey was conducted less than 2 years after the opening of the Spandana branches, it is still too early to determine the long-term consequences of microcredit on the basis of the Hyderabad experiment, and in particular, to what extent it increased household welfare and contributed to economic development.

Chapter Summary

The Demand for Credit in Developing Economies

Some sources of demand for credit in developing countries are farmers who need to purchase seed, fertilizer, and equipment, as their work generates revenue only after they harvest a crop. Small entrepreneurs are also in need of credit. Demands for consumer credit are less prevalent, even though households borrow in the case of income shocks or to finance expenditures for important ceremonies such as weddings.

The Theory of Credit Markets in Development

Informational problems associated with financial transactions are ubiquitous in credit markets and problems of moral hazard and adverse selection play a fundamental role in those markets. They play an even bigger role in developing countries because it is much more difficult to use collateral to alleviate these problems, given general weaknesses in property titling systems and legal institutions. Monitoring can be a substitute for collateral, but it increases interest charges, especially for small loans because the costs of monitoring loans are mostly fixed costs. Informational problems lead to credit constraints. Commitment problems are also a factor in developing credit markets as borrowers may

decide to default on their loans. In practice, however, borrowers rarely default on loans in developing countries, in part due to reputational concerns.

Credit Constraints in Developing Countries

Measuring how large credit constraints are is very difficult. When constraints are present, credit supply is smaller than credit demand, and credit demand is usually unobserved. Banking reforms in India that resulted in changes to the size of businesses targeted for preferential loans provide one of the few opportunities for precisely measuring credit constraints and they resulted in clear evidence for those constraints.

Microfinance

Microfinance is an institutional innovation that provides credit to the poor when collateral is not available. Microfinance relies on the joint liability of local communities as a substitute for collateral. Peer monitoring becomes a viable substitute for monitoring by a bank. Microcredit also allows borrowers who are more or less risk averse to self-sort into different risk groups. This alleviates the adverse selection problem in lending. Not all microfinance institutions are financially sustainable and many require subsidies to remain solvent.

Key Terms

collateral
credit constrained
credit elasticity
credit rationed
financial sustainability
group lending

intermediation margin
limited liability
microcredit
microfinance
operational sustainability
progressive lending

ration credit

risk averse

risk neutral

rotating savings and credit associations (ROSCAs)

serially correlated

strategic default

Review Questions

1. In this exercise, we examine the adverse selection issue discussed in the chapter. Call α_s the share of safe projects and $(1 - \alpha_s)$ the share of risky projects. Assume that a safe project yields a return of R_s with 100% probability. Assume that a risky project yields a return of R_r with probability p_r and a return of 0 with probability $(1 - p_r)$. Assume that the lender has perfect information about which projects are safe and which are risky. What is the minimum interest rate necessary to recover a loan of 1 with the safe project? What is the minimum interest rate necessary to recover a loan of 1 with the risky project? Assume that the lender cannot recognize which loans are safe and which are risky. What, then, is the minimum interest rate the bank must charge in order to recover a loan of 1? Above what interest rate would the safe projects stop demanding a loan?

2. This is an exercise on moral hazard in credit markets. Assume that a borrower must borrow 100 for an investment. The borrower can choose between a safe project yielding a return of R_s with 100% probability and a risky project yielding a return of R_r with probability p_r and a return of 0 with probability $(1 - p_r)$. Assume that the lender cannot observe or control the type of project chosen by the borrower. What are the conditions for the borrower to choose the risky over the safe project under limited liability? What is the minimum level of collateral that will lead the borrower to choose the safe project instead? Alternatively, assume that the borrower has some money of his or her own to invest in the project that costs 100. Assuming that the bank cannot collateralize the loan, what is the maximum amount of the loan such that the borrower will prefer the safe over the risky project?

3. Take the same assumptions as in the previous exercise on the returns and probabilities associated with the safe and risky projects. Assume that there are monitoring costs C to make sure the borrower chooses the safe over the risky project. If L is the size of the loan, what is the minimum interest rate the bank must charge as a function of the size of the loan and the monitoring costs?

4. This is an exercise on microcredit as a substitute for collateral. Take the same assumptions as in the previous two exercises on the safe and risky projects. Now assume that there are two borrowers, A and B. Assume that the size of the loan is 1 and that the interest rate is r. Also assume that A has limited liability. What is the minimum size of B's liability in case A defaults on his loan, so that B can convince A to choose the safe loan?

5. Download and read "Bank Credit and Business Networks," an article by Asim Ijaz Khwaja, Atif Mian, and Abid Qamar (http://dash.harvard.edu/bitstream/handle/1/4876870/RWP11-017_Khwaja_Mian_Qamar.pdf?sequence=1). What is the research innovation in this article? How would you explain the researchers' findings? How do they relate to the discussions in Chapter 14?

6. Read "Banking for the Poor: Evidence from India," an article by Robin Burgess, Rohini Pande, and Grace Wong, *Journal of the European Economic Association* 3 (2–3): 268–278.

Compare and describe the similarities and differences between the approach in this article to the Banerjee-Duflo article on credit constraints in India discussed in this chapter, and to the Banerjee-Duflo-Glennester article on microfinance, also discussed in this chapter.

7. Will the problems of credit markets disappear when developing countries become more affluent? Explain your answer.

8. How does monitoring alleviate informational asymmetries and what effect does it have on loans of different sizes?

9. Explain the different methods economists usually employ to measure credit constraints. What are the potential problems with these approaches?

10. What is progressive lending? How is it related to group lending? When is progressive lending less successful?

16

Health Care Delivery in Developing Countries

Why do many children in developing countries miss school? Many answers may come to mind: they have to help their parents farm the land, the distance to school is long, or the cost is too high. An answer that probably would not come up is parasitic worms: soil-transmitted helminths that include the genus *Schistosoma*, flatworms known as blood flukes.[1] Four hundred million children in developing countries suffer from chronic worm-related diseases with symptoms such as anemia, diarrhea, fatigue, and chronic abdominal pain, to name a few. These diseases, while not fatal, keep children away from school and can have significant long-term negative effects on them in terms of physical and mental development. It costs only 50 cents per child per year to deliver effective oral medication that kills 99% of known intestinal worms, yet 90% of children at risk in developing countries have not been treated. Can we measure the benefits of deworming? Edward Miguel and Michael Kremer, professors of economics at UC Berkeley and Harvard, respectively, conducted an evaluation of a deworming program implemented by the NGO International Child Support among 30,000 pupils in 75 primary schools in western Kenya, a region with high worm infection rates. This was a randomized controlled evaluation as is conducted in medical research. Some schools were randomly chosen to be part of the deworming program and others were not. Miguel and Kremer found significant benefits in terms of improved health for those who received the deworming drugs while school absenteeism was reduced by 25%. They also found that deworming is a very cost-effective health program at only $5 per **disability adjusted life year (DALY)** saved, which is the concept used by the World Health Organization to measure the benefits of health intervention. It corresponds to a year of healthy life that results from a health program and includes years of life saved but also years of disability prevented.[2] In comparison, vaccinations for measles, diphtheria, pertussis, or tetanus cost $12 to $17 per DALY saved. Following this research, deworming programs were expanded in Kenya and in 25 other countries and they now protect 7 million children. While there is still a long way to go in terms of improving health care in developing nations, economics research has important health policy impacts in those countries and it is the topic covered in this chapter. Improving health in developing countries is a major goal of development policies.

---

[1]Helminths are parasitic worms that usually find their way into human bodies through contaminated water and soil. These worms can easily infect people who are barefoot. Schistosomiasis, sometimes also called bilharzia, refers to the group of chronic diseases caused by the parasitic flatworms. Its effects include diarrhea, fevers, damage to the major organs, blood infections, and even seizures. After malaria, it is the most debilitating parasitic disease.

[2]We give the precise definition of DALY later in this chapter.

W e will first take a historical perspective and examine the health impact of the so-called epidemiological transition. The invention of antibiotics such as penicillin, antiviral medications, and DDT (yes, the highly toxic insecticide that is now prohibited in many countries) had major health effects worldwide, including in developing countries, on fighting diseases such as pneumonia, cholera, dysentery, yellow fever, influenza, and malaria. We will see how development economists measure human health in developing countries to evaluate the efficiency of health care interventions. We will then examine policy interventions meant to alleviate and eradicate diseases in developing countries. We also address the question of how to improve access to inexpensive drugs in developing countries. We then examine the dual interactions between health and economic development. Last but not least, we will look at institutions that provide health care in developing countries. How good is the quality of health care? What are the main problems faced by health care institutions in developing countries?

A Historical Perspective: The Epidemiological Transition

Major medical breakthroughs in the first half of the 20h century have had a powerful and lasting impact on health outcomes in both rich and poor countries. This worldwide improvement in health is called the **epidemiological transition**.

Several medical breakthroughs are critical to the epidemiological transition. The invention of antibiotics may be the most important development in the history of medicine. Penicillin, the first effective drug for killing bacteria, as well as other antibiotics such as streptomycin, became widely available in the 1950s. Once-fatal diseases such as pneumonia, dysentery, and cholera could now be treated.

A second major breakthrough was the use of the pesticide DDT in the years following World War II, which led to the eradication of malaria and yellow fever in many developing countries. Today, DDT is considered so toxic that its use is prohibited in many countries. However, it proved to be an extremely efficient tool for eradicating mosquito-borne diseases. For example, spraying the walls of a house with DDT repels or kills mosquitoes that carry the malaria parasite. Before the advent of DDT, malaria was much more widespread in tropical areas and even in the warm and humid climates of the southern United States.

A third major innovation was institutional: the establishment of the World Health Organization (WHO) in 1948, which launched worldwide campaigns to combat disease and to provide vaccinations that would ultimately result in the virtual eradication of highly communicable infections such as smallpox and polio.

Figure 16.1 illustrates the impact of the epidemiological transition on life expectancy and mortality. The evolution of life expectancy at birth (in logarithms) is shown for three different groups of countries in the 1930s that were initially, respectively, rich, middle income, and poor, before the advent of the major medical breakthroughs mentioned above. We can see that, during the epidemiological transition, life expectancy increased in all countries but

FIGURE 16.1   The Evolution of the Log of Life Expectancy at Birth for Initially Rich, Middle-Income, and Poor Countries

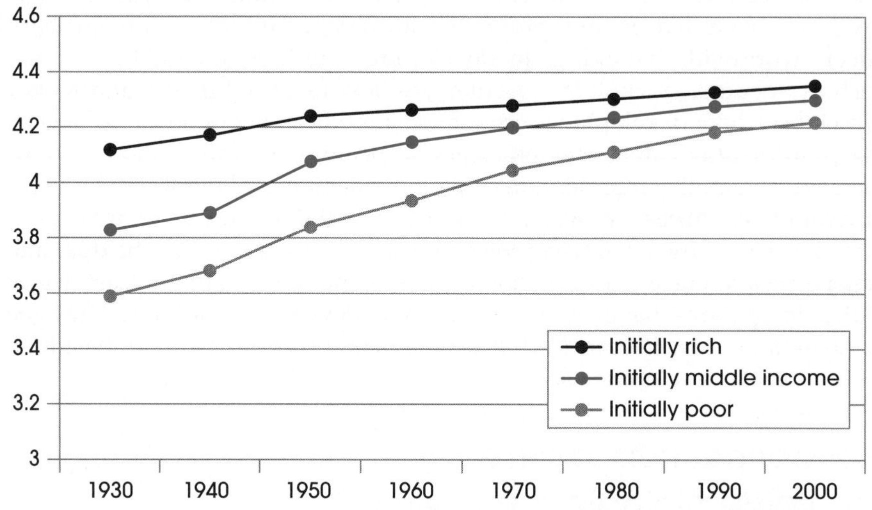

The invention of antibiotics, the pesticide DDT to fight malaria and other mosquito-borne diseases, and the establishment of the World Health Organization have increased life expectancy across the world and reduced, though not eliminated, the life expectancy gap between rich and poor countries.

Source: Daron Acemoglu and Simon Johnson, "Disease and Development: The Effect of Life Expectancy on Economic Growth," *Journal of Political Economy* 115, no. 6 (2007): 927.

especially in poor and middle-income countries. The gap in life expectancy between these three groups of countries decreased steadily. Nevertheless, poor countries still experienced a deficit in terms of life expectancy relative to the rest of the world.

The success of the epidemiological transition provides a reason to be optimistic about improving health in developing countries. History has shown that health can be improved in a major way. How do we measure health improvements as well as the effects of particular health policies?

Measuring Health

How do economists measure health levels in a given population? The ideal way is to perform a clinical evaluation of the health of representative samples of a population. However, this is extremely expensive and can usually be done only on a small scale. Given the weakness of health infrastructures in developing countries, it is a daunting task. Development economists have designed cheaper but nevertheless informative methods to measure health and, in this section, we will examine their advantages and drawbacks.

Self-Reported Health Status

Surveys done by economists ask respondents questions such as, "Generally speaking, would you say, on a scale from 1 to 5, you are in poor or good health?" The answer is often a good predictor of morbidity and mortality but it has obvious drawbacks. First of all, it is a very rough measure—people may be in bad health for different reasons. Reporting that your health is a 2 might mean many different things; you could have the flu at the time of the survey or suffer from heart disease. Second, this measure relies on people's perceptions, which might be biased. If a person lives in a village where most people are in poor health, but that person's health is slightly better than the majority in the village, the answer to the question might be too optimistic. There may also be cultural biases in people's answers as social norms may, for example, forbid them from talking negatively about their own health. Also, people may think they are in reasonably good health before a doctor examines them, after which they are then likely to report being in poor health, even if their health has improved because of the medicine the doctor has prescribed for them.

Self-Reported Symptoms

Surveys often ask more specific answers about health status such as whether someone has had fever, diarrhea, or respiratory problems in the last week or month. These kinds of questions are more precise and ask about objective symptoms, not subjective perceptions. However, this measure is not perfect either; if a disease or symptom is fairly common in a village, people may not consider that it warrants mention. In developing countries, researchers have found that more educated people give more accurate responses to these types of questions because they understand better the meaning of particular symptoms. The responses of less-educated people may therefore suggest that these individuals are healthier than are more-educated people, whereas this is not necessarily the case.

Reporting Daily Activities

If different people interpret particular symptoms differently, an alternative is to ask people whether they have had difficulties with daily activities considered normal for healthy people. They are asked if they have had difficulties walking certain distances, lifting weights, bending, or climbing stairs. A drawback of this approach is that the answers are more informative in terms of the health status of older people rather than of young adults who are usually able to perform all these activities normally while still having health problems. This approach can thus underestimate the health problems of young adults.

Nutrient Intake

Measuring an individual's nutrient intake is a more accurate measure of health than are surveys. Malnutrition is a major source of health problems in developing countries and people who are underfed usually cannot work as productively as those who are adequately nourished. However, this method is more demanding as it requires very detailed data collection.

How do economists measure nutrient intake? One method questions people about what food they have purchased and produced over a given period and then converts the answer into calories. A pound of rice or a pound of chicken will be translated into a certain number of calories. Researchers can rely on household expenditure surveys to calculate food purchases and on surveys about household farm production. The assumption is that no food is wasted, an expectation that is plausible for poor households. There is, however, the potential for measurement error. If guests are invited, they will share the household's food and the nutrient measure will, in this case, tend to overestimate real calories consumed. People will also eat when they are away from home, either as someone else's guests or when they travel. The poor who work as laborers could receive food on the job. In these situations, the nutrient measure will then tend to underestimate the calorie intake.

Another method that measures nutrient intake consists of asking people to recall exactly what they ate in the last 24 hours. This has the advantage of including food eaten outside the home, but it is also quite expensive in terms of survey time. Moreover, people's memories of ordinary activities like eating are not necessarily accurate; while we can remember what we ate, recalling specific quantities can be more difficult and sometimes inaccurate. Clearly, measures of nutrient intake are all imperfect, but more importantly, they only measure one aspect of an individual's health.

Anthropometric Measures

Another way to measure health is to use anthropometric measures: height, weight, and body-mass index (BMI). These measures are directly related to nutrition because they assess its result. For example, undernourished children will be shorter than average when they become adults. Obviously, people's heights vary as a function of their genetic background, but an individual's adult height also reflects the quality of his or her health and nutrition as a child.

Figure 16.2 gives measures of adult height in the United States, Brazil, Cote d'Ivoire, and Vietnam. The horizontal axis shows the year of birth, the vertical axis on the left measures the height of males (solid line) and the vertical axis on the right measures the height of females (dashed line). For example, a male born in the United States in 1950 has an average height of slightly less than 177 cm (5 ft., $9\frac{3}{4}$ in.), while a female born in 1950 in the United States has an average height of 163.5 cm (5 ft., $4\frac{3}{8}$ in.). A male born in Cote d'Ivoire in 1959 measures slightly above 169 cm (5 ft., $6\frac{1}{2}$ in.), while the corresponding figures for men from Brazil and Vietnam born in 1959 are 168 cm (5 ft., $6\frac{1}{8}$ in.) and 161 cm (5 ft., $3\frac{3}{8}$ in.), respectively. We see from Figure 16.2 that people in the United States as well as in developing countries have become taller over time. Increases in height have been the steepest for men in Cote d'Ivoire for births since the late 1920s, whereas women's heights in that nation increased sharply only for births after 1950. Note that Vietnam has experienced almost no increase in height for births from 1950 onward, a period that corresponds to its wars against the French and the Americans. In terms of height, those Vietnamese born in the late 1960s and early 1970s seem to have suffered the most significant deficits, as shown by a dip in height for men and women born around that period.

Weight is a more direct reflection of nutrition intake in the short run, but weight is a condition of height. This is why the body-mass index (BMI) is used to estimate weight. The index measures the ratio of weight (in kilograms, kg) to the square of height (in meters, m). Thus, a person weighing 70 kg (154 pounds) and measuring 1.75 m (5 ft., 9 in.) will have a body-mass index of $70/(1.75)^2 = 22.86$. A BMI less than 18 is considered very low while a BMI

FIGURE 16.2   Adult Height in the United States and in Some Developing Countries

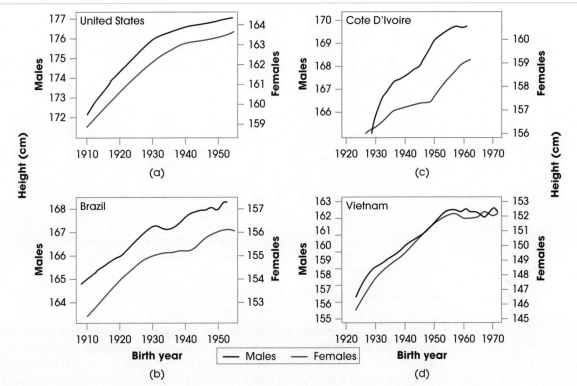

The average height of adult males and females has been increasing with birth year in the United States as well as in developing countries.

Source: Acemoglu, D. and S. Johnson (2007). "Disease and Development: The Effect of Life Expectancy on Economic Growth," *Journal of Political Economy* 115(6), 927. Printed with permission of American Economics Association.

above 30 indicates obesity. Figure 16.3 shows the correlation between BMI and the log of wages in Brazil and in the United States. We can see that there is a positive correlation between BMI and income in Brazil. In other words, Brazilians with a higher BMI have, in general, a higher income. The same is not true for the United States. There, people with a BMI of 24 have the highest wage. Above that BMI level, there is a negative correlation between BMI and income resulting in a non-monotonic relationship between BMI and income that is typical of developed countries.

Disability Adjusted Life Year (DALY)

When measuring the benefits of health interventions, a common measure used, and already introduced in the introduction to this chapter, is the DALY or Disability Adjusted Life Year. It is an indicator of a year of healthy life saved. How do researchers measure the DALY? The following formula is useful to understand how this method works,

$$DALY = (N \times L) + (I \times W \times D).$$

FIGURE 16.3   BMI and Income in the United States and in Brazil

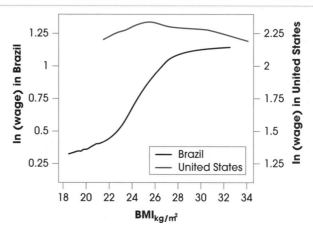

For a developing country such as Brazil, BMI rises with income. For a developed country such as the United States, there is a non-monotonic relationship: BMI first rises but then declines with income.

Source: Strauss and Thomas, "Health, Nutrition, and Economic Development" (1998): 774.

where N measures the number of deaths from a disease; L measures the life expectancy at the age of death; I measures the number of incidences of the disease; W is the disability weight, i.e., the percentage of disability as a consequence of the disease; and D is the average duration of the disease. The first element (N × L) measures the number of years lost to fatalities from the disease, while the second element (I × W × D) measures the years lost through disability. For example, if someone has a 10% disability from a disease that lasts 10 years, then W × D is equal to one year.

The DALY measure is useful because it makes comparisons of disease incidence possible. Suppose that a disease is not fatal but has debilitating effects on people's health. Take a second disease that is much less frequent but nearly always fatal. The DALY measure is the common standard measuring the health incidence of both diseases.

Diseases and Development

Some diseases are particularly widespread in developing countries. Table 16.1 gives the number of deaths from various diseases in the world and in low-income and high-income countries. By far the largest number of deaths occurs in low-income countries. Moreover, more than 30.2% of deaths in low-income countries represent children under age 4, while the corresponding figure for high-income countries is only 0.9%. In contrast, more than three-quarters of deaths from disease in developed countries occur among people above age 60. The corresponding figure for developing countries is only 34.2%. Diseases in developing countries thus affect mostly poor families and with frequent fatalities among young children.

Most of the deaths from the diseases reported in Table 16.1 can be avoided through prevention or medication. Respiratory infections such as pneumonia can be treated by antibiotics; perinatal deaths can be avoided by pre- and post-natal

TABLE 16.1 Diseases and Development

	Treatments and prevention	World	Low income	High income
Millions of deaths per year				
Respiratory infections	Antibiotics	3.96	2.90	0.34
HIV/AIDS	HAART	2.78	2.14	0.02
Perinatal deaths	Pre- and post-natal care	2.46	1.83	0.03
Diarrheal disease	Oral rehydration therapy	1.80	1.50	0.00
Tuberculosis	Public health: DOTS	1.57	1.09	0.01
Malaria	Partially treatable	1.27	1.24	0.00
DPT/measles/polio	Vaccinations	1.12	1.07	0.00
Percent of deaths				
Ages 0–4		18.4	30.2	0.9
Ages 60 and above		50.8	34.2	75.9

The overwhelming majority of deaths from disease occur in poor countries. Disease mortality is highest among young children in those countries. In contrast, it is higher among those over 60 in developed economies.

Source: WIDER Annual Lecture 10 Global Patterns of Income and Health: Facts, Interpretations, and Politics by Angus Deaton. This table is reproduced by permission of UNU-WIDER, who commissioned the original research and holds copyright thereon.

care; and diarrheal diseases can be treated very efficiently, especially in children with oral rehydration therapy using a simple solution of salts, glucose, and other substances. On the other hand, treating tuberculosis has become more challenging in recent years as new drug-resistant strains of the tuberculosis bacteria have appeared. The WHO strategy for dealing with tuberculosis is called DOTS, which stands for Directly Observed Treatment Short course. The DOTS strategy requires: 1) identification of TB cases in a community by using up-to-date bacteriology techniques for diagnosis (microscopy and culture of expectorated mucus, and drug susceptibility testing); and 2) treatment by directly observing medication intake for 6 to 8 months and monitoring the results. When properly followed, the DOTS strategy has a 95% success rate. When an infected patient is cured, he or she will not infect others. DPT (diphtheria, pertussis or whooping cough, and tetanus), measles, and polio have long been treated with vaccines. As for malaria, prevention is the best strategy, but there are now various drugs that can treat the parasite somewhat effectively. HIV treatment currently consists of highly active, antiretroviral therapy (HAART). This treatment does not cure a patient, but can be relatively effective in stabilizing the progression of the disease.

If these diseases can be prevented, cured, or at least stabilized, what does it take to reduce the incidence of them in developing countries to bring their levels closer to those observed in advanced countries? Besides the obvious health and social welfare benefits, what economic benefits can we expect from improved treatment of diseases in developing countries?

HIV

HIV (human immunodeficiency virus) causes the human immune system to fail, leading to various infections from which the infected person eventually dies. This failure of the immune system is called AIDS (acquired immunodeficiency syndrome). HIV spreads through unsafe sex, needles shared for drug use, and contaminated blood supplies. Figure 16.4 shows a map of HIV's prevalence throughout the world in 2007, the most recent year for which global data are available. The disease spread since the 1970s and the 1980s, and is a very serious health problem throughout the world.

We can see from Figure 16.4 that African countries suffer the most from HIV, especially the countries in the southern half of the continent where it has reached epidemic proportions. In Swaziland and Botswana, nearly 40% of the population aged 15–49 carries the HIV virus, while in Namibia and Zimbabwe, nearly 25% of the population is infected. In South Africa, Malawi, and Zambia, HIV infection rates are about 15%. The effects of HIV are enormous: whole villages have lost their young adult populations, leaving grandparents to rear surviving children, while millions of children are born with HIV and condemned to die from AIDS at an early age. Elsewhere, the countries with the highest rates of HIV infections are Haiti with 5.6%; Caribbean nations such as Trinidad and Tobago (3.2%), the Bahamas (3%) and Belize (2.4%) have slightly lower rates. The United States has a comparatively high HIV infection rate compared to other advanced industrialized countries, but is only at 0.6%. Most European countries are at 0.1%. Russia and Estonia score higher with 1.1%, slightly below Jamaica (1.2%). Thailand, at 1.5%, scores among the Asian countries with the highest rates. Apart from the terrible human tragedy, what are the economic consequences of HIV?

The long-term effects of HIV. Alwyn Young has a provocative answer to that question, suggesting that the long-term economic effects of HIV are positive.[3] Young draws a parallel between the AIDS tragedy in Africa and the Black Death pandemic of the 14th century in Europe, caused by several

FIGURE 16.4   Prevalence of HIV (% of Population Aged 15–49) in 2007

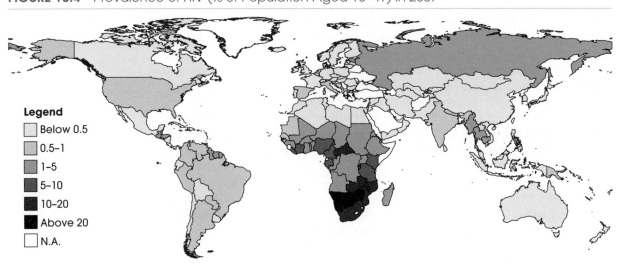

Legend
- Below 0.5
- 0.5–1
- 1–5
- 5–10
- 10–20
- Above 20
- N.A.

HIV is more prevalent in poor countries and has reached epidemic proportions in the southern half of Africa.

Source: The World Bank, World Development Indicators, 2007.

strains of the plague bacterium, *Yersinia pestis,* thought to have been carried by infected fleas on rats. The plague drastically reduced Europe's population, killing, by some estimates, over 100 million people; it is thought that the plague reduced the population of Britain by half. Although the plague was one of the greatest human tragedies of all times, some economic historians suggest that it had positive economic effects. Their argument is that the Black Death created a scarcity of labor, encouraged the rise of female participation in the labor force, and led to a reduction in fertility rates. Reduced fertility rates maintained labor scarcity and this led to a permanent and large increase in real wages.

Young argues that there might be a similar effect in Africa as a consequence of the AIDS epidemic. He points out that AIDS has reduced both the labor pool and fertility rates, which have declined as a direct result of so many women being infected by HIV and, as a result, having fewer or no children. There is also, however, an indirect effect. As labor scarcity gives women better opportunities and increased incomes on the labor market, the opportunity cost of having children also becomes higher. Higher real wages thus lead to a decrease in the fertility rate that, in turn, contributes to keeping labor scarce and real incomes high. Young argues that without AIDS, the population of South Africa would be at around 100 million in 2050, whereas because of the epidemic and the resulting decline in fertility, it will be around 50 million.

Young's findings have been challenged by other researchers. Using African data from 1985 to 2000, Sebnem Kalemli-Ozcan finds that AIDS increased fertility rates and reduced education levels.[4] Kalemli-Ozcan suggests a precautionary effect that leads to an increase in fertility rates: Because of the high AIDS death rate of young adults, people in this group are more uncertain about how many of their children will survive to adulthood. They therefore choose to have more children to be sure that enough of them will survive. For the same reason (lower expected survival rate of children), these young adults will also invest less in the education of each child because the potential for HIV infection will reduce the expected benefits of education. Kalemli-Ozcan estimates that AIDS will increase fertility by 2 more children per household, while there will be 38% lower school enrollment in Africa.

Similarly, Peter Lorentzen, John McMillan, and Romain Wacziarg found that an increase in mortality had a negative effect on economic growth because it not only led to an increase in fertility rates, but also to a reduction in investment and education.[5] Their argument is similar to Kalemli-Ozcan's: if people expect to die young and also expect their children to die young, they will save less and invest less in education. Using international data from 1960 to 2000, they found that increased mortality increases fertility rates. Note that the argument applies not only to AIDS, but to any cause of an increase in mortality.

[3]Alwyn Young, "The Gift of the Dying: The Tragedy of AIDS and the Welfare of Future African Generations," *The Quarterly Journal of Economics* 120, no. 2 (2005): 423–466.
[4]Sebnem Kalemli-Ozcan, "AIDS, 'Reversal' of the Demographic Transition and Economic Development: Evidence from Africa" (working paper, National Bureau of Economic Research, May 2006).
[5]Peter Lorentzen, John McMillan, and Romain Wacziarg, "Death and Development," *Journal of Economic Growth* 13, no. 2 (2008): 81–124.

Diarrheal Diseases

A major cause of child mortality in developing countries is diarrheal diseases, accounting for 20% of the mortality of children under the age of 5. Diarrheal diseases are primarily caused by the lack of access to safe water. Surface water that is used for drinking is often contaminated with bacteria, viruses, and parasites, which is the result of the water coming in contact with human and animal wastes. Many countries are too poor to provide their populations with safe sources of water and poor rural areas suffer the most from water contamination. Short of introducing expensive modern water and sanitation systems, what are some of the effective ways to fight diarrheal diseases?

Oral rehydration therapy is the most common form of treatment, often effectively complemented by micronutrient supplementation. In some situations, supplements of zinc and vitamin A may reduce parasitic infections.

There are other means of preventing diarrheal diseases. Breastfeeding is a very simple and effective method as it provides a more hygienic supply of food for infants, especially under the age of 6 months. Continued breastfeeding after that point can prolong significant protective effects.

Vaccines are very effective in preventing those diarrheal diseases caused by viruses. Roughly 20% of deaths from diarrheal diseases among children under the age of 5 are related to rotaviruses. Particles of these viruses are present in the feces of infected animals and people, and are spread by contaminated water and physical contact. New vaccines have been developed that are very effective against the gastroenteritis caused by rotaviruses.

An obvious preventive method is to change individual behavior with, for example, more frequent hand washing before and after handling children and food, after defecating, and before eating. In poor rural areas, education campaigns can help to explain the benefits of hand washing and distribute soap to households. When implemented, these programs are quite effective. Randomized evaluations of hand washing campaigns in Pakistan and Myanmar tend to show a roughly 40% decrease in diarrheal incidence.

Another method is called **point-of-use water treatment**, which involves various forms of water purification. Randomized evaluations have demonstrated that this method can reduce the incidence of diarrheal diseases by roughly 20%. Point-of-use water treatment, similar to hand washing, is critically dependent on behavioral changes. Irregular water disinfection and irregular hand washing will both be ineffective preventive measures. However, educating people about the benefits of behavioral change is costly and often more difficult among poorer people. Moreover, it is not clear what the best methods are to provide this education: Address households directly? Focus on community leaders? Target mothers of newborns?

Point-of-use water treatment also has disadvantages that people have to learn to accept. Water has a somewhat unpleasant taste when treated with disinfectant and filtration systems can reduce water flow. Moreover, households have to pay for point-of-use water treatment products. It is not clear what percentage of households would buy these products at market prices or even at subsidized prices.

Piping water into homes. How effective is the provision of piped water and improved sanitation practices in poor countries relative to other methods for preventing diarrheal diseases? S.A. Esrey and colleagues have gathered empirical evidence that suggests hygiene education or sanitation investments (sewage systems) result in nearly twice the median reduction of diarrheal incidence compared to improvement of water quality.[6] Clean water can be recontaminated when it is transported and stored unless people wash their hands and their water containers properly. Therefore, water quality improvements will not be effective unless the water arrives directly to a tap in people's homes. A recent study by Michael Kremer and his research associates in 175 Kenyan communities found somewhat different results. Their evidence suggests that few health improvements result from better rural water infrastructure (piped water).[7] Instead, they found that spring protection in the form of sealing off a water source so that it flows through a pipe instead of allowing it to seep from the ground was a very effective method to improve household water quality. They found also little evidence of quality deterioration of water at the transport and storage stage after a water source is sealed.

Overall, however, the majority of the literature on interventions to prevent diarrheal diseases seems to suggest that hand washing and point-of-use water treatment should be prioritized over programs to improve communal water infrastructure and to pipe water into people's homes.

Malaria

A typical infectious disease of the tropics, malaria is caused by mosquito-borne parasites. Malaria causes anemia, intense fever, chills, and chronic weakness. It can be fatal, especially among children. In addition, it can lead to brain damage, seizures, and other neurologic complications.

Figure 16.5 shows the global incidence of death from malaria between 2005 and 2010. It is clear that the greatest number of malarial deaths occur in sub-Saharan Africa. Fatalities from malaria are much lower in Central America and Brazil, as well as in the subtropical parts of Asia, including India.

Transmission of the malaria parasite occurs when a mosquito bites an infected person and ingests contaminated blood; when that same mosquito later bites an uninfected person, it transmits the parasite into a new host. The goal of campaigns to fight malaria has generally been not to kill all mosquitoes but rather to interrupt the transmission of the parasite long enough to let the existing populations of parasites die out. After World War II, the World Health

---

[6]S.A. Esrey, J.B. Potash, L. Roberts, and C. Schiff, "Effects of Improved Water Supply and Sanitation on Ascariasis, Diarrhoea, Dracunculias, Hookworm Infection, Schistosomiasis, and Trachoma," *Bulletin of the World Health Organization* 69, no. 5 (1991): 609–621.

[7]Michael Kremer, Jessica Leino, Edward Miguel, and Alix P. Zwane, "Spring Cleaning: Rural Water Impacts, Valuation, and Property Right Institutions," *The Quarterly Journal of Economics* 126, no. 1 (2011): 145–205.

FIGURE 16.5 Estimated Global Deaths from Malaria, 2005–2010

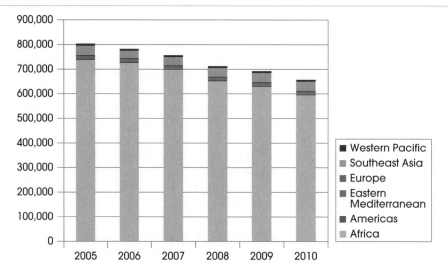

Although malaria is a tropical disease, it causes the greatest number of fatalities in sub-Saharan Africa.

Source: The World Bank, World Development Indicators.

Organization launched extensive campaigns to eradicate malaria by spraying DDT (dichlorodiphenyltrichloroethane), a complex and extremely toxic chemical whose insecticidal properties were discovered shortly before World War II. Walls of dwellings are sprayed with DDT to keep mosquitoes outside.

Effects of malaria control campaigns. Significant effects of malaria control campaigns were observed in countries such as Brazil, India, Vietnam, and Eritrea, as well as in at-risk regions of the American South. Hoyt Bleakley has examined the effects of these campaigns in the United States and in South America.[8] Pesticide spraying, draining swamps, and mass administration of quinine (a natural extract of the cinchona tree, found in the tropical forests of western South America, with analgesic and anti-inflammatory properties) completely eradicated malaria in the American South during the 20th century. After World War II, extensive Latin American campaigns using DDT led to a spectacular decrease in malaria cases.

Bleakley examined the economic effects of these campaigns by comparing the evolution of literacy and income levels in regions with initially high malaria infection rates to regions with lower initial infection rates. Malaria has particularly negative effects on children; because both physiological and human capital development take place during childhood, children infected with the parasite become physically weaker and, as a result, are frequently absent from school, which negatively impacts their education. The positive

---

[8]Hoyt Bleakley, "Malaria in the Americas: A Retrospective Analysis of Childhood Exposure," *American Economic Journal: Applied Economics* 2, no. 2 (2010): 1–45.

effects of malaria eradication campaigns on education and income levels was thus quite significant. Because the dates of the eradication campaigns were well known, these efforts provided the most benefits to those individuals who were born either after the campaigns began or shortly before they were initiated. In contrast, those individuals who were already adults at the time of the campaigns realized fewer benefits because of their age and the long-term negative impacts of the disease on their education. Bleakley found that malaria eradication campaigns had a significant effect on literacy rates and incomes in the American South and in Brazil, Mexico, and Colombia. Those individuals born after the campaigns began had, in general, higher literacy rates and a higher income level.

Figures 16.6a and 16.6b estimate the effects of the Brazilian eradication program on literacy levels. The horizontal axis represents an individual's year of birth and the vertical axis represents the coefficient of the effect of malaria (measured at the level of each Brazilian state) on the dependent variable (literacy and income). Each dot represents a coefficient for a given cohort (birth year). We see that the two-dimensional map of the malaria effects takes the form of a horizontal line until 1940, followed by a line with positive slope and then another, higher horizontal line after 1958. How should we interpret these data? Take into account that the DDT campaign in Brazil, which began in 1955, took several years to reach full implementation, at which point a significant drop in the number of malaria infections could be observed. The lower horizontal line shows the effects on earlier cohorts (measured by birth year) who were already old enough when the campaign started. We see a clear negative effect of malaria on literacy and income. The line with positive slope shows the effects of partial exposure to the campaign (those who were born after 1940 and were younger than 15 when the campaign started); the horizontal line after

FIGURE 16.6a The Effects of the Brazilian Malaria Eradication
Campaign on Literacy

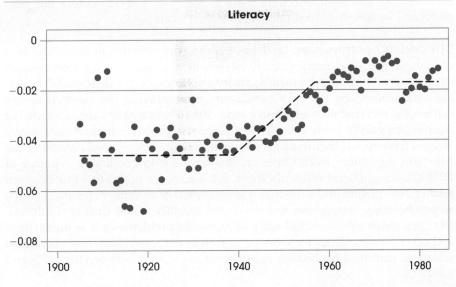

FIGURE 16.6b   The Effects of the Brazilian Malaria Eradication Campaign on Income

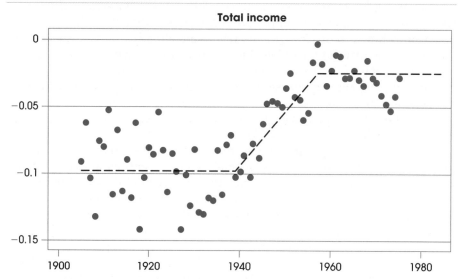

The horizontal axis measures an individual's year of birth and the vertical axis gives the coefficient of the effect of malaria (measured at the state level) on the dependent variable (literacy and income). Each dot represents a coefficient for a given cohort (birth year). The campaign to eradicate malaria in Brazil started in 1955; those who were born more than 15 years before that date in states with malarial infections had lower literacy and income levels than those in states with few or no infections. The negative effects were attenuated for those born after 1940 and became nearly equal to zero for those born after the start of the campaign.

Source: Hoyt Bleakley, "Malaria in the Americas: A Retrospective Analysis of Childhood Exposure," *American Economic Journal: Applied Economics* 2, no. 2 (2010): 17.

1958 shows the effect of being born after the malaria campaign began. It is evident that the economic effects of malaria were more severe before the campaign and were reduced to almost zero after the campaign.

DDT and its controversies. DDT has proved very effective in the eradication of malaria, but its extreme toxicity has resulted in widespread controversies over its use. Currently banned in many countries, it is considered "moderately hazardous" by the WHO. Indiscriminate spraying has resulted in this compound entering an ecosystem's food chain, threatening various species of wildlife, especially birds. It is also considered a probable human carcinogen. Studies have found that workers who handled DDT developed cancers of the liver and the biliary tract. Other studies have found conflicting evidence of DDT causing different types of cancer. Some research points to a link between fetal DDT exposure and subsequent neurological development problems, such as psychomotor retardation and decreased cognitive skills during childhood. DDT has also been associated with reproductive problems such as miscarriage and other fertility issues for women, as well as decreased semen quality. Most advanced countries banned the agricultural use of DDT between the 1970s and the 1990s.

There has been less use of DDT in Africa than in Latin America or Asia. Because it leaves stains on house walls when sprayed as well as a lingering unpleasant smell, many people in Africa avoid its use. It is reported to leave bedbugs alive, leading people to believe it is not effective. Donors of development aid often make the provision of funds contingent on prohibiting the use of DDT. The European Union has threatened to ban imports from countries that use DDT. Despite its toxicity, DDT is still considered by many scientists and the WHO to be the most effective instrument in the fight to eradicate malaria. There is growing concern, however, that in many countries using DDT (India being one of them), mosquitoes have become resistant to it.

Scientists and medical researchers are considering alternatives to DDT. An effective vaccine against malaria has not yet been developed so the best current alternative to its use appears to be bed nets treated with other, less toxic insecticides, but the insecticides must be renewed every 6 months for the bed nets to retain their effectiveness. For example, Jeffrey Sachs, director of the Earth Institute at Columbia University and special adviser to the UN Secretary General on the Millennium Development Goals, recommends widespread free distribution of bed nets across Africa. Critics have claimed that those who receive the nets for free are less likely to use them than those who pay a price, albeit subsidized. Stories also circulate about bed nets used for fishing and the toxic effects the insecticides have on fish, but this information is, as yet, anecdotal. In a randomized trial in Kenya, Jessica Cohen and Pascaline Dupas found that demand for bed nets is much larger when the price is reduced drastically.[9] In addition, they found that there was no difference in the use of bed nets by households who received them for free compared to those who paid for them. This research thus corroborates the view that free distribution of bed nets would be very effective in countries still suffering from malaria.

Worms

Various forms of parasitic worms have extremely damaging effects on human health. Unlike fleas and lice that can live on the human body, parasitic worms feed and reproduce inside the body and weaken or damage their host organism. The most infamous of these worms are the hookworm, the roundworm, the whipworm, and the flatworm. Usually very small, parasitic worms infect one in four people worldwide. Worm infections are particularly prevalent among school-age children in developing countries. Infections may not have severe effects, but in many cases they lead to more serious complications such as anemia, malnutrition, frequent abdominal pain, and listlessness, and they can be very debilitating. The flatworm causes schistosomiasis (also called bilharzia), which can cause damage to major organs such as the liver and spleen. Worm infections can spread through poor hygiene; infected children defecate in bushes around their houses or schools; worms present in the feces thus contaminate human environments and can come in contact with other children, repeating the cycle of infection. Schistosomiasis is usually contracted by

---

[9]Jessica Cohen and Pascaline Dupas, "Free Distribution or Cost-Sharing? Evidence from a Malaria Prevention Field Experiment," *The Quarterly Journal of Economics* 125, no. 1 (2010): 1–45.

bathing or swimming in contaminated fresh water in lakes, ponds, or streams. It can also be contracted by walking barefoot in puddles near infected water sources.

There are successful drug therapies to treat worm infections, but they must be taken every year or every 6 months because of the high rates of reinfection, especially among children. How effective are deworming programs? In the introduction to this chapter, we mentioned their health and education benefits, but measuring these effects is difficult. Simply studying the effects of a deworming program in a particular village may not be adequate as the prevalence of worm infestation in that village is likely to be different than in other villages. Moreover, there is a strong seasonal effect to consider because worms spread more easily during the rainy season. Thus, researchers must study deworming programs over a sufficiently long period of time and have reliable comparison groups. The best method is a randomized evaluation that can make a valid comparison between those individuals who are treated and those who are not.

However, conducting randomized trials within a village can also be challenging. Suppose that half of the children in a school are randomly treated for deworming and the other half are not. When comparing the effects of deworming on school absenteeism and school performance between those treated and those not, the results are likely to be disappointing and researchers may conclude that deworming programs do not have a significant effect on health and school performance. In fact, the externalities created by a deworming program must be recognized. For example, if half of the children in a school receive deworming medications, the other half will also benefit from it because a certain percentage of them are less likely to be infected. A randomized evaluation within schools would thus ignore this externality and underestimate the positive effects of deworming programs.

Miguel and Kremer analyzed the effects of a Kenyan deworming program in a study designed to take these externalities into account.[10] With the help of the NGO, International Child Support, they studied a program in the Busia district of western Kenya that was randomized and gradually phased in across several schools. Twenty-five of the 75 schools chosen for the project received free deworming treatments beginning in 1998, a second group started receiving treatment in 1999, and a third in 2001. In addition to the deworming treatment, schools also received prevention education on the importance of hand washing and wearing shoes, as well warnings about the dangers of swimming in infected waters.

Table 16.2 compares the effects of the treatment between group 1 and group 2, before group 2 got the treatment. Panel A shows that infection rates were lower by 25 percentage points in the treated group. Moderate to heavy infections from hookworms, roundworms, and schistosomes (flatworms) were significantly lower in the treatment group by a margin of 10 to 25 percentage points. There was no significant difference for whipworm infection because

---

[10]Edward Miguel and Michael Kremer, "Worms: Identifying Impacts on Education and Health in the Presence of Treatment Externalities," *Econometrica* 72, no. 1 (2004): 159–217.

TABLE 16.2 Deworming Effects in Treatment Group 1 and Control Group 2

	Group 1	Group 2	Group 1–Group 2
Panel A: Helminth Infection Rates			
Any moderate–heavy infection, January–March 1998	0.38	—	—
Any moderate–heavy infection, 1999	0.27	0.52	−0.25***
			(0.06)
Hookworm moderate–heavy infection, 1999	0.06	0.22	−0.16
			(0.03)
Roundworm moderate–heavy infection, 1999	0.09	0.24	−0.15***
			(0.04)
Schistosome moderate–heavy infection, 1999	0.08	0.18	−0.10*
			(0.06)
Whipworm moderate–heavy infection, 1999	0.13	0.17	−0.04
			(0.05)
Panel B: Other Nutritional and Health Outcomes			
Sick in past week (self-reported), 1999	0.41	0.45	−0.04**
			(0.02)
Sick often (self-reported), 1999	0.12	0.15	−0.03**
			(0.01)
Height for age, 1999 (low scores denote undernutrition)	−1.13	−1.22	0.09*
			(0.05)
Weight for age, 1999 (low scores denote undernutrition)	−1.25	−1.25	0.00
			(0.04)
Hemoglobin concentration, 1999	124.8	123.2	1.6
			(1.4)
Proportion anemic (Hb < 100g/L), 1999	0.02	0.04	−0.02**
			(0.01)
Panel C: Worm Prevention Behaviors			
Clean (observed by field worker), 1999	0.59	0.60	−0.01
			(0.02)
Wears shoes (observed by field worker), 1999	0.24	0.26	−0.02
			(0.03)
Days in contact with fresh water in past week (self reported), 1999	2.4	2.2	0.2
			(0.3)

Group 1 was treated with deworming medications and had significantly lower infection rates and better health outcomes than did group 2, which was not treated.

Notes: Hb denotes hemoglobin concentration, a measure of anemia. *p < .05; **p < .01; ***p < .001. Standard errors in parentheses

Source: Edward Miguel and Michael Kremer, "Worms: Identifying Impacts on Education and Health in the Presence of Treatment Externalities," *Econometrica* 72, no. 1 (2004): 173. Printed with permission of The Econometric Society.

the single dose of the drug used (albendazole) is known to be less effective against whipworms. Panel B displays the results in terms of health outcomes. Those in the treatment group reported having 4% fewer symptoms in the preceding week, and 3% fewer children reported frequent symptoms of illness. Height-for-age scores were 9% higher for the treatment group. Note that these scores represent deviation (measured in cm) from the average WHO score for that age. However, weight-for-age scores did not vary. There were 2% fewer anemic children in the treatment group compared to 4% in the control group. Panel C shows that worm-prevention behavior was not, however, found to be different between the treatment and control group, thus the positive health effects were apparently the result of the deworming treatment rather than preventive behaviors.

It is interesting to observe that students in the treated schools who did not receive the deworming medication (some pupils were absent and girls older than 13 did not receive a treatment) had rates of heavy infection that were 12% lower than in the untreated schools. This is a significant effect—nearly half the difference between treated and untreated schools—and underscores the externality effect mentioned above: when some children in a school receive deworming drugs, other untreated children also benefit because of the lowered probability of exposure and infection. Miguel and Kremer also found that deworming increased school attendance between 6% and 9 % and they calculated that an additional year of school participation in the deworming program would only cost $3.50!

Researchers have conducted studies on the effects of deworming programs in other regions of the world. In an Indian study, done in the slums of Delhi, on the effects of providing iron supplements and deworming drugs to children between the ages of 2 and 6 in preschools, Gustavo Bobonis, Edward Miguel, and Charu Puri-Sharma found that school attendance increased by 6% and children's weights increased by slightly over a pound as a consequence of the intervention.[11]

Tuberculosis

Tuberculosis is a contagious bacterial infection caused by virulent pathogens called mycobacteria that attack the lungs but can also damage the nervous system, the circulatory system, the bones, and the skin. While it can be treated with antibiotics, new, antibiotic-resistant strains of the bacteria have appeared in recent years and tuberculosis infections have steadily increased over the last 2 decades.

Figure 16.7 shows the incidence of tuberculosis across the world measured as the estimated deaths from the disease per 100,000 inhabitants in 2010. Sadly, sub-Saharan Africa is the region that suffers the most from tuberculosis, where Sierra Leone has the highest incidence with 146 deaths per 100,000 inhabitants. Cambodia has the second highest incidence in Asia with 61 deaths per 100,000 inhabitants. Haiti has the highest incidence in Latin America with 29 deaths per 100,000 inhabitants.

---

[11]Gustavo J. Bobonis, Edward Miguel, and Charu Puri-Sharma, "Iron Deficiency Anemia and School Participation," *Journal of Human Resources* 61, no. 4 (2006): 692–721.

FIGURE 16.7   Estimated Deaths in 2010 from Tuberculosis per 100,000 Inhabitants

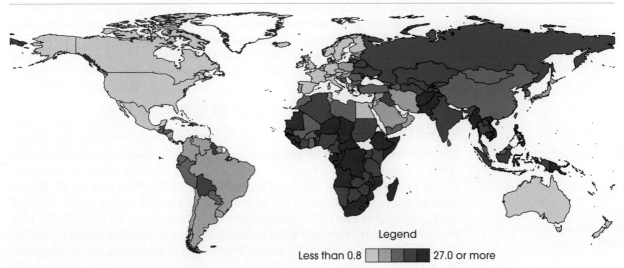

Deaths from tuberculosis are highest in Africa and Asia.

Source: The World Bank, World Development Indicators, 2012.

Those infected with the tuberculosis bacterium are usually adolescents or young adults and it is the world's greatest killer of women of reproductive age. Infection can result by inhaling droplets from the cough or sneeze of someone carrying the pathogen. Tuberculosis vaccines administered to children have significant preventative effects. Of great concern is the fact that HIV infection greatly increases the chance of getting tuberculosis as a result of the body's weakened immune system.

There are, as yet, few evaluations of the economic effects of fighting tuberculosis. A specialized study based on a randomized sample in Thailand found that the cost of treating someone for tuberculosis represented, on average, 15% of a household's annual income, while the disease itself reduced annual household income by 5%.[12]

Cheap Drugs and Development

As we have discussed in this chapter, drug therapies that treat the most serious diseases in developing countries can have substantial positive health effects. The problem is that poor people living on a dollar a day or less lack the means to purchase drugs at their market prices. HIV medications in the United States cost between $200 and $1,000 per month. Other drugs to treat the health problems we have discussed may cost less, but people who are not well educated about the efficiency of these treatments are often not willing to pay even those

---

[12]P. Kamolratanakul, H. Sawert, S. Kongsin, S. Lertmaharit, J. Sriwongsa, S. Na-Songkhla, S. Wangmane, S. Jittimanee, and V. Payanandana "Economic Impact of Tuberculosis at the Household Level," *The International Journal of Tuberculosis and Lung Disease* 3 no. 7 (1999): 596–602.

lower prices. The cost of a bed net is about $10, which for many Africans represents more than a third of their monthly income. Many NGOs raise money to provide free or subsidized medications to people in developing countries, but the funds only reach those populations targeted by specific projects. Governments in developing countries obviously do not have the adequate budgetary resources to provide free medicine for their people.

Why Pharmaceutical Companies Spend So Little on Developing Countries

The inability to provide an adequate supply of drugs for populations in developing countries is only part of the world's health problems. If there were a vaccine to prevent malaria, we could eradicate the disease once and for all, as was the case with smallpox many decades ago. Why is there yet no vaccine against malaria, arguably one of the most widespread diseases on the planet? The simple answer is that pharmaceutical companies are not spending much money on developing one. Less than 5% of the investment in research and development (R and D) by private industry on health issues is related to diseases specific to poor countries. While R and D spending does not guarantee that researchers will find the right drugs or vaccines for a particular disease, little or no spending virtually guarantees no medical progress. The reason pharmaceutical companies spend so little on R and D for diseases endemic to poor countries is purely economic: expenditures on R and D are a fixed cost and the companies can only recoup that money through profits on sales above a certain level. The market for drugs and vaccines in developing countries is simply not large enough. There could be an adequate market if governments from all developing countries would join forces and commit to spending a certain amount of money each year on drug and vaccine purchases. That, however, represents a huge collective-action problem. Even if it could be overcome, the commitment problems would still be significant. Suppose that pharmaceutical companies spend a substantial amount on a malaria vaccine with the expectation of receiving a steady stream of income from the governments of developing countries. Once the vaccine became available, those governments might be tempted to renege on their commitment and insist on paying only the marginal cost of the vaccine's production instead of the higher price they had agreed to pay. This commitment problem would deter pharmaceutical companies from spending on R and D for medications to treat or prevent diseases in developing countries.

An Advance Market Commitment

A potential solution to this commitment problem has emerged that could incentivize pharmaceutical companies to invest more in R and D expenditures for poor countries. Following the British government's initiative, the G8 (the governments of eight of the world's wealthiest nations) at its July 2006 summit in St. Petersburg, Russia, supported the idea of an "advance market commitment" for a malaria vaccine. The idea behind the advance market commitment is that a coalition of sponsoring countries or organizations precommits to purchase a quantity of vaccines from pharmaceutical companies at a predetermined price. The supplier, in turn, guarantees further sales at a reasonably low price or agrees to license its technology to other manufacturers. The purpose is to eliminate the market risk for suppliers. Companies will always face the risk that the R and D expenditures required do achieve the expected results, but this is a risk that is also present for R and D expenses related to the development of pharmaceuticals for markets in developed countries.[13] Nevertheless, eliminating the market risk represents an important step in creating a level playing field in terms of prioritizing R and D expenditures between poor and rich countries. An additional argument for this plan is the presence of the rule of law in developed nations that make this advance commitment, as it will better guarantee the likelihood that the agreement will be honored.

Designing an advance market commitment is challenging. Suppose there is an advance commitment and a pharmaceutical company develops the first malaria vaccine. Also suppose that after one year, a second company develops a better and cheaper vaccine. What should be done in terms of the initial advance market commitment? Continuing to purchase the first vaccine to honor the commitment would not be socially optimal once the second vaccine became available; while it would be better, both in terms of costs and in terms of health outcomes, to switch to the second vaccine, wouldn't that reduce the incentives for a company to invest in a vaccine in the first place? One solution to this commitment problem is to promise a higher price for certain quantities of the first vaccine with the provision of switching to a better and cheaper second vaccine if one is developed. This higher sum would certainly be justified, not only as an incentive to pharmaceutical companies, but also as a benefit to social welfare because the marginal value of a first vaccine would be quite high.

The Orphan Drug Act

One example of an advance market commitment is the U.S. Orphan Drug Act of 1983. It includes a promise to biopharmaceutical companies of 7 years of market exclusivity for drugs they may develop unless a clinically superior product appears. The Orphan Drug Act provides incentives to the first producers of a pharmaceutical to invest in R and D because they receive guaranteed market exclusivity until a better medication appears. It also gives other companies incentives to improve a first drug and it delivers the best available treatments to patients, which is optimal from a public health perspective. This type of market guarantee could be made for the development of vaccines to use in developing countries.

The Costs of Vaccine Commitments for Developing Countries

What would it cost to develop an advance market commitment for malaria, tuberculosis, and HIV vaccines that would provide sufficient incentives to pharmaceutical companies for R and D investments? Ernst Berndt and his

---

[13]Billions of research dollars have been spent on HIV and AIDS, and significant progress has been made controlling infections and managing their effects. However, there is still no vaccine to prevent HIV.

research colleagues have estimated what such a commitment would require.[14] A first factor is the average cost, which they found to be, over the life-cycle of the average product in advanced market economies, about $3.1 billion, taking into account lower marketing costs for developing countries. A second factor is the vaccine research done by entities other than pharmaceutical companies, such as governments and private foundations. For example, the Bill and Melinda Gates Foundation has been giving significant financial support to the Malaria Vaccine Initiative, an NGO. A third factor is the level of research development of vaccines for particular diseases. The more advanced the research, the less costly an advance commitment should be. Research on vaccines for HIV and tuberculosis is still in its early stages. On the other hand, there are already candidate vaccines for malaria at a more advanced stage of development. Finally, the development of a rotavirus vaccine is already in a very advanced stage of development.

Taking those factors into account, Berndt and his colleagues proposed a price commitment of $15 for the first 200 million malaria vaccines. They found that this represented a cost of less than $15 per disability adjusted life year (DALY) saved. Similarly, they proposed an estimate of $13 per dose for the first 200 million tuberculosis vaccines and a cost of $14 per dose for the first 200 million HIV vaccines. In the latter case, this represents a cost of $17 per DALY saved. If we add up the numbers for these three vaccines, it represents a bit less than $26 billion. The benefits would be enormous in terms of lives saved.

Health and Income

Health improvements are fundamental for social welfare in developing countries, but what is their economic impact in terms of growth? One answer to this question comes from Jeffrey Sachs, the Columbia economist, who has argued that eradicating malaria in sub-Saharan Africa could increase the continent's per capita growth rate by as much as 2.6% a year.

Does Better Health Lead to Higher Incomes?

If people are healthier, they can not only be more productive but they can also become better educated, which can make them even more productive. However, not all health improvements should have economic effects, even though their welfare effects are obvious. For example, think of a health improvement that helps people to live longer; it might not have measurable economic effects if the additional years of life it adds come after retirement age. It is beneficial to live longer, but in this case, it may not increase the actual supply of labor.

How can we identify a causal effect of health improvements on income? If we find a correlation between health and income, it might be because better health leads to better economic performance, but the causal effect could also

---

[14]Ernst R. Berndt, Rachel Glennerster, Michael. R. Kremer, Jean Lee, Ruth Levine, Georg Weizsäcker, and Heidi Williams, "Advanced Purchase Commitments for a Malaria Vaccine: Estimating Costs and Effectiveness," *Health Economics* 16, no. 5 (2007): 491–511.

operate in reverse: countries with a higher income are able to afford better and more expensive health care. How can we disentangle these two effects?

Daron Acemoglu and Simon Johnson have examined the causal effects of health on income by using the timing of the major medical breakthroughs associated with the epidemiological transition.[15] It is difficult to argue that these health breakthroughs resulted from a change in world income levels; the breakthroughs were largely exogenous to changes in GDP. They were also clustered in time (toward the end of World War II) and resulted from specific scientific discoveries, which are largely unpredictable. We saw earlier in this chapter that the epidemiological transition was associated with a very visible convergence in rates of life expectancy. However, this convergence in life expectancy has not been associated with a comparable convergence in income levels. Figure 16.8 shows the evolution of the log of GDP per capita for three different groups of countries: those that were, respectively, rich, middle-income, and poor in the 1930s, before the major medical breakthroughs of the epidemiological transition. It is clear that the gap between these three groups of countries has not decreased, contrary to what was the case for life expectancy, and this gap has remained remarkably stable. Because the epidemiological transition represents one of the most important health breakthroughs in modern times, the fact that it had no significant effect on GDP per capita is an important finding.

FIGURE 16.8 Log GDP Per Capita for Initially Rich, Middle-Income, and Poor Countries

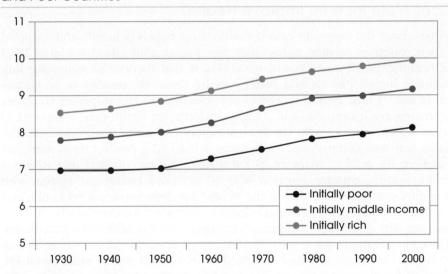

The epidemiological transition did not lead to a convergence of income per capita between poor, middle-income, and rich countries.

Source: Acemoglu and Johnson, "Disease and Development: The Effect of Life Expectancy on Economic Growth," 2007: 929.

---

[15]Daron Acemoglu and Simon Johnson, "Disease and Development: The Effect of Life Expectancy on Economic Growth," *Journal of Political Economy* 115, no. 6 (2007): 925–983.

How can we explain this finding? Increased life expectancy is equivalent to an increase in population. If people live longer, that means there are more people alive at any point in time. Indeed, Acemoglu and Johnson found that a 1% increase in life expectancy led to 1.35% increase in population. We can therefore use the tools of growth theory to understand what is happening. An increase in population, or an increase in the size of the labor force, has a positive effect on GDP because more labor leads to more output. However, because there is a diminishing marginal product of labor, more labor tends to decrease average productivity. Lower average labor productivity leads, in turn, to lower per capita income as the increase in output is not as large as the increase in the labor force. The result of Acemoglu and Johnson's findings, however, was not that increased life expectancy led to a decrease in GDP per capita—they found no significant effect for this. This means that the negative effect of increased life expectancy on GDP per capita must be partly compensated by a positive effect of better health on total factor productivity. As stated above, better health makes people more productive and also allows them to become better educated. This productivity effect is, however, not high enough to offset the negative effect of the diminishing marginal product of labor.

Overall, even if improvements in health in developing countries do not necessarily lead to higher growth rates, they are important developmental goals in themselves, and the economic effects of health improvements should be seen as second-order effects at best.

Does More Income Improve Health?

What about the opposite causal relationship between health and income? When countries become richer, they can presumably afford a higher level of health expenditures. Should we conclude that there is an automatic link between higher income and better health? There are reasons to be skeptical of such a link. Health outcomes are sometimes better in poorer countries with stronger institutions and a higher priority for health care, compared to some richer countries with weaker institutions and a low health care priority. Cuba is a poor country, but for decades it has had a health care system that has been the envy of many of its Latin American neighbors. Costa Rica is a middle-income country, but it is believed to have a health care system with a quality comparable to that of the richest developed nations. Sri Lanka and the Indian province of Kerala also have a reputation for excellent health care systems. However, other countries have neglected the health of their citizens. The United States is one of the richest countries in the world, but its health care system is nevertheless widely criticized by its citizens and by other countries. Russia's health care system has experienced significant deterioration since the early 1990s and the fall of Communism, and is widely considered to be appallingly bad. Life expectancy has declined year after year in Russia, especially for men. While South Africa is one of the richest countries in Africa, many of its health policies have been disastrous. In particular, the South African government has remained extremely passive in dealing with HIV, with calamitous effects on the life expectancy of its citizens.

Large spurts of economic growth do not necessarily lead to health improvements. China and India are good examples. Health improvements in China took place before the important economic reforms that initiated the Chinese growth miracle. In India, improvements in health care have actually slowed down since its economy experienced faster growth.

Institutions and the Provision of Health Care

In developing countries, the large variation in the availability and quality of health care provision might be due to institutional differences. We do not have systematic evidence about the quality of health care institutions in developing countries, but we do have a number of indicators for the quality of health care delivery.

Variable Quality of Health Care Systems

Similar to wealthy and middle-income nations, health care institutions in developing countries are, to a large extent, financed and managed by governments; as a result, the quality of those governments often affects the quality of health care delivery.

An indicator of health care quality is absenteeism among health care workers. Absenteeism is very costly because scarce public funds often pay medical personnel in excess of the services they actually perform. There may be multiple reasons for absenteeism: a lack of appropriate monitoring due to poor management, or a culture in which guilt and shame are not associated with various forms of moral hazard and upper levels of management will not bother to report absenteeism or can be bribed to look the other way.

Figure 16.9 shows rates of absenteeism in some developing countries based on different surveys done during surprise visits to hospitals, clinics, and health

FIGURE 16.9   Rates of Medical Personnel Absenteeism in Developing Countries

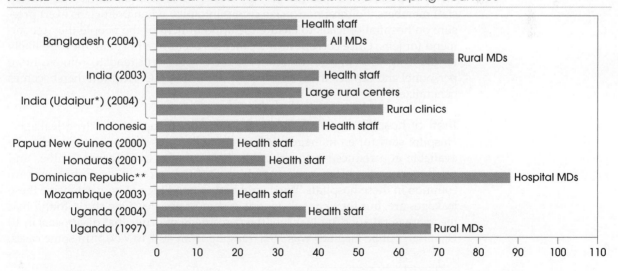

There is significant variation in the rates of absenteeism for health care personnel across countries. Absenteeism is measured during surprise visits to hospitals, clinics, and health dispensaries.

Source: Maureen Lewis, "Governance and Corruption in Public Health Care Systems" (working paper, Center for Global Development, 2006): 17.

dispensaries. These numbers were recorded at different times in the context of different studies, so they are not extremely accurate and possibly contain large measurement errors. We nevertheless can see a large variation in absenteeism rates for health personnel from a low of 19% in Papua New Guinea and Mozambique to over 60% in the Dominican Republic, Bangladesh, and Uganda.

Another indicator of poor-quality health care is the lack of supplies in hospitals. Patients are often asked to bring not only their own bed sheets and food, but also bandages, drugs, syringes, and other medical equipment. Many rural hospitals even lack basics such as thermometers, stethoscopes, and scales.

Corruption in the Health Care Sector

Figure 16.10 shows individuals' perceptions of corruption in the health care sector for various countries. These are subjective measures of corruption collected from surveys of the general public and of public officials and business executives. They vary greatly across countries; they are very high in Pakistan, Sri Lanka, and Tajikistan, where roughly 90% of those surveyed thought their country's health care sector was corrupt, but the perceptions of corruption are much lower in Kazakhstan, Peru, Bangladesh, and the Kyrgyz Republic.

Bribes for jobs and promotions. Corruption in the health care sector takes many forms. The first is buying positions and promotions in hospitals. When this happens, both the selection of doctors and their potential promotions are based on bribes to government officials instead of professional merit. As a result, incompetent and dishonest physicians are hired and promoted. Corrupt hiring practices sometimes take less overt forms than outright bribing; nepotism plays a role and jobs can also go to friends of hospital officials or current staff members. Political patronage comes into play when politicians exert pressure on hospital officials to ensure the appointment of the people they recommend for jobs. Once corrupt hiring practices occur in a hospital, they are likely to take root. Corrupt administrators and doctors will tend to remove more personnel and replace them with family and friends. Corruption then becomes generalized.

Theft of hospital supplies. A second form of corruption is "drug leakage." Hospital staff (often management) steal medications that are supposed to be available at a reduced price in public hospitals for low-income families and resell them on the black market at a high profit. As a result, drug shortages are common in these hospitals. We do not have a good idea of how extensive these leakages are, but they are substantial in some countries. One study found that the average rate of drug leakage (the percentage of drugs that disappear) in 10 Ugandan public facilities was 76%, ranging from 40% to 94%.[16] In some cases,

---

[16]Barbara McPake, Delius Asiimwe, Francis Mwesigye, Mathias Ofumbi, Lisbeth Ortenblad, Pieter Streefland, and Asaph Turinde, "Informal economic activities of public health workers in Uganda: Implications for quality and accessibility of care," *Social Science & Medicine* 49, no. 7 (1999): 849–865.

FIGURE 16.10   Perceptions of Corruption in the Health Care Sector

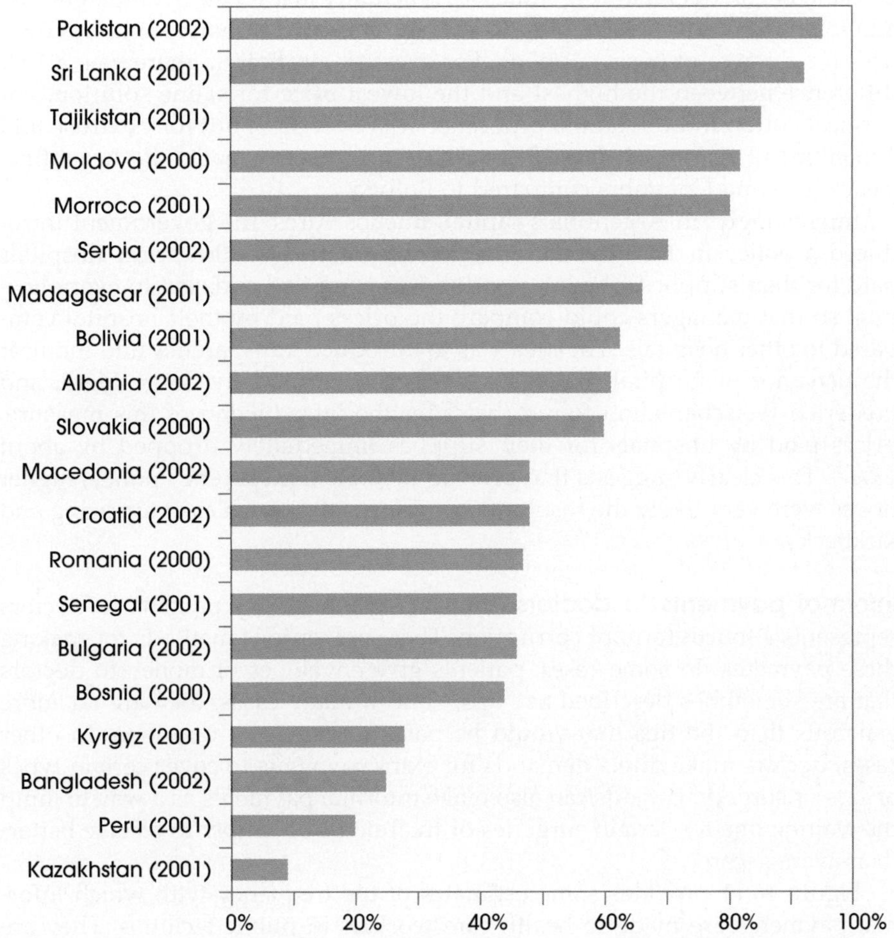

Perceptions of corruption, the percentage who think there is corruption in their health care sector, vary among developing countries. They are lower in Kazakhstan and Peru, and highest in Pakistan and Sri Lanka. The year in parentheses indicates when the survey was conducted.

Source: Lewis, "Governance and Corruption in Public Health Care Systems," 2006: 15.

government agencies responsible for delivering the drugs to hospitals sell them directly on the black market instead.

Overpricing and kickbacks. A third form of corruption is the vulnerability of a health system's supply chain to theft by its administrators. One strategy involves suppliers charging hospitals a higher price for drugs or equipment than these provisions actually cost and giving kickbacks to hospital managers. While it is difficult to provide evidence for these kickbacks, large differences in prices between hospitals should be indicative of overcharging. Rafael Di Tella and William Savedoff have looked at differences in purchase prices for very basic hospital supplies in various Latin American countries.[17] Even a 5% difference for basic supplies should be indicative of possible illegal overcharging, unless it is actually just gross incompetence by administrators. The researchers found significant differences within countries for a range of basic supplies. For example, in Bolivia there was a 15% difference between the highest and the lowest price for saline solution. For surgical cotton in Bolivia, the difference was over 35%, but for dextrose and penicillin, it was much less. Price differences were smaller in Argentina, Venezuela, and Colombia compared to Bolivia.

Interestingly, in Argentina's capital, Buenos Aires, the government introduced a policy in 1996 to centralize all information on the prices hospitals paid for their supplies. The information was compiled and sent to every hospital so that managers could compare the prices paid by their hospital compared to other hospitals. The idea was to introduce transparency and monitor the behavior of hospital managers. Ernesto Schargrodsky, Jorge Mera, and Frederico Weischenbaum found that after the introduction of this measure, prices paid by hospitals for their supplies immediately dropped by about 13%.[18] This clearly suggests that prior to the new transparency policy, higher prices were very likely the result of corrupt practices such as overpricing and kickbacks.

Informal payments to doctors. Informal payments by patients to doctors represents a fourth form of corruption. There are various methods for making these payments. In some cases, patients give envelopes of money to doctors that are sometimes described as "tips," but in many cases, they are far more generous than the tips that would be paid to waiters or doormen. In other cases, doctors make direct demands for extra payments to cover certain types of care or surgery. Patients can also make informal payments as a way to jump the waiting line for certain surgeries or treatments or simply to receive better-than-average care.

Figure 16.11 provides some estimates of the frequency with which informal payments are made to health care workers in public facilities. They are very low in Bulgaria, Kosovo, Peru, and Thailand, but quite high in Armenia, Kyrgyz Republic, Moldova, Pakistan, Sri Lanka, and Vietnam. Doctors often justify the practice of informal payments by invoking the low salaries paid in the public health system.

The body of evidence on institutional quality suggests that developing countries can bring about better health care provision with institutional improvements and the eradication of corruption.

---

[17]Rafael Di Tella and William D. Savedoff, eds., *Diagnosis Corruption: Fraud in Latin America's Public Hospitals* (Washington, DC: Inter-American Development Bank, 2001).

[18]Ernesto Schargrodsky, Jorge Mera, and Frederico Weinschelbaum, "Transparency and Accountability in Argentina's Hospitals," in Di Tella and Savedoff, *Diagnosis Corruption: Fraud in Latin America's Public Hospitals*: 95–122.

FIGURE 16.11   Percentage of Patients Who Make Informal Payments

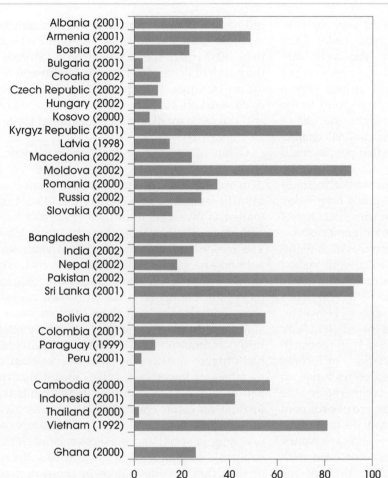

Surveys in various countries (the year is indicated in parentheses) asked patients if they make informal payments to doctors.

Source: Maureen Lewis, "Governance and Corruption in Public Health Care Systems," 2006: 28.

Social Networks, Caste, and Health

In India, caste (the country's hereditary system of social classes) is still a significant social reality and the caste system is thus an important institution in Indian culture. Does the caste system affect the demand for and provision of health care, and if so, how?

Traditionally, at the highest level of the Hindu caste system were the *Brahmins*, scholarly priests and intellectuals who sought the highest spiritual knowledge. Below them were the ruling and military elite, the *Kshatriya*. Next were the traders and merchants, the *Vaisya*, followed by the *Shudras*, farmers, workers, and artisans. At the very bottom of the social order were the "untouchables," the *Dalit* who were only allowed to do the most menial and degrading of jobs, such as cleaning streets and latrines. Within the castes, were the *jatis* that correspond to the different occupations; for example, the *jati* of goldsmiths or carpenters. A traditional characteristic of the caste system was that people could only marry within their caste, not into a higher or lower caste. Social networks were also traditionally confined to an individual's own caste. Therefore, different social norms and habits developed that were specific to different castes.

How can we measure differences in demand for health services between the different castes? We could simply look at the demand for those services by individuals from different castes and then analyze the differences. However, this would not be an accurate or efficient way to measure caste effects. Indeed, differences in behavior might be due to variations in income levels; individuals from higher castes have, on average, higher incomes and are therefore able to afford more health care than are poorer people from lower castes. How can we differentiate between caste and income effects? Nancy Luke and Kaivan Munshi have come up with an ingenious way to measure the specific effects of caste on investment in health expenditures.[19] They recorded the health expenditures of workers on tea estates in the mountainous areas at the border between the states of Tamil Nadu and Kerala. What was unique about their findings was that workers on those estates were from different castes but they all earned the same income. Moreover, they all had access to the same health and education facilities. It is quite unusual for lower-caste workers to have both the same income and the same medical and educational facilities as higher-caste workers.

Given these exceptional circumstances, it is possible to identify a "caste effect" on the demand for health services. What Luke and Munshi found is that workers from lower castes tended to invest more in their children's health and education than workers from higher castes. The reason had to do with the different social networks people from different castes had. While all workers on the tea estates were migrants, they still maintained links with their ancestral communities; they sent their children home to study and to marry, and they ultimately retired in those communities. Higher-caste individuals had "higher quality" social networks than did members of lower castes. This meant that they had both more opportunities in and obligations to their ancestral communities, such as giving presents, exchanging loans and transfers, and investing in social and business relationships as compared to people from lower castes. Because of this, they invested more in those networks and relatively less in their children's human capital. In contrast, lower-caste people with the same income, but who had lower-quality social networks, spent more on health and education for their children.

Chapter Summary

A Historical Perspective:
The Epidemiological Transition

The health gap between rich and poor countries has substantially narrowed since the second half of the 20th century following the epidemiological transition that brought penicillin and other antibiotics, and antiviral medications to treat and cure diseases such as dysentery, cholera, and yellow fever. The World Health Organization initiated worldwide vaccination drives to protect

---

[19]Nancy Luke and Kaivan Munshi, "Social Affiliation and the Demand for Health Services: Caste and Child Health in South India" *Journal of Development Economics* 83, no. 2 (2007): 256–279.

populations from diseases such as smallpox. The use of DDT eradicated malaria in many places in the world where it had been endemic, including the American South.

Measuring Health

There are advantages and drawbacks to the different methods used to measure health in developing countries: self-reported health status, such as illness in the past week or month, and difficulties with activities such as walking, bending, or climbing the stairs; measurement of nutrient intakes; and anthropometric measures such as height, weight, and body-mass index.

Diseases and Development

In order to overcome the health gap between rich and poor countries, significant efforts must be made to prevent and treat a small number of critical diseases: HIV, diarrheal diseases, malaria, parasitic worms, and tuberculosis. As yet, there is no consensus on the long-term economic effects of HIV, but most studies find that it leads to increased fertility rates and decreased investments in education.

Many policies are critical to preventing and treating diarrheal diseases: breast feeding for longer periods, campaigns to encourage more hand washing, and point-of-use water treatment. The most expensive policy, piping water into homes improves the quality of the water, but has minimal effects on diarrheal diseases because of the many other sources of potential infection.

Spraying DDT inside homes to kill or repel mosquitoes carrying the malaria parasite has traditionally been a very effective antimalarial treatment. DDT campaigns have been particularly weak in Africa where the incidence of malaria remains very high. DDT is controversial because of its toxic effects. While it is still considered to be the most effective strategy to prevent malaria, alternatives such as the use of bed nets sprayed with insecticide, are also producing good results. While there is skepticism about the effectiveness of bed nets, campaigns to distribute them at no, or a very low, cost have proved to work well.

Distribution of deworming drugs in schools has proven to be a very cost-effective way to deal with parasitic worm infections. Considering the significant negative health consequences of worm infections, $3.50 will pay for one additional school year of participation in a treatment program for one child.

Tuberculosis treatments are costly and represent, in many developing countries, a very high percentage of the annual incomes of the poor.

Cheap Drugs and Development

One of the big obstacles to better health in developing countries is the absence of vaccines or cheap drugs for diseases endemic to these countries, such as malaria. One reason for this is that the market is often not big enough for pharmaceutical companies to recover their investment in research and development on new drugs and vaccines. To offset this, "advance market commitments," whereby rich countries commit to purchase, in advance, vaccines for malaria, tuberculosis, or HIV in a certain amount and at a certain price, can create adequate incentives for pharmaceutical companies to engage in research and development that benefit the health of poor nations.

Health and Income

Improvements in health, while desirable in and of themselves, do not seem to have a long-term positive effect on economic growth. The epidemiological transition significantly improved health in developing countries, but it did not close the development gap with rich countries. Countries can afford better health care as they develop, but it is not an automatic relationship; much depends on the strength of a country's institutions.

Institutions and the Provision of Health Care

Persistent problems in the provision of quality health care is the absenteeism rates of health care personnel, corruption in the allocation of jobs in hospitals or clinics, and corruption in supply procurement for medical facilities. Countries with weaker institutions therefore tend to have more problems associated with the quality of their health care.

Key Terms

disability adjusted life year (DALY)
epidemiological transition

point-of-use water treatment

Review Questions

1. What are the best methods to prevent and to treat diarrheal diseases in developing countries? Find other documentation than that in the chapter on the costs and benefits of different methods.

2. Better infrastructure to improve water quality in developing countries has often had disappointing results in terms of reducing diarrheal diseases. Why?

3. Malaria was eradicated in many countries after World War II. How did this happen and what were the methods used? Find other documentation than that in the chapter on controversies surrounding different methods.

4. A malaria vaccine would be a safe method to eradicate the disease. What are the possible reasons for the absence of a malaria vaccine?

5. Read the article by Hoyt Bleakley, "Disease and Development: Evidence from Hookworm Eradication in the American South," *The Quarterly Journal of Economics* 122, no. 1 (2007): 73–117. Compare the method he uses to evaluate the effect of hookworm eradication with that used by Edward Miguel and Michael Kremer discussed in this chapter. What differences do you observe between the two methodologies? What information does Bleakley use to estimate the effect of deworming campaigns?

6. Download and read Paul Gertler and Orville Solon, "Who Benefits from Social Health Insurance in Developing Countries?" (Berkeley: University of California at Berkeley/ NBER and University of the Philippines, 1998) http://faculty.haas.berkeley.edu/gertler/ working_papers/philippines-6.pdf. What are the problems with mandated health insurance systems in developing countries identified in this article? Think of at least two scenarios for policy changes that would solve these problems, either partly or completely. Discuss the advantages and drawbacks of each scenario.

7. According to Alwyn Young, HIV will lead to lower fertility choices, whereas Sebnem Kalemli-Ozcan argues that HIV will lead to higher fertility choices. Use the economics of fertility choices analyzed in Chapter 3 to evaluate both arguments. Draw a two-dimensional diagram with the number of children on the horizontal axis and consumption on the vertical axis. Draw a budget line, indifference curves, and optimal fertility choice. Show how Young's argument affects fertility choices in this diagram. Do the same exercise for Kalemli-Ozcan's argument. Discuss which of the arguments seems more plausible and why.

8. Go to the World Health Organization's website (http://apps.who.int/ghodata/); on the left side of the page, select "World Health Statistics", select "Cause-specific mortality and morbidity" and download "Distribution of life years lost by broader causes" Find which diseases cause the largest reductions in years of life in Afghanistan, Argentina, Bangladesh, Brazil, Cambodia, China, the Democratic Republic of the Congo, Cuba, Egypt, Haiti, Mozambique, and Peru. Interpret your findings in the light of the themes of the chapter.

9. Some researchers argue that free bed nets will lead to lower rates of malaria, while others argue that the free nets will be used inefficiently. Use supply and demand arguments to make the case for the first argument. Then make the case for the second argument using what you have learned about moral hazard. In particular, assume that people are more or less willing to pay for bed nets and that there are costs associated with using the nets correctly. With these assumptions, develop an argument for free bed nets that would be more widely available, but also would be used less efficiently. Then develop arguments for why free nets would not be misused.

10. We found in this chapter that better health did not lead to higher income per capita. We saw that higher life expectancy amounts to an increase in population. Use the Solow model in Chapter 4 to show the effect of a variation of an exogenous increase in the size of population on income per capita. What do you conclude? Then show the effect of an exogenous increase in total factor productivity on income per capita due to better health. Use both effects to show why empirical research finds no effect on income per capita.

Delivering Education in Developing Countries

In India, nearly 100% of children are now enrolled in primary education. This reflects significant efforts by the Indian government to provide the country's 400 million poor children access to education. Despite these impressive numbers, illiteracy is still a large problem and roughly one out of three Indian children cannot read after attending primary school. A survey of schools in Mumbai in 2000 showed that 25% of children in grades 3 and 4 could not recognize letters and 35% could not recognize basic numbers. Teachers go formally through the curriculum and all children pass to the next grade, regardless of how well they master the material. As a result, many children fall behind and never acquire basic competencies.

In 2001, the Indian NGO, Pratham, which dedicates its efforts to improving education in that country, decided to establish a remedial program for children who were falling behind in school. Pratham provided tutors to children in grades 2, 3, and 4 who had not mastered the basic skills of grades 1 and 2, such as the ability to spell simple words, read a paragraph, recognize a number, count to 20, or perform single digit addition or subtraction. These children were pulled out of their regular classes and put in remedial classes consisting of 20 pupils each. The tutors, typically young women, were hired from the local community at a salary equivalent to $10–$15 per month, representing less than 10% of a regular teacher's salary. The tutors were required to have finished their secondary education and they received 2 weeks of additional training for the remedial program.

The program significantly improved the basic competencies of the children in remedial classes (by 27.1% for reading comprehension and by 68% for single-column addition problems) and substantially improved overall test scores (by 8% to 13%) in schools that implemented the remedial program. The program proved extremely cost effective, with costs estimated at $2.25 per student per year compared to an average per student education cost of $78 per year.[1]

T his remedial program is one of many designed to improve education in developing countries and we can estimate its effects with a good degree of precision thanks to **randomized evaluations** done by development economists. The schools in which the pilot program was introduced were chosen randomly, making it possible to draw meaningful comparisons of its effects with schools where it had not been introduced.

In this chapter, we will describe many of the studies done on programs to improve education. We start by documenting the education gap between

---

[1]To find out more about Pratham's remedial programs, go to MIT's poverty action lab website at: http://www.povertyactionlab.org/sites/default/files/publications/26_Policy_Briefcase_2.pdf.

developing and developed countries and we highlight the educational gender gap in developing countries. Measures of educational achievement in developing countries show that there are significant discrepancies in the quality and delivery of education services. We then examine the economic returns to education in developing countries, i.e., the additional income generated by education, a major topic in the economics of education.

We also discuss institutional issues of education, such as corruption in education; public funds for education are often diverted and end up in the pockets of dishonest politicians. Finally, we discuss educational reforms and review research that shows which reforms work and which do not. This is an exciting field of research that has produced many randomized evaluations in recent years. We discuss how best to fight teacher absenteeism and what incentives can improve teaching quality. We also consider these questions: Which policies work best to reduce the educational gender gap? What is the effect of decentralization that gives more power to local communities to monitor education? What do we know about experiments in developing economies with government-subsidized vouchers that allow children to attend private schools? We also discuss many experimental policies to reduce the costs of schooling and to enhance school participation, such as transfers to mothers to pay for their children's education, free school meals, free uniforms and textbooks, or grants for classroom improvements.

Measuring the Education Gap

The education gap between developing and developed countries is more important at the secondary (middle and high school) and at the tertiary level (college and higher education) than at the primary school level. How has the education gap evolved over time?

The Primary School Gap

Table 17.1 shows the gross enrollment rates for primary schools in different parts of the world between 1980 and 2010. These rates measure the number of students enrolled in primary school as a percentage of children of primary-school age. As we can see in Table 17.1, gross enrollment rates are often higher than 100%. Why is that? The rates are calculated by dividing the number of primary-school children by the number of children who are old enough to be in primary school. As a result, if children repeat certain classes and are still attending primary school when they are older than primary-school age, they will be counted in the numerator but not in the denominator. For example, assume that 100% of children attend primary school, that primary school is 4 years (which is the case in many countries), and that all children complete primary school in 5 years instead of 4. Finally, assume that the number of children in each age group is the same. In that case, because of grade repetition, the gross enrollment rate will be 125%.

Looking at Table 17.1, we can see that in 2005, gross primary-school enrollment rates were already above 100%, whether in low-income, middle-income, or high-income countries. However, this was not the case in 1980 when average

TABLE 17.1   Gross Enrollment Rates (% of Students of Primary-School Age)

Area	1980	1990	2000	2002	2005	2010
World	97	101	102	103	107	106
Country group						
Low-income	83	87	95	94	102	105
Middle-income	106	112	109	112	113	106
High-income	102	103	102	101	100	110
Region						
Sub-Saharan Africa	80	73	86	95	92	99
Middle East/North Africa	87	95	95	97	103	105
Latin America	105	104	130	123	118	114
South Asia	77	95	98	97	110	106
East Asia	111	119	106	113	114	110
Eastern Europe and Central Asia	99	98	94	98	102	100
Europe (Euro area)	106	105	104	104	104	105

Gross primary enrollment rates measure enrolled primary-school pupils as a percentage of children of primary-school age. The gap between rich and poor countries has generally been eliminated.

Source: The World Bank, World Development Indicators, primary gross enrollment rates, 2012.

enrollment rates for low-income countries stood at 83%. In the countries of sub-Saharan Africa, the poorest region of the world, gross enrollment rates in primary school were still only at 92% in 2005, but they stood at 99% in 2010. In 1980, the gross enrollment rate in that region stood at 80%, so progress has been made. However, South Asia (mostly India and the surrounding countries) has seen more rapid progress. The primary-school enrollment rates in 1980 were at 77%, but in 2005 they were already at 110%.

Grade repetition is not the only reason why gross enrollment rates may exaggerate actual school enrollment rates. The number of children of primary-school age is calculated using census data, whereas the number of children attending school is calculated on the basis of data provided by the schools. Schools may have a tendency to exaggerate their pupil numbers because the subsidies the schools receive depend on those numbers. For example, in India, 1993 school data gave an official enrollment rate of 104.5%, but data from household surveys on primary-school attendance showed a primary enrollment rate of only 95%.

Net enrollment rates subtract from the gross enrollment data the number of pupils who are older than the relevant age group. Unfortunately, data on net enrollment rates are not as widely available as data on gross enrollment rates, and we only have data for very recent years. Figure 17.1 gives net enrollment rates for various regions of the world in 2010. Net enrollment rates are generally above 90% except for sub-Saharan Africa, where they were at 76%. Even looking at net enrollment rates, we see that primary education is now more or less generalized in the developing world.

FIGURE 17.1   Net Primary-School Enrollment Rates in 2010

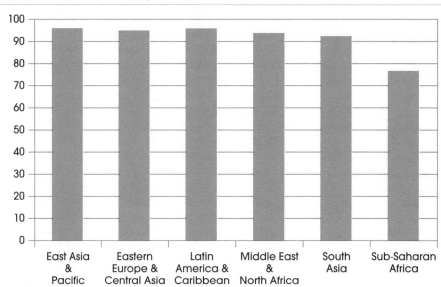

Net enrollment rates are above 90% in all regions of the world except sub-Saharan Africa.

Source: The World Bank, World Development Indicators, 2012.

The Secondary-School Gap

What about the gap in secondary-school education (middle and high school)? Figure 17.2 gives net secondary-school enrollment rates for different regions of the world in 2007.

There is clearly a larger gap for secondary than for primary education and countries from sub-Saharan Africa tend to have the lowest secondary-school enrollment rates. In 2007, Niger had a secondary-school enrollment rate of 9%, with Burundi at 9.3%, Mozambique at 10.5%, Burkina Faso at 12%, Mauritania at 16%, and Madagascar at 22%. The only country outside sub-Saharan Africa to have secondary-school enrollment rates below 30% is Afghanistan at 24%. Pakistan, Cambodia, and Laos have relatively low enrollment rates with, respectively, 32.7%, 35%, and 36%. South Asia as a whole has a secondary enrollment rate barely above 40%. Note that some successful developing countries have been making substantial investments in secondary education; South Korea has a gross enrollment rate of 95.2%, which is higher than that of the United States (91%)! Former socialist countries in Central and Eastern Europe have, in general, very high secondary-school enrollment rates that are comparable to those of the most advanced economies.

The Educational Gender Gap

The educational gender gap measures the difference in educational achievements between boys and girls. This is an important issue, as boys and girls are not necessarily treated equally across countries. In some countries, girls are discriminated against both by their families and by society at large. When this

FIGURE 17.2 Net Secondary-School Enrollment Rates in 2007 (%)

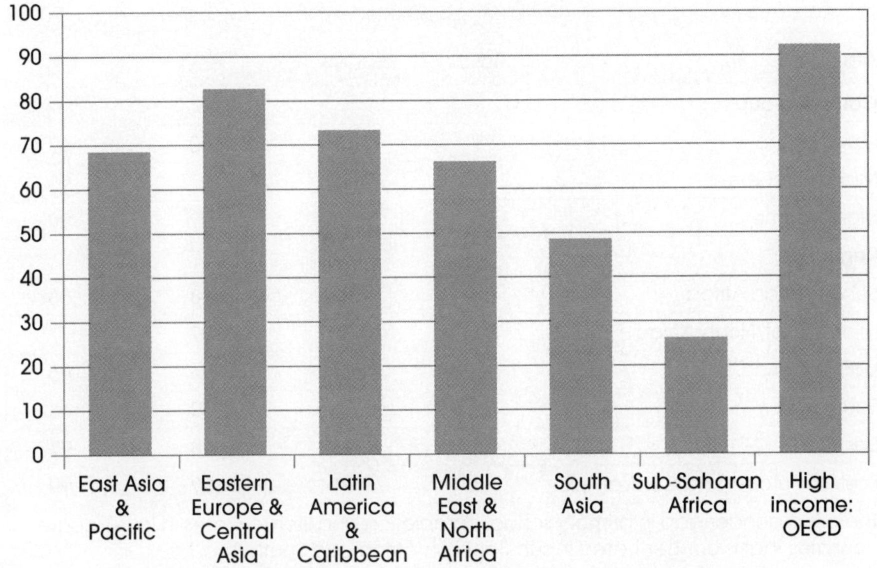

The secondary-school enrollment gap is large, with average enrollment rates in sub-Saharan Africa and South Asia below 50%.

Source: The World Bank, World Development Indicators, 2012.

is the case, parents tend to invest less in the education of their daughters than in that of their sons. Table 17.2 shows the differences in primary-school completion rates and literacy rates for boys and girls in 2005.

As we can see in 2005, there was still a 10% gender gap in primary education completion and an even larger gap in youth literacy rates. This gap is present mainly in sub-Saharan Africa and South Asia. We do not see it in Latin America and East Asia. The Middle East/North Africa (MENA) region has 86% primary-school completion rates for both boys and girls, but the literacy rate for girls is only 77% compared to 89% for boys, which suggests a gender gap in actual educational achievements.

Educational Achievements

Another way to look at the education gap is to compare measures of educational achievement. Table 17.3 shows a first measure: the average years of schooling for adults above age 15, a measure compiled and perfected at regular intervals by Robert Barro of Harvard University and Jong-Wha Lee of Korea University.

In 2010, adults in developing countries had 7.09 average years of schooling compared to 11.03 for advanced countries. This gap reflects the fact that secondary education is still not very widespread in many developing countries. Sub-Saharan Africa has the lowest average years of schooling (5.23 years) followed by South Asia with 5.24 years. Measured this way, the education gap is still quite significant, but it is much lower than it used to be in previous decades.

TABLE 17.2   Gender Disparities in Education

Area	Primary completion, 2005%		Youth literacy rate, 2005%	
	Boys	Girls	Boys	Girls
Country group				
Low-income	79	69	80	67
Middle-income	96	95	97	95
High-income	98	97	99	99
Region				
Sub-Saharan Africa	63	53	78	68
Middle East/North Africa	86	86	89	77
Latin America	98	99	96	96
South Asia	86	77	80	63
East Asia	98	98	98	97
Eastern Europe and Central Asia	93	91	99	99

There is a gender gap in primary school completion and literacy rates in low-income countries that is concentrated in sub-Saharan Africa and South Asia.

Source: The World Bank, World Development Indicators, 2012.

TABLE 17.3   Average Years of Schooling for Adults above Age 15

Area	1950	1960	1970	1980	1990	2000	2010
Income level							
Developed	6.22	6.81	7.74	8.82	9.56	10.65	11.03
Developing	2.05	2.55	3.39	4.28	5.22	6.15	7.09
Region							
Middle East and North Africa	0.76	1.07	1.78	3.04	4.58	5.9	7.12
Sub-Saharan Africa	1.28	1.52	2.02	2.76	3.93	4.62	5.23
Latin America	2.57	3.07	3.82	4.6	5.79	7.13	8.26
East Asia and Pacific	1.77	2.5	3.66	4.84	5.6	6.82	7.94
South Asia	1.02	1.16	1.59	2.1	3.41	4.22	5.24
Eastern Europe and Central Asia	4.83	5.56	6.69	7.88	8.85	9.13	9.65

Measured in average years of schooling, the education gap for adults in developed versus developing nations is still quite large even though it has declined significantly.

Source: Data from Robert J. Barro and Jong-Wha Lee, "A New Data Set of Educational Attainment in the World, 1950–2010" (working paper 15902, National Bureau of Economic Research, April 2010). The data can be downloaded from www.barrolee.com.

Moreover, the average years of schooling have increased every decade in every region of the world, which is certainly an optimistic trend.

How much progress has been made in the last decades? In 1950, the average years of schooling in low-income countries stood only at 2.05. Substantial progress has occurred in South Asia, where the average years of schooling went from 1.02 in 1950 to 5.24 in 2010. Progress has even been faster in the Middle East/North Africa region (MENA), where the average years of schooling went from 0.76 to 7.12 during the same period.

Another measure of educational achievement is the youth literacy rate (see Table 17.2). Primary-school enrollment does not automatically guarantee stable literacy rates in developing countries. What often happens is that after primary school, many children go to work and do not use the reading and writing skills that they acquired. They can then lose those skills especially if the skills were not firmly ingrained in the first place. As noted previously, in many countries, children also pass into higher grades automatically without having acquired the basic competencies of the lower grades.

Can we go beyond measuring educational achievement with literacy rates and look at more advanced skills that are taught in secondary school? A useful tool for that purpose is the PISA test for 15-year-olds. PISA stands for "Program for International Student Assessment." It is run by the Organisation for Economic Co-operation and Development (OECD) to compare the educational achievements of those students who are about to finish secondary school. It is a good indicator of education quality. The PISA test data do not represent as many countries as is the case for other measures of educational achievement. While the PISA database also includes more high- and middle-income countries than low-income countries, it is nevertheless quite useful. The tests measure reading and comprehension skills and are thus more specific than a simple literacy test. Table 17.4 gives PISA scores for reading and math skills for a representative sample of developed and developing countries in the database, most of which are middle-income countries.

The results show heterogeneity in reading and math scores, highlighting the difference in the quality of education across the world. There are several other striking observations we can make about the table's data: Korea, Hong Kong, and Singapore score very high, as does Japan. All these countries have scores that are far above the OECD average. The United States does reasonably well on reading scores (though it is only ranked in 17th place), but is below the OECD average on math scores, ranking in 31st place, which is somewhere in the middle, as the sample includes 65 countries. Apart from the East Asian countries cited above, developing countries generally have lower scores than developed countries; for example, Kyrgyzstan has the worst scores, lower than Peru. We thus see a clear difference between more-developed and less-developed countries in terms of education quality as measured by reading and math skills. The picture would even be clearer if we had scores for some of the poorest countries in the world.

To summarize, while remarkable progress in closing the primary-school education gap between developed and developing countries has been observed

TABLE 17.4   2009 PISA Scores for 15-Year-Olds

Country	Reading mean score (ranking in parenthesis)	Mathematics mean score (ranking in parenthesis)
South Korea	539 (2)	546 (4)
Finland	536 (3)	541 (6)
Hong Kong	533 (4)	555 (3)
Singapore	526 (5)	562 (2)
Canada	524 (6)	527 (10)
Japan	520 (8)	529 (9)
Poland	500 (15)	495 (25)
United States	500 (17)	487 (31)
Germany	497 (20)	513 (16)
France	496 (22)	497 (22)
U.K.	494 (25)	492 (28)
OECD average	493	496
Italy	486 (29)	483 (35)
Spain	481 (33)	483 (34)
Israel	474 (37)	447 (42)
Turkey	464 (41)	445 (43)
Russia	459 (43)	468 (38)
Chile	449 (44)	421 (49)
Mexico	425 (48)	419 (51)
Thailand	421 (50)	419 (50)
Colombia	413 (52)	381 (58)
Brazil	412 (53)	386 (57)
Tunisia	404 (56)	371 (60)
Indonesia	402 (57)	371 (61)
Argentina	398 (58)	388 (55)
Peru	370 (63)	365 (63)
Azerbaijan	362 (64)	431 (45)
Kyrgyzstan	314 (65)	331 (65)

Math and reading scores from the PISA tests in 2009 show a large variation across countries, with high scores in East Asia. Note that the best reading and math scores were obtained in Shanghai in China.

Source: Data from www.oecd.org/pisa.

in recent decades, the education gap at the secondary level remains quite significant and a critical gap in educational achievements remains.

The Issue of Education Quality

A major problem facing developing countries is the low quality of their educational systems. Table 17.5 shows a general quality indicator for which data exist on a worldwide level: class size or the pupil–teacher ratio.

TABLE 17.5   Class Sizes (Pupil–Teacher Ratio) in Primary School, 2010

Area	Pupil–teacher ratio: primary 2010
Country group	
Low-income	43
Middle-income	24
High-income	14
Region	
Sub-Saharan Africa	43
Middle East/North Africa	22
Latin America	22
South Asia	40
Eastern Asia	18
Europe and Central Asia	15
Euro Area	13

Class sizes in primary schools are more than twice as large in low-income countries compared to high-income countries. Sub-Saharan Africa and South Asia have the largest class sizes.

Source: The World Bank, World Development Indicators, 2012.

In primary school, there are 43 pupils per teacher in low-income countries, whereas the corresponding ratio in high-income countries is 14 to 1, less than a third as many pupils! In sub-Saharan Africa and in South Asia, primary schools have, on average, over 40 pupils per class, which represents large class sizes. In comparison, East Asia has much smaller class sizes with 18 pupils per teacher.

Another quality indicator is teacher training. In high-income countries, all teachers, as a rule, have received the required training to be a teacher. This is not always the case in developing countries. According to the World Development Indicators, only 80% of primary-school teachers in low-income countries have received teacher training. Obviously, lack of training has a negative effect on education quality.

Other factors also affect the quality of education such as a critical shortage or absence of resources. Not only do pupils lack textbooks, but many schools have no blackboards. For example, in 1998, 39% of primary-school classrooms in rural areas of Vietnam's Northern Uplands region did not have blackboards. Many schools do not have desks or benches—children have to sit on the ground, while other schools are without classrooms so that many classes take place outside.

We could argue that motivated teachers can, to some degree, overcome these adverse circumstances by passionately engaging with their pupils and inspiring them to learn. However, in many cases teacher motivation is an even greater problem than a lack of resources. Teacher absenteeism is a very widespread problem; children often walk for miles to go to school only to find that their teacher has not shown up. Surprise visits in primary schools in six developing countries showed that about 19% of the teachers were absent. Table 17.6

TABLE 17.6   Absenteeism Rates of Primary-School Teachers in Selected Countries

	Primary schools
Ecuador	14
India (average over 14 states)	25
Indonesia	19
Papua New Guinea	15
Peru	11
Zambia	17
Uganda	27

The absenteeism rate is the percentage of teaching staff who are supposed to be present in schools but have not come to work on the day of an unannounced visit. It includes staff whose absence is "excused."

Sources: Nazmul Chaudhury, Jeffrey Hammer, Michael Kremer, Karthik Muralidaran, and F. Halsey Rogers, "Missing in Action: Teacher and Health Worker Absence in Developing Countries," *Journal of Economic Perspectives* 20, no. 1 (2006): 91–116. Printed with permission of American Economics Association.

gives us the numbers of teacher absenteeism by country. Note the high rate in India and Uganda. In none of the countries in Table 17.6 is the absence rate lower than 10%.

Absenteeism rates tend to be higher in poorer regions. Headmasters often have higher absenteeism rates than teachers, which makes it impossible for them to supervise their teachers. Absenteeism is not the only form of shirking; minimal effort in educating children as well as social prejudice can also play important roles. Teachers who come from a higher social background tend to look down on the children in their classes who come from poorer families. Bad teacher behavior can also go to the extreme of outright extortion of pupils' families; there are cases of teachers who threaten to flunk a child unless the parents pay them bribes, extorting money for fair grading. Other teachers may pressure parents to pay for private tutoring.

The Returns to Education in Developing Countries

One of the main concepts used to determine the economic effects of education is that of the **returns to education**. According to the economic theory of human capital, education is similar to an investment except that it is a very special sort of investment, an investment in one's own human capital.

Figure 17.3 helps us to understand this theory. The horizontal axis measures age but also time. As the old saying goes, "time is money": no one wants to waste their time. The vertical axis measures earnings. Negative earnings represent the costs of education.

Consider an individual who must choose between going to work immediately or delaying his or her entry into the job market by investing in education

FIGURE 17.3 Investment in Human Capital and the Returns to Education

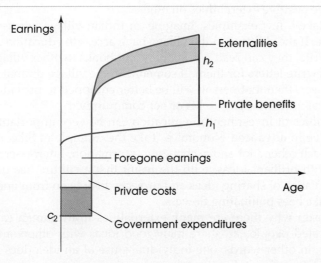

Curve h_1 represents the earnings over time of someone without education. Someone who invests in human capital will have earnings curve h_2 minus costs of education c_2. Because of externalities (the shaded area above h_2), the return to education is higher than the private return. This justifies the government funding portion of the cost of education (blue box next to c_2).

for a number of years. Going to work immediately has a payoff indicated by curve h_1 in Figure 17.3. An individual starts earning immediately and those earnings tend to rise with age following a concave curve. Earnings rise with age because people become more experienced at what they are doing. The choice of investing in human capital instead involves two components: a cost and an earnings profile. The cost is represented by c_2 in the negative part of the vertical axis. The earnings profile is represented by h_2, which has two properties compared to h_1. First, it starts taking positive values at a later age: people start earning money only after they finish their education. Second, once positive earnings kick in, they are higher than if the individual did not invest in human capital. When comparing the choice of investing in human capital instead of going to work immediately, we must thus take into account one benefit and two costs. The benefit is higher earnings. This is the area labeled "private benefits" in Figure 17.3 above h_1 and below h_2. The first cost is the cost of education c_2. The second cost is foregone earnings. During the period when the individual is investing in education, he or she foregoes potential earnings. The theory of human capital says that people will invest in human capital if the expected benefit in lifetime earnings exceeds the cost of education and the cost of foregone earnings. In Figure 17.3, the benefit is higher than the costs.

Externalities of Education

Comparing the private benefits and costs of investing in human capital is not the whole story. There are also externalities of investment in human capital that we must take into account. Externalities are the effects of economic choices of some economic agents on the welfare of other economic agents who were not involved in those choices. In the case of education, individuals' education choices have positive externalities on others.

Let us take a few examples. Imagine an Indian village whose inhabitants are illiterate. If the children in the village have access to education and learn to read and write, they can read newspapers and books to other village members or they can write letters for them. If someone in the village ultimately learns to be an engineer, then that person will be better equipped to provide all sorts of technological improvements to his or her community.

Externalities of investment in education can be very important and this is certainly true in advanced economies. Take the example of Silicon Valley. By talking to each other a lot and exchanging information, Internet-era innovators came up with brilliant ideas, with the result that a culture has developed in the Silicon Valley of sharing ideas and projects. People go from one firm to the other just like bees pollinating flowers.

One reason why there are many externalities from human capital is that better-educated people can share their good ideas with others and still keep those ideas; in other words, one individual's use of an idea does not prevent others from also using it. In economics terms, ideas are *nonrival* goods: an individual can still use ideas when sharing them or even selling them to others. Normal goods like cars are, instead, called *rival* goods.

Why do children from educated families often do better in school than children from less-educated families? They benefit from the conversations with their educated parents, who transmit their knowledge during family conversations, be it at the dinner table or in the car. The parents' education has positive externalities on their children. In Figure 17.3, the shaded area above curve h_2 shows the positive externalities that result from education.

Why do externalities matter? The main reason is that the total benefits from investment in human capital are higher than the private benefits. When an individual makes a choice of whether or not to invest in education, that individual only takes into account the private benefits and costs, but not the effects of externalities on others. This means that individual decisions to invest in education will lead to underinvestment from the point of view of society. Imagine an individual whose costs of investing in education are slightly above the expected benefits. The individual will thus rationally choose not to invest in education. However, if we add the externalities, then the expected benefits would outweigh the costs and it would be better from the point of view of society if that individual would decide to invest in education. This is very important in the development context, where education can play an important role aiding countries to grow out of poverty.

The Role of Government in Education

The solution to individual underinvestment in education is government investment in education. Ideally, if a government could figure out exactly the externalities of an individual's education investment, it could subsidize that individual for the amount of those externalities. Then, all individuals would make the right education decision from the point of view of social welfare. In reality, this is not possible, but public subsidization of education investments will lead more people to invest in education. In Figure 17.3, the shaded rectangle c_2 represents government expenditures that subsidize part of the cost of education.

Externalities are not the only reason governments want to play a prominent role in the provision of education services. Poor families are credit constrained and generally unable to cover the costs of education. In advanced economies, education of the poor is usually not financed by credit markets, so it is unreasonable to expect those markets to play a role financing education in poor countries.

Despite substantial government involvement in education in developing countries, there are often significant private costs involved as well, whether in the form of school fees, uniforms, or textbooks. These costs can be quite burdensome for poor families.

Empirical Estimates of the Returns to Education

What do we know about the returns to education in developing economies? Estimating these returns is not as straightforward as we might think. Ideally, we would like to compare two individuals, each of whom was randomly assigned to receive education (primary, secondary, or tertiary) and then compare the earnings profiles of the two. In reality, as we would expect from the theory of human capital explained above, investments in education are the result of individual and family choices. Take two people who can choose whether or not to go to university and assume that the costs are the same for both. If one of the two decides to go and not the other, presumably the former has a higher expected return to education than the latter. A comparison of their earnings profile later in life is likely to exaggerate the return to education because the one who chose to invest had a higher expected return than the one who chose not to invest. In other words, there is a selection effect. This would give a too-optimistic view of the returns to education, one that is biased upward.

Those who choose to invest in education are likely to come from richer families that are not credit constrained, from better-educated families (the positive externalities within the families we mentioned earlier), or they could also belong to communities in which people are more educated and intellectual activities are more valued. In sum, there are many reasons why those who choose to pursue more education differ from those who do not.

In the past, economists did not pay too much attention to these problems. Researchers who wanted to get an estimate of the returns to education in developing countries would typically do regressions of wages on years of schooling and these traditional studies would usually find very high rates of return. The estimated rates of return to primary, secondary, and tertiary (higher) education were typically around 26%, 20%, and 26%, respectively, for low-income countries (27.4%, 18%, and 19.3%, respectively, for middle-income countries). These numbers are higher than for high-income countries, where rates of return of 12% were typically found for secondary and tertiary education (given that 100% of people go through primary education in high-income countries, we have no estimates of the returns to primary education in those countries). There are reasons to be skeptical of these numbers because of the sample selection problem mentioned above. This is a serious issue: we would like to have unbiased estimates of the returns to education in order to evaluate correctly the payoff of aid and resources put into education. How can we solve this problem?

Esther Duflo developed a smart, unbiased method for estimating the returns to education.[2] She exploited a large-scale program of school construction in Indonesia from 1973 to 1974 and from 1978 to 1979. As one of the world's oil producers, Indonesia benefited from the sudden increase in revenues following these two big oil booms in the 1970s and spent part of its oil revenues on a vast expansion of school buildings. A total of 61,000 schools were built between 1974 and 1978. This addition to the total number of schools represents roughly 2 schools per 1,000 children aged 5 to 14 in 1971. This very sizeable program had a major effect on primary-school enrollment rates, which, for children ages 7 to 12, increased from 69% in 1973 to 83% in 1978.

The school construction program represents a good opportunity to study the returns to education. Children who were older than 12 in 1974 did not benefit from the program, but children who were younger than 12 in the same locality did. We can thus compare the returns to education of those who were able to benefit from the program using the returns of those who were not. Estimating returns to education this way is close to what we would obtain if we could randomly educate some children and not others. Indeed, the windfall oil revenues were completely exogenous to the circumstances of the Indonesian children. Some were lucky to benefit from the school expansion program because they were the right age at the right time, while others were unfortunately born earlier. Another fact that helps to identify the beneficiaries of the construction program is that some regions received more schools than others. These were regions where primary school enrollment was traditionally lower; as a result, the construction program was more intensive in these regions.

Table 17.7 shows the estimate of the returns to education using information about Indonesia's school construction program. It is based on the method of **difference in differences** explained in more detail in the Econometric Appendix. The first row in panel A has data on years of education and the log of wages for children ages 2–6 in 1974 who benefited from the program. The row below has data on those ages 12–17 in 1974 who did not benefit from the program. Moreover, individuals were classified according to whether or not they lived in regions where there was a higher rate of school construction. The average number of schools built per thousand children in the higher-rate regions was 2.44 compared to 1.54 in the lower-rate regions. As we can see, children who benefited from the program in higher-rate regions received an average of 8.49 years of education compared to 8.02 for those who did not benefit from it. There is thus an average difference of 0.47, roughly half a year more of education for the children who benefited from the program in those regions. In the regions where the construction rate was lower, the difference is only 0.36 more years. Note, however, that in those

[2]Esther Duflo, "Schooling and Labor Market Consequences of School Construction in Indonesia: Evidence from an Unusual Policy Experiment," *The American Economic Review* 91, no. 4 (2001): 795–813.

TABLE 17.7   The Results from the 1974–1978 Indonesian School Construction Program

	Years of education			Log wage		
	Level of program in region of birth			Level of program in region of birth		
	High (1)	Low (2)	Difference (3)	High (4)	Low (5)	Difference (6)
Panel A: Experiment of Interest						
Ages 2–6 in 1974	8.49	9.76	−1.27	6.61	6.73	−0.12
	(0.043)	(0.037)	(0.057)	(0.0078)	(0.0064)	(0.010)
Ages 12–17 in 1974	8.02	9.40	−1.39	6.87	7.02	−0.15
	(0.053)	(0.042)	(0.067)	(0.0085)	(0.0069)	(0.011)
Difference	0.47	0.36	0.12	−0.26	−0.29	0.026
	(0.070)	(0.038)	(0.089)	(0.011)	(0.0096)	(0.015)
Panel B: Control Experiment						
Ages 12–17 in 1974	8.00	9.41	−1.41	6.87	7.02	−0.15
	(0.054)	(0.042)	(0.078)	(0.0085)	(0.0069)	(0.011)
Ages 18–24 in 1974	7.70	9.12	−1.42	6.92	7.08	−0.16
	(0.059)	(0.044)	(0.072)	(0.0097)	(0.0076)	(0.012)
Difference	0.30	0.29	0.013	0.056	0.063	0.0070
	(0.080)	(0.061)	(0.098)	(0.013)	(0.010)	(0.016)

Children who were young enough to benefit from the school construction program had 0.12 more years of schooling and an average wage 2.6% higher. This represents a 2.6/.12 = 21.7% return per extra year of education.

Source: Esther Duflo, "Schooling and Labor Market Consequences of School Construction in Indonesia: Evidence from an Unusual Policy Experiment," *The American Economic Review* 91, no. 4 (2001): 798. (Note: The sample was taken from individuals who earn a wage.) Printed with permission of American Economics Association.

regions with lower rates of construction, the average in years of education is higher (9.76 for children who were young enough to benefit from the program and 9.4 years for those who were too old). If we compare the benefits of the program in regions with high construction rates compared to regions with lower rates, we have: 0.47 − 0.36 = 0.12 years. This is the "difference in differences," that is, the difference in years of education between those benefiting from the program (the difference in years of education between children ages 2–6 in 1974 and children ages 12–17 in 1974) in the regions where the program was implemented more intensively compared to regions where it was implemented less intensively. This difference in differences is thus 0.12 years.

Columns 3 to 6 in panel A do the same exercise for the log of wages. Note that we can interpret the difference between the log of wages as a percentage difference in wages. The difference in the difference of wages between the high- and low-intensity regions is 2.6%. Also note that those who were young enough to benefit from the program had a lower wage than those who were older. This is because, everything else being equal, wage increases with age.

Using the difference in differences results from Table 17.7, we can conclude that the Indonesian school construction program led to an increase in the average years of schooling of 0.12 years.[3] The estimated return per year of education obtained this way would thus be the wage increase divided by the difference in average years of schooling: 2.6%/.12 = 21.7%. This is somewhat lower than the 26% return generally estimated in the literature.

A useful exercise is provided in panel B of Table 17.7. Two age groups are compared: those ages 12–17 in 1974 and those ages 18–24 in 1974. Because neither of those two groups benefited from the program, we should not find any real effect either on average years of schooling or on earnings. Indeed, looking at the difference in differences for years of schooling, the result is 0.013 years and the difference in differences for wages is 0.7%. These estimates are much smaller. Moreover, they are not statistically significant.

Even though the results of the study provide somewhat lower estimates of the return to education compared to previous studies, the difference is not extremely large. The selection bias from the traditional studies on the returns to education does not appear to be too significant. However, we need many more studies in the Duflo style to measure the returns to education in developing countries more accurately.

Institutions and Education in Developing Countries

Our discussion now turns to some issues related to institutions in the context of education in developing countries. An important question is that of child labor, which is very prevalent in developing countries. Should child labor be banned so that all children can go to school instead of being sent to work by their families? We also discuss the role of India's caste system in education.

Why Is There Child Labor and Should It Be Banned?

Child labor is still a stark reality in many developing countries. Instead of sending their children to school to get an education, many parents in poor households make their children work on the family farm or send them to work in factories or in the service sector to earn a living to supplement their family's meager income. According to the International Labor Organization (ILO), 120 million children between the ages of 5 and 14 work full time and 130 million work half time. That makes 250 million children who work instead of going to school. Of those 250 million, roughly 153 million are in Asia, 80 million are in Africa, and 17 million are in Latin America. In terms of percentages, 41% of children between 5 and 14 in Africa work and the corresponding figures for Asia and Latin America are, respectively, 21% and 17%.

Child labor is often blamed on the parents. Children can only obey their parents, but forfeiting an education in order to supplement the household's income severely limits their opportunities in life. Many people in the West are

---

[3]Note that in Table 17.7, this difference is not statistically different from zero, but in more sophisticated regressions, Duflo does find a statistically significant effect of the school construction program.

appalled to learn that children work in factories for very low wages and there are campaigns to boycott products from companies using child labor. However, we should not forget that, in the 19th century and even in the early 20th century, child labor was pervasive in the United States and Europe. Even then, there were vigorous campaigns against child labor and bans on child labor were seen as necessary in order to secure universal primary education. As was the case in Europe more than 100 years ago, many developing countries have now taken steps to ban child labor; India took the bold step of banning child labor in 2006. Even when they are adopted, however, laws banning child labor are not always enforced. Is it a good thing to ban child labor? Can it hurt or help the cause of development?

There is a large body of literature on child labor. One of the most recent analyses of it is by Jean-Marie Baland and James A. Robinson.[4] They present a sophisticated examination of child labor and a good reason to ban it. Moreover, they argue that banning child labor can be good for development. Let us discuss their analysis.

When we think about child labor, it seems obvious that the children in question would be better off if they received an education in order to realize higher earnings later in life. If, instead, parents make their children work, the first reason for this decision that comes to mind is that they are selfish and only think about the children's contribution to the household income. Are things really that simple? Would altruistic parents never make their children work? Parents who place their children's welfare before their own would, in general, want to give their children an education, even if that requires great parental sacrifice. Most parents, however, are neither completely selfish nor completely altruistic: they care both about their children and about themselves. The best solution for partly altruistic parents is to pay for their children's education, but then to reduce the children's inheritance in order to make them share the costs of the education they have received. That way, the interests of both the parents and the children are taken into account: the children receive an education instead of working and the costs of education are shared between parents and children. This is, after all, what is done in many American families.

However, in many developing countries, parents might be too poor to reduce bequests to their offspring as a way of having the children share the costs of their education. Moreover, because of credit constraints, they are not in a position to borrow to pay for their children's education. Such loans would be ideal because they would help pass part of the costs of education to the children who would have to reimburse a portion of the loan after completing their education. Because of poverty and credit constraints, parents might not be able or willing to bear all the costs of their children's education without anything in exchange. That is why they may prefer to send their children to work rather than to school. Thus, even partly altruistic parents might make their children work and thus forfeit a better education.

Why might a ban on child labor help in such a situation? Baland and Robinson argue that a collective withdrawal of children from the labor market reduces labor supply, which has positive effects on the wages of adults, who

---

[4]Jean-Marie Baland and James A. Robinson, "Is Child Labor Inefficient?" *Journal of Political Economy* 108, no. 4 (2000): 663–679.

are thus better off as a result of the legal ban on child labor that leads to higher wages. If parents individually withdraw their children from the labor market in order to give them an education, there will be no effect on adult wages; there is only an effect if all parents do it at the same time. The collective-action problem of parents can only be overcome through an institutional constraint that bans child labor. Historical experience shows that child labor has disappeared only when it has been banned. In addition to a possible ethical argument against child labor, there is thus also an economic argument. As a result, a ban on child labor can benefit not only the children, but also their parents. Indeed, it can improve the welfare of all generations and of society at large.

This argument is not as simple as it may seem. Banning child labor without making sure that children receive an education might have negative effects. Parents may send their children to work in the underground economy or the children may even end up in human trafficking rings once child labor is illegal. Moreover, banning child labor itself might not be the best policy for social welfare. Very poor families may find themselves in dire straits if their children cannot work and the parents cannot afford to pay for their education. Education subsidies and government-sponsored loans to parents might be necessary complements to a ban on child labor to ensure that poor parents can send their children to school.

Ugandan Corruption in Education

In countries rife with corruption, unscrupulous officials and politicians often divert government funds from their intended use. This diversion is very difficult to measure because it is the result of clandestine activities. A very interesting study by Ritva Reinikka and Jakob Svensson of Ugandan schools was able to measure the diversion of funds intended for school grants.[5] These are called capitation grants, that is, grants proportional to the number of students in a school. These grants are earmarked for nonwage expenditures because teacher salaries are paid directly by the central government, and they were supposed to be managed by the local districts on behalf of the central government. In the framework of a survey by the World Bank, schools were asked how much funding they actually received from the capitation grants. This amount was then compared to the theoretical capitation grant, that is, the official per-student grant multiplied by the number of students. The results were quite striking. The study done in 1995 found that only 23.9% of the entitled capitation grants reached the schools, a diversion rate of 76.1%! More than half of the schools surveyed did not receive any money at all (a median share of entitled grants of 0%).

The story does not end there, however. The results of the research were so shocking that the information on the diversion was reported in the Ugandan media. The government decided to publish information on the monthly transfers of capitation grants in order to create transparency and keep the public informed. The changes that were a result of this decision were quite drastic, as can be seen in Table 17.8. By 2001, nearly 82% of the capitation grants were effectively transferred to the schools. Why did the number not jump

---

[5]Ritva Reinikka and Jakob Svensson, "Local Capture: Evidence from a Central Government Transfer Program in Uganda," *The Quarterly Journal of Economics* 119, no. 2 (2004): 679–705.

TABLE 17.8   Percentage of Ugandan School Grants as a Share of Entitled Grants before and after the Release of Anti-corruption Information

	Mean	Median	Standard deviation	Maximum	Minimum	Number of observations
All schools						
1995	23.9	0.0	35.1	109.8	0.0	229
2001	81.8	82.3	24.6	177.5	9.0	217

	1995	2001
Regions		
Central	24.3	92.8
North	26.7	102.4
Northwest	11.2	90.3
West	24.0	71.6
Southwest	21.1	83.3
East	20.1	62.4
Northeast	36.0	73.4

Data from 1995 show the percentage of capitation grants that schools effectively received. Data from 2001 show the percentage the schools received after the Ugandan media campaign that disclosed the capitation grants' rate of delivery.

Source: Data from Ritva Reinikka and Jakob Svensson, (2005). "Fighting Corruption to Improve Schooling: Evidence from a Newspaper Campaign in Uganda," *Journal of the European Economic Association* 3, no. 2-3 (2005): 262.

immediately to 100%? One reason is that access to newspapers in Uganda is not as widespread as it is in advanced countries. The other reason is that collective-action problems may hinder public protests. Overall, however, the Ugandan media disclosure did lead to many protests and investigations. This episode shows that media can be a very effective tool to expose and limit corruption. It is also quite telling both because of the volume of diversion before the World Bank investigation and because of the drastic change that followed the information campaign.

The Indian Caste System and Educational Choices

Historically, India's lower castes have been disadvantaged in all areas of economic and social life. The educational gap was significant between the upper and lower castes. By birth, lower castes were restricted in the type of occupation they could choose. This, together with the constraints of poverty, was a strong disincentive for lower-caste families to invest in education. From this perspective, the caste system has been an impediment to economic development because a lack of educational investment among lower-caste families perpetuates poverty. Are there prospects for change?

It turns out that globalization may offer unprecedented educational opportunities to the lower castes. Kaivan Munshi and Mark Rosenzweig have analyzed the effect of globalization on educational choices in Mumbai, given the traditional caste institutions.[6] They found that those disadvantaged under the traditional institutions, in particular girls from lower castes, were able to switch much faster to English-language education when the returns to that education increased dramatically in the 1990s.

Worker occupations in large cities like Mumbai have traditionally been divided into sub-castes, the *jati.* By custom, male networks dominated the labor market as women were confined to domestic chores. Munshi and Rosenzweig analyzed school choices between an education in English or in Marathi, the local language, for boys and girls between 1982 and 2001 in the different *jatis.* In the 1990s, the returns to English education increased quite strongly for both men and women, with increases over 50%.

Figures 17.4a and 17.4b show the evolution of the proportion of children over time receiving an English-language education among high-, medium-, and low-caste children.

Several striking facts from the study emerge. First of all, the share of an English-language education increases as the returns to it increase (starting from 1991 in Figures 17.4a and 17.4b). This is true for all castes. Second, the proportion of high-caste children receiving an English-language education is, in general, higher, which is not surprising given the fact that English has traditionally been the language of the elite in India. When looking at the data for boys only,

FIGURE 17.4a The Proportion of Boys Schooled in English among Different Castes

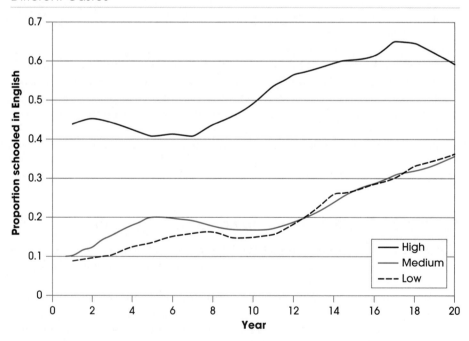

[6]Kaivan Munshi and Mark Rosenzweig, "Traditional Institutions Meet the Modern World: Caste, Gender, and Schooling Choice in a Globalizing Economy," *The American Economic Review* 96, no. 4 (2006): 1225–1252.

FIGURE 17.4b The Proportion of Girls Schooled in English among Different Castes

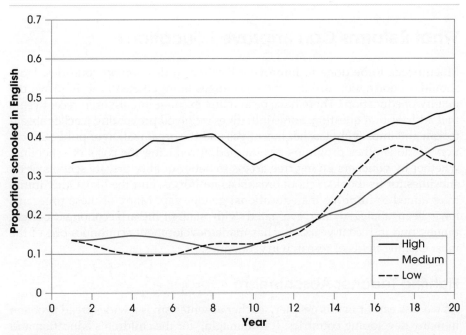

Over time (year 1 is 1982 and year 20 is 2001), the proportion of lower-caste girls learning English increased much faster than that for lower-caste boys. Moreover, it was nearly as high as for girls of higher castes.

Source: Kaivan Munshi and Mark Rosenzweig, "Traditional Institutions Meet the Modern World: Caste, Gender, and Schooling Choice in a Globalizing Economy," *The American Economic Review* 96, no. 4 (2006): 1228–1229. Printed with permission of American Economics Association.

we can see that the gap in the share of an English-language education between the higher castes and the middle or lower castes remains roughly the same. For girls, the finding is very different: the gap in the share of an English-language education between the high-caste girls and those from the middle and especially the lower castes narrows over time and nearly disappears.

Why were girls from the lower and middle castes better able than boys to seize the opportunity to receive an English-language education in the 1990s? Munshi and Rosenzweig explain this by network externalities among caste members. Social connections have always been important to secure jobs within a *jati* and investing in the *jati* network was thus very important. Boys in lower castes took less advantage of the opportunity provided by an English-language education because the local language, Marathi, has traditionally been more valuable than English in securing the social connections needed to get jobs. The network structure of caste can thus restrict job mobility. Girls, on the other hand, did not get traditional jobs within a *jati* and, by investing more in an English-language education, they were thus able to seize opportunities in the new economy and the service sector much faster than boys from the same castes. These new occupations do not rely on caste networks. It will be interesting to see if, over time, the effects of the caste system will become more diluted as the Indian economy continues its integration into the global economy. Only time will tell.

What Reforms Can Improve Education?

Much needs to be done to improve education in developing countries. How should a poor nation use its scarce resources more efficiently to improve the quality of education? There have been many exciting initiatives in recent years that address that question. Some initiatives involved preventing teacher absenteeism and improving teacher incentives and the organization of public education. Various other programs have aimed at reducing the costs of schooling, whether by vouchers giving free access to better-quality private schools or by subsidies for textbooks, school breakfasts, uniforms, and the like. Other initiatives aimed to improve the educational gender gap. Many of these programs have been analyzed and evaluated with state-of-the-art econometric techniques, and in recent years, this has made development economics one of the most exciting fields of research in economics.

Fighting Teacher Absenteeism

As we saw earlier in this chapter, teacher absenteeism is a widespread problem in many developing countries. It is damaging for the children's education and represents a waste of scarce resources. Various NGOs have come up with programs to prevent teacher absence.

In India, a randomized experiment using camera monitoring was implemented by the NGO, Seva Mandir, in the rural Udaipur district. Before the program was implemented, an inspection done in 2003 revealed a teacher absence rate of 44%, which is extremely high compared to the figures shown in Table 17.6. In 60 randomly selected schools, the organization gave the teacher a camera, with instructions to take a picture every day of him- or herself and the students at the beginning and end of the school day. The cameras had a tamper-proof date and time stamp. An incentive system was established with a bonus (or penalty) of 5% per day present (or absent) relative to a benchmark of 21 days of attendance per month. In other words, for every day a teacher attended school above 21 days, he or she received a bonus, while for every day of absence below that threshold there was a penalty. In 60 other schools, a more traditional method was used: teachers were threatened with dismissal if found to be absent and monthly unannounced visits were organized to measure the teacher absence.

Esther Duflo and Rema Hanna evaluated that program and found that in the schools with the camera monitoring treatment, the absence rate was cut in half.[7] The program eliminated extreme absenteeism (teachers who rarely ever showed up) and also increased the number of teachers with a perfect attendance record. As a result, children gained one-third more teaching days.

How cost effective is such a camera monitoring program? Duflo and Hanna found that the costs of the bonuses for additional attendance were nearly offset

---

[7]Esther Duflo and Rema Hanna, "Monitoring Works: Getting Teachers to Come to School" (working paper 11880, National Bureau of Economic Research, 2005).

by the penalties for absence. Note that bonuses and penalties were set relative to the benchmark of 21 days, which was an above-average attendance rate before the program was introduced. Otherwise, there might have been a cost in terms of higher bonuses. As a result, the only real cost was the cost of the cameras. Duflo and Hanna evaluated the cost of the program at $6 per student per year. This seemed quite cost effective. In contrast, because of the long distances between schools in the area, monitoring by unannounced visits is relatively expensive and is also not as effective in fighting absence, as the research has shown.

A different program to fight absenteeism was implemented in Kenya by International Child Support, another NGO. The headmasters of schools selected to participate in the program were asked to monitor teachers and received money to reward the good attendance records of teachers in their schools. The teacher with the best attendance record would win a bicycle at the end of the term. It was found that headmasters tended to over-report the presence of teachers in order to deliver the prize. There was thus collusion between headmasters and teachers, which is not too surprising. Note that the absence rate of headmasters also tends to be high. The lesson from the Kenyan program is that rules that can be bent work less effectively. The impersonal system of camera monitoring, because it creates a daily record and cannot be tampered with, tends to work better.

Are Incentives for Teachers Effective?

It is a commonly held view that education would be improved if teachers were incentivized, that is, if their salaries were dependent on the results of their teaching. Because students in many countries take various forms of standardized tests, it is possible to compare the results of one teacher's pupils with those of other teachers, making it feasible to evaluate teachers' performance and give teachers a bonus that increases with the positive test results of their pupils, or to offer them some other reward related to their pupils' test scores. Paul Glewwe, Michael Kremer, and Sylvie Moulin analyzed a program in Kenya that gave prizes to teachers whose pupils did well in tests.[8] The researchers found that the program encouraged teachers to do more practice sessions in preparation for tests. However, they also found no improvement in teacher attendance, nor did they find any reduction in student dropout rates or any changes in pedagogy and teaching methods.

This is not really surprising and we would be wrong to think that economists would, in general, be in favor of incentivized pay for teachers. Economists were actually among the first to point out its dangers. In 1991, Bengt Holmström and Paul Milgrom showed that incentives based on the test results of pupils distorted teacher incentives instead of improving teaching.[9] Most of

---

[8]Paul Glewwe, Michael Kremer, and Sylvie Moulin, "Textbooks and Test Scores: Evidence from a Prospective Evaluation in Kenya," Policy Research Group, The World Bank, 2001.

[9]Bengt Holmström and Paul Milgrom, "Multitask Principal-Agent Analyses: Incentive Contracts, Asset Ownership, and Job Design," *Journal of Law, Economics, & Organization* 7 (special issue, papers from the Conference on the New Science of Organization, January 1991): 24–52.

what a teacher does to educate children is not observable. If teachers' pay becomes dependent on test results, then teachers will allocate much more effort preparing their pupils for tests and divert a lot of effort away from the non-observable part of teaching. Paying teachers for test results leads to "teaching to the test" without necessarily improving overall education. The message from the research by Holmström and Milgrom is that if a job involves multiple tasks, some of which are observable (or whose results are directly observable such as tests) and some of which are not, conditioning the pay on the observable results will lead to diverting effort away from the non-observable tasks to the observable tasks. In that case, it might be better not to introduce incentive payments in order to avoid such distortions of effort. Most parents will prefer that their children be well educated rather than only well prepared for tests.

Decentralization

School systems are often very centralized. This is not surprising; the objective of most education systems is to give equal education to children, which means that the curricula and school administration are often centralized at the national level. However, while centralization has benefits, it also has disadvantages, one of which is that the monitoring of teachers is done only from above. If parents are dissatisfied with some aspect of their children's schooling, they cannot do much about it as their complaints would have to reach the higher levels of the school's administration and, as a result, would have less of a chance to be heard. Some countries have encouraged the decentralization of education in order to allow more control from below with the hope of improving the quality of teaching.

In some countries, local education committees have been set up that include parent participation to monitor and partially reward teachers. One such initiative is the EDUCO program (Educacion con Participacion de la Comunidad) in El Salvador in Central America. From 1980 until 1992, El Salvador experienced a bloody civil war and public education was disrupted, especially in rural areas. In response, local communities decided to take charge of the local schools, often with considerable success. In 1991, El Salvador's Ministry of Education decided to draw on this experience to expand primary education in rural areas by establishing the EDUCO program. The EDUCO schools are managed autonomously by community associations of elected parents. These associations play a key role in school management; they sign contracts with the teachers and maintain the schools. Research by the World Bank on the results of the EDUCO program found that while it was successful in expanding education, student performance was no better than in traditional schools. However, teacher absenteeism was somewhat lower.[10]

While EDUCO is deemed a relative success, the results of other such decentralization efforts are, in general, mixed, if not outright disappointing. For

---

[10]Emmanuel Jimenez and Yasuyuki Sawada, "Do Community-Managed Schools Work? An Evaluation of El Salvador's EDUCO Program," *World Bank Economic Review* 13, no. 3 (1999): 415–441.

example, Edward Miguel and Mary Kay Gugerty found that on the basis of a study in Tanzania and Kenya, there is a strong collective-action problem in ethnically heterogeneous communities.[11] These communities collect less money for schools, there is less community participation, and various indicators such as textbook availability and school maintenance suggest a lower quality of education in these heterogeneous communities.

In Kenya, ICS, the NGO mentioned above, experimented with parent participation. A school committee composed of parents was supposed to give a prize for the best teacher. Parents were given guidance about the criteria for choosing the best teacher. Michael Kremer and Christel Vermeersch found that the results were disappointing: no positive effects were found either on teacher absenteeism or on the children's school performance.[12]

Decentralization and control from below may work in some communities, but there is no guarantee that it will because local communities must first resolve their collective-action problems. Moreover, parents in rural communities are often illiterate and not well prepared to judge the quality of teaching.

Vouchers

Voucher programs for education have their advocates and opponents all over the world. The idea behind school vouchers is to create competition between private and public schools, and between different schools in general, by giving parents the option to choose their child's school, whether private or public, by using government-financed school vouchers. The idea is that if parents have more school choices, competition for admission between schools will create incentives to improve the quality of schooling in poorly performing public schools and improve the general level of education.

In the context of developing countries, the voucher idea is less applicable. School competition is limited in rural areas because children do not have a real choice of schools. There is only one school they can go to and they often have to walk quite a distance to do so. However, in urban environments, competition between schools is possible and various voucher programs have been implemented. We discuss two such programs, one in Colombia and one in Chile.

Joshua Angrist, Eric Bettinger, and Michael Kremer examined the Colombian program.[13] Vouchers were distributed by lottery to 125,000 students, creating a random experiment so as to avoid any selection bias in the data.[14] Data were then

---

[11]Edward Miguel and Mary Kay Gugerty, "Ethnic Diversity, Social Sanctions, and Public Goods in Kenya," *Journal of Public Economics* 89, no. 11-12: 2325–2368.

[12]Michael Kremer and Christel Vermeersch, "School Meals, Educational Achievement, and School Competition: Evidence from a Randomized Evaluation (policy research working paper 3523, World Bank, 2005).

[13]Joshua Angrist, Eric Bettinger, and Michael Kremer, "Long-Term Educational Consequences of Secondary School Vouchers: Evidence from Administrative Records in Colombia," *The American Economic Review* 96, no. 3 (2005): 847–862.

[14]If people could have chosen to participate in the program, the more motivated parents would have made that choice and their children would probably also have performed better than average, thereby creating an upward bias in the results.

collected from 1,600 students (mainly in Bogota, the capital) 3 years later, after the start of high school. The lottery winners appeared to be 15% to 20% more likely to be in private schools and performed the equivalent of one grade higher on tests compared to lottery losers. The reasons for this stronger performance are twofold: First, the private schools were deemed to provide a better education. Second, students had an extra incentive to succeed in order to keep the voucher benefits. Indeed, students who failed a grade would lose the vouchers they had received from the experiment, so there was an extra incentive not to fail. The cost to the government of paying for one student's voucher for private school for one year was only $24 higher than the cost of paying for that student's education in the public system. The benefit, in terms of improved education, was deemed much larger.

The evaluation of the Chilean experience by Hsieh and Urquiola led to more disappointing results.[15] Unlike the Colombian program, the Chilean voucher program was a nationwide initiative. In 1981, all Chilean students received vouchers that allowed them to attend the school of their choice. By 1990, 41% of students were in private schools compared to 22% in 1981. Similar to Colombia, there was a clear shift in Chile toward private schools.

However, was the competition introduced by the voucher system effective in increasing incentives in public schools? The answer is no; the voucher system led to a decline in test scores, an increase in grade repetition rates, and a drop in the socioeconomic status of students in public schools. In other words, vouchers allowed the better public school students to transfer to private schools, thereby producing negative externalities on those students who stayed in the public school system. Did the improvements for those who went to private school compensate for the reduction in education outcomes in public schools? Hsieh and Urquiola found that this was not the case. The higher private school outcomes for those who benefited from the voucher system did not improve the average test outcomes of the schools in the same municipality. These results thus suggest that vouchers did not increase the average quality of education, but merely led to a sorting of students: the better students went to private schools, leaving the poorer students behind in the public schools.

Reducing Education Costs

Poor parents end up paying substantial amounts, relative to their income, for their children's education, whether for textbooks, uniforms, or school supplies. Reducing the costs of schooling can thus help struggling parents. If education costs are cheaper, enrollment will be higher because many parents will decide to send their children to school instead of sending them to work. Different programs have been established to reduce the costs of schooling: conditional transfers, that is, payments to families that are contingent on parents sending their children to school; providing school meals to children; and supplying money for uniforms, textbooks, and classroom improvements. The effects of many of these programs have been evaluated by development economists.

Conditional transfers. The Mexican government established a program called Progresa that provided cash grants to families, with the condition that they

---

[15]Chang-Tai Hsieh and Miguel Urquiola, "The Effects of Generalized School Choice on Achievement and Stratification: Evidence from Chile's Voucher Program," *Journal of Public Economics* 90, no. 8-9 (2006): 1477–1503.

send their children to school. The program targeted poor families below a certain income level in rural locations and it also provided health benefits. The education component gave families the equivalent of $28 per month for each child in grades 3 through 9 if the child attended more than 85% of classes. It started in 1997 and was phased in randomly in rural communities. By 1999, it covered 40% of rural families in Mexico. This randomized phase-in made an accurate evaluation of the program's effects possible. Significant research has been done using data from the Progresa program. T. Paul Schultz, who evaluated the impact of the Progresa program, found that it resulted in an average 3.4% increase in enrollment for all students in grades 1 through 8.[16] The increase was largest among girls who had completed grade 6, with as much as 15.8% higher enrollment. The Progresa program was later introduced throughout the country on the basis of this success and is considered a model transfer program for development countries.

School meals. Vermeersch and Kremer evaluated an experiment in 25 Kenyan preschools where a free breakfast was introduced for children.[17] The results were compared to 25 similar schools without a breakfast program. They found that school attendance in the schools where the program was implemented was 30% greater. The provision of free breakfasts, however, cut into school time. Overall, test scores were 0.4 standard deviations greater in the program schools compared to schools without the breakfast program, but only if the teacher had been well-trained prior to the program's implementation.

Uniforms, textbooks, and classroom improvements. The NGO, International Child Support, also provided uniforms, textbooks, and classroom improvements to 14 Kenyan schools. The experiment was evaluated by Michael Kremer, Edward Miguel, and Rebecca Thornton.[18] Uniforms costs $6, but the per capita annual income in Kenya is around $340. A uniform thus represents 1.7% of annual income. Taking into account that per capita income in the United States is around $35,000, the cost of the same uniform would be the equivalent of roughly $600 for a U.S. student. In schools where the ICS program was implemented, dropout rates were much lower and students completed 15% more years of schooling. However, the researchers found that students from nearby schools transferred into the program schools, so that eventually, no measurable overall impact on test scores was observed.

Reducing the Educational Gender Gap

We saw that school enrollment of girls is lower in developing countries. Girls' school participation appears more responsive to different programs that cut education costs. If families cannot afford to send all their children to school,

---

[16]T. Paul Schultz, "School Subsidies for the Poor: Evaluating the Mexican Progresa Poverty Program," *The Journal of Development Economics* 74, no. 1 (2004): 199–250.

[17]Michael Kremer and Christel Vermeersch, "School Meals, Educational Achievement, and School Competition: Evidence from a Randomized Evaluation, Harvard University Working Paper, 2005.

[18]Michael Kremer, Edward Miguel, and Rebecca Thornton, "Incentives to Learn," *Review of Economics and Statistics* 91, no. 3 (2009): 437–456.

they will send boys first. Programs that reduce the costs of schooling thus often lead to more positive enrollment effects for girls than for boys.

Because reducing the educational gender gap is an important objective and because many education programs seem to work more effectively for girls, various programs target girls specifically as a way to reduce the educational gender gap in the most effective way. Indian NGO Seva Mandir initiated a program in Indian schools to hire a second teacher for each class so as to increase school attendance and the quality of teaching. The second teacher had to be a woman. The idea was that this would improve the quality of education, especially for girls. The program was indeed effective; it had some positive effects on the number of days a school was closed due to endemic teacher absenteeism. Schools with one teacher were closed 44% of the time, whereas schools with the two-teachers program were closed 39% of the time. While the difference is not huge, a more impressive result of the program is that girls' attendance increased by 50%. No significant effect was recorded on the attendance of boys.

In 2001, Kremer, Miguel, and Thornton conducted a randomized evaluation of the Girl's Scholarship Program (GSP) in rural Kenya that was designed to enhance girls' education.[19] Out of a set of 128 schools, half were randomly selected. The program provided merit-based scholarship to girls who scored in the top 15% on government-administered tests. These scholarships provided uniforms, partial school fees, and school supplies. The results were quite positive; there was higher school attendance in the schools where the program was implemented and significantly higher test scores were recorded. Interestingly, this program also generated positive externalities in the schools where it was implemented. First of all, a higher teacher attendance was observed, even though the teachers did not benefit directly from the program. Second, better school results were observed for boys, even though boys did not benefit from the program either. Third, girls who were not in the top 15% also performed better. This suggests that programs targeting only certain categories of pupils (in this case, the best female pupils) also benefited others in the class due to the overall stimulation provided. This is a clear example of externalities generated by education, as discussed earlier in this chapter.

Chapter Summary

Measuring the Education Gap

In developing countries, the average number of years of schooling is 7.09, whereas in advanced economies it is 11.03. Primary school enrollment in developing countries is still somewhat lower than in developed countries, especially in sub-Saharan Africa, but the situation has improved drastically in recent decades. Primary school enrollment is now found all over the world. Literacy rates in low-income countries have gone up, but a gap remains. The gap in secondary-school enrollment remains more important. There is also a substantial gender gap in education. Primary- and especially secondary-school enrollment tends to be lower for girls than for boys. There is also a quality gap in education. International test scores for 15-year-olds in secondary school show a substantial gap in the quality of secondary education between developing and developed countries. Class sizes are larger in developing countries, teachers are not as well

---

[19]Michael Kremer, Edward Miguel, and Rebecca Thornton, "Incentives to Learn," 2009, op. cit..

trained, teacher absenteeism is significant, and there is scarcity of teaching material, blackboards, classrooms, etc.

The Returns to Education in Developing Countries

The returns to education measure the net benefit of investment in education or human capital. These returns accrue not only to those who invest in education, but also to others because of externalities to education. The knowledge transmitted tends to spread and benefits others in local communities, businesses, and neighborhoods. Externalities from education and credit constraints for poor households justify the role of government in education.

Empirical research suggests that the returns per year of education are slightly above 20%.

Institutions and Education in Developing Countries

Child labor is a big issue in developing countries. Sending children to school improves families and society more than if children are forced to earn a living to supplement household income. The increases in family income from education compensate for the loss of income due to years of education and its costs. Moreover, withdrawing children from the labor market helps to sustain higher wages for adults in the economy. Nevertheless, child labor is still widespread because parents cannot borrow to pay for their children's education.

What Reforms Can Improve Education?

We have discussed at length the evidence on what works to improve education in developing countries. In India, the experimental introduction of cameras with a tamper-proof date and time stamp to take pictures of teachers and pupils at the beginning and end of each school day proved very effective in reducing teacher absenteeism. Experimental programs of incentives to provide higher pay to teachers with better attendance did not work as well, especially if these programs were administered by the headmasters. Experimental programs to involve parents more in monitoring school activities delivered mixed results, with few significant effects on student performance. Evidence on voucher programs that allow children to attend private schools in the urban areas of developed countries is also mixed. A lottery voucher program in Colombia had positive results on student performance, but the much larger voucher program introduced in Chile merely led to higher sorting of students, with the better students going to private schools and the poorer students staying behind in public schools without any observable improvement in overall school performance.

Various programs to reduce the costs of schooling have had a positive effect on school enrollment. These include conditional transfers giving parents cash grants that are contingent on the parents sending their children to school, free uniforms, or school meals such as free breakfasts. Various programs that provide textbooks and school supplies have proved to be somewhat disappointing. Programs designed to address the gender educational gap in developing countries have been quite successful. In an experimental remedial education program introduced in India, a second teacher was hired in certain schools in order to increase school attendance and the quality of teaching. The second teacher had to be a woman. The program had a very positive effect on the attendance of girls and led to less disruption of classes due to teacher absenteeism. Merit-based scholarships for girls introduced in Kenya proved to be very cost effective in increasing school performance for girls as well as for boys. Many rigorously designed experiments are taking place in developing countries to find out what are the most cost-effective ways of improving the provision of education. The results of those studies will have significant effects on policy choices in developing countries in years to come.

Key Terms

difference in differences
randomized evaluations

returns to education

Review Questions

1. How can we measure the gross enrollment rate in education? Why can it sometimes be higher than 100%? How can we correct it and calculate a net enrollment rate?

2. What are the usual estimates of returns to education in developing countries? How can we measure these returns? What is the potential problem with simple OLS (ordinary least squares) regression of wages on education? How does Esther Duflo's research in Indonesia avoid this problem?

3. Teacher incentives can be enhanced by giving them bonuses if their students do well in test scores. Discuss. What was the experience with teacher incentives in Kenya? Do some research on the same topic for other countries.

4. What is the experience in developing countries with parent involvement and bottom-up monitoring of schools?

5. Programs to reduce the costs of schooling lead to higher participation rates for girls than for boys. How do you explain this? How does it relate to the education gender gap? How does it relate to gender preferences of parents discussed in Chapter 3?

6. Private net returns to education could be negative. Use the data in Figure 17.3 on human capital investment discussed in this chapter to show how this can be the case. Why might this be the case?

7. Download and read the article, "The Impact of Children's Work on Schooling: Multi-Country Evidence based on SIMPOC Data" by Ranjan Ray and Geoffrey Lancaster. You can find this article on the website http://repec.org/esAUSM04/up.15362.1076562558.pdf.

   To understand the effect of child labor on school participation, why is a measure of child labor in terms of hours worked per week more satisfactory than a measure of child labor participation (whether a child works or not)? What does the article conclude about the effect of child labor hours on school participation? The authors find that the results in Sri Lanka are different. Do some research to find an explanation for the Sri Lankan experience.

8. Read the article by Joshua D. Angrist and Victor Lavy, "Using Maimonides' Rule to Estimate the Effect of Class Size on Scholastic Achievement," in *The Quarterly Journal of Economics* 114, no. 2 (1999): 533–575. Explain why Maimonides' rule is a good instrumental variable for class size. Without such an instrumental variable, if we regress pupil performance on class size with ordinary least squares, give one reason why the effect of class size may be underestimated and one reason why it may be overestimated. Can you think of another good instrumental variable for class size? Explain.

9. Go to the World Development Indicator website (http://data.worldbank.org). Scroll down the page and under "The World at a Glance," select the database on "Education" and download the data on the ratio of girls to boys in primary and secondary education for 2005. Find the 10 developing countries with the lowest ratio and the 10 developing countries with the highest ratio. What variables might explain the difference? Discuss.

10. Download the following article by Hongbin Li, Pak Wai Liu, Ning Ma, and Junsen Zhang: "Does Education Pay in Urban China? Estimating Returns to Education Using Twins." You can find the article at this website: http://www.econ.cuhk.edu.hk/~discusspaper/00013.pdf.

    Why is it interesting to use data on twins to estimate returns to education? Why is the estimate found by the authors lower than what ordinary least squares regression estimates typically give? How do these estimates compare to those for Indonesia discussed in the chapter? What is specific about Chinese educational institutions in the returns of high school, college, and vocational school education?

Delivering Infrastructure in Developing Countries

Back in 1960, Singapore's GDP per capita was lower than $400. It was not apparent then how successful this island city-state would become a few decades later. Today, Singapore's GDP per capita is close to $40,000, one hundred times higher, making it one of development's big success stories. Singapore is renowned for its modern infrastructure, which has contributed to this success. The port of Singapore is the world's busiest in terms of total shipping tonnage; a fifth of the world's shipping containers pass through Singapore as well as half of the world's annual supply of crude oil. Even though its total area is only 274 square miles, Singapore counts 1,940 miles of highways, all of them paved. Its road system is studied worldwide. Indeed, despite a high population density (more than 17,000 per square mile), traffic congestion is much lower than in a typical large Asian city such as Bangkok, Manila, or Djakarta. Traffic congestion is even lower than in many large American cities. Singapore has an excellent public transportation system, more than 2 million telephone lines, and 8 million cell phone subscriptions. Because of its excellent infrastructure and business-friendly environment, Singapore has been able to attract private investment from all over the world and has become one of the most successful development stories of recent decades.

Contrast Singapore with Niger in Africa. With a total area of 489,678 square miles, Niger has 4,225 miles of road, but while it is nearly 2,000 times larger than Singapore, Niger only has 350 miles of paved roads, less than 20% of Singapore's surfaced roadways. Niger has only 14,000 telephone lines. Poor infrastructure makes it difficult to transport goods across the country and when there are food shortages in some regions, this can be a significant contributor to famines. Unfortunately, the quality of infrastructure in many of the poor countries in the world is closer to Niger's than to Singapore's.

The difference between infrastructure development in Singapore and Niger relates, in part, to geography. Singapore is a small city-state surrounded by the sea. Because transporting goods by water has always been easier than transporting them by land, countries with access to the sea and easily navigable rivers can transport goods more cheaply. Low transportation costs attract economic activity and investment that make countries richer. In contrast, Niger is a landlocked country with no direct access to the sea. Geography gives an advantage to Singapore over Niger.

Being landlocked does not, however, condemn a country to remain poor. Switzerland is a landlocked and mountainous country, but has a very good infrastructure, high-quality institutions, and a prosperous economy. Along with weak governing institutions that exacerbate its infrastructure problems, what makes things really difficult for Niger is that its neighboring countries that have access to the sea, such as Nigeria, Benin, or Burkina Faso, are also poor with inferior infrastructure and unstable governance. Even if Niger could afford to improve its infrastructure, it would not be able to attract much private investment because of the substandard infrastructure of these neighboring countries.

We begin this chapter by documenting the state of infrastructure in developing economies in terms of access to water, electricity, sewage, and telecommunication services. The gap between the poorest countries and even middle-income countries is very large. There is a minimal presence of the private sector in the poorest countries and the quality of government regulation is low. We then explore the relationship between infrastructure and economic development. What kinds of infrastructure investments are the most effective in poor countries? Which infrastructure investments are ineffective and thus should be avoided? What is the role of private investment in infrastructure and how can foreign direct investment help?

Two factors play equally important roles in terms of explaining differences in the return to infrastructure investment: geography and institutions. Landlocked countries similar to Niger are at a disadvantage because they face higher transportation costs and therefore benefit less from international trade. However, infrastructure investment can only partly compensate for this disadvantage; disparities in the quality of institutions across developing countries are also a key factor in how effective infrastructure investment will be. We discuss the role of regulation, analyze the costs and benefits of fiscal decentralization as it relates to infrastructure decisions, and review the problems of corruption.

The State of Infrastructure in Developing Countries

In this section, we review some of the essential facts about the state of infrastructure in developing countries. For example, one of the most critical issues is that of inequality of access; the poorer countries and the poorest households within those poorer countries have very little access to infrastructure. Second, we discuss institutional issues in the provision of infrastructure. How involved is the private sector in infrastructure investment in developing countries? How effective are the regulatory agencies responsible for overseeing the private sector?

Inequality of Access to Infrastructure

The infrastructure gap between rich and poor countries is acute. There is significant inequality across countries in terms of access to infrastructure, but critical inequalities exist both across and within developing countries. Table 18.1 provides some relevant data.

We can see from Table 18.1 that the biggest difference in access to infrastructure is between the group of poor countries and more developed nations (lower-middle income to high income). In low-income countries, a group defined as having a gross national income per capita below $1,025 per year, only 23% of the population had, on average, access to electricity in 2009; for example, less than 10% of the population had access to electricity in Uganda and Malawi. A similar picture emerges for access to telephone lines. On average, there are only 12 telephone lines per 1,000 people in low-income countries, but that number jumps to 123 per 1,000 in lower-middle-income countries, roughly a fourth of the coverage of high-income countries. Access to improved water sources (household connection, public standpipe, borehole, protected

TABLE 18.1 Access to Infrastructure by Income Groups across the World in 2009

	Access to electricity (% of population)	Telephone lines per 1,000 people	Access to improved water sources (% of population)	Access to sanitation (% of population)
Low-income countries	23	12	65	36
Lower-middle-income countries	74	123	86	56
Middle-income countries	81	142	89	59
Upper-middle-income countries	97	222	92	71
High-income countries	100	444	100	100

There is marked inequality in access to infrastructure (electricity, telephone, water, and sanitation) between the poorest regions and more-developed regions.

Source: The World Bank, World Development Indicators, 2012.

dug well or spring, rainwater collection) is a fundamental necessity. A lot of progress has been made already; in 2009, 65% of the population of low-income countries already benefited from such access. Less than 10 years before, however, access was well below 50% in these countries. Less progress has been made on access to sanitation: only 36% of the population of low-income countries had access to it, whereas the equivalent number for lower-middle-income countries was 56%.

Table 18.2 provides data on access to infrastructure within countries with figures for the poorest 20% and the richest 20% of incomes in different country groups. The data are older and were collected before 2006. We can see that inequality of access to infrastructure within countries is quite substantial. In the low-income countries, among the 20% poorest, only 9.7% have access to electricity, only 41.1% have access to improved water sources, only 27.2% have access

TABLE 18.2 Access to Basic Infrastructure Services around 2006

Share of population	Electricity		Water		Sanitation		Telephone	
	Poorest 20%	Richest 20%	Poorest 20%	Richest 20%	Poorest 20%	Richest 20%	Poorest 20%	Richest 20%
Low-income countries	9.7	68.7	41.1	78.5	27.2	68.8	3.2	24.5
Lower-middle-income countries	79.5	99.3	64.5	86.6	48.2	78.7	21.2	66.1
Upper-middle-income countries	81.4	99.5	76.7	95.0	73.4	96.4	32	73.1

Columns 1 and 2: Percent of households reporting access to electricity; columns 3 and 4: percent of population with access to an improved water source; columns 5 and 6: percent of population with access to an improved sanitation facility; columns 7 and 8: Percent of households reporting access to a telephone.

Source: Antonio Estache, "Infrastructure: A Survey of Recent and Upcoming Issues" (World Bank, Annual Bank Conference on Development Economics, Tokyo, 2006): 6.

to sanitation, and only 3.2% have access to a telephone. Inequality of access is not as marked within lower-middle- and upper-middle-income countries.

Institutions for Infrastructure Provision

Infrastructure provision in developing countries is still primarily delivered by government, despite the privatization policies of the last 30 years. In poorer countries, the private sector usually plays less of a role in infrastructure investments. Table 18.3 provides data on the amount of private sector involvement in the provision of infrastructure. Less than 50% of developing countries (developing countries include low income to upper middle income countries) have benefited from the involvement of private capital in electricity generation (47%), electricity distribution (36%), water and sanitation (35%), and the railroad sector (36%). Only in the telephone sector do we see that 59% of countries have benefited from private capital investments. These numbers are even smaller for low-income countries, as we can see from Table 18.3. Overall, the private sector has contributed only about 20%–25% of the investment in infrastructure in developing countries. In Africa, the poorest continent, the contribution was less than 10%.

Table 18.4 provides data on the share of independent regulatory agencies in developing countries. The independence of regulatory agencies is indeed an important factor for ensuring that regulatory agencies function properly. Utility companies in most countries of the world tend to have a natural monopoly, that is, a situation in which fixed costs are so large that there is often no place in the market for more than one firm. In order to prevent monopoly pricing, economic theory recommends, in the case of natural monopoly, that utilities are either owned by the government or owned by private firms and subject to strong regulatory oversight. The two solutions are often assumed to be equivalent. In the case of government ownership, the government has direct control over the utility and gives orders on what the pricing and output levels should be. In the case of the regulated monopoly, the regulatory agency imposes constraints on the private firm such as a maximum price or a minimum output level. Regulators design and enforce these constraints. Regulatory agencies that function properly and efficiently are critical to achieving these objectives and to curbing monopolistic behavior in markets characterized by natural monopoly.

In that context, the independence of regulatory agencies is essential for a variety of reasons. First of all, regulatory agencies that are independent from

TABLE 18.3   Countries with Private Sector Investment in Infrastructure (% of Sample)

	Electricity generation (2004)	Electricity distribution (2004)	Water & sanitation (2004)	Railroads (2002)	Fixed-line telecoms (2004)
Low-income	41	29	18	34	50
Lower-middle-income	48	37	50	26	62
Upper-middle-income	58	48	47	60	72
Developing	47	36	35	36	59

The percentage of countries receiving private-sector investment in various types of infrastructure is lower for the poorer developing countries.

Source: Antonio Estache and Ana Goicoechea, "How Widespread Were Private Investment and Regulatory Reform in Infrastructure Utilities during the 1990s?" (policy research working paper 3595, The World Bank, 2005).

TABLE 18.4   Percentage of Countries in Different Income Groups with Independent Regulatory Agencies in Various Public Utilities

	Electricity (2004)	Water & sanitation (2004)	Railroads (2002)	Fixed-line telecoms (2004)
Low income	38	13	2	69
Lower-middle income	63	32	8	60
Upper-middle income	63	28	19	71
Developing	51	22	8	66

The percentage of developing countries with independent regulatory agencies is lower in poorer developing countries.

Source: Estache and Goicoechea, "How Widespread Were Private Investment and Regulatory Reform in Infrastructure Utilities during the 1990s?" 2005.

political meddling and government intervention can focus on their mission and have enough authority to effectively implement existing regulations. Second, it is important for regulatory agencies to have enough resources to remain independent from the private sector and to resist any pressure for leniency toward the large private utilities. As we can see from Table 18.4, the poorer developing countries are at an institutional disadvantage compared to lower-middle- and upper-middle-income developing countries. Only 2% of the low-income countries have an independent regulator for railroads and only 13% have an independent regulator for water and sanitation. Only in the telecom sector do we see, in general, a high percentage of countries with independent regulators. This is also a more modern sector that has experienced significant development in the last decades.

Development Effects of Infrastructure Investment

What are the development effects of infrastructure investment? Because enterprises cannot think of investing in a location where there are no roads or reliable electricity and telecommunications networks, let alone no functioning water supply or sewage systems, infrastructure investment is indispensable for development. Indeed, without infrastructure, the return on private investment will not be as high as it could be—infrastructure and private investment are complementary: in terms of quantity and quality, the better the infrastructure in a country, the higher the return on investment.

How precisely can we estimate the effects of infrastructure investments on growth? While general studies are useful, because infrastructure includes so many diverse categories, it is not easy to draw general conclusions. It is, however, important to measure the precise effect of particular types of infrastructure such as roads, electricity, or dams, as their effects are likely to be very different. In many cases, infrastructure investment is also often misspent and ultimately has negligible effects on development; some countries are notorious for poor returns on infrastructure investment. Our discussion then turns to the issue of "white elephants," or megaprojects that give a government public visibility, but are not particularly beneficial for development.

The Effect of Infrastructure Investment on Growth

Measuring the effect of infrastructure investment on growth is very difficult and it is nearly impossible to do properly at the international level because of what economists call **heterogeneity**, loosely speaking, the differences in economic conditions across countries. What this means is that if some countries invest more in infrastructure than other countries and have more growth performance as a result, there can be many other reasons besides the differences in infrastructure investment that can account for the higher growth due to all the other variations in economic conditions across countries. For example, there could be higher savings rates, higher export growth, or productivity improvements that can also impact the various economic conditions in different countries.

Heterogeneity is not the only difficulty in measuring the effect of infrastructure on development. There might also be other variables that affect both infrastructure investment and growth. If a country has better institutions for example, it is likely to have both better infrastructure and higher growth. In that case, part of the correlation between infrastructure investment and growth would be due to the quality of institutions. Regressing growth on infrastructure investment is then likely to exaggerate the effect of infrastructure.

Hadi Salehi Esfahani and María Teresa Ramírez have analyzed the influence of institutions on infrastructure investment and growth.[1] They performed an international study covering 75 countries that focused on the telecommunications and electricity sectors. They found that a variable expressing the quality of contract enforcement, as measured by the *International Country Risk Guide*, had a positive effect on the adjustment of infrastructure investment, not to be confused with the level of infrastructure investment. By adjustment, the researchers mean that different countries have target infrastructure investment levels that vary with economic fundamentals and the adjustment is the speed at which those countries move toward that target. They also found that more ethno-linguistic fractionalization and a larger informal economy had negative effects on infrastructure adjustment.

The researchers thus used those three institutional variables (quality of contract enforcement, ethno-linguistic fractionalization, and size of the informal economy) as instrumental variables for the adjustment of infrastructure investment. In other words, they regressed the adjustment of infrastructure investment on the three variables and regressed the growth of GDP per capita on the thus estimated infrastructure variable.

Esfahani and Ramírez found that if the growth rate of telephones per capita rises from about 5% per year as in Africa, to about 10% per year as in East Asia, the annual growth rate of GDP per capita would rise by about 0.4 percentage points. In the electricity sector, an increase of per-capita electricity production from a rate of 2% as in Africa, to 6% as in East Asia, can raise annual GDP growth rate by another 0.5 percentage points.

We must be cautious with these results because the instrumental variable methodology's validity is based on the assumption that institutions affect

---

[1]Hadi Salehi Esfahani and María Teresa Ramírez, "Institutions, Infrastructure, and Economic Growth," *Journal of Development Economics* 70, no. 2 (2003): 443–477.

growth only indirectly through infrastructure investment. However, institutions are likely to affect growth directly as seen in Chapter 4 on growth. Why is this important? Because then the estimate of the effect of infrastructure on growth cannot be accurately measured. In particular, the estimate may exaggerate the effect of infrastructure investment (see the Econometric Appendix for a discussion of this and for an explanation of instrumental variable regression). Nevertheless, the significant effect of institutional variables (the quality of contract enforcement, ethno-linguistic fractionalization, and the size of the informal economy) on infrastructure investment is worth noting.

The Benefits of Transportation Infrastructure

A more precise and recent study by Dave Donaldson examined the effect of railroad infrastructure in India.[2] Under colonial rule in India, railroads were the dominant form of British infrastructure investment. Although the study is based on just one country and on a single infrastructure sector, rail transport, measuring the economic effect of railroads is still difficult. We might reasonably think that railroads are built between cities that have the most potential for economic expansion. Yet regressing a measure of economic activity in cities after the railroad reaches them relative to economic activity before its construction might therefore exaggerate the effect of the railroad on economic activity. Indeed, the regression coefficient on railroads would also pick up the unmeasured variables related to the strong potential for expansion that is independent of railroads. Donaldson was nevertheless able to give quite convincing estimates of the effect of the railroads in India.

Before the railroad was introduced, most goods in India were transported on roads. When the roads were in good condition, carts pulled by bullocks transported the goods. A cart could typically cover 15 miles a day. However, in the monsoon season, roads became impassible due to flooding and goods were carried on the bullocks' backs, making transport considerably less efficient. Some goods moved along India's main rivers, but this was limited and, because of the current, boats going upstream had to be towed from the riverbanks. Compared to those traditional modes of transport, trains represented a technological revolution. They were capable of moving large amounts of goods over distances of up to 350 miles a day, and could meet reliable timetables in all seasons.

Railroad construction in India began around 1850 and continued during the Raj, the period of British colonial rule (1858–1947). While there were obvious commercial incentives (increasing trade between cities) as well as humanitarian goals (transporting food and medical supplies from one town to another in case of famine or disease outbreak), the primary motivation was military: railroads enabled the rapid transport of troops from one place to another to quell a revolt against the colonial rulers. The Indian rebellion of 1857 that started in north central India and quickly spread across the country, convinced the British colonial authorities that building an extensive railroad system to transport large numbers of troops rapidly was absolutely essential to maintaining

---

[2]Dave Donaldson, "Railroads of the Raj: Estimating the Impact of Transportation Infrastructure" (working paper 16487, National Bureau of Economic Research, 2010).

control of the Indian subcontinent. The first rail lines built for military purposes were along direct routes that connected India's major provincial capitals and the construction was unrelated to the economic prospects of the cities that would be connected. This is helpful from an econometric point of view if we want to measure the effect of the railroad on economic activity, for as we will see below, Donaldson also performed extra checks to be sure the choice of railroad lines was not motivated by economic prospects. Figure 18.1 shows the development of India's railroad network between 1860 and 1930, when it reached, more or less, its current size.

How was Donaldson able to measure accurately the amount by which railroad construction helped to reduce trade costs across India? Take the example of Kohat salt, a particular type of salt that was produced only in the salt mines in the Kohat region, now part of Pakistan. Differences between the price of Kohat salt in the Kohat region and its price in other regions should reflect costs of trade, mainly transportation costs. Thus the price of Kohat salt 500 miles away from Kohat should equal the price of salt in Kohat plus the transportation costs. By comparing the price of Kohat salt in a particular region before and after railroad construction, we can get an estimate of the effect of railroad construction on the transportation costs of salt. To be more precise, once the railroad was constructed, we have to estimate the lowest cost-effective route between the Kohat region and any other region. A complication arises in making this estimate because all of this distance may not have been covered by rail but may have involved transport by road or water. Transporting salt 500 miles by rail is thus not the same as transporting it 300 miles by rail and 200 miles by other modes of transport. Therefore, we must take into account which percentage of the lowest cost-effective route was covered by train, which percentage was covered by road, and which was covered by water or other methods of transportation.

Donaldson used annual data on retail prices for eight types of salt between 1861 and 1930 in 124 districts of northern colonial India. He found that transport by road was roughly 8 times more costly than transport by rail. Similarly, transport by river or along the coast was roughly 4 times more expensive than transport by rail. The introduction of railroads thus drastically reduced transportation costs.

This reduction in transportation costs led to a reduction in the prices of goods, which encouraged larger trade flows across India. Donaldson used over 1.3 million observations on trade flows for 17 commodities between 45 regions in India between 1880 and 1920. He found that a 1% reduction in trade costs led, on average, to a 3.8% increase in trade flows. This is quite an important effect. He also found that, on average, the arrival of the railroad raised real agricultural income by 16% because of the increase in trade flows resulting from the availability of rail transportation. This increase in the market for agricultural products led, in turn, to a substantial expansion of agricultural production.

As mentioned above, we might be concerned that railroads were built in areas where there was more potential for growth and we noted that the choice of railroad lines was determined by military strategy. Nevertheless, it is also useful to determine whether economic prospects played a role in the choice of railroad lines. Davidson did this by performing some "placebo" tests. What does this mean? In randomized medical drug trials, placebo drugs are given

FIGURE 18.1   The Development of India's Railroad Network during British Colonial Rule

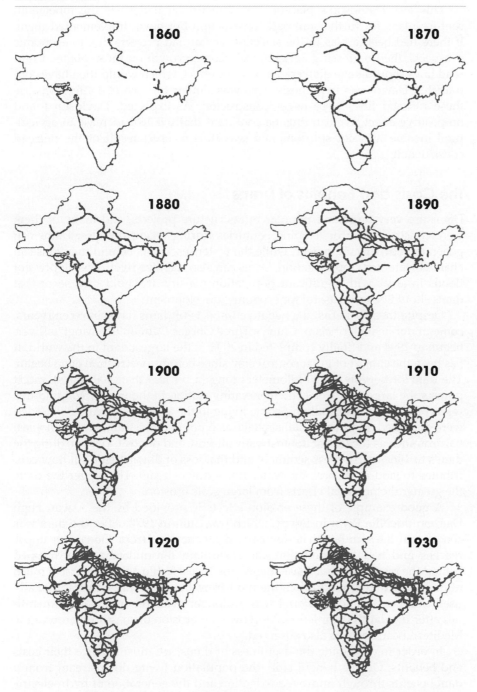

During their colonial rule in India, the British built a large railroad network between 1860 and 1930, when it reached the size it has today.

Source: Dave Donaldson, "Railroads of the Raj: Estimating the Impact of Transportation Infrastructure" (working paper 16487, National Bureau of Economic Research, 2010): 38. Printed with permission from Dave Donaldson.

to subjects instead of the test drug. Placebos have no effect on patients. In economics, a placebo test is designed to have no statistical effect.

This was Davidson's placebo test: The British had since the nineteenth century plans for further railroad construction but never implemented them. If there had been a bias in the selection of railroad projects due to economic prospects, then regressing agricultural income growth on those planned railroad lines should have delivered a positive effect, which would then have contradicted Davidson's hypothesis. This was similar to a placebo effect because those railroad lines were never constructed. As expected, Davidson found no positive effect. We can thus be confident that the 16% increase in agricultural income was not spurious and was thus a direct result of the railroad construction.

The Costs and Benefits of Dams

Dams are very large and popular infrastructure projects, and many of them were constructed in developing countries during recent decades. Dams can generate hydroelectric power, while the water reservoirs behind the dams can channel water for crop irrigation. Dams can also stabilize river flows to prevent floods in areas with significant population density. It would thus seem that dams should be quite useful for economic development.

Despite these benefits, the negative impacts of dams have, in recent years, come under heavy criticism. China's Three Gorges Dam on the Yangtze River, begun in 1994 and finally completed in 2006, is the largest dam in the world. It has been the subject of great controversy since before construction even began. The dam's reservoir is 600 kilometers long (a bit less than 400 miles) and it powers the largest hydroelectric generating station in the world. To build this reservoir, more than 1 million people living in the areas that would be flooded were displaced. Environmentalists have also pointed to a number of ecological hazards such as the loss of downstream silt flow and deposit. Water exiting the dam's turbines carries less sediment and that loss of downstream silt flow contributes to land erosion as the water flows downstream. The bigger the dam, the greater the potential effects from large-scale erosion.

A good example of these erosion effects is provided by the Aswan High Dam on the Nile River in Egypt, which was built in 1970. After the dam was completed, the rich silt that was carried all the way from the river's upper reaches and had fertilized the Nile floodplain for millennia, was trapped behind the reservoir. As a consequence, the Nile's fertile delta region lost much of its productivity. In addition, the mud from the delta that was traditionally used as a construction material was no longer available in adequate quantities after the dam's completion. Moreover, an erosion of coastlines around the Mediterranean Sea was also observed.

In order to determine the usefulness of dams, we must balance their costs and benefits. On the benefit side, the population living downstream from a dam benefits through improved irrigation and the generation of hydroelectric power. These are the two most important benefits. On the cost side, upstream populations are displaced due to areas flooded by a dam's reservoir. This entails not only substantial moving costs, but the displaced populations may have reduced economic opportunities after they have moved: fewer good jobs, less arable land to cultivate, etc. Another cost is related to the increased water-logging and salinity of the soil adjacent to a reservoir. Water from the reservoir seeps in the ground nearby and saturates it, making it too wet to till. Because water always carries mineral salts, seepage from the reservoirs eventually causes high levels of salinity in adjacent soils and reduces their fertility.

How can we measure the costs and benefits from dams? Esther Duflo and Rohini Pande have performed this analysis for India, which has the largest number of dams after the United States and China; thus, results from India should give us significant data about the costs and benefits of dams.[3]

To assess these costs and benefits, the idea that first comes to mind is to compare economic outcomes in regions with dams to regions without dams. This is, however, not an accurate way to estimate the effect of dams. Indeed, regions with and without dams are likely to differ in other measures such as agricultural productivity. For example, it is possible that richer Indian states are able to build more dams. By comparing economic outcomes in states with and without dams, our data would then pick up not only the effects of dams but also the states' economic differences that have nothing to do with dams and, as a result, the effect of dams would be exaggerated.

Duflo and Pande utilized the fact that dams could only be built in places where the river gradient was neither too steep nor too flat. A river's gradient is a good instrumental variable. On one hand, variation in the gradient is not directly correlated to economic outcomes, but on the other hand, it is a good explanatory variable for the presence of dams. Rivers with gradients that are too flat or too steep are unlikely locations for dams. If the gradient is too flat, the water flow will not be strong enough and very large reservoirs would have to be built to compensate for this. If the gradient is too steep, the water will tend to flow too fast which will create significant erosion in adjacent land. Moreover, in too steep terrain there will often not be enough reservoir capacity. A steep river gradient might thus be good only for hydroelectric power generation.

Figure 18.2 shows two maps of India. The left-hand map displays the number of dams in various districts. Darker areas have more dams, which are primarily located in west-central India in the provinces of Gujarat, Madhya Pradesh, and Maharashtra. The right-hand map shows average river gradients throughout India, with lighter-shaded areas having a low gradient and darker-shaded areas having a high gradient. Note that the gradients are quite steep in both the northwest and northeast regions of the country. Regions with average river gradients correspond quite closely to those areas with more dams. An average gradient is thus a good explanatory variable for the presence of dams.

By using the instrumental variable estimation technique with river gradient as an instrument, Duflo and Pande were able to measure more accurately a dam's economic effects. They found that agricultural production increased by 0.34% and agricultural yield by 0.19 % in districts downstream of a dam, but they found no effect on the district in which the dam was built. They also found that a dam had an effect on the substitution of downstream crop choices in favor of more water-intensive crops such as rice and sugarcane. An interesting

---

[3]Esther Duflo and Rohini Pande, "Dams," *The Quarterly Journal of Economics* 122, no. 2 (2007): 601–646.

FIGURE 18.2   River Gradients and the Number of Dams in India

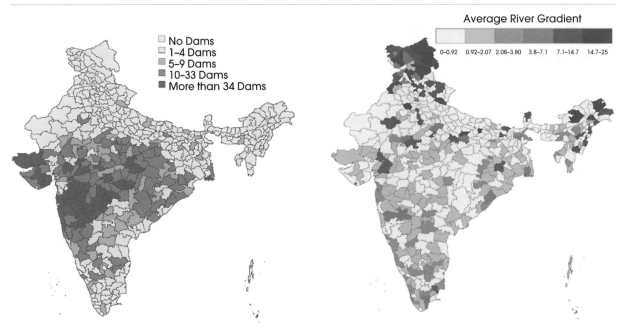

There are more dams in districts in central and west-central India (left-hand map). These are areas where river gradients are neither too flat nor too steep (right-hand map).

Source: Esther Duflo and Rohini Pande, "Dams," *The Quarterly Journal of Economics* 122, no. 2 (2007): 614, 618.

finding was that a dam increased the variance, that is, the volatility of production in the district where the dam was built because the effects of rainfall were amplified: as the ground adjacent to a dam's reservoir tended to be more saturated, rain often flooded fields in those areas more often.

The study found that a dam had no demographic effects. The displaced populations tended to relocate close to the submerged area of the reservoir. On the other hand, a dam increased poverty by 0.77% in the district where the dam was built and decreased poverty in the downstream districts by 0.26%. The latter effect is thus not strong enough to compensate for the increase in poverty in the dam's district. The effect on poverty was, however, halved in the districts where there had been historically no landlords (*zamindari*) to collect tax revenues during the time of British colonization (see Chapter 12 on property rights). A possible explanation for this is that the populations in those districts were more organized politically and could thus use that organization to reduce the poverty effects caused by the dam building in their districts. This result would suggest that better institutions for collective action yield better outcomes from dam construction because poverty effects in a dam's district were mitigated.

No significant effect on health outcomes were observed as a result of dam construction. In particular, there was no incidence of malaria, despite the higher water surface and humidity.

Overall, the study by Duflo and Pande seemed to show that the economic benefits from dams were not as significant as we might have assumed. It is not clear that the benefits outweighed the costs. This study in a large country such as India would seem to suggest not only that the net benefits of dams are marginal, at best, but that better cost-benefit analyses should also be done before launching large-scale dam projects in the developing world.

Opposition to dam construction is actually strong in many countries. In India, activist Medha Paktar is well known for her opposition to controversial dam projects such as the Narmada Dam in Gujarat. Protesters have claimed that the project was meant to benefit big construction companies and that it created environmental and social havoc, but did not bring significant improvement in terms of irrigation or flood control.[4] The World Bank has been actively supporting dam projects in recent decades, but the latest research on dams and their costs and benefits should certainly make it take a much closer look at future proposed dam construction.

White Elephants

Infrastructure investment may sometimes have a disappointing effect on economic performance in developing countries because of a phenomenon called "white elephants," which are infrastructure projects that are expensive but are either without benefit or quite inefficient from the point of view of economic development.

Where does the term "white elephant" come from? Traditionally, the kings of Southeast Asian countries such as Thailand (then called Siam) and Burma gave white elephants as presents to powerful nobles. White elephants are very rare in nature and thus considered very valuable. Moreover, they were considered sacred in Buddhism. The day before giving birth to the Buddha, his mother dreamed that a white elephant came to deliver her a lotus flower. Because they were sacred, white elephants could not be put to any use, but they still had to be cared for and fed. Receiving a white elephant was thus seen as both a blessing because of its sacred nature, but also a liability because of its expense and lack of utility.

There are many examples of infrastructure investments that turned out to be white elephants. One example is the Biblioteca Vasconcelos in Mexico City, a huge and prestigious library project. It was the largest infrastructure investment undertaken during the administration of President Vincente Fox (2000–2006). He inaugurated the library on May 16, 2006, a week before the planned finishing date, in order to include the library among the accomplishments of his presidency. He declared the library to be one of the most technologically advanced constructions of the 21st century, but by March 2007, the library had to be closed down because of structural failures. The next president, Felipe Calderón, had to pump an additional 3 million dollars into the structure to save it.

Another example is that of Thailand's first and only large aircraft carrier, the *Chakri Naruebet*. It was commissioned in 1997, but has seen little service due, in part, to a shortage of funds following the East Asian financial crisis. It has served mainly as vessel for surveillance, search-and-rescue, and disaster relief during the aftermath of the 2004 Indian Ocean tsunami.

White elephants can be found in developed countries, as well. One example is the Concorde, the jetliner that for 20 years flew passengers from Europe to

---

[4]See also Jacques Leslie , *Deep Water: The Epic Struggle over Dams, Displaced People, and the Environment*, (New York: Farrar, Strauss and Giroux).

the United States at supersonic speeds, but never realized a profit. A second example is the Millennium Dome in London, which was built to commemorate the year 2000. It staged an exhibition that received many fewer visitors than expected and authorities had a hard time finding a use for it once the Millennium celebrations were over.

Why are there so many occurrences of white elephant projects? A simple answer is governmental incompetence. However, these projects can also be politically motivated. Politicians may enjoy the notoriety they receive from promoting these projects while ignoring their costs and inefficiencies, but they may also use white elephant projects as a political strategy. James Robinson and Ragnar Torvik have a theory that white elephants act as clientelistic instruments.[5] **Clientelism** refers to the behavior of politicians who cater to their voter constituency. It can take many forms, such as politically motivated job creation or the construction of housing projects to reward faithful voters.

Why can white elephants be used as a clientelistic instrument? Suppose that a white elephant project is promoted by an incumbent politician to create jobs for his constituency. If the project has little or no positive economic and social returns, the incumbent's opponent is likely to stop the project if elected. However, the possibility that the project will be cancelled gives an extra incentive to those voters who would benefit from the project to support the incumbent and reelect him. Thus, white elephants are instruments to attract voters and create a loyal voter base for a politician. Consider the alternative: If the project is efficient, its construction will continue after the election and workers who benefit from it have less to fear from voting for the incumbent's opponent because they will still keep their jobs. According to Robinson and Torvik, politicians thus deliberately choose inefficient projects in order to assure their reelection. While this strategy is certainly Machiavellian, it is used by politicians in many cases.

Investment Risk and the Cost of Capital in Infrastructure

We have seen that private-sector involvement in the poorest developing countries remains limited. Many multinational firms have specialized in infrastructure investment and could help modernize the economies of poor countries, so why are their investments in these nations so limited?

The primary reason is that these firms believe the expected rate of return is too low to be worth the risk. Because the fixed costs of infrastructure investment are so large, risk is an especially important consideration. A company may invest hundreds of millions of dollars before it can make any profits. If there is political instability in a developing country or if a government makes decisions that have a negative effect on the private sector, the value of the fixed investments made may drop sharply. One way of measuring the risk for companies is to calculate hurdle rates: what is the minimum return below which a company would not be ready to invest?

---

[5]James A. Robinson and Ragnar Torvik, "White Elephants," *Journal of Public Economics* 89, no. 2-3 (2005): 197–210.

The Cost of Capital

To calculate a hurdle rate, firms consider their **cost of capital** by estimating the cost of financing investments through equity as well as the cost of debt in various countries, and including a risk premium that takes into account the level of risk. A higher estimated cost of capital means that a higher return to investment is expected in order to justify a specific investment. The cost of capital can thus be seen as the return hurdle for investment. Antonio Estache and Maria Elena Pinglo have estimated these hurdles in different groups of country for different infrastructure services (energy, water, railways, and ports).[6] They considered the weighted average cost of capital (WACC) given by the following formula:

$$WACC = [(1 - g)C_e] + [g(1 - T)C_d]$$

There are two components in this formula: the first relates to the cost of equity and the second relates to the cost of debt. Let us consider the different variables and parameters.

Variable g, present in both parts of the formula, stands for leverage or the weight of debt $D/(D + E)$, where D represents debt and E represents equity. Total financing is $(D + E)$ and g thus represents the share of debt in the financing of a firm. C_e stands for the **cost of equity**. It is calculated as the sum of three elements: the risk-free rate of interest plus an equity premium plus a country premium. Let us explain these elements in turn.

The **risk-free rate of interest** is typically the interest rate on government bonds. United States bonds are seen as risk free and those who buy U.S. government bonds generally do not fear default. Typically, the risk-free rate of interest is calculated by taking an average of rates on U.S. treasury bills.

The **equity premium** is the premium for choosing equity over debt. Risk-free debt pays an interest generated by the interest rate. The interest rate is known and usually does not vary. Equity is more risky than debt for two reasons. First, the income paid on equity is composed of dividends, which are much more variable than interest because dividends are only paid out when a firm makes enough profits. In a good year, dividends are higher than interest payments, but in a bad year, when the firm makes little or no profits, no dividends are paid. Second, equity has greater risk because the price of shares varies considerably. Because equity is more risky than debt, investors will only be prepared to hold equity if the expected return to equity is higher than that of debt—in other words, if equity holds a premium to account for its higher risk relative to equity.

The **country premium** takes into account the fact that some investments are more risky in some countries than in others. This is most often related to a country's quality of institutions: its courts, rule of law, regulatory quality, political stability, and the presence of corruption, among other variables. Institutional quality affects the degree to which an investment in a country faces the

---

[6]Antonio Estache and Maria Elena Pinglo, "Are Returns to Private Infrastructure in Developing Countries Consistent with Risks since the Asian Crisis?" (policy research working paper 3373, the World Bank, 2004).

chance of being expropriated. It also affects the probability that the currency of that country will sharply depreciate. The equity premium will affect variations in the cost of equity across countries, but the country risk premium will affect those variations even more.

Looking at the second part of the formula, C_d represents the **cost of debt**— the risk-free rate of interest plus a **debt premium** that takes into account the probability of default on debt. Two types of default risk must be considered here: default on debt by private companies and default on government debt, which is also called sovereign debt. Governments in advanced countries do not generally default on their debt, but it has happened repeatedly in developing countries and not necessarily among the poorest. To take a few examples, Russia defaulted on its government bonds in 1998, resulting in a serious economic crisis in the country. The government of Argentina defaulted on its debt in 2001, causing a significant downturn in the country's economy. Since the 1980s, there have been numerous other examples of sovereign default in developing countries.

Variable T stands for the nominal corporate income tax rate. To the extent that interest payments are tax deductible, the cost of debt is calculated after deducting for taxes.

Estimates of the Cost of Infrastructure Investment

Taking into account these variables, Figure 18.3 shows the estimate done by Estache and Pinglo for the weighted average cost of capital (WACC) for four infrastructure sectors (energy, water, railway, and ports) in different categories

FIGURE 18.3   Weighted Average Cost of Capital in Four Infrastructure Sectors

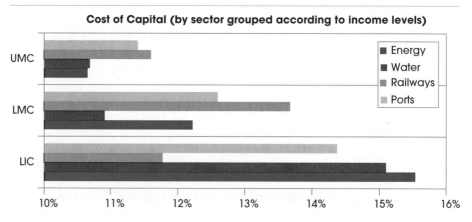

The weighted average cost of capital (WACC) is shown for infrastructure investment in energy, water, railways, and ports for low-income countries (LIC), lower-middle-income countries (LMC), and upper-middle-income countries (UMC). The cost of capital is generally higher in poorer countries because of higher country risk.

Source: Antonio Estache and Maria Elena Pinglo, "Are Returns to Private Infrastructure in Developing Countries Consistent with Risks since the Asian Crisis?" (policy research working paper 3373, The World Bank, 2004): 12.

of countries: low income, lower-middle income and upper-middle income. We can see that the estimates for low-income countries are much higher than those for lower-middle- and upper-middle-income countries. This is because private companies perceive much larger risks of investing in poorer countries. These higher risks are related mostly to higher country risks, which in turn are mostly related to the quality of institutions and the degree to which property rights are protected. This finding is in tune with one of the major themes in development economics: the idea that differences in institutions affect differences in growth and development.

Geography and Infrastructure

While good infrastructure can reduce trade costs and improve trade flows, geography can also affect trade costs. However, infrastructure can, to some degree, compensate for unfavorable geographical conditions. Countries that are landlocked are at a disadvantage compared to countries that have direct access to the sea. Transportation costs are lower by ship than by train or by road. Moreover, findings from a study by Nuno Limão and Anthony J. Venables indicate that these landlocked countries are at an even greater disadvantage when their goods must transit through countries that have poor infrastructure.[7]

The researchers used three different data sets to analyze the relationship between geography, infrastructure, and transport costs. A first data set represented the costs of shipping a standard 40-foot container from Baltimore, Maryland, to 64 cities worldwide, with 35 of those cities in landlocked countries. The first advantage of these data is that they were homogeneous because they measured the shipping cost for the same good. The second advantage is that the container's transportation was broken into component parts, including transport by both land and by sea. The researchers found that the average shipping cost from the median landlocked country was 58% higher than the median shipping cost from a country with access to the sea. Improvements to infrastructure in the median country to the level of the best 25th percentile in infrastructure performance among landlocked countries cut this cost penalty to 46%, a gain of 12 percentage points. Similar improvements to infrastructure in the country through which goods transited to reach the sea cut the cost penalty to 51% only, a gain of 7 percentage points.

A second data set was based on what is called the **cif/fob** ratio in the International Monetary Fund's database. Imports are measured by their free on board (fob) value and by their value including carriage, insurance, and freight (cif). The cif/fob ratio minus 1 thus represents the ratio of the transport cost over the free on board price of imports; in other words, it measures the transport cost rate of imports. The advantage of this measure is that data for it are available for many more countries than are shipping data. However, there is more measurement error involved and the goods transported are not homogeneous; some countries might systematically import goods that have higher or lower transport

---

[7]Nuno Limão and Anthony J. Venables, "Infrastructure, geographical disadvantage, and transport costs" (policy research working paper 2257, The World Bank, 1999). Note that transport by air is the most expensive for commodities.

costs than others, which would bias the estimates of transport costs. Based on those data, the median transport cost rate for a landlocked country was 42% higher than the median rate for a coastal country. In this case, improvement of infrastructure from the median to the best 25th percentile in infrastructure performance in the landlocked country reduced its extra cost to 32%, while with a similar improvement in the transit country, the extra cost only dropped to 36%.

The third data set directly compared the trade volume of different countries. The median landlocked country had only 30% of the trade volume of the median coastal country, a remarkable difference. An infrastructure improvement in the median landlocked country to the best 25th percentile improved trade flows by 8%, while a similar improvement in the transit country improved those flows by only 2%.

All in all, the study by Limão and Venables showed that the lower trade flows between landlocked countries and the rest of the world were due to the countries' geographical disadvantages. These disadvantages were compounded by bad infrastructure in both the landlocked countries as well as in the transit countries. The researchers found that geography and infrastructure explain why, as we discussed at the beginning of this chapter, countries from sub-Saharan Africa not only trade less with the rest of the world, but also within Africa.

Institutional Aspects of Infrastructure

Efficient infrastructure investment requires adequate institutions. Three issues have been the object of research in this area. The first is the role of ownership and regulation; the second is the effect of decentralization of authority on the efficiency of infrastructure; and the third is corruption, its importance, and how to deal with it.

Regulatory Reform

In the 1990s, major reforms took place in the infrastructure sectors of developing countries as part of structural reform programs. A large portion of these reforms took place in Latin American countries, where structural reform programs were in place as a consequence of the debt crises of the 1980s. Luis Andres, Jose Luis Guasch, and Stephane Straub studied the regulatory reforms in the infrastructure sector that were associated with the privatization of utilities.[8] They used data from over 1,000 concessions (contracts in which private firms run infrastructure services) granted in Latin America between the 1980s and 2000.

Because infrastructure firms usually operate under monopoly conditions, regulation aims to keep prices at the level of marginal costs. There are different ways of doing this. One is by imposing price caps; another is by rate-of-return regulation. In the former case, the price level is set at the estimated marginal

---

[8]Luis Andres, Jose Luis Guasch, and Stephane Straub, "Do Regulation and Institutional Design Matter for Infrastructure Sector Performance?" (policy research working paper 4378, The World Bank, 2007).

cost, while in the latter case, the regulator sets prices in such a way that a firm's rate of return is equalized to the cost of capital. How well this is done depends on regulatory quality. Andres et al., built an indicator of regulatory quality in which the value of the indicator increased if:

- The regulatory framework was established by law;
- The regulator had its own revenues from regulatory levy, did not depend directly on state budgets, and had an adequate budget;
- The regulator was independent and not directly appointed by the executive branch of government;
- There was a single, fixed term of appointment for a regulator;
- If regulatory decisions were taken collegially.

They then asked how these variables affected the difference between the rate of return and the cost of capital (WACC). They found that regulatory agencies with strong budgets were the only significant variable that affected this difference. The other variables were not significant. In other words, regulatory agencies with strong budgets are better at reducing the difference between the rate of return and the cost of capital.

Another issue in infrastructure regulation is opportunistic renegotiation of contracts, a form of the hold-up problem examined in Chapter 7 (see also Chapter 13 in the context of privatization). Latin American governments organized competition among private firms to receive government concessions to run infrastructure utilities. However, once concession contracts were signed, the contracts were often renegotiated either by governments or by the firms that obtained the contracts. In the former case, governments tried to renegotiate contracts once firms had incurred sunk costs. One example would be a government renegotiating a price cap downward to please voter constituencies, thereby hurting the firm. In the latter case of firms renegotiating, a firm would be able to extort additional resources from the government by threatening to close its operations if the contract was not renegotiated. For example, in 1997, the Mexican government was pressured to bail out private firms that had been operating the highway toll system at a financial loss despite initial plans to the contrary.

Andres et al., found that the existence of a regulatory agency significantly reduced opportunistic renegotiation. There are two reasons why this was the case. First, regulators are generally better able to design contracts than are politicians. Second, regulators are less prone to renegotiating contracts to please particular voter constituencies than are politicians. Interestingly, the researchers also found that there were more instances of renegotiation when there were price caps instead of rate-of-return regulations. The latter seem to be more flexible than price caps. Contracts never include all possible contingencies; unexpected contingencies thus also tend to lead to the renegotiation of existing price caps for non-opportunistic reasons.

Decentralization

In recent years, convincing arguments have been made for decentralizing authority in developing countries. One such argument is that decentralization of authority in democratic systems results in local authorities being more accountable.

Citizens can closely observe what local authorities do and react by either not reelecting them or by protesting against the authorities' actions or policies.

A second argument in favor of decentralization of authority is that it enables local leaders to act on the basis of local knowledge. Local leaders have better knowledge of the local conditions than do national leaders. They are thus able to make better decisions, provided they have the incentives to do so.

A third argument for decentralization is that a central government can use yardstick competition between various local authorities and reward those who perform best given certain criteria. Yardstick competition has been used extensively in China, where fiscal decentralization has provided local leaders with many policy instruments. Provincial leaders who managed to achieve the best growth performance have tended to earn faster promotion, while leaders of provinces where growth was more sluggish tended to be either demoted, sent into early retirement, or blocked for promotion. Yardstick competition can produce powerful incentives to perform well within some observable parameters. It also imposes risks on local leaders because not all factors of performance are under their control.

Decentralization also has its disadvantages. Pranab Bardhan and Dilip Mookherjee demonstrated that, under decentralization, local leaders may be more influenced by local elites such as the owners of large firms.[9] The decentralization of infrastructure provision is an example they used to illustrate their point. Under centralization, the policies of a central government might not be sufficiently responsive to local conditions, but the government will also be better able to resist pressures from local businesses to spend more than necessary on infrastructure investments. Let us take the case of dams discussed above. If decisions on a dam's construction must be made by local leaders, they might know better where to locate it. On the other hand, they are more likely to be influenced by, or to yield to the pressure of, local business leaders who may have a vested interest in building the dam in a place where the social costs exceed the benefits. When local accountability is weak, then local capture of authorities might be a very significant problem and decentralization might be less effective. The conclusion we can draw here is that there are no universal recipes for success with decentralization. We must measure its costs and benefits in their particular contexts.

Fighting Corruption in Road Construction

Corruption is a very relevant issue in the context of infrastructure. Large sums of money are involved in infrastructure projects, which means that there are also lucrative opportunities for corruption.

In the context of infrastructure, Benjamin Olken developed an ingenious way both to measure corruption and to evaluate which policies work best to prevent it.[10] Road construction in Indonesia is financed by the government, but implemented by local governments who spend the funds based on submitted projects. Olken organized a randomized experiment on corruption in road construction with the help of the World Bank. In certain villages, local authorities were

---

[9]Pranab K. Bardhan and Dilip Mookherjee, "Capture and Governance at Local and National Levels," *The American Economic Review* 90, no. 2 (2000): 135–139.

[10]Benjamin Olken, "Monitoring Corruption: Evidence from a Field Experiment in Indonesia," *Journal of Political Economy* 115, no. 2 (2007): 200–249.

randomly selected and told that they would be audited later for corruption on road construction. These individuals thus knew with certainty that they would be audited, whereas the normal probability of being audited was about 4%. In other villages, community participation for monitoring corruption in road construction was organized instead using two different methods. In some of the community participation villages, meetings were organized at which village officials had to explain how they spent the money for road construction. In other community participation villages, anonymous comment forms were distributed together with an invitation to the meeting so that villagers could report on corruption anonymously without fear of retaliation.

How was corruption measured? Olken went so far as to use experts to develop engineering estimates of the costs of road construction. He assembled a team of engineers and surveyors who, after the road projects were completed, dug core samples in each road to estimate the quantity of materials used, asked local suppliers to estimate prices, and interviewed villagers to determine the wages paid on the project. He was able to develop independent estimates of the road construction costs and estimate corruption by computing the difference between the real announced costs and the estimated costs suggested by the engineers. On average, he found that the announced was 24% higher than the estimated cost. Part of this may be due to measurement error, but nevertheless, this measure provides a rather good estimate of the diversion of funds in road construction.

How effective were the measures to fight corruption? Olken found that the announced audit reduced the cost differential by 8% (16% instead of 24%). He also found that the announced audits increased the jobs allocated to family members. This may seem counterintuitive because we often associate corruption with nepotism. In this case, however, the reason is probably due to the fact that village leaders had more trust in their family members not to divert money. Audits are, of course, costly. Nevertheless, Olken estimated the benefit of audits to be equal to 150% of their cost. The inclusion of audits in all future road projects would thus reduce the total costs of road construction thanks to the decrease in the diversion of funds.

In terms of community participation, he found that it had very little significant effect in reducing corruption and was much less effective than centralized auditing. This was not due to the fact that there was little participation. On the contrary, there was enthusiastic attendance at the village meetings, but the meetings did not prove to be effective in fighting corruption. Villagers took care to compare paid wages with planned wages, but had little to contribute about the costs of inputs. Informed auditors were thus more effective. In this case, centralized auditing, monitoring "from above," was more effective than community participation, or monitoring "from below."

Chapter Summary

The State of Infrastructure in Developing Countries

There is a significant infrastructure gap between developed and developing countries. In the poorest countries of the world, a majority of the population does not have access to electricity and sanitation, let alone to telephones, and a large percentage of the planet still does not have access to clean water. Inequality of infrastructure access is thus still very critical. Infrastructure investment is mainly provided by governments despite the privatization campaigns of the last decades.

Development Effects of Infrastructure Investment

Poor contract enforcement, a large informal economic sector, and extensive ethno-linguistic fractionalization are associated with a statistically significant lower level of infrastructure investment, and less infrastructure investment is associated with lower growth. Railroad investments in India under British colonial rule were estimated to have increased real agricultural income by 16%. Some large infrastructure projects yield less efficiency gains. The benefits of dam construction in India have not been much larger than the costs. Many large infrastructure projects are also called white elephants because of their inefficiency. One reason why politicians are willing to go ahead with white elephant projects is that they create jobs and voter constituencies to help reelect these officials.

Investment Risk and the Cost of Capital in Infrastructure

It is not easy to attract private capital to invest in infrastructure in developing countries. The main reason is that the cost of capital is very high: investors are only willing to fund infrastructure projects if they can get a return that is at least 2% to 4% higher than in richer countries. The main reason for the higher cost of capital is the higher risk perceived by investors due to the lower quality of institutions and/or the lower degree of property rights protection.

Geography and Infrastructure

Landlocked countries have higher trade costs due to their geographical disadvantages. This geographical disadvantage is often compounded by bad infrastructure, not only in the landlocked countries but also in the countries, through which goods transit to reach sea ports.

Institutional Aspects of Infrastructure

The costs and benefits of particular infrastructure projects can be impacted by the particular institutional context. Having an independent regulatory agency endowed with an adequate budget helps to curb the monopoly power of private firms that provide infrastructure services. A regulatory agency can also help to prevent the hold-up problems caused by governments or by private firms.

Fiscal decentralization facilitates holding local politicians more accountable because these officials are not distant from the electorate. Also, local officials have better information and it is possible to use yardstick competition between local officials to provide them with incentives for making honest and efficient decisions. A disadvantage of decentralization is that local politicians may be more easily captured or influenced by owners of big firms.

We examined some of the research done on corruption in infrastructure investment using the example of road construction in Indonesia. When local leaders responsible for building roads are told that they will be audited, diversion of funds is reduced by one-third. The benefits from auditing largely outweigh its costs. While auditing is effective, empowering villagers to monitor road construction, through village meetings or by distributing forms to report corruption anonymously, is much less effective.

Key Terms

cif/fob	country premium
clientelism	debt premium
cost of capital	equity premium
cost of debt	heterogeneity
cost of equity	risk-free rate of interest

Review Questions

1. Why is infrastructure investment important for development? Explain by giving some examples of infrastructure investment that help development.

2. What effect does income inequality have on access to infrastructure in development?

3. Define the weighted average cost of capital. How important is it for private investment in infrastructure in development?

4. A telecom company is considering investing in South Africa. Here are the data necessary to calculate the rate of return. The debt is 71% of equity. The risk-free rate of interest is 8%, the country premium is 12%, the return on equity is 18%, the return on debt is 11%, and the tax rate is equal to 0. Calculate the rate of return on the investment that would make it worthwhile to an investor.

5. Take the same numbers as shown in the previous exercise, but assume that debt is 42% of equity. What is the necessary rate of return to make the investment worthwhile? Explain why this rate of return differs from the answer to the previous exercise. Based on the variation of WACC as a function of the firm's debt-equity ratio, can you think of any criticism of the WACC formula? Explain.

6. Esfahani and Ramírez found that ethno-linguistic fragmentation and a large informal economic sector had a negative effect on infrastructure investment. Look at other chapters in the book and find what other effects these two variables have.

7. One problem with infrastructure concession contracts given to private firms in Latin America was the tendency for those firms to renegotiate the contracts in their favor. Explain this phenomenon in terms of the hold-up problem analyzed in Chapter 7.

8. Download the latest version of the World Competitiveness Report: http://www.weforum.org/reports?filter[type]=Annual%20Reports. Find the country ranking in terms of infrastructure quality. Find the countries that are better ranked than the United States. Among those, select the subset of developing countries. Why do you think some developing countries have a better infrastructure score than the United States?

9. Read the article "Does Decentralization Increase Spending on Public Infrastructure?" by Antonio Estache (policy research working paper 1457, The World Bank, 1995). Summarize the main findings. Can you make sense of these findings given the discussion on decentralization in this chapter? Explain. Do you draw additional lessons about decentralization after reading this chapter? Explain.

10. Go on the World Bank website (http://databank.worldbank.org/) and find data per country on Internet users per 100 inhabitants between 2005 and 2009. Find the countries in Latin America, Asia, and Africa that have the lowest and the highest number of Internet users for each continent. Find the country, worldwide, that has the highest number of Internet users for each of the 5 years. Construct a table to compare these numbers. Interpret the results.

19

Corruption

Mobutu Sese Seko (1930–1997) was president of Zaire (now the Democratic Republic of the Congo) between 1965 and 1997. He holds the sad record of having been the most corrupt leader in Africa. During his years in power, he is said to have stolen or embezzled US$5 billion, most of it placed in Swiss bank accounts. In the first years of his presidency, he diverted money given by U.S. government agencies and Western powers to support his fight against rebel movements backed by the Soviet Union. Later, he received kickbacks from royalties paid to Zaire by foreign companies that extracted the country's natural resources. He went on to accept bribes from any major business deal in Zaire. In later years, he personally diverted a significant portion of the government budget to his own accounts.

During his administration, the country became impoverished. Roads were neither built nor repaired, leading to a collapse of the country's transport infrastructure. The education system was left in ruins. The country had a wealth of natural resources such as copper, uranium, gold, and diamonds, but their extraction never benefited the population. When Mobutu was overthrown in 1997, income per capita in the country was a mere $160, roughly two-thirds less than when he seized power. Unfortunately, Mobutu was not the only corrupt leader in a developing country; others include Mohammed Suharto, the president of Indonesia between 1967 and 1998; Ferdinand Marcos, the president of the Philippines between 1966 and 1986; Jean-Claude Duvalier, the president of Haiti between 1971 and 1986; and Alberto Fujimori, president of Peru between 1990 and 2000.

The topic of corruption has become increasingly important in all discussions of development and foreign aid. There is a large body of evidence that significant amounts of foreign aid have been diverted because of corruption, though it is difficult to give exact figures.[1] The extent of corruption in a country is an indicator of the quality of its institutions. One of the main themes in development economics, and in this book, is that institutions are key to encouraging or, instead, hampering development.

Corruption involves the misuse of public office for private gain. Corrupt activities are not only illegal, but they are also covert in order to avoid detection.[2] Corrupt contracts are not legally enforceable. Because corrupt activities are clandestine, they imply minimal or no transparency in public and administrative

---

[1]See, for example, William R. Easterly, *The Elusive Quest for Growth: Economists' Adventures and Misadventures in the Tropics* (Cambridge, MA: MIT Press, 2002).

[2]Some corrupt activities that are illegal in certain countries are legal in others. For example, this is the case for laws regulating political campaign contributions, which vary greatly across countries. Some countries have very strict limits on campaign contributions while others do not.

decision making. The more corrupt a society is, the less enforcement of laws there will be. The problems do not stop there. As corruption increases, so do the forces that work to undermine formal institutions. In other words, corruption threatens not only the quality of formal institutions, but also their existence.

In this chapter, we first consider the different definitions of corruption because it is important to know exactly how corruption is defined in social sciences. Next, we review the existing measures of corruption. We then consider the consequences of corruption for economic development. Next, we will examine the evidence available on the effect of corruption on growth and ask why some countries are more corrupt than others. Corruption is a long-term phenomenon that can have deep roots. Societies do not become corrupt or law abiding simply as a result of policy changes. We will examine cultural explanations of corruption and finally ask why it is so difficult to fight it.

What Is Corruption?

The word *corruption* is used in many contexts and the boundaries between corrupt and honest behavior are not always clear. Nevertheless, in economics as well as in social sciences, it is generally accepted that corruption means the misuse of public office for private gain. The focus is thus on public-sector corruption. This definition includes the obvious case of a politician or a bureaucrat taking a bribe in exchange for favoring some special interests, such as a firm bidding to procure goods or services for a government agency or an industry lobbying against environmental legislation. Another example would be a bureaucrat taking a bribe to accelerate the delivery of a license or a permit to a small businessman. In these cases, corruption may lead to possible inefficiencies in public decision making—a government official signing a contract with a less-efficient company or failing to introduce well-crafted legislation. In the case of taking a bribe in return for a license, corruption may not necessarily lead to inefficiency, which can actually be reduced by the prompt, albeit corrupt, delivery of the license. Nevertheless, corruption still plays a role because of the misuse of public office for private gain. The bureaucrat is supposed to do his or her work efficiently without needing to be bribed. Thus, corrupt activities can, in some cases lead to less efficiency, while in other cases, they may result in more efficiency. We return to this distinction later in the chapter.

Illegal behavior, that is, breaking the law, is inherent in the definition of corruption as misuse of public office for private gain. As a result, a verdict that finds an individual or organization guilty of corruption will involve legal penalties. Being suspected of corruption can carry electoral or political costs. Note that this definition of corruption excludes corruption within the private sector. Thus, if two suppliers are competing for a contract to deliver some kind of goods to a firm, one of the suppliers may offer the manager of the firm a bribe in order to win the contract. In this case, the manager is bribed to make a decision that may not be in the best interests of the firm. Also, managers sometimes steal money from a firm's shareholders. These kinds of corrupt practices are not uncommon in the business world; although they are illegal and we can certainly consider them to be morally and ethically wrong, we will not focus on these cases in this chapter.

Note that corruption need not involve bribery. According to our definition, a tax collector who steals part of the revenues he collects is guilty of corruption. He does not receive bribes but diverts public funds. A borderline case would be a politician who receives illegal contributions to finance his party's election campaign. If the politician takes some of this money for his own use, it is an obvious case of corruption, but if all the money goes into the party's campaign fund, does this fit our definition of corruption as there is no obvious direct private financial enrichment? We can argue that this is a form of corruption because eventually the party and its elected officials can reap private gains from this activity. Indeed, if one political party engages in illegal campaign financing while others do not, this activity may give the party an unfair competitive edge that can result in an electoral victory. Party leaders will then garner personal benefits from an illegal activity, which qualifies as corruption. Whether specific political leaders directly benefit from these funds is rarely the primary issue in trials that focus on illicit campaign financing.

A case that does not fit the definition of corruption is clientelism or particularistic spending. This occurs when politicians give favors to particular voter groups in exchange for their electoral support. These favors often take the form of government jobs or public works projects in the voters' districts. In the United States, this is called pork-barrel spending. Particularistic spending may be associated with corruption; a firm that receives the contract for a public works project may give kickbacks to politicians who approved the project. However, we will not include particularistic spending in our definition of corruption.

Sometimes corruption is also confused with **rent-seeking**, trying to influence politicians in order to obtain economic favors. While corruption can be seen as a form of rent-seeking, this practice is not necessarily corrupt. In a democracy, rent-seeking is perfectly normal as different interest groups try to advance their interests. This is unavoidable and it would be naïve to think that rent-seeking could be eliminated. However, institutional rules can ensure that rent-seeking activities take place in a transparent and legal context.

As we mentioned above, because corruption involves breaking the law, corrupt activities will also be covert and because of this, their consequences will be hidden, as well. The more corruption there is, the less transparency there will be in government decisions.

Measuring Corruption

How can we measure corruption? Because it is a covert activity, it might seem that trying to measure it would be a hopeless endeavor that is necessarily doomed to fail. Moreover, not all acts of corruption are equal. A routine bribe to a policeman who will "fix" a traffic ticket is not the equivalent of a politician who pays criminal elements to eliminate a political opponent or to organize large-scale electoral fraud. Corruption at a higher level of power is considered more egregious than petty corruption.

There are two main methods used to measure corruption: objective measures quantify observed acts of corruption while subjective measures evaluate perceptions of corruption by those who are either confronted with it or with its consequences.

Objective Measures of Corruption

The most obvious objective measure of corruption is to count the number of criminal indictments for corruption. This can, however, be tricky because a country with fewer indictments for corruption can, in some cases, be more corrupt than one with numerous indictments. Indeed, fewer indictments can either mean that there is no corruption or that there is so much corruption that the country's police and judicial system do not prosecute those responsible. Thus, counting the number of indictments for corruption might not accurately reflect the actual degree of corruption.

Not all objective measures of corruption necessarily suffer from bad measurement. There are revealing objective corruption data for specific countries. For example, during the presidency of Alberto Fujimori in Peru, the head of the secret police, Vladimiro Montesinos, kept a very detailed record of all the bribes paid by the Fujimori administration to politicians, judges, and the media (see the box on page 514). There are other studies that also give us objective measures of corruption. For example, Benjamin Olken measured corruption in road construction in Indonesia by comparing the reported costs of the construction that were provided by local village authorities to the estimated costs that he received from independent engineers and surveyors.[3] He estimated that 24% of the construction funds had been diverted (see Chapter 18). Ritva Reinikka and Jakob Svensson studied corruption in the Ugandan educational system.[4] They compared the flows disbursed by the central government to the school districts with surveys done of the actual receipt of cash and supplies in those schools. They found that between 1991 and 1995, the schools received only 13% of the central government money they were promised. The rest of the money was apparently diverted by local officials and politicians (see Chapter 17). Rafael Di Tella and Ernesto Schargrodsky analyzed corruption in procurement for hospitals in Buenos Aires.[5] They found that prices for basic hospital inputs fell by 15% after a crackdown on corruption in 1996–1997, suggesting that the prices before the crackdown had been inflated because of corruption (see Chapter 16). Chang-Tai Hsieh and Enrico Moretti have also proposed estimates of the corruption related to the UN Oil for Food Program under Saddam Hussein.[6] This program was established after the first Gulf War to try to alleviate the suffering populace hurt by the post-war sanctions placed on Iraq. Under that program, the proceeds from the sale of Iraqi oil did not go directly to the Iraqi government, but into an escrow account. The use of that money was to be supervised by UN authorities. Hsieh and Moretti compared the official selling price of Iraqi oil with estimates of its market price. They then constructed an

[3]Benjamin Olken, "Monitoring Corruption: Evidence from a Field Experiment in Indonesia," *Journal of Political Economy* 115, no. 2 (2007): 200–249.

[4]Ritva Reinikka and Jakob Svensson, "Local Capture: Evidence from a Central Government Transfer Program in Uganda," *The Quarterly Journal of Economics* 119, no. 2 (2004): 679–705.

[5]Rafael Di Tella and Ernesto Schargrodsky, "The Role of Wages and Auditing during a Crackdown on Corruption in the City of Buenos Aires," *The Journal of Law & Economics* 46, no. 1 (2003): 269–292.

[6]Chang-Tai Hsieh and Enrico Moretti, "Did Iraq Cheat the United Nations? Underpricing, Bribes, and the Oil for Food Program," *The Quarterly Journal of Economics* 121, no. 4 (2006): 1211–1248.

estimate of the kickbacks from oil buyers who would pay a lower official price, but give kickbacks to the Iraqi government in the amount of the difference between the market price and the official price. The researchers estimated that $1–$4 billion in bribes were collected by the Iraqi government, which is between 2% and 10% of total spending under the auspices of the Oil for Food program.

These microeconomic measures of corruption are very useful, but they are relatively scarce and only measure certain aspects of corruption without allowing for international comparisons of corruption that are very useful.

Who Received the Biggest Bribes from Peru's Fujimori Government?

John McMillan and Pablo Zoido have studied the records kept by Vladimiro Montesinos, the head of Peru's secret police under President Alberto Fujimori, that document the bribes paid by the Fujimori government to politicians, judges, and the media.[7] The amount of bribes paid to various agents is indicative of an indirect reflection of checks and balances on the executive in the sense that those who need to be bribed the most are those who have more powers to check actions of the executive branch of government.

Among politicians, the largest bribes went to opposition leaders of the Peruvian Congress who were bribed to join Fujimori's party. They received higher bribes than those recipients from Fujimori's party. To demonstrate the value of muzzling the opposition, McMillan and Zoido found that the costs of bribes to politicians to obtain a majority of votes in the Congress were about $300,000 per month.

Among judges, those on the national election board received the largest bribes, but on average, bribes to judges were somewhat lower than those to politicians; the total bribes paid to judges were about $250,000 per month.

By far the largest bribes went to the news media. Two newspaper directors received payments between 1 and 1.5 million dollars over 2 years. However, the most costly bribes went to television channels, in the amount of $3 million per month, an amount far greater than that paid to politicians and judges.

Why did television broadcasters receive the biggest bribes? One possible explanation is that they were richer to begin with and needed more money to be silenced. However, they were carrying significant debt and could, theoretically, have been bought off more easily. Another, potentially more convincing, reason is that television is a powerful tool for exposing the abuses of incumbent politicians and mobilizing the citizenry against them. In other words, it is a key instrument to overcome the collective-action problem of citizens (see Chapter 7) in fighting a corrupt regime. Mobilized citizens are the ultimate check against dishonest politicians and this underscores the importance of free media as a vital institution in a healthy democracy. Another, more subtle, explanation might be that TV broadcasters had more bargaining power in extracting bribes than did judges or politicians. All the country's TV channels had to be bribed in order not to expose the corruption and abuse, but not all politicians needed to be bribed to achieve a majority in congress. As a result, each TV channel had significant bargaining power that allowed it to extract huge bribes.

---

[7]John McMillan and Pablo Zoido, "How to Subvert Democracy: Montesinos in Peru," *The Journal of Economic Perspectives* 18, no. 4 (2004): 69–92.

Subjective Measures of Corruption

Subjective measures of corruption do not suffer from some of the main problems encountered with objective measures. Subjective measures are more comprehensive and are constructed so as to make international comparisons possible. Their disadvantage is that they are based on perceptions of corruption and this can be problematic if those perceptions are biased by different kinds of prejudice. A country with a past history of corruption might be perceived to be more corrupt than it really is. Citizens who are distrustful of their government might underestimate the effects of a campaign against corruption. Very often, the indices of corruption are developed from diverse independent sources in order to try to minimize these kinds of prejudices, but there is no guarantee that the results will be free from bias.

One of the first surveys on corruption was produced by the *International Country Risk Guide* (ICRG; http://www.prsgroup.com/countrydata.aspx). This publication is produced by a private company that attempts to measure country risk for firms that are considering investments in a particular country. The corruption index measures a) the likelihood that high government officials will demand special payments; and b) the extent of illegal payments expected by the various tiers of the country's government. However, the composite indicator produced by the ICRG also mixes corruption with the political risk produced by corruption. The data that result are usually sold to private firms and then published online several years later.

A very well-known survey of corruption is the Corruption Perceptions Index, published each year since 1995 by Transparency International. Transparency International's Corruption Perceptions Index measures the perceived level of public sector corruption in countries and territories around the world. In a given year, this organization collects 18 different polls from 12 different institutions for different countries. The criteria for including a poll or indicator in the Corruption Perceptions Index are: a) to be consistent across all countries and thus to enable a ranking across countries; and b) to cover the overall extent of corruption and not combine it with other issues. Questions included are related to the level of kickbacks in public procurement, the bribing of bureaucrats, and the level of public-funds embezzlement. An interesting feature of the index is that respondents to the different surveys included are from various backgrounds: residents of the country, whether nationals or expatriates from multinational firms, and nonresidents such as international experts and international businessmen. Note that there is, in general, a high correlation between the different surveys used.

Figure 19.1 displays the Corruption Perceptions Index for 2011. The darker colors denote higher levels of corruption. The least-corrupt countries are New Zealand, the Scandinavian countries, Singapore, Netherlands, Australia, and Canada. This chapter's appendix (see page 534) reveals that the United States ranks 24th. Note that Chile has a better score than the United States. Among the most corrupt countries are Somalia, North Korea, Myanmar (Burma), Afghanistan, Uzbekistan, Turkmenistan, and Sudan. Russia and many of the former Soviet republics also have very high scores for corruption along with many African countries. The chapter appendix gives a ranking of all countries for 2011 together with country scores, as well as the number of surveys used for each country's score and a country's standard deviation.

FIGURE 19.1   Transparency International's 2011 Corruption Perceptions Index

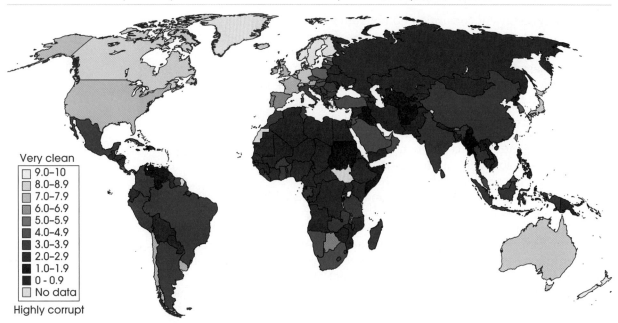

According to the Transparency International index, countries with darker colors and lower Corruption Perceptions Indices (CPI) have a higher level of corruption.

Source: http://www.transparency.org/cpi2011 Transparency International's Corruption Perceptions Index measures the perceived level of public sector corruption in countries and territories around the world. © Transparency International 2011. All Rights Reserved.

The World Bank produces the other well-known measure of corruption. It is a variable called "coasasntrol of corruption" and is derived from a larger set of indicators than the Corruption Perceptions Index. It includes up to 32 surveys from 30 differenasast organizations as well as the ICRG index. From 1996 until 2004, it was published every 2 years; since 2004, it has been updated every year. Even though it is calculated by a different method than the Corruption Perceptions Index, it is closely correlated with that index.[8] This is not surprising because both measures use many of the same sources. Most of the studies on corruption in recent years have used one of the subjective perception indices (ICRG, Transparency International, or World Bank).

While the subjective measures of corruption are more comprehensive than the objective measures, the question of how precise these measures are remains open. One reason why they might have a relatively high degree of accuracy is that if a corruption index is computed from many different indicators, each of which is derived from different sources, the measurement error in these different sources is likely to be independent. As we know from

---

[8]For details, see Daniel Kaufmann, Aart Kraay, and Massimo Mastruzzi, "Governance Matters: Aggregate and Individual Governance Indicators for 1996–2005," (policy research working paper 4012, The World Bank, 2006).

statistics, if we add many independent variables, we are likely to get more accurate results. In other words, the aggregate measurement error is likely to be smaller than the measurement error of each of the original sources. But there are reasons to be cautious. It is possible that many of the different indicators used by Transparency International or the World Bank overlap in terms of data sources. Adding data to different indicators that come from the same source does not increase accuracy, which may exaggerate the precision of the corruption indices. Caution is required in any case.

There is another problem related to the corruption data: they are subjective perceptions that may be contaminated by other variables such as observations of bad performance. For example, take two hypothetical countries with the same level of corruption, but assume that one country performs better economically than the other. When observers are asked to evaluate the corruption in these countries, their judgment might be influenced by their observations of economic performance. Because of good economic performance, they might infer that corruption is not as widespread as what they observed, or vice versa observation of bad economic performance may lead to an exaggerated perception of the overall degree of corruption in a country. If this is the case, then the subjective data on corruption might be contaminated by economic performance, in which case we should be very careful using statistics to analyze the relation between corruption and economic performance. We might erroneously find a correlation between corruption and economic performance, which would be, at least in part, due to the measurement error resulting from subjective perceptions of corruption that are contaminated by observed economic performance.

Greasing the Wheels or Rotting the Fruit Basket?

We now turn to the main topic of this chapter: the relationship between corruption and development. Ever since economists have studied corruption in the context of development, two opposing views have come forth. The first emphasizes the positive effects of corruption on efficiency, while the second emphasizes its negative effects.

According to the first view, corruption "greases the wheels" of an economy. The idea is that if there are many bureaucratic obstacles to trade and production, a certain amount of corruption that breaks inefficient rules may actually enhance efficiency. This idea was quite widespread during the era of central planning. As we discussed in Chapter 8, in a pure central planning system, firms were not allowed to trade with each other outside the plan. Think of a situation in which two firms would participate in a mutually beneficial trade and would bribe a bureaucrat to look the other way. This was seen as "greasing the wheels." In a free market system, we can find similar examples. Consider a situation in which there are restrictions on the number of taxi licenses issued to keep the prices for licenses up and the number of taxis down. Bribes paid to buy extra licenses should be economically beneficial because they help increase market entry and competition. Another argument often invoked in favor of the "greasing the wheels" approach is that bribes are an inducement to accelerate administrative procedures. Those who are more willing to pay to speed up procedures will pay a bribe to do so.

The general idea behind this benign view of corruption is that if agents can bargain freely, efficient outcomes will be the result. This is often referred to as Coasian bargaining and is based on the ideas of Nobel Prize–winner Ronald Coase about property rights and bargaining (see Chapter 7). In this case, corruption is seen as breaking rules that prevent efficient bargaining.

The second view on the efficiency effects of corruption is more negative. It is predicated on the fact that a corruption contract cannot be enforced in a court. Therefore, all the problems identified in Chapter 7 that formal institutions are supposed to solve (in particular, the hold-up and commitment problems) will be present. A corrupt bureaucrat, who extracts bribes from law-abiding citizens and whose powers in a corrupt environment are unchecked, will behave arbitrarily. He will increase the size of the bribes he demands when he feels he can do so and will leave citizens vulnerable and fearful. The argument for speeding up administrative procedures must then be reinterpreted in a more pessimistic way. Bureaucrats may purposefully delay or paralyze normal procedures in order to extract bribes from citizens and businesses.

Because corruption is associated with breaking the law, it is important to emphasize here that there is a fundamental difference between the economic effect of taxation and the economic effect of corruption. If we take a benign view of corruption, we could indeed claim that corruption is not any worse than taxation. We could argue that paying a tax or a bribe can lead to the same distortions in allocations. The difference between taxation and bribes is that tax rates are, in principle, established and implemented within a set of laws that are known to all. Tax rates may change and these changes may sometimes be unpredictable. However, there are legal procedures for making these changes; usually, changes in tax rates are decided by a legislature. A citizen who thinks that he or she is being taxed abusively can mount a defense by invoking tax laws. If citizens collectively decide they are being taxed too much, they may vote to replace the politicians with others who are less pro-taxation.

With corruption, the situation is quite different; there are no rules for setting the price of a bribe. It depends on the bargaining power and on the arbitrary decision-making power of a bureaucrat or a politician. Bribes are therefore not as predictable. Those who extract bribes are much more predatory because they are less accountable.[9] In the absence of rules that constrain the stronger party and protect the weaker party to a transaction, when corruption is the norm, the "law of the jungle" or the Hobbesian "state of nature" will prevail. High-ranking government officials will abuse their power and oppress the weak. Moreover, the uncertainty generated by the absence of rule will deter investment, whether from domestic or foreign sources.

Because corruption breaks the law, it weakens the formal institutions that are supposed to protect property rights and contracts. Corruption is then seen as "rotting the fruit basket." Observation of corruption, especially if the

---

[9]Of course, the difference between taxation and bribes becomes less significant if all branches of government are corrupt and dysfunctional.

corruption is unpunished, will encourage further corruption, which then will spread; the observation of widespread unpunished corruption leads people to accept corruption as inevitable. The institutionalist view is particularly critical of corruption because of its damaging effect on institutions.

While the two views of corruption have had equal numbers of proponents for a long time, in recent years, the consensus has moved toward the second view. This is, to a certain degree, due to the fact that economists have changed their view of the economy from one where markets emerge spontaneously and create efficient outcomes in the absence of red tape, to one where institutions are important for the protection of property rights and efficient transactions.

Corruption and Growth

Does corruption inhibit economic growth? This question is directly related to our discussion in the previous section: If corruption is primarily about greasing the wheels, then we should expect it to have a positive effect on growth. On the other hand, if the view that corruption rots the fruit basket is true, we might expect it to have a negative effect on growth.

Inefficiencies associated with corruption do not necessarily result in lower growth. They might only result in a lower static output level and have no effect on growth. This distinction is important: increases in efficiency may increase output, but not necessarily the growth of output. In order to show an effect on growth, one must show that corruption must affect either population growth, accumulation of physical or human capital, or total factor productivity (see Chapter 4). However, it is possible to argue that this is the case. Corruption may hinder investment by firms, and thus capital accumulation, because firms fear being held up by government bureaucrats. Firms may also avoid more productive but irreversible investment, and pursue less irreversible investments that may not be as economically productive, but may protect them from bureaucratic holdup. The choice to enter the informal sector to hide from corrupt bureaucrats is also likely to lead to the adoption of less efficient technologies. Firms may allocate more time for bribing bureaucrats in order to obtain monopoly positions than they do investing in productive technologies. An individual may decide to become a corrupt bureaucrat instead of a productive entrepreneur, which would be bad for economic growth.

What does the evidence suggest? There is some micro-evidence that implies negative effects of corruption on growth, but the macro-evidence is less conclusive. Raymond Fisman and Jakob Svensson estimated the effect of corruption on firm growth in Uganda between 1995 and 1997.[10] They found that a 1 percentage point increase in the bribe rate led to a reduction in firm growth of 3 percentage points, whereas an increase of 1 percentage point in the tax rate only led to a 1 percentage point decrease in firm growth. This finding tends to confirm the idea discussed above that corruption is more distortionary than taxation.

---

[10]Raymond Fisman and Jakob Svensson, "Are Corruption and Taxation Really Harmful to Growth? Firm Level Evidence," *Journal of Development Economics* 83, no. 1 (2007): 63–75.

Paolo Mauro was the first to analyze the effect of corruption on growth in an international comparative framework.[11] He used corruption data from a firm called Business International that was related to the Economist Intelligence Unit (EIU). These were data on subjective perceptions of corruption. He found that corruption had a negative effect on the investment rate, that is, the ratio of investment over GDP. This was true in ordinary least square regression as well as in an instrumental variable regression in which ethno-linguistic fractionalization was taken as an instrument for corruption (see the Econometric Appendix on instrumental variable regression).

Ethno-linguistic fractionalization measures the probability that two randomly matched people in a country will not belong to the same ethnic or linguistic group. This fractionalization may be a possible cause of corruption because in countries where it is present, government is jointly managed by representatives of these different groups who do not trust one another, or trust one another less than they would if they were from the same ethno-linguistic group. Because there is less cooperation between the groups, representatives from each feel entitled to divert common resources for their own personal enrichment or for that of their own ethnic group. Because no ethno-linguistic group feels responsible for government as a whole, there is less moral stigma resulting from the diversion of government funds. In Mauro's research, while the effect of corruption on investment seemed quite significant, the effect of corruption on growth was less robust. Mauro's work leads to the conclusion that corruption mainly affects investment and, thus as a result, it may have indirect effects on growth via its effects on investment.

Shang-Jin Wei examined the effect of corruption on foreign direct investment (FDI).[12] He used the same corruption variable as Mauro, as well as the ICRG and the Transparency International data mentioned above. His basic finding was that the effect of corruption on foreign direct investment was very significant. An increase in a host government's corruption level from that of Singapore's (ranked as no. 5 at the time in the Transparency International index, with a very low level of corruption) to that of Mexico's much higher level (ranked no. 70 at the time), had the same negative effect on the inward FDI as raising the marginal tax rate by 42 percentage points.

The evidence we have on corruption both at the microeconomic and at the macroeconomic level thus tends to favor the pessimistic view of corruption rather than the benign "grease the wheels" interpretation.

Why Are Some Countries More Corrupt than Others?

The fact that some countries are more or less corrupt than others is an important question that is hard to answer in a fully satisfactory way because it requires a true grasp of the precise mechanisms that cause corruption. There are many possible mechanisms as we have discussed above and they are difficult to disentangle. Corruption may be due to local culture that considers it

[11]Paolo Mauro, "Corruption and Growth," *The Quarterly Journal of Economics* 110, no. 3 (1996): 681–712.

[12]Shang-Jin Wei, "How Taxing Is Corruption on International Investors?" *The Review of Economics and Statistics* 82, no. 1 (2000): 1–11.

acceptable to pay and receive bribes. It may also be due to very low wages for civil servants, as well as bad governance and inadequate selection of civil servants, among other causes. Moreover, it is also difficult to distinguish between the causes and the consequences of corruption.

Development and Corruption

One of the strongest correlations we find in all studies of corruption is the link between development and corruption. Countries with a lower GDP per capita tend to have a higher level of corruption. There are several interpretations of this finding: one is that poverty tends to breed corruption; another is that corruption is bad for development; a third and perhaps more plausible interpretation is that there are certain underlying variables such as institutions that cause both more corruption and less development. In an article synthetizing the causes of corruption found in the literature, Daniel Treisman highlighted the correlation between contemporary measures of corruption (the World Bank's measure of control of corruption mentioned above) and GDP per capita going as far back as 1820.[13] Table 19.1 shows the correlation Treisman found between economic historian Angus Maddison's series of GDP per capita since 1500 and control of corruption in 2005. The p-value is a statistical indicator for the probability that the coefficient is equal to zero. The lower the p-value is, the higher the probability that the coefficient is significantly different from zero. Table 19.1 shows that until 1700, there is no correlation between income per capita and corruption today. However, income per capita in 1820 is already correlated with control of corruption today and the correlation is very significant. This means that richer countries in 1820 were likely to be less corrupt today. The correlation is quite striking and suggests that there are long-term effects at play in the determination of corruption. It is plausible that these effects could be related to institutions rather than to short-term policies. Of course, we must keep in mind that the rich countries in 1820 are still the rich countries today; in other words, the ranking of different countries' income has not changed significantly over time.

TABLE 19.1 Correlation of 2005 Perceived Control of Corruption and Maddison's Estimates of GDP Per Capita, 1500–1950

	1500	1600	1700	1820	1900	1950
World Bank control of corruption 2005	−0.47	0.145	0.228	.599**	.791**	.441**
p-value	.835	.52	.308	.000	.000	.000
Number of countries	22	22	22	46	42	146

There is a correlation between corruption in 2005 and the level of development in 1950, 1900, and even as far back as 1820. Countries that were richer in 1820 are less corrupt today. Note that ** indicates significant at the 1% level.

Source: Daniel Treisman, "What Have We Learned about the Causes of Corruption from Ten Years of Cross-National Empirical Research?" *Annual Review of Political Science* 10 (2007): 211–244.

---

[13]Daniel Treisman, "The Causes of Corruption: A Cross-National Study," *Journal of Public Economics* 76, no. 3 (2000): 399–457.

The correlation between level of development and corruption is very strong and it is still present and quite significant when we control for other variables that could affect corruption, such as ethno-linguistic fractionalization and geographical variables such as latitude, region, religion, culture, democracy, trade openness, inequality, inflation, and government policies.

Political Institutions and Corruption

Not surprisingly, there is a relationship between political institutions and corruption. This is a topic that has been the subject of a large body of research. A first-order effect is that of democracy and political rights on perceived corruption. Countries with democratic institutions tend to be less corrupt. However, the relationship is not mechanical: an improvement or deterioration of the Freedom House democracy index or the polity score (see Chapter 9) does not necessarily lead to an automatic deterioration or improvement in the corruption score. Here again, the long term seems to matter a lot. Treisman's 2007 study, cited above, found that the duration of a democracy impacts its level of corruption: countries that have been democracies since 1950 are less likely to be corrupt. He also found that freedom of the press has significant impact on corruption levels, a result that echoes the large bribes Peru's Fujimori administration paid to the directors of Peru's TV channels (see box on page 514). A greater circulation of daily newspapers also has a negative effect on perceived corruption.

An important distinction among democratic regimes is found between presidential and parliamentary systems mentioned in Chapter 9. Studies by Ugo Panizza and by Jana Kunicova and Susan Rose-Ackerman have found that, controlling for income, democracies with a directly elected president tend to be more corrupt than parliamentary democracies.[14] They reason that most existing presidential regimes are characterized by a president with a high degree of executive power. In contrast, power is more diluted in a parliamentary government. However, in terms of the effect of a powerful presidential regime on corruption, the studies primarily focus on the fact that Latin American regimes, which are all presidential, have higher corruption scores. The effect of presidential regimes on corruption ceases to be significant if a "Latin America" dummy variable (taking a value of 1 if the country is in Latin America and 0 otherwise) is included, or if a Catholicism variable (percentage of Catholics in a country) is included because it is the predominant religion in Latin America.[15] It is thus difficult to tell whether the presidential regime actually causes more corruption or whether corruption in this region has something to do with elements of Catholic culture or with other variables that are specific to Latin American societies.

Another important distinction among democratic regimes, also analyzed in Chapter 9, is the effect of electoral rules. Scholars have argued that corruption

---

[14]Ugo Panizza, "Electoral Rules, Political Systems, and Institutional Quality," *Economics and Politics* 13, no. 3 (2001): 311–342; and Jana Kunicova and Susan Rose-Ackerman, "Electoral Rules and Constitutional Structures as Constraints on Corruption," *British Journal of Political Science* 35, no. 4 (2005): 573–606.

[15]Dummy variables are variables that can take only two values: 1 or 0.

should be lower in countries with electoral rules that make politicians more accountable. In terms of those rules, one important distinction is between those that are closed list and those that are open list. With closed-list electoral rules, a candidate's place on the electoral list determines the probability of whether he or she is reelected, whereas with an open-list system, the probability of a candidate's reelection depends only on the number of votes he or she receives. Thus, under closed-list electoral rules, it is possible for a politician to be reelected without getting many votes. In other words, voters cannot vote out a corrupt politician who is placed high on the list. This effect is potentially more present under proportional electoral rule, where more than one representative is elected per district (see Chapter 9). Closed lists should thus favor more corruption, in contrast to open lists.

In systems with open-list electoral rules, what are the effects of proportional electoral rule and plurality rule? Two effects are possible. On one hand, it is difficult for new parties to participate in elections under plurality rule because the seat in a district goes to the party with the most votes. It is thus quite a challenge for a new party to win seats because it must garner the most votes in a district to do so. With entry being more difficult and costly, there generally are only two parties competing nationally and it is very rare for a third party to emerge as a significant player. The electorate will vote strategically for one of the two most important parties and will rarely waste their votes on a third party. This should favor corruption because it is possible for corrupt parties to continue to compete with each other without being threatened by a new party. It would take exceptional circumstances and strong coordination among voters for them to shift their votes to a new, uncorrupt party (see Chapter 7 on coordination problems).[16] There is, however, an opposite effect: Competition is stiffer under plurality rule because it is a "winner-take-all" electoral system. This could reduce incentives for corruption, which could be more severely punished electorally.

What does the evidence suggest? Torsten Persson, Guido Tabellini, and Francesco Trebbi found international evidence for these three effects (closed list versus open list, higher costs of entry versus stiffer competition) under plurality rule compared to proportional rule.[17] Overall, the difference between the effects of proportional and plurality rule on corruption is, however, not very large. The study cited above by Kunicova and Rose-Ackerman also found that closed-list proportional rule had poorer results in terms of corruption than did majoritarian electoral rule. However, according to Treisman's 2007 study cited above, these electoral rule effects were not extremely robust.

In terms of corruption, another distinction between political institutions is found in the comparison of centralized political systems and federal systems, where political and fiscal authority is decentralized to lower levels of government. One argument suggested by Andrei Shleifer and Robert W. Vishny is that under centralization, bribes are also centralized, while under decentralization, a "tragedy of the commons" effect can occur when different levels of government

---

[16]See, for example, Roger B. Myerson, "Effectiveness of Electoral Systems for Reducing Government Corruption: A Game-Theoretic Analysis," *Games and Economic Behavior* 5, no. 1 (1993): 118–132.

[17]Torsten Persson, Guido Tabellini, and Francesco Trebbi, "Electoral Rules and Corruption," *Journal of the European Economic Association* 1, no. 4 (2003): 958–989.

try to extract bribes from the same businesses.[18] Empirically, no significant link has been found between federalism or fiscal decentralization and the degree of corruption, and this is not really surprising because the argument is not about decentralization per se. The reasoning on centralization and decentralization only holds if there is some confusion of powers between the different levels of government. If those levels do not have overlapping jurisdiction, then the Shleifer and Vishny argument will not hold.

Legal Institutions and Corruption

The quality of a country's legal system may also affect corruption. In Chapter 10, we discussed the differences between civil-law and common-law systems; we also presented measures of legal formalism and bureaucratic regulation. The 2000 Treisman study found that measures of legal formalism (such as the time it takes to evict a tenant who does not pay his rent or to indict somebody who passes a bad check) are correlated with corruption. Treisman also found that the number of days it takes to register a new business has a significant positive correlation with corruption. However, it is not clear in which direction the causality is going. High levels of legal formalism might lead to more corruption because more red tape invites more opportunities for extracting bribes. On the other hand, corruption might lead to a deterioration of the legal system and to a slowing of the judicial and administrative systems. When testing for the causality between formalism and corruption by using the legal origin (civil law or common law) as an instrumental variable for formalism (see the Econometric Appendix on instrumental variables), there appears to be no significant effect at all between formalism and corruption.

Natural Resources, Trade, and Corruption

Some have suggested that countries with more natural resources have more corruption. The idea is that if a country has large oil reserves or other valuable natural resources such as gold, its government officials and bureaucrats will have more opportunities to enrich themselves by grabbing rents from those resources, as was the case with Mobutu in Zaire. On the other hand, countries that are more open to trade and face competitive economic conditions in the global marketplace, including competition from imports, are less likely to be prone to corruption because there will be less rents to grab. Alberto Ades and Rafael Di Tella found international evidence to support these ideas. They identified a positive association between corruption and the share of fuels and minerals in total exports, and a negative association between corruption and the share of imports in GDP as a measure of openness to trade.[19] Treisman found that the effect of openness took time to kick in.[20] Countries that liberalized earlier in time therefore had lower corruption scores.

---

[18]Andrei Shleifer and Robert W. Vishny, "Corruption," *The Quarterly Journal of Economics* 108, no. 3 (1993): 599–617.

[19]Alberto Ades and Rafael Di Tella, "Rents, Competition, and Corruption," *The American Economic Review* 89, no. 4 (1999): 982–993.

[20]Treisman, "What Have We Learned about the Causes of Corruption from Ten Years of Cross-National Empirical Research?" 2007.

To summarize, countries that have been developed for a long time and have an established history of democracy have less corruption. Independent and vigorous media are an important anticorruption factor. Natural resources tend to engender more corruption, while openness to trade is associated with less corruption. As we can see, corruption is primarily determined by long-term factors that correlate with economic prosperity and democracy.

Culture and Corruption

Because the long term seems to matter for corruption and because culture changes very slowly over time (see Chapter 11), corruption might be closely related to culture and to people's beliefs and value systems. We now examine the links between culture and corruption.

Different Cultures, Their Various Social Norms, and Corruption

We usually associate corruption with acts that are "morally wrong." However, this need not always be the case. Think of stories about German businessmen who hid Jews in their factories during World War II and bribed Nazi authorities to look the other way. These were acts of corruption, but undoubtedly they represented high moral values that were praiseworthy. Similarly, in today's world, no one would fault bribing a North Korean border guard to help a political opponent of the regime escape its oppression. In any country ruled by a dictatorship, examples like these would not be unusual. If an act is seen as morally correct, then there is no social opprobrium associated with it. As a result, society may accept or even encourage such acts.

However, what is considered morally correct or reprehensible can vary across countries. In many countries around the New Year, municipal sanitation workers or firefighters come to people's homes to collect annual tips. This is usually not seen as a form of corruption but it is not easy to argue otherwise. People may for example feel they must give the municipal sanitation workers a tip because otherwise they might find part of their garbage spilled on the ground. Now consider the case of people who stand in line to get a passport or another official document and then tip the employee who assists them. We would certainly consider it corruption because it is something that is not usually done. But how different is it from tipping municipal sanitation workers? It is conceivable that in some countries, the social norm dictates that municipal clerks must receive tips. Social norms on tipping vary greatly across countries. In the Unites States, tipping a waiter is not only morally acceptable, it is a social obligation. In most other advanced industrial countries, tipping in restaurants is not a social norm; for example, Europeans feel uncomfortable having to pay tips in American restaurants.[21] Of course, we can argue endlessly about different cases

---

[21]Another perspective on bribing is the frequent flyer miles individuals earn each time they fly for their companies. It is well understood that this creates an incentive for loyalty to an airline company that can then charge its passengers higher prices.

of conflicting social norms, but the basic point is that they are different across cultures. What is considered socially correct in one culture might be considered socially reprehensible in another. These differences therefore imply that cultural attitudes about corruption vary from culture to culture.[22] The practice of giving gifts is a long-standing obligation in many cultures. Gifts seen as bribes in certain cultures are seen only as acts of politeness in others. In many African and Central Asian countries, kinship and clan loyalties take precedence over any social norm for obeying the law. If someone gets a job as a government official, it is considered his or her absolute duty to use this position to favor fellow clansmen with jobs, funds, and other perks. Western values condemn such behavior, but how do we view the congressman who brings home pork for his constituents? Is this behavior less morally reprehensible?

This discussion of cultural differences in social norms does not mean we should be more tolerant of corruption in different countries. However, understanding these differences in social norms helps us to understand better why certain countries may be more prone to corruption than others.

Different attitudes about corruption are not only related to social norms. They are also rooted in different historical experiences with government. The Western way of thinking about corruption is rooted in the Western concept of government that, in the last several centuries, has evolved with the emergence of nation-states and the rule of law, a process that predates the establishment of democratic regimes. Western concepts of government are rooted in the modern idea of the law, which is predicated on obeying specific rules. Citizens are supposed to be equal before the law and the law is supposed to be applied equally to all citizens. Corruption conflicts with that concept because it suggests that people can pay to be exempt from the law. If officials are corrupt, it means they are not fulfilling their responsibility to treat all citizens equally according to the law, but are, instead, using their official position for their own private gain and possibly for the gain of those who bribe them.

In many other countries, the government and the rule of law did not have the chance to develop as they did in the Western world. When people were subject to the despotic rule of a feudal lord, they were victimized by all sorts of predatory behavior; as a result, they tried to please the feudal lord and avoid his wrath by giving in to his wishes and offering him gifts. If this has been the only type of relationship people have ever experienced with their government, then corruption has another meaning: it is the normal state of affairs, the way things are done because the powerful abuse their power and are expected to do so. For those countries that have known colonial rule under which the colonial authorities governed with the help of local feudal lords, corruption is more the normal state of affairs than the exception. It is not a dysfunction of government, it is how government functions.

The concept that government should collect taxes in order to provide public services is also relatively modern and linked to Western concepts of government. In many cultures, it was the social duty (*noblesse oblige*) of the aristocracy and other wealthy citizens to do good deeds and provide charity in the form of roads, schools, hospitals, and so forth. In Chapter 11, we discussed the

---

[22]See, for example, Pranab Bardhan, "Corruption and Development: A Review of Issues." *Journal of Economic Literature* 35, no. 3 (1997): 1320–1346.

tradition of the *waqf* in Islamic countries that calls for affluent private citizens to organize and fund public services for society at large. If most public services are privately funded, payments from private citizens to other private citizens who are providing those services are not considered corrupt. Just as commissions are expected in private contracts, why should they be inappropriate when private citizens provide public services?

While we recognize that different cultures have different social norms, there is not enough understanding in the Western world of other cultures, their value systems and beliefs, and the historical experiences that have influenced them. It is not only important that we understand other cultures, but it is critical that we do so without paternalistic and condescending attitudes. It would be completely wrong to think that the cultural history of other nations is nothing more than just one long path toward Western values. Just as we appreciate food from other cultures, as globalization progresses, we must strive to engage in more cultural exchange and increase our knowledge and appreciation of the world's diverse cultural norms.

Disentangling Culture from Other Institutional Causes of Corruption

It is extremely challenging to disentangle the various causes of corruption, many of which are linked. For example, what are the effects on corruption of legal and political institutions as well as culture? If a given culture is more permissive of corruption, it is likely that this will also be reflected in its legal system. Disentangling legal and cultural effects would thus be very difficult.

Ray Fisman and Edward Miguel have done some interesting and ingenuous research to disentangle cultural effects on corruption from other institutional effects.[23] Because the United Nations is headquartered in New York City, diplomatic personnel from around the world are stationed there. These diplomats and their families benefit from diplomatic immunity, which, until November 2002, even exempted them from paying parking fines. In their research, Fisman and Miguel examined the differences between diplomats from different countries in terms of illegal parking behavior. They used the extent of illegal parking behavior as a measure of a culture of corruption. Because diplomatic immunity protected the diplomats from legal sanctions, parking behavior was entirely driven by social norms. Those who abided by the law did so not because of monetary incentives (fines), but because of social norms that prohibit corrupt behavior and encourage people to abide by the law not only because they fear punishment, but also because they believe that this is morally correct behavior. In cultures that are more accepting of corruption, breaking the law could be the result of a social norm that places some individuals "above the law." Because of New York's scarce parking spaces, observing the social norm obviously had a cost. If culture did not matter at all and only financial incentives guided behavior, the researchers should have observed similar behavior across countries, with all diplomats parking illegally.

---

[23]Ray Fisman and Edward Miguel, "Corruption, Norms, and Legal Enforcement: Evidence from Diplomatic Parking Tickets," *Journal of Political Economy* 115, no. 6 (2007): 1020–1048.

Remarkably, Fisman and Miguel found a pattern of parking violation among the diplomats that strongly correlated to the subjective measures of corruption discussed earlier in this chapter. Figure 19.2 shows, on the vertical axis, the relation between the log of a country's annual per diplomat New York City parking violations and, on the horizontal axis, the World Bank country corruption measure (a higher score in the figure means more corruption because the index for control of corruption was inverted by the researchers).[24] The relationship is quite strong and gives some reassurance about the use of the subjective perception indices. On the other hand, it also shows that culture matters for corruption. As a result, cultural factors play a very important role when compared to other institutional factors. Note that the relation between the World Bank corruption index and parking violations holds when controlling for income per capita, the number of cars registered with different consulates, and other control variables. Note also that as diplomats stayed longer in New York, those from countries with a high tolerance for corruption had more parking violations over time, while those from countries with a low tolerance also tended to have more violations, but with a lower rate of increase. This suggests that even though diplomats knew that parking violations would go unpunished, cultural norms still played an important role in predicting the number of parking violations a particular diplomat incurred.

FIGURE 19.2   Parking Violations and the Corruption Index

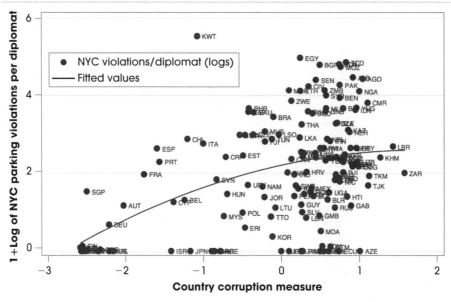

The horizontal axis measures country corruption and is derived from the World Bank corruption data described above. Here though, a higher score means more corruption. The vertical axis measures the log of (1+ a country's annual-per-diplomat New York City parking violations).

Source: Ray Fisman and Edward Miguel, "Corruption, Norms, and Legal Enforcement: Evidence from Diplomatic Parking Tickets," *Journal of Political Economy* 115, no. 6 (2007): 1038. Printed with permission from University of Chicago Press.

[24]Because this is a log, 1 is added to the number of violations so as to avoid the log taking very negative values and, possibly, minus infinity in case there are no violations.

The fact that culture appears to play an important role in corruption is consistent with a constant theme in this chapter: corruption is a long-term phenomenon. Cultural norms are slow to change and if corruption is, to a large extent, driven by culture, it can only experience consistent improvement over time if social norms change by establishing moral prohibitions against corrupt practices.

The Difficulty of Fighting Corruption

That corruption seems to be determined by long-term factors is corroborated by the reality that it is very difficult to fight corruption; anticorruption programs are usually not successful.

The most common methods for fighting corruption are 1) to devote more resources to the legal apparatus to identify and punish corruption and 2) to launch anticorruption campaigns. The idea is that more rules, better enforcement of those rules, and stricter monitoring will deter corruption. This is often more difficult than it may initially seem. If corruption has permeated all levels of government, how can we assume that by giving more resources to some levels of government, there will be less corruption? It is possible that those authorities who are asked to fight corruption are themselves corrupt. As an example, Jonathan Hay and Andrei Shleifer found that when elite units of the Russian police received better weapons to fight the Russian Mafia, police officers quickly resold those weapons on the black market, primarily to the Mafia, but at a higher price.[25]

Few Success Stories, but Can We Generalize?

Two success stories in the fight against government corruption that are often cited are Hong Kong since the 1970s, and Singapore since the 1980s. A common element in both examples is that a powerful independent anticorruption agency was set up with enormous authority: the Independent Commission Against Corruption (ICAC) in Hong Kong and the Corrupt Practices Investigation Bureau (CPIB) in Singapore.[26] These agencies were given powers that would not, however, be acceptable in democratic regimes, such as shifting the burden of proof from the prosecutor to the accused. Similar reforms have usually been recipes for the abuse of power. In Singapore, civil servants' pay was increased, their jobs were rotated often to prevent them from forming collusive and corrupt ties with clients, they received rewards for turning in clients who offered bribes, and much of the bureaucratic red tape that invites corruption was scrapped. In both Hong Kong and Singapore, a strong commitment to fight corruption paid off.

South Korea is often cited as another positive case study. The regime of dictator Syngman Rhee (1948–1960) is usually cited as having been very corrupt

---

[25]Jonathan R. Hay and Andrei Shleifer, "Private Enforcement of Public Laws: A Theory of Legal Reform," *The American Economic Review* 88, no. 2 (1998): 398–403.

[26]Robert Klitgaard, *Controlling Corruption* (Berkeley: University of California Press, 1988).

and predatory, while the regime of the next dictator, Chung-Hee Park (1961–1979), is often seen as much less corrupt.[27] However, controversy has arisen in the light of the East Asian financial crisis and some scholars have argued that corruption was still quite prevalent under Park.[28] In any case, progress in the fight against corruption in South Korea was not as spectacular as in Hong Kong or Singapore.

Higher Pay for Civil Servants: Does It Work?

Researchers have tried to determine whether higher pay for civil servants was, in general, a good strategy for fighting corruption. The idea is appealing: if civil servants are paid well, they will be more fearful of losing their jobs if they are caught taking bribes and will therefore have more incentives to fulfill their responsibilities honestly. On the other hand, poorly paid civil servants will have no shame and no fear of taking bribes. This is a version of the efficiency wage theory of incentives, according to which paying workers higher wages gives them a greater incentive to work hard.[29] However, international studies did not find significant evidence of such an effect. James Rauch and Peter Evans as well as Treisman found no effect, whereas Caroline Van Rijckeghem and Beatrice Weder did.[30] Di Tella and Schargrodsky, in their study of hospitals in Buenos Aires, found that higher wages had a deterrent effect, but only if there was sufficient monitoring.[31] Thus, it seems that higher wages alone are not effective to fight corruption and should be combined with more monitoring.

The alternative to fighting corruption from above is to combat it from below. Citizen access to information; a strong, free media; transparency of public decisions; and public participation in the decision-making process are tools to ensure citizen enforcement and monitoring. However, these measures are thoroughly institutionalized, they should not be seen as a panacea because grassroots initiatives are usually subject to the collective-action problems discussed in Chapter 7. Moreover, citizens may frequently have reasons not to denounce a case of corruption. They will have an incentive to denounce bureaucrats who expect bribes for a service that they should, in principle,

---

[27]Peter B. Evans, *Embedded Autonomy: States and Industrial Transformation* (Princeton: Princeton University Press, 1995).

[28]See, for example, David C. Kang, *Crony Capitalism: Corruption and Development in South Korea and the Philippines* (Cambridge, UK, and New York: Cambridge University Press, 2002).

[29]Carl Shapiro and Joseph E. Stiglitz, "Equilibrium Unemployment as a Worker Discipline Device," *The American Economic Review* 74, no. 3 (1984): 433–444; and Samuel Bowles, "The Production Process in a Competitive Economy: Walrasian, Neo-Hobbesian, and Marxian Models," *The American Economic Review* 75, no. 1 (1985): 16–36.

[30]James E. Rauch and Peter B. Evans, "Bureaucratic Structure and Bureaucratic Performance in Less Developed Countries," *Journal of Public Economics* 75, no. 1 (2000): 49–71; Daniel Treisman, "The Causes of Corruption: A Cross-National Study," 2000; and Caroline Van Rijckeghem and Beatrice Weder, "Bureaucratic Corruption and the Rate of Temptation: Do Wages in the Civil Service Affect Corruption, and by How Much?" *Journal of Development Economics* 65, no. 2 (2001): 307–331.

[31]Op. cit. 2003.

provide for free. However, in the case of bribes paid by citizens to bureaucrats and policemen as a reward for them to ignore actions that break the law, there will be very little incentive on either side to report these practices to anticorruption authorities.

Why Is Fighting Corruption So Difficult?

One reason why fighting corruption is so difficult is related to the coordination problems discussed in Chapter 7. This has been studied in a model by Jens Andvig and Karl Ove Moene.[32] They found that if the probability of being detected when taking a bribe declined along with the number of corrupt officials, then there were two possible coordination equilibria: one honest and one corrupt. If all officials were honest, the incentive to stay honest would be strong because there would be a high probability of being caught when acting dishonestly. There would thus be no incentive to deviate and everybody would be honest. If, on the other hand, all officials were corrupt, there was no disincentive to be corrupt because the probability of being caught would be low due to so many others being corrupt.

In a situation where corruption is widespread, it is thus very difficult to change the behavior of corrupt officials. It would take a very intense campaign to convince these bureaucrats that there is a high probability that they will be caught. However, if corruption is indeed widespread, it is very difficult to find enough honest and incorruptible officials to engage in such a campaign. Moreover, it may also be quite a challenge to find the necessary fiscal resources to fund an anticorruption campaign within a corrupt government, where funds are routinely pocketed by bureaucrats at all levels.

Another argument made in a model by Jean Tirole is that a reputation for corruption persists and is difficult to repair.[33] Because reputations endure, an administration that would launch a vigorous anticorruption campaign would incur the campaign's costs, but might not reap its benefits for a long time. Indeed, if a country keeps its reputation of corruption even while it fights to repair that reputation, foreign investors would still shy away from investing in that country. Even domestic investors might not give credit to the government's efforts and, as a result, would fail to invest or enter the economy's formal sector. It would only be after observing a long period of honest behavior by the government and its officials that economic agents would start to change their expectations. Precisely because the private sector and foreign investors might fail to react positively to an anticorruption campaign, an anticorruption government might be seen to have excessively high costs and low immediate benefits. The persistence of the reputation for corruption might thus create a "corruption trap": once a country falls in, it is difficult to get out. A country that has been corrupt is thus likely to stay corrupt because of the effects of the negative reputation, while a country that has been honest, but briefly lapses into corruption, might get stuck in its trap.

---

[32]Jens C. Andvig and Karl Ove Moene, "How Corruption May Corrupt," *Journal of Economic Behavior & Organization* 13, no. 1 (1990): 63–76.

[33]Jean Tirole, "A Theory of Collective Reputations (with Applications to the Persistence of Corruption and to Firm Quality)," *The Review of Economic Studies* 63, no. 1 (1996): 1–22.

Chapter Summary

What Is Corruption?

Corruption is defined as abuse of public office for private gain. It includes bribes, diversion of public money, and abuse of power to benefit a public official. Because it is illegal, corruption tends to be covert.

Measuring Corruption

Objective measures of corruption quantify observed acts of corruption such as indictments for corrupt activities. These measures might severely underestimate corruption in countries where police and courts are themselves corrupt and do not prosecute other corrupt officials. Subjective measures of corruption such as the Transparency International index or the World Bank index of control of corruption are more comprehensive and comparable across countries. These measures might however be contaminated by observed economic performance. Countries might wrongly be perceived as more corrupt because of bad economic performance.

Greasing the Wheels or Rotting the Fruit Basket?

The benign view of corruption is that it helps overcome inefficient regulations and works to improve efficiency. The more pessimistic view that has become more prevalent these days is that corruption creates insecurity of property rights and corrodes formal institutions of the rule of law.

Corruption and Growth

Empirical studies tend to confirm the view that corruption has a negative effect on economic performance and growth. International studies have found that corruption has a negative effect on growth through a negative effect on investment, both domestic and foreign.

Why Are Some Countries More Corrupt than Others?

Countries that were more developed as early as 1820 are less corrupt today. There is thus a long-term negative correlation between corruption and development. Corruption correlates with the absence of a long-standing tradition of democratic political institutions, little or no media independence, a lack of transparency in public and administrative decision making, weak or absent civil rights, and insufficient accountability by elected officials and civil servants. The presence of natural resources in a country tends to engender more corruption, while openness to trade is associated with less corruption.

Culture and Corruption

Diverse cultural norms lead to different moral judgments on forms of corrupt behavior. A country's cultural norms and the quality of both its government and that government's interaction with the citizenry play an important role as long-term determinants of corruption. There is empirical evidence suggesting a specific role for culture in explaining corruption.

The Difficulty of Fighting Corruption

It is not easy to fight corruption because it is a long-term phenomenon and it should not occur in isolation but in conjunction with other institutional reforms and cultural movements. Citizens must develop cultural norms that prohibit corruption and be able to mobilize against it. Eliminating corruption can succeed even in the absence of democracy, as shown by the evidence from Hong Kong and Singapore. However, respect for the rule of law is a critical precondition for successful administrative campaigns against corruption.

Key Term

rent-seeking

Review Questions

1. Explain why discussions about corruption can become politicized. Give some examples to show the possible policy consequences of different ideological views on corruption in developing countries. What is your view?

2. The extent of corruption in a country is an indicator of the quality of its institutions. Explain. How do you see the link between corruption and institutions?

3. Does corruption always lead to inefficiency? Why could corruption lead to improved efficiency? What is your view?

4. Why is corruption more distortionary than taxation? Do we have some evidence to support this view? Explain.

5. Give examples of two acts that are identical in terms of corruption, but one is morally reprehensible and the other is not.

6. Call x the proportion of people in a country who decide to behave in a corrupt and dishonest way. Assume that when people are honest, their payoff is L. Assume that when they behave in a corrupt way and are caught, their payoff is 0, but if they are not caught, their payoff is $C > L$. Assume that p is the probability of being caught when corrupt and that p is a negative function of x with $p(0) = 1$ and $p(1) = 0$. Show that there are two Nash equilibria, one where all people behave in a corrupt way and one where all are honest. Explain why these are Nash equilibria. Is there a third equilibrium? Explain how these equilibria come about.

7. Using the previous exercise, assume that the same competitive game can be played twice. Assume that in the beginning of the second period people can observe how people behaved in the first period. Does the analysis of the second period game change relative to what it was in the previous exercise? Explain.

8. Go to the following website that ranks the 10 most corrupt world leaders: http://www.infoplease.com/ipa/A0921295.html.

   Do you detect any empirical patterns from this list's data? Find and identify commonalities and differences between these leaders and describe any possible correlation between variables on the list.

9. Read the following article by Benjamin Olken and Patrick Barron: "The Simple Economics of Extortion: Evidence from Trucking in Aceh," *Journal of Political Economy* 117, no. 3 (2009): 417–452. The researchers examined the effect of market structure on the level of bribes paid by truckers to pass through checkpoints. How do the results of this study relate to basic principles of industrial organization on pricing by monopoly and oligopoly? How do the results of this study relate to the hold-up problem studied in Chapter 7? Give another example of possible hold-up problems that might involve corruption.

10. Download the following article by the United Nations Office on Drugs and Crime that references corruption in the Afghan government: http://www.unodc.org/documents/data-and-analysis/Afghanistan/Afghanistan-corruption-survey2010-Eng.pdf.

    The report lists in detail different forms of bribery. Using the report, draw up a list of the forms of bribery that may be efficiency enhancing and another list of those that have a negative economic effect. Which bribes might belong to both categories? Justify your classification.

APPENDIX

Transparency International's 2011 Corruption Perceptions Index

Country Rank	Country/Territory	CPI 2011 Score	Surveys Used	Standard Deviation
1	New Zealand	9.5	9	0.05
2	Denmark	9.4	8	0.05
2	Finland	9.4	8	0.07
4	Sweden	9.3	9	0.08
5	Singapore	9.2	12	0.13
6	Norway	9.0	9	0.07
7	Netherlands	8.9	9	0.11
8	Australia	8.8	11	0.12
8	Switzerland	8.8	8	0.22
10	Canada	8.7	9	0.15
11	Luxembourg	8.5	8	0.25
12	Hong Kong	8.4	11	0.17
13	Iceland	8.3	8	0.27
14	Germany	8.0	10	0.18
14	Japan	8.0	12	0.27
16	Austria	7.8	10	0.24
16	Barbados	7.8	4	0.40
16	United Kingdom	7.8	10	0.15
19	Belgium	7.5	9	0.21
19	Ireland	7.5	8	0.23
21	Bahamas	7.3	3	0.11
22	Chile	7.2	11	0.21
22	Qatar	7.2	7	0.79
24	United States	7.1	12	0.40
25	France	7.0	10	0.27
25	Saint Lucia	7.0	3	0.26
25	Uruguay	7.0	6	0.28
28	United Arab Emirates	6.8	8	0.46
29	Estonia	6.4	10	0.29
30	Cyprus	6.3	5	0.37
31	Spain	6.2	9	0.28
32	Botswana	6.1	7	0.19
32	Portugal	6.1	8	0.42

(Continued)

Country Rank	Country/Territory	CPI 2011 Score	Surveys Used	Standard Deviation
32	Taiwan	6.1	10	0.31
35	Slovenia	5.9	8	0.39
36	Israel	5.8	7	0.27
36	Saint Vincent and the Grenadines	5.8	3	0.73
38	Bhutan	5.7	4	0.28
39	Malta	5.6	5	0.23
39	Puerto Rico	5.6	4	0.48
41	Cape Verde	5.5	5	0.29
41	Poland	5.5	12	0.30
43	South Korea	5.4	13	0.23
44	Brunei	5.2	4	0.59
44	Dominica	5.2	3	0.26
46	Bahrain	5.1	6	0.67
46	Macau	5.1	3	0.74
46	Mauritius	5.1	6	0.37
49	Rwanda	5.0	6	0.72
50	Costa Rica	4.8	6	0.59
50	Lithuania	4.8	9	0.44
50	Oman	4.8	6	0.82
50	Seychelles	4.8	3	0.97
54	Hungary	4.6	11	0.41
54	Kuwait	4.6	6	0.66
56	Jordan	4.5	9	0.29
57	Czech Republic	4.4	12	0.29
57	Namibia	4.4	7	0.30
57	Saudi Arabia	4.4	5	0.86
60	Malaysia	4.3	12	0.31
61	Cuba	4.2	4	0.49
61	Latvia	4.2	7	0.30
61	Turkey	4.2	11	0.22
64	Georgia	4.1	7	0.43
64	South Africa	4.1	11	0.21
66	Croatia	4.0	10	0.21
66	Montenegro	4.0	5	0.50
66	Slovakia	4.0	10	0.36
69	Ghana	3.9	10	0.28
69	Italy	3.9	9	0.19
69	FYR Macedonia	3.9	6	0.21

(Continued)

Country Rank	Country/Territory	CPI 2011 Score	Surveys Used	Standard Deviation
69	Samoa	3.9	3	0.35
73	Brazil	3.8	10	0.24
73	Tunisia	3.8	7	0.67
75	China	3.6	12	0.26
75	Romania	3.6	10	0.17
77	Gambia	3.5	6	0.65
77	Lesotho	3.5	6	0.44
77	Vanuatu	3.5	3	0.92
80	Colombia	3.4	9	0.29
80	El Salvador	3.4	7	0.10
80	Greece	3.4	8	0.26
80	Morocco	3.4	8	0.37
80	Peru	3.4	9	0.16
80	Thailand	3.4	11	0.15
86	Bulgaria	3.3	10	0.27
86	Jamaica	3.3	7	0.18
86	Panama	3.3	6	0.23
86	Serbia	3.3	7	0.20
86	Sri Lanka	3.3	8	0.23
91	Bosnia and Herzegovina	3.2	6	0.12
91	Liberia	3.2	6	0.34
91	Trinidad and Tobago	3.2	5	0.32
91	Zambia	3.2	8	0.31
95	Albania	3.1	8	0.18
95	India	3.1	13	0.12
95	Kiribati	3.1	3	0.56
95	Swaziland	3.1	5	0.08
95	Tonga	3.1	3	0.17
100	Argentina	3.0	10	0.21
100	Benin	3.0	7	0.18
100	Burkina Faso	3.0	7	0.31
100	Djibouti	3.0	3	0.59
100	Gabon	3.0	4	0.29
100	Indonesia	3.0	12	0.27
100	Madagascar	3.0	7	0.40
100	Malawi	3.0	8	0.18
100	Mexico	3.0	11	0.13
100	Sao Tome & Principe	3.0	3	0.19
100	Suriname	3.0	3	0.37

(Continued)

Country Rank	Country/Territory	CPI 2011 Score	Surveys Used	Standard Deviation
100	Tanzania	3.0	8	0.18
112	Algeria	2.9	7	0.16
112	Egypt	2.9	7	0.21
112	Kosovo	2.9	3	0.10
112	Moldova	2.9	8	0.13
112	Senegal	2.9	10	0.15
112	Vietnam	2.9	11	0.17
118	Bolivia	2.8	7	0.18
118	Mali	2.8	7	0.20
120	Bangladesh	2.7	9	0.34
120	Ecuador	2.7	6	0.22
120	Ethiopia	2.7	9	0.18
120	Guatemala	2.7	7	0.19
120	Iran	2.7	7	0.35
120	Kazakhstan	2.7	9	0.37
120	Mongolia	2.7	8	0.13
120	Mozambique	2.7	8	0.16
120	Solomon Islands	2.7	3	0.28
129	Armenia	2.6	8	0.16
129	Dominican Republic	2.6	7	0.19
129	Honduras	2.6	7	0.19
129	Philippines	2.6	12	0.19
129	Syria	2.6	6	0.16
134	Cameroon	2.5	9	0.19
134	Eritrea	2.5	4	0.56
134	Guyana	2.5	5	0.10
134	Lebanon	2.5	7	0.15
134	Maldives	2.5	3	0.15
134	Nicaragua	2.5	7	0.21
134	Niger	2.5	5	0.17
134	Pakistan	2.5	10	0.13
134	Sierra Leone	2.5	6	0.15
143	Azerbaijan	2.4	8	0.19
143	Belarus	2.4	4	0.10
143	Comoros	2.4	3	0.37
143	Mauritania	2.4	6	0.18
143	Nigeria	2.4	10	0.14
143	Russia	2.4	11	0.22
143	Timor-Leste	2.4	5	0.26

(Continued)

Country Rank	Country/Territory	CPI 2011 Score	Surveys Used	Standard Deviation
143	Togo	2.4	5	0.08
143	Uganda	2.4	9	0.13
152	Tajikistan	2.3	7	0.28
152	Ukraine	2.3	10	0.10
154	Central African Republic	2.2	4	0.05
154	Congo Republic	2.2	6	0.10
154	Côte d'Ivoire	2.2	8	0.15
154	Guinea-Bissau	2.2	4	0.10
154	Kenya	2.2	9	0.12
154	Laos	2.2	4	0.16
154	Nepal	2.2	6	0.10
154	Papua New Guinea	2.2	6	0.16
154	Paraguay	2.2	6	0.17
154	Zimbabwe	2.2	8	0.37
164	Cambodia	2.1	10	0.15
164	Guinea	2.1	6	0.11
164	Kyrgyzstan	2.1	8	0.09
164	Yemen	2.1	6	0.12
168	Angola	2.0	8	0.10
168	Chad	2.0	6	0.05
168	Democratic Republic of the Congo	2.0	5	0.09
168	Libya	2.0	6	0.13
172	Burundi	1.9	6	0.14
172	Equatorial Guinea	1.9	3	0.07
172	Venezuela	1.9	9	0.10
175	Haiti	1.8	5	0.14
175	Iraq	1.8	4	0.09
177	Sudan	1.6	6	0.08
177	Turkmenistan	1.6	3	0.12
177	Uzbekistan	1.6	6	0.11
180	Afghanistan	1.5	4	0.10
180	Myanmar (Burma)	1.5	4	0.26
182	North Korea	1.0	3	0.24
182	Somalia	1.0	4	0.23

Conflict

The Democratic Republic of Congo (DRC) is one of the world's poorest countries with a GDP per capita no higher than $300 per year. The country has been at war since 1996, when dictator Mobutu Sese Seko was overthrown. The subsequent leader of the country, Laurent-Désiré Kabila, was assassinated by one of his own bodyguards in 2001, but he had been challenged by rival politicians as soon as he came to power. While it has been the bloodiest conflict ever known in Africa, Western media have done little reporting on it. Nearly 6 million people have died directly or indirectly as a consequence of the conflict, including nearly 3 million children. Some call it Africa's World War because many countries have been involved, some in support of the incumbent Congolese government (Zimbabwe, Angola, Namibia, Chad, Libya, and Sudan) and others (Rwanda, Burundi, Uganda) in support of rebel groups. Although it is impoverished and has suffered the ravages of interminable conflict, the DRC is also endowed with enormous natural resources. Along with significant exports of tropical woods, it has rich deposits of copper, gold, diamond, tin, and coltan, a rare metal that is increasingly used in consumer electronics but is virtually unknown outside Silicon Valley. The U.S. Department of Defense classifies coltan as a strategic mineral. It is very easy to mine and its presence in the DRC whetted the appetite of different rebel groups trying to gain control of resource-rich territories in the eastern parts of the country in order to fund their military campaign. For the people of the DRC, their country's natural resources have been more of a curse than a blessing.

Unfortunately, the sad history of the DRC is not unique. Between 1990 and 2001, roughly 60% of the 50 poorest countries on the planet have experienced war or civil conflict. Being born in a poor country does not only mean living in poverty, it also means you will very likely be exposed to deadly conflict. Most of the armed hostilities since the end of World War II have involved developing countries and, since 1945, out of 47 civil wars, only 2 took place in developed countries.[1] Of 59 wars since World War II, all took place in the developing world. Out of these conflicts, 11 were wars of independence against colonial powers, 11 involved aggression or intervention by rich countries (the United States in 8 cases), while the remainder occurred between developing countries. Civil wars are often lengthy, with guerilla movements in total or partial control of certain territories for long periods of time. This is the case in Colombia, where the ongoing civil war dates back to at least 1964 and the Revolutionary Armed Forces of Colombia, known as the FARC, have controlled portions of the country for decades. The civil war in Nepal, which began in 1996 between the government and Maoist forces who controlled parts of the mountainous country lasted more than 10 years.

---

[1]The first is the Greek civil war in the aftermath of World War II between 1946 and 1949, and the second is the Northern Ireland conflict from about the mid-1960s to 1998.

Conflict is one of the most serious problems facing developing countries, yet peace is one of the most fundamental dreams any human being can have. Developed countries are fortunate that none have had a war on sovereign soil since the end of World War II and since then have had an unprecedented period of prosperity and exceptional improvements in living standards and life expectancy. What can be done about conflict in developing countries? In order to answer that question in this chapter, we will need to examine closely many complex questions.

A first issue has to do with why conflicts persist at all. If war destroys human life and material wealth, why are the parties in a conflict unable to negotiate a solution that would avoid these losses? We will explore two different reasons why negotiated outcomes may fail to materialize: informational asymmetries between parties (lack of information about the other party's strength) and commitment problems (the inability of parties to a conflict to abide by peace treaties they have signed). Remember that informational asymmetries and commitment problems were discussed in Chapter 7 when we examined the problems that institutions can help to solve. However, international institutions such as the United Nations have usually been too weak to be effective in resolving conflict situations.

After examining theories of why there are conflicts, we look at some of the empirical research on the causes of conflict. Contrary to common perceptions, civil wars are less often the consequence of ethnic or religious divisions than of fights over natural resources. We will indeed examine to what extent civil wars are associated with greed (attempts to seize regions that are rich in natural resources) or grievance (a history of conflict between different groups that, among other causes, results from ethnic and religious divisions).

Does lack of development lead to conflict or, on the contrary, does conflict lead to a lack of development? It seems difficult to disentangle these two causal chains. Development researchers have found ingenious ways of proving empirically that there is a causal effect from adverse economic shocks on conflicts. We will also discuss the aftermath of conflict; for example, we will consider the long-term economic effects of conflict such as the fate of child soldiers, a phenomenon that is unfortunately far too frequent in developing countries and, in particular, Africa.

Theoretical Explanations of Conflict

From the point of view of economic theory, understanding why conflicts happen at all appears to be a very puzzling question. This may sound strange, given that so many conflicts have economic stakes such as natural resources, disputed territories, or access to vital water sources. Because conflicts are so destructive and could be avoided through efficient bargaining between opposing parties, why would those parties not pursue peaceful negotiations so as to avoid the loss of precious lives and resources? Suppose party A is stronger than party B and is likely to win a war, but at a great cost. In that case, party A would certainly be better off pursuing a deal in which it would receive the resources from party B minus the losses it would have incurred in a war. Similarly, party B would be better off giving to party A the resources it wants and avoiding the likelihood of losses from war. In other words, because war brings destruction to both parties, why are they not able to strike a rational bargain and split the bigger pie in a way that avoids overall losses and ultimately makes each party better off?

We must include some numbers in this discussion. Suppose that two countries are bargaining over the division of 100. For a cost of 20 each, they can go to war and each side has a 0.5 probability of winning 100 and a 0.5 probability of losing with a payoff of 0. The expected value of war is then $(0.5 \times 100 + 0.5 \times 0) - 20 = 30$. We assume that the parties are risk neutral for the sake of a simple calculation.[2] Given that the expected payoff to war is 30, neither country should be willing to accept less than 30 in a peacefully negotiated bargain. But if each of them gets 30, there is still 40 that they can share, the sum of the costs of war for both. As long as there are costs of war, both parties are better off bargaining. This would be the case even if one party had a 100% chance of winning because the same outcome would be reached and the costs of war would be avoided. Indeed, the winning party would get at least 80 by bargaining and the losing party would always be better off avoiding a war. Historically, when an army besieged a city, the citizens often preferred to surrender rather than to incur the costs of a long blockade.

Our example of the two countries is theoretical, but in reality, conflicts continue to create "inefficient" losses for the parties involved, so there must be something missing in our reasoning. One explanation could be that the parties to a conflict are not rational, but this is not an extremely satisfactory explanation. People are able to reason; if they can make rational choices in situations that involve far fewer costs and benefits than does a war, they should surely be able to think rationally about the costs and benefits that result from war. This is not to say that wars are never started for irrational reasons, but the argument that conflict is always the result of irrational thinking is not very convincing.

For many years, researchers devoted considerable thought to explaining why countries may choose war over negotiation. They have come up with two classes of explanations about why conflicts take place despite the opportunity to avoid their associated losses: one class is based on informational asymmetries and the other is based on the inability to make binding commitments. Note that these two issues were central to our discussion of the role of institutions in Chapter 7.

Misjudging Your Rival

It seems reasonable to think that informational problems might be a cause for war. Remember that the United States went to war against Iraq in 2003 on the claim that Saddam Hussein had weapons of mass destruction, yet none were ever found. Perhaps the Bush administration knew he had no weapons of mass destruction, but decided to use them as a justification to invade Iraq for some other strategic purpose. On the other hand, perhaps the administration really did believe WMDs were stockpiled in the country and it was misled by faulty

---

[2]Risk neutrality means that an individual makes decisions based on their expected payoff, that is, the sum of the payoffs in the different states of the world (or contingencies) weighted by the probabilities that those contingencies will occur.

intelligence. The interesting point is that Saddam Hussein acted as if he did have the weapons because he thought that a belief in their existence would deter an invasion of Iraq. In other words, he wanted to exaggerate his military strength in order to prevent an attack. This happens all the time in wars; information plays a key role and each party tries to control it and to provide misinformation to the other side. Thus, in most if not in all cases, each side may lack accurate information about the strength and resolve of the other side. Diplomacy may be possible, but the incentives to misrepresent information are very strong. Each side will want to mask its military strength and readiness, but will also want reliable intelligence about the capabilities of its opponents. Although espionage may sometimes resolve certain informational asymmetries, it cannot eliminate them all.

What types of informational asymmetries can lead to conflict? An obvious case is a situation in which one of the parties exaggerates its expected gain from war because of imperfect information about the strength of the other party. In other words, war would be the result of a rational miscalculation by one of the parties due to inaccurate information. Both sides may misjudge their relative power because of informational problems and therefore fail to agree on a negotiated solution. This would then lead to a conflict. A slightly different type of asymmetry occurs when one one party engages in a limited intervention, say to seize some territory on the other side of its borders, in the expectation that there will be no retaliation, but the other party does retaliate and war breaks out between the two. This could be an explanation for World War II, when Hitler invaded Austria and Czechoslovakia in 1938. At the time, France and Great Britain did not retaliate and Hitler likely thought that they were too weak to do so. However, when the Nazis invaded Poland in 1939, France and Great Britain declared war on Germany. Another way to think about these events is that each side may not have known how committed the other side was to fight.

Explanations based on informational asymmetries are not always satisfactory for explaining why conflicts occur and why many of them continue for long periods of time. We might be inclined to think that information would improve over time and, in many cases, we might argue that once a conflict starts and both sides gain better information about each others' strength, they might have an incentive to negotiate a bargain that benefits both. Why, then, do conflicts continue? Theories of conflict based on informational asymmetries provide no obvious answer.

Deals That Aren't Worth the Paper on Which They Are Written

A simpler and maybe more convincing explanation of war is based on the inability of the different parties to commit to a deal. Commitment is very difficult to enforce between countries. Lack of commitment could thus easily lead to a breakdown of a negotiated solution based on efficient bargaining. In particular, countries may not be willing to commit to a bargained negotiation if they perceive that their future military strength might improve.

Some numbers are useful to illustrate the essence of this argument. Assume that the military strengths of two countries, A and B, vary over time. Each has a wealth of 500 and the winner in a conflict will acquire the wealth of the loser. The cost of war is assumed to be equal to c for each country. Country

A is assumed to have an 80% chance of winning today (period 1), but would have a 20% chance tomorrow (period 2). (We assume two periods to keep the argument simple.) Also assume that country B would have a 20% chance of winning today and an 80% chance tomorrow. On average, each has a 50% chance of victory over time and they could peacefully negotiate an efficient bargain if they were able to commit to it. Now, assume for simplicity that country A has all the bargaining power and is able to get all the surplus from bargaining. This means that country B is left indifferent between war and a bargained solution. Country B can get $0.2(500 + 500) - c = 200 - c$ in period 1 if there is a war because it would have a 20% probability of winning. The alternative is to pay country A a sum of $300 + c$. Indeed, in that case, country B's payoff would be $500 - (300 + c) = 200 - c$. Country B is then indifferent between war and bargaining, and country A has all the surplus from bargaining. In period 2, country B can get $0.8(500 + 500) - c = 800 - c$ if there is a war, or receive a sum of $300 - c$ from country A, achieving an equal payoff of $500 + 300 - c$. Over the 2 periods, in the bargaining solution, country A receives $300 + c - (300 - c) = 2c$. Country A thus gains $2c$ from bargaining instead of going to war and has a total payoff of $500 + 2c$, assuming no discounting across periods. However, country A could decide not to commit to a negotiated deal made in advance and, instead, go to war in period 1 for two reasons: 1) to benefit from its superiority; and 2) avoid further conflict in period 2 because if country A wins in period 1, country B cannot go to war in period 2. In that scenario of a war in period 1, country A would then receive $0.8(500 + 500) - c = 800 - c$. This is preferable to the negotiated deal if $800 - c > 500 + 2c$, that is, as long as $c < 100$. In other words, if $c < 100$, country A would prefer to renege on a deal made in advance and go to war in period 1 to benefit from its temporary superiority. However much country B may be willing to offer A so as not to start a war, after receiving country B's payment, country A will always be tempted to break the deal and start the war because of the expected gains from it.

This is only an example and we can construct other similar examples, but the value of this one is that it demonstrates how the absence of commitment may make efficient bargains impossible to achieve. Lack of commitment seems to be a plausible and simple explanation for why wars take place. There is no international framework that is strong enough to be able to enforce negotiated deals between countries or between conflicting parties within a country. In light of our discussion in Chapter 7 about institutions, stronger international organizations might help. The United Nations is clearly not strong enough for that purpose and there are many political obstacles to making it more powerful. As long as this situation persists, there will continue to be conflicts in the world.

The Empirical Determinants of Conflict

We will now turn to the empirical research on the determinants of conflict. The existing literature does not ask why conflicts happen, but instead examines the principal motives behind them.

The first study that examines the causes for the onset of civil war finds that, contrary to popular belief, ethnic, cultural, and religious differences are not significant, whereas variables that explain state weaknesses are quite important. A second study attempts to distinguish between economic and grievance motives for war. As we will see, the evidence from international analysis as well as from specific countries such as Nepal is more consistent with economic motives.

Why Do Civil Wars Start?

In a highly regarded study, James Fearon and David Laitin analyzed the reasons for which civil wars start.[3] Figure 20.1 shows the trend in civil wars between 1945 and 1999. We can notice a steady increase since 1945, a significant increase around 1990, and a steep fall thereafter. How can we explain the upward-sloping trend after 1945? It was not due to an increase in the outbreak of civil wars, the rate of which was fairly constant at 2.31 per year. The reason for the upward trend was the fact that each year, there were fewer wars that ended compared to the wars that started. The rate for wars that ended is only 1.85 per year. It might seem that the end of the Cold War, around 1989, should have been a major cause of the increase in conflicts as the world had become more unstable. While there was an increase in conflicts after 1989, there was also a sharp reduction in conflicts a few years later. The decline in the number of wars in the 1990s is yet not well explained, but hopefully it is a trend that will continue.

FIGURE 20.1 Number and Percentage of Countries with Ongoing Civil Wars, 1945–1999

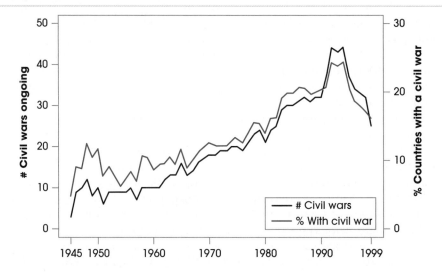

While the number of ongoing civil wars increased steadily between 1945 and the early 1990s, it has declined since then. The increase is primarily due to the fact that wars start more frequently than they finish.

Source: Copyright © 2003 American Political Science Association. Reprinted with the permission of Cambridge University Press.

---

[3]James D. Fearon and David D. Laitin, "Ethnicity, Insurgency, and Civil War," *The American Political Science Review* 97, no. 1 (2003): 75–90.

Table 20.1 provides a regression analysis of the onset of civil war that shows the effect of different potential variables that could explain why such a conflict begins. It is a **logit regression**. This is a regression in which the dependent variable takes either a value of zero or 1. Indeed, a civil war either starts in a given year or it does not. In the former case, the dependent variable takes a value of 1 and in the latter case, it takes a value of 0.

Columns 1 and 3 show the onset of civil wars in general. The columns differ in that column 3 includes a few more explanatory variables. Column 2 represents the onset of civil wars that are ethnic or partially ethnic in character. Column 4 refers to anticolonial wars and column 5 uses the Correlates of War database started at the University of Michigan to gather data on wars (COW, http://www.correlatesofwar.org). We must consider which variables are significant and which are not. Coefficients with 3 asterisks are significant at the 0.1% level. They have a p-value of less than 0.1%. This means that the probability of making the mistake of statistically rejecting the hypothesis that the coefficient is different from 0 is less than 0.1%. Similarly, a coefficient with 2 asterisks means a significance level lower than 1% and a coefficient with one asterisk means a significance level lower than 5%. The lower the "significance level," the more confident we can be that the coefficient is different from 0.

We see from the table that prior wars have a negative impact. In other words, if there had been a prior war in a country the year before, it decreases the likelihood that a civil war will start. Per capita income also has a significant negative effect on the outbreak of war. In other words, richer countries are less likely to experience a civil war. This is one of Fearon and Laitin's main findings and they give two reasons for why a lower income per capita makes a civil war more likely. First, poorer countries have weaker financial, administrative, and military resources. They are less able to build roads to transport the troops and supplies quickly to regions occupied by insurgent forces. Therefore, it is easier for antigovernment forces to sustain a guerilla campaign in a poor country. A second reason has to do with the opportunity costs of guerilla fighters. Recruiting them is easier and cheaper when young men do not have many economic opportunities. In richer countries, the same young men would have to be paid much more to give up their civilian lives to fight and hide in the mountains.

We also see that a civil war is more likely to occur in larger countries (measured here by the log of the population) primarily because they are proportionally more costly to administer than are small states. Note, however, that this variable should not be interpreted as a measure of ethnic diversity because other variables, discussed below, reflect that effect. We see that the presence of mountainous terrain has a positive effect on the likelihood of civil war because it is easier for guerilla forces to hide in mountainous terrain such as that of Afghanistan, where the Taliban have been hiding since 2001. Civil wars are also more likely to break out in countries that export oil. High revenues from natural resources incentivize those groups who would like to seize power and control these natural resources, oil being a particularly hot commodity. We will talk further about the role of natural resources in conflict later in this chapter.

The onset of civil war is also much more likely in new states, a variable that takes a value of 1 for countries in the first two years after their independence and a value of 0 otherwise. This is because new states have not had the time to develop a modern administrative apparatus. Moreover, the military strength

TABLE 20.1　Causes for the Onset of Civil War

	Civil war (1)	Ethnic war (2)	Civil war (3)	Civil war (including in colonial empires) (4)	Civil war (COW) (5)
Prior war	−0.954**	−0.849*	−0.916**	−0.688**	−0.551
	(0.314)	(0.388)	(0.312)	(0.264)	(0.374)
Per capita income[a,b]	−0.344***	−0.379***	−0.318***	−0.305***	−0.309***
	(0.072)	(0.100)	(0.071)	(0.063)	(0.079)
Log (population)[a,b]	0.219**	0.389***	0.272***	0.267***	0.223**
	(0.085)	(0.110)	(0.074)	(0.069)	(0.079)
Log (% mountainous)	0.443	0.120	0.199*	0.192*	0.418***
	(0.274)	(0.106)	(0.085)	(0.082)	(0.103)
Noncontiguous state	0.858**	0.481	0.426	0.798**	−0.171
	(0.279)	(0.398)	(0.272)	(0.241)	(0.328)
Oil exporter	0.858**	0.809*	0.751**	0.548*	1.269***
	(0.279)	(0.352)	(0.278)	(0.262)	(0.297)
New state	1.709***	1.777***	1.658***	1.523***	1.147***
	(0.339)	(0.415)	(0.342)	(0.332)	(0.413)
Instability[a]	0.618**	0.385	0.513*	0.548*	0.584*
	(0.235)	(0.316)	(0.242)	(0.225)	(0.268)
Democracy[a,c]	0.021	0.013			
	(0.017)	(0.022)			
Ethnic fractionalization	0.166	0.146	0.164	0.490	−0.119
	(0.373)	(0.584)	(0.368)	(0.345)	(0.396)
Religious fractionalization	0.285	1.533*	0.326		1.176*
	(0.509)	(0.724)	(0.506)		(0.563)
Anocracy[a]			0.521*		0.597*
			(0.237)		(0.261)
Democracy[a,d]			0.127		0.219
			(0.304)		(0.354)
Constant	−6.731***	−8.450***	−7.019***	−6.801***	−7.503***
	(0.736)	(1.092)	(0.751)	(0.681)	(0.854)
Observations	6327	5186	6327	6360	5378

The onset of civil war is lower in countries with a higher income per capita and higher in larger countries, oil exporting countries, and new states. Ethnic and religious motives do not play a significant role.

Note: The dependent variable is coded "1" for country years in which a civil war began and "0" in all others. Standard errors are in parentheses.
* $p < .05$; ** $p < .01$; *** $p < .001$.
[a] Lagged one year
[b] In 1,000s
[c] Polity IV; varies from −10 to 10
[d] Dichotomous
Source: Copyright © 2003 American Political Science Association. Reprinted with the permission of Cambridge University Press.

of a new state is usually untested because there is less information available to estimate its capabilities. Note also that political instability (taken from the Polity IV database; see Chapter 9) also has a positive effect at the 10% significance level. The term *anocracy* is used to indicate regimes that have had swings between democracy and autocracy; anocracy is a form of institutional instability, and this variable is also significant at the 5% level.

Equally, if not more, interesting are the "nonresults." Variables that represent ethnic and religious fractionalization are not significant and this is surprising because we might easily think the opposite. Fearon and Laitin tried different measures and found that ethnic and religious heterogeneity are not a significant factor for civil war. Note also that democracy is not significant, meaning that democracies are, everything else being equal, neither more nor less likely to have a civil war than are autocracies.

The primary finding of Fearon and Laitin's study is that countries that are culturally, ethnically, or religiously more diverse are not more likely to experience a civil war. On the contrary, the variables related to the weakness of the state apparatus, such as a low income per capita, a large population, and the presence of rugged terrain are better predictors of the onset of civil wars.

Greed versus Grievance

Paul Collier and Anke Hoeffler also studied the determinants of civil wars and identified two fundamental motives for these conflicts: greed and grievance.[4] The greed motive is an economic cause: one group fights to seize power because it wants to take control of a country's natural resources. We have already mentioned the example of oil, which is a driving force for Nigeria's ongoing guerrilla campaign in the Niger River delta, where large deposits of oil are being extracted. The Movement of Emancipation of the Niger Delta (MEND) has destabilized the entire region and, after the movement took foreign employees of the Royal Dutch Shell company hostage, the company suspended its operations for a time. Oil also played a big role in the long Angolan civil war (1975–2000) after that country ceased to be a Portuguese colony. Significant diamond deposits have been the motivation as well as a funding source for conflicts in Angola and also as in Sierra Leone. Similarly, drugs have played an important role in Colombia's civil unrest. We have already mentioned the role Congo's deposits of the valuable mineral coltan plays in its civil war and we could compile a very long list of other examples of greed as the motivation for conflict.

The grievance motive refers to retaliation for harm done, oppression, demand for ideological or political change, or hatred for other groups. A possible example of the grievance motive would be the violent secessionist movement of the Tamil Tigers that began in the mid-1970s on the island of Sri Lanka off India's southeastern coast. The movement fought for a breakaway Tamil state in the island's northern and eastern regions because of its dissatisfaction with the policies of the Sri Lankan government. The government subsequently crushed the Tamil resistance in 2009.

---

[4]Paul Collier and Anke Hoeffler, "Greed and Grievance in Civil War," *Oxford Economic Papers* 56, no. 4 (2004): 563–595.

Other examples of the grievance motive could be the 1959 Cuban revolution against the dictatorship of Fulgencio Batista, or the Sandinista rebellion in Nicaragua against dictator Anastasio Somoza, from 1978 to 1979. In both cases, leftist-inspired revolutionary groups rebelled against right-wing autocratic regimes. Modern Cuba is still a Communist state. However, after the Sandinistas overthrew Somoza and seized power in Nicaragua, they subsequently lost the country's national elections in 1990, but in 2006, Sandinista leader Daniel Ortega was reelected president. An additional example would be the Eritrean secessionist movement in Ethiopia between 1979 and 1993. Eritrea had been an independent state, but in the aftermath of Italian colonization in North Africa, the UN revoked its autonomy in 1950 and it became part of Ethiopia.

These two different motives, greed and grievance, entail quite different predictions about the determinants of civil war. Significant determinants for the greed motive (think of armed thugs fighting a war for booty) in a particular country would be:

- a higher share of natural resource exports, meaning the stakes are relatively high, especially in poor countries;
- more mountainous terrain, making it easier for rebel forces to hide, and higher geographic dispersion of the population, making government control more difficult;
- a lower per capita income interpreted mainly as a lower opportunity cost of organizing a guerilla campaign (recall that Fearon and Laitin also interpreted it as lower state capacity);
- less fractionalizalization, as it is easier to organize a rebellion that is more socially homogeneous;
- a history of conflict that makes it easier to motivate the people to overthrow its government. We can argue that this variable is more relevant to the grievance motive, but it is, nevertheless, a determinant for the greed motive.

Collier and Hoeffler also argued that in terms of size, larger countries should have a higher probability of experiencing at least one territorial conflict.

Determinants for civil war caused by the grievance motive would be somewhat different than those for greed. They would be:

- inequality of wealth and income that incite the poor to revolt against the rich;
- ethnic fractionalization leading some ethnic groups to organize and revolt either to secede or to improve their status in the country; here, fractionalization is predicted to have a positive effect on the likelihood of a conflict.
- a low level of political rights that leads those without rights to fight in order to obtain them. Note that a low level of rights is not an automatic cause for a civil war because the oppressed groups face a collective-action problem. This can be partially mitigated if a country has a well-organized diaspora abroad that can finance and help the guerilla forces.

Similar to Fearon and Laitin, Collin and Hoeffler performed a logit regression in order to estimate the probability of a civil war, In their regression, the dependent variable took a value of 1 if a country experienced a civil war during a given period of time, and a value of 0 otherwise. Periods of time are defined as 4-year periods between 1960 and 1999. The greed model, for which results are shown in Table 20.2, worked relatively well. The share of primary commodity exports had a significantly positive effect. There was also a quadratic effect of that variable that was negative, which tended to show that the effect of primary commodity exports was nonlinear and had a positive but concave effect. In other words, a higher share of primary commodity exports in GDP led to a higher likelihood of a civil war; however, this effect became weaker as that share increased. GDP per capita and male secondary education

TABLE 20.2 The Greed Model

	1	2	3	4	5
Male secondary schooling	−0.036***	−0.037***	−0.028**	−0.027**	
	(0.011)	(0.011)	(0.012)	(0.012)	
log (GDP per capita)					−0.822***
					(0.288)
(GDP growth − 3* population growth)$_{t-1}$	−0.080**	−0.074**	−0.084**	−0.086**	−0.101***
	(0.036)	(0.036)	(0.036)	(0.036)	(0.035)
Primary commodity exports/GDP	34.088**	34.109***	32.147***	32.058***	22.923***
	(8.186)	(8.423)	(8.497)	(8.465)	(6.903)
(Primary commodity exports/GDP)^2	−67.792***	−67.172***	−62.307***	−62.091***	39.192***
	(18.683)	(18.679)	(18.954)	(18.962)	(14.710)
Log population	1.026***	0.960***	0.832***	0.832***	0.574***
	(0.191)	(0.194)	(0.198)	(0.197)	(0.146)
Social fractionalization	−0.0002***	−0.0003***	−0.0003***	−0.0003***	−0.0003***
	(0.0001)	(0.0001)	(0.0001)	(0.0001)	(0.001)
Geographic dispersion	−3.517**	−3.888***	−3.384***	−3.289***	−1.568
	(1.142)	(1.181)	(1.200)	(1.180)	(1.051)
Mountainous terrain	0.019**	0.013	0.014	0.015	0.012
	(0.009)	(0.009)	(0.010)	(0.010)	(0.009)
Previous war		1.016***	0.252		
		(0.405)	(0.527)		
Peace duration			−0.004**	−0.004***	−0.004***
			(0.002)	(0.001)	(0.001)
Observations	691	691	688	688	747
Number of wars	43	43	43	43	47

In the greed model, war occurs if there are resources to loot and if the opportunity cost of organizing a guerilla movement is smaller. The first factor is captured by a significant coefficient for the share of primary commodities in exports, reflecting resource abundance. The second factor is captured by a lower level of education, a lower GDP per capita, and a country's larger population.

Note: Standard errors are in parentheses.
* p < .1; ** p < .05; *** p < .01.
Source: Paul Collier and Anke Hoeffler, "Greed and Grievance in Civil War," *Oxford Economic Papers* 56, no. 4 (2004): 563–595.

had a negative effect that corroborated the idea of the opportunity cost of participating in the guerilla movement.[5]

A variable in Collin and Hoefler's study that looked at the difference between GDP per capita and population growth (multiplied by 3 to put a large weight on population growth) had the same interpretation as GDP per capita and was also significant. The size of the country as measured by the log of the population also had a positive effect, as predicted, and social fractionalization had a negative effect, also as predicted. Similarly, the occurrence of a previous war or a peace of short duration was also more likely to lead to a higher probability of civil war.[6] The variable for mountainous terrain was not significant and geographic dispersion had a negative effect, meaning that more geographical dispersion led to a lower probability of civil war. This was the opposite of the expected effect. We might indeed think that a more dispersed population would be harder to control and thus lead to a greater likelihood of rebellion, but this is not what the data suggest.

Let us now examine the results of the grievance model shown in Table 20.3. The results are not as clear. Both income and land inequality have no effect, nor do measures of social fractionalization or ethnic dominance. This is similar to the findings in Fearon and Laitin's study. Only two variables appear to be significant: peace duration and democracy. A longer duration for peace has a negative effect on civil war, which is consistent with the grievance results. Similarly, the more democratic a country is, the less likely it is to experience civil conflict. Note that democracy was not significant in the Fearon and Laitin study.

Overall, Collier and Hoeffler conclude that the greed model works better than the grievance model for predicting the likelihood of civil conflict.

Nepal's Civil War

In the same vein as the studies by Fearon and Laitin, and Collier and Hoeffler, Quy-Toan Do and Lakshmi Iyer studied the Nepalese civil war.[7] One advantage of focusing on a single country instead of multiple countries is that there is less heterogeneity in the data. Nicaragua, Sri Lanka, and Eritrea are all very different along dimensions and variables that are not recorded. Studying different regions in one country is more like a controlled experiment; it may give a clearer interpretation of the determinants of conflict. This is what Do and Iyer did in their study of Nepal. Between 1996 and 2006, a Maoist rebellion was active in Nepal, primarily in the mountainous regions of the Himalayas. More than 13,000 people were killed in this country of 29 million inhabitants. In particular, the researchers asked whether the civil war should be interpreted as a lower-caste revolt, supported by Maoist ideology, or whether it was fueled more by poverty.

---

[5]GDP per capita and education are taken separately as they are quite correlated and should thus not be put together in the same regression. Columns 1–4 have male secondary schooling as a regressor and column 5 has the log of GDP per capita as a regressor.

[6]Note that Fearon and Laitin found a different result. In their regression, a country that had a war the previous year had a decreased likelihood for the onset of a civil war thereafter. Collier and Hoeffler were, however, measuring something different: the existence of a prior conflict in the country at any time.

[7]Quy-Toan Do and Lakshmi Iyer, "Poverty, Social Divisions, and Conflict in Nepal," *Journal of Peace Research* 47, no. 6 (2010): 735–748.

TABLE 20.3   The Grievance Model

	1	2	3
Social fractionalization	0.00003	0.00000	0.00008
	(0.00007)	(0.00009)	(0.00009)
Ethnic dominance (45%–90%)	0.263	0.534	0.567
	(0.290)	(0.342)	(0.374)
Democracy	−0.117	−0.091**	−0.138***
	(0.046)***	(0.051)	(0.052)
Geographic dispersion	0.095	−0.276	−0.152
	(0.787)	(0.958)	(1.039)
Mountainous terrain	0.015**	0.011	0.015
	(0.006)	(0.008)	(0.006)**
Income inequality		0.014	
		(0.016)	
Land inequality			−0.150
			(1.159)
Peace duration	−0.005***	−0.004***	−0.005***
	(0.001)	(0.001)	(0.001)
Observations	884	614	620
Number of wars	57	40	38

In the grievance model, social fractionalization and ethnic dominance should be a determinant of war, but they are not significant. A longer duration of peace and the presence of democracy have a significant negative effect on wars, which is consistent with the grievance model.

Note: Standard errors are in parentheses.
* $p < .1$; ** $p < .05$; *** $p < .01$.
Source: Collier and Hoeffler, "Greed and Grievance in Civil War," 2004.

We cannot regress the onset of the war on explanatory variables, as there was no variation in the onset of violence there: the civil war was present in all regions at the same time. However, there was variation in the level of violence, with conflict more intense in some regions than in others. Do and Iyer used the number of casualties as an indicator of the level of violence. They looked at both the deaths caused by the Maoists and the deaths caused by the government.

Do and Iyer found that, in general, there were more deaths in areas with higher elevation and in forested areas. For example, the Maoist strongholds were primarily located in mountainous regions. The border between Nepal and India crosses the very large Terai jungle and Maoist guerillas passed into and out of Nepal through India using the jungle for cover. The regression results confirmed that there was more violence both in the mountains and in the areas with dense jungle vegetation. Violence was also more prevalent in areas where poverty and illiteracy were higher. On the other hand, caste variables (the proportion of advantaged castes as well as caste polarization) were not significant. The researchers concluded that violence was more associated with poverty.

If we consider these results in terms of the greed and grievance motives of Collier and Hoeffler, the absence of results for caste would appear to be a rejection of the grievance motive. The fact that higher poverty is associated with more violence and more deaths is quite consistent with the greed motive, according to which it is easier to recruit poorer people. Therefore, the guerilla forces would be more prevalent in areas where there are poor people. However, there are other possible reasons why there might have been more deaths in poorer regions. Poor people are less able to protect themselves from both the Nepalese army and the Maoists. The government might also spend more resources to protect the richer areas. One dimension in which Nepal does not fit the greed story well is that it is not resource rich. Its main income is from tourism so it does not fit neatly in either the grievance or greed narrative.

What Is the Causal Link between Conflict and Development?

The previous studies we have considered found a strong correlation between low income per capita and conflict. However, in what direction does the causality go? Is there a causal link from low GDP per capita to conflict, or is it the other way round, that is, does conflict cause poverty? Because both causal chains appear reasonable, how can we identify an accurate causal effect between these two variables?

Edward Miguel, Shanker Satyanath, and Ernest Sergenti proposed such a causal empirical analysis by employing instrumental variable analysis.[8] They used rainfall as an instrument for economic growth.[9] Rainfall affects economic outcomes in agrarian societies; droughts are catastrophic for crops, so more rain (to a point) is thus generally good for crops. Rain, however, is not correlated to conflict. The instrumental variable method allowed the researchers to compare the effect on conflict of the variation in economic growth due to rainfall. In other words, using rainfall as an instrument for economic growth allowed them to estimate the causal effect of economic growth on conflict.

Their analysis was limited to Africa because it is on that continent that rainfall was expected to have the most real economic effect. Conflict data were from the Peace Research Institute in Oslo (PRIO). This study included a larger number of small conflicts than the studies previously considered. It included any conflict with over 25 deaths. The researchers measured the weather data by taking the normalized difference in vegetation levels from satellite imagery that showed photosynthetic activity. This was not a direct measure of rainfall, but rather a measure of the consequences of rainfall. It had, however, a very significant 0.9 correlation with rainfall. Data from rainfall stations did exist, but were less numerous.

Table 20.4 shows the results of the analysis. In all specifications in the five columns, economic growth had a significant negative effect on conflict, which

---

[8]Edward Miguel, Shanker Satyanath, and Ernest Sergenti (2004). "Economic Shocks and Civil Conflict: An Instrumental Variables Approach," *Journal of Political Economy* 112, no. 4 (2004): 725–753.

[9]See the Econometric Appendix for an explanation of instrumental variable analysis.

TABLE 20.4 The Effect of Economic Growth on Conflict in Africa

	Conflict with more than 25 civilian deaths				Conflict with more than 1,000 deaths
	OLS (1)	OLS (2)	IV (3)	IV (4)	IV (5)
Annual economic growth	−0.58** (0.28)	−0.48** (0.25)	−2.27** (0.98)	−.208** (0.96)	−2.17** (0.78)
Democracy (Polity IV score), lagged one period	−.003 (0.005)		−.003 (0.005)		
Ethno-linguistic fractionalization	0.21 (0.27)		0.21 (0.27)		
Oil-exporting country	0.01 (0.19)		0.01 (0.20)		
Log (mountainous terrain)	0.074* (0.040)		0.975* (0.039)		
Log (population), lagged one period	0.073 (0.048)		0.71 (0.49)		
Country fixed effects	No	Yes	No	Yes	Yes
R^2	0.11	0.55			
Number of observations	647	647	647	647	647

Higher economic growth associated with more rainfall led to a lower level of conflict in Africa.

Note: Standard errors in parentheses, significant at the 1% level (*), 5% (**), and 10% (***). *Source*: Edward Miguel, Shanker Satyanath, and Ernest Sergenti (2004). "Economic Shocks and Civil Conflict: An Instrumental Variables Approach," *Journal of Political Economy* 112, no. 4 (2004): 725–753. Printed with permission from University of Chicago Press.

was stronger in the instrumental variable (IV) estimates (columns 3–5) than in the ordinary least squares (OLS) regressions (columns 1 and 2). We also see that mountainous terrain had a positive effect on conflict, but similar to the other studies, measures of ethno-linguistic or religious fractionalization had no effect. Democracy had no effect either, nor did the fact that a country exported oil. Note that in contrast to the two previous international studies, this research covered only Africa, which could explain the difference in the results.

The Economic Effects of Conflict

If economic variables affect conflict in developing countries, how do the economic effects of conflict impact development patterns in the long term? In this section, we examine the long-term effects of war in Japan, Vietnam, and Sierra

Leone for which there is ample recent research. We also examine the effects of the wartime abduction of children who become child soldiers. What happens to them when they return to civilian life?

The Long-Term Effects of War

The social welfare effects of war are clearly devastating and among the most catastrophic that can afflict a population: death, grievous injury, and destruction. However, what effects does conflict have over the long term? Does it lead countries to become permanently impoverished or not?

From one perspective, we can think of war as having many long-term economic effects. It destroys lives and human capital that took years to build up. It destroys costly material capital and infrastructure, and it disrupts schooling, preventing children from receiving a normal education. Modern weapons, from chemical to nuclear arms, tend to have increasingly significant potential negative effects on the environment. War can damage the social fabric, leaving indelible scars on people from both sides of a conflict, and it endangers civil liberties as basic freedoms are often curtailed for the duration of hostilities. It displaces populations that flee battle scenes, bombing raids, and marauding gangs of soldiers who loot, rape, and massacre civilians. War can create health crises and famines. Any one of these devasting effects could have negative long-term effects on a country's development.

From another perepective, we might be able to present arguments for the positive long-term effects of wars. First, war may encourage technological progress as many inventions often originate from advances in military technology. In the ancient world, the wheeled chariot was a technological breakthrough in weaponry. The road construction that flourished in the Roman empire and in the United States during the Eisenhower administration was initiated for military purposes, but ultimately resulted in significant economic benefit. The steam engine might not have been invented if cannons had not been invented before. Nuclear energy would not have been invented without nuclear weapons technology. The GPS system that many people use in their cars initially had only military applications.

War may also encourage nation-building. Historian Charles Tilly showed that wars in Europe many centuries ago had a major influence on the advent of the modern nation-state.[10] Wars may also result in social and political progress. For example, after the U.S. Civil War or after World War I, government officials feared that armed, demobilized soldiers who had endured the horrors of battle might engage in insurrection against the politicians who sent them to war. In a preemptive move to calm rising waves of discontent, voting rights were substantially expanded, which gave more political power to the people. Enhanced politicial participation can lead to the enhanced provision of public services, in terms of education and health, for example. In Europe, universal suffrage was associated with the development of the welfare state.

As we can readily see, there are arguments for both the long-term negative or positive effects of war. Thus, empirical analysis is necessary to determine

---

[10]Charles Tilly, *The Formation of National States in Western Europe* (Princeton: Princeton University Press, 1975).

which effect is dominant. In the following sections, we discuss three empirical studies that consider this question: the long-term effects of the United States' detonation of atom bombs over Hiroshima and Nagasaki in Japan in 1945, the U.S. bombing of Vietnam, and the civil war in Sierra Leone.

The Long-Term Effect of Hiroshima and Nagasaki

The deadliest weapons ever used in war were nuclear weapons. They not only have a destructive power far superior to all other conventional weapons, but they also have powerful radiation effects that, over time, can kill people, cause cancer and birth defects, and have devastating environmental effects. The atomic bomb was invented during World War II and was tested for the first time on July 16, 1945, in the desert of New Mexico. On August 6, 1945, an atomic bomb was dropped on Hiroshima from the Enola Gay, a B-29 bomber. About 90% of the city was destroyed and 70,000 people were killed on impact. A second atomic bomb was dropped on the city of Nagasaki on August 9, 1945, killing between 25,000 and 40,000 people. Including those who ultimately succumbed from their injuries or from radiation poisoning, roughly 200,000 people died as a consequence of the bombings. This was not only one of the deadliest military strikes in world history, but it heralded the dawn of the nuclear age and the buildup of weapons with the capacity to destroy our planet several times over. The horrific effects of those first bombs were so great that nuclear weapons have never been used since. The constant threat of nuclear war, the possiblity of "mutually assured destruction," was the single most important feature of the decades of the Cold War between the United States and the Soviet Union, from 1945 until 1991, when the Soviet Union collapsed, and was a signficant deterrent to the two superpowers actually engaging in armed conflict that could escalate into shared annihilation.

Because of the nearly complete destruction of Hiroshima and Nagasaki, and the residual nuclear contamination of the environment around them, we might think that any survivors would relocate elsewhere. Conversely, who would want to move to a place that had been devasted by a nuclear bomb? Donald Davis and David Weinstein were interested in research on the determinants of city locations and wanted to examine the effects of the Hiroshima and Nagasaki bombings on the growth of Japanese cities.[11] Figure 20.2 shows the most sriking finding of their research: Hiroshima and Nagasaki recovered their long-term population trends in 20 to 30 years. In other words, 20 years after the bombing of Nagasaki and 30 years after the bombing of Hiroshima, their total population size was the same as it would have been if the cities had not been bombed! While this finding has implications for theories of the economics of urban agglomeration, what is most interesting here is that these cities recovered in a matter of decades from the most extreme destruction ever visited on a city in human history. This is a very surprising finding. Of course, this does not mitigate the destruction of so many lives, but it does clearly suggest that there were no long-term negative population effects from the bombings.

---

[11]Donald R. Davis and David E. Weinstein, "Bones, Bombs, and Break Points: The Geography of Economic Activity" *American Economic Review* 92, no. 5 (2002): 1269–1289.

FIGURE 20.2   Population Trends in Hiroshima and Nagasaki

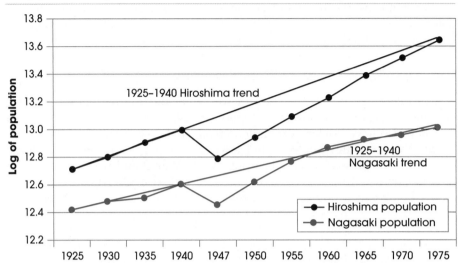

After the 1945 atomic bombing that destroyed Hiroshima and Nagasaki, the population trends in those cities returned to their pre-war levels within 20 to 30 years.

Source: Donald R. Davis and David E. Weinstein, "Bones, Bombs, and Break Points: The Geography of Economic Activity" *American Economic Review* 92, no. 5 (2002): 1282. Printed with permission of American Economics Association.

The Long-Term Effects of Bombing Vietnam

Another very interesting study considers the U.S. bombing of Vietnam during the Vietnam War, from the early 1960s to 1975. Even though no nuclear bombs were dropped on Vietnam, the war involved the most intense bombardment in all of world history. It is estimated that the United States dropped 6,162,000 tons of explosives on North and South Vietnam during the conflict. This represents roughly 3 times the total of all U.S. bombing during World War II in Asia and Europe, 13 times the total U.S. bombing during the Korean War (1950–1953), and roughly 100 times the equivalent of the combined bombings of Hiroshima and Nagasaki.

Moreover, the bombing was very concentrated in certain areas. These were primarily the region around the 17th parallel, the border between North and South Vietnam, and the Mekong Delta, just to the north of Saigon, South Vietnam's capital. North Vietnamese soldiers coming from Laos and Cambodia to attack Saigon passed through the delta and were repeatedly bombed by U.S. forces.

The area around the 17th parallel in Quang Tri province was by far the most bombed of any region during the war and Figure 20.3 clearly shows this: all the blue dots represent bombing impacts.

Edward Miguel and this author have analyzed the long-run effects of bombing in Vietnam by exploiting the fact that there was so much variation in

FIGURE 20.3   Bombing Intensity in Quang Tri Province

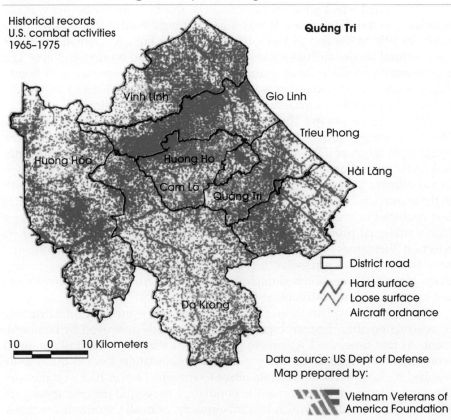

Quang Tri Province, at the border between North and South Vietnam, was the region that was bombed the most during the Vietnam War. All the blue dots indicate bomb impacts.

Source: Printed with permission from Vietnam Veterans of America Foundation.

bombing across regions.[12] This makes it possible to check whether the regions that were bombed suffered more in the long run than did regions that were bombed less. Of course, the bombing was not random. Ordinary least square regressions of bombing on long-run economic variables might thus result in a biased measurement of the effects of the bombing. If the regions that were bombed more were poorer rural areas, then these regions might still be poorer today for reasons that have nothing to do with the bombing. A simple correlation between more or less bombing during the war and poverty today might thus give a false impression of an effect of bombing on poverty. The researchers thus took an area's distance to the 17th parallel as an instrumental variable for the intensity of the bombing and looked at the bombing's effects not only on the area's population, as in the Davis and Weinstein study, but also on poverty,

[12]Edward Miguel and Gérard Roland, "The Long-Run Impact of Bombing Vietnam," *Journal of Development Economics* 96, no. 1 (2011): 1–15.

literacy rates, infrastructure, consumption, and growth. An area's distance to the 17th parallel was a good instrumental variable because the border was not correlated to these outcomes. It was a geographical border that was set arbitrarily in 1954 at the end of Vietnam's war against French colonialism. It was not a natural border such as a river that could have had economic effects. The instrumental variable estimation thus gave the effect of the variation in bombing on economic outcomes that was explained by an area's distance to the 17th parallel. This was thus a measure of the causal effect of bombing.

What were the results? There was no significant effect on population trends. Moreover, the study did not find any significant negative long-run effect of the bombing in terms of impact on poverty, as measured in 1999, or on consumption levels in 1992 or 1998. There was a slightly higher growth in consumption in the districts that were bombed more, suggesting somewhat higher growth in those districts. This is consistent with the Solow growth model that predicts that countries or regions that are poorer will grow faster because they have a higher marginal product of capital (see Chapter 4). The study also found no effect on Vietnamese literacy rates in 1999, when households in regions that were bombed had a somewhat higher rate of access to electricity, suggesting that regions that were bombed might have benefited from post-war investment in a more modern infrastructure.

How can one explain those findings? There was significant infrastructure reconstruction after the war, especially in the regions destroyed by bombardment. At that time, the Vietnamese government was still a centrally planned economy and it reallocated investments and population toward the heavily bombed regions. Because the Vietnamese Communist forces had won the war, there was a large mobilization of the population to rebuild the country as rapidly as possible, some of which was involuntary, as in all Communist regimes, and some of it voluntary, as a patriotic response. The government later engaged in an economic reform and transition process to introduce a market economy and that process has been quite successful.

The examples of Japan and Vietnam show an extraordinary resilience in response to some of the world's most devasting wartime destruction ever inflicted on a population. This does not mean that we should underestimate the human cost and suffering caused by these conflicts. It is nevertheless surprising to see that post-war economic recovery can take place in a few short decades.

Sierra Leone's Civil War

The examples of Japan and Vietnam were conflicts between countries, although the Vietnam War was, in part, a civil war between North and South Vietnam. Has civil war on other continents resulted in greater devastation? John Bellows and Edward Miguel studied the effects of the civil war that took place in Sierra Leone between 1991 and 2002.[13] This conflict provided the background for the 2006 movie, *Blood Diamond*. In 1993, Sierra Leone was the second-poorest country in the world, ruled by dictators who enriched

---

[13]John Bellows and Edward Miguel, "War and Institutions: New Evidence from Sierra Leone," *American Economic Review* 96, no. 2 (2006): 394–399.

themselves through diamond dealing. In 1991, the Revolutionary United Front (RUF), a rebel army of Sierra Leoneans hiding in neighboring Liberia, crossed the border and began to take control of many regions of Sierra Leone. The motives of the RUF were unclear; the group may have wanted to remove the corrupt incumbent regime or it may have wanted to control the country's diamond resources.

In the case of Sierra Leone, diamonds were extracted from dried river beds and no sophisticated technology was necessary for removing them. Once the regime in power or the RUF controlled a given territory, it had access to the diamonds in that region. Violence was constant when the RUF took over a village, yet there was no ethnic targeting of that violence. There was also no specific socioeconomic targeting within villages except for the households of chiefs who were consistently victimized by the RUF. Those chiefdoms with more diamond mines were attacked more often. Eventually, British and UN troops brought the war to an end in 2002 after a particularly brutal attack by the RUF on Freetown, the capital of Sierra Leone.

Bellows and Miguel found no lasting effects from violence during the civil war on economic variables such as consumption and household expenditures, income status (wage earner or not), or asset ownership. This is in line with the results from Vietnam, albeit in a different context. They found no effects of violence on trust or religiosity. A very interesting finding coming out of their research was that individuals whose households experienced violence were, after the war, more likely to be politically active. They found that these individuals had a 5.7% higher attendance rate at community meetings and were 2.4% more likely to register to vote, controlling for their age, gender, education, and authority status in the household. These mobilization effects were stronger at the individual level than at the village level. Villages that had more violence did not demonstrate much more political participation, but for individuals, the effect was significantly positive. This suggests that violence and victimization had a transformative effect on individuals, but we must be careful when interpreting this result. It might be that the increased political activity of individuals was triggered by hatred for those groups who had perpetrated the violence.

Abduction and the Effects of Being a Child Soldier

In many African civil wars, up to a third of young males, many of them still children, have been involved in active combat. Being a child soldier is certainly much worse than being a child forced to labor in order to supplement family income. We have all heard horror stories about child soldiers, boys abducted from their villages by guerrilla movements who are forced to kill family members, fight alongside the guerillas, and participate in the atrocities these forces inflict on local populations. Casual observations by journalists and other witnesses emphasize either the ongoing traumatization of former child soldiers or, on the contrary, their extraordinary resilience.

Christopher Blattman and Jeannie Annan surveyed former child soldiers in northern

(Continued)

Uganda to analyze the consequences of their experiences.[14] In 1988, a guerilla movement called the Lord's Resistance Army (LRA) emerged in northern Uganda. With little popular support, it maintained itself by constantly looting the villages of the Acholi tribe in the region. Guerrilla activity increased in 1996 when the LRA received the support of neighboring Sudan to the north. Large-scale and indiscriminate abduction of children by the LRA followed. It is estimated that a total of 66,000 youths were kidnapped. Except for age, there was no specific targeting among the youth in terms of socioeconomic characteristics. Abductees were primarily between the ages of 10 and 24, so not all were children.

They were beaten, tied, and forced to carry pillaged loot and military equipment. After a few months, those who did not escape were trained as child soldiers. They were forced to kill, sometimes members of their own families. Overall, 80% of abductees eventually escaped; the length of abduction was between 10 days and 10 years, with an average of 8 months. When they were able to return to their villages, they were welcomed and granted amnesty because it was understood that they were more victims than perpetrators.

While there is significant casual evidence on the traumatizing effects of having been a child soldier, there is little systematic evidence. Surprisingly, Blattman and Annan found that the principle effect of being a child soldier was a loss in education (0.78 years on average) compared to those children who were not abducted. This loss roughly corresponds to the duration of abduction (0.68 years on average). Abductees were twice as likely to be illiterate when compared to nonabductees. Missing 1 year out of 7 in terms of primary education thus had

potentially signficant effects. Former abductees were not necessarily more likely to be unemployed but they only qualified for unskilled jobs, with wages 32% lower than comparable youth who were not abducted and received more education. The former child soldiers were more likely to be politically active; they were 25% more likely to have voted and 2 times more likely to become low-level community leaders. This is a striking finding that resonates with Bellows' and Miguel's results from Sierra Leone. Experiencing violence appears to push people toward political activism.

There were moderate effects of more aggressive behavior demonstrated by former abductees. They were more likely to report having been in a fight or acting aggressivly. These effects were not, however, significant and there was no evidence of social exclusion. This does not mean that there were no important psychological effects experienced by the former child soldiers, but these effects were concentrated in a small subset of the abductees. Of 19 reported symptoms of depression or traumatic stress, the average youth had 3.9 and the average abductee had 4.4. This difference is not clinically important. However, the abductees were nearly 3 times as likely to be in the top quartile of psychological distress. In other words, among the top 25% of those experiencing symptoms of trauma, former abductees were present 3 times more affected than nonabductees in the population. This clearly suggests some serious cases of significant anxiety, which Blattman and Annan found resulted more from the number of violent acts experienced than from the abduction experience itself. Abduction did not necessarily lead to psychological distress, but participation in continuing acts of violence as an abductee did.

---

[14]Christopher Blattman and Jeannie Annan, "The Consequences of Child Soldiering," *Review of Economics and Statistics* 92, no. 4 (2010): 882–898.

Chapter Summary

Theoretical Explanations of Conflict

Some theories explaining why conflicts arise ascribe an important role to informational asymmetries. The different parties in a conflict do not have information about the military strength of their opponents and can overestimate the benefits of going to war. Other theories insist on the lack of commitment as a cause for rational players to go to war. The parties in a conflict will not commit to a negotiated agreement if one of them believes it may have an unexpected military advantage or opportunity at some time in the future. In that case, at least one of the parties may find it profitable to engage in a military conflict.

The Empirical Determinants of Conflict

Ethnic, cultural, and religious tensions do not appear to play as important a role in conflicts as do economic motives such as the effort to control natural resources, the inability of governments to fight rebel movements, or prior adverse economic shocks in poorer countries. Governments in poor countries often do not have the state capacity to effectively fight guerilla movements, a situation that can be compounded by the presence of mountainous or jungle terrain. Research has identified a causal effect of economic shocks on conflict in Africa when lower-than-average rainfall leads to lower crop production, which in turn exacerbates conflicts over scarce resources.

The Economic Effects of Conflict

Research on the consequences of the nuclear bombing of Hiroshima and Nagasaki by U.S. forces in 1945 or on the consequences of the U.S. bombing of Vietnam from the early 1960s until 1975, has found that within a period of 20 to 30 years, pre-war trends of economic development could be regained. In terms of the consequences of being a child soldier abducted by the guerrilla forces of the Lord's Resistance Army, the most important effect detected was on the labor market. The abductees lost years of schooling that they were usually not able to recover and because of this, they were only able to find unskilled, low-wage jobs. These labor market effects tended to be more significant than the psychological effects of abduction, but those abductees who had repeatedly been confronted with, or participated in, extreme violence experienced more psychological trauma than did those abductees not exposed to that violence.

Key Terms

logit regression

Review Questions

1. Assume two countries, A and B, are considering going to war with each other. Each has initial resources of 100. In case of war, the winner gets the resources of the losing country, but pays a cost of war c_A or c_B. Call p_A the probability that country A wins (the probability that B wins is thus $1 - p_A$). Assume that there is full information available and both parties can commit to an agreement. Also assume that country A has all the bargaining power and can impose an agreement, making country B indifferent between going to war or not. How large is the payment country A imposes on country B in such an agreement? What is the gain of country A in such an agreement over its expected payoff in a war?

2. Given the same assumptions as in the previous exercise, assume now that country A thinks that the probability of either party winning is 50%, but country B thinks that its probability of winning is 75% and country A does not have

this information. Will the proposed agreement made by country A work? Explain.

3. Under the same assumptions as in question 1 (however, assume for simplicity that $c_A = c_B = c$), suppose that there are 2 periods and that the probability that country A wins in period 1 is 70%, while it is 30% in period 2 (the probability that country B wins is then 30% in period 1, but 70% in period 2). If both parties can commit to a negotiated agreement over both periods, how much payment can country A extract from country B over the 2 periods? Now assume a lack of commitment in which country A may, after signing an agreement, exploit its advantage in period 1. How much would country B have to pay country A in order to prevent a conflict in that case?

4. Do some research and find an example of a conflict in a developing country due primarily to greed. Explain the circumstances of the war.

5. Do some research and find an example of a conflict in a developing country due primarily to grievance. Explain the circumstances of the war.

6. What is the difference between the interpretation given by Fearon and Laitin, on one hand, and by Collier and Hoeffler, on the other, of the important correlation between income per capita and conflict?

7. What difficulty do we encounter when attempting to understand the effect of income per capita on conflict? How do Miguel, Satyanath, and Sergenti deal with this problem?

8. Conflict can have an effect on civil participation. Explain.

9. Read the following article by Massimo Guidolin and Eliana La Ferrara on how private firms can benefit from conflict: http://research.stlouisfed.org/wp/2005/2005-004.pdf. Explain how the authors were able to identify the private firms that were benefiting from the war. Suggest another example of a private firm listed on the stock market that could benefit from a conflict and describe how the firm might do so.

10. Some countries, such as Costa Rica, have no army. On the Internet, find the list of countries that have no standing army. Using that information, identify the factors that allow these countries to forego maintaining an army. Discuss your findings in class, including what advantages these countries derive from having no army.

Econometric Appendix

This appendix should help the reader understand in more depth some of the tables presented in the textbook. While the explanations in the tables are usually intuitive enough for students to grasp their insights, some students may be curious to know more about the statistical and econometric techniques that are used in many of the tables presented. This appendix provides explanations for all of the different techniques used in the book. For students who have had an introductory econometrics course, this appendix is probably not necessary. However, some introductory econometrics courses do not cover all the relevant material covered here.

Our aim is to familiarize students with some of the very basic research tools used in development economics. The use of these tools, such as randomized evaluations, difference-in-differences estimations, or instrumental variable regressions, is now very widespread. A reader will be unable to grasp the exciting new insights in development economics without understanding these techniques and how they contribute to improving our scientific understanding of development issues. The good news is that these techniques are relatively easy to understand. In the information age, understanding basic econometric techniques has become part of economic literacy. My view is that while graduate students in economics must learn to use econometric techniques in a creative way, undergraduate students should learn to understand these techniques and to understand research results based on these techniques. It is, of course, impossible in such a short appendix to explain all the relevant econometrics needed to understand the papers cited fully. Often, we simply state some statistical properties without proving them. The reader should then consult econometrics textbooks for a more complete exposition. This appendix should therfore be seen more as a reader's guide in understanding the basic econometric techniques used in development economics. The fact that it is short is intended to make it as readable and accessible as possible.

We first start by introducing some fundamental statistical concepts such as the mean, the variance, and the standard deviation and their basic properties. We then explain how to estimate these concepts on the basis of sampled data. We also use the concepts to explain the covariation between two different statistical distributions and measures of this covariation such as the covariance, correlation coefficients, and regression analysis.

We then tackle the very important subject of causal inference. This is the area where most progress has been made in applied econometrics in the last 15 to 20 years. Economists now take causal analysis very seriously and no longer satisfy themselves with regression analysis where causality issues have not been clarified carefully. We explain the selection bias problem in causal inference, which was not taken seriously enough in the past by practitioners. We explain how randomized evaluations, such as in medicine, solve the selection bias and allow the use of basic regression techniques in an easy but correct way. We explain the omitted variable problem that is ubiquitous in applied econometrics. We introduce the reader to panel regression analysis, which allows the joint analysis of data variation across time and across individuals or across space. In many cases, fixed-effect and difference-in-differences analysis yield rigorous estimations of causal effects when randomization is absent. Finally, we introduce the topic of instrumental variables, which also allows us to analyze data as if they had been generated by a randomized experiment. These techniques are used in many of the chapters of the book and must be understood in order to follow modern research in development eonomics.

Some Basic Statistical Concepts

Econometrics uses statistical techniques to study how economic variables affect each other. For example, we may be interested in knowing how economic growth affects conflict or how education affects wages, but before trying to understand how economic variables relate to one another, we must first understand some basic properties of a single variable. Therefore, we must first understand some basic definitions such as the mean, the variance, and the standard deviation. We explain them in terms of a statistical distribution and then explain how they are measured using statistical samples. We then explain relations between two or more variables, such as covariance and correlation. We explain how they are measured and how regression analysis can measure their relation.

Mean, Variance, and Standard Deviation

Let us start by thinking of a statistical distribution. Call X an economic variable, such as, for example, the height of men around the world. If we think of the height of men as a statistical distribution, this means that there will be certain properties to this distribution. These properties will answer basic questions we might have such as what the average height is, how much dispersion and variation there is in height, and so forth. Ideally, we can discover the properties of this distribution by measuring all men on earth. In reality, such an exercise would be too impractical and costly, so we take samples. We must therefore distinguish between the **true distribution** (the actual statistical distribution based on all men on earth) which we will call X, and a **sample** (a set of observations drawn from a limited number of men) of n observations, say $x_1, x_2, \ldots, x_n$. We will make inferences about the true distribution using sampled data. In order to do this, it is important to distinguish between the true distribution and sample data. Because X has statistical properties, we also call it a **random** or **stochastic variable**, a variable that takes on random values drawn from its statistical distribution. The toss of a coin is a random variable that takes only two values, heads or tails, with 50% probablility for each. When sampling a person's height, we are similarly drawing at random from the distribution of heights.

$E(X) = \mu_x$ is the expected height or **mean** height, i.e., average height, in the true distribution of all possible heights. $E(X)$ is sometimes also called the

mathematical expectation of X. The expectations operator has some mathematical properties which are useful:

First of all, the expectation of a sum of random variables is the sum of their expectations:

$$E(X + Y) = E(X) + E(Y)$$

Second, the expectation of the sum of a random variable and a constant is equal to that constant plus the expectation of the random variable:

$$E(X + c) = E(X) + c.$$

Third, the expectation of a random variable multiplied by a constant is equal to that constant multiplied by the expectation of the random variable:

$$E(aX) = aE(X)$$

These properties are useful because the expectations operator is an operator that is used quite often in performing calculations on random variables.

As stated above, when measuring a variable such as height, we never have the luxury of observing the distribution of the whole population (and because the expectation is a function of the true distribution, we do not observe the true mean height). Instead, we draw samples. Let us say we take the height of n men drawn at random. We will have observations: $x_1, x_2, \ldots, x_n$.[1]
We can calculate the **mean** of the sample defined as follows:

$$\bar{x} = \frac{1}{n} \sum_{i=1}^{n} x_i$$

The mean of a sample, $\bar{x}$, drawn at random, is an approximation of $E(X)$. The larger the sample n, the better the approximation and the more precise the estimation. It is very important, however, that we draw the sample at random. Otherwise, the mean of the sample might be a biased estimate of $E(X)$. Suppose, for example, that we picked the tallest men in a crowd. The sample would be biased for that reason and the mean height of the samples of men's heights would likely be higher than $E(X)$.

Another very important notion is that of **conditional expectation**, the expected value of a stochastic variable, conditional on the distribution of another variable. Instead of asking what the average height of men is, we could ask what the expected height is, conditional on age. This is noted $E(X \mid \text{age})$. Expected height will be different for a 10-year-old boy than for a 20-year-old man.

Another important property of a distribution is its **variance**. It is a measure of how much variation there is in the true distribution. It is noted $\text{Var}(X)$, or σ_x^2, and is equal to $E[X - E(X)]^2$.

---

[1]Throughout this appendix, we note random variables with capital letters X or Y and observations with lowercase letters and an observation-specific index such as x_i and y_i. In some cases, random variables will also be indexed when necessary for better comprehension.

How does the variance σ_x^2 relate to the average of the distribution μ_x? Let us do some operations using the properties of the expectations operator.

$$\begin{aligned}\text{Var}(X) = E[X - E(X)]^2 &= E[(X - E(X))(X - E(X))]\\ &= E[(X^2 - 2X.E(X)) + (E(X)^2]\\ &= E(X^2) - 2\mu_x E(X) + E(\mu_x)^2 = E(X^2) - 2\mu_x^2 + \mu_x^2\\ &= E(X^2) - \mu_x^2\end{aligned}$$

Note that we made use of the fact that μ_x is a constant. Therefore, $2E(X.E(X)) = 2\mu_x E(X)$ and $E(\mu_x)^2 = \mu_x^2$.

A useful property that we can easily derive is the following (a and b are constant parameters):

$$\text{Var}(aX + b) = a^2 \text{Var}(X)$$

To know the true variance of the distribution, we would again need to know the whole distribution. This is usually impossible and therefore we calculate a variance from the random sample that we drew. The usual formula for the variance of a sample is:

$$s_x^2 = \frac{1}{n}\sum_{i=1}^{n}(x_i - \bar{x})^2 = \frac{1}{n}\sum_{i=1}^{n}x_i^2 - \bar{x}^2$$

The variance is the sum of the squares of the deviation of an observation from its mean divided by n. We take the square because some deviations are positive and others are negative. By adding up deviations without squaring them, they could cancel out and not give a true picture of the variation in the distribution. An average squared deviation is, however, not necessarily easy to interpret. The standard deviation s_x is the square root of the variance. It gives a rough idea of the average deviation of data from the mean and thus has an intuitive interpretation.

Covariation between Two Variables

Now that we have an idea of the basic properties of a single variable, we can introduce concepts that relate one variable to another. The **covariance** between two variables, say X and Y, gives us an idea of how much two variables move together. It is defined in the following way:

$$\text{Cov}(X, Y) = E[(X - \mu_x)(Y - \mu_Y)]$$

Again, using the properties of the expectations operator, we get:

$$\text{Cov}(X, Y) = E[XY - X\mu_Y - \mu_x Y + \mu_x\mu_Y] = E(XY) - \mu_x\mu_Y$$

Note again that we used the properties of the expectations operator in order to calculate the formula. Note also that if X and Y are statistically independent, then $E(XY) = E(X)E(Y) = \mu_x\mu_Y$ and thus $\text{Cov}(X, Y) = 0$.

When drawing observations $x_1, x_2, \ldots x_n$ and $y_1, y_2, \ldots y_n$ from both distributions, the sample covariance is computed in the following way:

$$s_{xy} = \frac{1}{n}\sum_{i=1}^{n}(x_i - \bar{x})(y_i - \bar{y}) = \frac{1}{n}\sum_{i=1}^{n}(x_iy_i - x_i\bar{y} - y_i\bar{x} + \overline{xy}) = \frac{1}{n}\sum_{i=1}^{n}x_iy_i - \overline{xy}$$

We can also calculate what is called a **correlation coefficient**, a statistic that measures the degree to which two variables move together. It is calculated by dividing the covariance by the product of the standard deviations of both variables.

$$r_{xy} = \frac{s_{xy}}{s_x s_y}$$

We can show that a correlation coefficient is always included in the interval $[-1, 1]$. Note that two variables that are statistically independent will not be correlated.

Bivariate Regression Analysis

Now that we have seen that we can correlate variables, we can introduce regression analysis between two variables, called **bivariate regression analysis**. Suppose that two random variables are related in the following way:

$$Y = \alpha + \beta X + \varepsilon$$

where ε is an error term, a random variable such that $E(\varepsilon) = 0$. One usually calls Y the dependent variable and X the independent variable. To better understand the role that ε plays, let us consider the relationship between schooling and earnings. It is reasonable to assume that more years of schooling would positively affect an individual's wage and so we would expect the dependent variable to be earnings while the independent variable would be schooling. In a model without the error term, ε, we would have the relationship, "*earnings* $= \alpha + \beta$ *schooling*." This model suggests that education alone determines a person's level of earnings. Unfortunately, data and common sense would suggest otherwise because many other factors determine earnings such as geography, gender, race, and even luck. If we include the error term, ε, in our model, then it would allow for other factors, such as the ones stated above, to determine wage.

We can easily see when using the expectations operator that $E(Y) = \beta E(X)$. If we know β, then we can make predictions on $E(Y)$ based on $E(X)$.

The big question is then: how do we know β? How can we estimate β using sample distributions $x_1, x_2, \ldots x_n$ and $y_1, y_2, \ldots y_n$?

Call b our estimate of β. Call $e_i = y_i - a - bx_i$ the residual of a regression with estimates of parameters a and b. We can call e_i the estimation error. We would like to choose an estimate of β that corresponds to a regression line that fits the data well, in other words, that minimizes the estimation errors. Figure A.1 depicts $e_i = y_i - a - bx_i$ graphically.

FIGURE A.1 Estimation Errors and the Regression Line

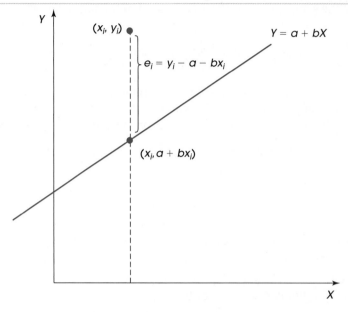

The regression line $Y = a + bX$ minimizes the distance between the observation (x_i, y_i) and the estimate of $Y(x_i, a + bx_i)$, in other words, it minimizes $e_i = y_i - a - bx_i$.

The method of ordinary least squares (OLS) is based on the idea that we want to minimize the sum of the square of errors from the estimation:

$$\min \sum_{i=1}^{n} e_i^2 = \min \sum_{i=1}^{n} (y_i - a - bx_i)^2$$

Coefficients a and b are derived by taking the derivative of that expression with respect to parameters a and b, respectively. We then have the two following equations:

$$-2\sum_{i=1}^{n}(y_i - a - bx_i) = 0$$

$$-2\sum_{i=1}^{n}(y_i - a - bx_i)x_i = 0$$

Dividing the elements of the first equation by n, we get:

$$a = \bar{y} - b\bar{x}$$

Replacing this in the second equation and distributing x_i, we get:

$$\sum_{i=1}^{n}(y_ix_i - \bar{y}x_i + b\bar{x}x_i - bx_i^2) = 0$$

Dividing by n, distributing, and rearranging we get:

$$b = \frac{s_{xy}}{s_x^2}$$

In other words, the regression coefficient b is estimated as the covariance between the two variables divided by the variance of the regressor. We interpret coefficient b as the share of the variance of X that can be explained by the covariance between X and Y. This is an intuitive explanation that helps us understand regression results.

From the way it is derived, the regression coefficient is estimated to minimize the estimation error of the relation between variables Y and X.

In regressions with multiple dependent variables, we can estimate regression coefficients using the same method. Their formula is more complex, but their interpretation remains roughly the same.

When reading a regression table, the standard error for the coefficient is usually in parentheses below the coefficient. It indicates the possible variation of the coefficient. Some coefficients are estimated with precision and have a very small standard error while other coefficients are estimated with less precision. It often happens that coefficients are estimated with so little precision that we cannot be sure they are significantly different from zero. Typically, when dividing the coefficient by the standard error, the rule of thumb is that if we obtain a number greater than 2, then it is significantly different from zero. Regression tables often give a percent level of significance, 10%, 5%, 1%, etc. If a coefficient is significant at the 5% level, this means that we can be 95% confident that the coefficient is different from zero. Regressions sometimes give **t-statistics** instead of standard errors. T-statistics are computed by dividing the coefficient by its standard error.

We lack the space to say much more about the ordinary least square model. However, it is important to emphasize the basic assumptions underlying the OLS model.

Take again our basic model:

$$Y = \alpha + \beta X + \varepsilon$$

Not only do we require that $E(\varepsilon) = 0$ as stated above, but we also require that $E(\varepsilon \mid X) = 0$. In other words, X and ε are assumed to be uncorrelated. This is very important as we will see below. The other assumption is that samples from the distribution of X and Y must be drawn independently and randomly.

Causal Inference

When performing regression analysis between variables, it is tempting to make causal inferences of the type "Y is caused by X." In these situations, we must be very careful. Running a regression does not mean that we have found a causal relationship. Causality can go in many different directions. Suppose we find a correlation between war and GDP. Is a low GDP causing war or is war damaging the economy? Moreover, regressions can sometimes be spurious. Suppose that we observe a positive correlation between drownings in swimming pools and ice cream sales. Can we claim that ice cream sales cause drownings? No, of course not. In this case, both ice cream sales and drownings are caused by another underlying variable, heat waves.

The Treatment Effect and Selection Bias

Suppose we want to understand the effect of a malaria vaccine on health. Let us note the treatment variable by $D_i = \{0, 1\}$, where a value of 1 is given to individuals who received the vaccine and a value of 0 to those who did not. Let us now use Y_{1i} as the health outcome variable for individual i who got the treatment. Let us call Y_{0i} the health outcome variable for the *same* individual i if that person was not included in the treatment group. These variables are called "potential outcome" variables. What does this mean? An individual can have two potential outcomes depending on whether that person receives the treatment or not. In reality, we do not observe two health outcomes for the same individual. Some are treated and some are not. However, the causal effect we are really interested in is $Y_{1i} - Y_{0i}$. This represents the difference between treatment and nontreatment for individual i. If an individual is treated, we want to know the difference in his or her health outcome relative to a situation in which that same individual would not be treated. Similarly, if an individual is not treated, we would want to know the difference in health outcome in a counterfactual situation in which that individual would be treated. The problem is that we have only one observation for each individual, the health outcome. We observe the health outcome of those treated and the health outcome of those not treated.

Based on observations on health outcomes and the identity of who was treated and who was not, we can find $E(Y_i \mid D_i = 1) - E(Y_i \mid D_i = 0)$. This is the *observed difference in health outcome for those treated compared to those not treated*. This is also by definition equal to $E(Y_{1i} \mid D_i = 1) - E(Y_{0i} \mid D_i = 0)$. Adding and subtracting $E(Y_{0i} \mid D_i = 1)$, we get

$$E(Y_i \mid D_i = 1) - E(Y_i \mid D_i = 0) =$$
$$[E(Y_{1i} \mid D_i = 1) - E(Y_{0i} \mid D_i = 1)] + [E(Y_{0i} \mid D_i = 1) - E(Y_{0i} \mid D_i = 0)].$$

The first term $[E(Y_{1i} \mid D_i = 1) - E(Y_{0i} \mid D_i = 1)]$ represents the **treatment effect** or the effect of the treatment on the individuals who were treated. This is the causal effect we are interested in. The second term $[E(Y_{0i} \mid D_i = 1) - E(Y_{0i} \mid D_i = 0)]$ is the **selection bias**. It represents the difference in expected health between those who were treated and those who were not. Suppose that those who received the malaria vaccine are more health-conscious than those who did not. We can thus expect those people to be healthier in general because they are more concerned with their health. Because the difference in health between those treated and those who were not treated is what we observe, if there is a selection bias, this observed difference will exaggerate the treatment effect. The malaria vaccine will no doubt make a difference and improve people's health. However, those who chose to take the malaria vaccine might generally be in better health. Therefore, the presence of a selection bias will exaggerate the real effect of the treatment. In other words, the treatment effect will, in this case, be smaller than what the observations tell us. As a result, we must be careful in measuring treatment effects to avoid including selection bias.

Randomized Evaluations

How, then, can we accurately measure a treatment effect so as to avoid a possible selection bias? The answer is randomized assignment of treatments. As we have seen in various chapters of the book, the generalization of randomized evaluations in developing countries has been one of the most exciting new directions in development economics research. Randomized evaluations have been done in medicine for quite a while and they are now increasingly used in economics.

The idea is to randomize the treatment so that the potential health outcome of someone treated would be the same as that of someone not treated:

$$E(Y_{0i} \mid D_i = 1) = E(Y_{0i} \mid D_i = 0).$$

Randomized evaluation thus solves the selection bias and gives unbiased estimates of the treatment effect. For more on how to do randomized evaluations, see Esther Duflo *et al.*, or Joshua Angrist and Jörn-Steffen Pischke.[2]

Ordinary Least Squares and Causal Inference

Ordinary least squares, the regression technique analyzed above, is the appropriate regression method when performing a randomized evaluation.

Look at the following regression model:

$$Y = \alpha + \rho D + \eta,$$

where Y is the outcome variable and D is a treatment variable taking the value of 0 or 1. In the regression equation, ρ is the treatment effect. Think of the malaria example above. The error term is η.

Using this equation, we have that $E(Y \mid D = 1) = \alpha + \rho + E(\eta \mid D = 1)$. Similarly, we have that $E(Y \mid D = 0) = \alpha + E(\eta \mid D = 0)$. Therefore, taking the difference between the two equations, we get:

$$E(Y \mid D = 1) - E(Y \mid D = 0) = \rho + E(\eta \mid D = 1) - E(\eta \mid D = 0).$$

As we can see, this expression is the same as the one above summing the treatment effect and the selection bias. The difference between the expected health for those treated and the expected health for those not treated is equal to the treatment effect plus the selection effect.

---

[2]Esther Duflo, Rachel Glennerster, and Michael Kremer, (2007) "Using Randomization in Development Research: A Toolkit" (discussion paper 6059, Centre for Economic Policy Research, 2007); and Joshua D. Angrist and Jörn-Steffen Pischke, *Mostly Harmless Econometrics: An Empiricist's Companion* (Princeton: Princeton University Press, 2008).

The selection effect will be equal to zero if $E(\eta \mid D = 1) = E(\eta \mid D = 0)$. This will be the case if the error term is uncorrelated with the independent variable, here the treatment variable. This is one of the basic assumptions of OLS as seen above (the relevant assumption being $E(\varepsilon \mid X) = 0$). Therefore, in the presence of randomized evaluations, OLS will give us an unbiased estimator of the treatment effect. This will thus enable us to draw causal inferences about the relationship between the treatment variable or the independent variable and the dependent variable.

If we now assume that there is more than one independent variable, then OLS will still give correct estimates as long as the dependent variables are not correlated with the error term and are drawn randomly. Now consider the following model:

$$Y = \alpha + \rho D + \beta X + \eta$$

As long as X is not correlated with η, there is no problem. However, we must now add an additional assumption to be sure that OLS will give us an unbiased estimate: D should also not be correlated with X.

Bias from Omitted Variables

In many cases, the assumptions underlying the OLS model are violated. A first example is that of omitted variables. Suppose we want to estimate earnings Y as a function of the years of schooling S and run a regression based on the following model:

$$Y = \alpha + \beta S + \varepsilon$$

Suppose that the true relation is the following:

$$Y = \alpha + \beta S + \gamma A + \varepsilon,$$

where A is the variable measuring a person's ability, which differs across individuals. In this case, we have what is called omitted variable bias. This is a very frequent problem in econometric estimation because many variables are often not measured. For example, we do not have direct measures of individual ability.

What is the problem with omitted variables? Supose we estimate the model of earnings as a function of schooling alone. The estimate of β will then be, following the formula developed above, $\dfrac{\text{cov}(Y, S)}{\text{var}(S)}$. Now replace Y by its true model and develop the expression, using the properties of the expectations operator. This gives us:

$$\frac{\text{cov}(\alpha + \beta S + \gamma A, S)}{Var(S)} = \beta \frac{\text{var}(S)}{\text{var}(S)} + \gamma \frac{\text{cov}(S, A)}{\text{var}(S)} = \beta + \gamma \frac{\text{cov}(S, A)}{\text{var}(S)}$$

We thus see that if Cov(S, A) is positive for example, the estimate of the effect of schooling will be biased upward. Omitting variables in a regression can thus result in a biased estimate.

In relation to the assumptions of OLS regression, this bias will be due to the fact that we violate the assumption that the error term is uncorrelated with the dependent variable. Indeed, if A is an omitted variable, the error term will pick up the ability variable. Indeed, the error term from the wrong model estimating earnings on schooling, $Y - \alpha - \beta S$, will be equal to $\gamma A + \varepsilon$. If A is correlated with S, that is, if $cov(S, A)$ is different from zero, then the assumption of the OLS model of noncorrelation between the error term and the dependent variable will be violated.

The omitted variable problem is a very serious one and researchers are likely to encounter this problem very frequently.

Panel Regressions

When performing regressions, we often have two kinds of data series: cross-sectional data and times-series data. Cross-sectional data will analyze a phenomenon across individuals, regions, or countries for a specific time period. If, for example, we try to understand the effect of a malaria vaccine on individuals' health, we will have a regression of the form presented above:

$$y_i = \alpha + \rho d_i + \beta x_i + \eta_i,$$

where y_i is the outcome observation for individual i, x_i is the control variable observation for that individual, and d_i is the observation for the treatment dummy variable. The variation in the data is across individuals indexed by i. The health measure of individuals is likely to have taken place some time after the malaria treatment, but the variation in the data is across individuals.

A times series analysis would be one in which we would, for example, follow the health of an individual before and after the malaria treatment, possibly over a number of years. All variables would be for the same individual, but across time. The regression would then have the following form:

$$y_t = \alpha + \rho d_t + \beta x_t + \eta_t$$

As we can see, here the variation in the data is variation across time indexed by t. The dummy for the treatment would take a value of 0 before the treatment and a value of 1 after the treatment. Control variable observations x_t would be for the same individual across time and so would the health measures.

In some cases, we are lucky to have data including both cross-sectional and time variation. These are called **panel data** and we can analyze them with panel data regression. In terms of our example, we could analyze the health of many different individuals over time to analyze the effect of the malaria treatment. The typical panel data regression would then take the following form:

$$y_{it} = \alpha_i + \alpha'_t + \rho d_{it} + \beta x_{it} + \eta_{it}$$

Note that in the term for the regression constant, we have both individual-specific constants and time-specific constants. This will prove very useful for causal inference. Let us now explain what we can do with panel data.

Fixed Effects and Difference-in-Differences Estimation

Suppose we want to perform a regression analysis using panel data. Suppose that the treatment was not based on randomization. We might thus have selection effects. Moreover, we might also have omitted variables that affect an individual's health but that we have not measured. Indeed, suppose that the true model takes this form:

$$Y_{it} = \alpha_i + \alpha'_t + \rho D_{it} + \beta X_{it} + \gamma_0 Y_{0it} + \gamma_1 Y_{1it} + \ldots + \gamma_n Y_{nit} + \eta_{it}$$

where $Y_{0it}, Y_{1it}, \ldots, Y_{nit}$ are omitted variables. One way of dealing with the problem of omitted variables in panel regression is to estimate what are called **fixed effects**, i.e., a constant coefficient specific to each individual i. Because we have variation across individuals and across time, the constants we estimate for each individual, α_i in the panel regression above are called individual fixed effects. These fixed effects can capture omitted variables because they capture the variation *across* individuals. For example, consider running a regression in which the dependent variable is test scores and the independent variable is the amount of time that a student spends studying. Such a regression would suffer from omitted variable bias because the time that a student spends studying is not the only determinant of her score. We might plausibly believe that some students have a natural affinity for a particular subject and it causes them to have higher scores than their classmates for the same amount of studying. This innate ability would not be captured if we simply ran a regression of test scores on time spent studying. If we are willing to believe that each student has his or her own affinity for a subject and that this ability does not change over time, then we can include individual fixed effects to account for the ability variable that we fail to observe. The fixed effect, or constant estimated for each individual, is thus supposed to absorb the effect of all omitted variables that do not vary over time.

This is reassuring and panel regressions are very useful when we work with data that are not based on randomized treatment and do not satisfy the conditions for ordinary least squares. The important restriction is that fixed effects will capture this unobserved heterogeneity only to the extent that the sum of these omitted variables does not vary across time. In other words, this will be the case if $Y_{0it}, Y_{1it}, \ldots, Y_{nit}$ (or at least their sum) are time invariant, that is, if $Y_{0it} = Y_{0i}, Y_{1it} = Y_{1i}$. Unobserved heterogeneity that would vary across time would not be picked up by the individual fixed effect. In the case of unobserved heterogeneity, we thus have to make a good case that the omitted variables do not vary across time. Suppose that we estimate the effect of a malaria treatment on the population and that the treatment was not done in a randomized way. Suppose that the individuals vary in their health due to where they live, genetic factors, etc. It seems reasonable to argue that all these unobserved variables are constant and will be captured in the fixed-effect coefficient. Assume however, that there have been improvements in hygiene over time after the malaria treatment was administered as well as economic improvements that affect people's health positively. Those variables would not be well captured in the fixed effect. To repeat, when there are time-varying unobserved variables, fixed effects cannot capture them appropriately.

Is there a way we could pick up the effect of time-varying omitted variables? If there are unobserved variables that vary over time in a similar way for all individuals (say that they vary in sync with the business cycle, for example), then time fixed effects can capture those variables. Time fixed effects can be dummy variables for years or months, depending on the frequency of collection of the observations. This is the role played by α'_t in the panel regression on the previous page.

When estimating a panel regression, we can estimate the first difference of the dependent variable:

$$\Delta y_{it} = \Delta \alpha'_t + \rho \Delta d_{it} + \beta \Delta x_{it} + \Delta \eta_{it}$$

Note that the individual fixed effect has been eliminated because it is time invariant. To the extent that the omitted variables are correctly assumed to be time invariant, the first difference regression will give us the same result as with a panel regression with individual fixed effects.

Panel regressions are also very useful to estimate difference-in-differences effects. What is a **difference-in-differences estimation**? It is an econometric technique to estimate a treatment effect, exploiting data before and after a particular treatment. Let us assume that there are two time periods, $t = 1, 2$, at which surveys are done. Assume that the treatment and its effects occur in period 2. Assume that the true model has the following form (we leave out the indices assuming that the model is the same across individuals):

$$Y = \alpha + \rho D + \beta X + \eta$$

If the treatment has not been done in a randomized way, we can use the fact that it occurred in period 2 and use the survey from period 1.

Because there was no treatment in period 1, the true equation for period 1 should be:

$$Y = \alpha + \beta X + \eta$$

Let us take our first period sample and separate it between those who were treated one period later and those who were not. We can then estimate ρ, using the difference between the two periods and the difference between the treatment and the control group. Calling the OLS estimate $\hat{\rho}_1$, we get:

$$\hat{\rho}_1 = E(Y \mid D_2 = 1) - E(Y \mid D_2 = 0) =$$
$$\alpha + \beta E(X \mid D_2 = 1) + E(\eta \mid D_2 = 1) - \alpha - \beta E(X \mid D_2 = 0) - E(\eta \mid D_2 = 0) =$$
$$\beta E(X \mid D_2 = 1) - \beta E(X \mid D_2 = 0)$$

If we do a regression for the second period, our OLS estimate $\hat{\rho}_2$ of ρ will be:

$\hat{\rho}_2 = E(Y \mid D_2 = 1) - E(Y \mid D_2 = 0) =$

$\alpha + \rho + \beta E(X \mid D_2 = 1) + E(\eta \mid D_2 = 1) - \alpha - \beta E(X_i \mid D_2 = 0) - E(\eta \mid D_2 = 0) =$

$\rho + \beta E(X \mid D_2 = 1) - \beta E(X \mid D_2 = 0)$

Taking the difference between estimates for both periods, we get:

$$\hat{\rho}_2 - \hat{\rho}_1 = \rho$$

In other words, the difference-in-differences estimator gives us an estimate of the treatment effect. Why is this? Suppose there is a selection effect. This means that there will be a difference between $\beta E(X \mid D_2 = 1)$ and $\beta E(X \mid D_2 = 0)$. The estimate $\hat{\rho}_2$ for the second period will include both the estimate of the treatment effect and of the selection effect. However, the estimate of the effect before the treatment should pick up only selection effects. The difference between the two estimates (the estimate after the treatment minus the estimate before the treatment) should thus be equal to the treatment effect. Note that this will be true only if $\beta E(X \mid D_2 = 1) - \beta E(X \mid D_{i2} = 0)$ is the same in period 1 and period 2.

We thus see that even if a treatment has not been done randomly, it is sometimes possible to estimate the true treatment effect by exploiting the time dimension before and after the treatment.

Instrumental Variables

In many cases, causal inference can be very difficult because it is not possible to do randomized evaluations. One obvious reason is that we cannot redo experiments from the past. This is valid for all historical data. Another problem is that fixed effects estimates are only convincing if unobserved heterogeneity between treated and untreated does not vary over time and this is often not the case. Fortunately, there is another method to estimate causal effects in an unbiased way that is widely used: instrumental variables. Throughout the book, we have cited many studies reporting instrumental variable estimates of causal effects. We first explain how it works and then provide the explanation for what it does.

Assume the following regression model:

$$Y = \alpha + \beta X + \eta$$

Assume that X and η are *not* uncorrelated (i.e., assume $E(\eta \mid X) \neq 0$). This violates the assumptions of the OLS model and will likely lead to biased estimates as seen above. This will be due either to a selection effect, omitted variables, or possibly even to reverse causality. We have already discussed the selection effect and the omitted variable problem; now we will consider reverse causality in more detail.

If bad economic outcomes cause conflict, then conflict could also cause bad economic outcomes. Thus, if there is two-way causality, the OLS estimate will be biased. Indeed, if X measures economic prosperity and Y measures conflict, and if the causality can go both ways, then Y will also cause X and because Y depends on η, then X will be correlated to η. The estimated coefficient of regression will therefore exaggerate the effect of the economy on conflict as it will pick up two-way causality.

What do we do in all those cases where the independent variable and the error term are likely to be correlated? The instrumental variable method provides a solution. Take a variable Z such that the following relation holds:

$$X = \gamma + \delta Z + \varepsilon$$

As we can see from that equation, X is correlated with Z. We also assume that η and Z are uncorrelated, which means that Y and Z are also uncorrelated. We call the latter assumption the *exclusion restriction*. It says that there is no *direct* link between Y and Z, only an indirect link that works through the channel of X. *A good instrumental variable must thus fulfill two conditions: it must be correlated with the independent variable but uncorrelated with the dependent variable.*

With the instrumental variable method, the estimated coefficient b_{IV} for β in the bivariate regression case will be the following:

$$b_{IV} = \frac{s_{zy}}{s_{zx}}$$

This formula for the estimated coefficient for the instrumental variable method gives us a readily apprehended interpretation of the estimation technique. The coefficient is estimated by taking the ratio of the covariance of the instrumental variable with the dependent variable and the covariance of the instrumental variable with the independent variable. In other words, we look at the covariation between Z and Y relative to the covariation between Z and X.

Let us think about instrumental variable estimation in the context of our example of the relationship between conflict and economic performance. We saw in Chapter 20 that rainfall was a good instrument for economic performance. Rainfall affects crops in poor countries. On the other hand, we cannot argue that rainfall is directly correlated with conflict. Rainfall is thus a good instrument for economic performance. *Intuitively, the instrumental variable regression will thus give an estimate of the effect of economic performance on conflict that is explained by the effect of rainfall on economic performance.*

Let us come back to the malaria vaccine example to elaborate further on instrumental variable regression. Assume that initially, we wanted to set up a randomized treatment to evaluate a malaria vaccine, but that the experiment was badly implemented and that only a portion of those individuals randomly selected for treatment took the vaccine. In this case, we would suspect that a selection effect is present. Let us call Z the *intention to treat variable* that takes a value of 0 or 1. Let us now call $D(Z)$ the treatment value as a function of the value of Z. Thus, $D(0)$ is the treatment value if there was no intention to treat and $D(1)$, the treatment value if there is an intention to treat. Remember that D only takes the value of 0 or 1. Call Y the outcome variable. As before, we need to think of counterfactuals in order to estimate the treatment effect correctly. The advantage of counterfactuals is that we not only can look at observed outcomes but we can also consider outcomes that could have occurred but were not observed. Therefore, let us call $Y(Z, D)$ the counterfactual outcome. Given that Z and D each take 2 values, there are four counterfactuals $Y(Z, D)$: $Y(1, 1)$, $Y(1, 0)$, $Y(0, 0)$, and $Y(0, 1)$. The assumption that Z and Y are uncorrelated means that $Y(Z, D) = Y(D)$. Let us pause to understand what this means. Take a person who was randomly selected for treatment, but for some reason, was not treated. The outcome for that person should not be different than for a person who was not selected. In other words, only the treatment affects the health outcome. This seems natural with a random selection of Z. Another way of saying it is that Z itself does not affect Y. This property will prove useful below.

The assumption that Z and X are correlated means that $E(D(1))$ is not equal to $E(D(0))$. In other words, the expectation of being treated depends on whether the individual was initially selected or not. This assumption will be automatically satisfied if those treated are only those initially selected ($Z = 1$), but even if that is not the case, it is reasonable to assume that this assumption holds. Without this assumption, Z would obviously play no role at all and we could forget about it entirely.

With these assumptions, we can identify three causal effects: 1) the causal effect of Z on D: $D(1) - D(0)$; 2) the causal effect of D on Y: $Y(1) - Y(0)$; and 3) the causal effect of Z on Y: $Y(D(1)) - Y(D(0))$.

Thus, suppose that individuals were selected randomly for the malaria treatment and that these individuals were surveyed. Also suppose that random disruption in the delivery of malaria vaccines in certain regions prevented those selected from receiving the vaccine. Let us then derive an easy interpretation of the instrumental variable coefficient.

Note first that the covariance between Z and Y can be simplified:

$$Cov(Z, Y) = E(ZY) - E(Z)E(Y)$$

Taking into account the fact that Z and Y are uncorrelated and that Z only takes two values, we get:

$$E(Y \mid Z = 1)E(Z = 1) - E(Y)E(Z = 1) = [E(Y \mid Z = 1) - E(Y)]E(Z = 1) =$$
$$\{E(Y \mid Z = 1) - [E(Y \mid Z = 1)E(Z = 1) + E(Y \mid Z = 0)E(Z = 0)]\}E(Z = 1)$$

Taking into account the fact that

$$E(Y \mid Z = 1) - E(Y \mid Z = 1)E(Z = 1) = E(Y \mid Z = 1)E(Z = 0),$$

we get:

$$\{E(Y \mid Z = 1) - E(Y \mid Z = 0)\}E(Z = 0)E(Z = 1)$$

Similarly, we can derive

$$Cov(Z, D) = [E(D \mid Z = 1) - E(D \mid Z = 0)]E(Z = 0)E(Z = 1)$$

We thus get:

$$b_{IV} = \frac{E(Y \mid Z = 1) - E(Y \mid Z = 0)}{E(D \mid Z = 1) - E(D \mid Z = 0)}$$

The numerator is the expected health effect for those intended to be treated relative to those not intended to be treated. The denominator is a correction that takes into account the difference between expected treatment for those selected versus for those not selected. In our example, because $E(D \mid Z = 0) = 0$, we look at the difference in health outcomes for those selected corrected for the fact that only a proportion of those selected were treated.

So far, we have only considered very stylized examples. The expression above for the instrumental variable regression is the one computed in the case of a bivariate regression. We can express the problem in much more general terms than what we have used here. However, the interpretations are essentially the same for multivariate regressions.

Let us conclude by comparing the interpretation of the OLS coefficient of regression with that of IV (instrumental variable) coefficient of regression. The OLS coefficient gives the part of the variance of the independent variable that can be explained by the covariation between the independent and the dependent variable. The IV coefficient gives the part of the covariation between the independent variable and the instrumental variable that can be explained by the covariation between the dependent variable and the instrumental variable. In contrast to the OLS coefficient, the IV coefficient only looks at the variation between the instrumental variable and the independent variable, not at the whole variation of the independent variable. For that reason, we often call the IV estimate the local average treatment effect (LATE), that is, we explain the part of the treatment that covaries with the instrument. The OLS estimate, on the other hand, gives the average treatment effect because it takes into account the whole variation of the independent variable.

While it takes some time to understand how IV estimation works, in reality, good instruments are very hard to find and requires considerable ingenuity on the part of researchers to identify them. The exclusion restriction is often not satisfied and even if it is, the correlation between the instrumental variable and the independent variable is often too weak. Researchers have become increasingly more demanding of IV estimations. In this book, we have provided some of the best examples of IV estimations in development economics. However, given these difficulties, it is safer to use randomized evaluations whenever possible. Unfortunately, that is often impossible and instrumental variable estimation, similar to fixed effect estimation, remains a very useful tool for researchers.

A Regressions Table

Now, let us use our understanding of the material presented above to interpret the regression table shown in Table A.1. The regressions in the table attempt to explain the effects of economic growth on civil conflict in sub-Saharan Africa. Each regression is given its own column and so, for instance, the regression of civil conflict on the annual economic growth rate with country fixed effects is presented in column (3). The dependent variable is usually in the top row. As

TABLE A.1   A Regression Table: The Effect of Economic Growth on Conflict

	Dependent Variable:				
	Civil conflict ≥ 25 deaths PRIO				Civil conflict ≥ 1,000 deaths, PRIO
	OLS	OLS	IV	IV	IV
Explanatory Variable	(1)	(2)	(3)	(4)	(5)
Annual Economic Growth Rate	−0.58**	−0.48*	−2.27**	−2.08**	−2.17***
	(0.28)	(0.25)	(0.98)	(0.96)	(0.78)
Democracy (Polity IV), time $t-1$	−0.003		−0.003		
	(0.005)		(0.005)		
Ethno-linguistic fractionalization	0.21		0.21		
	(0.27)		(0.27)		
Religious fractionalization	−0.26		−0.27		
	(0.24)		(0.24)		
Oil-exporting country	0.01		−0.01		
	(0.19)		(0.20)		
Log (mountainous)	0.074*		0.075*		
	(0.040)		(0.039)		
Log (national population), time $t-1$	0.073		0.71		
	(0.048)		(0.49)		
Country fixed effects	No	Yes	No	Yes	Yes
R^2	0.11	0.55	—	—	—
Number of observations	647	647	647	647	647

Table A.1 notes: 1) Huber robust standard errors in parentheses. Significantly different than zero at 90% (*), 95% (**), and 99% (***) confidence.

we can see, in columns (1)–(4), the dependent variable is the number of civil conflicts with more than 25 deaths from the PRIO (Peace Research Institute in Oslo) database, whereas in column (5), the dependent variable is the number of conflicts with more than 1,000 deaths. The regression method is outlined at the top of each column. Thus, columns (1) and (2) are regressions using ordinary least squares (OLS) while columns (3) through (5) use instrumental variable (IV) regression. The explanatory variables are listed in the leftmost column: Annual economic growth rate, the Polity Democracy index lagged by 1 year, ethno-linguistic fractionalization, whether or not a country is an oil exporter, the log of the percentage of a country that is mountainous, the log of the population lagged by 1 year, and whether or not there are country fixed effects. The regression coefficient in a given column that corresponds to the row of the dependent variable expresses the estimate of the effect of the explanatory variable on the dependent variable. Thus, the first coefficient in the first regression (−0.58) is the effect of annual growth on conflict: 1% more growth reduced the number of conflicts by −.58. The most important thing to consider when looking at coefficient estimates is the level of significance, which is indicated by the number of stars next to each coefficient. Three stars means significant at the 99% level. This means that there is a 99% chance that the coefficient is different from zero. Two stars indicate significance at the 95% level and 3 stars indicate significance at the 90% level. Usually, when a coefficient is significant below the 90% level, we do not consider the precision of the estimate is high enough to be significant. How do we compute the level of significance of a coefficient? Below the coefficient estimate, the standard error of the estimation appears. The smaller the standard error, the higher the precision of the estimate and the higher the level of significance. It turns out that if we take the estimate of the coefficient divided by its standard error, it behaves according to a statistical distribution called the "Student's t-distribution." We do not have the space to explain the properties of this distribution, but a rule of thumb used by many researchers is to see if the ratio of the regression coefficient and its standard error is larger than 2. If that is the case, the coefficient is significant. Standard statistical packages such as STATA automatically give levels of significance. Finally, the last rows in a regression table provide some information such as the number of observations or the R^2, which is a measure of how well the regression explains the dependent variable. The higher the R^2 the better, but it is often small. Below the table, explanatory notes for the reader appear.

The regression table above is also useful when considering the difference between OLS and IV regression. A simple regression with civil conflict as the dependent variable and annual economic growth as the independent variable would suffer from the problem of endogeneity. A higher level of conflict might lead to a lower level of growth because of the disruptions in the economy. The causality would then go in the other direction. It might also suffer from a problem of omitted variables. For example, a more stable government might reduce the level of conflict and also have a positive effect on economic growth. To address these concerns, we can use rainfall as an instrument for economic growth. This is a good instrument because rainfall affects economic outcomes in agrarian societies but it is not correlated with conflict. The instrumental variable regressions are presented in columns (3), (4), and (5). Each of these regressions shows that annual economic growth rate has a negative and significant effect on civil conflict. This is evidence that even when we account for endogeneity, there is a causal effect of economic growth on civil conflict.

Definitions

Adversarial system   System of adjudication in the common-law system where each party brings evidence to court. The prosecution presents evidence against the defendant and the defense offers evidence in favor of the defendant.

Adverse selection   A situation caused by informational asymmetries in which reputable agents and sellers leave the market to disreputable agents, resulting in a possible market collapse.

Age distribution   The percentages of the population in a country belonging to different age groups.

Age-specific fertility rates   The number of children born to a woman of a certain age. Fertility rates are only counted for women's childbearing ages, generally consider to be 15 to 44.

Age-specific mortality rates   The percentage of deaths in a particular age group.

Arab Spring   Wave of protests in the spring of 2011 that began in Tunisia and spread all over the Middle East and North Africa, ultimately leading to regime change in Tunisia, Egypt, Libya, and Yemen, political changes in Morocco, and civil war in Syria.

Asset specificity   See *relationship specific*.

Asymmetric information   A situation in which one party to a transaction possesses information that the other party does not have.

Autocracy   A government in which all power resides in a single person such as a dictator, monarch, or supreme religious leader.

Automatic stay on the assets   Bankruptcy rule preventing assets of a firm from being claimed by creditors.

Average labor productivity   National output divided by total employment in the economy, or output per worker or per hour worked.

Average productivity   Output produced per unit of labor, units of labor being measured either in hours worked or in number of full-time employed workers.

Backward linkages   Effects of economic events in downstream sectors on upstream sectors that play the role of suppliers for those sectors.

Balanced growth   A growth process in which all economic sectors grow at the same rate.

Bank run   A situation in which a bank's customers make massive withdrawals of their deposits, usually causing the bank to close because it cannot satisfy these demands for deposit withdrawals.

Big push theories   Theories stating that economic development can only be successful based on policies to expand, simultaneously, various sectors on a very large scale.

Bilateral trade negotiations   Negotiations held between two countries to reduce trade barriers between them.

Birth rate   The number of babies born per 1,000 inhabitants in a given year in a country.

Black-market transactions   Illegal transactions in the planned economy that enrich participants in the transaction.

Bright-line rules   Precise descriptions of prohibited actions.

Calorie counting   The minimal economic cost of 2,000 calories worth of food per day, the average daily number of calories humans need.

Capital account convertibility   Refers to flows of capital in and out of a country that are unrestricted. In other words, anyone can buy and sell any amount of the domestic currency against foreign currencies without restriction.

Capital flight   Investment decision of domestic capital owners to transfer a portion or the totality of their capital holdings abroad instead of leaving it in the domestic economy.

Capital intensity   The quantity of capital per worker in an economy or in a firm.

cif/fob ratio   Ratio of imports including carriage, insurance, and freight costs (cif) over exports measured by their free on board (fob) value. The cif/fob ratio minus 1 measures the transport cost rate of imports.

Civil society The network of diverse voluntary associations.

Civil society development Situation in which citizens are more organized in various associations, political parties, unions, etc. In other words, citizens increase their ability to overcome collective-action problems.

Civil-law systems Legal systems derived from ancient Roman civil law that rely mostly on recorded legal statutes. Legal arguments in the civil-law system are made on the basis of the consistency or inconsistency of a decision with the principles laid down in statutory law.

Clientelism Behavior of politicians who cater to their voter constituency using public money. It can take many forms, such as politically motivated job creation or the construction of housing projects to reward faithful voters.

Collateral Assets that a borrower contractually permits a creditor to seize in case the loan is not repaid.

Collective action A joint action by individuals to achieve a particular goal.

Collective action failure A situation in which individuals fail to take an action that would be in their joint interest because they can free-ride on the actions taken by others.

Collective-action problem Situation in which people fail to undertake a collective action even though it is in their joint interest to do so. It has the game-theoretic structure of the cooperation problem and the prisoner's dilemma.

Commitment problem Situation in which one party can renege on prior commitments made to another party in the course of joint transactions.

Common-law system Legal system developed in England and other Anglo-Saxon countries, based on customary Saxon law, the law that existed in England before the Norman invasion of 1066. Legal arguments in the common-law system rely heavily on legal precedents, decisions made in past court cases.

Comparative advantage If two countries have different cost structures in different sectors, the comparative advantage of a country lies in those sectors where its opportunity cost of production, i.e. the

cost of producing one good, and not producing other goods, is lower compared to other countries.

Complementarities Complementarities between two objects exist when the objects must be combined in certain fixed proportions in order to be effective.

Congestion effects Excessive use of public services, such as health, education, and various types of infrastructure (water, sewer, transportation, etc.) related to the fact that the population using these public services is higher than the population numbers for which the services were planned.

Conspicuous consumption Consumption dictated by the desire to show one's wealth and status rather than by the useful characteristics of the good consumed.

Constant returns to scale If each factor of production is multiplied by the same number z, output is also multiplied by that number z.

Conventions Set of agreed-upon norms of behavior in a society to which people conform because members of the society are expected to exhibit these norms of behavior.

Convertibility The freedom to convert one currency into another currency.

Cooperation problem A situation that arises when individuals follow their self-interest in making their choices and when the outcomes of these choices are less than optimal for all parties, but would be improved upon if all parties collaborated to enhance joint payoffs.

Coordination problems Problems that occur when economic agents make independent decisions that affect all agents. Agents can coordinate on a good equilibrium leading to good payoffs for all or on a bad equilibrium leading to bad payoffs for all.

Copenhagen Accord Agreement signed in December 2009 at the United Nations. The agreement failed to provide binding commitments by participating countries to reduce their carbon emissions.

Corporate governance Rules by which a company is managed and supervised.

Corporatism An economic system in which access to markets and competition are severely restricted so as to favor established industries and the financial status quo. There are, however, other meanings of corporatism in other contexts.

Cost of capital The cost of financing investments through equity as well as through debt. A higher estimated cost of capital means that a higher return to investment is expected in order to justify a specific investment. The cost of capital can thus be seen as the return hurdle for investment.

Cost of debt The risk-free rate of interest plus a debt premium.

Cost of equity Usually calculated as the sum of three elements: the risk-free rate of interest plus an equity premium plus a country premium.

Country premium Risk premium that takes into account the riskiness of investments in a particular country. The country risk is most often related to a country's quality of institutions: its courts, rule of law, regulatory quality, political stability, and the presence of corruption, among other variables.

Credibility A party's ability to uphold the commitments it makes.

Credit constrained A firm is credit constrained if it wants to borrow more than *all possible* lenders are willing to lend at a given interest *r*.

Credit elasticity Measure of by what percent demand for credit drops when the interest rate increases by one percentage point.

Credit rationed A firm is credit rationed if it wants to borrow more than a lender is willing to lend at a given interest *r*.

Credit rationing See *credit rationed*.

Creditworthiness Property of a borrower that refers to his or her willingness or ability to fulfill a debt contract.

Culture The set of beliefs and values passed down from generation to generation. Beliefs concern nature, interactions between humans and nature, and interactions among humans in a society. Values reflect what people in a culture consider important in and give meaning to their lives. Culture is mostly transmitted vertically from parents to children.

Currency board A currency board is a system that allows a country's central bank to print quantities of the local currency only in proportion to the amount of foreign reserves that come in. When Argentina had a currency board, the Argentinean peso was linked to the dollar in a 1:1 ratio; additional pesos could be printed only if there were an inflow of U.S. dollars.

Currency peg Policy whereby the fixed exchange rate of a country is linked to a particular foreign currency, such as the dollar, the yen, or a basket of currencies.

Death rate The number of deaths per 1,000 inhabitants in a given year in a country.

Debt premium Interest rate premium that takes into account the probability of default on debt, both default on debt by private companies and default on government debt.

Decreasing returns to scale If each factor of production is multiplied by the same number z, output is multiplied by a number smaller than z.

Democracy Political regimes where political leaders are selected through free, fair, and competitive elections in which all adult citizens have the right to vote and all political parties have the right to participate in elections and governance. Democracy is founded on the premise that all citizens enjoy fundamental rights such as freedom of expression, freedom of association, and freedom of movement.

Demographic transition The transition from a stabilized global population with high birth and high mortality rates to a stabilized population characterized by low birth and low mortality rates. During the transition, mortality rates decline faster than birth rates, leading to a fast increase in the world population.

Demographic trends The evolution of populations over time.

Devaluation A change in the exchange rate that makes foreign exchange more expensive.

Development banks Banks that specialize in giving long-term loans for development purposes. Development banks often support the growth of export-oriented industrial firms.

Development gap The differences in economic development between the advanced economies of the world and the poorer developing economies.

Difference in differences Econometric method that analyzes the difference between a treatment and a control variable before and after the treatment took place.

Diminishing marginal productivity The marginal productivity of a factor of production decreases as more units of that factor are used in the production process.

Direct sales   Sales between a buyer and a seller without competition from multiple buyers, as in auctions.

Disability adjusted life year (DALY)   Concept used by the World Health Organization to measure the benefits of health intervention. It corresponds to a year of healthy life that results from a health program and includes years of life saved as well as years of disability prevented.

Disclosure rules   Legal rules forcing one party to a contract to disclose information to another party to the contract.

Dispersed ownership   Situation in which shares in an enterprise belong to a very large number of shareholders with no single shareholder holding a significant number of shares.

Distortionary   Describes policies such as taxes that modify the economic decisions of economic agents.

District magnitude   The average number of seats for elected representatives in a district.

Divided government   Situation in which the executive and the legislative branches of government are each controlled by another party or coalition.

Dominant strategy   A situation in a game-theoretic context in which the same action is optimal for one player and independent of what the other player chooses.

Dual-track liberalization   Method of price liberalization used in China in the 1980s. Under dual-track liberalization, only part of a firm's output is liberalized, while the other part remains under the control of the central planning system.

Economic development   Improvements in living standards and in the quality of life in a country.

Economic growth   Growth in economic production, usually measured as Gross Domestic Product (GDP) or Gross National Product (GNP).

Ejido   Land system in Mexico that originated during the Aztec Empire, in which peasants collectively owned an area of communal farmland that they could work but could not sell.

Elasticity of the tax base   The percentage by which the tax base declines if the tax rate increases by 1%.

Encomienda   Legal system established by the Spanish conquistadores in Latin America that forced local Indian populations to work for specific Spanish landlords and subjected them to highly exploitative conditions often amounting to slavery.

Endogenous growth theory   A growth theory emphasizing that economic growth is generated by endogenous technical change resulting from entrepreneurial innovation.

Entitlement set   All the goods an individual can obtain with the resources he or she commands, given the laws of his or her society.

Epidemiological transition   Major medical breakthroughs in the first half of the 20th century that have had a powerful and lasting impact on health outcomes in both rich and poor countries.

Equity premium   Premium for financing an investment through equity instead of debt.

Excludable good   A good that the seller can exclude others from consuming.

Expected payoff   The sum of payoffs in different contingencies or states of the world where each payoff is weighed by its probability of occurrence.

Export promotion   Policies that tend to help domestic firms increase market shares on international markets.

Export promotion strategies   Development strategies focusing on developing competitive sectors for the successful export of products to the world market.

Externalities   The impacts that economic transactions have on others who are not part of those transactions.

Extractive or predatory institutions   Institutions set up to plunder a country's resources. Predatory institutions were established by colonial powers in many countries, such as the Congo in Africa or by Spanish colonizers in Latin America.

Factor abundance   The relative availability of a certain factor of production relative to other factors of production. Certain countries are more capital-abundant while others are more labor-abundant.

Factor mobility   Degree to which factors of production can move across borders, for example, in response to tax rates.

Factor productivity   The contribution of each factor of production to output.

Factor shares   The share of national income used as payment for the share of capital (or labor) in production.

Factors of production   The fundamental inputs to the production process in an economy. Factors of production are labor, capital, and land.

Fallowing   Leaving a field idle during a growing season to let the soil retain nutrients and moisture for future crops.

Fascist   Describes the dictatorial regime established in Italy by Benito Mussolini in 1922 that exalted similar values to Nazism: nationalism, corporatism, the cult of violence, and of the supreme leader, *Il Duce*.

Financial convertibility See *capital account convertibility*.

Financial industrial groups   Large conglomerates set up in Russia in the 1990s that were able to finance their activities internally and work together.

Financial repression   Policies undertaken by governments that make domestic returns to capital artificially low. Under financial repression, there will be underdevelopment of the financial sector.

Financial sustainability   Describes a firm with enough profits to cover its operating costs as well as the cost of capital.

Fiscal institutions   The rules and means by which government assures fiscal revenue.

Fixed exchange-rate regime   Exchange rate regime in which the price of a country's currency remains fixed in terms of other currencies.

Fixed wage   Wage paid by the hour, independent of the work actually performed.

Floating exchange-rate regime   Exchange-rate regime in which the exchange rate for a currency varies on a daily basis, in line with the supply and demand for that currency. The exchange rate is then a market price.

Focal point   A solution to a coordination problem that most people will find without having to communicate.

Forced substitution   Form of substitution in a shortage economy in which firms substitute goods in shortage for available inputs, which are not necessarily of adequate quality.

Formal institutions   Rules codified in writing that are generally more precise than unwritten rules.

Forward linkages   Effects of economic events in upstream sectors on downstream sectors that are clients for those sectors.

Free ride   Benefiting from the actions of others while not incurring any of the costs of taking action.

Functionalist fallacy   Fallacy that mistakes an object's function for the cause of its existence.

Game theory   Theory that studies the decisions of agents whose payoffs depend on the actions of other agents.

Gini coefficient   A number between 0 and 1 measuring income inequality. It is calculated as twice the area between the diagonal line and the Lorenz curve.

Gray-market transactions   Illegal transactions in the planned economy that serve the purpose of fulfilling the plan.

Gross domestic product (GDP) per capita   A measure of output per inhabitant in a country. It is a good approximation of average annual per capita income.

Group lending   Lending by a bank to a group of people in a village or neighborhood. The composition of the group is usually decided by the villagers or the neighborhood residents. The members of the group are then jointly responsible for paying back the loan.

Growth accounting   The decomposition of an economy's growth rate into various components: that which is explained by the growth rate of the labor force, that which is explained by the growth rate of the capital stock, and that which is the residual attributed to total factor productivity.

Growth rate   The increment in value of a given variable (say GDP) at time t between time t and time $t - 1$ as a percentage of the value of that variable at time $t - 1$.

Growth rate of the population   The increase in a population over a given time period as a percentage of the existing population at the beginning of that time period.

Growth rate of total factor productivity   Increase in total factor productivity as a percentage of total factor productivity.

Hacienda   Large land estate in Spanish-speaking countries, primarily in Latin America.

Harris-Todaro model   Model of migration from rural areas to urban areas. The model explains why people may migrate from rural to urban areas even when there is urban unemployment.

Heterogeneity   Differences in conditions across space or across individuals for a given variable.

Hoarding demand   Behavior under shortage: if a buyer expects goods to be in short supply in the future, he will increase today's demands relative to a situation in which he expects no shortages.

Hold-up problem   A situation in which a business partnership requires an investment from one of the parties that is specific to the transaction in question. Once the investment has been made, however, the other partner "holds up" the party that made the investment in order to renegotiate the deal.

Hukou   System of residence registration for households in China that limits migration of rural residents to the cities because they will not enjoy the same rights and benefits as urban residents.

Human capital   The knowledge and skills embodied in people. Human capital is positively related to the level of education.

Import quotas   Quotas that limit the total volume of imports to a country at a given moment in time. A government can implement them through the allocation of the licenses required to import goods from abroad.

Import substitution   Replacement of imports by domestic production.

Import substitution strategies   Development strategies focusing on the development of a country's domestic industry with the objective of a gradual decline in imports of industrial products while the domestic industrial sectors expand.

Import tariffs   Taxes on imported goods.

Income convergence   Convergence of income per capita of poor countries to the level of rich countries, obtained by the higher growth of the former. The Solow model of economic growth predicts income convergence.

Income-elasticity of demand   The growth rate of demand as income grows by 1%. Industrial goods have a higher income-elasticity than basic commodities.

Increasing returns to scale   If each factor of production is multiplied by the same number z, output is multiplied by a number higher than z.

Industrial frontier   A situation in which the most advanced technologies in the world are used in various industrial sectors.

Infant industries   Newly established firms that do not have a foothold in the global marketplace or the experience and knowledge of long-established industries.

Infant mortality rate   The number of children dying before age 1 per 1,000 live births in the same year. Divide this rate by 10 to compute the probability a child will die before age 1.

Inferior good   Good for which demand decreases as income increases.

Influence activities   Biased information supplied by interest groups to policy makers in order to influence them in the interest group's favor.

Informal institutions   Rules that are not legally codified; they are based on social norms (or conventions), the accepted and expected standards of behavior. These rules are enforced in an informal way using peer pressure, feelings of guilt, and moral obligations.

Informal sector   Sector of economic activity that is not registered, not subject to laws of registered companies, or not subject to taxation.

Informational intermediaries   Economic agents such as chain stores or other firms that gather information about the products they sell before offering them for sale in their stores.

Inquisitorial system   System of adjudication in the civil-law legal system where an investigative judge, who is in charge of instructing the case before the trial opens, collects all the evidence for both parties.

Institution   A constraint placed by law and/or *social norms* on human behavior.

Intermediation margin   The difference between rates on loans and rates on deposits.

Intersectoral linkage   The effects that conditions in one sector of the economy have on other related economic sectors.

Investment specificity   Investments that are specific to a given production relationship and do not have value, or have little value, outside that relationship.

Knowledge The stock of knowledge as it exists in books, files, archives, patents, computer code, and in various other forms that humans can store. In principle, knowledge can grow boundlessly and can accumulate indefinitely. The only constraint to the accumulation of knowledge is that it has to be produced through research.

Kyoto Protocol The Kyoto Protocol, signed in 1997, required 36 developed countries to reduce their greenhouse gas emissions by 5% relative to their 1990 levels.

Land reform Redistribution of land from large landholders to small farmers.

Large blockholders Shareholders who own a sufficiently large number of shares so as to have strong incentives to monitor the firm.

Life expectancy The average number of years a newborn infant would live if health and living conditions at the time of his or her birth remained the same throughout its life. Life expectancy reflects the health conditions in a country and the quality of health care its people receive.

Limited liability Financial liability of a company that is limited to the investment in the company.

Logit regression Regression in which the dependent variable takes only two values, usually 0 and 1. Also called logistic regression.

Lorenz curve A curve that plots the cumulative share of total income in a country of different quantiles for the whole range of income distribution, starting from the lowest quantile to the highest quantile.

Majoritarian rule Electoral rule also called "first past the post," "plurality rule," or "single-member district." With majoritarian rule, only one representative—the candidate with the most votes—is elected per legislative district. All that a candidate needs is to have more votes than the other candidates.

Marginal productivity The output increase caused by an additional unit of a factor of production in the production process.

Marginal productivity of capital The output increase caused by an additional unit of capital in the production process.

Marginal productivity of labor The output increase caused by an additional unit of labor in the production process.

Market integration Markets are integrated when the same good is sold at the same price in different markets. If transport costs are sufficiently high, markets are integrated if prices on different markets move in the same way at the same time.

Market track In the context of dual-track price liberalization, the firm's output above the plan track is sold freely at market prices.

Mass privatization Rapid privatization methods implemented in Eastern Europe in the 1990s that involved giveaway schemes to the population or to managers and workers of state-owned enterprises.

Microcredit Small loans made available to poor households and villages. Microcredit does not require collateral, but instead uses peer pressure from the local community to enforce loan repayment.

Microfinance Institutional innovation that has emerged in developing economies in response to the pervasiveness of credit constraints faced by small firms and poor households. See *microcredit*.

Monopoly rents Extra profits derived from monopoly status.

Monopsonies Single buyers on a market, in contrast to monopolies that are single sellers.

Monsoon Seasonal reversal of winds accompanied by significant changes in precipitation characterized by heavy rains. Term used mostly in India and neighboring countries of South Asia.

Moral hazard Possibility of unobservable actions that one of the contracting parties (the agent) can take that will hurt the interest of the other contracting party (the principal).

Most favored nation clause Principle of international trade according to which if a country grants a favor to another country in terms of trade, it must extend that favor to all other countries. Also, once an imported good is on a domestic market, it must be treated in the same way as domestic products.

Multilateral trade negotiations Negotiation held between multiple countries simultaneously to reduce trade barriers between them. Multilateral trade negotiations have been an important feature of international trade since the end of World War II.

Multiple equilibria   Situation with multiple Nash equilibria that is present in coordination problems.

Nash equilibrium   Outcome in a game-theoretic situation in which each agent has chosen an action that is optimal given the action of the other agent. In other words, no player wants to deviate from his or her actions given the actions of the other.

National treatment clause   Rule of international trade that treats foreign goods as domestic goods and is designed to prevent nontariff barriers, for example the technical specifications for products, such as specific labeling, that are designed to protect domestic goods from competition by foreign goods.

Natural monopoly   Market with economies of scale that are so large there is only space for one firm.

Nazism   German totalitarian regime that began in 1933 under Adolph Hitler's leadership and was based on an ideology asserting the superiority of the Germanic races and the supremacy of the *Führer*, the leader. It lasted until 1945, when the combined Soviet and Western Allied forces defeated the Nazis at the end of World War II.

Net migration rate   The difference between the number of persons entering and leaving a country per 1,000 inhabitants.

Nondiscrimination   Principle of international trade according to which trade agreements between two countries may not lead to trade discrimination against a third country.

Nongovernmental organizations (NGOs)   Voluntary private associations pursuing nonprofit motives such as promoting health, education, or peace. They are mainly funded through gifts and grants.

Non-rival good   A good that can still be consumed by the seller after it is sold. Most normal economic goods are rival goods; once they are sold, the seller can no longer consume them.

Non-tradables   All goods in an economy that are not exported and imported.

Normal good   A good for which consumption increases as income increases.

Old-age dependency ratio   The ratio of the retired population above the age of 65 over the active population defined as those from ages 16 to 64.

Oligarchs   Refers to individuals in Russia and Eastern Europe who became immensely rich in a short period of time by gaining control over a large number of enterprises and wielding economic and political influence.

Operational sustainability   Ability of a firm to generate enough revenue to cover operating costs.

Opportunity cost   Cost of doing something instead of something else given available resources.

Panel regression   An econometric regression technique that analyzes data variation across space (countries or regions) and across time.

Parliamentary regime   Usually, a form of political democracy in which the executive branch is appointed by a parliamentary majority. In a parliamentary regime, the legislative branch can routinely vote down an executive for political reasons through a vote of no confidence.

Patronage   The creation of inefficient jobs or inefficient public spending activities as a way to buy votes.

Peg   See *Currency peg*.

Plan track   In the context of dual-track price liberalization, part of a firm's output is still produced and allocated within the central planning system.

Planning from the achieved level   Firms' plans under central planning were usually computed by taking the previous year's output as the initial level of production and then adding some growth rate to it.

Point-of-use water treatment   Methods for purifying water from wells or other untreated sources to make it safe and potable.

Political economy of trade liberalization   Political conflicts between sectors and firms that become winners and losers as a result of trade liberalization policies.

Population growth rate   The difference between the birth rate and the death rate (we divide the birth and death rates by 10 to get a percentage growth rate) adjusted for the net migration rate.

Poverty gap   The poverty gap counts people below the poverty line and weighs them according to their distance from the line so that poorer people have a higher weight than those closer to the poverty line.

Poverty headcount   The number of people in a given population who are below the poverty line.

Poverty headcount ratio   The proportion of the population that is below the poverty line.

Poverty line   The income required to purchase 2,000 calories of food, taking into account food habits and preferences. Those families or individuals with income below the poverty line are considered poor, whereas those with income above that line are not.

Poverty trap   A situation in which economic agents or a country cannot escape poverty due to a lack of resources that could otherwise be invested as a means to grow out of poverty.

Prebisch-Singer hypothesis   Hypothesis that states that countries specializing in exports of primary commodities (raw materials, agricultural products) are doomed to experience a decline in their terms of trade. It is based on the idea that as the world economy develops, demand for primary commodities will fall behind the demand for manufactured goods.

Presidential regime   Usually, a form of political democracy in which the president, who heads the executive branch, is directly elected by voters.

Price ratio   Ratio between the prices of different goods.

Price signals   Information on prices that is the mechanism guiding coordination between supply and demand.

Primary commodities   Goods that have not yet undergone industrial processing: raw materials, agricultural products, and unprocessed goods in general.

Primogeniture   Inheritance rule whereby the oldest son inherits the business (or land) of his father.

Prisoner's dilemma   A situation in which two suspects have been arrested by the police and are interrogated in an attempt to extract confessions to a joint crime. Each prisoner is in a separate cell and cannot communicate with the other. They face a cooperation problem and each prefers to confess individually whereas they would both be better off if neither confessed.

Privatization   The transfer of firm ownership from the state sector to the private sector.

Production function   A mathematical expression of the joint effect of the factors of production on output. Call K_t the stock of capital in the economy during year t, call L_t the amount of labor, and call Y_t output in the economy. The production function is: $Y_t = F(K_t, L_t)$.

Production possibility frontier   The maximum that can be produced of one good for a given quantity produced of another good.

Progressive lending   Usually present in the context of microcredit. The size of the loan a group receives can become larger over time as the group demonstrates its reliability when it pays back the original loan amount.

Proportional rule   Electoral rule in which the share of seats for the different parties is allocated proportionally to the share of votes parties receive.

Protectionism   Policies that put in place barriers to international trade in order to protect a country's domestic industries.

Public offering   Floating (or sale) of a firm's shares on the stock market.

Purchasing power parity (PPP)   Purchasing power parity is a principle used to calculate exchange rates between different currencies such that the same basket of goods in one country has the same dollar value in all countries.

Purchasing power parity (PPP) exchange rates   Exchange rates calculated on the basis of purchasing power parity.

Quantile measures   Division of a population into equal groups, ranking them according to a certain variable, usually income. Particular examples of quantiles are quartiles (4 groups), quintiles (5 groups), and deciles (10 groups).

Quantile ratio   Ratio of the average income in the highest quantile over the average income in the lowest quantile. For example, the ratio of the richest decile over the poorest decile measures the ratio of the average income of the top 10% of incomes over the average income of the bottom 10% of incomes.

Quantity signals   Coordination between supply and demand occurs within hierarchies through direct information on quantities available and needed.

Randomized evaluations   Evaluation of development programs involving randomized choice of program subjects/locations.

Ratchet effect The ratchet effect is an incentive problem that appears 1) when a principal and an agent are in a repeated relationship; 2) when there is asymmetric information about how productive the agent can be; and 3) when the principal cannot commit to a pre-established incentive scheme. In this case, the principal cannot commit not to exploit the information learned after the first period about the agent's type. This absence of commitment is not good because it induces the worker to hide capacity.

Rating agencies Agencies that rate the quality of firms, lenders, or borrowers.

Ration credit See *credit rationed*.

Reciprocity Rule of international trade according to which if a country reduces its trade barriers, other countries must reciprocate. In other words, concessions from one country must be matched by concessions from others.

Regional trade agreements Multilateral trade agreements between a subset of countries in the world.

Regulation of access or entry Rules that govern entry into and the practice of a profession, and require a candidate to earn a qualified diploma or pass an exam as a means to screen out unqualified people.

Regulatory barriers Domestic regulations that have the effect of limiting imports. For example, specifications for product standards can be deliberately established or modified to favor domestic producers or to hurt foreign producers.

Regulatory capture Situation in which the regulators, who are supposed to monitor a private firm in the public interest, are "captured" by that firm.

Relational contracting Describes a situation in which institutions are weak and firms tend not to trust businesses they do not know well, preferring to maintain trusted business relationships.

Relationship specific Describes a situation in which an investment only has value in the context of a specific partnership with another firm.

Relative factor endowments See *factor abundance*.

Rent-seeking Trying to influence politicians in order to obtain economic favors.

Rents Return in excess of a normal market return under competitive conditions.

Residual return The return that is left from an investment after all the costs, including labor costs and rental costs of capital, have been paid.

Return policies Policies that allow a buyer to bring purchased goods back to the seller within a specified time after their purchase.

Returns to education Return on the investment in the education of an individual; it is related to the theory of human capital.

Risk averse Describes the risk preferences of an individual who puts less weight on the upside payoff than on the downside payoff for given probabilities.

Risk neutral Describes the risk preferences of an individual who values upside and downside payoffs equally and weighs them according to their probability.

Risk-free rate of interest Rate of interest on bonds with no expectation of default. Typically, the risk-free rate of interest is calculated by taking an average of rates on U.S. Treasury bills.

Rotating savings and credit associations (ROSCAs) Credit institutions in developing countries in which a group of people, usually women, decide to save money together and then lend to the different group members on a rotating basis: one individual receives a loan from the group first; after repayment of the first loan, a second individual receives a loan, and so on. An individual's place in the rotation scheme is often chosen at random.

Search frictions Situation in which buyers and sellers on markets, or investors and entrepreneurs in need of finance, do not find each other immediately and must incur search costs before finding the right partner.

Secondary school enrollment rates The number of pupils enrolled in secondary school as a ratio of the population in the theoretical age group for secondary education.

Sectoral composition The weight of each sector in the economy's total output, i.e., the weight of agriculture, the steel industry, the textile industry, etc.

Sectoral growth The expansion of specific sectors of the economy.

Secularization hypothesis Hypothesis that states as countries become richer, the influence of religion in society declines.

Selection bias   Problem in statistical and econometric analysis when the "treatment" variable does not have similar characteristics to the nontreated or "control" variables. For example, if firms being privatized are more profitable than firms not being privatized, then a regression of profits on privatization might attribute a higher profit to privatization itself when, in fact, the effect is actually because the most profitable firms were selected for privatization.

Sellers' markets   Markets with excess demand: sellers have all the bargaining power as buyers are competing for their scarce products.

Separation of ownership and control   Situation where the owners of a firm are not directly overseeing its activities and use professional managers for that purpose.

Sequential transactions   Transactions that do not take place at the same time but rather in a certain order.

Serially correlated   Describes a variable whose realization in the past, present, and future profits is correlated.

Shortage   A situation in which demand exceeds supply.

Signaling   An economic term that means taking certain actions to provide other parties in a transaction with credible information.

Sin of usury   Centuries-old prohibition by the Catholic Church that prevented its members from charging interest on a loan, claiming the practice was a sin.

Social norms (conventions)   Norms of behavior that are expected from individuals and to which they are supposed to conform. Social norms are enforced through peer pressure.

Soft-budget constraint   A term coined by Janos Kornai to describe agents (or firms) that expect to be bailed out or refinanced if they incur losses.

Specialization   Concentration of resources on some sectors or activities as opposed to diversification of resources.

Stationary population   A population that does not grow over time.

Steady state   A situation in which an economic variable remains constant over time.

Strategic default   A situation in which the borrower is able to fulfill his debt obligations but decides not to.

Structural change   A situation in which some sectors in an economy expand while others shrink.

Sunk cost   A cost that cannot be recovered once it has been incurred.

Supply multiplier   Economic mechanism in the planned economy related to shortage. Higher shortages tend to dull worker incentives because they will not be able to use all the extra money earned to buy goods and services. This results in a reduction in their productivity, which then would lead to a lower supply of goods and, in turn increases in shortages.

Survey   A sampling of data based on questionnaires addressed to a limited but representative subset of the population to be assessed.

Tax base   The base to which tax rates apply. For example, total income is the tax base for income taxes.

Tax distortions   Change in allocative decisions brought about by taxation. See *distortionary*.

Terms of trade   A country's terms of trade measure the evolution of the prices of its exports relative to the prices of its imports.

Theory of comparative advantage   Theory developed by economist David Ricardo (1772–1823). It explains that countries gain from specializing in sectors for which they have a comparative advantage.

Time inconsistency   Circumstance that occurs when the optimal choice for one of the contracting parties at one point in time is no longer optimal at a later stage.

Total factor productivity   The part of output that labor and capital productivity cannot explain. It is usually thought to be the result of technological progress.

Total fertility rate   The average number of children born to a woman of childbearing age.

Totalitarian   Describes a dictatorial regime that seeks to influence and control all aspects of citizens' lives.

Trade convertibility   Also called current account convertibility, it means that importers and exporters are free from restrictions on exchanging the proceeds of trade from one currency into another.

Trade diversion   Trade flows between countries that would not take place under full multilateral liberalization.

Trade openness   Economic concept related to how open a country's economy is to international trade. It is measured by the share of exports (or by the average of exports and imports) in GDP.

Trade shares   The trade share of a region (or sector) represents the share of that region's (sector's) exports as a percentage of total world exports. A region's (sector's) increasing trade share means that it has had faster export growth than that of the rest of the world.

Transaction costs   Costs associated to simple transactions such as buying or selling merchandise, borrowing money, or investing in a business.

Unbalanced growth   A growth process in which sectors grow at different rates.

Universal bank   A financial institution that both lends money to firms and also holds equity in industrial enterprises.

Urbanization rate   The percentage of a country's population living in urban areas as opposed to rural areas.

Value added   The value of output minus the value of inputs used in production.

Value-added tax (VAT)   Tax that is only levied on the value added of a product. In other words, the value of the purchased inputs is deducted from the sales figure.

Values   What people consider important in and give meaning to their lives. Values, derived usually from existing religious and philosophical beliefs, determine social norms in society.

Vertical integration   A situation in which two firms working together as supplier and client merge into a single firm.

Voluntary export restraints   Voluntary and unilateral decisions to limit exports to a certain country, usually out of fear of being hit by import quotas from that country to which its goods are exported.

Warranty   Obligation by a seller to guarantee the quality of a product. It can involve a return policy if the product's quality is inadequate.

Yardstick competition   Competition between agents for the highest ranking on some common measure of performance. Some incentive schemes are associated with such a ranking.

Zamindari   Intermediaries in India under British colonial rule who collected tax revenues for the British and extracted large rents from tenants for their own enrichment.

Index

Numbers

1-dollar-a-day poverty standard, of World Bank, 35–36

A

Accountability of leadership, in autocracies and democracies, 241

Accounting, growth accounting, 87–88

Acemoglu, Daron, 105–108, 255–257, 260, 445–446

acquired immunodeficiency syndrome. See AIDS (acquired immunodeficiency syndrome)

Ades, Alberto, 522

Administrative constraints, comparing taxation in developed and developing countries, 283–284

Advanced economies. See Developed countries; OECD high income countries

Adversarial system, common-law system as, 266

Adverse selection
  compared with moral hazard, 398
  credit rationing and, 398–400
  as informational problem, 179–180, 396

Africa. See also MENA (Middle East and North Africa); Sub-Saharan Africa
  anticolonial movement in, 259
  communal ownership of land in, 324–325
  conflicts affecting economic growth, 552
  development gap, 3
  economic growth, 16–17
  education gap, 10
  GDP per capita, 4–5
  gender biases, 72
  geography and growth in, 104
  growth rate in, 59–60
  HIV prevalence in, 430
  income inequalities changing over time, 52–53
  land ownership in, 316
  land reform examples, 331–333
  life expectancy, 7–8
  monopsonies common in, 378
  population growth, 56–57
  poverty gap, 6–7
  privatization in, 360
  right-wing dictatorships, 251
  ROSCAs (rotating savings and credit associations), 413–414
  sex ratio in, 71
  tuberculosis in, 440–441
  urbanization rate, 11
  values regarding corruption and trust, 291
  values regarding economic interventionism, 290
  values regarding thrift and work, 292

Age distribution, of population
  demographic trends and, 62–63
  effect of, 61–62
  growth rates and, 60
  population growth and, 74

Age-specific fertility rates, 60

Age-specific mortality rates, 60

Aghion, Philippe, 97

Agricultural economy, transition to industrial economy, 114

AIDS (acquired immunodeficiency syndrome). See also HIV (human immunodeficiency virus)
  life expectancy in Africa and, 7–8
  overview of, 429–431

Aker, Jenny, 382–383

Akerlof, George, 179–180

Aleem, Irfan, 403

Allende, Salvador, 251, 334, 353

Andres, Luis, 502–503

Andvig, Jens, 529

Angrist, Joshua, 479

Annan, Jeannie, 558–559

Anocracy, instability causing move between democracy and autocracy, 545

Anthropometric measures, of health, 426–427

Antibiotics, in epidemiological transition, 423–424

Anticorruption campaigns, 527, 529

Antivirals, in epidemiological transition, 423

Aquinas, Saint Thomas, 304–305

Arab Caliphate, 23–24

Arab Spring, 344

Árbenz, Jacobo, 334

Argentina
  currency board, 170–171
  economic decline of, 4, 22–23

Asia. See also Central Asia; East Asia; South Asia
  anticolonial movement, 259
  Communist regimes following World War II, 249
  development gap, 3
  economic growth, 14–15
  education gap, 10
  GDP per capita, 4–5
  geography and growth in, 104
  growth rate, 59–60
  HIV prevalence, 430
  income inequalities changing over time, 50–53
  income inequality and economic growth and, 49
  land ownership, 316
  life expectancy, 8
  population growth, 56–57
  poverty gap, 6–7
  privatization in, 359–360
  right-wing dictatorships, 251
  ROSCAs (rotating savings and credit associations),
    413–414
  savings impacting steady state, 94
  sex ratio in, 71–72
  tuberculosis in, 440–441
  urbanization rate, 11–12
Asian growth miracle
  export promotion and, 135–138
  savings and investment and, 94
Asian tigers
  developing economies, 15
  from nationalization to privatization, 352–353
Asset giveaway
  mass privatization via, 360
  as privatization method, 357
Asset specificity, hold-up problem and, 186
Asymmetric information
  adverse selection, 179–180, 396
  informal solutions, 183–185
  as informational problem, 179
  institutional solutions, 181–183
  moral hazard, 180, 396
  reasons for conflicts, 539–540
Atomic bomb, long-term effects of Hiroshima and
    Nagasaki, 553–554
Auctions, privatization methods, 356–357
Australia
  values regarding corruption and trust, 291
  values regarding economic interventionism, 290
  values regarding thrift and work, 292
Autocracies. See also Political institutions
  anocracy as swing between democracy and
    autocracy, 545
  Communist regimes, 249–250
  defined, 233
  famines and, 390
  Nazi and Fascist regimes, 250
  Polity IV database of, 234–235
  right-wing dictatorships, 251
  theory of, 236–237
  vs. democracy, 240–243
Automatic stay on assets, creditor rights and, 270
Autonomy, norms of governance and, 300–301
Average labor productivity, 85

B

Backward linkages, sectoral growth strategy, 129–130
Balanced growth, sectoral growth strategy, 128–130
Baland, Jean-Marie, 471
Banerjee, Abhijit, 336, 337, 405–408, 418
Bangladesh
  credit needed for agricultural diversification, 394
  poverty gap and poverty headcount ratio in, 32–33
Bank runs, East Asia crisis (1997), 168
Banks
  benefits and trade-offs in use of, 285
  credit rationing by, 180, 399–400
  dealing with loan default, 403–404
  group lending, 409
  in microfinance, 415
  monitoring variation in interest rates, 402
  use of collateral to mitigate moral hazard, 400–401
Bardhan, Pranab, 504
Bargaining, corruption and efficiency of, 516
Barone, Enrico, 205
Barro, Robert J., 48, 254, 307, 459–460
Barter, in short-term adjustment to shortage, 216
Batista, Fulgencio, 546
Becker, Gary, 67–68
Becket, Thomas, 267
Beliefs. See also Social norms
  culture and, 288
  informal institutions based on, 177–178
Bellows, John, 558
Berndt, Ernst, 443–444
Besley, Timothy, 324–325, 335
Bettinger, Eric, 479
Bias, statistical
  from omitted variables, 570–571
  selection bias in, 568–569
Big push strategies
  coordination problem and, 196
  East Asia miracle as example of, 131–132
  overview of, 130–131
Bilateral trade negotiations, 161

Bill and Melinda Gates Foundation, 444
Binswanger, Hans, 329, 330, 333
Birth rates
    demographic transition and, 58
    population growth and, 60–61
Bivariate regression analysis, 565–567
Black Death, 430–431
Black-market transactions, 216
Blanchard, Olivier J., 373
Blattman, Christopher, 558–559
Bleakley, Hoyt, 434
BMI (body-mass index), 426–427
Bobonis, Gustavo, 440
Body-mass index (BMI), 426–427
Boundless knowledge-based growth, 97–98
Boys. See Men
Branding (brand recognition), institutional solutions
        to informational problems, 182–183
Brazil. See also Latin America & Caribbean, 4–5
Bribes. See also Corruption
    centralized vs. decentralized political systems and,
        521–522
    corruption in health care sector, 448
    in Corruption Perception Index, 513
    culture and acceptability of, 518–519
    frequent flyer programs as, 523
    greasing the wheels of development, 515–516
    objective measures of corruption and, 511
    from Peru's Fujimori government, 512
    winning contracts via, 509
Bright-line rules, in civil law system, 265
Burgess, Robin, 335
Business International Corporation, 271
Business networks
    importance of long-term relationships in
        developing countries, 370–371
    as solution to monopsony problem, 379
Business start-up costs, by region, 345
Byzantine Empire, 24

C

Calderón, Felipe, 497
Calorie counting, as measure of poverty, 29
Campaign contributions, corruption and, 510
Canada. See also North America
Canada, urbanization rate in, 11
Capital
    accumulation in modern sector of economy (Lewis
        model), 117
    average and marginal productivity of, 85
    capital mobility restrictions by governments, 167

cost of, 499–501
    diminishing marginal productivity, 86
    as factor of production, 83
    factor shares, 86
    growth rate of, 88
    human capital, 95
    scarcity of capital in developing countries, 120
Capital account convertibility (financial
        convertibility), 166
Capital flight, investing worldwide vs. locally, 122
Capital intensity
    labor productivity as function of, 85
    in Solow growth model, 89
    technological progress and, 93
Capitalism
    falling output in transition to, 372–374
    transitioning from socialism to, 367–368
Cárdenas, Lázaro, 331
Caribbean. See Latin America & Caribbean
Caste system, in India
    impact on education, 473–476
    impact on health care, 451–452
Castro, Fidel, 249
Catholicism, religious taboos on interest, 304–305
Causal inference
    bias from omitted variables, 570–571
    fixed effects and difference-in-differences
        estimation, 572–574
    instrumental variables, 574–577
    ordinary least squares and, 569–570
    overview of, 567–568
    panel regression, 571–572
    randomized evaluations, 569
    regression table analysis, 577–579
    treatment effect and selection bias, 568–569
Cell phones, improving market integration, 383
Central America, forms of land ownership in, 316
Central Asia. See also Asia
    business start-up costs, 345
    education and income inequality, 45
    education gap, 10, 457–460
    geography and growth in, 104
    Gini coefficient indicating income inequalities,
        43–44
    life expectancy, 7–8
    population growth, 16–17
    poverty in, 38
    secondary school enrollment, 10
    trade share of, 147
Central Europe. See also Europe
    central planning experiment, 208
    effects of institutions on property rights, 347–349

Central Europe (*continued*)
   income inequalities changing over time, 50
   output falling in transition to capitalism, 372–374
   privatization in, 360–363
   property rights, investment and market
      development, 349–352
Central planning
   complexity, coordination, and slow demise of,
      222–224
   debate regarding, 204–205
   experiment in Soviet Union, Central Europe, and
      China, 208
   Hayek's critique of, 207–208
   as hierarchical approach to economic coordination,
      203–204
   hoarding demand creates shortages, 217–218
   Lange rebutting argument against central
      planning, 206–207
   long-term adjustments to shortages, 218–219
   managerial incentives, 208
   medium-term adjustments to shortages, 216–218
   plan-fulfillment bonus system, 208–209
   ratchet effect, 210–211
   review and key terms, 230–231
   short-term adjustments to shortages, 215–216
   shortages and, 213–215
   soft-budget constraint, 211–213
   success indicator problem in, 209
   theoretical argument against, 205–206
   wage setting and wage drift, 221–222
   worker behavior, 220–222
Chavez, Hugo, 203, 335
Chen, Shaohua, 36–38
Children
   consequences of child soldiers, 558–559
   effects of ban on child labor, 471–472
   infant mortality. See Infant mortality
   population growth and. See Fertility rates
   reasons for child labor, 470–471
   shift in cost of raising, 64–65
   traditional role as insurance policy for elderly,
      69–70
China. See also Asia
   agricultural to industrial transition, 114–115
   central planning experiment in, 208
   Communist regime following World War II, 249
   comparative advantage example, 151–153
   Cultural Revolution as example of totalitarianism,
      250
   dual-track liberalization in, 374–375
   economic catch-up, 18

   economic decline in history of, 21–22
   economic development in, 3
   economic growth of, 14
   family planning in, 76
   famine (1959–1961) in, 388
   gender biases impacting male to female population
      ratio, 72
   income inequalities changing over time, 50–53
   institutional strength, 139
   life expectancy, 8
   old-age dependency ratio, 75–76
   population growth, 16
   regulatory obstacles to market integration, 386
   road construction in, 84
   role in reduction of poverty in East Asia and
      Pacific, 37
   savings and investment in, 94, 288
   Three Gorges Dam project, 494
   transportation improvements support market
      integration, 384–386
   urban migration impacting development, 121–122
   urban migration policies, 127
   urbanization rate, 12
   worker output compared with U.S., 102–103
Chinese Revolution (1949), 330–331
cif/fob ratio, IMF (International Monetary Fund),
     501–502
Cities, size in developing countries, 12
Civil law systems
   comparing with common-law, 265–268
   controversies regarding, 272–275
   countries using, 264–265
   creditor rights, 269–271
   historical origins, 267
   law enforcement quality, 271–272
   shareholder protections, 268–269
   as type of legal systems, 177
Civil servants, increasing pay as means of reducing
     corruption, 528
Civil society, democratization and, 261, 297–299
Civil wars
   greed vs. grievance as motives for, 545–549
   Nepal example, 548–550
   reasons for, 542–545
   Sierra Leone example, 557
Classrooms, reducing costs of education, 481
Clientism
   compared with corruption, 510
   politics of white elephant investments, 498
Coase, Ronald, 200, 229, 516
Coasian bargaining, 516

Cobb-Douglas production function
    calculating factor shares, 87
    expressing effect on output, 84–85
    in growth accounting, 87–88
Coffee, example of export price risk, 154–155
Cohen, Jessica, 437–440
Cold War, 554
Collateral
    "emergency funds" as, 413
    microfinance based on peer pressure instead of
        collateral, 395
    in mitigation of moral hazard, 400–401
Collective-action problem
    democracy and, 194, 241–242
    fighting corruption and, 528
    institutional solutions to preservation of commons,
        194
    Olson's role in developing concept of, 200
    prisoner's dilemma illustrating, 192–193
    privatization goals and problems, 354
Collectivism
    contract enforcement and, 302–303
    egalitarian norms and, 303–304
Collier, Paul, 545–548
Colombia. See also Latin America & Caribbean
    civil war in, 537
    export price risk related to coffee, 154–155
Colonialism
    correlation between institutions and growth and,
        108
    democracy and decolonialization, 259
    famines and, 390
Commitment problem
    comparing autocracies and democracies, 243
    consequences of lack of commitment, 188
    default due to, 403
    informal solutions, 189
    institutional solutions, 188–189
    negotiation breakdown caused by lack of
        commitment, 540–541
    overview of, 187–188
    prisoner's dilemma as, 190–193
Commitment, to caring for elderly, 70–71
Commodities
    developing countries specializing in export of
        primary commodities, 148
    income-elasticity of demand, 134–135
Commodities, exporting primary, 133
Common law systems
    comparing with civil-law, 265–268
    controversies regarding, 272–275

countries using, 264–265
creditor rights, 269–271
historical origins, 267
law enforcement quality, 271–272
shareholder protections, 268–269
types of legal systems, 177
Commons
    institutional solutions to preservation of, 194
    tragedy of overexploitation and failure of
        cooperation, 192
Commons, John R., 200
Communal ownership
    adverse effects on investment, 312
    economic properties of, 318
    ejido system, 331–332
    patterns of land ownership in Africa, 312
    properties of land contracts, 323
    as type of land ownership and tenancy, 316
    vs. private ownership, 324–326
Communication
    obstacles to market integration, 382–383
    problems of market development in poor
        countries, 368
Communist regimes. See also Central planning
    famines and, 388, 390
    from nationalization to privatization, 352–353
    overview of, 249–250
Comparative advantage
    advantages of specialization, 150–151
    examples, 151–152
    export price risk and, 154–156
    factor endowments as basis for specialization,
        152–153
    patterns of trade explained by, 154
    theory of comparative advantage (Ricardo),
        148–150
Comparative economics, 208
Competition, solutions to monopsony problem,
    379–380
Complementarities, between economic sectors,
    130–131
Conditional expectation, in statistical analysis, 563
Conflict
    child soldiers, 558–559
    development and, 550–551
    economic effects of, 551–552
    empirical causes, 541–542
    failure to negotiate a deal, 540–541
    greed vs. grievance as motives, 545–549
    informational asymmetries causing, 539–540
    long-term economic effects, 552–553

Conflict (*continued*)
  long-term effects of bombing Vietnam, 555–558
  long-term effects of Hiroshima and Nagasaki, 553–554
  overview of, 537–538
  reasons for civil wars, 542–545
  review and key terms, 559–560
  Sierra Leone example of civil war, 557
  theoretical explanations of, 538–539
Congestion effect, negative externalities, 78
Congo. See also Africa
  GDP per capita, 4
  poverty gap and poverty headcount ratio in, 32–33
  war in, 537
Conspicuous consumption (Veblen), 199–200
Constant returns to scale, production function and, 84
Constitutional government, comparing autocracies and democracies, 243
Consumer goods, cost impacting fertility choices, 64–66
Contracts
  bribes and, 509
  corrupt contracts unenforceable in courts, 516
  hold-up problem and, 185–186
  labor contracts, 320–321
  land contracts. See Land contracts
  opportunistic renegotiation of, 503
  role of culture in enforcing, 301–303
  solutions to commitment problem, 188–189
  solutions to hold-up problem, 186, 229–230
Conventions. See also Social norms
  cultural, 198
  types of informal institutions, 177
Cooperation problem
  coordination problem compared with, 195–196
  informal solutions, 194–195
  institutional solutions, 193–194
  overview of, 190
  tragedy of commons and, 192
Coordination
  between economic sectors, 131
  markets and hierarchies in coordination of economic activity, 203–204
Coordination problem
  big push strategies and, 196
  cooperation problem compared with, 195–196
  informal solutions, 197–198
  institutional solutions, 197
  overview of, 195
  stag hunt game example, 197

Copenhagen Accord, 191
Corporate governance, 354
Corporatism, 250
Correlation coefficient, in measuring covariance, 565
Corrupt Practices Investigation Bureau (CPIB), 527
Corruption
  culture and social norms and, 523–525
  difficulty in fighting, 527–529
  disentangling causes of, 525–527
  infrastructure development and, 504–505
  legal institutions and, 522
  measuring, 510
  natural resources and trade and, 522–523
  objective measures, 511–512
  overview of, 508–509
  political institutions and, 520–522
  positive and negative relationships to development, 515–517
  reasons for differences by country, 518–519
  regulatory capture, 355
  relationship to development, 519–520
  relationship to growth, 517–518
  review and key terms, 530–531
  subjective measures, 513–515
  Transparency International Corruption Perception Index, 532–536
  Uganda example of corruption in education, 472–473
  what it is, 509–510
  World Values Survey (WVS), 290–291
Corruption, in health care sector
  bribes, 448
  informal payment to doctors, 450–451
  overpricing and kickbacks, 449–450
  theft, 448–449
Corruption Perception Index, of Transparency International, 513–515, 532–536
Cost of capital
  estimating infrastructure investments, 500–501
  overview of, 499–500
Cost of debt, 500
Cotton, example of U.S. protectionism, 160–161
Country premium, in determining cost of capital, 499
Covariance, between two variables, 564–565
CPIB (Corrupt Practices Investigation Bureau), 527
Credibility, consequences of lack of commitment, 188
Credit constrained firms, 406–408
Credit elasticity, 417
Credit markets
  adverse selection and credit rationing, 398–400
  constraints in developing countries, 404

default management, 403–404
demand for credit in developing economies, 395–396
difficulty of measuring credit constraints, 404–405
evaluating microfinance, 418–419
example of financing entrepreneur in Mumbai, 396–398
how microfinance works, 409–410
imperfections, 49–50
incentives in microfinance, 410–413
microfinance, 409
monitoring variation in interest rates, 402
moral hazard and collateral, 400–401
moral hazard and monitoring, 401–402
overview of, 394–395
priority lending program in India, 405–408
profitability of microfinance, 415–418
review and key terms, 419–421
theory of role in development, 396
types of microfinance, 413–415
Credit rationed firms, 406–407
Credit rationing
adverse selection and, 398–400
by banks, 180
measuring, 406
Creditor rights, 269–271
Criminal organizations, commitment problem and, 189
Cross-sectional analysis, of income inequality, 47–48
Cuba. See also Latin America & Caribbean, 249
Cultural Revolution, in China, 76
Culture
caring for elderly and, 70–71
contract enforcement and, 301–303
conventions and, 198
corruption and, 518–519, 523–525
effects on contemporary world, 306
effects on institutions, 297
egalitarian norms and development, 303–304
Hofstede's Index of individualism and collectivism, 294–297
human behavior and, 199–200
informal institutions based on, 177–178
Islam and inheritance laws, 305–306
measuring, 289
norms of governance and, 300
obstacles to economic development, 303
overview of, 288
pitfalls to avoid when researching, 309–310
quality of democracy and, 297–299
religion's effect on economic growth, 307–308
religious beliefs and trust, 308–309
religious taboos on interest, 304–305
review and key terms, 310–311
Schwartz's cultural mapping, 292–293
thrift and, 308–309
World Values Survey (WVS), 289–292
Currency board, Argentina, 170–171
Currency convertibility, 166–168
Czechoslovakia. See also Central Europe, 361–362

D

DALY (Disability Adjusted Life Year)
applied to development of drugs for developing countries, 444
as measure of health, 427–428
Dam projects, investing in, 494–497
Dantzig, George B., 206
Dasgupta, Amil, 402
Davis, Donald R., 554–555
DDT
alternatives to, 437
controversy regarding, 436–437
epidemiological transition and, 423–424
malaria eradication programs, 433–434
de Roover, Raymond, 304–305
de Soto, Hernando, 341, 343
de Tocqueville, Alexis, 299
Death rates, population growth and, 60–61
Debt burden, suicide of Indian farmers due to, 394
Debt premium, in determining cost of capital, 500
Decentralization
of infrastructure, 503–504
of school systems, 478–479
Decentralized political systems, variables in corruption, 521–522
Decreasing returns to scale, production function and, 84
Default
management, 403–404
reputation and, 413
Deininger, Klaus, 48, 330, 333
Demand. See Supply and demand
Democracies. See also Political institutions
anocracy as swing between democracy and autocracy, 545
civil society and democratic institutions, 297–299
collective-action problem, 194
commitment to redistribution in, 258–259
corruption and, 520
decentralization of power/authority in, 503–504
defined, 233

Democracies (*continued*)
  economic effects of democratic institutions,
      246–249
  education in, 255–256
  electoral rules in, 245–246
  famines in, 390
  Freedom House criteria for, 233–234
  income and, 254–255
  income inequality and democratization, 260–262
  inequality and social conflict in, 257–258
  political institutions of, 176–177
  Polity IV database of, 234–235
  presidential and parliamentary types, 244–245
  revolutionary threats and democratization process,
      259–260
  separation of powers, 244
  theories of democratization, 254
  theory of democracy, 237–240
  vs. autocracy, 240–243
  waves of democratization, 251–253
Democratic Republic of Congo. See Congo
Democratization
  revolutionary threats and, 259–260
  theories of, 254
  waves of, 251–253
Demographic transition
  fertility rates and, 73–76
  growth rate and, 58–59
  overview of, 56
Demographic trends, stationary population, 62–63
Devaluation of currency, by fixed-rate regime, 171
Developed countries. See also OECD high income
      countries
  age distribution in, 61–62
  demographic transition in, 73
  development gap and, 3
  factor abundance in, 83
  land ownership inequality and, 314–315
  relative absence of conflict in, 538
  taxation compared with developing countries,
      275–279, 283–285
  trade openness in, 146
Developing countries
  age distribution in, 61–62
  city size in, 12
  composition of exports, 149
  credit constraints in, 404
  demand for credit in, 395–396
  demographic transition in, 74
  development gap and, 3
  diseases in. See Diseases, in developing countries
  evolution of development gap, 13–14

  exchange-rate policies, 165–166
  factor abundance in, 83
  family planning in, 76
  famines and, 388
  fixed vs. floating exchange rates in, 170–171
  infrastructure in, 486
  monopsonies in, 378–379
  pegging currency to currency of major country,
      169–170
  population growth, 55
  prevalence of conflicts in, 537
  privatization methods in, 356–357
  problems with market development in poor
      countries, 368–370
  right-wing dictatorships, 251
  scarcity of capital in, 120
  shift from industrial to service economy, 114
  specialization of trade in, 148
  taxation compared with developed countries,
      283–285
  taxation in, 275–279
  terms of trade for, 133
  trade openness in, 146
Development banks, in East Asia, 131
Development gap
  defined, 3
  economic decline and, 21–24
  economic growth and, 14–16
  education gap, 10–11
  evolution of, 13–14
  health gap, 7–9
  history of catch-up in Japan and Germany, 18–21
  important questions regarding, 24–25
  income gap, 4–6
  overview of, 1–4
  population growth and, 16–17
  poverty gap, 6–7
  reasons for, 13
  review and key terms, 25–26
  urbanization gap, 11–13
Di Tella, Rafael, 449–450, 511, 522, 528
Diarrheal diseases
  overview of, 432–433
  prevalence of, 429
Dictatorships
  military dictatorships overthrowing
      democracies, 260
  political institutions of, 176–177
  right-wing dictatorships, 250–251
Difference-in-differences estimation
  estimating returns to education, 468
  estimating using panel regression, 573–574

Diminishing marginal productivity
  factor productivity, 86
  in Solow growth model, 89–90
Diplomacy, informational asymmetries causing
    failure of, 539–540
Diplomatic immunity, social norms and, 525–526
Direct sales, as privatization method, 356
Directly Observed Treatment Short (DOTS) course,
    WHO program for TB, 429
Disability Adjusted Life Year (DALY)
  applied to development of drugs for developing
      countries, 444
  as measure of health, 427–428
Disaster response, political institutions and, 232
Disclosure rules, institutional solutions to
    informational problems, 181
Diseases, in developing countries
  diarrheal diseases, 432–433
  HIV, 429–431
  malaria, 433–437
  overview of, 428–429
  tuberculosis, 440–441
  worms, 437–440
Dispersed ownership, privatization goals and
    problems, 354
Distortionary effects, of taxes, 280–282
District magnitude, measuring proportionality in
    electoral rules, 246
Divided government, in presidential regimes, 245
Do, Quy-Toan, 548
Dominant strategy, in game theory, 190
Donaldson, Dave, 491–494
DOTS (Directly Observed Treatment Short) course,
    WHO program for TB, 429
"Drug leakage," theft as corruption in health care
    sector, 448
Drug therapies
  issues in R&D of drugs for developing countries,
      442–444
  for treating worms, 438
Dual-track price liberalization
  in China, 374–375
  lessons regarding market development, 376
Duflo, Esther, 405–408, 418, 468–469, 476, 495–497
Dupas, Pascaline, 437–440

E

East Asia. See also Asia
  business start-up costs, 345
  development banks in, 131
  economic growth and, 14, 17

  education and income inequality, 45
  education gap and, 10, 457–460
  export promotion in, 138
  Gini coefficient indicating income inequalities,
      43–44
  infant mortality rates in, 9
  land ownership inequality and, 314
  land reform in, 332
  life expectancy in, 7–8
  reduction of poverty in, 37
  secondary school enrollment, 10
  trade share increasing, 147
  values regarding corruption and trust, 291
  values regarding economic interventionism, 290
  values regarding thrift and work, 292
East Asia crisis (1997), 167–168
East Europe. See also Europe; Russia
  business start-up costs, 345
  changes in income inequalities over time, 50
  Communist regimes following World War II, 249
  development gap with richer economies, 3
  effects of institutions on property rights, 347–349
  falling output in transition to capitalism, 372–374
  GDP per capita, 4–5
  privatization in, 360–363
  property rights, investment and market
      development, 349–352
  trade share of, 147
Easterly, William, 139–141, 508
Ebenstein, Avraham, 72
Echeverria, Luis, 331
Economic decline
  Argentina, 4
  development gap and, 21–24
Economic development
  comparing autocracies and democracies, 241
  conflict and, 550–551
  corruption and, 515–517, 519–520
  economic growth compared with, 82
  effects of investment on, 489
  egalitarian norms and, 303–304
  markets and hierarchies in coordination of, 203–204
  obstacles to, 303
Economic effects
  of democratic institutions, 246–249
  of legal institutions, 268
Economic effects, of conflict
  long-term, 552–553
  long-term effects of bombing Vietnam, 554–557
  long-term effects of Hiroshima and Nagasaki,
      553–554
  overview of, 551–552

Economic growth
   boundless knowledge-based growth, 97–98
   causal effect of institutions on growth, 108–111
   corruption and, 517–518
   development gap and, 14–16
   effect of conflict on economic growth in Africa, 552
   effects of investment of, 490–491
   effects of land reform on, 335–336
   empirical analysis of, 102–103
   endogenous growth theory, 97
   equilibrium in Solow growth model, 90–91
   factor productivity, 85–86
   factor shares, 86–87
   factors of production, 83–84
   geography and, 104–105
   growth accounting, 87–88
   human capital and, 95
   income convergence, 96–97
   and income inequality, 49
   institutions and, 105–108
   knowledge as non-rival good, 98–99
   overview of, 82
   production function, 84–85
   property rights protection, 101–102
   religion's effect on, 307–308
   returns to scale and diminishing marginal products, 89–90
   review and key terms, 111–112
   Romer model, 100–101
   savings rates and, 94
   Solow growth model, 88
   steady state, 91–92
   technological progress and steady state, 93
Economic interventionism, WVS and, 290
Economic systems analysis, 208
Economics
   family planning and, 78–79
   of fertility choices, 63–64
Economies
   advanced. See Developed countries
   developing. See Developing countries
Economies of scale
   in court role in market development, 368
   wage laborers and, 321
Educacion con Participacion de la Comunidad (EDUCO), 478–479
Education
   caste system in India and, 473–476
   child labor and, 470–472
   comparing measures of achievement, 459–464
   corruption example, 511
   decentralizing school systems, 478–479

   democracies and, 255–256
   education gap, 10–11
   effect of migration on rural education, 126–127
   externalities of, 465–466
   gender gap, 458–459
   government role in, 466–467
   incentives for teacher effectiveness, 477–478
   income inequality and, 44–45
   institutions and, 470
   measuring education gap, 456
   overview of, 455–456
   primary school gap, 456–458
   reducing costs of, 480–481
   reducing gender gap, 481–482
   reducing teacher absenteeism, 476–477
   reforms, 476
   returns to education, 464–465, 467–470
   review and key terms, 482–484
   secondary school gap, 458
   voucher programs, 479–480
EDUCO (Educacion con Participacion de la Comunidad), 478–479
Egalitarian norms, economic development and, 303–304
Egypt. See also MENA (Middle East and North Africa), 24
Ejido system, land reform and, 331–332
Elderly
   population growth and aging populations, 74
   traditional role of children as insurance policy for, 69–70
Electoral rules
   in democracies, 245–246
   variables in corruption, 520–521
Electricity, infrastructure gap and, 487–489
Embeddedness, norms of governance and, 300–301
"Emergency funds," as collateral, 413
Emigration, negative externalities, 78–79
Encomienda system, of land ownership in Latin America, 321, 330
Endogenous growth theory
   boundless knowledge-based growth, 97–98
   intellectual property rights and technology transfers, 101–102
   knowledge as non-rival good, 98–99
   overview of, 97
   Romer model, 100–101
Energy, cost of capital for infrastructure sectors, 500
Engerman, Stanley L., 327–328
Enrollment rates
   primary school, 457
   secondary school, 10–11

Entitlement sets, in Sen's analysis of famine, 388–389
Environment
    controversy regarding use of DDT, 436–437
    cooperation problem in protection of, 191
    impact of dam projects on, 494
Epidemiological transition, 423–424
Equilibrium, in Solow growth model, 90–91
Equity premium, in determining cost of capital, 499
Esfahani, Hadi Salehi, 490
Esrey, S.A., 432
Estache, Antonio, 499–500
Ethnicity, insignificant variables in civil war, 545
EU (European Union), 193
Europe. See also Central Europe; East Europe
    development gap and, 3
    education and income inequality, 45
    education gap and, 10, 457–460
    evolution of trade specialization, 148–149
    GDP per capita, 4
    Gini coefficient indicating income inequalities, 43–44
    growth rate in, 59–60
    HIV prevalence in, 430
    income inequalities changing over time, 50
    infant mortality rates in, 9
    land ownership in, 316
    life expectancy in, 8
    population growth in, 16–17, 57–58
    poverty gap and, 7
    poverty in, 38
    secondary school enrollment, 10
    sex ratio in, 71
    trade share of, 147
    values regarding corruption and trust, 291
    values regarding economic interventionism, 290
    values regarding thrift and work, 292
Evans, Peter, 528
Exchange rates
    basing on PPP (purchasing power parity), 4–5
    currency convertibility options, 166–168
    fixed exchange rates, 168–169
    fixed vs. floating rates in developing countries, 170–171
    floating exchange rates, 169
    pegging currency of developing country to major currency, 169–170
    policies in developing countries, 165–166
    poverty line and, 33–34
Excludable goods, knowledge as, 98
Executive branch, separation of powers in democracy, 244
Expectation operators, in statistical analysis, 563

Expected payoff, in adverse selection example, 179–180
Export promotion. See also Import substitution vs. export promotion
    Asian miracle, 135–138
    institutions and, 138
    protectionism and, 137
    why it worked in East Asia, 138
Exports
    composition by developing countries, 149
    import quotas restricting, 159–160
    nontariff barriers to trade, 159–160
    price risk, 154–156
    primary commodities, 133
    trade openness as share of exports to GDP, 146
    voluntary restraints, 160
Expropriation risk
    correlation between institutions and growth, 106–107
    settler mortality correlated with, 109–111
Externalities
    definition of, 78
    of family planning, 78–79
    returns to education and, 465–466
Extractive (predatory) institutions, 108

F

Factors of production
    factor abundance, 83
    factor endowment as basis for specialization in trade, 152–153
    factor productivity, 85–86
    factor shares, 86–87
    production function expressing effect on output, 84–85
    technological progress and, 93
Fafchamps, Marcel, 368, 370
Fallowing method, for improving productivity of land, 325
Family planning
    externalities and economics of, 78–79
    policies, 77
Famines
    analysis of, 388
    democracy and, 390
    in North Korea, 390–391
    overview of, 388
Farmer ownership
    basic types of land ownership and tenancy, 316
    economic properties of, 317–318
    incentive effects, 321–323

Farmer ownership (*continued*)
    plantations compared with family-owned farms, 328–329
    sharecropping compared with, 326–327
    vs. communal ownership, 324–326
Fascist regimes, 250
Fearon, James, 542–545
Feder, Gershon, 330, 333
Federal political systems, variables in corruption, 521–522
Fertility rates
    commitment and cultural values impacting, 70–71
    demographic transition and, 73–76
    economics of fertility choices, 63–64
    financial security and, 70
    institutional factors in fertility choices, 69
    population growth and, 60–61
    shift in cost of consumer goods and, 64–66
    shift in cost of raising children and, 64–65
    shift in income and, 66–67
    shift in preferences and, 67–69
    social norms and gender biases impacting, 71–73
Field, Erica, 345–346
Financial convertibility (capital account convertibility), 166
Financial industrial groups, privatization in Russia and, 362
Financial markets
    in common-law and civil-law countries, 272
    development in 20th Century, 273
Financial repression, capital mobility restrictions by governments, 167
Financial sector, underdevelopment of, 284
Financial security, impact on fertility rates, 70
Financial sustainability, measuring profitability of microfinance, 416–417
FINCA (Foundation for International Community Assistance), 415
Firms
    transactions within (Coase), 200
    vertical integration vs. subcontractors, 228–229
Fiscal institutions
    comparing taxation in developed and developing countries, 283–285
    determinants of tax structure, 280–283
    overview of, 275
    review and key terms, 285–287
    taxation in developing countries, 275–279
    value-added taxes, 280
Fiscal policy, in presidential and parliamentary regimes, 246–249
Fisman, Raymond, 517, 525–526

Fixed effects, dealing with omitted variables in panel regression, 572–574
Fixed exchange rates
    overview of, 168–169
    vs. floating rates in developing countries, 170–171
Fixed land rental
    basic types of land ownership and tenancy, 316
    economic properties of, 318–319
    properties of land contracts, 323
    sharecropping compared with, 327
Fixed wages, labor contracts, 320–321
Floating exchange rates
    overview of, 169
    vs. fixed exchange rates in developing countries, 170–171
Focal point concept (Schelling), 197
Fogel, Robert W., 327–328
Food
    availability. See also Famines, 389
    impact of food prices on people living at or near poverty line, 30
    nutrient intake as measure of health, 425–426
Forced substitution, short-term adjustment to shortage, 215
Foreign aid
    conclusions regarding, 141
    controversy regarding, 139
    Sachs argument for, 140
    skeptical views on, 140–141
Formal institutions. See also Institutions
    interactions with informal institutions, 178
    legal. See Legal institutions
    obstacles to entry in formal sector, 343–345
    overview of, 176
    political. See Political institutions
Forward linkages, sectoral growth strategy, 130
Foundation for International Community Assistance (FINCA), 415
Fox, Vincente, 497
Franco, Francisco, 250
Free riding, collective-action failures and, 192–193
Freedom House, Political Rights index, 256
Freedom of the press, impact on corruption, 520
Fujimori, Alberto, 511–512
Functionalist fallacy, 198–199

G

Gabre-Madhin, Eleni, 368
Game theory
    coordination problem and, 195
    prisoner's dilemma and, 190

Gandhi, Indira, 76
GATT (General Agreement on Trade and Tariffs), 161
GDP (gross domestic product) per capita
    changes in income inequalities over time, 51
    comparing North and South Korea, 203
    comparing richest and poorest nations, 4–6
    correlation with education gap, 10
    global comparisons of annual growth rates, 14
    income convergence and, 96–97
    income inequality and economic growth and, 49
    Kuznets curve mapping, 47
    relationship to corruption, 519
    relationship to life expectancy, 445–446
    relationship to population, 16
    trade openness as share of exports to, 146
Gender biases, fertility choices and, 71–73
Gender gap
    measuring education gap, 458–459
    reforming education gap, 481–482
General Agreement on Trade and Tariffs (GATT), 161
Geography
    economic growth and, 104–105
    investing in infrastructure and, 501–502
    variables in likelihood of war, 543
Germany. See also Europe
    example of protecting infant industries, 135
    history of economic catch-up in, 19–21
Gerschenkron, Alexander, 20
Gertler, Paul, 336
Ghatak, Maitreesh, 336
Gift giving, social norms and, 524
Gini coefficient
    changes in income inequalities over time, 51–52
    income inequality and, 45–46
    land ownership inequality and, 45–46, 313–315
    in measuring income inequality, 40–42
    real-world examples, 42–44
Girls. See Women
Glennerster, Rachel, 418, 444
Glewwe, Paul, 477
Globalization, democratization and, 262
Goldschmidt, Chanan, 300
Goldstein, Markus, 325–326
Goods
    income-elasticity of demand, 134–135
    inferior and normal, 67
    knowledge as non-rival good, 98–99
Gordon, Roger, 284–285
Governance, measures of good, 300–301
Governments. See also Central planning
    role in coordination of economic activity, 203–204
    role in education, 466–467

role in infrastructure development, 488
spending in presidential and parliamentary
    regimes, 247–248
Western concept of rule of law and, 524
Grameen Bank, 395, 409
Gray-market transactions, short-term adjustment to
    shortage, 216
Great Depression, 206
Greed, causes of war, 545–549
Greif, Avner, 301–303
Grievance, causes of war, 545–549
Group lending
    borrowers self-sorting by risk groups, 412
    features of microfinance, 409
Group tax, forms of microfinance, 413
Growth accounting, production function in, 87–88
Growth rate of population, 58–60
Growth rate of total factor productivity, 88
Guasch, Jose Luis, 502–503
Guerilla forces, variables in likelihood of war, 543
Gugerty, Mary Kay, 479
Guiso, Luigi, 308
Gupta, Nandini, 363

H

Haciendas
    land ownership in Latin America, 321
    land reform and, 331
    obstacles to land reform, 333
Haiti. See also Latin America & Caribbean
    impact of changes in food prices on impoverished
        people, 30
    income inequalities in, 27
Ham, John, 363
Hand washing, in preventing diarrheal diseases, 432
Hanna, Rema, 476
Harris, John R., 123
Harris-Todaro model
    implications of, 126–127
    migration equilibrium in, 123–126
    of rural to urban migration, 123
Hay, Jonathan, 527
Hayek, Friedrich August, 207–208, 266
Health care delivery
    anthropometric measures of health, 426–427
    better health leading to higher income, 444–446
    corruption in health care sector, 448–451, 511
    DALY (Disability Adjusted Life Year) as measure of
        health, 427–428
    diarrheal diseases, 432–433
    diseases in developing countries, 428–429

Health care delivery (*continued*)
  drug therapies, 441–443
  epidemiological transition, 423–424
  higher income not necessarily creating better
     health, 446–447
  HIV, 429–431
  institutions in, 447
  malaria, 433–437
  measuring health, 424
  nutrient intake as measure of health, 425–426
  overview of, 422–423
  quality of health care system, 447–448
  review and key terms, 452–454
  self-reported health status, 424–425
  tuberculosis, 440–441
  vaccines, 443–444
  worms, 437–440
Health gap
  differences in infant mortality, 8–9
  differences in life expectancy, 7–8
  overview of, 7
Heckscher-Ohlin (neoclassical) theory of
     international trade, 152
Height, anthropometric measures of health,
     426–427
Heterogeneity, measuring effect of infrastructure
     investment on growth and, 490
Hierarchies
  central planning. See Central planning
  price signals vs. quantity signals, 224–228
  review and key terms, 230–231
  role in coordination of economic activity, 203–204
Hiroshima, 553–554
Hirschmann, Albert, 129
Hitler, Adolph, 250
HIV (human immunodeficiency virus)
  cost of medications for, 441
  issues in R&D of drugs for developing countries,
     442–444
  long-term effects of, 430–431
  overview of, 429–430
  prevalence of, 429
Hoarding, shortages created by, 217–218
Hoeffler, Anke, 545–548
Hofstede, Geert, 294–296
Hold-up problem
  informal solutions, 187
  institutional protections mitigating, 229–230
  institutional solutions, 186
  opportunistic renegotiation of contracts, 503
  overview of, 185–186

  rural markets and monopsony problem, 377–378
  Williamson's role in developing concept of, 200
Holmström, Bengt, 477–478
Honda Motors, 137
Honda, Soichiro, 137
"Household Responsibility System," China's urban
     migration policies, 127
Howitt, Peter, 97
Hsieh, Chang-Tai, 480, 511
Hukou, China's urban migration policies, 127
Human capital, in Solow growth model, 95
Human immunodeficiency virus. See HIV (human
     immunodeficiency virus)
Huntington, Samuel, 251
Hussein, Saddam, 511, 539–540
Hydroelectricity, China Three Gorges Dam project, 494
Hygiene, in disease prevention, 432–433

I

ICAC (Independent Commission Against
     Corruption), 527
ILO (International Labor Organization), 470
IMF (International Monetary Fund)
  cif/fob ratio, 501–502
  on currency convertibility, 166
  East Asia crisis (1997) and, 167–168
  on pegging currencies, 169
Import substitution vs. export promotion
  export promotion and the Asian miracle, 135–138
  industrialization and protection of infant
     industries, 134–135
  overview of, 132–133
  Prebisch-Singer hypothesis, 133–134
Imports
  import quotas, 159–160
  tariffs on, 158–159
Income
  better health leading to higher income, 444–446
  democracies and, 254–255
  GDP per capita as measure of, 4–5
  higher income not necessarily creating better
     health, 446–447
  positive impact of malaria eradication campaign
     on, 435–436
  relationship to fertility choices, 66–67
  relationship to likelihood of war, 543
Income convergence, in Solow growth model, 96–97
Income effect, cost of raising children and, 64
Income-elasticity of demand, for industrial goods vs.
     commodities, 134–135

Income gap, 4–6
Income inequality. See also Poverty
    comparing equal vs. unequal income distributions,
        40
    cross-sectional analysis of, 47–48
    democratization and, 260–262
    economic growth and, 49
    education and, 44–45
    Gini coefficient, 40–44
    increase/decrease over time, 50–53
    Kuznets hypothesis, 46–47
    land ownership and, 45–46
    linking democracy to, 257
    Lorenz curve, 39–40
    measuring, 38–39
    panel regression applied to analysis of, 48
    quantile measures of, 39
Income redistribution
    in democracies, 258–259
    median voter theorem and, 240
    politics and economics and, 50
Increasing returns to scale, production function and,
        84
Independent Commission Against Corruption
        (ICAC), 527
India. See also Asia
    anticolonial movement in, 259
    caste system impact on education, 473–476
    caste system impact on health care, 451–452
    cost/benefit analysis of dams, 495–497
    debt burden of farmers in, 394
    economic catch-up in, 18
    economic development in, 3
    family planning in, 76
    gender biases impacting male to female population
        ratio, 72
    import substitution, 136
    income inequalities changing over time, 52
    literacy in, 456
    population growth and, 16
    poverty in, 37–38
    priority lending program in, 405–408
    purchasing power of rupees, 4
    railroad construction impact on growth, 491–494
    regulatory obstacles to market integration,
        386–387
    shift from industrial to service economy, 114
    urbanization rate in, 12
Indifference curves, comparing preferences for
        consumption vs. children, 68–69
Indirect taxes, 280

Individualism
    contract enforcement and, 302–303
    egalitarian norms and, 303–304
    Hofstede's index of cultural values, 295–296
Industrial economy
    structural change across industrial sectors, 115
    transition from agricultural economy to, 114
    transition to service economy from, 114–115
Industrial frontier, 21
Industrial goods, income-elasticity of demand, 134–135
Industrialization (industrial revolution)
    development of German economy and, 19–20
    economic development and, 47
    growth rate and, 58
    population growth increasing during, 56
    protection of infant industries, 134–135
    urbanization and, 11
Inequality, in democracies, 257–258
Infant industries, protecting, 135
Infant mortality
    diarrheal diseases as major cause of, 432
    as indicator of health gap, 8–9
Inferior goods, supply and demand and, 67
Influence activities, problems arising from
        privatization policies, 355
Informal institutions
    compensating for weakness of formal institutions,
        368
    interactions with formal institutions, 178
    overview of, 177–178
    solutions to commitment problem, 189
    solutions to cooperation problem, 194–195
    solutions to coordination problem, 197
    solutions to hold-up problem, 187
    solutions to informational problems, 183–185
Informal sector, of economy
    hidden nature of, 285
    high transaction costs in, 342–343
    institutional obstacles to entry in formal sector,
        343–345
    institutional quality and, 347–349
    overview of, 121
    property rights and, 341–342
Informational intermediaries, 183
Informational problems
    adverse selection as, 179–181, 396
    informal solutions, 183–185
    institutional solutions, 181–183
    moral hazard as, 181, 396
    overview of, 179
    reasons for conflicts, 539–540

Infrastructure
    cost of capital, 499–501
    dam project investment, 494–497
    decentralization of, 503–504
    development effects of investment in, 489
    fighting corruption, 504–505
    geography and, 501–502
    inequality of access to, 486–487
    institutions and, 502
    institutions in provision of, 488–489
    investment effect on growth, 490–491
    investment risks, 499
    overview of, 485–486
    regulatory reforms and, 502–503
    review and key terms, 505–507
    state of in developing countries, 486
    transportation system investment, 491–494
    white elephant investments, 497–498
Infrastructure gap, 486–487
Inglehart, Ronald, 289
Inheritance laws
    in Islam, 305–306
    primogeniture, 306
Innovation, monopoly rents from, 99
Inquisitorial system, civil-law system as, 266
Institutions
    adverse selection as informational problem, 179–181
    causal effect on economic growth, 108–111
    commitment problem, 187–188
    cooperation problem, 190
    coordination problem, 195–196
    culture's effect on, 297
    definitions, 175–176
    economic growth and, 105–108
    educational, 470
    epidemiological transition and, 423
    export promotion by, 138–139
    extractive or predatory types, 108
    fast and slow rates of change in, 300
    fertility choices and, 69
    fiscal. See Fiscal institutions
    formal. See Formal institutions
    functionalist fallacy, 198–199
    health care delivery by, 447
    hold-up problem, 185–186
    inefficient institutions, 198
    informal. See Informal institutions
    informational problems, 179
    infrastructure development and, 488–489, 502
    interactions between, 178
    land inequalities and, 329–330
    land reform and, 337–338
    leaders in institutionalism, 199–200
    legal. See Legal institutions
    market development and, 367, 370
    moral hazard as informational problem, 181
    obstacles to entry in formal sector, 343–345
    overview of, 175–176
    political. See Political institutions
    prisoner's dilemma as commitment problem, 190–193
    quality of in informal sector, 347–349
    review and key terms, 200–202
    role in Lewis model, 122
    solutions to commitment problem, 188–189
    solutions to cooperation problem, 193–195
    solutions to coordination problem, 197–198
    solutions to hold-up problem, 186–187
    solutions to informational problems, 181–185
    trade. See Trade institutions
Instrumental variables
    applying to analysis of cause of conflicts, 551
    in causal inference, 574–577
Intellectual property rights
    monopoly rents from innovations, 98–99
    technology transfers and, 101
    WTO insistence favors rich nations, 165
    WTO protection of, 101–102
Interest rates
    bank profit and, 399
    monitoring variations in, 402
    religious taboos on, 304–305
    risk-free rate of interest, 499
    suicide of Indian farmers due to debt burden, 394
Intermediation margin, as measure of
    competitiveness of banking sector, 402
International Country Risk Guide
    creditor rights and, 271
    measures of good governance, 301
    measuring effect of infrastructure investment on growth, 490
    survey of corruption, 513
International Labor Organization (ILO), 470
International Monetary Fund. See IMF (International Monetary Fund)
International trade
    advantages of multilateral trade liberalization, 161–162
    advantages of specialization, 150–151
    benefits of exchange, 150
    bilateral and multilateral negotiations, 161

collective action failures, 157
comparative advantage and patterns of trade, 154
comparative advantage example, 151–152
currency convertibility options, 166–168
diversity of trade performance across regions, 147
exchange-rate policies in developing countries, 165–166
export price risk, 154–156
factor endowments as basis for specialization, 152–153
fixed exchange rates, 168–169
fixed vs. floating rates in developing countries, 170–171
floating exchange rates, 169
nontariff barriers to, 159–161
pegging currency of developing country to major currency, 169–170
politics of, 156
politics of multilateral trade agreements, 162–163
politics of trade liberalization, 157–158
protectionism and tariffs, 158–159
review and key terms, 172–174
specialization in developing countries, 148
theory of comparative advantage (Ricardo), 148–150
trade openness in developed and developing economies, 146
trends in, 145
winners and losers, 156–157
WTO (World Trade Organization), 163–165
Internet, as marketing tool in developing countries, 366
Intersectoral linkage, sectoral growth strategy, 129–130
Investment
    capital flight and, 122
    communal ownership and, 318
    corruption inhibiting, 517–518
    dam project investments, 494–497
    development effects of infrastructure investments, 489
    in domestic economy vs. global economy, 120–121
    farming related, 312
    fixed land rental and, 319
    growth effects of infrastructure investments, 490–491
    impact of savings on steady state, 94
    long-term adjustments to shortages in centrally planned economies, 218–219
    property rights and, 324–325, 349–352
    risk of infrastructure investments, 499
    transportation system investments, 491–494
    white elephant investments, 497–498

Investment specificity, 374
Islam
    inheritance laws, 305–306
    religious taboos on interest, 305
Italy, study of relationship of civil society to democratic institutions, 297–299
Iyer, Lakshmi, 337, 548

J

Japan. See also Asia
    big push theories, 132
    comparative advantage example, 151–152
    development gap with poorer economies, 3
    economic catch-up in, 18–19, 21
    export promotion, 136–137
    intersectoral linkages in, 130
    land reform in, 332
    life expectancy in, 7
Johnson, Simon, 105–108, 255, 445–446
Judicial branch
    common-law systems and, 266
    separation of powers in democracy, 244
Justinian code, 267

K

Kalemli-Ozcan, Sebnem, 430–431
Kantorovich, Leonid, 206
Kickbacks
    corruption in health care sector, 449
    corruption in Iraq Oil for Food program, 512
    in Corruption Perception Index, 513
Kim Il Sung, 390
Kim Jong Il, 390
Kinnan, Cynthia, 418
Klaus, Václav, 361
Knowledge-based growth
    boundless knowledge-based growth, 97–98
    knowledge as non-rival good, 98–99
Kornai, Janos, 211, 361
Kozeny, Viktor, 361
Kremer, Michael, 373, 433, 438–439, 444, 477, 479, 481–482
Kunicova, Jana, 520, 521
Kuran, Timur, 305–306
Kuznets hypothesis
    applied to income inequality, 46–47
    cross-sectional analysis and, 47–48
    panel regression and, 48

Kuznets, Simon, 46–48
Kyoto Protocol, example of cooperation problem, 191

L

Labor
    average and marginal productivity of, 85
    diminishing marginal productivity, 86
    distortionary effect of taxes and, 280–282
    as factor of production, 83
    factor shares, 86
    growth rate of, 88
    marginal product of labor in agriculture, 116–117
    relationship to capital intensity, 89
    shortages in centrally planned economies, 220–221
    transferring from traditional to modern sector of economy, 118–120
Labor contracts
    basic types of land ownership and tenancy, 316
    economic properties of, 320–321
    properties of land contracts, 323
Labor unions, 193
Laffont, Jean-Jaques, 327
Laitin, David, 542–545
Land contracts
    economic effects of, 323–324
    economic properties of, 316–317, 323
    incentive effects, 321–322
    institutions and patterns of land inequality and, 329–330
    land distribution and, 313–316
Land distribution, 313–316
Land (property) ownership. See Property rights
Land reform
    effects of, 335–338
    obstacles to, 333–335
    overview of, 330–333
Land-titling programs, 345–346
Lange, Oskar, 206–207
Language, culture and, 300–301
Latin America & Caribbean
    cross-sectional analysis of income inequality, 48
    development gap, 3
    economic growth and, 16–17
    education and income inequality, 45
    education gap, 10, 457–460
    evolution of trade specialization, 148–149
    GDP per capita, 4–5
    geography and growth in, 104
    Gini coefficient indicating income inequalities, 43–44
    growth rate in, 59–60

    HIV prevalence in, 430
    income inequality and economic growth and, 49
    infant mortality rates in, 9
    land ownership in, 316
    land ownership inequality, 314–315
    life expectancy in, 7–8
    obstacles to land reform and, 334–335
    population growth in, 56–57
    poverty gap and, 7
    poverty in, 37–38
    privatization in, 357–359
    right-wing dictatorships, 251
    secondary school enrollment, 10
    sex ratio in, 71
    trade share of, 147
    urbanization rate in, 12
    values regarding corruption and trust, 291
    values regarding economic interventionism, 290
    values regarding thrift and work, 292
Law enforcement
    corruption and, 509, 516
    difficulty of fighting corruption, 527
    institutions and, 175
    quality of, 271–272
    trust and, 308
Lee, Jean, 444
Legal codes, in civil law system, 265
Legal institutions
    common-law vs. civil-law, 265–268
    controversies regarding, 272–275
    corruption and, 522
    court-related problems of market development in poor countries, 368
    creditor rights, 269–271
    economic effects of different systems, 268
    law enforcement quality, 271–272
    overview of, 177, 264–265
    review and key terms, 285–287
    shareholder protections, 268–269
    solutions to hold-up problem, 229–230
    solutions to commitment problem, 188–189
    solutions to hold-up problem, 186
    solutions to informational problems, 181–183
Legislative branch, separation of powers in democracy, 244
Lenin, Vladimir, 205
Levine, Ruth, 444
Lewis, Arthur, 116
Lewis model
    applying, 120–122
    overview of, 116

role of institutions in, 122

traditional and modern sectors in, 116–117

transferring labor from traditional to modern sector, 118–120

Li, Hongbin, 68

Li, Wei, 284–285

Li, Zhigang, 383, 386–387

Licht, Amir, 300

Life expectancy

    epidemiological transition and, 423–424

    as indicator of health gap, 7–8

    relationship to GDP, 445–446

Limão, Nuno, 501–502

Limited liability, credit risk and, 397–398

Lipset, Seymour, 254

List, Friedrich, 135

Literacy

    democracy and, 256

    impact of malaria eradication campaign on, 435

    in India, 456

Logit regression, analysis of onset of civil wars, 543

Long-term relationships, solutions to monopsony problem, 379

Lord's Resistance Army (LRA), 558

Lorentzen, Peter, 430–431

Lorenz curve

    comparing equal vs. unequal income distributions, 40

    Gini coefficient, 40–44

    graphical representation of income distribution, 39–40

LRA (Lord's Resistance Army), 558

M

Maddison, Angus, 18, 519

Magna Carta, 267

Majoritarian rule

    in election of legislators, 245–247

    fiscal policy and, 246–249

    social welfare and, 248

    variables in corruption, 521

Malaria

    campaigns to control, 434–436

    DDT and controversy regarding, 436–437

    DDT in prevention of, 423–424

    issues in R&D of drugs for developing countries, 442–444

    overview of, 433–434

    prevalence of, 429

Malaria Vaccine Initiative, 444

Malthus, Thomas, 56

Manager incentives, in central planning systems

    overview of, 208

    plan-fulfillment bonus system, 208–209

    ratchet effect, 210–211

    soft-budget constraint, 211–213

    success indicator problem, 209

Marginal productivity

    factor productivity, 85–86

    of labor in agricultural economy, 116–117

Market development

    business networks in, 370–371

    communication obstacles to market integration, 382–383

    danger of taking markets for granted, 367–368

    dual-track liberalization in China, 374–375

    falling output in Central and Eastern Europe, 372–374

    famines and, 388–391

    lessons from transition economies, 376

    market integration, 381–382

    monopsonies in developing countries, 378–379

    monopsony and hold-up problem, 377–378

    overview of, 366–367

    in poor countries, 368–370

    property rights and, 349–352

    regulatory obstacles to market integration, 386–388

    review and key terms, 391–393

    rural markets and monopsony problem, 376–377

    solutions to monopsony problem, 379–381

    in transition economies, 371–372

    transportation obstacles to market integration, 383–386

Market integration

    communication obstacles to, 382–383

    overview of, 381–382

    regulatory obstacles to, 386–388

    transportation obstacles to, 383–386

Market track, dual-track price liberalization in China, 374–375

Marketing cooperatives, solutions to monopsony problem, 380–381

Markets

    danger of taking for granted, 367–368

    financial market development in 20th Century, 273

    financial markets in common-law and civil-law countries, 272

    firm boundaries and, 228–229

    Hayek's critique of central planning, 207–208

    price signals vs. quantity signals, 224–228

    review and key terms, 230–231

    role in coordination of economic activity, 203–204

    rural markets and monopsony problem, 376–377

Markets (*continued*)
  theoretical arguments against central planning,
    205–206
  vertical integration vs. subcontractor debate, 228–230
Marx, Karl, 204–205
Mass privatization
  Czechoslovakian example, 361–362
  overview of, 360–361
Mathematical expectation, in statistical analysis, 563
Matoussi, Mohamed Salah, 327
Mauritius, dual-track price liberalization in, 376
Mauro, Paolo, 518
McCleary, Rachel, 307
McMillan, John, 361, 430–431, 512
Mean, in statistical analysis, 562–563
Measuring
  credit constraints, 404–405
  credit rationing, 406
  culture, 289
  good governance, 300–301
  income, 4–5
  income inequality, 38–42
  standards of weights and measures, 370
  success, 209
Measuring corruption
  objective measures, 511–512
  overview of, 510
  subjective measures, 513–515
Measuring education gap
  comparing measures of achievement, 459–464
  gender gap, 458–459
  overview of, 456
  primary school gap, 456–458
  secondary school gap, 458
Measuring health
  anthropometric measures of health, 426–427
  DALY (Disability Adjusted Life Year) as measure of
    health, 427–428
  nutrient intake as measure of health, 425–426
  overview of, 424
  self-reported health status, 424–425
Measuring poverty
  calorie counting as measure of, 29
  poverty gap, 6–7, 31–33
  poverty line as, 29–31
  surveys for, 28
Mechanization, farmer ownership and, 317
Median voter theorem, of democracy, 238–240
Men
  gender biases impacting fertility choices, 71
  gender biases impacting male to female population
    ratio, 72

Hofstede's index of masculinity, 295
impact of Indian caste system on education, 474
measuring education gap, 458–459
reducing gender gap in education, 481–482
MENA (Middle East and North Africa). See also
    Africa
  Arab Spring protests, 344
  business start-up costs, 345
  economic growth and, 14, 16–17
  education and income inequality, 45
  education gap and, 10, 457–460
  evolution of trade specialization, 148–149
  gender biases impacting male to female population
    ratio, 72
  Gini coefficient indicating income inequalities, 43–44
  infant mortality rates in, 9
  land ownership inequality and, 314
  life expectancy in, 7–8
  population growth and, 16
  reduction of poverty in, 37
  secondary school enrollment, 10
  trade share of, 147
  values regarding corruption and trust, 291
  values regarding economic interventionism, 290
  values regarding thrift and work, 292
Menchú, Rigoberta, 335
MEND (Movement of Emancipation of the Niger
    Delta), 545
Menem, Carlos, 357
Mexican Revolution, 331
Microfinance
  evaluating, 418–419
  how it works, 409–410
  incentives in, 410–413
  overview of, 409
  peer pressure replaces collateral in loan repayment,
    395
  profitability of, 415–418
  types of, 413–415
Middle East and North Africa. See MENA (Middle
    East and North Africa)
Migration equilibrium, in Harris-Todaro model, 123–126
Migration, rural to urban, 123
Miguel, Edward, 438–440, 479, 481–482, 525–526, 551,
    554, 557
Milgrom, Paul, 477–478
Military dictatorships
  in Latin America, 251
  overthrowing democracies, 260
Millennium Development goals, 36
Minority rights, comparing autocracies and
    democracies, 242–243

Mobutu Sese Seko, 251, 508
Modern sector, of economy (Lewis model)
    capital accumulation in, 117
    overview of, 116–117
    transferring labor from traditional sector to, 118–120
Moene, Karl Ove, 529
Mohamad, Mahathir, 353
Monitoring
    as means of preventing moral hazard, 401–402
    teacher absenteeism, 476
    variations in interest rates and, 402
Monopoly rents, from innovation, 99
Monopsonies, in rural markets
    developing countries and, 367, 378–379
    hold-up problem and, 377–378
    overview of, 376–377
    solutions, 379–381
Monsoons, farming related risks, 329
Montesinos, Vladimiro, 511–512
Mookherjee, Dilip, 504
Moral hazard
    collateral mitigating, 400–401
    compared with adverse selection, 398
    due to asymmetric information, 180
    as informational problem, 181, 396
    microcredit preventing, 410
    monitoring as means of preventing, 401–402
Morales, Juan Evo, 334
Moretti, Enrico, 511
Mortality rates
    demographic transition and, 58
    population growth and, 60–61
Mosquito-borne diseases, 433
Most favored nation clause, WTO rules for trade liberalization, 163
Moulin, Sylvie, 477
Movement of Emancipation of the Niger Delta (MEND), 545
Multilateral trade negotiations
    economic advantages of, 161–162
    overview of, 161
    politics of, 162–163
Multiple equilibria, coordination problem and, 195
Munshi, Kaivan, 473–475
Mussolini, Benito, 250

N

NAFTA (North American Free Trade Agreement), 331
Naga City (Philippines), success story in urban development, 13

Nagasaki, 553–554
Napoleonic code, 265, 267
Nash equilibrium
    applied to game theory, 190
    coordination problem and, 195
Nation-building, wars encouraging, 553
National treatment clause, WTO rules for trade liberalization, 163
Nationalism, in Nazi and Fascist movements, 250
Nationalization, to privatization, 352–353
Natural monopolies, justifying state-ownership, 353
Natural resources
    corruption and, 522–523
    as a negative externality, 78
Nazi regimes, 250
Negotiations
    conflict resulting from failure to reach a deal, 540–541
    multilateral trade negotiations, 161–163
    opportunistic renegotiation of contracts, 503
    reasons for choosing conflict over, 539
Nehru, Jawaharlal, 259
Neoclassical (Heckscher-Ohlin) theory of international trade, 152
Nepal, civil war in, 537, 548–550
Net migration rate, growth rates, 60
New Zealand
    values regarding corruption and trust, 291
    values regarding economic interventionism, 290
    values regarding thrift and work, 292
Newman, Mark, 1
NGOs (nongovernmental organizations)
    deworming program, 438
    education improvement programs, 456
    education reform and, 476–477, 479, 481–482
    institutional solutions to cooperation problems, 193
    Malaria Vaccine Initiative, 444
    policies to fight poverty, 28
    role in microfinance, 415
Nkrumah, Kwame, 331
Non-rival goods, 98–99
Non-tradable goods
    exchange rates and poverty line and, 33–34
    PPP (purchasing power parity) and, 34–35
Nondiscrimination, WTO rules for trade liberalization, 163–164
Nontariff barriers to trade, 159–160
Normal goods, 67
North Africa. See MENA (Middle East and North Africa)

North America. *See also* United States
  forms of land ownership, 316
  growth rate in, 59–60
  infant mortality rates in, 9
  life expectancy in, 8
  population growth in, 57–58
  sex ratio in, 71
  urbanization rate in, 11
  values regarding corruption and trust, 291
  values regarding economic interventionism, 290
  values regarding thrift and work, 292
North American Free Trade Agreement (NAFTA), 331
North, Douglass, 105, 176, 200
North Korea
  comparing GDP of North and South Korea, 203
  famines in, 390–391
Norway, 4
Nuclear weapons, 553–554
Nutrient intake, as measure of health, 425–426
Nyerere, Julius, 331

O

Oceania. *See also* Pacific
  growth rate in, 59–60
  population growth in, 57
  sex ratio in, 71
OECD high income countries
  business start-up costs, 345
  education and income inequality, 45
  education gap and, 457–460
  Gini coefficient indicating income inequalities, 43–44
  infant mortality rates, 8–9
  population growth, 16–17
  secondary school enrollment, 10
  trade openness in, 146
OECD (Organization for Economic Co-operation and Development)
  about, 146
  overview of, 8
  PISA (Program for International Student Assessment), 461–462
Oil, greed as motive for conflict, 545
Old-age dependency ratio, 75–76
Oligarchs, privatization in Russia and, 362
Olken, Benjamin, 504–505, 511
OLS (ordinary least squares)
  bias from omitted variables, 570–571
  in causal inference, 569–570
  estimation errors and, 566–567

Olson, Mancur, 200, 236
One-child policy, China, 72, 76
Operational sustainability, measuring profitability in microfinance, 416
Opportunity cost
  of capital, 86
  of production, 151
Ordinary least squares. *See* OLS (ordinary least squares)
Orphan Drug Act (1993), 443
Ortega, Daniel, 546
Ossa, Ralph, 163
Oster, Emily, 72
Ostrom, Elinor, 194
Ottoman Empire (Turkey), 22
Overexploitation
  of commons, 192
  solutions for preservation of commons, 194
Ownership
  land ownership. *See* Property rights, in rural areas
  privatization goals and problems, 354–355

P

Pacific. *See also* Oceania
  business start-up costs, 345
  economic growth in, 14, 17
  education and income inequality, 45
  education gap in, 10, 458
  Gini coefficient indicating income inequalities, 43–44
  infant mortality rates in, 9
  land ownership inequality in, 314
  life expectancy in, 8
  poverty gap in, 6–7
  reduction of poverty in, 37
  secondary school enrollment, 10
  trade share of, 147
  values regarding corruption and trust, 291
  values regarding economic interventionism, 290
  values regarding thrift and work, 292
Pande, Rohini, 326, 495–497
Panel regression
  applied to income inequality, 48
  in causal inference, 571–572
  dealing with omitted variables, 572–573
  estimating difference-in-differences effects, 573–574
Panizza, Ugo, 520
Parasitic diseases
  Schistosomiasis, 422
  worms, 437–440

Park, Chung-Hee, 528
Parliamentary regimes
    corruption and, 520
    electoral rules in, 246
    fiscal policy, 246–249
    types of democracies, 244–245
Particularistic (pork-barrel) spending, 510
Patronage, politician buying votes via, 122
Pegging currencies of developing countries, to major
        currencies, 169–170
Penicillin, 423
Peron, Juan, 251
Persian Empire, 24
Persson, Torsten, 245–248, 253, 521
Pharmaceutical companies, issues in R&D of drugs
        for developing countries, 442–444
Pinglo, Maria Elena, 499–500
Pinochet, Augusto, 251, 334, 353
PISA (Program for International Student
        Assessment), 461–462
Plan-fulfillment bonus system, managerial incentives
        under central planning, 208–209
Plan track, dual-track price liberalization in China,
        374–375
Planning from the achieved level, 222
Planning theory, mathematics of, 206
Plantations
    privately owned family farms compared with,
        328–329
    slave labor and, 327–328
Plurality rule. See Majoritarian rule
Point-of-use water treatment, in preventing diarrheal
        diseases, 432
Policies
    corruption and, 509
    exchange-rate policies in developing countries,
        165–166
    family planning policies, 77
    in fight against poverty, 28
    infant mortality and, 9
    one-child policy in China, 72, 76
    privatization policies, 355
    return policies, 182
    urban migration policies in China, 127
Policy makers, applying poverty rates, 36
Political economy constraints, 284
Political economy of trade liberalization, 156
Political institutions
    autocracy vs. democracy, 240–243
    commitment to redistribution in democracies,
        258–259

Communist regimes, 249–250
    corruption and, 520–522
    economic effects of democratic institutions, 246–249
    education and democracy, 255–256
    electoral rules in democracies, 245–246
    income and democracy, 254–255
    income inequality and democratization, 260–262
    inequality and social conflict in democracies,
        257–258
    institutional solutions to preservation of commons,
        194
    Nazi and Fascist regimes, 250
    overview of, 176–177, 232–233
    presidential and parliamentary democracies,
        244–245
    rate of change and, 300
    review and key terms, 262–263
    revolutionary threats and democratization, 259–260
    right-wing dictatorships, 251
    separation of powers in democracy, 244
    theories of democratization, 254
    theory of autocracy, 236–237
    theory of democracy, 237–240
    types of political regimes, 233–235
    waves of democratization, 251–253
Political parties, institutional solutions to cooperation
        problems, 193
Political power, role of institutions in allocation of, 233
Political regimes
    autocracies. See Autocracies
    democracies. See Democracies
    types of, 233–235
Politics
    corruption and, 509–510
    economics and, 50
    of multilateral trade agreements, 162–163
    patronage and, 122
    white elephant investments and, 498
Politics, of international trade
    failures of collective action, 157
    give and take in politics of trade liberalization,
        157–158
    overview of, 156
    winners and losers, 156–157
Polity IV, 256–257
Population growth
    age distribution, 61–63
    commitment and cultural values impacting fertility
        choices, 70–71
    demographic transition and, 56, 74
    demographic transition and fertility choices, 73–76

Population growth (*continued*)
  determinants of, 60
  development gap and, 16–17
  economics of fertility choices, 63–64
  exponential nature of, 56–57
  externalities and economics of family planning,
    78–79
  family planning policies, 77
  fertility, mortality, and birth and death rates, 60–61
  financial security and, 70
  growth rates, 58–60
  institutional factors in fertility choices, 69
  overview of, 55
  review and key terms, 79–81
  shift in cost of consumer goods and, 64–66
  shift in cost of raising children and, 64–65
  shift in income and, 66–67
  shift in preferences and, 67–69
  social norms and gender biases impacting fertility
    choices, 71–73
Population growth rate, 60
Pork-barrel (Particularistic) spending, 510
Ports, cost of capital for infrastructure sectors, 500
Poverty
  calorie counting as measure of, 29
  challenges of international surveys, 35
  Chen and Ravallion's study, 36–38
  conflicts and, 537
  credit market imperfections and, 49–50
  cross-sectional analysis of income inequality, 47–48
  economic growth and income inequality, 49
  education and income inequality, 44–45
  equal vs. unequal income distributions, 40
  exchange rates and poverty line, 33–34
  Gini coefficient in measuring, 40–44
  increase/decrease of inequality over time, 50–53
  Kuznets hypothesis applied to income inequality,
    46–47
  land ownership and income inequality, 45–46
  land reform's impact on, 335–336
  levels of, 33
  local assessments of, 28–29
  Lorenz curve in measuring, 39–40
  measuring income inequality, 38–39
  measuring poverty, 28
  overview of, 27–28
  panel regression applied to income inequality, 48
  policy makers applying poverty rates, 36
  politics and economics and, 50
  poverty gap and, 31–33
  poverty line and poverty headcount, 29–31

PPP (purchasing power parity) and, 34–35
  quantile measures, 39
  review and key terms, 53–54
  urbanization and, 12–13
  World Bank's 1-dollar-a-day methodology, 35–36
Poverty gap, 6–7, 31–33
Poverty headcount, 29, 32–33
Poverty line
  in Chen and Ravallion's study, 37
  exchange rates and, 33–34
  impact of changes in food prices on, 30
  as measure of poverty, 29–31
Poverty trap, 140
Power
  decentralization of, 503–504
  power distribution in Hofstede's index of cultural
    values, 295
  separation of, 243–244, 248
PPP (purchasing power parity)
  in Chen and Ravallion's study, 37
  comparing richest and poorest nations, 4–6
  non-tradable goods and, 34–35
PR (proportional rule). See Proportional rule (PR)
Prebisch-Singer hypothesis, 133–135
Precedents, in common law system, 265
Predatory (extractive) institutions, 108
Presidential regimes
  corruption and, 520
  electoral rules in, 246
  fiscal policy, 246–249
  types of democracies, 244–245
Price signals vs. quantity signals, in market
    coordination
  case illustrating superiority of price coordination,
    227–228
  case illustrating superiority of quantity
    coordination, 226–227
  how price and quantity signals work, 225–226
  mistakes due to, 224–225
  overview of, 224
Prices
  liberalization in Central and Eastern Europe,
    372–374
  liberalization in China, 374–375
  overpricing in health care sector, 449
  price ratios in analysis of comparative advantage,
    151–153
  volatility of farm commodity prices, 317
Primary commodities
  developing countries specializing in export of, 148
  exporting (Prebisch-Singer hypothesis), 133

Primary schools. See also Education
    class size as quality indicator, 463
    measuring education gap, 456–458
Primogeniture, in inheritance law, 306
Prioritization, short-term adjustment to shortage,
    215–216
Priority lending program, in India, 405–408
Prisoner's dilemma
    collective-action problem as example of,
        192–193
    inefficiency of pure self-interest maximization,
        191–192
    overview of, 190–191
Private ownership. See Farmer ownership
Privatization
    in Africa, 360
    in Asia, 359–360
    in Central and Eastern Europe, 360–363
    of economic activities, 204
    goals and problems, 353–355
    in Latin America, 357–359
    methods in developing countries, 356–357
    moving from nationalization to, 352–353
    problems arising from privatization policies, 355
    of water in Bolivia, 358
Production
    factors of, 83–84
    international productivity ratios by country, 103
    long-term adjustments to shortages in centrally
        planned economies, 218
    opportunity cost of, 151
Production function
    in analysis of factor productivity, 85
    cross-derivative of marginal product with respect
        to labor, 86
    factors of production and, 84–85
    in growth accounting, 87–88
Production possibility frontier, 152–153
Professional associations, collective-action and, 194
Program for International Student Assessment
    (PISA), 461–462
Progresa program, reducing costs of education, 481
Progressive lending
    features of microfinance, 410
    incentives of microfinance, 411–413
Property rights
    institutions for protecting, 347–349
    investment and, 324–325
    North on, 200
    protection of, 101–102
    relationship to market development, 366

Property rights, in rural areas
    communal ownership, 318
    communal vs. private ownership, 324–326
    economic effects of land contracts, 323–324
    economic properties of land contracts, 316–317, 323
    effects of land reform, 335–338
    evolution of property rights system in Ghana, 326
    farmer ownership, 317–318
    fixed land rental, 318–319
    institutions and patterns of land inequality, 329–330
    labor contracts, 320–321
    land distribution and land contracts, 313–316
    land reforms, 330–333
    obstacles to land reforms, 333–335
    overview of, 312–313
    plantations and slave labor, 327–328
    plantations vs. privately owned family farms,
        328–329
    review and key terms, 338–339
    sharecropping, 320
    sharecropping vs. fixed rental contracts, 327
    sharecropping vs. private ownership, 326–327
Property rights, in urban areas
    economic effects of legal titles, 345–346
    high transaction costs in informal sector, 342–343
    informal sector and, 341–342
    institutional obstacles to entry in formal sector,
        343–345
    institutional quality and informal sector, 347–349
    investment and market development and, 349–352
    moving from nationalization to privatization,
        352–353
    overview of, 340–341
    privatization goals and problems, 353–355
    privatization in Africa, 360
    privatization in Asia, 359–360
    privatization in Central and Eastern Europe, 360–363
    privatization in Latin America, 357–359
    privatization methods in developing countries,
        356–357
    review and key terms, 364–365
Proportional rule (PR)
    in election of legislators, 245–247
    fiscal policy and, 246–249
    social welfare and, 248–249
    variables in corruption, 521
Protectionism
    export promotion, 137–138
    nontariff barriers, 159–161
    protection of infant industries, 134–135
    tariffs and, 158–159

Protestant ethic, 255, 288
Przeworski, Adam, 254
Public offerings, privatization methods, 356
Public services, comparing autocracies and
      democracies, 241
Purchasing power parity. See PPP (purchasing power
      parity)
Puri-Sharma, Charu, 440
Putin, Vladimir, 203
Putnam, Robert, 297–299

Q

Qatar, 4
Quality
      balancing supply and demand in centrally planned
            economies, 223
      poor-quality goods due to supply/demand
            mismatch, 213
Quantile measures, of income inequality, 39
Quantity-quality theory (Becker), in fertility choices,
      67–68
Quantity signals. See Price signals vs. quantity
      signals, in market coordination

R

Ragan, Raghuram C., 273–275
Railroads
      cost of capital for, 500
      improving market integration in China, 384–385
      infrastructure gap and, 488–489
      measuring effect of investment in, 491–494
Rainfall, geography and growth and, 104
Ramírez, María Teresa, 490
Random (stochastic) variables, 562
Randomized evaluations
      in causal inference, 569
      of education systems, 456
Ratchet effect, managerial incentive problems under
      central planning and, 210–211
Rating agencies, institutional solutions to
      informational problems, 183
Rauch, James, 528
Ravallion, Martin, 35, 36–38, 389
Raw materials
      developing countries specializing in export of, 148
      exporting primary commodities, 133
      as factor of production, 83
Real estate. See Property rights
Reciprocity principle, WTO rules for trade
      liberalization, 163–164

Redistribution of income. See Income redistribution
Reforms, educational
      creating incentives for teacher effectiveness, 477–478
      decentralizing school systems, 478–479
      overview of, 476
      reducing costs, 480–481
      reducing gender gap, 481–482
      reducing teacher absenteeism, 476–477
      voucher programs, 479–480
Reforms, land
      effects of, 335–338
      obstacles to, 333–335
      overview of, 330–333
Reforms, regulatory, 502–503
Regional trade agreements, 162
Regression analysis
      applying to onset of civil wars, 543
      bivariate regression analysis, 565–567
      causal inference and, 567
      dealing with omitted variables in panel regression,
            572–573
      instrumental variables and, 574–577
      OLS (ordinary least squares) for randomized
            evaluation, 569
      panel regression, 571–572
      regression table analysis, 577–579
Regulation
      of access or entry rules, 181
      obstacles to market integration, 386–388
      regulatory reforms, 502–503
Regulatory capture, problems arising from
      privatization policies, 355
Rehydration therapy, for diarrheal diseases, 432
Reinikka, Ritva, 472–473, 511
Relational contracting
      informal solutions to informational problems,
            183–185
      in trade when formal institutions are weak, 370
      trust, 351
Relationship specific investments, hold-up problem
      and, 186
Relative factor endowments, comparative advantage
      based on, 152–153
Religion
      beliefs and trust and, 308–309
      effect on economic growth, 307–308
      informal institutions and, 177–178
      insignificant variables in civil war, 545
      taboos on charging interest, 304–305
Rent-seeking
      compared with corruption, 510
      overview of, 274–275

Rents, due to tariffs, 158–159
Reputation
    default and, 413
    fighting corruption and, 529
    relational contracting and, 184–185
Residual return, from fixed land rental, 318–319
Return policies, institutional solutions to informational
    problems, 182
Returns to education
    empirical analysis of, 467–470
    externalities of, 465–466
    government role in, 466–467
    overview of, 464–465
Returns to scale
    constant, increasing, and decreasing, 84
    in Solow growth model, 89–90
"Reversal of fortune" (Acemoglu, Johnson, and
    Robinson), 105
Revolutionary threats, democratization and, 259–260
Rhee, Syngman, 527
Ricardo, David, 148
Right-wing dictatorships
    emerging in developing countries, 251
    Fascist regimes, 250
Riots, examples of collective-action, 195
Risk averse
    in adverse selection example, 179–180
    investment selection and, 397
Risk-free rate of interest, 499
Risk neutral
    in adverse selection example, 179–180
    applying to analysis of causes of conflict, 539
    investment selection and, 396
Risks
    dividing borrowers by risk group in microfinance,
        410–412
    farm size and, 329
    farmer ownership and, 317
    farming related, 312
    fixed land rental and, 319
    investing in infrastructure and, 499
    investment selection and, 396–397
    labor contracts, 321
Road construction
    corruption example, 511
    factors of production in developed and developing
        countries, 83–84
    fighting corruption (Indonesian example), 504–505
Robinson, James A., 105–108, 255, 257, 260, 471, 498
Rodrik, Dani, 374–375
Roland, Gérard, 248, 300, 373–374, 555
Roman Empire, 24

Roman law, 267
Romer model, 100–101
Romer, Paul, 97
ROSCAs (rotating savings and credit associations),
    413–414
Rose-Ackerman, Susan, 520, 521
Rosenzweig, Mark, 68, 329, 473–475
Rotating savings and credit associations (ROSCAs),
    413–414
Rousseau, Jean Jacques, 197
Roving bandit vs. stationary bandit, in
    understanding autocracies, 236–237
Rule of law
    comparing autocracies and democracies, 243
    cultural attitudes about corruption and, 524
Rural areas
    effect of migration on rural education, 126–127
    monopsonies. See Monopsonies, in rural markets
    property rights. See Property rights, in rural areas
    rural to urban migration, 123
Russia. See also East Europe
    balancing supply and demand in Soviet Union,
        222–223
    central planning experiment in Soviet Union, 208
    Communist regime established in 1917, 249
    early success of central planning in Soviet Union,
        206
    effect of inefficient use of savings and investment
        in Soviet era, 94
    falling output in transition to capitalism, 372–374
    GDP per capita, 4–6
    geography and growth in, 104
    HIV prevalence in, 430
    life expectancy in, 8
    poverty in, 37–38
    privatization in, 362
    worker behavior in Soviet Union, 220–222
Russian mob, solutions to commitment problem, 189
Russian Revolution (1917), 330–331

S

Sachs, Jeffrey, 104, 140, 360
Sala-i-Martin, Xavier, 51
Salazar, Antonio de Oliveira, 251
Salinas, Carlos, 331, 357
Samples, vs. true distribution in statistical analysis,
    562
Sanitation, infrastructure gap and, 487–489
Sapienza, Paola, 308
Satyanath, Shanker, 551
Savedoff, William, 449–450

Savings
   in China, 288
   impact of saving rate on steady state, 94
   thrift as cultural value, 308–309
Schargrodsky, Ernesto, 511, 528
Schelling, Thomas, 197
Schistosomiasis, 422, 437–438
Schools. See Education
Schultz, T. Paul, 481
Schumpeter, Joseph, 99, 207
Schwartz, Shalom, 293–294, 300
Schwartz's cultural mapping, 292–293
Search frictions, causes of falling output after price
      liberalization, 374
Secession of regions, comparing autocracies and
      democracies, 242
Secondary schools. See also Education
   enrollment rates, 10–11
   measuring education gap, 458
Sectoral ministries, balancing supply and demand in
      centrally planned economies, 223
Sectors, of economy
   balanced and unbalanced growth, 128–130
   big push theories, 130–131
   inefficiency of, 121
   informal sector, 121
   sectoral growth strategy, 128
   structural change across industrial sectors, 115
   traditional and modern, 116–117
   transferring labor from traditional to modern
      sector, 118–120
Secularization hypothesis (Weber), 307
Selection bias
   in causal inference, 568–569
   privatization and, 363
Self-interest maximization, prisoner's dilemma and,
      191–192
Self-reported health status, 424–425
Seller's market, for labor in central planning systems,
      220–221
Sen, Amartya, 72, 388–390
Separation of ownership and control, in large
      privatized enterprises, 354
Separation of powers
   comparing autocracies and democracies, 243
   in democracies, 244
   in presidential and parliamentary regimes, 248
Sequential transactions, commitment problem and,
      187
Sergenti, Ernest, 551
Serially correlated profits, credit constraints
      and, 405

Service economy, transition from industrial economy
      to, 114–115
Settler mortality, extractive or predatory institutions
      and, 108–109
Sewage systems, in disease prevention, 433
Shaban, Radwan Ali, 326–327
Sharecropping
   basic types of land ownership and tenancy, 316
   economic properties of, 320
   fixed rental contracts compared with, 327
   incentive effects, 321–323
   private ownership compared with, 326–327
   properties of land contracts, 323
Shareholder protections, 268–269
Sharia law, 305–306
Shleifer, Andrei, 268, 360, 521–522, 527
Shortages, in central planning systems
   demand/supply mismatches, 213–215
   hoarding demand creating, 217–218
   long-term adjustments, 218–219
   medium-term adjustments, 216–218
   overview of, 213
   short-term adjustments, 215–216
Sierra Leone example of civil war, 557
Signaling, institutional solutions to informational
      problems, 182
Singapore
   GDP per capita, 4
   infrastructure development and, 485
Slave labor
   plantations and, 321
   productivity and efficiency of, 327–328
Social conflict, in democracies, 257–258
Social mobility, comparing autocracies and
      democracies, 241
Social norms
   caring for elderly and, 71
   corruption and, 523–525
   culture and, 288
   demographic transition and, 73
   diplomatic immunity and, 525–526
   egalitarian norms, 303–304
   fertility choices and, 71–73
   human behavior and, 199–200
   informal solutions to hold-up problem, 187
   institutions and, 175
   solutions to coordination problem, 197–198
   types of informal institutions, 177
Social security, old age and, 70
Social welfare
   long-term effects of conflict, 552
   majoritarian systems and, 248

Socialism. See also Central planning
    attraction vs. failings of, 203
    market development in transitioning to capitalism, 367–368
    Marx and, 204–205
    mathematical theory of planning and, 206–207
Soft-budget constraint, managerial incentive problems under central planning and, 211–213
Solow growth model
    endogenous growth theory as alternative to, 97
    equilibrium in, 90–91
    growth inside and outside of, 92–93
    human capital and, 95
    income convergence, 96–97
    overview of, 88
    returns to scale and diminishing marginal products, 89–90
    Romer model compared with, 100–101
    savings rates and, 94
    steady state, 91–92
    technological progress and steady state, 93
Solow, Robert, 88
Somosa, Anastasio, 546
South Africa, land reform in, 332–333
South Asia. See also Asia
    business start-up costs, 345
    economic growth and, 14
    education gap and, 10, 457–460
    evolution of trade specialization, 148–149
    GDP per capita, 4–5
    gender biases impacting male to female population ratio, 72
    infant mortality rates in, 8
    land ownership inequality and, 314–315
    life expectancy in, 7–8
    population growth and, 16
    poverty gap and, 6–7
    privatization in, 359
    reduction of poverty in, 37–38
    secondary school enrollment, 10
    trade share of, 147
    values regarding corruption and trust, 291
    values regarding economic interventionism, 290
    values regarding thrift and work, 292
South Korea
    big push theories, 132
    comparing GDP of North and South Korea, 203
    land reform in, 332
    structural change across industrial sectors, 115
Soviet Union. See Russia

Specialization, of trade
    advantages of specialization, 150–151
    in developing countries, 148
    export price risk and, 154–156
    factor endowments as basis for, 152–153
Speculation, fixed vs. floating rates and, 171
Spencer, Percy, 198
Squire, Lyn, 48
Stag hunt game example, coordination problem, 197
Standard deviation, in statistical analysis, 564
Standards
    1-dollar-a-day poverty standard of World Bank, 35–36
    coordination problems and, 197
    of weights and measures, 370
State-ownership, privatization goals and problems, 353–354
Stationary population, demographic trends and, 62–63
Statistics
    bivariate regression analysis, 565–567
    covariation between two variables, 564–565
    mean, variance, and standard deviation, 562–564
    overview of, 562
Steady state
    effect of savings rates on, 94
    growth inside and outside of, 92–93
    in Solow growth model, 91–92
    technological progress and, 93
Stiglitz, Joseph, 164
Stochastic (random) variables, 562
Stock market capitalization, in common-law and civil-law countries, 274
Strategic defaults, 403–404
Straub, Stephane, 502–503
Stroessner, Alfredo, 251
Structural change, as development strategy
    across industrial sectors, 115
    from agricultural to industrial economy, 114
    applying Lewis model, 120–122
    balanced and unbalanced growth, 128–130
    big push theories, 130–131
    export promotion and the Asian miracle, 135–138
    foreign aid controversy, 139–141
    Harris-Todaro model of rural to urban migration, 123
    implications of Harris-Todaro model, 126–127
    import substitution vs. export promotion, 132–133
    from industrial to service economy, 114–115
    industrialization and protection of infant industries, 134–135
    Lewis model of, 116

Structural change, as development strategy (*continued*)
  migration equilibrium in Harris-Todaro model, 123–126
  overview of, 113
  Prebisch-Singer hypothesis, 133–134
  review and key terms, 142–144
  role of institutions in Lewis model, 122
  sectoral growth strategy, 128
  traditional and modern sector in Lewis model, 116–117
  transferring labor from traditional to modern sector, 118–120
Sub-Saharan Africa. See also Africa
  business start-up costs, 345
  economic growth and, 14, 16–17
  education and income inequality, 45
  education gap and, 10, 457–460
  evolution of trade specialization, 148–149
  Gini coefficient indicating income inequalities, 43–44
  infant mortality rates in, 9
  land ownership inequality and, 314–315
  population growth and, 16–17
  poverty in, 37–38
  secondary school enrollment, 10
  trade share of, 147
Subcontractors
  institutions and, 229–230
  trade-off between efficiency and hold-up, 229
  vs. vertical integration, 228–229
Substitution effect, cost of raising children and, 64
Success indicator problem, in measuring economic performance, 209
Suharto, 251
Supply and demand
  balancing in centrally planned economies, 222–223
  credit rationing and, 399–400
  distortionary effect of taxes on labor supply, 280–282
  falling output in transition to capitalism, 373–374
  hoarding demand creating shortages, 217–218
  income-elasticity of demand, 134–135
  inferior and normal goods and, 67
  long-term adjustments to shortages in centrally planned economies, 218–219
  medium-term adjustments to shortages in centrally planned economies, 216–217
  mismatches in central planning, 213–215
  for normal goods demand increases as income increases, 67
  problems of market development in poor countries, 368–369

  short-term adjustment to shortages in centrally planned economies, 215–216
  shortages creating uncertainty of supply, 215
Supply multiplier, 221
Surveys
  challenges of international surveys, 35
  local assessments of poverty, 28–29
  for measuring poverty, 28
  self-reported health status, 424–425
Svejnar, Jan, 363
Svensson, Jakob, 472–473, 511, 517

T

Tabellini, Guido, 245–248, 253, 521
Taiwan, land reform in, 332
Tariffs
  GATT (General Agreement on Trade and Tariffs), 161
  on imports, 158–159
Taxation
  comparing developed and developing countries, 283–285
  composition of taxes, 279
  determinants of tax structure, 280–283
  in developing countries, 275–279
  income redistribution and, 50
  tax distortions, 275
  tax elasticity, 282–283
  value-added taxes, 280
Teachers
  absenteeism rates, 464
  incentives for effectiveness of, 477–478
  quality indicators in education systems, 463
  reducing absenteeism, 476–477
Technology
  problems of market development in poor countries, 370
  technological progress and steady state in Solow growth model, 93
  wars stimulating technological progress, 553
Telephone, infrastructure gap and, 487–489
Tenancy reforms, 336
Terms of trade, for developing countries, 133–134, 155–156
Textbooks, reducing costs of education, 481
Thatcher, Margaret, 353
Theft, corruption in health care sector, 448
Theory of comparative advantage (Ricardo), 148–150
Thornton, Rebecca, 481–482
Three Gorges Dam project, China, 494

Thrift. See also Savings
   as cultural value, 308–309
   WVS and, 290
Tilly, Charles, 553
Time inconsistency, commitment problem and, 187–188
Tipping, social norms and, 523–524
Tirole, Jean, 529
Titles, economic effects legal titling of property, 345–346
Todaro, Michael P., 123
Torvik, Ragnar, 498
Total factor productivity, 85, 88
Total fertility rate, 60
Totalitarianism
   China's Cultural Revolution as example, 250
   of Communist regimes, 249
Touré, Ahmed Sékou, 331
Township village enterprises (TVEs), in China, 127
Trade
   barriers. See Protectionism
   convertibility, 166
   corruption and, 522–523
   diversion, 162
   international. See International trade
   openness in developed and developing economies, 146
   regulatory obstacles to market integration, 386
Trade institutions
   bilateral and multilateral negotiations, 161
   economic advantages of multilateral trade liberalization, 161–162
   politics of multilateral trade agreements, 162–163
   WTO (World Trade Organization), 163–165
Trade liberalization
   bilateral liberalism resulting in trade diversion, 162
   failures of collective action, 157
   give and take in politics of, 157–158
   political economy of, 156
   WTO rules for, 163–165
Trade-Related Intellectual Property (TRIPS) agreement, 165
Trade shares, regional decomposition (1960–2008), 147
Trade unions, 193
Traditional sector, of economy (Lewis model)
   overview of, 116–117
   transferring labor to modern sector, 118–120
Transaction costs
   in informal sector, 342–343
   institutions role in reducing, 175
   religious taboos on interest increasing transaction costs, 304

Transactions, legal and institutional aspects of, 200
Transition economies
   effects of institutions on property rights, 347–349
   lessons regarding market development, 376
   market development in, 371–372
   understanding market development and, 367
Transparency International
   Corruption Perception Index, 513–515, 532–536
   measures of good governance, 301
Transportation
   factors in cost of, 104
   investing in infrastructure, 491–494
   obstacles to market integration, 383–386
   problems of market development in poor countries, 368
Treatment effect, in causal inference, 568–569
Trebbi, Francesco, 521
Treisman, Daniel, 519, 522, 528
TRIPS (Trade-Related Intellectual Property) agreement, 165
Tropical disease, geography and growth and, 104
True distribution, vs. samples in statistical analysis, 562
Trust
   relational contracting and, 351
   religious beliefs and economic growth and, 308–309
   role business networks in developing countries, 370–371
   WVS and, 290–291
Tuberculosis
   issues in R&D of drugs for developing countries, 442–444
   overview of, 440–441
   prevalence of, 429
Tunisia, 55
TVEs (township village enterprises), in China, 127

U

Udry, Christopher, 325–326
Uganda, 472–473
Unbalanced growth, sectoral growth strategy, 128–130
Uncertainty tolerance/avoidance, Hofstede's index of cultural values, 295
Unemployment, effect of urban migration on, 127
United Arab Emirates, 4
United Kingdom. See also Europe
   history of cycles of development and decline, 24
   industrialization of British economy, 17–18
   privatization in, 353

United Nations, institutional solutions to cooperation
    problems, 193
United States. See also North America
    changes in income inequalities over time, 50–53
    comparing worker output vs. China, 102–103
    development gap with poorer economies, 3
    evolution of trade specialization, 148
    example of protectionism, 160–161
    GDP per capita, 4
    geography and growth in, 104
    HIV prevalence in, 430
    life expectancy in, 8
    Orphan Drug Act (1993), 443
    population growth and aging populations, 74
    urbanization rate in, 11
Universal bank, development of German economy
    and, 19–20
Urban areas/urbanization
    effect of migration on development, 121–122
    impact on norms calling for large families, 73
    migration and urban planning, 126
    property rights. See Property rights, in urban areas
    rural to urban migration, 123
Urbanization gap, 11–13
Urquiola, Miguel, 480
Usury, sin of, 304
Utility maximization hypothesis, 235

V

Vaccines
    in disease prevention, 429
    issues in R&D of drugs for developing countries,
        442–444
    in treating diarrheal diseases, 432
    tuberculosis, 441
Value-added, factors of production and, 83
Value-added taxes (VAT), 280
Values. See also Culture; Social norms
    culture and, 288
    informal institutions based on, 177–178
Van Rijckeghem, Caroline, 528
Variance
    bias from omitted variables, 570–571
    bivariate regression analysis, 565–567
    covariation between two variables, 564–565
    dealing with omitted variables in panel regression,
        572–573
    instrumental variables, 574–577
    random (stochastic) variables, 562
    in statistical analysis, 563–564

Veblen, Thorstein, 199–200
Venables, Anthony J., 501–502
Verdier, Thierry, 373–374
Vermeersch, Christel, 481
Vertical integration
    good legal institutions support less vertical
        integration, 229–230
    informal solutions to hold-up problem, 187
    trade-off between efficiency and hold-up, 229
    vs. subcontractors, 228–229
Videla, Jorge Rafael, 251
Vietnam, 554–557
Vishny, Robert W., 521–522
Voluntary export restraints, 159–160
von Mises, Ludwig, 205
von Neumann, John, 129
Voucher programs, 479–480

W

WACC (weighted average cost of capital)
    estimating cost of infrastructure investments,
        500–501
    formula for, 499
    regulatory variables impacting, 503
Wacziarg, Romain, 430–431
Wages
    egalitarian drift in centrally planned economies,
        221–222
    famine and, 389
    labor contracts, 320–321
    setting in centrally planned economies, 221
Warranties, institutional solutions to informational
    problems, 182
Water
    benefits of piped water systems in disease
        prevention, 433
    cost of capital for infrastructure sectors, 500
    infrastructure gap, 487–489
    point-of-use water treatment for disease
        prevention, 432
    privatization in Bolivia, 358
Weber, Max, 255, 288, 307
Weder, Beatrice, 528
Wei, Shang-Jin, 518
Weight, anthropometric measures of health, 426–427
Weighted average cost of capital. See WACC
    (weighted average cost of capital)
Weinstein, David, 554–555
Weitzman, Martin, 224
Weizsäcker, Georg, 444

Welfare loss, due to tariffs, 158–159
White elephants, infrastructure investments as, 497–498
WHO (World Health Organization)
  DDT and controversy regarding, 436–437
  epidemiological transition and, 423–424
  malaria eradication programs, 433–434
  strategy for dealing with tuberculosis, 429
Williams, Heidi, 444
Williamson, Oliver, 194, 200
Wolfe, Philip, 206
Wolpin, Kenneth, 68
Women
  gender biases impacting fertility choices, 71
  gender biases impacting male to female population ratio, 72
  impact of Indian caste system on education, 474–475
  measuring education gap, 458–459
  microfinance providing opportunities for, 413
  reducing gender gap in education, 481–482
Work ethic, WVS and, 290
Worker behavior, in central planning systems
  ineffective labor-discipline campaigns, 222
  overview of, 220
  seller's market for labor, 220–221
  wage setting and wage drift, 221–222
World Bank
  1-dollar-a-day methodology, 35–36
  control of corruption variable, 514–515
  on currency convertibility, 166
  Doing Business project, 344
  measures of good governance, 301
World Health Organization. See WHO (World Health Organization)
World Trade Organization. See WTO (World Trade Organization)

World Values Survey (WVS)
  overview of, 289–292
  religious beliefs and trust, 308
Worms
  DALY (Disability Adjusted Life Year) measure of cost of deworming, 422
  effects of deworming, 439–440
  types and diseases related to, 437–438
  types and effects of, 437–438
WTO (World Trade Organization)
  protection of property rights by, 101–102
  replacing GATT in 1995, 161
  rules for trade liberalization, 163–165
WVS (World Values Survey)
  overview of, 289–292
  religious beliefs and trust, 308

Y

Yakuza, solutions to commitment problem, 189
Yared, Pierre, 255
Young, Alwyn, 94, 430–431
Yunus, Muhammad, 395, 409

Z

Zaibatsu, 18, 21
Zamindari
  abolishing intermediaries, 335
  land reform and, 332
  persistence of past arrangements impacting land reform, 337
Zhang, Junsen, 68
Zhu, Yi, 68
Zimbabwe, 333
Zingales, Luigi, 273–275, 308
Zoido, Pablo, 512